Writing That Works

Communicating Effectively on the Job

EIGHTH EDITION

Writing That Works
Communicating Effectively on the Job

Walter E. Oliu
U.S. Nuclear Regulatory Commission

Charles T. Brusaw
NCR Corporation

Gerald J. Alred
University of Wisconsin–Milwaukee

Bedford/St. Martin's
Boston ♦ New York

For Bedford/St. Martin's

Developmental Editor: Ellen Thibault
Assistant Editor, Publishing Services: Maria Burwell
Production Supervisor: Yexenia Markland
Senior Marketing Manager: Richard Cadman
Project Management: Books By Design, Inc.
Cover Design: Zenobia Damania
Cover Art: © Lisette Le Bon/SuperStock
Composition: Pine Tree Composition, Inc.
Printing and Binding: RR Donnelley & Sons Company

President: Joan E. Feinberg
Editorial Director: Denise B. Wydra
Editor in Chief: Karen S. Henry
Director of Marketing: Karen Melton Soeltz
Director of Editing, Design, and Production: Marcia Cohen
Manager, Publishing Services: Emily Berleth

Library of Congress Control Number: 2003103952

Manufactured in the United States of America.

9   8   7   6   5
f   e   d   c

For information, write: Bedford/St. Martin's, 75 Arlington Street, Boston, MA 02116 (617-399-4000)

ISBN: 0-312-40853-6

Acknowledgments
Acknowledgments and copyrights are continued at the back of the book on page 754, which constitutes an extension of the copyright page.

Preface

Writing That Works, Eighth Edition, is designed to help students of varied academic backgrounds and occupational interests develop the skills they need to write and communicate successfully on the job. The book offers practical coverage of the writing process, clear guidelines for specific types of workplace writing—such as memos, reports, proposals, presentations, and more—supported by a wealth of sample documents, hundreds of helpful projects and writing assignments, and the most current advice for using technology in today's workplace. Following is a description of the established features of *Writing That Works*. For a detailed description of what's new to this edition, see pages vii–viii.

■ About This Book

Practical Advice for Writing at Work

Writing That Works is a comprehensive text with flexible enough organization to accommodate a variety of teaching approaches and a range of business and professional writing courses. Its thorough coverage also makes it a book that students can use long after the course is over as a reference tool on the job. Advice throughout the book is supported by more than 200 sample documents, each now annotated to highlight rhetorical and design choices, that students can apply to their own writing. Divided into four parts, the book is structured so that it begins with the basics of the writing process and then moves into more complex tasks and types of business writing.

Part One: The Writing Process (Chapters 1 through 5) guides students through the steps of planning, organizing, drafting, and revising memos and other types of writing. These chapters emphasize the questions a writer must ask when approaching any writing task. What is my purpose in writing? Who is my audience? How much information do I need to provide? How can I best persuade my readers? How can I make my writing more organized, clear, and concise?

Part Two: Essential Skills (Chapters 6 through 8) helps students develop additional communication and writing skills. The chapter on collaborating includes advice on how to peer review and edit shared documents; the research chapter covers primary, print, and online research, with guidelines for documenting sources; the design chapter offers concrete advice and examples for creating effective visuals and integrating them into documents and presentations.

Part Three: Writing at Work (Chapters 9 through 17) applies the skills learned in Parts One and Two, guiding students through the many types of writing and communications they will face in any workplace, with detailed advice on routine correspondence—e-mail, letters, and memos—informal and formal reports, instructions, and proposals, all illustrated by effective model documents. These chapters also cover creating and delivering presentations, conducting meetings, and writing for the Web. The chapter on finding a job includes a variety of résumés and helpful advice for succeeding at the job interview.

Part Four: A Writer's Handbook provides help with grammar, punctuation, mechanics, spelling, and vocabulary, and it includes a section tailored to students for whom English is a second language.

Easy to Use, with the Latest on Using Workplace Technology

Writing That Works provides a number of reference features that make the book especially accessible. Handy checklists and tips boxes throughout the text highlight important information and include Writer's Checklists, ESL Tips, and new checklists for Considering Audience and Purpose and Designing Your Document. Digital Shortcuts provide the latest advice for using workplace technology and cover such topics as managing e-mail, sending e-mail attachments, and using software for writing collaboratively. The presentations chapter (Chapter 15) includes specific advice for using PowerPoint software. Research—how to conduct, evaluate, and document it—is covered in detail in Chapter 7, Researching Your Subject. This chapter shows students how to use databases and other resources available at college library Web sites, and how to find useful, reliable sources on the Internet that students can incorporate into their researched writing.

Focused on Success in the Real World

To connect the book's advice with the real world, each chapter opens with brief commentaries called Voices from the Workplace. These popular interviews—featuring both experienced professionals and those who are new to the workplace—provide firsthand experience and advice for writing, communicating, facing challenges, and succeeding on the job. In this edition there are thirty-four commentaries, two-thirds of which are new, and each voice features a photo of the speaker.

To prepare students for the real demands of professional life, *Writing That Works* offers advice for writing successfully, even under the pressure of a tight deadline. The book's popular Meeting the Deadline sections offer practical help for approaching time-sensitive memos, proposals, and, new to this edition, presentations (see below for a description).

■ New to This Edition

As with each edition of *Writing That Works,* this revision has been guided by the thoughtful reviews and suggestions of business and technical writing instructors across the country. In response to this feedback, and to better meet the needs of the variety of courses in which *Writing That Works* is taught, we have made the following improvements:

- **New and updated examples of workplace writing**—including proposals, informal reports, and résumés—reflect a variety of occupations and provide excellent models for writing. **New annotations** to each sample document help students understand specific rhetorical and design choices.

- **New and expanded coverage of audience, purpose, document design, and technology.** New Considering Audience and Purpose checklists offer clear advice and prompt students to keep their readers and goals in mind throughout the writing process. Coverage of document design, now integrated into the writing process chapters (Part One), is reinforced throughout the text with helpful new Designing Your Document checklists. New and updated Digital Shortcuts for using technology in the workplace now include tips for using templates and collaborating electronically on documents.

- **A new chapter—Writing for the Web**—covers basic rhetorical principles for writers crafting content for the Web and provides plenty of helpful examples of Web documents.

- **A new section titled Meeting the Deadline: The Time-Sensitive Presentation** gives advice for creating and practicing a presentation under pressure and includes sample PowerPoint notes and slides.

- **An updated research chapter** reflects today's research environment, offering more concise advice for conducting primary, Internet, and library research; evaluating sources; and avoiding plagiarism. The chapter includes new Web screens that illustrate the research process, and the documentation section provides the latest APA and MLA guidelines for citing sources.

- **New reference features** include chapter-opening images that offer snapshots of the types of documents to be covered. New color tabs highlight the most referenced sample documents. The Writer's Handbook in Part Four, now streamlined and easier to use, opens with a menu of entries for quick reference.

- **New Web links** throughout the margins of the book point students to specific business writing resources and activities at the companion Web site. The site itself, now easier to navigate, also provides an extensive online Instructor's Manual.

- **Updated Voices from the Workplace**—two-thirds of which are new to this edition—reflect a diversity of professions and levels of experience and offer helpful tips for succeeding on the job.

■ Ancillaries

Book Companion Web Site

<bedfordstmartins.com/writingthatworks>

The companion Web site for *Writing That Works* (illustrated on the back cover of this book) offers a variety of resources for students, including access to the Web links included in the book, a gallery of sample documents, and additional advice and resources for finding a job or an internship.

Online Instructor's Manual

<bedfordstmartins.com/writingthatworks>

This comprehensive online Instructor's Manual provides chapter overviews and teaching tips, suggested responses to the assignments and projects in the book, helpful handouts, a gallery of model documents, course-planning help, and sample syllabi.

Additional Resources for Business and Technical Writing

<bedfordstmartins.com/bustech>

This site provides helpful resources for students—access to a *Web Design Tutorial* by Mike Markel and to *Research and Documentation Online,* a reference guide by Diana Hacker for finding and documenting sources in multiple disciplines.

■ Acknowledgments

We would like to thank Lisa-Anne Culp of the University of South Florida for her thoughtful work on the Eighth Edition's writing assignments and projects, the companion Web site, and the online Instructor's Manual. We are grateful to Marcia Muth of the University of Colorado at Boulder for her suggestions for improving the handbook section of the book. We thank Sandy Petrulionis of Pennsylvania State University and her students Susan Litzinger, Shana L. Richardson, and Eric Shoop for the formal report, trip report, and sales proposal included in this book. We are grateful to Suzanne Karberg of Purdue University both for her contributions to the new Meeting the Deadline coverage in the presentations chapter and for her work on the writing assignments and projects.

For her contributions to previous editions of this book, we would like to thank Candy Henry of Pennsylvania State University for her ESL advice and work on the book's writing assignments and companion Web site. We are grateful to Sandy Fuhr, research librarian at Gustavus Adolphus College, for her contributions to the research chapter, and to Kate Williams of Oglethorpe University for developing the advice for finding a job or an internship provided at the book's Web site.

We also wish to thank the following instructors who have substantially strengthened the Eighth Edition by generously sharing their helpful comments and recommendations: Luann Adams, Mid-State Technical College; Laura Albritton, University of Miami; David Beach, George Mason University; Kristen O'Dell Brumfield, Radford University; Basil A. Clark, Saginaw Valley State University; John Early, Minnesota State University, Moorhead; Laura Garren, Clemson University; Jan Gerzema, Indiana University Northwest; Charla B. Greene, Clemson University; Husne Jahan, Santa Clara University; Eileen Landis-Groom, Kutztown University; Michelle Manning, University of Central Florida; Scott McKelvie, University of Missouri–St. Louis; Paul William Murphey, Southwest Wisconsin Technical College; Pamela W. Payne, Palm Beach Atlantic College; Sandy Petrulionis, Pennsylvania State University, Altoona; Julliana Probst, Trenholm State Technical College; Dirk Remley, Kent State University; David Sidore, Macon State College; Scott Weeden, Indiana University–Purdue University, Indianapolis; and Sarah Zahm, University of Nebraska at Omaha.

For kindly sharing their experiences of writing and communicating at work and for contributing to our Voices from the Workplace feature, we would like to thank James Bates, U.S. Department of Housing and Urban Development; Diane Bernard, Freelance Researcher; Kate Bishop, Blackboard, Inc.; Beth Blazon, St. Joseph's Hospital; Alvin Blunt, Nuclear Regulatory Commission; Steve Bramlage, Vectren Energy of Ohio; Malorye Branca, *BioItWorld* Magazine; Sheree Crute, SCL Health and Medical Communications; Hélène Ducros, University of North Carolina; Corey Ann Eaton, Wachovia Securities; Anna Rose Eckenrode, Charter Communications; Liz Goodwin, Melrose Public Library; Paul B. Greenspan, Interland, Inc.; Terry Kalna, International Speedway Corporation; Ted Kalo, U.S. House of Representatives; Susan U. Ladwig, Reinhart Boerner Van Deuren; Eduardo Lapetina, Cato Research; Mark Lin, GlaxoSmithKline Pharmaceuticals; Colleen McDonough, Hobart and William Smith Colleges; Susan McLaughlin, Paragon Alliance; David Noyes, Neumann Monson Wictor Architects; C. J. Pascarella, Deloitte & Touche, LLP; Sherri Pfennig, University of Wisconsin–Milwaukee; Judy Prono, Los Alamos National Laboratory; Emily Rankin, Bedford/St. Martin's; Joseph G. Rappaport, Transport Workers Union; Kezia Scales, Communities in Schools; Jonathan Spiegel, Trustcompany Bank; William M. Tammick III, Lifeline Systems, Inc.; Annika Tamura, Boston.com; Adam Thompson, *Denver Post;* Tobin H. Van Pelt, Icosystem Corporation; Larrell Walters, Edison Material Technology Center; and Claire Zulkey, Ebel Dunnell Merrick, Inc.

We are also greatly indebted to the leadership of Bedford/St. Martin's, beginning with Joan Feinberg, president; Charles Christensen, retired president; Denise Wydra, editorial director; Karen Henry, editor in chief; and Leasa Burton, executive editor, for helping us to re-imagine our approach to key facets of this edition and for their un-stinting support throughout the revision process. We thank Emily Berleth, who, with the help of Herb Nolan at Books By Design, oversaw the difficult task of producing this book. We are grateful to Claire Seng-Niemoeller for her creative design, and to Kathleen Benn McQueen and Barbara Jatkola for their careful copyediting and proof-reading. Finally, we were *again* especially fortunate to work with Ellen Thibault, our developmental editor at Bedford/St. Martin's. She sets and adheres to the highest professional standards, and this edition is stronger throughout because of her ex-pertise, creativity, and unfailing tact in working with us and in coordinating the work of the many contributors acknowledged in this Preface.

Walter E. Oliu
Charles T. Brusaw
Gerald J. Alred

About the Authors

Walter E. Oliu, Charles T. Brusaw, and Gerald J. Alred are coauthors of *The Business Writer's Handbook,* Seventh Edition (Bedford/St. Martin's 2003), the *Handbook of Technical Writing,* Seventh Edition (Bedford/St. Martin's 2003), *The Business Writer's Companion,* Third Edition (Bedford/St. Martin's 2002), and *The Technical Writer's Companion,* Third Edition (Bedford/St. Martin's 2002).

Walter E. Oliu until recently served as Chief of the Publishing Services Branch at the U.S. Nuclear Regulatory Commission. He is a communications consultant in the Washington, D.C., area and has provided publications and Web consulting services to the Russian and Ukrainian governments. He has taught at Miami University of Ohio and Slippery Rock State University.

Charles T. Brusaw is a business writing consultant for corporations worldwide. He worked for twenty years as a technical writer for the NCR Corporation and has also worked in advertising, public relations, and curriculum development.

Gerald J. Alred is professor of English at the University of Wisconsin–Milwaukee, where he teaches courses in professional writing and directs the Graduate Certificate Program in International Technical Communication. In addition to coauthoring the titles listed above, he is author of *The St. Martin's Bibliography of Business and Technical Communication* (Bedford/St. Martin's 1997). His recent articles include "Essential Works on Technical Communication," published in the fiftieth anniversary issue of *Technical Communication* (November 2003).

Brief Contents

Contents

Chapter 3   Writing the Draft   63

Chapter 4   Revising for Essentials   102

PART THREE Writing at Work: From Principle to Practice   303

Chapter 9   Understanding the Principles of Business Correspondence   305

Chapter 12   Writing Formal Reports   417

Chapter 13   Writing Instructions   455

Chapter 14   Writing Proposals   477

PART FOUR   A Writer's Handbook   633

Section A   Grammar, Punctuation, and Mechanics   635

Writing That Works

Communicating Effectively on the Job

PART ONE

The Writing Process

1

In Part One, you will learn techniques for developing, drafting, and revising letters, memos, and a wide array of other on-the-job writing tasks. Using these strategies will help you produce clearly written, well-organized documents, because effective on-the-job writing always reflects the writer's attention to the work that goes on before the finished memo or letter emerges from the printer.

◆ **Determining Audience and Purpose.** Chapters 1 through 3 provide discussion and exercises to help you clearly define your reader's needs and the message you intend your document to convey.

◆ **Brainstorming and Gathering Information.** Chapter 1 includes detailed examples and discussion of methods you can use to generate ideas and collect and begin to organize information.

◆ **Outlining.** Chapter 2 describes how you can organize your information into an outline that is appropriate to your purpose and audience. It also offers examples of a wide range of outline styles.

◆ **Writing the Draft.** Chapter 3 discusses and offers examples of the process through which writers turn an outline into a successful rough draft.

◆ **Revising.** Chapters 4 and 5 describe the kinds of problems you need to evaluate when you revise your draft. You will learn how to review your draft to see how well it communicates to its intended audience; to be sure it emphasizes key ideas; to check information for factual accuracy; to consider the ethical implications of your writing; to scrutinize language for grammatical correctness, consistency, and preciseness; and to proofread for punctuation and spelling.

1 Determining Your Audience and Purpose

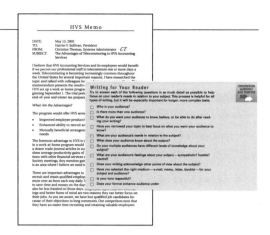

C hristine Thomas was aware of a potential opportunity at HVS Accounting Services, where she worked as the company's Systems Administrator. The company was prospering. In just the past year, Harriet Sullivan, the President and founder of the small company, hired five new employees to handle the increasing workload of tax preparation, financial planning, and investment services. HVS now had 12 full-time employees, about half of whom commuted over an hour each way. Christine was also aware that the company recently lost several promising job applicants because they did not wish to spend two or more hours a day driving to and from work.

With this information in mind, for the past several months Christine had carefully reviewed several management magazines and Web sites about the benefits of telecommuting for companies and their employees. Companies that offered this option to their employees had a happier workforce, less absenteeism, and greater productivity per employee. Such a program would also benefit the local community by reducing traffic congestion and air pollution.

So, with all the information in hand and confident of the value of her suggestion, Christine wrote an e-mail message to Harriet Sullivan (Figure 1–1). Two days later, Christine received the following terse return e-mail from Harriet: "Not right for HVS." Christine was not only disappointed but also puzzled. She knew that her suggestion was timely and reasonable because she had checked all the facts before writing the e-mail. Yet she had failed to convince Harriet Sullivan.

■ Using a Systematic Approach to Writing

In writing her e-mail message, Christine Thomas committed the most common of all mistakes made by people who write on the job: She lost sight of the purpose of her message and overlooked the needs of her audience. Christine was so convinced of the value of her suggestion that she did not realize that Harriet was not familiar with the information her research had produced and could not see the situation from her perspective. Had she kept her primary purpose and her reader

Voices from the Workplace

Sheree Crute, SCL Health and Medical Communications

Sheree Crute is President of SCL Health and Medical Communications, where she develops brochures and writes feature articles for publications such as *Consumer Reports on Health* and nonprofit organizations such as the Centers for Disease Control and Prevention.

Understanding and writing to her audience is crucial, says Sheree. "Before you pick up a pen or flip on the computer to write, make sure you understand the reader you are trying to reach. You cannot produce information that's on target if you are unsure of the interests or needs of your audience. Readers want their health information delivered in a succinct and accessible way. They want news they can use — and bring into their daily lives. For this type of reporting, it doesn't matter how eloquent you are — if you don't understand your audience's needs, you will never be heard or understood."

Colleen McDonough, Hobart and William Smith Colleges

Colleen McDonough is the Assistant Director of Annual Giving at Hobart and William Smith Colleges. As a fund-raiser, Colleen is called upon not only to express enthusiasm for her alma mater but also to persuade other alumni to contribute to the colleges.

Colleen says: "Having excellent writing skills is essential to succeeding in a job like mine where I deal with people and their individual concerns every day. Persuasive writing skills are easy to develop, but difficult to fine-tune. I must know how to address different audiences. I have to remember that the similarity between alumni groups is often only that they have graduated from the same school. Era of attendance, current age, race, politics, gender, and geographic location also come into play. Needless to say, the scope of my writing has to have quite a range; soliciting support from a man who graduated in 1955 would take quite a different angle than when addressing a group of 23-year-old women. Having the ability to convey facts, be persuasive, and be flexible enough to craft the same basic thoughts in different ways to appeal to different groups are valuable skills which come with much practice and dedication."

Visit Hobart and William Smith Colleges online at <hws.edu>.

clearly in mind, Christine would then have been able to generate ideas, establish her scope, and organize her thoughts in a way that ultimately might have achieved her objective.

The last three steps are important: Even with her reader and her purpose clearly in mind, Christine would still not have been ready to write her e-mail to Harriet. She would simply have established a framework in which to develop her message. Once they have identified their purpose and their audience, some writers don't know what to do next and stare at a blank page or computer screen waiting for inspiration.

A systematic approach helps writers over this hurdle. Before beginning to write, careful writers not only identify their purpose and audience but think seriously about the content of their writing and about how to organize and present it

To: Harriet V. Sullivan, President
From: Christine Thomas, Systems Administrator
Date: May 5, 2003
Subject: Telecommuting and HVS Accounting Services

I believe that HVS Accounting would benefit greatly if we permitted our employees
to telecommute one or more days a week. A growing number of companies, large
and small, permit employees to perform company work at home on a schedule they
jointly agree to. The companies can communicate with these employees during the
workday in a variety of ways—by phone, e-mail, and fax.

There are many advantages to such a policy that would help HVS and our employees. Employees would save the time and expense necessary to commute every day.
They would also suffer less stress and be in a better frame of mind to tackle their
work. This would result in greater worker productivity. Finally, our community would
benefit because fewer commuter cars on the road means reduced traffic congestion
and cleaner air. Please consider my suggestion that we offer our employees the opportunity to perform their HVS work at home one or more days a week.

Christine

Figure 1–1   First Proposal (E-mail)

for ease of understanding. This process involves first listing all the ideas and facts
the writer might wish to include, then refining the list by examining each item in it
from the perspectives of audience and purpose, and finally organizing the resulting list in a way that satisfies the writer's primary purpose and the audience's needs.

Planning Your Document

WRITER'S
CHECKLIST

- ☐ Determine your purpose.
- ☐ Determine your audience's needs.
- ☐ Generate, gather, and record ideas and facts.
- ☐ Organize your ideas in a list.
- ☐ Establish the scope of coverage for your topic.
- ☐ Organize the list based on the needs of your purpose and audience.

Determining Your Purpose

Everything you write has a purpose. You want your reader to know, to believe, or
to be able to do something when he or she has finished reading what you have
written. Determining your purpose is the first step in preparing to write; unless
you know what you hope to accomplish by your writing, you cannot know what
information you should present.

Purpose, then, gives direction to your writing. The more precisely you can
state your primary purpose at the outset, the more successful your writing is likely

to be. (You may also have a secondary purpose, such as to motivate or reassure.) Christine Thomas might have said that her purpose was "to allow HVS employees to telecommute"—but permitting employees to telecommute was the *result* she wanted; it was not the precise purpose of her memo. Further thought would have led Christine to recognize the more specific goals of the e-mail itself.

To make sure that your purpose is precise, put it in writing. In most cases, you can use the following formula to guide you:

■ My primary purpose is to _____ so that my audience _____.

Using this formula, Christine Thomas might have come up with the following statement of purpose:

■ My primary purpose is to explain the advantages of telecommuting so that my reader, Harriet Sullivan, will be persuaded that the idea has enough merit for the company and its employees that she will permit it at least for a trial period.

W **On the Web**
For online resources for determining audience and purpose, go to Chapter 1, bedfordstmartins.com/ writingthatworks

With this statement of purpose, Christine would have recognized that her purpose was more complicated than it had at first appeared and that she would have to present persuasive evidence to be effective.

Determining Your Audience's Needs

Remember that your job as a writer is to express your ideas so clearly that your audience cannot misinterpret them and that an important element of the purpose formula is the phrase "so that my audience . . ." Simply identifying the response you would like is very different from actually achieving it. Although a purpose statement addresses a problem from the writer's point of view, the audience's needs must also be taken into account if you are to be persuasive. Yet many writers often forget that they have an audience and they write essentially to themselves, focusing solely on their own purposes.

After you have stated your purpose, ask yourself, "Who is my audience?" Often you will know the answer. For example, if you are writing a memo to your boss attempting to persuade him or her to fund a project, you know who your reader is. In another situation, however, you might be writing a letter to someone you do not know in another company. In this case, you would try to imagine your reader, taking into consideration what you know about that company, your reader's position in the company or department, and his or her responsibilities regarding the topic you are writing about. You could not know what your reader's needs were until you knew at least that much about him or her.

Obviously, when you know enough about your reader that you can actually picture him or her responding to what you have written, you have an advantage. However, even when you know your audience very well, a little reflection is necessary. Without careful thought, Christine Thomas might have answered the question "Who is my reader?" from only one point of view:

■ My reader is Harriet Sullivan, and she's been my boss for ten years. We've worked together since she founded the company, so she'll no doubt understand that I have her best interests in mind.

Had Christine carefully analyzed Harriet as the reader of her e-mail, she would have considered Harriet's role in the company, her lack of familiarity with the topic, and her anxiety about taking such a step. Bearing these concerns in mind, Christine might have answered the question differently.

■ My reader is Harriet Sullivan, president of HVS Accounting Services. Harriet founded HVS ten years ago with modest savings and a substantial loan. Cautious, industrious, and a stickler for detail, Harriet has built HVS into a sound business and is now beginning to see some return on her investment. Harriet is also a hands-on executive. She puts in long hours at the office and is in frequent contact with the staff by e-mail, telephone, and face-to-face conversations. In addition to a regularly scheduled staff meeting every Wednesday, she holds informal meetings several times a week. She may strongly resist the loss of hands-on access to her staff when they work at home. She values computer technology and purchased laptop computers for the accountants and financial analysts to help them as they visit clients around the metropolitan area. However, although she uses e-mail regularly, she does so reluctantly and prefers memos.

Writing for Your Reader

CONSIDERING
AUDIENCE
AND PURPOSE

Try to answer each of the following questions in as much detail as possible to help focus on your reader's needs in relation to your subject. This process is helpful for all types of writing, but it will be especially important for longer, more complex tasks.

- ☐ Who is your audience?
- ☐ Is there more than one audience?
- ☐ What do you want your audience to know, believe, or be able to do after reading your writing?
- ☐ Have you narrowed your topic to best focus on what you want your audience to know?
- ☐ What are your audience's needs in relation to the subject?
- ☐ What does your audience know about the subject?
- ☐ Do your multiple audiences have different levels of knowledge about your subject?
- ☐ What are your audience's feelings about your subject — sympathetic? hostile? neutral?
- ☐ Does your writing acknowledge other points of view about the subject?
- ☐ Have you selected the right medium — e-mail, memo, letter, booklet — for your subject and audience?
- ☐ Is your tone respectful?
- ☐ Does your format enhance audience understanding?

Based on this analysis, Christine is better prepared to provide the information that Harriet needs to understand, agree with, and act on Christine's proposal.

Generating, Gathering, and Recording Ideas and Facts

When you have determined your purpose and analyzed your reader's needs, you must decide what information will satisfy the demands of both. There are several techniques you can use for gathering and recording this information.

Brainstorming

A good way to start generating ideas and gathering information is to interview yourself so that you can tap into your own knowledge and experience. You may find that you already have enough information to get started. This technique, commonly known as *brainstorming,* may also suggest additional ways of obtaining information.

To begin, create a list containing as many ideas as you can think of about the general subject of the document you plan to write and jot them down as they occur to you. (Keep in mind that this type of research may be performed especially effectively by a group of writers or project team members.) Jot down what you know and, if possible, where you learned of it, using a computer, a dry-erase board, a pad of paper, or notecards.

Reporters and other writers have long used the following questions as a guide to ensure that they have answered the questions their audience is likely to have about a particular story: *What* happened? *Why* did it happen? *When* did it happen? *How* did it happen? *Where* did it happen? *Who* was involved? Rarely will you be able to apply all these questions to any single on-the-job writing situation, but the range of information they cover can be useful in helping to start your thinking.

Once you have assembled a list of ideas, examine each item and decide whether it contributes to your purpose or satisfies your audience's needs. Then mark the item with a *P* for purpose or an *A* for audience. Some items will satisfy both your purpose and your audience, others will appear to satisfy only one, and still others will appear to have nothing to do with either. The items of no relevance can be crossed out.

When you have finished marking your list, cross out any item that is not marked. Be sure to reconsider an unmarked item from the perspectives of both your purpose and your audience, making certain that the item fits neither before eliminating it. Ideally, you will have a comprehensive list of items beside which you have placed both a *P* and an *A*. The more common ground your purpose and your audience's needs share, the more effective your writing will be.

As you review your list, you will find that items relating clearly to both your purpose and the needs of your audience are easiest to work with. Items that your audience might need but that would get in the way of your purpose are trickier. Harriet Sullivan, for example, needs to know that after the program begins, she will have less direct access to employees working from home. Because she's a "hands-on" manager, this break with her customary practice will be difficult for

Harriet to accept. Christine, however, might be reluctant to mention this fact because it appears to undermine her purpose, which is to persuade Harriet to support telecommuting. However, to reconcile Harriet's interests and her own, Christine would have to point out this aspect of the program. To have credibility, you need to acknowledge opposing points of view when they are relevant; doing so allows you to respond to your audience's objections rather than leaving them unanswered.

Turning a writer's list of ideas into a reader's list of information should be neither difficult nor mysterious; thoroughness is the key. Christine Thomas, for example, might have generated the well-balanced list shown in Figure 1–2, using one or more of the methods described here. Such a list will give you an idea of the content of the project. The list will probably be sketchy or missing information, but that's actually helpful in showing where additional research is needed. It will also give you a framework for where to integrate the details of the additional research.

Using Other Sources of Information

Brainstorming may not produce all the information you need. Christine, for example, read about this new way of working by reviewing trade journals and Web sites in the field. To get enough information to meet the needs of your audience, you may have to conduct formal, systematic research into your subject. In such cases, you should have some idea of how thoroughly you will cover your subject. To consult the appropriate sources, you will have to know how much detail is required. If you know what you are looking for and where to find it, research presents few problems.

The library provides books, articles, reference works, and other material for your research. The Internet, used carefully, provides access to vast amounts of information from commercial, educational, governmental, and other sources. A personal interview with an expert can provide you with up-to-date information not readily available in printed material. A questionnaire permits you to obtain the views of a group of people and requires less time and money than numerous personal interviews. These different sources of information are discussed in detail in Chapter 7, "Researching Your Subject."

Establishing Your Scope

Having refined your list of ideas and facts, you must review it once again to establish the scope of coverage for your topic. Your *scope* is the degree of detail you decide is necessary to cover each item in your list, and you must determine it based on your purpose and the needs of your audience. As you contemplate each item, ask yourself, "How much information should I include to support my purpose? to satisfy my audience's needs? Have I omitted only unnecessary information that gets in the way of meeting my purpose and my audience's needs?" Often you will find that you are omitting important facts or figures and you will have to research

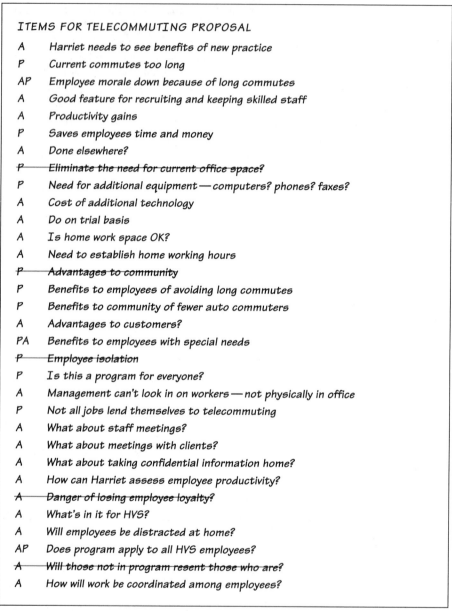

ITEMS FOR TELECOMMUTING PROPOSAL

A   *Harriet needs to see benefits of new practice*
P   *Current commutes too long*
AP   *Employee morale down because of long commutes*
A   *Good feature for recruiting and keeping skilled staff*
A   *Productivity gains*
P   *Saves employees time and money*
A   *Done elsewhere?*
P   ~~*Eliminate the need for current office space?*~~
P   *Need for additional equipment — computers? phones? faxes?*
A   *Cost of additional technology*
A   *Do on trial basis*
A   *Is home work space OK?*
A   *Need to establish home working hours*
P   ~~*Advantages to community*~~
P   *Benefits to employees of avoiding long commutes*
P   *Benefits to community of fewer auto commuters*
A   *Advantages to customers?*
PA   *Benefits to employees with special needs*
P   ~~*Employee isolation*~~
P   *Is this a program for everyone?*
A   *Management can't look in on workers — not physically in office*
P   *Not all jobs lend themselves to telecommuting*
A   *What about staff meetings?*
A   *What about meetings with clients?*
A   *What about taking confidential information home?*
A   *How can Harriet assess employee productivity?*
A   ~~*Danger of losing employee loyalty?*~~
A   *What's in it for HVS?*
A   *Will employees be distracted at home?*
AP   *Does program apply to all HVS employees?*
A   ~~*Will those not in program resent those who are?*~~
A   *How will work be coordinated among employees?*

Figure 1–2   Brainstorming List for a Proposal

your subject further. At other times, you will find that your list is cluttered with un-necessary detail.

Had Christine Thomas drawn up the list shown in Figure 1–2 and then reviewed it to establish her scope, she would have discovered that some of the items on her list needed detailed information to satisfy Harriet Sullivan's concerns. Entries such as "Cost of additional technology" would tell her that she had to either provide detailed figures for the cost of this equipment or explain why no additional expense is necessary. However, other items requiring more detail might be more difficult to identify: "How can Harriet assess employee productivity?" indicates Christine's sense that evaluating productivity would present a cost-conscious person like Harriet with a challenge. She would want to know how this could be done effectively. Figure 1–3 shows the list in Figure 1–2 after the scope has been established.

Be careful when establishing your scope. Writers who know a lot about a subject tend to unload information on audiences who have no time or need to wade through a boring catalog of topics or a mass of details to get to the point. Understand, too, that establishing your scope in the classroom may be different from doing so on the job. The scope of topics for classroom assignments must often be limited because of accessibility of information, the goals of the course, or other learning objectives. Consider these limitations as part of the purpose of an assignment. In whatever context you establish the scope of your writing, always be guided by your purpose and your audience's needs.

POINTS TO COVER

- *Good feature for recruiting and keeping skilled staff*
- *Productivity gains — note industry data*
- *Saves employees time and money*
- *Our competitors permit telecommuting*
- *Costs of additional technology and types needed — although HVS is set up well right now*
- *Do on trial basis — recommend three months, two days/week*
- *Need to establish home working hours*
- *Advantages to community — less congestion and pollution*
- *Advantages to customers — maybe?*
- *Benefits to employees with special needs — two HVS employees can use now!*
- *Employee morale down because of long commutes*
- *Management can't look in on workers — not physically in office*
- *Not all jobs lend themselves to telecommuting — such as receptionist*
- *Scheduling staff and client meetings*
- *Need to protect confidential information when home*
- *Show how Harriet can assess employee productivity*
- *Possible danger of losing employee loyalty*
- *Address possibility that employees will be distracted at home*

Figure 1–3   Notes for Proposal

Organizing Your Ideas

Once you have established your scope, you should have a list of the ideas and facts to be included in your writing. Examine this list and look for relationships among the items in it. Group the related ideas and arrange them under headings—short phrases that identify the kind of items in each group. As you group the related ideas, consider the following questions: Is the time sequence among items important? If so, organize them chronologically. Do you need to compare the features of one item with those of one or more other items? Organize accordingly. Should you present the most important information first or, instead, build a case that ends with the most important information? Organize items by decreasing order of importance or by increasing order of importance, respectively. As you assemble and arrange the groups of ideas, rework the items in your groups; add, delete, and move ideas around until you feel that you have the best possible organization.

As she prepared to organize her information, Christine thought again about Harriet as her reader. Harriet is a practical businessperson concerned about money and wary of change. Christine realizes that she must organize her ideas first to convince Harriet of the advantages of such a program before going on to point out the potential disadvantages from Harriet's perspective. Figure 1–4 shows Christine's organization of the list in Figure 1–3. To organize larger and more complex subjects, a more formal outline is often helpful. Chapter 2 discusses outlining techniques in detail.

From the groups of items in Figure 1–4, presented in the order shown, Christine can now write a rough draft and revise it into a final form that not only will achieve its purpose but also will demonstrate Christine's skill and effectiveness in presenting a proposal.

■ Writing for Success

Soon after she received the disappointing response to her e-mail, Christine found the courage to step into Harriet's office. Christine explained, "I've really investigated the situation, and I'm sure my suggestion would be in our best interests. Perhaps if I gave you more information, you'd reconsider my suggestion." Harriet thought for a moment and then said, "All right. Give me the major benefits and any associated disadvantages and costs by next Monday. If they are convincing, I'll meet with you and Fred Sadowski, our Controller, as soon as I get the chance. And, by the way, give me the information in a memo. An e-mail is too informal for what you're suggesting." Christine Thomas left Harriet Sullivan's office both relieved and determined that this time she would convince Harriet.

After writing a statement of purpose; determining the general needs of her reader; generating, gathering, and recording ideas and facts; and establishing her scope, Christine organized the items she wanted to cover and wrote the rough draft of her memo. Note that the first draft is less concerned with creating a coherent, correct, and persuasive memo than it is with getting all the needed information down in a reasonably organized manner.

1. **COMPANY BENEFITS**
   - Productivity gains
   - Done elsewhere—by competitors
   - Advantages to customers?
   - Special-needs employees
   - Do on trial basis only—low risk
   - Worker recruitment and retention

2. **COMPANY CONCERNS**
   - Need for additional equipment
   - Need to establish home working space and hours
   - Employee isolation?
   - Not for all jobs/employees
   - Can't observe workers firsthand
   - Staff meetings
   - Client meetings
   - Confidential information
   - Assessing productivity
   - Employee loyalty
   - Distractions at home
   - Coordinating work

3. **EMPLOYEE BENEFITS**
   - Help special-needs employees
   - Improve morale—less time on the road
   - Save time and expenses

4. **COMMUNITY BENEFITS**
   - Less air pollution
   - Less traffic congestion

Figure 1–4   Revised Notes for Proposal

Christine put the draft aside for an afternoon, then reread her work the next morning to discover problems with clarity, coherence, and correctness. (See Chapters 4 and 5 for discussions of specific revision techniques that writers use to evaluate and improve their drafts.) She also e-mailed the draft to a trusted coworker and asked for suggestions. The coworker said that Christine had obviously researched her subject with care and that she presented the appropriate information about starting the new program, but that she needed to do a better job of anticipating some of Harriet's questions. The coworker suggested also that Christine might rephrase and reorganize the memo with a sharper eye for Harriet's needs. She noted, for example, that the memo would benefit from headings to introduce subtopics. She also advised Christine that Harriet would not appreciate being told that Christine plans to work independently with Fred Sadowski without Harriet's permission. However, Harriet would appreciate reading that the new program would benefit both the company and its employees. Finally, she told Christine that the writing was too choppy because of too many short sentences and needed to be smoothed out. She handed Christine a draft that included her handwritten suggestions (Figure 1–5).

Memo

DRAFT

Date: May 9, 2003
To: Harriet V. Sullivan, President
From: Christine Thomas
Subject: Telecommuting and HVS Accounting Services

Make subject line more descriptive

Sentences too choppy— smooth out

I believe that HVS Accounting Services and its employees would benefit if we permit our professional staff to telecommute two days a week. Telecommuting is becoming increasingly common throughout the U.S. I suggest that we try the program for three months. That would give us a trial basis. I suggest that we begin on September 1. That would be before our busy end-of-year and winter tax-preparation period.

Add topic headings for readability

Include list of articles and publications they appear in?

There are a lot of advantages to HVS from such a program. The biggest advantage is that employee productivity could increase. I looked at a dozen trade-journal articles and they show average gains of from 15–30%. I spoke with other financial services companies at monthly Accounting Society meetings. They mention gains in the 20–30% range. We need to pull even with the competition.

Reasons?

Name one or two specific competitors doing this?

This would also benefit out employees. They save time and money on the days they work at home. They also wind up being less frazzled. Employees say that the time savings and better frame of mind are two reasons why they can better focus on their jobs. Also, the competition is doing it. They say they have an easier time recruiting and keeping employees. This is an important option that we can offer to our employees. The current job market is very competitive.

The program would also be good for Bill Mayhue and Mabel Chong. Bill is having a hip replacement next month. He will be away from work for up to 6 weeks. Part of this time away could be used productively if he's allowed to work at home. Mabel's baby is due in September. She plans to spend 3 months at home after the birth and wants to keep up with

Figure 1–5   Draft Proposal (with Notes from Coworker) (continued)

page 2

her projects. Instead of losing their services, we would all mutually benefit. This would be a great boost for employee morale, too.

Note that staff has well-defined tasks

Will the program work in practice? One key issue is keeping track of employees working away from the office. HVS currently has details on staff productivity by billable hours. This system would apply to work-at-home employees. I will work with Fred Sadowski to set up and maintain measurable goals for those in the program. We would then review these goals in the middle and at the end of the 3-month trial period with you.

I wouldn't approach Fred w/o Harriet's permission

OK for all jobs at HVS?

Long-distance calls?

I believe that Mondays and Fridays would be ideal work-at-home days. That would leave Tuesday through Thursday as core business days. Keeping in touch with employees at home will not be difficult. Everybody has a telephone. Our staff also has home desktop computers with Internet access. They also have fax machines and printers. Several also have small copiers. HVS has secure electronic information exchange. That's how we send and receive confidential client information electronically. Those in the program can be given password access to this information with their current remote-access software. In other words, they can log into and work on their office computer from their home computer. Finally, we can put home e-mail addresses and phone and fax numbers on our internal Web site. We can give that information to clients, also.

Who pays for paper? Other supplies?

Any costs to HVS?

Will employees mind sharing their info?

Everyone I have spoken with already maintains a home office. So, they have access to private work space at home already. They also believe that they would not lose touch with everyone else at HVS if they're only gone for a day or two a week. Our staff has a proven record of getting the job done. This makes them well suited to a work-at-home program.

Any evidence?

Maybe auditors?

Figure 1–5 **Draft Proposal (with Notes from Coworker)** (continued)

Christine considered the suggestions noted in the text of her draft, reviewed the brainstorming lists she'd written earlier, and then developed her introduction and conclusion and reworked the body of the memo. The extra attention she gave to Harriet's needs provided a helpful point of focus she could use to restructure and polish her writing. She also heeded the format advice about adding topic headings to guide Harriet through the proposal. When she finished her revisions, she printed out and proofread her work for mechanical errors and sent the final version of the memo to Harriet Sullivan (Figure 1–6). Note that the content and style of the finished memo reflect the suggestions made by Christine's coworker. (For detailed guidance on memo format, see Chapter 9, pages 330-332.)

Christine's story had a happy ending: Harriet was persuaded by Christine's final memo and started the work-at-home program on a trial basis that September.

DIGITAL SHORTCUTS

Writing On-Screen

☐ Avoid the temptation of writing first drafts on your computer without any planning.

☐ Use the outline feature to brainstorm and organize an initial outline for your topic. As you create the draft, you can use the cut-and-paste feature to try alternative ways of organizing the information.

☐ Practice freewriting on the computer to overcome writer's block. Type your thoughts as quickly as possible without stopping to correct mistakes or to complete sentences; concentrate on polishing your writing when you revise. Before you begin freewriting, turn down the monitor brightness so you can't see the text you're typing. When you finish the first draft, turn the screen brightness up and review, revise, and reorganize as appropriate.

☐ Use the Find-and-Replace command to find and delete wordy phrases such as "that is," "there are," "the fact that," "to be," and unnecessary helping verbs such as "will."

☐ Use a spelling or grammar checker and other specialized programs to identify and correct typographical errors, misspellings, and grammar problems.

☐ Print a double-spaced paper copy of each draft; reread your drafts and mark them for major revisions and reorganizations. (Viewing your writing on the screen makes it difficult to catch all the errors in your draft.)

☐ Always proofread your final copy on paper.

☐ Print out and distribute or e-mail a copy of your document for your peers to comment on before making final revisions (as Christine Thomas does to good effect).

☐ Use the Find command, this time to find technical terms and other data that may need further explanation for some readers or inclusion in a glossary.

☐ Practice effective document design by highlighting major headings and subheadings with bold or italic print, by using the Copy command to create and duplicate parallel headings throughout your text, and by inserting blank lines in your text to allow extra white space to set off examples and illustrations.

☐ Frequently save your text to the hard drive during long writing sessions. Routinely create an extra, or backup, copy of your documents on duplicate disks for safekeeping.

☐ Keep the standard version of certain documents, such as your résumé and application letters, on file so you can revise them to meet the specific needs of each new job opportunity.

HVS Memo

DATE: May 13, 2003
TO: Harriet V. Sullivan, President
FROM: Christine Thomas, Systems Administrator *CT*
SUBJECT: The Advantages of Telecommuting

Memo heading

I believe that HVS Accounting Services and its employees would benefit if we permit our professional staff to telecommute one or more days a week. Telecommuting is becoming increasingly common throughout the United States for several important reasons. I have researched the topic and talked with colleagues here and among our competitors. This memorandum presents the results of my findings and proposes that HVS set up a work-at-home program on a three-month trial basis beginning September 1. The trial period would occur well before our busy end-of-year and winter tax-preparation period.

Introduction to proposal for a new program

What Are the Advantages?

Heading signals an upcoming topic

The program would offer HVS several important advantages:

- Improved employee productivity
- Enhanced ability to recruit and retain good employees
- Mutually beneficial arrangements for employees with special needs

List of key points focuses attention on advantages to company

The foremost advantage to HVS is that employee productivity for those in a work-at-home program would very likely increase. I have reviewed a dozen trade-journal articles in our field and several Web sites that show average productivity gains of from 15 to 30 percent. In conversations with other financial-services companies at monthly Accounting Society meetings, they mention gains in the 20 to 30 percent range. This is an area where I believe we need to pull even with the competition.

Development of key points

There are important advantages to the staff that would help us also to recruit and retain qualified employees. Several of our employees commute over an hour each way daily. Telecommuting would permit them to save time and money on the days they worked at home. They would also be less frazzled on those days. Employees report that the time savings and better frame of mind are two reasons they can better focus on their jobs. As you are aware, we have lost qualified job candidates because of their objections to long commutes. Our competitors note that they have an easier time recruiting and retaining valuable employees

Advantages to employees

Figure 1–6   Final Proposal (continued)

Harriet V. Sullivan   2   May 13, 2003

when they offer telecommuting as an option. This is an important benefit that we can offer to our employees, especially in the current competitive job market.

The program would also be strongly beneficial to HVS and two employees in particular: Bill Mayhue and Mabel Chong. Bill is scheduled for a hip replacement in two months and will be away from work for up to six weeks. Part of this time away could be used productively if he's allowed to work at home. Mabel's baby is due in September. She plans to spend three months at home after the birth and would also be a good candidate for this program. Instead of losing their services for extended periods—and their ongoing contacts with their clients—we would all benefit. This would be a great boost for employee morale, too.

How Will Telecommuting Work at HVS?

Any new program of this kind raises questions about how well it will work in practice. I believe that the key questions are the following:

List focuses attention on company concerns

- How can we track the work of those in the program?
- Should everyone participate?
- Which days of the week would work best?
- Are there startup or ongoing costs to HVS?

Development of key points

HVS Accounting Services is in an ideal position to be able to keep track of employees working away from the office. Each member of the professional staff has well-defined tasks in financial and estate planning for families, in tax preparation and auditing for financial and estate planning for families, and in tax preparation and auditing for families and small businesses. As you know from our monthly reports, HVS currently maintains detailed information that quantifies staff productivity by billable hours. This system would apply equally well to work-at-home employees. Also, with your approval, I will work with Fred Sadowski to set up and maintain measurable goals for those in the program. We would then review these goals in the middle and at the end of the three-month trial period with you. Not all jobs at HVS would be suitable for the program. The receptionist, mail staff, several of our temporary employees, and I need to be at the office during business hours, so we would not participate.

I believe that Mondays and Fridays would be ideal work-at-home days. That would leave Tuesday through Thursday as core business days for staff meetings, client conferences, and other activities better done at the office. Even on Mondays and Fridays, keeping in touch with em-

Figure 1–6   Final Proposal (continued)

Harriet V. Sullivan 3 May 13, 2003

ployees at home will not be difficult in this electronic era. In addition to telephones, everyone eligible for the program already has home desktop computers with Internet access, fax machines, and printers. Several also have small copiers. Essentially, there are no startup expenses for HVS associated with the program. The staff can keep a log of long-distance business calls and bring in their telephone bill monthly for reimbursement.

Can We Protect Customer Confidentiality?

Customer confidentiality would also be protected. HVS has secure electronic information-exchange software that allows us to send and receive client confidential information electronically. Those in the program can be given password access to confidential and other client information at home using pcEverywhere, their current remote-access software. In other words, the software allows employees to connect to and work on their office computer from their home computer. Finally, I can post the home e-mail addresses and phone and fax numbers for everyone in the program on our internal Web site and provide that information to the appropriate clients. I will also program everyone's phone speed-dial feature with the home numbers of participants.

Everyone I have spoken with already maintains a home office, so having access to private work space at home is not a hindrance. Having this space also minimizes the possibility of interruptions or other disturbances during the day while still permitting employees to schedule home-repair visits rather than having to leave work to meet a repair person, as happens now. The staff also believes that they would not lose touch with everyone else at HVS if they're gone for only a day or two a week. As you know, the auditing staff is periodically away from the office for a week or two at a time at client sites until an audit is completed. Working away from the office is customary to them and causes few disruptions. Finally, everyone in the program would keep the same business hours, minus the commute, of course. Another indirect benefit of telecommuting is it allows us to help do our part to reduce air pollution and traffic congestion in the area.

Can We Make It Happen?

Our staff has a proven record of getting the job done regardless of where they are working, which I believe makes them well suited to a work-at-home program. I look forward to discussing this option with you at your convenience.

Heading signals shift in topic

Closing

Figure 1–6 Final Proposal (continued)

> ## CHAPTER 1 SUMMARY: Determining Your Audience and Purpose
>
> Successful writing on the job is the result of careful preparation. Review the following checklist, based on the information covered in this chapter, which contains the steps essential to ensure that your writing assignments — in the classroom and on the job — are adequately planned.
>
> ☐ Have I determined the purpose of my writing?
>
> ☐ Have I considered my audience's needs and perspectives?
>
> ☐ Have I gathered and recorded all of the ideas and facts necessary for my scope of coverage?
>
> ☐ Have I organized my ideas into related groups and determined the best sequence to link these groups based on my audience's needs?
>
> ☐ Have I established the scope of coverage essential for my purpose and audience's needs?
>
> ☐ Have I reviewed my draft for problems with clarity, coherence, and correctness?
>
> ☐ Have I revised the draft to emphasize the points most important to my audience?
>
> ☐ Have I formatted the final draft to highlight key ideas?

■ Exercises

1. Select a problem at your place of employment (past or present) or on your campus. Using the pattern suggested in this chapter, create a statement of purpose for a memo you could write about this topic. Your reader should be able to make a decision regarding your suggestion. Give the reader's name and position in your statement of the objective.

   a. Brainstorm a list of items for the subject selected. Try to list 15 to 20 items; even if they seem inappropriate, just keep listing. Mark the items with a *P* for purpose or an *A* for audience.

   b. Eliminate the items in your list from 1a that clearly do not meet the audience's needs or contribute to your objective. Then establish your scope and rewrite the list, grouping the items into three or more categories. Next, arrange the items in each category in sequence.

   c. Using the groups of items created in 1b, write the memo suggesting a solution to the problem.

2. For three of the following topics, or topics of your own choosing, list the topic, the audience, one possible purpose for a document, and the information needed to meet that objective. (List kinds of information, not sources of information.) Because the following topics are broad, you will need to select some particular aspect of the topic that you choose.

Topics	Occupations
Banking	Office procedures
Computer programming	Personal computers
E-commerce	Photography
Electronics	Printing
Health care	Real estate
Highway construction	Small businesses
The Internet	Sports
Marketing	Television
Music	Welding

The following is a sample list:

Topic	Internet faxing
Audience	The average computer user
Purpose	To instruct the average computer user on how to set up and send a fax message to a friend, fellow student, coworker, or instructor.
Kinds of information	Required hardware, Internet access, e-mail address, fax number, location (Web address) of one or more Internet faxing services, detailed instructions on how to send and receive faxes over the Internet

3. Using the techniques described in this chapter, write a memo explaining how to perform your job (or a job you've had) for an employee who will be replacing you while you are on vacation. Write two versions of this memo: Write one to a temporary employee hired through a temporary job agency and write a second to an employee who works in your department but not in the same job. (See Chapter 9 for memo-format examples.)

4. Write a memo to your manager asking for tuition reimbursement to attend this or another course. Assume that the memo will be sent elsewhere for further approval. Use the course and text descriptions and the syllabus to prepare your memo. This memo will be most successful if you help your audience see the value of this course. You may wish to attach supporting material (within reason). (See Chapter 9 for memo-format examples.)

5. Using the list of topics in Exercise 2, select a product or service and write a complaint letter about a problem you, the consumer, have had with this product. Before writing, consider the purpose of your letter, the exact nature of your complaint, the audience you are addressing, and what you want the company to do about the problem or what you think the resolution to the problem should be. Bring your letter to class.

6. Keeping in mind this chapter's discussion of clarifying your purpose before writing, list five specific features a company or other employer would need to have to make you interested in working for them. Next, list what you would want to gain from your work experience.

7. Your boss has asked you to report on the in-house food-service vendors that your company uses. Because you do not have enough information to begin your assignment, create a list of questions to ask your boss to clarify your assignment. Include details about purpose and priorities.

■ Collaborative Classroom Projects

1. Discuss similarities and differences between writing for the audience in Exercise 3 and writing for the audience in Exercise 4.

2. Discuss similarities and differences between writing on the job and writing in the classroom.

3. Divide into groups of four to six students. For 20 to 25 minutes, brainstorm and develop a list of problems that make studying on campus difficult. Then take 15 minutes to revise the list into two versions: (1) a list for the Dean's office committee whose assignment it is to make studying on campus easier and (2) a list for the residence-hall planning committee in charge of designing a new dormitory on campus. Discuss how the different purposes and audiences affected your lists.

4. In small groups, choose and recommend a recreational activity for an end-of-semester celebration with an activity or theme that will please the majority of your classmates. After 20 minutes, a spokesperson from each group will present each group's ideas. Discuss the ideas generated by all the groups and, if desired, select the best one.

5. Exchange your complaint letter from Exercise 5 with that of another student. Using the ideas listed in the chapter summary, evaluate your classmate's letter. Comment on your classmate's letter, detailing what makes the letter successful or what could be done to improve the letter.

6. Revise your complaint letter from Exercise 5, based on your exchange in Collaborative Classroom Project 5. Exchange letters with a different classmate and write a reply to his or her complaint letter as if you were the person receiving the complaint.

■ Research Projects

1. Find an article on a subject of interest to you in two different types of publications—for example, a newspaper and a newsmagazine, a magazine such as *Discover* and a technical journal. After you have read the two articles, do the following:

   a. Identify the target audience of each article. Compare the approaches taken in each article toward the intended audience. Look specifically for indicators of the audience's knowledge of the subject, such as the presence or absence of technical terms and the kind and number of illustrations used.

   b. Create statements of purpose for each article, as if you had been the writer.

   c. Discuss how well the writers met the needs of their audiences. (Respond only after you have completed a and b.)

2. Using the pattern described in Exercises 1 and 2, prepare a five- to seven-page double-spaced proposal recommending a recycling program for a specific facility within your college or place of work. Estimate the volume of the wastepaper, glass, cans, and plastic generated annually at that location, the potential environmental impact, and the steps necessary to implement the program to recycle this waste.

3. Find someone in a position that you imagine holding five years from today and interview that person about the amount and type of writing he or she does on the

job. Then write a memo to your instructor describing what you learned. (*Note:* Before you begin, read the section on interviewing in Chapter 7, Researching Your Subject.)

4. Choose a topic of interest to you—related to the workplace—as the subject for a research paper. Establish your audience and purpose, and refer to Considering Audience and Purpose on page 7. Get instructor approval before you start. Interview experts as part of your research and use at least three different types of sources for your information (journal articles, books, newspapers, etc.) and document all information appropriately (see Chapter 7 for models for documenting works cited).

5. Write a five- to seven-page research paper about the company that you think you would like to work for. (You can use your research from Web Project 3 and your memo from Web Project 4 as the basis of your paper.) Gather and analyze materials about the company you've chosen—from interviews and at least three print sources. Explain your reasons for wanting to work for this company, documenting all sources appropriately.

Web Projects

1. Suppose that the company you work for provides a paid week's vacation package as a reward to the Employee of the Year and his or her immediate family. Your boss has asked you to select this year's vacation package at a location that has educational value. You have a budget of $4,000. Using the Web, compare and contrast different vacation packages and then outline your reasons for your recommendation. Keep the Writer's Checklist on page 5 and Considering Audience and Purpose on page 7 in mind as you write a concise memo to your boss.

2. Once you have selected the vacation package in Web Project 1, research the Web to find out as much as you can about the location you have chosen. Your purpose is to help the winner learn about the place he or she will be visiting. Make a list of the Web sites referenced and provide a brief description (no more than two or three sentences) of each site's content and include its Web address. Your description should make clear why these particular sites are helpful.

3. Select a topic from the list provided in Exercise 2 (or choose your own) and think of a product that specifically relates to your topic. (For example, if you choose the topic of personal computers, a related product could be a particular brand of personal computer.) Your goal is to write an advertisement about that product. Using the Web, find as much product information as you can and build a list of as many different features of the product as possible (for example, some features of a particular brand of personal computer might include memory capacity and the software it comes with). Use at least four different sites and note the Web address (URL) of each, keeping track of what information came from each site.

4. Search the Web to identify three companies that you would like to work for. In a one-page, single-spaced memo to your instructor, explain why you chose these companies and make a persuasive case for the employer that you view as the best match for you. Detail why that employer is more attractive than the others. When preparing your memo, keep in mind the Chapter 1 Summary, on page 20, and the components that you listed in Exercise 6

2 Organizing Your Information

When a motion picture is being filmed, the scenes are usually shot out of the sequence in which they will eventually appear. Different shooting locations, actors' schedules, weather conditions, and many other circumstances make shooting out of sequence necessary. If it were not for a skilled film editor, the completed film would be a jumble of randomly shot scenes. The film editor, following the script, carefully splices the film together so that the story moves smoothly and logically from one event to the next, as the screenwriter and director planned. Without a plan, no such order would be possible: The editor would have no guide for organizing the thousands of feet of film.

Organizing a movie and organizing a written document are obviously different tasks, but they have one element in common—both must be planned ahead of time. For a film, planning means creating a script. For a written document, it means organizing the information into a sequence appropriate to the subject, the purpose, and the audience.

■ Outlining

Organizing your information before you write has two important advantages. First, it forces you to reexamine the information you plan to include to be sure that you have sufficient facts and details to satisfy your audience's needs and achieve the purpose of your writing. Second, it forces you to order the information logically, so that your audience understands it as clearly as you do.

The importance of these advantages emerged from a study of the writing habits that separated good from poor writers in a corporate setting. According to the researcher, more than three times the number of good writers as compared with poor writers use a written outline. Whereas none of the good writers denied using an outline or plan for their reports, 36 percent of the poor writers said they never use an outline or plan, either written or mental.[1]

W On the Web
For online resources for outlining, go to Chapter 2, bedfordstmartins.com/writingthatworks

---

[1]Christine Barabas, *Technical Writing in a Corporate Culture: A Study of the Nature of Information* (Norwood, N.J.: Ablex Publishing Corp., 1990), p. 188. "Good" and "poor" writers were so classified by their readers within the corporation.

Voices from the Workplace

Steve Bramlage, Vectren Energy of Ohio

Steve Bramlage is Director of Energy Delivery for Vectren Energy Delivery of Ohio, a Midwest gas and electric utility serving a three-state area. He is responsible for the delivery of natural gas to 500,000 customers in eastern Indiana and west-central Ohio. In this effort he is accountable for 400 employees and the management of over $35 million of capital and operating budget. Because the energy-delivery business is so closely governed, Steve must be sure that daily operations meet state and federal regulations.

The scope of Steve's job and the many demands on his time require him to be extremely organized, especially when he approaches writing. Because Steve does not have time to work through several drafts, he decides what he wants to say *before* he sits down to write. "If you don't organize your thoughts before you hit the keyboard," he says, "you're sure to end up writing several drafts instead of getting it right the first time. In today's business world you can't afford inefficiency in communication. There just isn't time."

Adam Thompson, the *Denver Post*

Adam Thompson is a sportswriter for the *Denver Post*. As a journalist, Adam must think about how to organize the information in his news stories to attract and hold his readers' attention. Adam carefully considers his method of organization; as he says, "a good news story keeps you until the final period."

Journalists often use the Inverse Pyramid theory. "This school of writing, commonly applied in straight Associated Press stories, says that the most important information should go up top, with the rest of the facts placed in descending order of importance." As an alternative, Adam prefers what he refers to as the bread-crumb theory. "I start off with a strong hook. From there, I like to leave a trail of information — or crumbs — doling out my good bits a little at a time throughout the piece to keep the reader biting.

"As you go from highlight to highlight, try to use transition sentences that connect one to the next. It creates a much smoother flow. Save a zinger for the end — to reward the readers or listeners who stayed with you. You want to guide your readers, taking them down the path of your choice — it takes conscious effort to keep your readers interested. Some careful thought about how you place your points takes little time and can make all the difference in the world."

Read the *Denver Post* online at <denverpost.com>.

Not every piece of writing benefits from a full-scale outline, of course. For relatively short items, such as memos and letters, you may need only to jot down a few notes to make sure that you haven't left out any important information and that you have arranged the information in a logical order. These notes then guide you as you write the draft. For example, note how Christine Thomas organized her ideas for the memo to Harriet Sullivan in Chapter 1 (see Figure 1–4).

Longer documents generally require more elaborate planning, such as a formal outline. In addition to guiding your first draft, the outline can be circulated for review by your colleagues and superiors. They can easily see in the outline the scope of information you plan to include and the sequence in which it is organized. Their reviews can help you find and fix major problems before you've committed a great deal of time to writing your draft. Any outline, including one you circulate, is tentative and represents your best thinking at that point. It need not be labored over for page after page so that it becomes virtually an end in itself. This chapter introduces conventions for creating simple and complex outlines and provides techniques for verifying that your outline is sound.

Roman Numeral Outline

The most common type of outline emphasizes topics and subtopics by means of Roman numerals, letters, and Arabic numbers in the following sequence of subdivisions:

I. Major section
   A. First-level subsection
      1. Second-level subsection
         a. Third-level subsection
            1) Fourth-level subsection

Creating a Roman numeral outline permits you to recognize at a glance the relative importance of topics and subtopics within your subject. Your subject will seldom require four subdivisions, but dividing it this way allows for a highly detailed outline if one is necessary. Stop at the level at which you can no longer subdivide into two items. For every Roman numeral *I*, you should have at least a Roman numeral *II*. For every *A*, you should have at least a *B*, and so on.

When you are ready to write, you should know your topic well enough to be able to identify its major sections. Begin your outline by writing them down. Then consider them carefully to make sure that they represent the logical divisions of the subject. For example, assume that you are writing an article about the development of the Internet for a company magazine. You might start with the following major sections.

I. History of the Internet
II. Growth of Internet technology and future societal issues for the Internet

After a moment's reflection, you decide that the first-level heading is actually the overall topic of the article. After reviewing your research notes you realize that the topic of the first section should be the background and developments that led to Internet technology, so you revise the outline accordingly.

I. Background of Internet technology
II. Growth of Internet technology and future societal issues for the Internet

You quickly decide, however, that you have put too many topics in your second major section, so you make another effort.

    I. Background of Internet technology
   II. Growth of Internet technology
  III. Future societal issues for the Internet

Now you are satisfied that you have appropriately identified the major sections for your topic.

Once you have established your major sections, look for minor divisions within each section. For example, you might first arrive at the following minor divisions within your major sections.

    I. Background of Internet technology
      A. Pioneers
      B. Later developments
   II. Growth of Internet technology
      A. Network technology
      B. Improvements in network technology
  III. Future societal issues for the Internet
      A. E-commerce and intellectual stakeholders
      B. Domain space
      C. "Digital divide"
      D. Privacy issues

This outline is a start, but it is weak. The second-level divisions are too vague to be useful. After considering these weaknesses, you might produce the following revision:

    I. Background of Internet technology
      A. Pioneering communications technology
      B. Development and evolution of network technology
   II. Growth of Internet technology
      A. Competing network techniques and protocols throughout the mid-1970s and early 1980s
      B. Improvements and standardization of techniques and protocols with increased users in the mid-1980s
      C. Transition from a community of scholars, scientists, and defense contractors to widespread infrastructure in the late 1980s and early 1990s
      D. Expansion of Internet in business, academic, and government institutions from late 1990s and beyond.
  III. Future societal issues for the Internet
      A. E-commerce and intellectual stakeholders to drive evolution and innovation
      B. Contending stakeholders to vie for control of domain space
      C. Protection of privacy to continue as a challenge
      D. "Digital divide" between developed and developing worlds to narrow

Now you are ready to insert any information that you compiled during your research under the appropriate major and minor divisions, as shown in Figure 2–1. When you have finished, you have a complete outline. However, although the outline looks final at this point, you still may need to revise it. Make sure that corresponding divisions present material of equal importance (i.e., that major divisions are equal to one another and minor divisions are equal to one another in importance).

NOT

II. Growth of Internet technology
    A. Competing network techniques and protocols throughout the mid-1970s and early 1980s
    B. Improvements and standardization of techniques and protocols with increased users in the mid-1980s
    C. Transition from a community of scholars, scientists, and defense contractors to widespread infrastructure in the late 1980s and early 1990s
    D. Future societal issues for the Internet

BUT

II. Growth of Internet technology
    A. Competing network techniques and protocols throughout the mid-1970s and early 1980s
    B. Improvements and standardization of techniques and protocols with increased users in the mid-1980s
    C. Transition from a community of scholars, scientists, and defense contractors to a widespread infrastructure in the late 1980s and early 1990s
III. Future societal issues for the Internet

Make sure that every head is divided into at least two parts if it is to be divided at all. Subtopics are typically divided into at least two parts (for every 1 there must be a 2), although doing so may not always be possible.

NOT

    A. Pioneering communications technology
        1. Morse and telegraph, calculating machines, silicon chip, and remote-access computers

BUT

    A. Pioneering communications technology
        1. Morse and telegraph
        2. Calculating machines
        3. Silicon chip
        4. Remote-access computers

Finally, review your outline for completeness, determining whether you need additional information. If you find that your research is not really complete, return to your sources and locate the missing material.

HISTORY OF THE INTERNET

I. Background of Internet technology — *Major topic*
   A. Pioneering communications technology — *First-level subsection*
      1. Morse and telegraph
      2. Calculating machines — *Second-level subsection*
      3. Silicon chip
      4. Remote-access computers
   B. Development and evolution of network technology — *First-level subsection*
      1. Galactic Network envisioned by John Licklider of the Dept. of Defense's DARPA (Defense Advanced Research Projects Agency) in 1962
      2. Packet-switching theories published by Leonard Kleinrock of MIT in 1961
      3. First wide area computer network developed by Lawrence Roberts and Thomas Merrill of MIT in 1965 — *Second-level subsection*
      4. Computer networks, packet-switching networks, and packet networks research presented at 1967 conference by three groups whose research took place without knowledge of each other
         a. MIT
         b. RAND Corp. — *Third-level subsection*
         c. National Physical Laboratory (UK)
      5. Interface Message Processor (IMP) developed by Bolt, Beranek & Newman — *Second-level subsection*
      6. ARPANET created with the connecting of four host computers at UCLA, Stanford Research Institute, UC Santa Barbara, and University of Utah (1969)
         a. Person-to-person communication (e-mail) introduced in 1972
         b. Host-to-host protocols developed in early 1970s
         c. Transmission control protocol/Internet protocol (TCP/IP) developed in 1974
II. Growth of Internet technology — *Major topic*
   A. Competing network techniques and protocols throughout the mid-1970s and early 1980s — *First-level subsection*
   B. Improvements and standardization of techniques and protocols with increased users in the mid-1980s and the early 1990s
      1. TCP/IP adopted as standard protocol in 1984
      2. Domain Name System (DNS) introduced in 1984
      3. U.S. Congress funds national research and infrastructure improvement through High Performance Computing Act — *Second-level subsection*
      4. World Wide Web browser/editor program released to public in 1991, simplifying global information sharing
      5. Mosaic browser created in 1993, making Internet easier to use and graphically richer
   C. Transition from a community of scholars, scientists, and defense contractors to widespread infrastructure in the late 1980s and early 1990s
      1. Governments encourage use of Internet throughout higher education system
         a. JANET serves British universities (1984)
         b. NSFNET serves U.S. universities (1985), eventually becoming the backbone of the Internet

Figure 2–1   Sample Outline (continued)

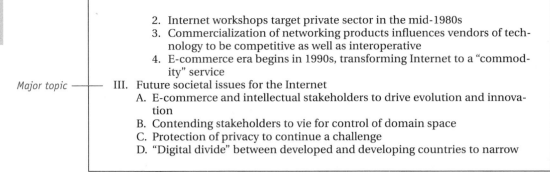

Major topic

2. Internet workshops target private sector in the mid-1980s
3. Commercialization of networking products influences vendors of technology to be competitive as well as interoperative
4. E-commerce era begins in 1990s, transforming Internet to a "commodity" service

III. Future societal issues for the Internet
   A. E-commerce and intellectual stakeholders to drive evolution and innovation
   B. Contending stakeholders to vie for control of domain space
   C. Protection of privacy to continue a challenge
   D. "Digital divide" between developed and developing countries to narrow

Figure 2–1   Sample Outline (continued)

Decimal Numbering System Outline

The sample outlines shown to this point use a combination of numbers and letters to differentiate the various levels of information. Many science and technology authors use a decimal numbering system instead, such as the following, to develop their outlines.

1.   MAJOR IDEA
1.1 Supporting idea for 1
1.2 Supporting idea for 1
1.2.1   Example or illustration of 1.2
1.2.2   Example or illustration of 1.2
1.2.2.1 Detail for 1.2.1
1.2.2.2 Detail for 1.2.1
1.3 Supporting idea for 1
2.   MAJOR IDEA

This system should not go beyond the fourth level because the numbers get too cumbersome past that point. In many technical articles and reports, the decimal numbering system is carried over from the outline to the final version of the document for ease of cross-referencing sections. Typical uses for the decimal outline include procedural manuals, mathematical texts, and scientific and technical material of many kinds. For a discussion of how this system applies to formal reports, see Headings in Chapter 12, beginning on page 436.

Remember that the outline is only a means to an end, not an end in itself. Don't view it as being cast in concrete. Outlines are preliminary by their nature. If you suddenly see a better way to organize your material while you are writing the draft, depart from your outline and follow the better approach. The main purpose of the outline is to bring order and shape to your information before you begin to write the draft.

Creating an Outline

- [ ] Complete your research and know your topic well enough to write about it.
- [ ] Break a large topic into its major divisions and write them down. Does the sequence fit the method of development you have decided to use? (See pages 34–53 for methods of development.) If not, resequence and label the topics with Roman numerals (I, II, III, etc.).
- [ ] Repeat the process for each major topic. Break each into its logical subtopics and list them under each major topic. Then sequence the subtopics to fit your method of development and label them with capital letters (A, B, C, etc.).
- [ ] If necessary, repeat the process for each subtopic, breaking each into its logical sub-subtopics and list them under each subtopic. Sequence them to fit your method of development, and label them with Arabic numbers (1, 2, 3, etc.).
- [ ] Now go to your notes and key each one to the appropriate place in your outline (for example, placing *II-C* beside any note the topic of which fits the portion of your outline labeled *II-C*).
- [ ] Merge your notes and your outline, placing every note under the appropriate head, subhead, or sub-subhead in your outline. Then organize the notes under each head in the most logical sequence.
- [ ] To convert your detailed outline into your first draft, put the first head on your computer screen and expand the notes listed under it into sentences and paragraphs.

■ The Influence of Audience and Purpose

As Christine Thomas learned in Chapter 1, the kinds of information and organization that shape your outline will vary according to your purposes for writing and according to the decisions you make about your audience's needs. Let us say, for example, that a writer needs to prepare two documents about the Lifemaker System, a home gym that combines ten Nautilus machines into a compact weight-and-cable exercise system. The first document will be a sales brochure directed toward potential purchasers of the Lifemaker; the second document will be a maintenance manual written for customers who have already purchased the system.

The two documents share the following aspects of audience and purpose:

1. Both documents will describe the design and structure of the Lifemaker System, although they will do so in different ways and for different reasons. Much of the information gathered and used for brainstorming and outlining will be useful for both the sales brochure and the maintenance manual.

2. The audience for both the brochure and the manual is composed of non-specialists, so both documents should contain a minimum of technical language and should not use terms that would be accessible only to technicians, engineers, and sales representatives.

3. The writer might assume that the readers, whether they are potential or current customers of Lifemaker, will know some things about the design features common to Nautilus-type exercise systems, so descriptions of the exercise equipment for either document need not be too detailed.

However, the documents reflect different purposes in two important ways.

1. Following is a written statement of purpose for the sales brochure:

   ■ My primary purpose for writing is to describe the benefits and features of the Lifemaker System so that my readers will want to purchase it.

   The writer of such a brochure will need to select and organize the information so that it persuades the reader to purchase the system. The brochure's outline, then, should offer more general comments about the design and structural features of the system and specific comments about the benefits of buying it.

2. Following is a written statement of purpose for the maintenance manual:

   ■ My primary purpose for writing is to explain the maintenance of the Lifemaker System so that the customer knows exactly how to put it together and take care of it.

   Because the manual will be directed toward readers who have already purchased the system, the writer will not be concerned with organizing information so that it forms a persuasive argument. Instead, the writer will want to create an outline that will eventually lead to clearly written, step-by-step instructions on how to assemble and maintain the Lifemaker. References to structural features will be very specific and more technical than they would be for the sales brochure. Because the audience is still a nonspecialist one, however, the writer still needs to keep the use of technical terms to a minimum and might refer in the outline to diagrams that will eventually appear in the manual as clarifying illustrations.

The outline for the sales brochure (Figure 2–2) notes specific design details (cast-iron plates, adjustable cables, 4-ft. by 7-ft. size), but the information is organized to support the brochure's persuasive purpose: The Lifemaker is a compact, well-designed, and affordable home gym system. (See Chapters 3 and 4 for drafts and revisions of this sales brochure.)

The purpose of the maintenance manual is to instruct rather than to persuade the audience, so the manual's organization would differ from that used for the brochure. Figure 2–3 is an excerpt from the outline for the maintenance manual. This outline follows a step-by-step organization of information (see pages 34–38), which is an ideal method to use when instruction, rather than persuasion, is the major purpose for writing. In contrast, the outline for the sales brochure uses a general-to-specific sequencing of information (see pages 47–49), which is

LIFEMAKER:
The Compact, Affordable Home Gym

I. General benefits of owning Lifemaker
  A. More compact than other systems
  B. Provides better training programs than other systems
  C. Lower-priced and easier to assemble and maintain than other systems

II. Design benefits/features
  A. Multiple stations so two people can work out at the same time
  B. Takes up minimal space (measures only 4' by 7')
  C. Designed to work all muscle groups (40 different combinations of exercises)

III. Structural benefits/features—weights
  A. Dual weight stacks that total 200 pounds of cast-iron plates
  B. Adjustable weight stacks with resistance range of 10 to 150 pounds
  C. Varied individual weights with resistance adjustable in 5-, 10-, and 15-pound increments

IV. Structural benefits/features—cables
  A. Adjustable cables that increase tension at stations working strongest muscle groups
  B. Reconfigurable weight stacks (cables permit reconfiguring of weights without dismantling entire system)
  C. Reversible tension (cables can increase/decrease tension in mid-set)

V. Financial and maintenance benefits
  A. More reasonably priced than leading system: $999.99
  B. Two-year guarantee for all parts
  C. Easy maintenance (no oiling or solvents necessary)

Organized to compare benefits with other systems

Organized by division of features, according to function in system

Organized to compare benefits with other systems

Figure 2–2   Outline for a Sales Brochure

MAINTAINING YOUR LIFEMAKER

I. Maintenance and troubleshooting
  A. Inspect and safeguard all parts each time you:
    1. Inspect parts for wear
      a. Check cables for fraying
      b. Check weights for cracks
      c. Replace worn parts immediately
    2. Tighten tension on cable #1
      a. Find end of 125" cable (#43 on diagram)
      b. Turn end of cable clockwise
      c. Thread cable farther into weight tube (#35 on diagram)
    3. Tighten tension on cable #2
      a. Find end of 265" cable (#46 on diagram)
      b. Turn end of cable clockwise
      c. Thread cable farther into weight tube (#35 on diagram)
    4. Clean parts
      a. Clean with damp cloth
      b. Use nonabrasive detergent
      c. Use no solvents or oils

Maintenance steps organized sequentially

Figure 2–3   Outline for Instructions in a Maintenance Manual (Excerpt)

more appropriate when the purpose for writing is to persuade the audience with a general argument supported with special details. Thus, although both documents are drawn from the same source and speak to nontechnical audiences, their different purposes call for different methods of organization, as shown by the outlines in Figures 2–2 and 2–3 and the variety of outlines presented in the following section.

DIGITAL SHORTCUTS

Formatting Your Outline

Using the outline feature of your word-processing software permits you to:

- format your outline automatically
- fill in, rearrange, and update your outline
- experiment with the organization and scope of information
- rearrange sections and subsections far more easily on-screen than cutting and taping the paper version
- create Roman numeral or decimal numbering outline styles

■ Methods of Organization

The choice of a method of organization comes naturally for some types of writing. Instructions for how to process an invoice or operate a piece of machinery are arranged step by step. A trip report usually follows a chronological sequence. When a subject does not lend itself to one particular sequence, you can choose the best sequence or combination of sequences by considering your purpose in writing and your audience's needs. Suppose, for example, that you report on a trip to several offset-printing companies to gather information on the most efficient way to arrange equipment to improve workflow through the printing shop where you work. You would probably organize the report of the trip chronologically, but your description of the various shop layouts, emphasizing the physical locations of the equipment, would be organized spatially. If you went on to make recommendations about the most workable arrangement for your shop, you would present the most efficient arrangement first, the second most efficient arrangement next, and so on. Thus the recommendations portion of the report would be organized according to decreasing order of importance.

Table 2–1 lists and describes the most common ways to organize, or sequence, information in on-the-job writing.

Sequential

In the sequential method of organization, you divide your subject into steps and then present the steps in the order in which they occur. This arrangement is the most effective way to describe the operation of a mechanism, such as a digital photocopier, or to explain a process, such as cardiopulmonary resuscitation

Table 2–1   Methods of Organization

Method	Description
Sequential	Consecutive order of steps, not connected to a specific time
Chronological	Sequence of steps or events related to time
Spatial	Description from top to bottom, front to back, etc.
Division and classification	Division into parts and grouping of parts by class
Decreasing order of importance	Order beginning with the most important item and leading to the least important item
Increasing order of importance	Order beginning with the least important item and leading to the most important item
General to specific	Order leading from an overview to a detailed explanation
Specific to general	Order leading from the details of a topic to a broad overview or conclusion
Comparison	Assessment of traits or characteristics of two or more items to determine their relative value

(CPR). Sequencing is also the logical method for writing instructions. For example, the instructions for installing printer software on a desktop computer follow a step-by-step sequence.

■ To install printer software:

1. Make sure that your printer is plugged in and connected to your computer.

2. Turn your computer on.

3. When you see the "New Hardware Found" screen, insert the Printing Software CD-ROM in the CD-ROM drive.

4. The printer's installation software loads automatically, so follow the instructions on the screen.

The greatest advantage of presenting your information in sequential order is that it is easy for your reader to understand and follow the process because the sequence of steps in your writing corresponds to the order of the process being described. Sequential and chronological methods of organization overlap because each describes steps in a process. If you were to write instructions for the proper way to download files from a digital camera for e-mailing, for example, you would present the information in a step-by-step sequence (Figures 2–4 and 2–5).

When you present your information in steps, you must carefully consider the needs of your audience. Do not assume that your readers are as familiar with your subject as you are; if they were, they wouldn't need your instructions. Even for a simple process, be sure that you list all steps and that you explain in adequate detail how each step is performed. Sometimes you must also indicate the purpose or function of each step.

In some instructions or process descriptions, the steps can be presented in one sequence only. For example, the steps for installing printer software must be

OUTLINE:
How to E-mail a Picture from a Digital Camera

1. Transferring photos from camera to computer
   a. Connect camera to computer by plugging the camera cable into the computer port.
   b. Click on Camera icon on desktop to view images stored in the camera.
   c. Decide which photos you want to transfer.
2. Saving photos on computer
   a. Create and name a folder on your hard drive or on your desktop.
   b. Open and view images (as described in step 1).
   c. Select images you wish to save; drag them to the designated folder or save by using imaging software.
   d. Delete images from camera.
   e. Back up images on a zip disk.
3. Modifying photos
   a. Crop, change resolution, or add effects, using imaging software.
   b. Save the edited image by using the Save As or Export command, renaming the image to reflect changes.
4. Attaching photos to an e-mail
   a. Open e-mail box and click on Attachment icon.
   b. Locate designated folder and click on file to be sent.
   c. Before sending, check with recipient about file size restrictions.

Figure 2–4 **Outline for Sequential Instructions**

INSTRUCTIONS:
How to E-mail a Picture from a Digital Camera

Introduction

Most digital cameras come with easy-to-install software that enables you to connect your camera to your computer via a cable, download your photo images, and edit and crop them for output to a printer, for posting to a Web site, or for sending as attachments to your e-mails. The following step-by-step instructions describe how to transfer images from your camera to your computer, save them, and then e-mail the images to your friends, relatives, or business colleagues.

1. How to Transfer Your Photos from the Camera to the Computer

Instructions organized by sequence in which steps must occur

Connect the cable from the camera to your computer at the USB, or serial port, to make the camera serve as its own disk drive. If your digital camera includes a docking station, place the camera in the docking station cradle to automatically connect it to the computer. In most cases, an icon of your camera or a folder for it will appear on your screen after you hook it to your computer. Typically, you can treat this icon or folder like any folder on your computer. Double-click on the icon to open and view the image files stored on your camera.

Figure 2–5 **Sequential Instructions** (continued)

2. How to Save Your Photos on the Computer

To save your images to your computer, create and name a folder on your hard drive. If you're working on an ongoing project that will have many images, include the dates of the images or other useful identifying information. After you create the folder, open and view the images stored on your camera as described in step 1, select the files you wish to save, highlight them, and drag them into the folder you've created on your hard drive. You now have a copy of your images. If you wish to delete the images from your camera, you can do so now. Finally, you can also save the images in software, such as Adobe's PhotoShop™, using the software's File/Open command to select a file directly from your digital camera. Many users prefer, however, to copy the files from the camera directly to their hard drive.

Most digital cameras will default to save images in either GIF or JPEG format. However, if yours does not, then the imaging software that came with the camera should provide a way to save the image in either of these formats.

If your camera also stores images on a floppy or zip disk, or on a memory stick, you can remove them from the camera for use as a backup to your hard drive or delete the images to re-use them for new photos.

3. How to Modify Photos

Use imaging software, such as Adobe's PhotoShop™, to crop your image, to change the resolution, and to add other effects. Once you're done making changes to your image, use the File/Save As command or, in some imaging programs, the File/Export command, to make a copy of the image. At this point you can give the image a more useful name than that which your camera will have given the file because digital cameras typically assign images a number.

4. How to Attach Your Photos to an E-mail Message

To attach the file to an e-mail message, open your outgoing e-mail box and click on the Attachment icon or box. When your file directory opens, select the folder where your photo images are stored, highlight the file you wish to send, and click Open. Your photo file is now attached to your e-mail box. However, before e-mailing an image, check with your recipients to ensure that their e-mail program can accept a file of the size you're sending. Some recipients have mailbox quotas that may not accommodate your image. E-mail attachments are sometimes used to transmit computer viruses, so letting recipients know in advance that you intend to send an image makes them feel more comfortable opening the attachment.

Figure 2–5   Sequential Instructions (continued)

carried out in the sequence in which they are listed. In many other instructions or process descriptions, however, the steps can be presented in the sequence that the writer thinks is most effective. The steps in the process by which a company solicits proposals for new equipment from vendors, for example, may vary in sequence from the steps a company uses to solicit proposals for services.

Chronological

In a chronological sequence, you focus on the order in which the steps or events occur in time, beginning with the first event, going on to the next event, and so on, until you have reached the last event. Trip reports, work schedules, minutes of meetings, recipes, laboratory test procedures, and certain accident reports are among the types of writing in which information may be organized chronologically.

In the outline and memo shown in Figures 2–6 and 2–7, a retail-store manager describes the steps taken over a one-year period to reduce shoplifting at his store.

OUTLINE

I. Task force established
   A. Salespeople, buyers, department managers, executives
   B. Four meetings in January and two in March
II. Mark IV Surveillance System
   A. Installed in April
   B. Includes closed-circuit TV
   C. Helps detect suspicious customer patterns
III. Employee training
   A. Held workshops in May and June
   B. Conducted by Security, Inc.
IV. Other steps
   A. Remodeled some areas to improve merchandise visibility
   B. Hired extra security guards for the holidays

Figure 2–6   Outline for a Chronological Process Description

Spatial

In a spatial sequence, you describe an object or a process according to the physical arrangement of its features. Depending on the subject, you may describe the features from top to bottom, from side to side, from east to west (or west to east), from inside to outside, and so on. Descriptions of this kind rely mainly on dimension (height, width, length), direction (up, down, north, south), shape (rectangular, square, semicircular), and proportion (one-half, two-thirds). Features are described in relation to one another:

■   One end is raised six to eight inches higher than the other end to permit the rain to run off.

Memo

To: Joanna Sanchez, Vice President for Marketing
From: Larry Brown, Manager, Downtown Branch   *LB*
Date: September 9, 2003
Subject: Reducing Shoplifting at the Downtown Store

Over the past year, my staff and I have taken a number of measures to reduce the amount of shoplifting in the downtown store. As you know, we've spent much time, effort, and money on the problem. In preparation for the Christmas shopping season, we have taken the following steps.

January–March 2003: Established Task Force
We formed a task force of salespeople, buyers, managers, and executive staff to recommend ways of curtailing shoplifting and methods of implementing our recommendations. We met four times during January and twice in March to reach our final recommendations. During the meetings . . .

All steps are dated to inform audience of the sequence of events

April 2003: Installed Mark IV Surveillance System
In early spring, we installed a Mark IV System, which uses closed-circuit TV cameras at each exit. The cameras are linked with our security office and are capable of taping signals from all exits simultaneously. The task force felt the Mark IV System might be useful in detecting a pattern of specific individuals entering and leaving the store. This system, which was operational on April 20, has been very helpful in . . .

Clear headings allow readers to see major steps at a glance

May–June 2003: Trained Employees
At the beginning of the summer, we held workshops for employees on detecting shop-lifters. We used the consulting firm of Security, Inc., which provided not only lectures and tips on spotting shoplifters but also demonstrations of common techniques used to divert store personnel. All those who attended the workshops thought they were quite helpful. . . .

July–August 2003: Remodeled Store
Because the task force determined that certain items were particularly vulnerable to shoplifters, we decided in July to restructure some of the display areas. Our purpose was to make these areas less isolated from the view of clerks and other store personnel and thus less vulnerable. The remodeling was completed over the summer months.

September–December 2003: Added Security
For the fall and holiday sales, we have hired extra security guards. These guards, also from Security, Inc., should deter first-time shoplifters . . .

January 2004: Evaluate Methods
We believe the steps we have taken will substantially reduce theft. Of course, after we've reviewed the figures at the end of the year, the task force intends to meet again in January to assess the effectiveness of the methods we have used. If you need more details, please let me know.

Figure 2–7   A Chronological Process Description

Features are also described in relation to their surroundings:

■ The lot is located on the east bank of the Kingman River.

The spatial method of organization is commonly used in descriptions of buildings and laboratory equipment, in proposals for landscape work, in construction-site progress reports, and, in combination with a step-by-step sequence, in many types of instructions.

Figure 2–8 presents an outline and Figure 2–9 a description for a house inspection using a bottom-to-top, clockwise (south to west to north to east) sequence, beginning with the front door.

OUTLINE

    I. Ground floor
       A. Front hall and stairwell
       B. Dining room
       C. Kitchen
       D. Bathroom
       E. Living room
    II. Second floor
       A. Hallway
       B. Southwest bedroom
       C. Northwest bedroom

Figure 2–8   Outline for Spatial Description

Division and Classification

An effective way to organize information about a complex subject is to divide it into manageable parts and then discuss each part separately. You might use this approach, called *division,* to describe a physical object, such as the parts of a fax machine; to examine an organization, such as a company; or to explain the components that make up the Internet global computer network. The emphasis in division is on breaking down a complex whole into a number of like units—because it is easier for an audience to consider smaller units and to examine the relationship of each to the other.

If you were a financial planner describing the types of mutual funds available to your investors, you could divide the variety available into three broad categories: money-market funds, bond funds, and stock funds. Although this division is accurate, it is only a first-level grouping of a complex whole. These three can, in turn, be subdivided into additional groups based on investment strategy. The second-level grouping could lead to the following categories:

Money-Market Funds
• taxable money-market funds
• tax-exempt money-market funds

Bond Funds
- taxable bond funds
- tax-exempt bond funds
- balanced funds — mix of stocks and bonds

Stock Funds
- balanced funds — mix of stocks and bonds
- equity-income funds
- growth and income funds
- domestic growth funds
- small capitalization funds
- specialized funds

DESCRIPTION:

Interior of Two-Story, Six-Room House

Ground Floor

Front hall and stairwell. The front door faces south and opens into a hallway seven feet deep and ten feet wide. At the end of the hallway is a stairwell that begins on the right-hand (east) side of the hallway, rises five steps to a landing, and reverses direction at the left-hand (west) side of the hallway.

Dining room. To the left (west) of the hallway is the dining room, which measures 15 feet along its southern exposure and ten feet along its western exposure.

Kitchen. North of the dining room is the kitchen, which measures ten feet along its western exposure and 15 feet along its northern exposure.

Bathroom. East of the kitchen, along the northern side of the house, is a bathroom that measures ten feet (west to east) by five feet.

Living room. Parallel to the bathroom is a passageway the same size as the bathroom and leading from the kitchen to the living room. The living room (15 feet west to east by 20 feet north to south) occupies the entire eastern end of the floor.

Second Floor

Hallway. On the second floor, at the top of the stairs, is an L-shaped hallway, five feet wide. The base of the L, over the door, is 15 feet long. The vertical arm of the L is 13 feet long.

Southwest bedroom. To the west of the hall is the southwest bedroom, which measures ten feet along its southern exposure and eight feet along its western exposure.

Northwest bedroom. Directly to the north, over the kitchen, is the northwest bedroom, which measures 12 feet along its western exposure and ten feet along its northern exposure.

Figure 2–9   Spatial Description

Specialized funds can be further subdivided as follows:

Specialized Funds
- communications
- energy
- financial services
- technology
- environmental services
- gold
- worldwide capital goods
- health services
- utilities

After you have divided the variety of mutual funds into accurate categories, you could classify them by their degree of relative risk to investors. To do so, you would reorganize your original categories based on the criterion of risk. Depending on how risk is defined, this classification might look as follows:

Low-Risk Funds
- taxable money-market funds
- tax-exempt money-market funds

Low- to Moderate-Risk Funds
- taxable bond funds
- tax-exempt bond funds
- balanced funds
- equity-income funds
- growth and income funds

High-Risk Funds
- domestic growth stock funds
- international growth stock funds
- aggressive growth funds
- small capitalization funds

High- to Very High-Risk Funds
- specialized stock funds

The process by which a subject is classified is similar to the process by which a subject is divided. While division is the separation of a whole into its parts (such as a piece of equipment, a company's organization, the U.S. budget), *classification* is the grouping of a number of units into related categories (such as the population of New York City, allergens affecting people in Hawaii, types of virus-checking software for desktop computers).

When dividing or classifying a subject, you must observe some basic rules of logic. First, divide the subject into its largest number of equal units. The basis for division depends, of course, on your subject and your purpose. If you are describing the *structure* of a four-cycle combustion engine, for example, you might begin by dividing the subject into its major parts—the pistons, the crankshaft, and the housing that contains them. If a more detailed explanation were needed, each of these parts, in turn, might be subdivided into its components. A discussion of the *function* of the same engine, however, would require a different logical basis for the division; such a breakdown would focus on the way combustion engines operate: (1) intake, (2) compression, (3) combustion and expansion, and (4) exhaust.

Once you have established the basis for the division, you must apply and express it consistently. Put each item in only one category so that items do not overlap categories. An examination of the structure of the combustion engine that listed the battery as a major part would be illogical. Although it is part a vehicle's ignition system (which starts the engine), the battery is not a part of the engine itself. A discussion of the parts of the ignition system in which the battery is not mentioned would be just as illogical.

An outline provides a clear expression of classification and is especially useful in preparing a breakdown of any subject at several levels. In the following example, two Canadian park rangers classify typical park users according to four categories; the rangers then discuss how to deal with potential rule-breaking by members of each group. The rangers could have classified the visitors in a variety of other ways, of course: as city and country residents, backpackers and drivers of recreational vehicles, U.S. and Canadian citizens, and so on. However, for law-enforcement agents in public parklands, the size of a group and the relationships among its members were the most significant factors (Figures 2–10 and 2–11).

OUTLINE

I. Types of campers
   A. Family groups
   B. Small groups
   C. Large groups
   D. Hostile groups
II. Dealing with groups of campers
   A. Groups A and B
     1. One on one
     2. Courses of action
   B. Groups C and D
     1. Large groups
        a. Make the leader responsible
        b. Course of action
     2. Hostile groups
        a. Make the leader responsible (once determined)
        b. Course of action

Figure 2–10   Outline for Division and Classification

Memo

To: All Employees
From: Canadian National Park Service, Office of Rangers
Date: June 15, 2003
Subject: Dealing with Campers in Violation of National Park Rules

To respond to campers breaking National Park Rules and Codes for Safety and Conduct, first, recognize the various types of campers. They can be categorized as follows:

A. Family groups
B. Small groups (up to six well-acquainted members)
C. Large groups or conventions (organized, but not always well-acquainted)
D. Hostile groups (may not have an evident leader)

Groups divided into major categories

Groups A & B
Persons in groups A and B can often be dealt with on a one-on-one basis. For example, suppose a member of the group is picking wildflowers, which is an offense in most of our park areas. Two courses of action are open. You could either issue a warning or charge the person with the offense. In this situation, a warning is preferable to a charge. First, advise the person that this action is an offense, but, more important, explain why. Point out that the flowers are for all to enjoy and that most wildflowers are delicate and die quickly when picked.

Each group is then classified according to specific criteria

Group C
For large groups, other approaches may be necessary. Every group has a leader. For a large group or convention, find out who the event organizer is (this is likely to be the person who reserved the campsite). Hold the group's leader responsible for the group's behavior and take action—issue a warning or charge the leader with the offense—according to the guidelines of the National Park Rules and Codes for Safety and Conduct.

Group D
For hostile groups without an obvious leader, observe the group's behavior to learn which person(s) assumes control of the group's actions, and try to deal with that person. Ultimately, it is best to regain control over a group through one or two individuals within the group. In a potentially hostile environment, always request backup of at least one other ranger on duty. Issue a warning or charge the leader or the group with the offense according to the guidelines of the National Park Rules and Codes for Safety and Conduct. If necessary, eject the group from the premises, as outlined in the Codes.

Figure 2–11   Division and Classification

Decreasing Order of Importance

When you organize your information in decreasing order of importance, you begin with the most important fact or point, then go on to the next most important, and so on, ending with the least important. Newspaper audiences are familiar with this sequence of information. The most significant information usually appears first in a news story, with related but secondary information completing the story. Minor details go last, where they may be cut to accommodate a last-minute need for column space.

Decreasing order of importance is an especially appropriate method of organization for a report addressed to a busy decision-maker, who may be able to reach a decision after considering only the most important points — and who may not even have time to read the entire report. This sequence of information is useful, too, for a report written for a variety of audiences, some of whom may be interested in only the major points and others in all the points. The outline and memo shown in Figures 2–12 and 2–13, respectively, present an example of such an approach.

OUTLINE

I. Most-qualified candidate: April Jackson, Acting Chief
    A. Positive factors
        1. Twelve years' experience in claims processing
        2. Thoroughly familiar with section's operations
        3. Strong production record
        4. Continually ranked "outstanding" on job appraisals
    B. Negative factors
        1. Supervisory experience limited to present tenure as Acting Chief
        2. Lacks college degree required by job description
II. Second-most-qualified candidate: Michael Bastick, Claims Coordinator
    A. Positive factors
        1. Able administrator
        2. Seven years' experience in section's operations
        3. Currently enrolled in management-training course
    B. Negative factors
        1. Lacks supervisory experience
        2. Most recent work indirectly related to claims processing
III. Third-most-qualified candidate: Jane Fine, Administrative Assistant
    A. Positive factors
        1. Skilled administrator
        2. Three years' experience in claims processing
    B. Negative factors
        1. Lacks broad knowledge of claims procedures
        2. Lacks supervisory experience

Figure 2–12 Outline for a Memo Organized by Decreasing Order of Importance

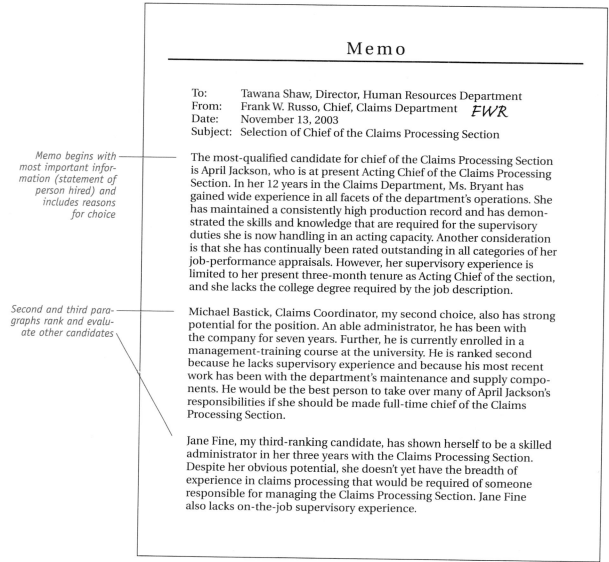

Memo

To: Tawana Shaw, Director, Human Resources Department
From: Frank W. Russo, Chief, Claims Department *FWR*
Date: November 13, 2003
Subject: Selection of Chief of the Claims Processing Section

Memo begins with most important information (statement of person hired) and includes reasons for choice

The most-qualified candidate for chief of the Claims Processing Section is April Jackson, who is at present Acting Chief of the Claims Processing Section. In her 12 years in the Claims Department, Ms. Bryant has gained wide experience in all facets of the department's operations. She has maintained a consistently high production record and has demonstrated the skills and knowledge that are required for the supervisory duties she is now handling in an acting capacity. Another consideration is that she has continually been rated outstanding in all categories of her job-performance appraisals. However, her supervisory experience is limited to her present three-month tenure as Acting Chief of the section, and she lacks the college degree required by the job description.

Second and third paragraphs rank and evaluate other candidates

Michael Bastick, Claims Coordinator, my second choice, also has strong potential for the position. An able administrator, he has been with the company for seven years. Further, he is currently enrolled in a management-training course at the university. He is ranked second because he lacks supervisory experience and because his most recent work has been with the department's maintenance and supply components. He would be the best person to take over many of April Jackson's responsibilities if she should be made full-time chief of the Claims Processing Section.

Jane Fine, my third-ranking candidate, has shown herself to be a skilled administrator in her three years with the Claims Processing Section. Despite her obvious potential, she doesn't yet have the breadth of experience in claims processing that would be required of someone responsible for managing the Claims Processing Section. Jane Fine also lacks on-the-job supervisory experience.

Figure 2–13   Memo Organized by Decreasing Order of Importance

Increasing Order of Importance

When you want the most important of several ideas to be freshest in your readers' minds at the end of your writing, organize your information by increasing order of importance. This sequence is useful in argumentative or persuasive writing when you wish to save your strongest points until the end. The sequence begins with the least important point or fact, then moves to the next least important, and builds finally to the most important point at the end. You build your case inductively (reasoning from the particular to the general).

Writing organized by increasing order of importance has the disadvantage of beginning weakly, with the least important information. Your readers may become impatient or distracted before reaching your main point. However, for writing in which the ideas lead, point by point, to an important conclusion, increasing order of importance is an effective method of organization. Reports on production or personnel goals are often arranged by this method, as are oral presentations. Figures 2–14 and 2–15 present an outline and a memo, respectively, that show the use of increasing order of importance as a method of organization.

General to Specific

In a general-to-specific sequence, you begin your writing with a general statement and then provide facts or examples to develop and support that statement. For example, if you begin a report with the general statement "Companies that diversify their products or services are more successful than those that do not," the remainder of the report would offer examples and statistics that prove to your reader that companies that diversify are, in fact, more successful than companies that do not.

A memo or report organized in a general-to-specific sequence discusses only one point. All other information in the memo or report supports the general statement (Figures 2–16 and 2–17). Examples and data that support the general statements are frequently accompanied by charts and graphs providing data to support your general point. Guidelines for creating and presenting illustrations are given in Chapter 8.

OUTLINE

    I. Staffing problem
        A. Too few qualified electronics technicians
        B. New recruiting program necessary
    II. Apprentice program
        A. Providing insufficient numbers
        B. Enlistment bonuses tempting the high school graduates into the military services
    III. Technical school
        A. Enrollment at area and regional technical schools up, but fewer students studying electronics
        B. Keen competition from the military services for high school graduates
    IV. Military veterans
        A. Relied heavily on veterans in the past
        B. Military reenlistment bonuses have all but removed this source
    V. Strategy to compete with the military services

Figure 2–14 Outline for Information Organized by Increasing Order of Importance

> # Memo
>
> To: Phillip Ting, Vice President, Operations
> From: Harry Mathews, Human Resources Department *HM*
> Date: May 19, 2003
> Subject: Recruiting Qualified Electronics Technicians
>
> As our company continues to expand, and with the planned opening of the Lakeland Facility late next year, we need to increase and refocus our recruiting program to keep our company staffed with qualified electronics technicians. In the past five years, we have relied on our in-house apprentice program and on local and regional technical schools to fill our needs.
>
> Although our in-house apprentice program provided a qualified pool of employees in the past, military enlistment bonuses are tempting graduating high school seniors to join a branch of the military services rather than join our apprentice program or attend the technical schools. This is particularly tempting to graduating high school students because the military services often send them to a technical school free of charge while they are in the service. Even our most vigorous Career Day recruiting at the high schools has yielded disappointing results.
>
> We have also in the past relied on recruiting skilled veterans from all branches of the military services. With the military now offering very attractive reenlistment bonuses, however, this source of technicians has all but disappeared.
>
> I would like to meet with you soon to devise a strategy for competing with the military services' enlistment and reenlistment bonuses.

The point-by-point description of the dilemma leads the reader to the urgency of the conclusion

Final paragraph states the memo's most important message

Figure 2–15   Memo Organized by Increasing Order of Importance

---

OUTLINE

The company needs to locate additional suppliers of computer chips because of several related events.

   I. The current supplier is reducing output.
  II. Domestic demand for our laptop computers continues to increase.
 III. We are expanding into the international market.

Figure 2–16   Outline for Information Organized from General to Specific (Excerpt)

LOCATING COMPUTER-CHIP SUPPLIERS

On the basis of information presented at the supply meeting on April 14, we recommend that the company locate additional suppliers of computer chips. Several related events make such an action necessary.

Our current supplier, ABC Electronics, is reducing its output. Specifically, we can expect a reduction of between 800 and 1,000 units per month for the remainder of this fiscal year. The number of units should stabilize at 15,000 units per month thereafter.

Domestic demand for our computers continues to grow. Demand during the current fiscal year is up 25,000 units over the last fiscal year. Sales Department projections for the next five years show that demand should peak next year at 50,000 units and then remain at that figure for at least the following four years.

Finally, our expansion into England and Germany will require additional shipments of 5,000 units per quarter to each country for the remainder of this fiscal year. Sales Department projections put computer sales for each country at double this rate, or 40,000 units in a fiscal year, for the next five years.

General statement

Supporting information includes specific details

Figure 2–17   Document Organized from General to Specific (Excerpt)

Specific to General

When you organize information in a specific-to-general sequence, you begin with specific information and build to a general conclusion. The examples, facts, and statistics that you present in your writing support the general conclusion that comes at the end. For example, if your subject were highway safety, you might begin with details of a specific highway accident, go on to generalize about how that accident was similar to many others, and then present recommendations for reducing the probability of such accidents. If your purpose is to persuade a skeptical audience by providing specific details, this method is useful because it suspends the general point until your case has been made. This method of organization is somewhat like increasing order of importance in that you carefully build your case and reach your conclusion at the end, as shown in Figures 2–18 and 2–19.

Comparison

When you use comparison as a method of development, you evaluate the relative merits of the items you are considering. Comparison works well in determining which of two or more items is most suitable for some specific purpose, such as selecting the best product, determining the least-expensive messenger service for your company, or finding the most-qualified job applicant for your job opening.

OUTLINE

   I. Study of 4,500 accidents involving nearly 7,200 adult front-seat passengers showed only 20 percent of the vehicles equipped with passenger-side air bags

  II. Study shows adult front-seat passengers in vehicles without air bags twice as likely to be killed as those in vehicles with air bags

     A. Children riding as front-seat passengers can be killed by deployment of air bags

     B. Children should ride in backseat

  III. Estimated 40 percent of adult front-seat passenger vehicle deaths could be prevented if passenger-side air bags were installed

  IV. Survival chances for adults in an accident greater with passenger-side air bags

Figure 2–18   Outline for Information Organized from Specific to General

To be sure that your choice will be the best one, you must determine the basis (or bases) for making your comparison. For example, if you were comparing bids from among contractors for a remodeling project at your company, you most likely would compare such factors as price, availability, projected schedule, previous experience, personnel qualifications, and professional references, as shown in Table 2–2.

Once you decide on the bases important to your comparison, you can determine the most effective way to structure your comparison: whole by whole or part

FACTS ABOUT AIR BAGS

Statistical details build the case for the final paragraph

Recently, a government agency studied the use of passenger-side air bags in 4,500 accidents involving nearly 7,200 front-seat passengers of the vehicles involved. Nearly all these accidents occurred on routes that had a speed limit of at least 40 mph. Only 20 percent of the adult front-seat passengers were riding in vehicles equipped with passenger-side air bags. Those not riding in vehicles equipped with passenger-side air bags were more than twice as likely to be killed as passengers riding in vehicles that were so equipped.

General conclusion

A conservative estimate is that 40 percent of the adult front-seat passenger vehicle deaths could be prevented if all vehicles came equipped with passenger-side air bags. Children, however, should always ride in the backseat because other studies have indicated that a child can be killed by the deployment of an air bag. If you are an adult front-seat passenger in an accident, your chances of survival are far greater if the vehicle in which you are riding is equipped with a passenger-side air bag.

Figure 2–19   Document Organized from Specific to General (Excerpt)

Table 2–2   Tabular Layout for a Comparison

Comparison of Contractors Being Considered for Remodeling Project

Contractor	Price	Projected Schedule and Completion Date	Personnel Qualifications	References
A	_____	_____	_____	_____
B	_____	_____	_____	_____
C	_____	_____	_____	_____
D	_____	_____	_____	_____
E	_____	_____	_____	_____

by part. In the whole-by-whole method, all the relevant characteristics of one item are discussed before those of the next item are considered. In the part-by-part method, the relevant features of each item are compared one by one. The outline (Figure 2–20) and discussion (Figure 2–21) of typical woodworking glues, organized according to the whole-by-whole method, describe each type of glue and its characteristics before going on to the next type.

As is often the case when the whole-by-whole method is used, the purpose of this comparison is to weigh the advantages and disadvantages of each glue for certain kinds of woodworking. The comparison of woodworking adhesives first

---

OUTLINE

    I. White glue
        A. Best for light construction
        B. Weakened by high temperature, moisture, and stress
        C. Takes about 30 minutes to set
    II. Aliphatic resin glue
        A. Strong and resistant to moisture
        B. Used at temperatures above 50°F
        C. Takes about 30 minutes to set
    III. Plastic resin glue
        A. Strongest of the common wood adhesives
        B. Moisture resistant
        C. Sold in powder form—must be mixed with water
        D. Used in temperatures above 70°F
        E. Takes four to six hours to set
    IV. Contact cement
        A. Very strong
        B. Bonds very quickly
        C. Ideal for mounting plastic on wood
        D. Most brands are flammable
        E. Fumes can be harmful if inhaled

Figure 2–20   Sample Outline for a Comparison: Whole-by-Whole Method

Type of glue being compared

COMMON WOODWORKING ADHESIVES

White glue is the most useful all-purpose adhesive for light construction, but it should not be used on projects that will be exposed to moisture, high temperature, or great stress. Wood that is being joined with white glue must remain in a clamp until the glue dries, which will take about 30 minutes.

Aliphatic resin glue has a stronger and more moisture-resistant bond than white glue. It must be used at temperatures above 50 degrees Fahrenheit. The wood should be clamped for about 30 minutes.

Plastic resin glue is the strongest of the common wood adhesives. It is highly moisture resistant—although not completely waterproof. Sold in powdered form, this glue must be mixed with water and used at temperatures above 70 degrees Fahrenheit. It is slow setting and the joint should be clamped for four to six hours.

Contact cement is a very strong adhesive that bonds so quickly it must be used with great care. It is ideal for mounting sheets of plastic laminate on wood. It is also useful for attaching strips of veneer to the edges of plywood. Because this adhesive bonds immediately when two pieces are pressed together, clamping is not necessary, but the parts to be joined must be very carefully aligned before being placed together. Check the label before you work with this adhesive. Most brands are quite flammable and the fumes can be harmful if inhaled. For safety, work in a well-ventilated area, away from flames or heat.

Detailed description of characteristics provides basis for comparison

Figure 2–21   Sample Comparison: Whole-by-Whole Method

OUTLINE

Rating adhesives by bonding strength, moisture resistance, and setting times.

  I. Bonding strength
     A. Contact cement and plastic resin glue bond very strongly
     B. Aliphatic resin glue bonds moderately strongly
     C. White glue bonds least effectively
 II. Moisture resistance
     A. Plastic resin glue and contact cement are highly resistant to moisture
     B. Aliphatic resin glue is moderately resistant
     C. White glue is least resistant
III. Setting times
     A. Contact cement dries immediately and requires no clamping
     B. White glue and aliphatic resin glue must be clamped for 30 minutes
     C. Plastic resin glue is strongest and must be clamped for four to six hours

Figure 2–22   Sample Outline for a Comparison: Part-by-Part Method

CHARACTERISTICS OF WOODWORKING ADHESIVES

Woodworking adhesives are rated primarily according to their bonding strength, moisture resistance, and setting times.

Bonding strength is categorized as very strong, moderately strong, or adequate for use with little stress. Contact cement and plastic resin glue bond very strongly, while aliphatic resin glue bonds moderately strongly. White glue provides a bond that is least resistant to stress.

Moisture resistance of woodworking glues is rated as high, moderate, and low. Plastic resin glue is moderately moisture resistant. Aliphatic resin glue is moderately moisture resistant, and white glue is least moisture resistant.

Setting times for these glues vary from an immediate bond to a four- to six-hour bond. Contact cement bonds immediately and requires no clamping. Because the bond is immediate, surfaces being joined must be carefully aligned before being placed together. White glue and aliphatic resin glue set in 30 minutes; both require clamping to secure the bond. Plastic resin, the strongest wood glue, sets in four to six hours and also requires clamping.

Characteristics that distinguish different kinds of glue

Comparison of glue characteristics organized by most effective to least effective

Figure 2–23   Sample Comparison: Part-by-Part Method

focused on the relative strength of the glue, then noted constraints on its use (conditions such as moisture and temperature), and finally discussed clamping.

However, if your purpose were to consider, one at a time, the various characteristics of all the glues, the information might be arranged according to the part-by-part method (Figures 2–22 and 2–23). Note that this method of comparison emphasizes the subdivided part or characteristics rather than the main types. Your emphasis can be further highlighted by syntax (word order) and mechanical highlighting (*italics,* **boldface,** or underlining).

Organizing Information

Organize your writing from the perspective of your audience and purpose. Keep in mind that some types of writing lend themselves logically to only one kind of organization and will best convey information to your reader by that method.

☐ **Sequential** organization takes your reader step by step through the stages of a process in the order in which the process occurs. (Example: instructions in a user's manual)

☐ **Chronological** organization takes your reader step by step through the stages of a process as they occur *in time* from beginning to end. (Example: a trip report)

☐ **Spatial** organization describes physical objects, areas, and phenomena at the level of detail necessary for your reader to envision their appearance or how they occurred. (Example: an incident report)

☐ **Division** is a way of organizing information about a complex whole by breaking it down into smaller units for your reader, making it easier to understand. (Example: a description of the parts of a computer)

☐ **Classification** is a way of organizing information that groups disparate units into categories recognizable to your audience. (Example: a description of different types of vacation packages)

☐ **Decreasing order of importance** introduces your reader to your main or important points at the beginning of your writing, followed by background information that supports your main points. (Example: a news story or formal report for busy readers)

☐ **Increasing order of importance** leads your reader through the thought process and details that support conclusions you reach at the end of your writing. (Example: a persuasive presentation)

☐ **General-to-specific** organization of information introduces your reader to the main or general point you wish to make at the beginning of your writing and leads your reader through the facts and other supporting information that describes how you reached your general point. (Example: a memo or proposal that begins with a recommendation)

☐ **Specific-to-general** sequence leads your reader through the facts and other supporting information you use to build your case for reaching the conclusion you state at the end of your writing. (Example: a report that begins by giving the details of an event)

☐ **Comparison** allows your reader to evaluate the relative strengths of the items that are under evaluation after you establish the basis for the comparison. (Example: a memo that considers a variety of options)

CHAPTER 2 SUMMARY: Organizing Your Information

Before you begin to write, consider the following questions as you organize your information into a logical sequence.

☐ Will I need a brief list or a full-scale outline to organize my information?

☐ Will I need to circulate the outline to colleagues or superiors?

☐ Is the outline divided into parts and subparts that reflect the logical divisions of the topic?

☐ Will my word-processing software structure the outline automatically?

☐ Does the topic lend itself naturally to one of the following methods of development?

  ■ sequential

  ■ chronological

  ■ spatial

  ■ division and classification

  ■ decreasing order of importance

  ■ increasing order of importance

  ■ general to specific

  ■ specific to general

  ■ comparison

☐ Does the topic need to be organized by more than one method of development?

■ Exercises

1. Create an outline for one of the following topics, organizing it sequentially. Using the outline, write a paper of assigned length on the topic.

   • Preparing a household budget
   • Tuning a guitar
   • Setting up a personal computer
   • Applying for a personal loan
   • Finding an apartment to rent
   • Repairing a broken window
   • Maturing of a monarch butterfly egg to an adult
   • Preparing your favorite meal
   • Purchasing a product on the Internet
   • Buying a car

2. Create an outline for one of the following topics, organizing it chronologically. Using the outline, write a paper of assigned length on the topic.

   • Report on an accident
   • Describe the life cycle of a typical fruit, from blossom to ripe fruit
   • Describe the job-search process

- Report on the steps involved in completing a research assignment
- Explain how to build a campfire
- Explain how to perform a specific aspect of a sport or activity

3. Create an outline for one of the following topics, organizing it spatially. Using the outline, write a paper of assigned length on the topic. Without relying on illustrations, describe the topic clearly enough so that a classmate, if asked, could create an accurate drawing or diagram based on your description.

- The layout of your apartment or of a floor in your home (as it is, or as you would like it to be)
- The layout of the reference room or other area of the school library
- The dimensions and pertinent features of a public park or building
- The layout of a garden
- The layout of the shop, office, or laboratory where you work
- Instructions for disinfecting a hospital room or painting or wallpapering a room

4. Create an outline for one of the following topics, organizing it by a decreasing-order-of-importance sequence. Using the outline, write a paper of assigned length on the topic.

- Your job qualifications
- The advantages of living in a particular city or area of the country
- The importance of preventive maintenance of a specific machine or piece of equipment
- The importance of preventive care in one health-related area (diet, exercise, dental care, and so on)
- Your career goal
- The advantages of having your paycheck directly deposited into your account, of having savings automatically deducted from your paycheck, or of using on-line banking
- The advantages of recycling
- The advantages of owning life insurance
- The advantages of carpooling

5. Create an outline for one of the following topics, organizing it by an increasing-order-of-importance sequence. Using the outline, write a paper of assigned length on the topic.

- The three to five college courses most important to your career
- Why smoking should or should not be permitted in restaurants
- The advantages of learning to pilot a small airplane
- The reasons you deserve a pay raise
- The advantages of alternatively fueled vehicles
- A proposal to change a procedure where you work

6. For this exercise, use a general-to-specific sequence. Choose one of the following statements, then support it with pertinent facts, examples, anecdotes, and so on. Outline the information and write a paper of assigned length based on the outline.

- Volunteer jobs and internships provide valuable experience in the working world.
- For families living within limited means, budgeting is essential.
- Capable managers are willing to delegate authority.

- Post–high school education or technical training is essential in today's job market.
- Ongoing computer education is fundamental in today's workplace.
- A sound management training program pays off for companies.

7. For this exercise, use a specific-to-general sequence. Choose one of the following sets of data, study the trends or patterns that are presented, draw your own conclusions, and state the conclusions in a plausible general statement. Outline the information that supports your main point, and write a paper of assigned length based on your outline. Alternatively, you may select other information from lists and tables in current yearbooks, almanacs, or newspapers for this exercise.

- Number of students enrolled in business programs

Year	Number of Students
1992	47,087
1993	45,582
1994	44,599
1995	41,508
1996	39,250
1997	38,150
1998	40,716
1999	41,817
2000	43,065
2001	43,013
2002	44,471

- Apartments completed in the United States in buildings with five or more units

Year	Apartments with 5 or More Units
2002	291,800
2001	273,900
2000	247,100
1999	251,300
1998	212,400
1997	154,900
1996	124,800
1995	155,200
1994	216,500
1993	294,400

8. Create a topic outline for one of the following topics, organizing it by division and classification. Using the outline, write a paper of assigned length on the topic.

- Personal digital assistants (including pocket PCs)
- Conventional and alternative medical therapies
- Weight-loss strategies and programs
- Home exercise equipment
- Bicycles (e.g., racing, mountain)
- Cameras
- Cable TV channels

9. Create a topic outline for one of the following topics, organizing it by the comparison method of development. Using the outline, write a paper of assigned length on the topic.

- The features of two or more word-processing or spreadsheet software programs

- U.S. intellectual property laws (e.g., copyright law, trademark law, and patent law)
- Features of at least five specialized library databases (e.g., InfoTrac, Clearinghouse, Health AtoZ, Thomas Legislative Information, Zip Code Lookup)

10. Revise the following list on the advantages and disadvantages of flexible work schedules, eliminating any unrelated notes or repetition and combining any closely related items.

- Advantageous to working parents
- More satisfied employees
- Workers not always available when needed
- Must have core hours when everyone must be at work
- Starting time from 7:00 a.m. to 10:00 a.m.
- Quit any time from 3:00 p.m. to 6:00 p.m.
- Personal lives easier to schedule
- Carpooling more difficult
- Cafeteria hours would have to be expanded
- Extended workday would increase utility bills
- Time-zone differences across the country become a potential problem
- Morning and afternoon people can take advantage of their best hours
- Daylight saving time
- Day care made easier
- Easier for employees to schedule medical appointments
- Employees can take advantage of daylight hours
- Bus schedules
- Greater efficiency
- Employees can work their most productive hours
- Employees are more productive
- Employees gain more control over their lives
- Could result in decreased control by managers and supervisors
- Could produce healthier employees
- Could result in cheating
- Could decrease or eliminate tardiness

11. Prepare an outline for a report to your boss from the list of notes you created in Exercise 9. Identify the method of organization you used in your outline.

12. Using the outline you created in Exercise 10, write a short report to your department manager recommending that flexible hours be adopted by your department.

13. Identify the method of organization that would be most effective for each of the following topics and explain how consideration of audience and purpose might affect your decision.

- Instructions for performing (CPR) cardiopulmonary resuscitation
- A police report of the results of a stakeout
- A report on the different kinds of programs on prime-time television
- A report on the differences among the major personal computer manufacturers
- Instructions for preparing a five-course meal, including recipes
- A report on the different types of media coverage of a world event
- A report on the results of a governmental election and its importance
- Instructions for buying or selling a house

14. Determine the best method of organizing each of the following topics—sequential, chronological, spatial, division and classification, decreasing order of importance, increasing order of importance, general to specific, specific to general, or comparison. You will use some of the methods more than once and at least one method not at all. It is possible for a topic to fit more than one method. Be prepared to defend your choice.

- Explaining how to register for classes
- Supporting an argument against smoking
- Describing different types of dogs at a dog show
- Determining the job that is right for you
- Explaining how to get the job you want
- Describing the most important room in your house
- Announcing the winners of a contest
- Describing the fire-escape route for a building
- Determining the best computer to buy
- Describing the nine planets in our solar system
- Explaining the changing educational system in your state
- Supporting an argument for environmental-protection laws

■ Collaborative Classroom Projects

Projects followed by the symbol Ⓦ are continued at **bedfordstmartins.com/writingthatworks**, Chapter 2.

1. Following is an example of a poorly developed outline. In small groups and within the allotted time frame, revise this outline, following the guidelines provided in this chapter. Select a spokesperson from your group to present your outline to the class.

Company Sports
   I. Intercompany sports
      A. Advantages to the company
         1. Publicity
         2. Intercompany relations
      B. Disadvantages
         1. Misplaced emphasis
         2. Athletic participation not available to all employees
   II. Intracompany sports
      A. Wide participation
      B. Physical fitness
      C. Detracts from work
      D. Risks injuries

2. In small groups and within the alloted time frame, select the three major heads in column B on the next page and place them in the appropriate sequence in column A. Then do the same for the minor heads. When your group has completed this task, choose a representative to share your outline with the class.

Report on Energy Efficiency of a House, with a Plan for Improvement

Column A	Column B
I. _____	Insulation
A. _____	Introduction
B. _____	Heat loss through conduction (transmission through solid materials)
C. _____	Scope of the report
II. _____	Storm doors and windows
A. _____	The solutions
B. _____	Procedure used to prepare the report
III. _____	Heat loss through air infiltration (transmission through cracks or other openings)
A. _____	The problems
B. _____	Weather stripping
C. _____	Purpose of the report
D. _____	Caulking

3. Rejoin your group (for Activity 2). Use the notes provided at the *Writing That Works* Web site to build more information into your outline. Ⓦ Select another spokesperson to present your revised outline to the class.

4. Bring five common tools to class (a can opener, a pencil sharpener, etc.). In small groups, outline a narrative description of one or more of the tools, keeping in mind the particular function of the tool(s). When finished, exchange papers and critique one another's outlines based on whether the outline effectively describes the tool.

5. In small groups, identify the three greatest barriers facing small businesses in the United States today. Then in 30 minutes (or the allotted time period) create an outline with these three subheadings (go to the third or fourth level as needed). A group spokesperson will briefly present (in three minutes or so) the outline to the class.

▨ Research Projects

1. Locate a government, business, or industry report or an article in a professional journal. Analyze the organization of information in the report or article, and write an outline that mirrors the organization. Develop the outline to the level of detail of the outline shown on page 28, or to the level of detail specified by your instructor. Then assess the report or article for its use of the methods of organization described in this chapter, citing specific sections or paragraphs in which each method is demonstrated. Finally, describe how the organization of the report or article made it easier or more difficult to understand its content.

2. Gather and review all sources, notes, and other research material that you have been collecting for your term project or current writing assignment. Brainstorm for 20 minutes on how to organize the material by writing down as quickly as possible the key points, main ideas, and subtopics that seem most important. Don't stop to evaluate the data; simply write the ideas down as fast as you can. Take a break; then organize the list into a structure that satisfies the logic of the topic,

your audience's needs, and your purpose. In a transmittal memo to your instructor, write down the outline and explain any gaps in it and give an estimate for completion of the remaining stages of the writing project.

3. As the information and marketing person for a small business, you have been asked to help plan your company's first Web site. Decide what your company does or sells and give your company a name. Gather information from at least three print sources about the business, then draft an outline about your company's business and the goods and services it provides. Based on your outline, make a list of what other information consumers would be interested in knowing about your company. (*Note:* This project is continued in Web Projects 3 through 6. Ultimately you will provide your company's graphic designer with an outline and complete information for the site.)

4. Your boss has asked you to interview a successful businessperson of your choice for your company's newsletter. Prepare an outline to use during your 30-minute interview.

5. In 30 to 45 minutes, interview the person you selected for Research Project 4 using your outline as a guide. Then, create a new outline using the information you obtained during the interview.

■ Web Projects

Projects followed by the symbol Ⓦ are continued at **bedfordstmartins.com/ writingthatworks**, Chapter 2.

1. Visit five or more credible Web sites and analyze the variety of ways that information is organized at each site; use specific examples to support your analysis. Write one to three paragraphs that detail the effectiveness or ineffectiveness of how information is presented at each site. Compare the sites. Write another one to three paragraphs explaining how other methods of organization and the use of outlining (as discussed in this chapter) could improve each of these sites.

2. Select a current event or news story that interests you and read about it on at least five well-known news sites on the Web. (You may want to print out the material that you find.) Develop an outline for an essay that would compare and contrast the different perspectives offered by different news sites. What conclusions can you draw about the coverage of this event? Your outline should indicate a clear method of organization. (Be sure to record the URLs of the sites you researched.)

3. Using the outline from Research Project 3, search the Internet to locate at least three Web sites relevant to your company's business — these can include sites run by your competitors (be sure to bookmark these sites for later use). Note the different ways that information is organized at these sites. Is a clear style of organization evident? What style of outline might have been used to create each site? In two or three paragraphs, compare the organization of these sites with the organization you have planned for your company's Web site and detail why the organization that you have planned for your site is appropriate.

4. Using the paragraphs from Web Project 3, consider in more detail what information should be included at your company's first Web site. List facts about your company that you want to include, resources you want to provide for your

audience or customers, and a plan showing how this information should be organized. Create an outline for your Web site, organizing it in whichever method of organization presented in this chapter seems logical for your topic. Refer to the sample Web sites you researched as you put together the plan for your company's Web site, and consider what you liked best about these sites and what seemed most effective to you.

5. Using your outline from Web Project 4, return to the Internet to find the information that you need to complete your outline for your company's Web site. Document all sites that you will use in your outline.

6. Based on the information you have found on the Internet for Web Project 5, finalize a detailed outline of your company's first Web site. Your outline should be detailed enough so that the graphic designer will understand what information you wish to include. Sketch a rough map of how you would like the site to look. The layout should make the site's organization obvious.

3 Writing the Draft

WRITER'S CHECKLIST

Writing a Rough Draft

- [ ] Set up a quiet writing area with the necessary equipment and materials, then hang out the "Do Not Disturb" sign.
- [ ] Remind yourself that you are beginning a draft that no one else will read.
- [ ] Remember past writing projects — you have completed something before, and you will this time.
- [ ] Start with the section that seems easiest or most interesting to you.
- [ ] Give yourself a 10- or 15-minute time limit in which you write continually, regardless of how good or bad your writing seems to you. The point is to keep moving.
- [ ] Stop writing when you've finished a section or before you're completely exhausted and give yourself a small reward.
- [ ] Reread what you have written when you return to your writing. Often, seeing what you have written will trigger the frame of mind that was producti...

When you have gathered and recorded enough information to meet your purpose, audience's needs, and scope, as described in Chapter 1, and when you have organized your information into an outline, as described in Chapter 2, you are well prepared to write a rough draft. Yet, even with the best preparation, writing the draft remains a chore—if not an obstacle—for most people. This chapter describes proven techniques for successfully writing your draft as well as staying connected to your audience and developing your information as you do so. It also guides you through the process of writing effective openings and closings and continues the development of the Lifemaker brochure introduced in Chapter 2 (page 31).

■ Getting Started on Your Draft

One technique experienced writers use to get started is to think of writing a rough draft as simply transcribing and expanding the notes from the outline into paragraphs without worrying about grammar, style, or such mechanical aspects of writing as spelling. Refinement will come with revision, a process discussed in Chapters 4 and 5.

W On the Web
For online resources for drafting and revising, go to Chapter 3, bedfordstmartins.com/ writingthatworks

Imagine a typical reader sitting across the desk from you as you explain your topic to him or her. This will make your writing more direct and conversational. If you are writing instructions or procedures, visualize your readers actually performing the actions you are describing. This should help you envision the steps they must perform and ensure that you provide adequate information in the right sequence and level of detail. If you are writing a sales letter, think of your arguments from the reader's point of view. Imagine how the features you describe can best be translated into benefits for a prospective customer.

Whatever technique you use, don't worry about a good opening—that can wait until you've constructed your paragraphs. Just start. Concentrate on ideas without attempting to polish or revise. Writing and revising are different activities. Keep writing quickly to achieve unity, coherence, and proportion.

As you write your rough draft, remember that the first rule of good writing is to help your audience by clearly communicating certain information to them. Write in a plain and direct style that is comfortable and natural for both you and your audience.

Also keep in mind your audience's level of knowledge of the subject. Doing so not only helps you write directly to your readers but also helps you decide which terms you must define. See Defining Terms and Concepts (pages 84–87).

Above all, don't wait for inspiration to write the rough draft — treat writing the draft as you would any on-the-job task.

The most effective way to start and to keep going is to use a good outline as a springboard and a map for your writing. The outline also serves to group related facts and details. Once these facts are grouped, you are ready to construct unified and coherent paragraphs — the major building blocks of any piece of writing.

Experienced writers use the tactics described in this chapter to start, keep moving, and get the job done; you will discover which ones are the most helpful to you.

■ Developing Confidence

On-the-job writers face the constant pressure of deadlines, which cause a great deal of anxiety. Nothing builds a writer's confidence more than adequate preparation. If you haven't done enough research to feel comfortable with the material, for example, you will no doubt face great anxiety — perhaps even "writer's block" — as you begin the draft. Furthermore, if you start without an adequate outline, you will also be frustrated by how much time it will take to produce your first draft.

Keep in mind that writing and revising are two very different tasks. When you write the draft, your goal is to communicate with your audience; when you revise, your objective is to become your own toughest critic. Trying to write something perfectly the first time puts pressure on you — pressure that can become self-defeating. In fact, any attempt to correct or polish your writing only stimulates the internal critic and undermines your ability to complete your draft.

Keep in mind that first drafts are necessarily rough and unpolished. Remember: You are the only person who will ever read your first draft. Far from criticizing yourself for not being able to write a smooth, readable sentence the first time, bear in mind that it is natural for first drafts to be clumsy and long-winded. Don't worry about precise word choices, usage, syntax, grammar, or spelling. Instead, concentrate entirely on getting the message down; concentrate on *what* you are writing, not on *how* you are writing it.

Next, put your thoughts into the draft without delay. You cannot afford to wait for inspiration; doing so is often an excuse for stalling. Be wary of such diversions as checking your e-mail, watching the clock, or making phone calls. They may be simply ways of avoiding work.

Diane Bernard, Researcher for Documentary Films

As a footage researcher, Diane Bernard's responsibilities are to find and license film footage and stills for use in documentary television and film productions. She works with directors and editors to decide on the archival footage that will work best for their films. Obtaining the footage "involves a lot of letter writing," Diane explains, to footage archives, libraries, and individual collectors. As she drafts and revises her letters, Diane makes sure she is as specific as possible in describing the material she's requesting. "We don't want a confused archivist running around looking for footage of neighborhoods in the state of New York, when what we need are neighborhoods in New York City — especially when I'm working under a tight deadline. You can waste a lot of time when you leave out a detail."

To gain permission to use the footage, Diane must write to copyright holders. "This can be tricky since not every company or individual is open to letting you use their material. And conversely, a film studio is all too happy to let you do so if, of course, you're willing to pay a huge amount of money for it. For these letters you have to choose your words and formulate your approach carefully." Diane writes multiple drafts, revising carefully with her reader in mind. "I always write a few drafts before I send out a final version, and when I'm writing to negotiate a fee, I have my producers read the draft, too. First, I think about my audience: Is it a big studio that charges a lot of money? Is it an individual who's reluctant to lend his or her personal property? With the audience in mind, I describe our program in the best possible light and highlight aspects of it that might appeal to the powers that be. You've got to hone your powers of persuasion and make sure your tone is appropriate and communicates respect for your audience and also for your own project.

"Once I needed to license footage from a classic Orson Welles film. Knowing that the footage would cost twice our entire budget, I wrote a letter to the film studio that highlighted our director's respect for Welles and talked up our film as a 'goodwill mission' that would reach a wide audience but was operating on a small budget. A few weeks later, the studio offered a fee that was a fraction of their normal asking price."

Jonathan Spiegel, The Trustcompany Bank

Jonathan Spiegel is a full-time law student and a part-time paralegal in the general counsel's office at The Trustcompany Bank. One of his most common writing tasks is drafting legal memoranda. "The legal memo is a direct communication between legal professionals that explains a particular area of the law and how it applies to real-life situations." It also is a memo that must be drafted quickly: "I can't devote more time than necessary in writing a memo — and the audience of the memo can't spend too long reading it." This fact, however, does not prevent him from revising his work.

"I will go through at least three or four drafts before reaching a final product," Jonathan explains. "[I] begin with a legal issue, find out what the relevant rule of law is, apply the rule to the facts at hand, and conclude with how the law affects the facts in question." From the start of his writing process, Jonathan makes it a priority to meet the needs of his readers. "Many times, lawyers read memos on the run and need them to be as succinct as possible. Brevity is a key part of the writing process. I can't stress enough the importance of brief, clear, and informative sentences." When drafting the body of his memo, he considers what his readers already know and expect: "Since the audience of the legal memo is usually a legal professional, I don't need to explain fundamental legal concepts or jargon in great detail, but it is important to provide accurate research citations." Finally, Jonathan drafts his final paragraph so that his readers "can take away the gist of the memo without reading the whole thing."

Jonathan comments on writing under pressure. "I like the pressure of writing a memo under the gun. It keeps me focused and my writing clear. Every time I write a new memo, I learn something new, and I find my writing skills getting better and better."

To learn more about The Trustcompany Bank of New Jersey, visit its Web site at <trustcompany.com>.

■ Using Time-Management Tactics

Because on-the-job writers must work not only under constant deadlines but also with several assignments at once, managing time is an essential part of the writing process.

Allocating Your Time

One effective time-management practice is to keep a calendar on your desk or computer that indicates various deadlines for projects, appointments for interviews, and time periods for gathering information. Your daily calendar should also include "writing appointments," times set aside for writing that you must keep (without interruptions) as if you had an appointment with another person.

Begin small. Within the deadlines set by teachers, managers, and others, set your own short-term, manageable deadlines for completing sections of a draft and other tasks. Concentrating on such subgoals can help you meet the overall deadline, and it can also relieve some of the pressure of writing the draft. Some professional writers think of the completion of subgoals as building a draft one brick at a time.

List these goals, together with your other job tasks; then schedule each task for a specific time. As you set your schedule, remember that time-management experts advise working on the most difficult or unpleasant tasks during the time of day when your mind is keenest.

DIGITAL SHORTCUTS

Drafting on Your Computer

- Freewrite your ideas, keyboarding quickly without stopping to correct mistakes or to complete sentences.

- If a difficult section hinders your progress, use the highlighting feature to make note of it and move on.

- Save each draft separately so that you can return to earlier versions if necessary.

Preparing Your Work Environment

Another useful time-management strategy for writing the draft is to prepare your writing environment and assemble your materials before you begin. Find an isolated place or a method of isolating yourself for writing the draft; then hang out the "Do Not Disturb" sign. Especially when a deadline is in jeopardy, finding a quiet area, away from phones and meetings, can be effective.

Put order into your writing environment by arranging your materials and supplies. Use whatever writing technology (pen and pad, computer, or tape recorder) is most comfortable for you. You may even discover that certain props will help you get started. Sitting in a favorite chair, opening computer files, or placing a reference book on your desk may symbolize your commitment to yourself and your work.

Remaining Flexible

Start with the outline as a guide, but remember that it is not cast in concrete. Feel free to improve your organization as you work. Consider starting with the easiest or most interesting part just to get moving and build some momentum. You may find that just writing out a statement of your purpose will help you to get started.

Once you are rolling, keep going. You may even wish to write comments to yourself while you are writing the rough draft if that tactic keeps you moving. When you reach landmarks (such as the subgoals described earlier) or feel powerfully tempted to start revising, you may need to take a break. When you do, leave a signpost, such as a printout of an unfinished section or a note in the outline recording the date and time you stopped, so you will not waste time searching for your place when you resume work. When you finish a section, reward yourself with a cup of coffee, a short walk, or another small diversion. Physical activity serves as an excellent break for writers. If possible, avoid immersing yourself in another mental activity while you are on your break. If you are not under mental pressure, you may even discover a solution to a nagging writing problem.

When you resume, reread what you have written so that you can recall your frame of mind. Some writers also like to change their writing tools or environment when they resume writing the draft. (For guidelines on writing three types of time-sensitive documents, see Meeting the Deadline: The Time-Sensitive Memo on pages 332–334, Meeting the Deadline: The Time-Sensitive Proposal on pages 507–509, and Meeting the Deadline: The Time-Sensitive Presentation on pages 536–540.)

■ Analyzing Your Audience

When writing the draft, focus on communicating with your readers. Think of your subject from your readers' perspective. How do you determine that perspective? Begin with Christine Thomas's successful analysis of her reader, Harriet Sullivan, in Chapter 1. Christine asked:

1. What information does Harriet need to understand what I'm writing about?
2. What is her basic attitude likely to be toward what I'm writing about?

These questions—which might be rephrased as "What does my reader probably know?" and "What are my reader's feelings about the subject—sympathetic? hostile? neutral?"—always repay the effort required to think about them.

Suppose you work for a manufacturer and your purpose is to explain your plan for dealing with periodic production bottlenecks caused by malfunctioning equipment. If your reader were the company's director of the maintenance department, these questions would be easier to answer than if your reader were the president of your company, someone you probably know only by name and title. In the first case, your reader understands the equipment, the terminology you will use, and the production system. In the second case, your reader is a decision-maker primarily interested in the big picture—the impact of the problem on production schedules and the feasibility of your plan to correct the problem. The company president probably would not know the technical details of the day-to-day operation of your production system. Therefore, a memo to that person would focus not on a detailed explanation of the problem but on the effect of the bottlenecks on production, alternative ways to fix the problem, and estimates of the costs and schedules for each alternative. After reading your explanation, the president would have to decide whether to choose from the several alternatives or to investigate the plan further.

Determining Your Audience's Point of View

Whether your reader is a coworker, a customer, or a company president, he or she is interested in the problem you are addressing more from his or her point of view than from yours. Imagine yourself in your reader's position. One way to do so is to visualize your reader performing a set of activities or taking certain actions based on your writing. Taken together with what you know about your reader's background, this picture will help you predict your reader's needs and reactions. This process should ensure that all the information your reader needs is clearly stated.

For instance, suppose you work for a bicycle manufacturer and you need to write a set of assembly instructions so that people who buy your new model 1050J can get from opening the carton to riding the bicycle with a minimum of frustration. You would have to break down the assembly process into a sensible series of easy-to-follow steps. You would avoid technical language and anticipate questions that your audience would be likely to have. You would make it unnecessary for them to consult other sources to follow your directions. You would not explain the engineering theory that is responsible for the bicycle's unique design; your audience would be more interested in riding the bicycle than in reading such details, however fascinating they might be to you. If you ventured into theory at all, it would be for a specific reason, such as to explain why a particular step in the assembly process had to be completed before the next step. You would also include assembly diagrams, a list of parts, and a list of the tools necessary for assembly.

You would approach the situation differently if you were preparing assembly instructions for a bicycle dealer. You could use standard technical terms without defining them, and you would probably reduce the number of steps necessary for assembly by combining related steps because your audience, the dealer, would be familiar with bicycle assembly and would be able to follow a more sophisticated set of instructions. Your audience would not need a list of tools required for assembly; the dealer's shop would no doubt have all the necessary tools, and the dealer would know which ones to use. You might well, in a separate section, include some theoretical detail, too. The dealer could possibly use this information to explain to customers the advantages of your bicycle over a competitor's.

Establishing Your Role and Voice as the Writer

Writers must also assume roles. If you are an on-the-job writer, you may need to assume the role of a teacher who guides the audience through the process of learning a new task. In this case, you must do more than explain—you must anticipate your audience's reactions and growing understanding of the subject. You must be alert to questions that your audience might ask, such as "Why do I need to read this document?" "Is this subject easy to learn?" "How much time must I spend to read it?" and "Where can I find a quick answer to my problem?" By anticipating that the audience will ask such questions, you will be more likely to answer them in your draft.

You may discover that an audience's interests do not always coincide with its needs. Some audiences, for example, would prefer not to read your document at all; however, they are interested in completing a task or solving a problem as quickly as possible. You must demonstrate how your document links the audiences' interests with their need to read the document.

As you write the draft, consider which voice your audience should hear. Should it be authoritative or friendly, formal or accessible, provocative or reassuring—or somewhere in between? Determine the voice you adopt by considering what is appropriate to your specific purpose. The guidelines shown in Figure 3–1 are intended for respiratory-care therapists when they assess patients to develop a plan of care. The writer's voice is slightly formal (the guidance is in the imperative mood) yet caring in tone, as befits the subject.

By contrast, the audiences of newsletters may expect a voice that is fast-paced and reportorial. Consider the attention-getting approach used in the opening of an article in a customer newsletter (Figure 3–2).

Writing for Varied Audiences

When you write for an audience similar in background and knowledge—all sales associates, for example, or all security officers—you should picture a typical representative of that group and write directly to that person. Occasionally, however, you may need to write a document for an audience with widely different work environments, technical backgrounds, or professional positions. For example, you

---

RESPIRATORY-CARE PLAN

1. Let the patient know exactly what is being done.
2. Maintain a good rapport; answer questions the patient may ask to allay fear.
3. Maintain the privacy and dignity of the patient at all times.
4. Be prepared. A stethoscope, a watch with a sweep second hand or a stopwatch, and a pen are basic items essential to this process.
5. Document your findings as soon as time permits; otherwise, you may forget important points.

Authoritative voice instructs yet reassures

Figure 3–1 Formal Voice (in Medical Instructions)

*Conversational voice
directly engages
audience*

SHAPING THE YEAR TO COME:
The Project Manager's Calendar Can Be a Scheduler's Dream Come True

Ahhh, it's a project manager's fantasy—to get a glimpse into all your work for the coming year and schedule it evenly over the next 12 months. Unfortunately, that only happens in dreamland. But if anything comes close to making that scenario a reality, it's the project manager's calendar.

Formulated for the entire upcoming year, the calendars are a sneak preview for each task of the projects you are juggling. . . .

Figure 3–2   Conversational Voice (in a Customer Newsletter)

might write a technical report that would be used by company executives, field-service engineers, and sales associates. In such a situation, you could address each audience separately in clearly identified sections of your document: an executive summary for the executives, an appendix for the service engineers, and the body of the document for the sales associates. (See Chapter 12 for an explanation of how the different parts of a formal report address the needs of different audiences.) When you cannot segment your writing this way, determine who your primary audience is, and make certain that you meet all of that audience's needs. Then try to meet the needs of your other audience—only if you can do so without placing a burden on your primary audience.

For example, if your primary audience is an executive and your secondary audience is a technical specialist, you should not include technical details that would obscure the main points for the executive, even though the technical specialist might find such details of interest. Instead, you could include a separate section titled "Technical Analysis"—optional for the executive but geared toward the specialist—containing detailed technical information.

Figures 3–3 and 3–4 are from a technical-assessment report that describes to an organization the advantages of acquiring media streaming technology. The first part of the report (Figure 3–3) provides an overview of the topic for policy-makers who may be unfamiliar with this technology and its uses. The second part (Figure 3–4) is targeted at technical experts who must understand the hardware and software requirements for the system.

The report's overview of a technology (Introduction) is aimed at the broadest possible audience. It is written with the assumption that decision-makers are unfamiliar with media streaming technology (MST) and need an introduction to what it is and what it can do. The section shown in Figure 3–4 occurs later in the report and is clearly aimed at a technical audience familiar with the details of the technology. Note the frequent use of technical terms and acronyms. The author assumes that the technical audience in this field will be familiar with them. GIF and JPEG, for example, are abbreviations that refer to common file formats for coding and exchanging graphic images on the Internet. This section also refers the audience to detailed cost information in an appendix to this report.

INTRODUCTION

This report demonstrates how the Office of the Chief Information Officer can improve the distribution of agency information and enhance communications with the staff, the nuclear industry, other federal agencies, the media, and the public by using media streaming technology (MST). This report explains this emerging technology and its advantages to our organization, details the resources necessary to deploy it, and recommends a course of action to achieve these goals.

Media streaming is the receipt of audio and video broadcast media over the Internet at one's desktop computer. The advantages of providing this capability to the agency are threefold:

- To enhance the agency's ability to collaborate with the nuclear industries, the states, other federal agencies, the public, and other agency stakeholders.

- To provide desktop delivery of training, commission meetings, public meetings at remote locations, staff safety programs, nuclear industry standards, and much else.

- To build partnerships with government and private-sector organizations.

This report provides no single solution to deploying media streaming technology. Agency requirements are not static and will require alternative configurations over time at headquarters and the regional offices.

Accordingly, the coverage includes necessary background information for decision-makers in the following areas:

- Business requirements for and cost of supporting media streaming technology.

- Technology cost alternatives based on a variety of agency program requirements.

- A new internal Web site focusing on media streaming technology to assist management and staff in determining how the technology can be used to improve agency programs and customer relations.

Overview and purpose of report

Definition of a key term

List of high-level advantages to organization

Statement defines intended audience (decision-makers)

Statement of scope of report

Figure 3–3   Introduction to a Report (for a General Audience)

ARCHITECTURE OF THE REAL SYSTEM

Real System G2 is a client-server application that delivers live and on-demand MST content across TCP/IP networks. The Real System architecture has three main components: Real Server, Real Player, and content publishing tools. Real Server streams live and on-demand Real Audio, Real Video, Real Flash animation, Real Pix (GIF and JPEG images), and Real Text content across the Internet and NGN. Real System G2 supports most other existing media file formats, such as ASF, AVI, JPEG, MPEG, VIV, and WAV. The Real Player is used on client workstations to play the MST content. Real System publishing tools, such as the Real Producer and Real System G2 Authoring Tool, are used to create MST content. . . .

Technical vocabular and abbreviations expert audience

Figure 3–4   Subsection of a Report (for a Technical Audience)

CONSIDERING AUDIENCE AND PURPOSE

Preparing to Write a Draft

When preparing to write a draft, ask yourself the following questions:

☐ What is my purpose in writing this document? What action do I want my reader to take after reading it?

☐ Who are my readers? Is there a secondary audience? What do my readers know and how do they feel about the subject I'm addressing or the idea I'm proposing?

☐ Why do my readers need to read this document or e-mail message? (To perform a task? To obtain basic information? To investigate a problem? To make a decision?)

☐ How much information will my readers need to understand the subject or to be persuaded by my idea? What is the best way to clearly present this material?

☐ What objections might my readers have to the subject or proposed idea?

☐ What medium would be most appropriate? (E-mail? Memo?) What voice would best convey my message? (Authoritative? Friendly? Provocative? Reassuring?)

Persuading Your Audience

Suppose you and a friend are arguing over whether the capital of Maine is Portland or Augusta. The issue is a simple question of fact that easily can be checked in an almanac or an atlas. (It's Augusta.) Now suppose you are trying to convince management at your company that it ought to adopt flexible working hours for its employees or to upgrade software in order to improve communications with its customers. A quick look in a reference book will not settle the issue. Like Christine Thomas in Chapter 1, you will have to persuade management that your idea is a good one. To achieve your goal—to convince your company to accept your suggestions and act on them—you will probably have to put your recommendations in writing.

In all on-the-job writing, it is important to keep your reader's needs, as well as your own, clearly in mind. This is especially true in persuasive writing, in which your purpose may often be to ask your reader to change his or her working procedures or habits. You may think, as Christine Thomas did, that most people would automatically accept a recommendation for an improvement in the workplace, but improvement means change, and people tend to resist change. ("We've always done it this way. Why change?"). Your proposed idea may be a threat to a staff member's pet project, or it may make the accumulated knowledge and experience of a veteran employee seem out of date. To overcome their resistance, you'll have to show the need for your recommendation and support it with convincing, hard evidence.

Keep in mind, as you seek to persuade your audience, that the way you present your ideas is as important as the ideas themselves. Respect your audience's opinions by applying some basic manners in your writing. Avoid sarcasm and a hostile tone that will offend your audience. Also avoid exaggeration or being overly enthusiastic. Your audience may interpret such an attitude as insincere or presumptuous. Of course, you should not conceal genuine enthusiasm; just be careful not to overdo it.

The memo in Figure 3–5 was written by an MIS (management information systems) administrator to persuade her staff to accept and participate in a change to a new computer system. Notice that not everything in this memo is

Memo

TO: Engineering Sales Staff
FROM: Bernadine Kovak, MIS Administrator   *BK*
DATE: April 8, 2003
SUBJECT: Plans for Changeover to NRT/R4 System

As you all know, our workload has jumped by 30 percent in the past month. It has increased because our customer base and resulting technical support services have grown dramatically. This growth is a result, in part, of our recent merger with Datacom.

Background of problem

This growth has meant that we have all experienced the difficulty of providing our customers with up-to-date technical information when they need it. In the next few months, we anticipate that the workload will increase another 20 percent. Even a staff as experienced as ours cannot handle such a workload without help.

Statement of problem

To cope with that expansion, in the next month we will be installing the NRT/R4 mainframe and QCS enterprise software with Web-based applications and global sales and service network. The system will speed processing dramatically as well as give us access to all relevant company-wide databases. It should enable us to access the information both we and our customers need.

Statement of solution

The new system, unfortunately, will cause some disruption at first. We will need to transfer many of our existing programs and software applications to the new format. And all of us need to learn to navigate in the R4 and QCS environments. However, once we have made those adjustments, I believe we will welcome the changes.

Candid acknowledgment of disruption

I would like to put your knowledge and experience to work in getting the new system into operation. Let's meet in my office to discuss the improvements on Friday, April 12, at 1:00 p.m. I will have details of the plan to discuss with you. I'm also eager to get your comments, suggestions, and—most of all—your cooperation.

Call for cooperation

Figure 3–5   Persuasive Memo

presented in a positive light. Change brings disruption, and the writer acknowledges that fact.

For persuasive communications outside the company, you must take equal if not greater care in the choice of medium and the way you present information. In the letter in Figure 3–6, the writer is disappointed because she did not expect the response she got, but she further attempts to persuade her audience. (See also Persuasive Writing in Chapter 14, page 480.) Instead of responding with anger or sarcasm ("Your fee is highway robbery!"), the writer compliments the publisher on the prompt response and gets quickly to the point: her concern for the high fee and her wish to have it reduced. She indicates that using the poem is certainly desirable, but as "nontechnical" or "ancillary" material it is not essential. She explains her project's budgetary constraints and completes her explanation with a counter offer. Throughout, her tone and language are courteous and respectful. She ends her letter by leaving the door open for the publisher: "I look forward to hearing from you."

When writing to persuade your audience, do not overlook opposing points of view. Most issues have more than one side, and you should acknowledge them, as does the writer proposing a disruptive change in Figure 3–5. It would be a mistake for the writer to overlook the added time and work required to transfer to a new computer system and to learn its navigation. It is most effective to admit that, in the short term, work will increase—and to then show that the added burden would be more than compensated for by an improved work environment in which employees can better manage their workloads and meet the needs of their customers. By including differing points of view, you gain several advantages. First, you show your audience that you are honest enough to recognize opposite views when they exist. Second, you can demonstrate the advantage of your viewpoint over those of others. Third, by anticipating and bringing up opposing views *before* your coworkers do, you may be able to blunt some or all of their objections.

WRITER'S CHECKLIST

Writing a Rough Draft

- ☐ Set up a quiet writing area with the necessary equipment and materials, then hang out the "Do Not Disturb" sign.
- ☐ Remind yourself that you are beginning a *draft* that no one else will read.
- ☐ Remember past writing projects — you have completed something before, and you will this time.
- ☐ Start with the section that seems easiest or most interesting to you.
- ☐ Give yourself a 10- or 15-minute time limit in which you write continually, regardless of how good or bad your writing seems to you. The point is to keep moving.
- ☐ Stop writing when you've finished a section or before you're completely exhausted and give yourself a small reward.
- ☐ Reread what you have written when you return to your writing. Often, seeing what you have written will trigger the frame of mind that was productive.

Commuter Aircraft Corporation
7328 Wellington Drive
Partridge, Ohio 45424

March 7, 2003

Adele Chu, Permissions Editor
Poet's Press, Inc.
One Plaza Way, Suite 3
Boston, MA 02116

Dear Ms. Chu:

Thank you for responding so quickly to my request for permission to reprint the poem "Flight" in the pilot's manual for our new Aerosoar 100 Commuter.

Complimentary and courteous opening

I am writing to express concern about the fee you have requested for the use of this selection. It is much higher than we expected. Because the manual is an instructional booklet distributed to pilots free of charge, the budget for this project is strictly limited, particularly for nontechnical, ancillary materials such as poetry. We continue to feel that the poem would interest and even inspire our readers, however, and we would like to ask you to consider lowering your fee to make this possible. To meet the demands of our budget, we are able to pay no more than $300 for each selection in the manual—considerably less than the $900 you have requested.

Statement of problem, its basis, and counteroffer

I hope you understand our position and that you will consider reducing your fee for the use of this material. Thank you for considering my request. I look forward to hearing from you.

Restatement of request and respectful closing

Sincerely,

J. T. Walters

J. T. Walters
Publications Manager

cc: Legal Department

**(890) 321-1231
Fax (890) 321-5116**   **commair.com**

Figure 3–6   Persuasive Letter

Finally, use the appropriate medium for communicating with your audience. As Christine Thomas learned in Chapter 1, a brief e-mail message to her boss was not the appropriate means to present her proposal. Her boss wanted the formality and readability that a memo permits. As you plan your writing and prepare the draft, consider how you want to package your finished communication. For a description of options available to help you make this decision, see Selecting the Appropriate Medium in Chapter 9, pages 306–310.

■ Using Methods of Development

The following methods for developing your writing are strategies that will help you not only to convey information but also to present evidence in order to persuade your audience:

- **Explaining a process:** tells how something works or how something happened
- **Describing information:** describes how something looks or is planned to look
- **Defining terms and concepts:** tells what your audience needs to know in order to understand
- **Explaining cause and effect:** explains why something happened

Although this section focuses on each method separately, they are often used in combination. For investigative and accident reports, for example, the writer must state exactly what happened (explaining a process), which may also require the writer to physically describe people, places, or equipment (describing information), and to provide meanings for language or ideas that the audience may not understand (defining terms and concepts). Finally, the writer must try to explain why the event or accident happened (explaining cause and effect). A skillful integration of these methods to present evidence will do much to convince your audience of your findings and recommendations.

Explaining a Process

When you explain a process, you tell your audience how something works or how something is done. The process you explain might be an event that occurs in nature (the tidal pull of the moon), a function that requires human effort (conducting a marketing survey), or an activity in which people operate machinery to produce goods or services (automobile assembly-line production).

Just as it is essential for you to be familiar with a task before you can write clear instructions for carrying it out, so you must thoroughly understand a process yourself before you can explain it to your audience. The explanation of a process is composed of steps—steps that should be as clear, accurate, and complete as possible and may also include illustrations that show the process from beginning to end.

As in all on-the-job writing, you must aim your writing at a level appropriate to your audience's background. Beginners require more basic information and less technical vocabulary than do experienced workers.

In your opening paragraph, tell your audience why it is important to become familiar with the process you are explaining. Before you explain the steps necessary to form a corporation, for example, you could cite the tax savings that incorporation would permit. To give your audience a framework for the details that will follow, you might present a brief overview of the process. Finally, you might describe how the process works in relation to a larger whole of which it is a part. In explaining the air-brake system of a large dump truck, for example, you might note that the braking system is one part of the vehicle's air system, which also controls the throttle and transmission-shifting mechanisms.

A process explanation can be long or short, depending on how much detail is necessary. The following explanation of the way a camera controls light to expose photographic film, intended for beginning photographers, fits into one paragraph. Note the writer's choice of words and definitions that are designed to communicate the ideas to an audience unfamiliar with the subject. The writer uses simple language and defines specialized terms.

■   The camera is the basic tool for recording light images. It is simply a box from which all light is excluded except that which passes through a small opening at the front. Cameras are equipped with various devices for controlling the light rays as they enter this opening. At the press of a button, a mechanical blade or curtain, called a shutter, opens and closes automatically. During the fraction of a second that the shutter is open, the light reflected from the subject toward which the camera is aimed passes into the camera through a piece of optical glass called the lens. The lens focuses, or projects, the light rays onto the wall at the back of the camera. These light reflections are captured on a sheet of film attached to the back wall.

The passage in Figure 3–7 explains the process by which drinking water is purified. It provides essential background information in the context of a discussion of how drinking water may be contaminated as it is treated before distribution to homes. The information is intended for the average homeowner, but the vocabulary does assume an elementary familiarity with biological and chemical terms. The description is enhanced by a step-by-step illustration that complements the pattern of the writing by providing an overview image (first panel in Figure 3–8) and then three more-detailed drawings of the water-treatment process (remaining three panels in Figure 3–8). Note that the title (or heading) for the process accompanies the explanation and that a citation for the source follows.

Describing Information

When you give your audience information about an object's size, shape, method of construction, or other features of its appearance, you are describing it. The kinds of description you write will vary—engineers must describe products they design according to corporate specifications; marketing professionals must

DRINKING WATER TREATMENT PROCESS

Background to process

After it has been transported from its source to a local water system, most surface water must be processed in a treatment plant before it can be used. Some groundwater, on the other hand, is considered chemically and biologically pure enough to pass directly from a well into the distribution system that carries it to the home.

Overview of steps in the process

Although there are innumerable variations, surface water is usually treated as follows: First, it enters a storage lagoon where a chemical, usually copper sulfate, is added to control algae growth. From there, water passes through one or more screens that remove large debris. Next, a coagulant, such as alum, is mixed into the water to encourage the settling of suspended particles. The water flows slowly through one or more sedimentation basins so that larger particles settle to the bottom and can be removed. Water then passes through a filtration basin partially filled with sand and gravel where yet more suspended particles are removed. (See "Drinking Water Treatment Process" illustration.)

Definition of key term

At that point in the process, the Safe Drinking Water Act has mandated an additional step for communities using surface water. . . . [W]ater is to be filtered through activated carbon to remove any microscopic organic material and chemicals that have escaped the other processes. Activated carbon is extremely porous—one pound of the material can have a surface area of one acre. This honeycomb of minute pores attracts and traps pollutants through a process called adsorption. . . .

Basis for importance of the process

The final stage of water treatment is disinfection, where an agent capable of killing most biological pathogens is added to the water. Until the chlorination process was developed, devastating epidemics—such as the outbreak of typhoid and cholera that took 90,000 lives in Chicago in 1885. . . .

Figure 3–7   Explanation of a Process   *Source: Indoor Pollution* by S. Coffel and K. Feiden (New York: Fawcett Columbine, 1990), pp. 127–130. Reprinted by permission of Ballantine Books, a division of Random House, Inc.

describe the products they are marketing to potential customers; software developers face the daunting task of describing something the audience cannot see; police must describe accident scenes, and so on. The key to writing an effective description is to accurately present details. To select appropriate details, determine what your audience will use the description for—to identify something? to assemble or repair the object being described?

Your description may be of something concrete, such as a machine, or of something abstract, such as computer software. Figure 3–9 is a description of the format of a computer disk.

When describing a physical object or system, first become thoroughly familiar with it and give an overview before describing its parts in detail.

Descriptions can be brief and simple, or they can be highly complex. Simple descriptions usually require only a simple listing of key features. A purchase order, shown in Figure 3–10, is a typical example of simple descriptive writing. Purchase-order descriptions should be clear and specific. An inaccurate or omitted detail may result in the delivery of the wrong item. Even an order for something as

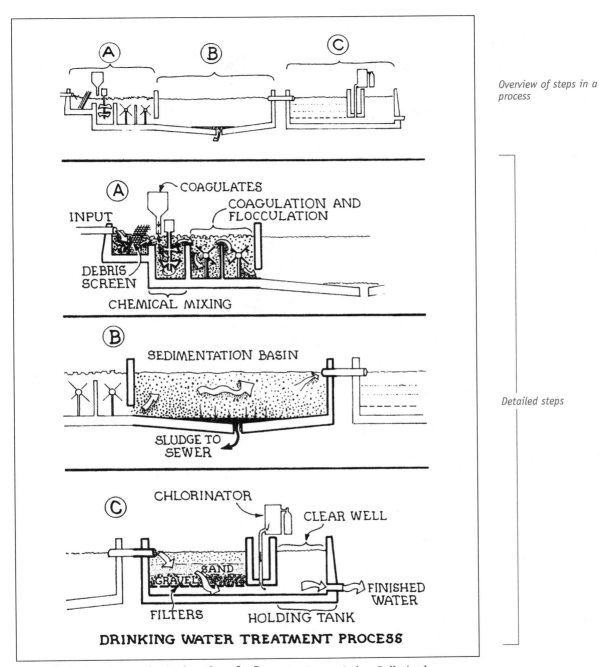

Overview of steps in a process

Detailed steps

Figure 3–8 Illustration for Explanation of a Process   *Source: Indoor Pollution* by S. Coffel and K. Feiden (New York: Fawcett Columbine, 1990), pp. 127–130. Reprinted by permission of Ballantine Books, a division of Random House, Inc.

Detailed description of a computer disk (partial segmentation)

When the disk initializer prepares a disk for use, it sets the disk to a predefined format, which includes reserving those software areas required by the operating system. Of the available 8,192 sectors, approximately 1,154 sectors, shown as follows, are reserved for disk information, system software, and system use. The remaining sectors are available to the user. Initialization of the disk reserves the areas as shown in this figure.

a.	Disk Volume Header	5 Sectors
b.	Monitor Boot	6 Sectors
c.	Skip Area	41 Sectors
d.	Disk Directory	20 Sectors
e.	System Storage	41 Sectors
f.	System-Software Overlays	801 Sectors
g.	Work Storage	240 Sectors

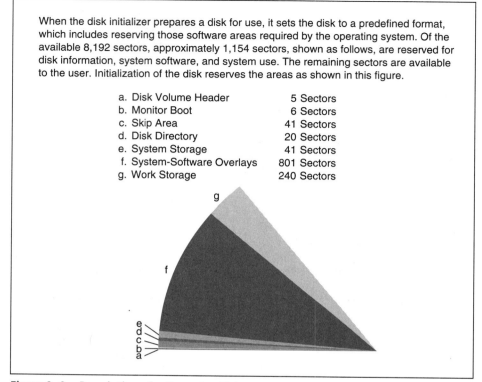

Figure 3–9   Description of a Computer Disk

ordinary as trash-compactor bags needs, in addition to the part number, four specific descriptive details.

Complex descriptions, of course, require more detail than simple ones. The details you select should accurately and vividly convey what you are describing. If it is useful for your audience to visualize an object, for instance, include details—such as color and shape—that appeal to the sense of sight. The example that fol-

Specifications for trash-compactor bags

PURCHASE ORDER		
Part No.	Description	Quantity
GL/020	Trash-compactor bags, 31″ × 50″ tubular, nontransparent, 5-mil thickness, including 100 tie wraps per carton	5 cartons@ 100 per carton

Figure 3–10   Simple Description

lows is a description of the leaf abnormalities that occur when trees are planted in soil lacking the necessary minerals. The writer, a forester writing for other foresters, offers precise details of the changes in color that were observed.

■ Foliage of the black cherry trees showed striking and unusual discolorations in mid-August. Bright red margins extended one-half the distance to the midrib and almost to the tip of the leaf. Nearly all leaves were similarly discolored and showed a well-defined line of demarcation between the pigmentation and the normal coloration. By late September, the pigmentation margins had widened and extended to the tips of the leaves. The red deepened in intensity and, in addition, blue and violet hues were apparent for the first time.

The description of leaf abnormalities concentrates on appearance—it tells the audience what the discolored leaves look like. Sometimes, however, you may want to describe the physical characteristics of an object and at the same time itemize the parts that go into its makeup. If you intended to write a description of a piece of machinery, for example, you would probably find this approach, called the whole-to-parts method, the most useful for your purpose. You would first present a general description of the device, because an overall description would provide your audience with a frame of reference for the more-specific details that follow—the physical description of the various parts and the location and function of each in relation to the whole. The description would conclude with an explanation of the way the parts work together to get their particular job done.

The text for Figure 3–11 describes a body harness tethered to a line that protects ironworkers from falls as they walk on beams high above the ground at building construction sites. The illustration is intended for occupational safety officials who must assess such devices as they seek ways to protect worker health and safety on the job.

Illustrations can be powerful aids in descriptive writing, especially when they show details too intricate to explain in words, as in Figure 3–12, which describes and illustrates the operation of a computer disk unit that uses multiple platters. Note that each illustration appears immediately after the text that discusses it. All illustrations should be positioned as close to the text they illustrate as possible.

Do not hesitate to use an illustration with a complex description if the illustration creates a clearer image. Detailed instructions on the use of illustrations appear in Chapter 8.

Approximately 50 ironworkers fall to their deaths each year in the United States. The latest fall-protection system may change all this. The following illustration shows a system that protects ironworkers from falls without interfering with their work. This system complies with the Occupational Safety and Health Administration's strict fall-protection requirements.

Specific details of system components and operation

Known as the Beamwalker, the system consists of two stanchions that clamp to a standard I-beam. A 40-foot line, to which workers can attach their lifelines, runs between the stanchions. The Beamwalker is installed while the beam is on the ground.

The Beamwalker

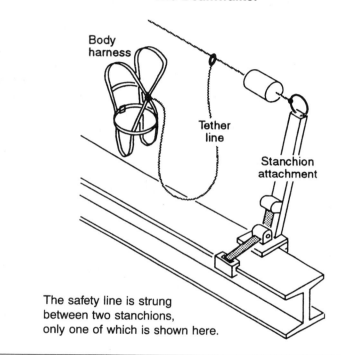

Body harness

Tether line

Stanchion attachment

Subsystem detail

The safety line is strung between two stanchions, only one of which is shown here.

Figure 3–11   Illustration to Aid Description

The disk pack contains six recording surfaces, each plated with cobalt-nickel to provide long disk life and a high-density magnetic recording surface. Each of the six surfaces is serviced by 12 read/write heads; therefore, each pack is serviced by 72 read/write heads. Of these 72 heads, 64 are available to the user and 8 are reserved for use by the hardware.

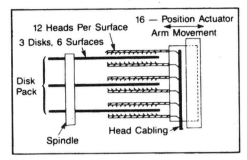

- The area of the disk covered by one read/write head during a revolution is called a track.
- A total of 64 tracks are available in any one of the 16-actuator positions.
- A total of 1,024 tracks are available over the entire 16 positions.

Illustrations of a system at three levels of specificity (general to specific)

Tracks

A track is the area covered by one read/write head during one complete rotation of the disk. Since 64 read/write heads are available to the user, there are 64 tracks for reading or recording data in each of the 16 positions. Therefore, over the entire recording surface, there are 1,024 tracks available for data.

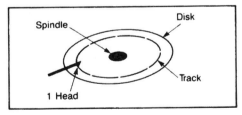

Sectors

Each track of the disk is divided into eight addressable units called sectors. Since there are 64 available tracks in an actuator position, 512 sectors are available in each of the 16 positions of the actuator. Therefore, over the entire 16 positions, 8,192 sectors are available for storage. Each sector may contain up to 512 characters.

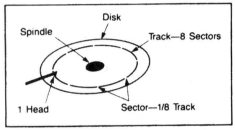

- Each track is divided into eight sectors.
- Each of 16 positions has 512 sectors.
- Each pack has 8,192 sectors.
- Each sector may contain 512 characters.
- Each pack may contain 4,194,304 characters.

Figure 3–12   Detailed Descriptions (with Illustrations)

Defining Terms and Concepts

Accurate definitions are crucial to many kinds of writing, especially for an audience unfamiliar with your subject. Depending on your audience's needs, your definition can be formal, informal, or extended.

Formal Definitions

A *formal definition* is a form of classification. In it, you place a term in a class of related objects or ideas and show how it differs from other members of the same class.

Formal Definitions

Term	Class	Difference
spoon	eating utensil	that consists of a small, shallow bowl on the end of a handle
auction	public sale	in which property passes to the highest bidder through successive increased offers
annual	plant	that completes its life cycle, from seed to natural death, in one growing season

Informal Definitions

In an *informal definition,* a familiar word or phrase is used as a synonym for an unfamiliar word or phrase.

- An invoice is a bill.

- Plants live in a symbiotic, or mutually beneficial, relationship with certain kinds of bacteria.

- The system is controlled by a photoelectric (optical) sensing device.

Informal definitions permit you to explain the meaning of a term with a minimum of interruption in the flow of your writing. Informal definitions should not be used, however, if the completeness of a formal, or extended, definition is needed to make the term easier to understand.

Extended Definitions

An *extended definition*—used when more than a phrase or a sentence is needed to explain an idea—explores a number of qualities of what is being defined. Some extended definitions may take only a few sentences, while others may run for several paragraphs, depending on the needs of your audience and the complexity of the subject. An audience familiar with a topic or an area might be able to handle a long, fairly technical definition, whereas a newcomer to a topic would require simpler language and more basic information.

Compare the language and detail provided in the following two definitions, which explain the chemical concept of pH. The first definition is intended for people in the graphic arts who need a general understanding of the concept but not a detailed explanation of the principles underlying the concept.

■ **pH.** A number used for expressing the acidity or alkalinity of solutions. A value of 7 is neutral in a scale ranging from 0 to 14. Solutions with values below 7 are acid, above 7 are alkalines.[1]

The second definition of pH, from an article about hydrogen ion activity in human blood, is intended for chemistry students and clinical laboratory technicians. The author assumes that the audience is familiar with chemical symbols (H^+), abbreviations (mol/liter), and terms (ions).

■ About 90 years ago, the pH scale was devised to express hydrogen ion concentration in convenient numbers. The pH value, the exponent of the H^+ concentration in mol/liter with the sign changed from minus to plus, increases as hydrogen ion concentration increases. The normal pH of blood lies between 7.38 and 7.42 and a small change in pH can mean a big change in the H^+ concentration. For example, when pH changes from 7.4 to 7.0, the H^+ concentration increases 2½-fold, from 4×10^{-8} to 10×10^{-8} mol/liter.[2]

Clarifying Definitions

Perhaps the easiest way to define a term is to give specific examples of it. For a land-use analysis of a regional park, a landscape architect needed to explain a number of abstract concepts, such as form, line, and color, that are used by landscape architects in precise ways not necessarily corresponding to their everyday use. Without an understanding of these concepts, Parks Department officials for whom the report was prepared, would be unable to understand the analysis. With this audience in mind, the architect used easy-to-picture details to bridge the gap between him and his audience, as in this definition of form.

■ Form, which is the shape of landscape features, can best be represented by both small-scale features, such as trees and shrubs, and by large-scale elements, such as mountains and mountain ranges.

Another way to define a difficult concept, especially when you are writing for nonspecialists, is to link the unfamiliar to the familiar by means of an analogy (comparison). Defining radio waves in terms of their length (long) and frequency (low), a writer develops an analogy to show why a low frequency is advantageous.

■ The low frequency makes it relatively easy to produce a wave having virtually all its power concentrated at one frequency. Think, for example, of a group of people lost in a forest. If they hear sounds of a search party in the distance, they all will begin to shout for help in different directions. Not a very efficient process, is it? But suppose that all the energy that went into the production of this noise could be concentrated into a single shout or whistle. Clearly the chances that the group will be found would be much greater.

---

[1] International Paper Company, *Pocket Pal—A Graphic/Arts Production Handbook*, 16th ed. (New York: International Paper Company, 1995), p. 200.

[2] John A. Lott, "Hydrogen Ions in Blood," *Chemistry* 51 (May 1978): 6.

Some terms are best defined by an explanation of their causes. Writing in a professional journal, a nurse describes an apparatus used to monitor blood pressure in severely ill patients. Called an indwelling catheter, the device displays blood-pressure readings on an oscilliscope and on a numbered scale. Users of the device, the writer explains, must understand what a dampened wave form is.

■   ˙The dampened wave form, the smoothing out or flattening of the pressure wave form on the oscilliscope, is usually caused by an obstruction that prevents blood pressure from being freely transmitted to the monitor. The obstruction might be a small clot or bit of fibrin at the catheter tip. More likely, the catheter tip has become positioned against the artery wall and is preventing the blood from flowing freely.

The most significant point about the occurrence of a dampened wave form is that it is usually the result of a potentially dangerous obstruction. The definition therefore emphasizes cause and indicates what factors may, in turn, produce the obstruction in blood-pressure transmission.

Some writers make a formal definition easier to understand by breaking a concept into manageable parts.

FORMAL DEFINITION	Fire is the visible heat energy released from the rapid oxidation of a fuel. A substance is "on fire" when the release of heat energy from the oxidation process reaches visible light levels.
DIVISION INTO COMPONENT ELEMENTS	The classic fire triangle illustrates the elements necessary to create fire: oxygen, heat, and burnable material or fuel. Air provides sufficient oxygen for combustion; the intensity of the heat needed to start a fire depends on the characteristics of the burnable material or fuel. A burnable substance is one that will sustain combustion after an initial application of heat to start it.

The techniques for dividing the elements of a concept follow the guidelines discussed in Division and Classification in Chapter 2.

Under certain circumstances, the meaning of a term can be clarified and made easier to remember by an exploration of its origin. Because they sometimes have unfamiliar Greek and Latin roots, scientific and medical terms benefit especially from an explanation of this type. Tracing the derivation of a word can also be useful when you want to explain why a word has favorable or unfavorable associations — particularly if your goal is to influence your audience's attitude toward an idea or activity.

■   Efforts to influence legislation generally fall under the head of *lobbying,* a term that once referred to people who prowl the lobbies of houses of government, button-holing lawmakers and trying to get them to take certain positions. Lobbying today is all of this, and much more, too. It is a respected — and necessary — activity. It tells legislators which way the winds of public opinion are blowing, and it helps inform them of the implications of certain bills, debates, and resolutions they must contend with.[3]

Sometimes it is useful to point out what something is *not* to clarify what it *is*. A what-it-is-not definition is effective only when the reader is familiar with the item with which the defined item is contrasted. If you say *x* is not *y*, your audience must understand the meaning of *y* for the explanation to make sense. In a crane operator's manual, for instance, a "negative definition" is used to show that, for safety reasons, a hydraulic crane cannot be operated in the same manner as a lattice boom crane.

■ A hydraulic crane is not like a lattice boom crane in one very important way. In most cases, the safe lifting capacity of a lattice boom crane is based on the weight needed to tip the machine. Therefore, operators of friction machines sometimes depend on signs that the machine might tip to warn them of impending danger. This is a very dangerous practice with a hydraulic crane. . . .[4]

Avoiding Problems in Definitions

When you use a definition as a means of presenting your material, keep in mind a few pitfalls that may result in confusing, inaccurate, or incomplete definitions.

Avoid circular definitions, which merely restate the term to be defined and therefore fail to clarify it.

INCORRECT	Spontaneous combustion is fire that begins spontaneously.
CORRECT	Spontaneous combustion is the self-ignition of a flammable material through a chemical reaction such as oxidation and temperature buildup.

Avoid "is when" and "is where" definitions; such definitions overlook what is essential to formal definition — they do not classify the term being defined.

INCORRECT	A contract is when two or more people agree to something.
CORRECT	A contract is a binding agreement between two or more people.

Avoid definitions made up of terms your audience won't understand. Even informally written material will occasionally require the use of a term in a special sense unfamiliar to your audience; such terms should be defined, too.

■ In these specifications, the term *safety can* refers to an approved container of not more than five-gallon capacity, having a spring-closing spout cover designed to relieve internal pressure when exposed to fire.

---

[3] Bill Vogt, *How to Build A Better Outdoors* (New York: McKay, 1978), p. 93.

[4] *Operator's Manual* (Model W-180), Harnischfeger Corporation.

Explaining Cause and Effect

When your purpose is to explain why something happened, or why you think something will happen, cause-and-effect analysis is a useful writing strategy. For instance, if you were asked to report on why the accident rate for the company truck fleet rose by 30 percent this year over last year, you would use cause-and-effect analysis. In this case, you would be working from an effect (higher accident rate) to its cause (bad driving weather, inexperienced drivers, poor truck mainte-nance, and so on). However, if your purpose were to report on the possible effects that the switch to a four-day workweek (ten hours per day) would have on the of-fice staff, you would also use cause-and-effect analysis—but this time you would start with cause (the new work schedule) and look for possible effects (changes in morale, in productivity, in absenteeism, and the like).

The goal of cause-and-effect analysis is to make the relationship between a situation and either its cause or its effect as plausible as possible. The conclusions you draw about the relationship will be based on the evidence you have gathered. Evidence is any pertinent fact or argument that helps explain the circumstances of an event. Because not all evidence will be of equal value to you as you draw con-clusions, it's a good idea to keep some guidelines in mind for evaluating evidence.

Evidence Should Be Pertinent

The facts and arguments that you gather should be pertinent, or relevant, to your topic. That is, even if the evidence you collect is accurate, you should be careful not to draw a conclusion that your evidence does not lead to or support. You may have researched some statistics, for example, that show that an increasing num-ber of Americans are licensed to fly small airplanes. However, you cannot use this information as evidence that there is a slowdown in interstate highway construc-tion in the United States—the evidence does not lead to that conclusion. Other, more relevant evidence is available to explain the decline in interstate construc-tion—greatly increased construction costs, opposition from environmen-tal groups, new legislation that transfers highway construction funds to mass transportation, and so on. Statistics on the increase in small-plane licensing may be relevant to other conclusions, however. You could argue that the upswing has occurred because small planes save travel time, provide easy access to remote areas, and, once they are purchased, are economical to operate.

Evidence Should Be Sufficient

Incomplete evidence can lead to false conclusions.

FALSE
CONCLUSION   Driver-training classes in the schools do not help prevent auto acci-dents. Two people I know who completed driver-training classes were involved in accidents.

Although the evidence cited to support the conclusion may be accurate, there is not enough of it here to even justify making a statement about the driver-training program at one school. A thorough investigation of the usefulness of driver-training classes in keeping the accident rate down would require many more than two examples. It would require a comparison of the driving records of those who had completed driver training with the records of those who had not.

Evidence Should Be Representative

If you conduct a survey to obtain your evidence, be sure that you do not solicit responses only from individuals or groups whose views are identical to yours—that is, be sure you obtain a representative sampling. A survey of backpackers in a national park on whether the park ought to be open to off-road vehicles would more than likely show them overwhelmingly against the idea. Such a survey should include opinions from more than one interested group.

Evidence Should Be Plausible

Two events that occur close to each other in time or place may or may not be causally related. Thunder and black clouds do not always signal rain, but they do so often enough that if we are outdoors when the sky darkens and we hear thunder, we seek shelter unless we're prepared to get wet. However, if you walk under a ladder and shortly afterward sprain your ankle on a curb, you cannot conclude that walking under a ladder brings bad luck—unless you are superstitious. Although the two events occurred close to each other in time, the first did not cause the second. Merely to say that x caused y (or will cause y) is inadequate. You must demonstrate the causal relationship with pertinent facts and arguments.

For example, a driver lost control of his car one summer day and crashed into a tavern. He told the police that the accident had occurred because his car had been in the sun so long and absorbed so much solar energy that he could no longer control it. The cause the driver gave for the accident cannot be taken as either plausible or objective. A careful examination of the event would probably reveal that the driver had been a patron of the tavern shortly before the crash took place, but even this explanation would have to be demonstrated with convincing facts. The police would have to interview other tavern patrons and test the driver to determine breath- and blood-alcohol levels. If the patrons identified the driver as a recent customer in the tavern, and if the breath and blood tests showed intoxicating levels of alcohol in his system, the evidence would be sufficient to explain why the car had hit the tavern.

Evidence Should Link Causes to Effects

To show a true relationship between a cause and an effect, you must demonstrate that the existence of the one requires the existence of the other. It is often difficult to establish beyond any doubt that one event was the cause of another event. More often, a result will have more than one cause. As you research your subject, your task is to determine which cause or causes are most plausible.

When several probable causes are equally valid, report your findings accordingly, as in the following excerpt from an article on the use of an energy-saving device called a furnace-vent damper. The damper is a metal plate fitted inside the flue or vent pipe of natural-gas or fuel-oil furnaces. When the furnace is on, the damper opens to allow the gases to escape up the flue. When the furnace shuts off, the damper closes, thus preventing warm air from escaping up the flue stack. The dampers are potentially dangerous, however. If the dampers fail to open at the proper time, they could allow poisonous furnace gases to back up into the house and asphyxiate anyone in a matter of minutes. Tests run on several dampers showed a number of probable causes for their malfunctioning.

■ One damper was sold without proper installation instructions, and another was wired incorrectly. Two of the units had slow-opening dampers (15 seconds) that prevented the [furnace] burner from firing. And one damper jammed when exposed to a simulated fuel temperature of more than 700 degrees.[5]

The investigator located more than one cause of damper malfunctions and reported on them. Without such a thorough account, recommendations to prevent similar malfunctions would be based on incomplete evidence.

■ A Sample Rough Draft

Figures 2–2 and 2–3 (page 33) offer examples of outlines written for a sales brochure and a maintenance manual for the Lifemaker home gym. Figure 3–13 shows a rough draft for the sales brochure, which follows the gist of the outline. It uses many of the drafting techniques and considers the methods of development discussed in this chapter.

Nevertheless, the draft is quite rough—loosely organized, lacking in transitions and punctuation, ungrammatical, inconsistent in upper- and lowercase letters and point of view, and cluttered with jargon and unnecessary phrases. Still, as drafts go, this one reflects a strong start for the writer. Not only has she followed the basic organization of her outline, but she has managed also to work through so-called writer's blocks and to jot down the new idea of emphasizing financial incentives. She can now go on to write a second draft, develop an opening and closing that will help her tighten her focus, and then revise the entire document by using the techniques covered in Chapters 4 and 5. A marked-up version of a later draft of this memo, along with a revision, can be found in Figures 4–2 and 4–3.

---

[5] Don DeBat, "Save Energy But Save Your Life, Too," *Family Safety,* Fall 1978, p. 27.

LIFEMAKER:
The Compact Exercise System You Can Afford

For opening—say something about how owning a Lifemaker will give you healthy bones and teeth, straighten your hair, improve your love life . . . no . . . Whether you are young or young at heart, male or female, developing well-conditioned muscles will help your body perform better, look better, and help you maintain an ideal level of fitness (Needs work!! Keep going, go back to it later. Get to the muscle of the matter.)

Tentative cause-and-effect linkage

(*Description*) The Lifemaker design more compact than leading competitor's, eliminates hassle and expense of going to health club to work out. The Lifemaker fits easily into small space—4 × 7 ft living room can accommodate the Lifemaker with more ease than many home gym systems, offers more stations and more exercises because of its multiple stations. What's the point I'm making? More compact than many fancy systems, offers 40+ exercises, more than most systems priced at a comparable level—comparably priced and sized systems. OK OK, don't compromise your exercise needs with an overpriced or ineffective system. The integration of an exercise program to suit your lifestyle and budget is possible with Lifemaker.

Tentative description of system compared with competitors' systems

I'm writing all over the place and I sound like I'm making a coronation speech—don't pick, THINK. Headings, use headings you used in outline.

Cast-Iron Weight Stack

Dual weight stacks total 200 pounds of cast-iron plates. You can arrange stacks to offer a resistance range of 10 to 150 pounds and they are adjustable in 10-pound increments.

Physical description

Adjustable Cables

Resistance can be increased—no—The unique cable system is engineered to increase resistance at the stations that work the strongest muscle groups. The cables can quickly be redesigned—restructured—reconfigured without taking apart the entire system. Just pulling the center rod permits adding or removing as many plates as needed.

Combined process and physical description

The cable tension is also adjustable within sets to make sure that your muscles get the most resistance from each exercise for maximum efficiency and results.

Process description

(*Closing*) Heading? Low Maintenance—Easily Affordable
Best of all, no it's not best of all, think later about transition. . . . The Lifemaker is easy to assemble and requires little maintenance. And at $999.99, it is priced lower than the leading competitor.

Need to emphasize financial perks—mention low-interest monthly payment plan. Lifemaker will fit your back and your budget.

Figure 3–13   Draft of a Sales Brochure (with Writer's Notes)

■ Writing an Opening

As discussed earlier in this chapter, you do not need to begin your draft by writing the opening; however, understanding the purposes of an opening and the strategies for writing one can help you start the draft. The opening statement of your writing should (1) identify your subject and (2) catch the interest of your audience.

Most audiences of on-the-job writing are preoccupied with other business when they begin to read a memo, a letter, a report, or even an e-mail message; therefore, it is a good idea to catch their interest and focus their attention on the subject you are writing about. Even if your audiences are required to read what you've written, catching their interest at the outset will help ensure that they pay close attention to what follows. If you are attempting to persuade your audience, you must catch their interest if your writing is to succeed. The author of the customer newsletter article (see Figure 3–2) did this quite well.

To catch your audience's interest, you first must know your audience's needs (as discussed in Chapter 1). An awareness of those needs will help you to determine which details your audience will find important and thus interesting. Consider the opening from a memo written by a human resources manager to her supervisor (Figure 3–14). This opening not only states the subject of the report but also promises that the writer will offer solutions to a specific problem. Solutions to problems are always of interest to audiences.

Another, less-obvious problem is that of shaping the sales brochure for the Lifemaker home gym. According to the purpose of the brochure, the audience is

---

Memo

To: Paul Route, Corporate Relations Director
From: Sondra L. Rivera, Human Resources Manager   *SLR*
Date: November 1, 2003
Subject: Decreasing Applications from Local College Graduates

Concise statement of problem sets stage for proposed solution

This year only 12 local college graduates have applied for jobs at Benson Tubular Steel. Last year over 30 graduates applied, and the year before 50 applied. This decline in applications is occurring despite increasing enrollments at each school. After talking with several college counselors, I am confident that we can solve the problem of decreasing applications from local colleges.

First, we could resume our advertisements in local student newspapers. . . .

Figure 3–14   Opening to a Memo

spending too much time and money working out at health clubs or has found home exercise machines oversized or inadequate. The Lifemaker System 40, with its compact design, multiple stations, and affordable payment plan, offers a solution. Thus, an initial revision of the brochure's opening section would not address the general benefits of exercise but should state the specific problem and solution, as shown in Figure 3–15.

LIFEMAKER SYSTEM 40:
The Compact, Affordable Home Gym Designed for Maximum Fitness Conditioning

Home gyms were designed to eliminate the hassle and expense of going to a health club to work out. But most home gyms are too bulky to fit either your home or your budget and do not offer a comprehensive workout program. The Lifemaker System 40 was designed to meet the needs of a limited living space and a limited budget and offers more exercises than the leading home system.

Figure 3–15 Opening to a Brochure

For most types of writing done in offices, shops, and laboratories, openings that simply get to the point are more effective than those that provide detailed background information. Furthermore, the subject line of a memo or the title of a report is often, by itself, enough to catch the audience's interest. The following openings are typical; however, do not feel that you must slavishly follow these patterns. Rather, always first consider the purpose of your writing and the needs of your audience and then tailor your opening accordingly. Notice that all these openings get directly to the point; they do not introduce irrelevant subjects or include unnecessary details. They give the audience exactly what they need to focus their attention on what is to follow. (For examples of openings for special types of writing, such as application letters, complaint letters, and formal reports, refer to specific entries in the Index.)

Opening to Correspondence

Dear Mr. Whittier:

You will be happy to know that we have corrected the error in your bank balance. The new balance shows . . .

Opening to a Progress Report Letter

Dear Dr. Chang:

To date, 18 of the 26 specimens you submitted for analysis have been examined. Our preliminary analysis indicates . . .

Opening to a Progress Report Memo

Memo

To: David Diehl, Director of Athletics
From: Marylynn Scott, Project Engineer   *MS*
Subject: Progress Report on Rewiring the Sports Arena
Date: August 22, 2003

The rewiring program at the Sports Arena is continuing ahead of schedule. Although the cost of certain equipment is higher than our original bid had indicated, we expect to complete the project without exceeding our budget because the speed with which the project is being completed will save labor costs.

Work Completed

As of August 15, we have . . .

■ Writing a Closing

A good closing is concise and ends your writing emphatically, making it sound finished. It not only ties your writing together but also may make a significant point. A closing may recommend a course of action, offer a value judgment, speculate on the implications of your ideas, make a prediction, or summarize your main points. Even if your closing only states, "If I can be of further help, please call me" or "I would appreciate your comments," you are showing consideration for your audience and thereby gaining your audience's goodwill.

The way you close depends on the purpose of your writing and the needs of your audience. For example, the purpose of the sales brochure for the Lifemaker System 40 is to persuade the audience to purchase the system. The closing, then, could summarize the benefits described throughout the brochure and then cap the summary with a specific financial incentive.

■   Lifemaker, Inc., is offering this state-of-the-art, compact home gym for only $999.99. You can also purchase the Lifemaker System 40 on a monthly payment plan, because we believe that an exercise program should strengthen your back, not flatten your wallet. Call 1-800-933-7800 to talk with us about purchasing a Lifemaker today or visit our Web site for more information at ‹lifemaker.com ›.

A document written with a different kind of purpose might be a report studying a company's annual sales; an effective closing for the report might offer a judgment about why sales are up or down. A report for a retail department store about consumer buying trends could end by speculating on the implications of these trends, perhaps even suggesting new product lines that the store might carry in the future. A lengthy report could end with a summary of the main points covered to pull the ideas together for the audience. The following figure shows a typical closing.

Closing of a Progress Report Memo

Memo

To: David Diehl, Director of Athletics
From: Marylynn Scott, Project Engineer *MS*
Subject: Progress Report on Rewiring the Sports Arena
Date: August 22, 2003

The rewiring program at the Sports Arena is continuing ahead of schedule. Although the cost of certain equipment is higher than our original bid had indicated, we expect to complete the project without exceeding our budget because the speed with which the project is being completed will save labor costs.

Work Completed

As of August 15, we have . . .

Opens with prediction

Although my original estimate on equipment ($20,000) has been exceeded by $2,300, my original labor estimate ($60,000) has been reduced by $3,500. Therefore I will easily stay within the limits of my original bid. In addition, I see no difficulty in having the arena finished in time for the December 23 Christmas program.

Ends with summary of costs and final prediction

Any of the methods for closing can be effective, depending on the purpose of your writing and the needs of your audience. Be careful, however, not to close with a cliché or a platitude, such as "While profits have increased with the introduction of this new product, the proof of the pudding is in the eating" or "Please feel free to contact us at your earliest convenience," when the contents don't call for a response of any kind. Also be careful not to introduce a new topic in your closing. A closing should always relate to and reinforce the ideas presented in the opening and body of your writing.

CHAPTER 3 SUMMARY: Writing the Draft
(continued)

Gathering the details you need (see Chapter 1) and grouping them in an outline (see Chapter 2) will enable you to write a good rough draft. When writing the draft, remember that your task is to produce only a working document, not a polished piece of writing. Polish will come with revision (see Chapters 4 and 5).

Use the following guidelines as you write the draft:

- [ ] Concentrate solely on getting your draft written.
- [ ] Do not confuse writing with revising; they are different tasks, and each requires a different frame of mind.
- [ ] Avoid revising as you write — do not worry about perfection at this point in the writing process. Focus on *what* you are writing, not on *how* you are writing.
- [ ] Allocate your time efficiently.
- [ ] Prepare a comfortable work environment.
- [ ] Sustain momentum once you begin writing.
- [ ] Take brief breaks after reaching certain milestones.
- [ ] Keep your intended readers actively in mind, visualizing them if possible, and address your topic from their point of view.
- [ ] Consider the voice your readers should hear — concerned, neutral, authoritative.
- [ ] Be persuasive:
  - Take your readers' feelings into account.
  - Avoid a hostile tone.
  - Appeal to your readers' good sense.
  - Acknowledge other points of view where an issue is controversial.

Consider the following kinds of writing:

- [ ] Explain a process:
  - Ensure that you understand the process thoroughly.
  - Introduce the process with information about its purpose and significance.
  - Divide the process into steps.
  - Present each step in its proper sequence.
  - Illustrate steps and procedures when this aids clarity.
  - Present the information at a level appropriate to your readers' background.
  - Write concisely.
- [ ] Describe information:
  - Select details carefully based on what use your readers will make of the description.
  - Ensure that you are thoroughly familiar with what you are describing.
  - Provide a brief explanation of the function of any physical objects you describe, such as equipment.
  - Do not overwhelm your readers with unnecessary details.
  - Add illustrations where they add clarity.

☐ Define terms and concepts:
  ■ For formal definitions, state which grouping or class the term belongs to and show how it differs from all other members of that class.
  ■ For informal definitions, substitute familiar words and phrases for unfamiliar terms.
  ■ Avoid circular and "is when" and "is where" definitions.
☐ Explain cause and effect:
  ■ Establish a plausible relationship between an event and its cause.
  ■ Evaluate evidence for the relationship carefully:
    – Is it pertinent?
    – Is it sufficient?
    – Is it representative?
    – Is it plausible?
  ■ Do not overstate conclusions.
☐ Write an opening that identifies your subject to focus your readers' attention.
☐ Get to the point first, even when providing essential background information in the opening.
☐ Create closings that reinforce, summarize, or tie together the ideas in the body of your writing.
☐ Do not introduce ideas in the closing that have not been discussed elsewhere in your writing.

■ Exercises

1. If you have not already started drafting a class assignment, use the following focused freewriting technique to get started. Gather your resource material—which may include, for example, a project plan, an outline, research notes, an audience analysis—and then review it. Focus on your role and voice as the writer who must communicate with a specific audience by considering the larger needs of your audience (reread Establishing Your Role and Voice as the Writer on page 69). After you have thought of the most important thing your audience wants to know, begin a focused freewrite on the subject by using the process described in this exercise. This process works especially well with a computer and a blank screen, but you can also use a pen and a pad of paper.

    W On the Web For an online quiz on composing and revising, go to Chapter 3, bedfordstmartins.com/ writingthatworks

    a. You will have 15 minutes. Time yourself by setting a timer or alarm or by writing down the time you start and glancing at the clock.
    b. Write for 15 minutes without stopping about the most important thing your audience needs to know about your topic or document. If you are using the computer, turn the monitor brightness down so that you cannot see what you are writing.
    c. Write whatever pops into your head and write as fast as you can. If you can't think of anything to say, just keep writing "I can't think of anything to say" over and over until something else comes into your head.

d. Don't stop to read what you have written or to correct or revise. Just keep writing.

e. Don't worry about making mistakes or incomplete sentences or paragraphs; just keep writing as much as possible while staying focused on the topic.

f. When the time is up, finish your last thought and then stop. Take a break, and then come back to read what you've written. Consider the most important point you uncovered in the freewriting and where you need to go next. Focusing on your next point or idea, repeat the process. When done, repeat the process one more time. By now, you should have written several pages.

g. Let your writing sit for a long period—at least overnight—and then reread what you have written. Write a brief assessment of the technique and turn in your assessment and freewriting to your instructor.

2. Write an opening paragraph for two of the following topics to the audience specified in parentheses.

   • My favorite instructor (to someone nominating him or her for a teaching award)
   • Ways to improve employee motivation (to the president or head of the organization that employs you)
   • Ways to improve student advising at your school (to the dean of students or someone in an equivalent position)
   • What to look for in a first apartment (to a friend who is looking)
   • Important features to consider when purchasing a new automobile, cellular phone, or personal computer (to a friend who is looking)
   • The advantages of setting up your budget or checking account on your personal computer (to a spendthrift friend)

3. Building on Exercise 2, write a closing for the same topics and audiences.

4. Interview three people who write as a major part of their jobs, such as technical writers, professors, or managers. Ask them about the techniques that they find especially useful in writing their first drafts, then present your findings to the class.

5. Using the Lifemaker compact exercise system as your topic (see Figure 3–13), write three different opening paragraphs for a Lifemaker System 40 sales brochure geared toward each of the following audiences (one paragraph for each):

   • college students
   • retired persons
   • industry executives

6. Building on Exercise 5, write three different closing paragraphs for a Lifemaker System 40 sales brochure geared toward each of the following audiences (one paragraph for each):

   • college students
   • retired persons
   • industry executives

7. Summarize in a list all of the differences you had to be aware of when writing for different audiences and for different purposes in Exercises 5 and 6 (for example, time constraints, mobility constraints, and so forth).

8. Write a letter to a prospective student from your hometown who is interested in learning more about your chosen course of study. With your audience and pur-

pose in mind, draft a letter that includes an effective opening, specifies important elements of the program and other relevant details in the body, and uses an appropriate closing. Use correct business-letter format when preparing your letter. (See Chapter 9 for format.)

9. Assume that your university is planning to purchase a city block next door to the business school. A grocery store, a print shop, a snack shop, and two apartment buildings have all been asked to sell their properties to the university. The property owners feel their businesses would not survive farther from campus. Without knowing any more details, write a letter of support—either for the property owners who do not want to sell or for the university, which feels expansion is necessary. After you have completed your letter, make a list of specific types of information that would have helped you write a more effective letter.

Collaborative Classroom Projects

1. Assume that your school has adopted a new policy that you and your classmates are dissatisfied with. In small groups, brainstorm ideas for a letter that your class would send to the dean. Refer to Considering Audience and Purpose on page 72 to outline and draft the letter.

2. Choose a spokesperson for your group and share with the class your group's letter from Project 1. As a class, decide which letter or letters are most persuasive. Discuss why. Then, in your small group, analyze your own letter, comparing it to the ones you heard from your classmates. Was your outline sufficient? Was your letter written for the intended audience (see page 72)? As a group, review your role and voice as writer. Did your opening identify your subject and catch the attention of the audience? Did it tie the writing together? Finally, analyze your closing.

3. Bring to class an advertisement from a magazine for a personal computer, a cellular phone, a fax machine, or a similar item. Create an outline and then draft a brief narrative describing the product and its technology to a person who knows nothing about this product. Or, draft a letter or memo aimed at a particular type of consumer whom you would like to persuade to purchase this product. Begin by assessing your audience and creating a brief outline.

Research Projects

1. Research a business or technological advancement that you are curious about. Narrow your topic to one particular aspect of that field and write a rough draft of a paper entitled "Recent Breakthroughs in _____ [a particular field]: _____ [specific breakthrough]." Analyze the topic and support your analysis with information that you've researched. For example, if you decided to write about a new medical procedure, your analysis might be that the risks do or do not outweigh the benefits; you would then support your opinion with the findings that persuaded you.

    a. Submit a four- to five-page draft with an outline to your instructor.

    b. Meet with your instructor to discuss his or her suggestions for revision.

    c. Conduct further research if necessary.

    d. Write a second draft and do any further revisions necessary.

Save this draft, as you will be asked to refer to it at the end of Chapter 4.

2. Gather three sales brochures (from direct-mailing campaigns or retail stores) that promote the same product or service.

    a. Write a two- to three-page paper in which you compare and contrast the opening paragraphs of the brochures.

      • In the first part of your paper, address whether the brochures differ in their purposes or audience focus. Support your analysis with examples from the brochures.

      • In the second part of your paper, read only the opening paragraph of each brochure. Then explain which brochure is your favorite. Support your choice with examples from the opening text of that brochure.

    b. Write a two- or three-page paper in which you compare and contrast the closing paragraphs of the brochures. In your paper, address the issues in Research Project 2a, considering only the closing paragraphs of the brochures.

3. Write your own sales brochure. You may use the same general topic you researched in Research Project 2, or you may select a different topic. Refer to the Chapter 3 Summary, on pages 96–97, keeping in mind the importance of the opening and closing paragraphs. Begin by drafting an outline.

4. Gather samples of correspondence, brief articles, or reports, using books, newspapers, magazines, and materials that you receive in the mail. Find an example of each of the following types of closings:

    • polite but helpful
    • recommends a response
    • makes a prediction
    • offers a judgment
    • summarizes

Based on the closing, what is the purpose of each writing sample and the target audience for each? Support your conclusions with examples.

5. You have the opportunity to apply for a semester's paid tuition because of your interest in and dedication to your prospective field of study. To apply for the funds, you need to submit a letter to the tuition committee describing the job opportunities available in your field and outlining your professional goals. After researching the different job opportunities, draft a letter to the committee. Keep your readers in mind, especially as you develop the opening and closing of your letter.

■ Web Projects

Projects followed by the symbol W are continued at **bedfordstmartins.com/ writingthatworks**, Chapter 3.

1. Locate the home page of the Web site of at least three companies you are familiar with, such as Chrysler, Procter & Gamble, or IBM, or any company of potential ca-

reer interest to you. Take note of the product information, warranty information, sales information for consumers, and employment information. List the common purpose your companies have when providing information on the Internet. Then choose one common type of information provided by all three companies—for example, product information—and write an opening paragraph on that topic for each company.

2. Visit the Web site of the U.S. Census Bureau and read about a particular aspect of the 2000 Census that affects or interests you personally. Prepare an outline and draft a brief summary of your findings. W

3. Research a particular project being carried out by a U.S. government agency or read the findings of a study that interests you. Prepare an outline and draft a brief summary of the project or report. W

4. Use the Web to research an individual in your professional field whom you admire. Gather advice that the individual may have about writing on the job, giving presentations, or performing some other specific aspect of his or her work. Draft a paper in which you briefly describe that person's professional achievements; explain the relevance of those achievements to you; and detail the useful advice or information that you have gathered during your research. Also describe how you might apply this advice or information to your own career.

5. Locate at least three companies on the Web that hire business or technical writers. For example, what companies in the area of medicine, technology, or advertising hire writers? What kinds of documents or other materials do writers for these companies produce? (Search the companies' Web sites for documents produced by their professional writers). How would the information covered in Chapter 3 apply to the writing required by these companies? Prepare a brief draft of your reply.

4 Revising for Essentials

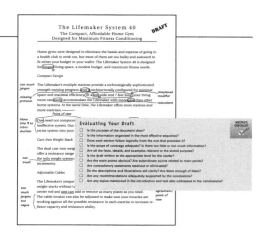

One of the enduring legends of American history is that President Abraham Lincoln wrote the Gettysburg Address as he made the train trip from Washington, D.C., to Gettysburg, Pennsylvania. The address is a remarkable accomplishment, even for a writer as gifted as Lincoln. It is the eloquent testimony of a leader with a powerful intellect and a compassionate heart.

The facts of how the Gettysburg Address was composed do not support the legend, however. Lincoln actually worked on the address for weeks and revised the draft many times.[1] What Lincoln was doing on the train to Gettysburg was nothing more than what any of us must do before our writing is finally acceptable: He was revising. What is remarkable about the address is that Lincoln made so many revisions of a speech of well under 300 words. Obviously, he wanted it to fit the occasion for which it was intended, and he knew that something written hastily and without reflection would not satisfy his purpose and audience.

This principle is as true for anyone who writes on the job (which, of course, is what the president was doing) as it was for Lincoln. Unlike the Gettysburg Address, however, most on-the-job writing should not strive for oratorical elegance; the more natural a piece of writing sounds to the audience, the more effort the writer has probably put into revising it.

This chapter introduces the elements essential to revising any draft piece of writing, such as:

- How to put yourself in the right frame of mind as you begin
- How to review the draft's organization for logic
- How to ensure that the scope of coverage is adequate to your purpose and audience
- How to evaluate the draft for accuracy
- How to test for effective sentences

---

[1] Tom Burnam, *The Dictionary of Misinformation* (New York: Perennial Library, 1986), pp. 93–94.

- How to ensure that the language throughout is precise, concise, unbiased, free of affectation, and grammatically correct
- How to proofread for punctuation and spelling errors

Finally, the chapter concludes with two annotated revisions of the Lifemaker sales brochure that use the points covered in this chapter as a guide.

■ Strategies

Have you ever found after writing a first draft that you knew it wasn't the best you could do, but that you did not know how to improve it? If your answer is yes, you are not alone. All writers — even professional writers — have the same problem at some time or another.

W On the Web
For online resources for revising for essentials, go to Chapter 4, **bedfordstmartins.com/ writingthatworks**

The problem has a simple explanation. Immediately after you write a rough draft, the ideas are so fresh in your mind that you cannot read the words, sentences, and paragraphs objectively. That is, you cannot sufficiently detach yourself from them to be able to look at the writing critically. To revise effectively, you must be critical. You cannot allow yourself to think, "Because my ideas are good, the way I've expressed them must also be good." The first step toward effective revision, then, is to develop a critical frame of mind — to become objective.

As professional writers have learned, there are a number of ways to put distance between yourself and your writing and become objective.

1. Allow for a cooling period. Wait a day or two (or even a few hours) between writing a rough draft and revising it — you will be able to look at the writing itself more objectively.

2. Pretend that a stranger has written your draft. This will help you to see the faults of the draft. If you can look at your writing and ask, "How could I have written that?" you are in the right frame of mind to revise.

3. Revise your draft in multiple passes. Don't try to find everything that is wrong all at once. Make a first pass, looking at only one aspect of your writing, such as organization. During the second pass, look at a different aspect, such as wordiness. Continue to make passes until you are satisfied with your draft.

4. Be alert for your most frequent problems. Be sure that you are aware of the errors you typically make, and watch for them as you revise.

5. Read your draft aloud. Some people find that this enables them to distance themselves from their writing so that they can become more objective about it.

6. Ask someone else to read and critique your draft. Someone who is fresh to your draft can see it objectively and identify problems that you need to address as you revise.

Voices from the Workplace

Eduardo Lapetina, Cato Research

As a senior scientist at Cato Research, a contract pharmaceutical research company, Eduardo Lapetina has researched and written more than 200 articles for prominent scientific journals. Above all, Eduardo says, "scientific writing has to be precise." To achieve both accuracy and clarity, Eduardo oversees a process that involves many people — from the first draft, through several revisions, to the final product.

"Writing scientific papers takes considerable time, and we go through many different drafts." For Eduardo and his colleagues, collaboration is the key to the revision process. "The first draft is written and polished by peer scientists who provide input on technical parts of the manuscript and make changes to improve the scientific language." Once the team has agreed upon the final draft, Eduardo checks the scientific content of the manuscript, revising it as needed. The content is further revised by a scientific editor who checks the accuracy of the language. "At this point," Eduardo says, "I read the manuscript again to be sure that the science and the scientific language are accurate and that there is stylistic consistency." Finally, the manuscript is sent out for publication in a scientific journal, where it may be further revised before publication.

Visit Cato Research on the Web at <cato.com>.

William M. Tammick III, Lifeline Systems, Inc.

William M. Tammick III is a senior customer service specialist for Lifeline Systems, Inc., a company that supplies and monitors personal emergency response systems. William is responsible for a variety of writing tasks — from writing daily correspondence to customers and coworkers to creating process and procedure documents and developing training manuals. When reworking drafts of his writing, William rereads and edits with his audience and purpose in mind.

"Revising is an important part of the writing process because initially you are just putting ideas and thoughts onto paper. It also allows you to fine-tune your message. When I am revising, I ask myself a few questions: Who is my audience — am I addressing a new employee or a customer? Is my vocabulary appropriate for my intended audience? I can use words and language when addressing a colleague that may not be appropriate when communicating with a customer. What are my key points? I will often start with these points and then work around them to fill out a letter during my revision. This way I ensure that my point is clear."

Visit Lifeline Systems, Inc., on the Web at <lifelinesys.com>.

Of course, you may discover your own methods of becoming objective. One student, for example, finds that she can be more critical if she writes her first draft on yellow paper. Another student creates his first draft on a computer because he cannot be critical when looking at his own handwriting. Some students like to revise with a felt-tip pen; others prefer using colored pencils. Experiment and find out what helps you. The particular methods that work for you are not important. What is important is that you develop some technique for evaluating your writing — and then use it as the basis of your revision.

■ Organization and Content

The more experienced you become as a writer, the more you will tend to view revision as a whole-text task, involving changes to the structure and content of a piece of writing as well as changes at the sentence level. The instructions about revising in passes in this chapter emphasize this point by indicating the sequence most commonly used by experienced writers in revising their drafts. They begin with the global issues—organization and scope of coverage—before proceeding to the details of grammar and punctuation.

The easiest way to test the soundness of your organization is to write an outline of your rough draft, a technique most useful for longer drafts but helpful with smaller ones, too. The advantage of doing so is that the outline breaks down the blocks of text to the essential ideas and makes the sequence of these ideas easy to see. Does this outline conform to the outline from which you wrote the draft? It may not because you probably rethought some ideas or added or deleted information as you wrote. If you find a problem with the logic of the sequence or with the amount or type of information included or omitted, revise the outline—and then your draft—to reflect the solution.

A review of the relevant information in Chapters 1, 2, and 3 will be especially helpful as you reassess the effectiveness of your draft when it comes to these larger issues. Review in Chapter 1 the sections titled Establishing Your Scope (page 9) and Organizing Your Ideas (page 12). Further evaluate the logic of your organization by reviewing the material in Chapter 2 on testing the difference between major and subordinate ideas (pages 24–31). See Chapter 3 for guidance on ensuring that you address the right audience in the right voice (pages 67–76). Once you complete this review, you are ready to tackle the smaller, more detailed steps of the process described in the remainder of this chapter.

Evaluating Your Draft

WRITER'S CHECKLIST

☐ Is the purpose of the document clear?

☐ Is the information organized in the most effective sequence?

☐ Does each section follow logically from the one that precedes it?

☐ Is the scope of coverage adequate? Is there too little or too much information?

☐ Are all the facts, details, and examples relevant to the stated purpose?

☐ Is the draft written at the appropriate level for the reader?

☐ Are the main points obvious? Are subordinate points related to main points?

☐ Are contradictory statements resolved or eliminated?

☐ Do the descriptions and illustrations aid clarity? Are there enough of them?

☐ Are any recommendations adequately supported by the conclusions?

☐ Are any topics mentioned in the introduction and text also addressed in the conclusions?

Chapter 5 describes the final revision stage. This stage encompasses evaluating paragraph unity, length, and coherence; knitting together the various components of your draft with a variety of transitional devices; and achieving emphatic writing—emphasizing important ideas and downplaying secondary ideas.

■ Accuracy and Completeness

Above all else, your information must be accurate. Although accuracy is important in all types of writing, it takes on special significance when you write on the job. One misplaced decimal point, for example, can create a staggering budgetary error. Incorrect or imprecise instructions can cause injury to a worker. At the very least, if your writing is not accurate you will quickly lose the confidence of your readers. They will be annoyed, for example, if a figure or fact in your writing differs from one in a chart or graph. These kinds of inaccuracies are easily overlooked as you write a first draft, so you must correct them during revision.

Revision is the time to insert any missing facts or ideas. When you finish your draft, check it against your outline. If any of the main ideas or supporting details you listed are missing from your draft, rewrite your sentences and paragraphs as necessary to incorporate the missing information.

In revising your draft for completeness, you may also think of new information that you failed to include when you were preparing and writing your outline. Always carefully consider such new information in the context of your audience and purpose. If the information will help satisfy your audience's need and accomplish the purpose of your writing, by all means add it now. However, if the information—no matter how interesting—does not serve these ends, it has no place in your writing.

DIGITAL SHORTCUTS

Revising Your Draft

- Print out a double-spaced copy of your draft. Write notes and revisions on this draft before returning to the computer to enter the corrections.
- Copy or move blocks of text as needed.
- Use the Find command to locate inappropriate diction such as *a lot;* wordy phrases such as *that is, there are, the fact that,* and *to be;* and unnecessary helping modifiers or verbs such as *very* and *will.*
- Use the Find command to locate technical terms that may need further explanation and define them in the text or in a glossary.
- Use the Find command to locate your most commonly misused words.
- Use the spell and grammar checkers, and reread for accuracy.

■ Effective Sentences

An effective writing style communicates precisely, clearly, and concisely. To achieve this style, review each sentence for problems that can obscure precision, clarity, and conciseness, such as unconventional sentence structure, unclear subjects, and imprecise verbs. The conventional structure of a sentence in English is subject-verb-object: "Marketing research improved sales." The majority of your sentences should follow this pattern, because your audience subconsciously expects that pattern.

In an effective sentence, subjects and verbs are clear and obvious. An effective sentence states the doer of the action in the subject and the action in the verb. Although that advice may seem too simple to be necessary, business writing abounds in sentences that do not identify the doer of the action that is being expressed. Consider the following sentence from a training manual:

AMBIGUOUS   This command enables sending the entire message again if an incomplete message transfer occurs.

This sentence contains no subject for the verb *sending*. The reader doesn't know who or what is doing the sending. (*This command* is the subject of *enables*, not *sending*.) Improve such a sentence by providing the missing subject:

CLEAR   This command enables you to send the entire message again if the message is incompletely transferred.

The doer of the action may also be buried someplace other than in the subject:

AMBIGUOUS   Decisions on design and marketing strategy are made at the managerial level.

For your sentence to be effective, you must make sure that the doer of the action is stated in your subject:

CLEAR   Managers make design and marketing decisions.

Analyze your draft for nominalizations, which occur when you indicate the action of a sentence or clause with a noun ("to perform an audit") instead of using the verb form of the noun ("to audit"). Although nominalizations are not grammatically wrong, their repeated use makes writing sluggish under the weight of all those formal-sounding nouns and redundant verbs. Whenever a sentence seems particularly fuzzy, look for the action being expressed; if it is expressed with a noun instead of a verb, try revising the sentence to state the action in a verb:

■ The Legal Department will ∧*conduct an investigation of* the charge.
                      investigate

ESL TIPS

Using Common Sentence Patterns

1. **Subject + Verb**
   The meeting + began.
2. **Subject + Verb + Direct Object**
   The chairperson + began + the meeting.
3. **Subject + Verb + Subject Complement** (renames or describes the subject)
   The meeting + was + effective.
4. **Subject + Verb + Indirect Object + Direct Object**
   The secretary + gave + the accountant + the pay schedule.
5. **Subject + Verb + Direct Object + Object Complement** (renames or describes the direct object)
   The chairperson + considered + the merger + a success.

■ Basics

Grammatical errors, like inaccurate facts or incomplete information, can confuse or irritate your readers and cause them to lose confidence in you. Even worse, many of the errors discussed in this chapter are so severe that they can actually alter the meaning of a sentence. Therefore, you must check for grammatical correctness in revising your draft.

Following is a summary of common grammatical errors: agreement, consistency, dangling modifiers, misplaced modifiers, and sentence problems. Each type of error is described briefly here and is then explained in detail in Part Four: A Writer's Handbook. (See Section A, Grammar, Punctuation, and Mechanics,

ESL TIPS

Constructing Sentences

Declarative sentences follow the subject-verb-object/complement word order.

subject verb object complement
■ Edward arrived late this morning.

Interrogative sentences add a question word and invert the subject and the first auxiliary verb (auxiliary verb-subject-main verb-object).

auxiliary verb subject main verb
■ Will Edward arrive on time?
                            —*object*

Adjectives precede nouns.

■ *my* book
■ *seven* files
■ *contented* coworkers

An adverb is often placed at the end of the sentence.

■ Edward arrived *late*.

An adverb should never separate a verb from its object.

                              immediately
■ Edward phoned ~~immediately~~ his boss.
                                ^

When adverbs of time, manner, and location are present, the adverb of time may appear at the beginning and adverbs of manner at the end of the sentence:

■ *Tomorrow,* Edward will arrive *late at his office.*

or the adverbs of manner, location, and time may appear at the end:

■ Edward will arrive *late at his office tomorrow.*

Frequency adverbs generally follow the verb *to be* or the first auxiliary verb and precede the main verb.

■ Vacations are *always* too short.
■ Vacations *always* fly by too quickly.

pages 635–730, and Section C, English as a Second Language (ESL), pages 736–753.) If you find it helpful, use the following summary as a checklist for grammatical revisions.

Agreement

Agreement means that the parts of a sentence, like the pieces of a jigsaw puzzle, fit together properly. The following discussion points out how problems of agreement often occur.

Subject-Verb Agreement

A verb must agree with its subject in number. A singular subject requires a singular verb; a plural subject requires a plural verb. Do not let intervening phrases and clauses mislead you. (See Section 4.11 of the Handbook.)

■   The *use* of insecticides, fertilizers, and weed killers, although they offer unquestion-
    able benefits, often *result* in unfortunate side effects.

Do not make the verb agree with the noun immediately preceding it if that noun is not its subject. This problem is especially likely to occur when a modifying phrase containing a plural noun falls between a singular subject and its verb.

■   Only *one* of the emergency lights *was* functioning when the accident occurred.

For additional coverage of subject-verb agreement, see Section 4.11 of the Handbook.

ESL TIPS

Forming the Third-Person Singular Present Tense

The third-person singular present tense must end in an *-s* or *-es*. This tense is formed when the subject of the verb is either a singular noun or one of the following pronouns: *he, she,* or *it.*

- ■ He *walks* every day.
- ■ She *does* her homework.
- ■ It *takes* too long.

Pronoun-Antecedent Number Agreement

A pronoun must agree with its antecedent, the noun to which it refers, in number (singular or plural). (See Section 2.13 of the Handbook.

■   Although the typical *engine* runs well in moderate temperatures, ~~they~~ *it* often stall in extreme cold.

Pronoun-Antecedent Gender Agreement

A pronoun must also agree with its antecedent in gender — masculine, feminine, or neuter. (See Section 3.2.2b of the Handbook.)

■ *Mr. Lin* acknowledges *his* responsibility for the misunderstanding, but *Ms. Barkley* should acknowledge *her* responsibility for it also.

Understanding Agreement (Pronouns)

ESL TIPS

The pronouns *he, she, it, his, hers,* and *its* must agree in number and gender with their antecedents — the words, phrases, or clauses that they *refer to — not* to the words they modify.

> *her*
■ The *lawyer* won all ~~its~~ cases.
>   ^
>   *her*
■ The *woman* brought ~~his~~ brother a cup of soup.
>   ^
>   *his*
■ *Robert* sent ~~her~~ mother flowers on Mother's Day.
>   ^

Each and *every* take singular pronouns, even in compound antecedents.

■ *Each* business has *its* own logo.
■ *Every* book and article was included on the list with *its* title and date of publication.

All and *some* can take singular or plural pronouns, depending on whether the nouns they modify are count nouns or mass nouns.

■ *All* of the chocolate melted; *it* was stored near a furnace.
■ *Some* of the prisoners escaped; *they* were left unattended.

A possessive pronoun agrees with the subject (*father*), not the object (*son*).

■ The *father* watches *his* son.

The phrase *one of the* takes a singular pronoun even though the noun that follows must be plural. The pronoun refers to *one.*

■ *One* of the accountants lost *her* luggage.

The relative pronoun *who* is used for people; *which* and *that* are used for objects.

■ The *man who* spoke is the company's largest investor.
■ Mr. Geoff invests in ExxonMobil *stocks, which* have increased in value.
■ The boss wants the *folder that* he left on his desk.

Collective nouns rarely end in *-s,* but they take plural pronouns.

■ Those *people* are interested only in seeing *their* investment grow.

Some singular nouns end in *-s,* but they take singular pronouns.

■ The *United States* asked *its* allies to support the effort.

Consistency of Person and Tense

Much like agreement errors, illogical shifts in person or tense can confuse the reader. You would be confused, for example, if someone wrote to you: "If you show the guard your pass, one will be allowed to enter the gate" (shift in person) or "When the contract was signed, the company submits the drawings" (shift in tense). Your confusion would disappear, however, if the sentences were revised as follows:

■ If you show the guard your pass, you will be allowed to enter the gate.

■ When the contract was signed, the company submitted the drawings.

Person

Person refers to the forms of a personal pronoun that indicate whether the pronoun represents the speaker, the person spoken to, or the person (or thing) spoken about. If the pronoun represents the speaker, the pronoun is in the first person. (See Section 2.9 of the Handbook.)

■   *I* could not find the answer in the manual.

If the pronoun represents the person or persons spoken to, the pronoun is in the second person.

■   *You* are going to be a good supervisor.

If the pronoun represents the person or persons spoken about, the pronoun is in the third person.

■   *They* received the news calmly.

Identifying pronouns by person helps you avoid illogical shifts from one person to another. A common error is to shift from the third person to the second person.

■   People should spend mornings on work requiring mental effort, because ~~your~~ mind *their* *s*
      ~~is~~ freshest then. *are*

Tense

Tense refers to the forms of a verb that indicate time—past, present, or future. Be consistent in your use of tense; an unnecessary and illogical change of tense within a sentence confuses the reader. (See Section 4.9 of the Handbook.) The following sentence changes from the past tense (*installed*) to the present tense (*cleans*).

■   Before he *installed* the circuit board, he ~~cleans~~ the contacts. *cleaned*

To be both correct and logical, the sentence must be written with both verbs in the same tense. The only acceptable change of tense within a sentence records a real change of time.

■   After you *have assembled* Part A [past tense, because the action occurred in the past], *assemble* Part B [present tense, because the action occurs in the present].

Dangling Modifiers

Modifiers are words that describe, explain, or qualify an element in a sentence. They can be adjectives, adverbs, phrases, or clauses. A *dangling modifier* is a phrase that does not clearly refer to another word or phrase in the sentence. As you will see in the next section, misplaced modifiers can result in ambiguity; dangling modifiers, by contrast, result in illogical sentences. (See Section 4.9 of the Handbook.)

ILLOGICAL   While eating lunch in the cafeteria, my computer experienced a power surge and shut down.

Although the idea of a computer eating lunch in a cafeteria is ridiculous, that is what the sentence actually states. With the dangling modifier corrected, the sentence reads as follows:

CORRECT   While I was eating lunch in the cafeteria, my computer experienced a power surge and shut down.

Dangling modifiers can cause such confusion that your reader misinterprets the meaning of your sentence completely. One way to correct a dangling modifier is to add a noun or pronoun for the phrase to modify.

■ After finishing the research, *we found that* the job was easy. [The phrase *after finishing the research* has nothing to modify without the pronoun *we* that tells the audience who finished.]

A dangling modifier can also be corrected by making the phrase a clause.

ILLOGICAL   *After finishing the research* [phrase], the job was easy.
CORRECT   *After we finished the research* [clause], the job was easy.

(See Sections 9 and 10 of the Handbook, respectively, for definitions of *phrase* and *clause*.)

Misplaced Modifiers

Another source of ambiguity occurs in the placement of modifiers. The simple modifiers most likely to create ambiguity are *only, almost, just, hardly, even,* and *barely.* When you use one of these terms in a sentence, be sure that it modifies the word or element that you had intended it to. In most cases, place the modifier directly in front of the word it is supposed to qualify.

■ We *almost* lost all of the parts. [The parts were *almost* lost but were not.]

■ We lost *almost* all of the parts. [Most of the parts were in fact lost.]

(See Section 11.19 of the Handbook for a more extensive discussion of modifiers.)

Sentence Problems

A number of errors can make a sentence ungrammatical. The most common such errors are sentence fragments and run-on sentences.

Fragments

A sentence that is missing an essential part (subject or predicate) is called a *sentence fragment*.

SENTENCE   He quit his job. [*He* is the subject; *quit his job* is the predicate.]

FRAGMENT   And left for Australia. [The subject is missing.]

Having a subject and a predicate does not automatically make a group of words a sentence, however; the word group must also make an independent statement. *If I work* is a fragment because the subordinating conjunction *if* turns the statement into a dependent clause. (See Section 11.18 of the Handbook.)

Understanding Sentence Structure   ESL TIPS

- A sentence must start with a capital letter.
- A sentence must end with a period, a question mark, or an exclamation point.
- A sentence must have a subject.
- A sentence must have a verb.
- A sentence must express an idea that can stand on its own (called the main, or independent, clause).

- A sentence must conform to subject-verb-object word order (or inverted word order for questions or emphasis).

Run-on Sentences

A *run-on sentence*, sometimes called a *fused sentence*, is made up of two or more independent clauses (sentence elements that contain a subject and a predicate and could stand alone as complete sentences) not separated by punctuation. (See Section 11.17 of the Handbook.)

INCORRECT   The new manager instituted several new procedures some were impractical.

Run-on sentences can be corrected in the following ways:

1. Create two separate sentences.
   - The new manager instituted several new procedures. Some were impractical.
2. Join the two clauses with a semicolon if they are closely related.
   - The new manager instituted several new procedures; some were impractical.
3. Join the clauses with a comma and a coordinating conjunction.
   - The new manager instituted several new procedures, *but* some were impractical.
4. Subordinate one clause to the other.
   - The new manager instituted several new procedures, some of which were impractical.

5. Join the two clauses with a conjunctive adverb preceded by a semicolon and followed by a comma.

■ The new manager instituted several new procedures; *however,* some were impractical.

ESL TIPS

Understanding the Subject of a Sentence

Every sentence, *except* commands, must have an explicit subject.

He established
■ *Ozzie* worked fast. ~~Established~~ the parameters for the project. [*He* is the subject.]

In commands, the subject *you* is understood and is used only for emphasis.

■ Wait! [*You* is understood.]
■ Show up at the airport at 6:30. [*You* is understood.]
■ *You* do your homework, young man. [*You* is for emphasis.]

The subject of a sentence can be a noun (*the office*), a pronoun (*he*), a noun clause (*what the manager reported*), a gerund (*working*), or an infinitive (*to attend*).

■ *The office* was closed.
■ *He* offered to work on the project.
■ *What the manager reported* did not agree.
■ *Working* late made the employees angry.
■ *To attend* the conference was a wonderful opportunity.

The subject of a sentence may be either a noun *or* a pronoun.

■ *The meeting it* was adjourned.
or
It
■ ~~*The meeting it*~~ was adjourned.

If you move the subject from its normal position (subject-verb-object), you may need to replace the subject with an expletive (*there, it*). In this construction, the verb agrees with the subject that follows it.

■ *There are* two files on the desk. [The subject is *files.*]

Time, distance, weather, temperature, and environmental expressions use *it* as their subject.

■ *It* is ten o'clock.
■ *It* is ten miles down the road.
■ *It* never snows in Florida.
■ *It* is hot in Jorge's office.
■ *It* gets stuffy in here quickly.

■ Mechanics

Comma Errors

The most common punctuation problem is misuse of the comma. This is understandable because the comma has such a wide variety of uses: It links, it encloses, it separates, and it indicates omissions. (For a complete discussion of the comma, see Section 13 of the Handbook. Other marks of punctuation are covered in the Handbook as well.) The following guidelines will help you to use the comma correctly and effectively.

When two independent clauses are joined with only a comma, the error is known as a *comma splice.* (See Section 13.11 of the Handbook.)

■ It was 500 miles to the facility, we made arrangements to fly.

Like a run-on sentence, a comma splice can be corrected in several ways. The most common way is to join the two clauses with a comma and a coordinating conjunction:

■ It was 500 miles to the facility, *so* we made arrangements to fly.

When correcting a comma splice, be sure that the solution you choose correctly conveys the intended emphasis of the original sentence.

Do not place a comma everywhere you pause. Although commas usually signal pauses, *pauses do not necessarily call for commas.* A number of common errors involve placing commas where they do not belong. (See Section 13.12 of the Handbook.)

Spelling Errors

Use your computer spell checker as a first step to finding spelling errors. The software will locate misspelled words, repeated words (*the the*), words with numbers instead of letters (*will* with two *1*'s rather than two *l*'s), and common errors in capitalization made during keying (*THere* for *There*).

Although the spell checker is an important tool for on-screen proofing, it cannot identify whether you meant *their* or *there* in a given context. It recognizes both words as correctly spelled and so will pass over each whenever it occurs, regardless of whether you intended one instead of the other. It will not help you with numbers or the special characters in chemical or mathematical equations. You still must print a paper copy of your document and proof it carefully to catch all keying mistakes. (Section C of the Handbook provides instructions that will strengthen your knowledge of English spelling conventions.)

■ Preciseness

The following sign once hung on the wall of a restaurant:

■ CUSTOMERS WHO THINK OUR WAITERS ARE RUDE SHOULD SEE THE MANAGER

After several days, the sign was removed because customers continued to chuckle at the sign's unintended suggestion: that the manager was even ruder than the waiters.

Writing in a Direct Style

- ☐ Get to the main point as quickly as possible.
- ☐ Support the point with specific evidence.
- ☐ Provide a clear transition between supporting points.

- ☐ Use precise words and sentence structure.
- ☐ Make sure each sentence has a specific purpose.

ESL TIPS

ESL

In the case of the sign, of course, the customers understood the point that the restaurant owner had wanted to make. However, in many types of job-related communication—a report or a letter, for instance—the audience may have difficulty deciding which of several possible meanings the writer had intended to convey. When a sentence (or a passage) can be interpreted in two or more ways and the writer has given the audience no clear basis for choosing from among the alternatives, the writing is ambiguous. Such lack of preciseness is a common source of miscommunication in on-the-job writing.

Precise writing is so clear that your audience should have no difficulty understanding exactly what you want to say. In checking for precision, look for three likely trouble spots that may lead to misinterpretation by your audience: faulty comparisons, unclear pronoun reference, and imprecise word choice.

Faulty Comparisons

When you make a comparison, be sure that your audience understands what is being compared.

- *does.*
  Ms. Jones values rigid quality-control standards more than Mr. Johnson. [The original could mean either that Ms. Jones values the standards more than she values Mr. Johnson or that she values the standards more than Mr. Johnson values them.]

When you compare two persons, things, or ideas, be sure they are elements that can logically be compared with each other.

- *textbook*
  The accounting textbook is more difficult to read than the office management. [A textbook cannot logically be compared with a field of study.]

Unclear Pronoun Reference

A *pronoun* is a word that is used as a substitute for a noun. The noun that the pronoun substitutes for or refers to is called its *antecedent*. When you use a pronoun, be sure that your audience knows which noun (or nouns) the pronoun refers to. When you revise your sentences to correct unclear pronoun references, look especially for three types of errors:

- ambiguous reference
- general (or broad) reference
- hidden reference

(For a further discussion of pronoun reference, see Section 2.14 of the Handbook.)

Ambiguous Reference

In an ambiguous reference, there is uncertainty as to which of two or more nouns a pronoun is referring.

■ Jim worked with Tom on the report, but ~~he~~ *Tom* wrote most of it. [Tom, not Jim, wrote most of the report.]

General (or Broad) Reference

In a general (or broad) reference, the pronoun—which is frequently a term such as *this, that, which,* or *it*—does not replace an easily identifiable antecedent. Instead, it refers in a general way to the preceding sentence or clause.

GENERAL   Mr. Bacon recently retired, which left an opening in the accounting department. [The pronoun *which* refers to the entire preceding clause.]

IMPROVED   Mr. Bacon's recent retirement left an opening in the accounting department. [Revising the sentence to eliminate the pronoun makes the meaning clear.]

Hidden Reference

In sentences that contain a hidden reference, the antecedent of the pronoun is implied but never actually stated.

UNCLEAR   Despite the fact that our tractor division had researched the market thoroughly, we didn't sell many. [The pronoun *many* has no stated antecedent in the sentence. The writer assumes that the audience understands that *many* refers to tractors.]

IMPROVED   Despite the fact that our tractor division had researched the market thoroughly, we didn't sell many tractors. [Revising the sentence so that *many* becomes an adjective modifying *tractors* makes the meaning clear.]

Imprecise Word Choice

As Mark Twain once said, "The difference between the right word and almost the right word is the difference between 'lightning' and 'lightning bug.'" Precision requires that you choose the right word. (See Section B. 36, of the Handbook.)

When you write, be alert to the effect that a word may have on your audience—and try to avoid words that might, by the implications they carry, confuse, distract, or offend your audience. For example, in describing a piece of machinery that your company recently bought, you might refer to the item as cheap—meaning inexpensive. However, because "cheap" often suggests "of poor quality" or "shoddily made," your audience may picture the new piece of equipment as already needing repairs.

Choosing General or Specific Terms

In selecting the appropriate word, you will want to keep in mind the *context*—the setting in which the word appears. Suppose instead of "cheap" you call the new machine "inexpensive" or "moderately priced." Your audience may ask, "What does the writer mean by inexpensive?" A desktop computer at $1,000 might be inexpensive; a small printing press at $80,000 could also be a good buy. The exact meaning of inexpensive would depend on the context. For an audience unfamiliar with the cost of printing machinery, it might be surprising to learn that an $80,000 press was reasonably priced. It would be up to you, the writer, to provide your audience with a context—to let them know, in this case, the relative costs of printing equipment.

The context will also determine whether a word you choose is specific enough. When you use the word *machine,* for instance, you might be thinking of an automobile, a lathe, a cash register, a sewing machine. *Machine* is an imprecise word that must be qualified, or explained, unless you want to refer in a general way to every item included in the category *machine.* If you have a particular kind of machine in mind, then you must use more precise language.

■   The maintenance contract covers all ~~the machines~~ in Building D.
                                    network printers ^

Depending on the context, you might need to choose a term even more specific than network printers. Figure 4–1 illustrates just how specific a particular context might require you to be. The terminology goes from most general, on the left, to most specific, on the right. Seven levels of specificity are shown; which one would be appropriate depends on your purpose in writing, your audience, and the context in which you are using the word.

For example, a person writing a company's annual report might logically use the most general term, *assets,* to refer to all the property and goods owned by the firm: Shareholders would probably not expect a further breakdown. Interoffice memos and e-mails between the company's accounting and legal departments would appropriately call the firm's holdings *real estate* and *inventory.* To the company's inventory-control department, however, the word *inventory* is much too broad to be useful; a report on inventory might contain the more specific categories *equipment* and *parts in stock.* To the assistant inventory-control manager in charge of equipment, that term is still too general; he or she would speak of several particular kinds of equipment—*office furniture, office machines,* and *factory equipment.* The breakdown of the types of office machines for which the inventory-control assistant is responsible might include *copiers; computer printers, monitors,* and *servers; fax machines;* and *graphing calculators.*

However, even this classification wouldn't be specific enough to enable the company's purchasing department to obtain service contracts for the normal maintenance of its printers. Because the department must deal with different

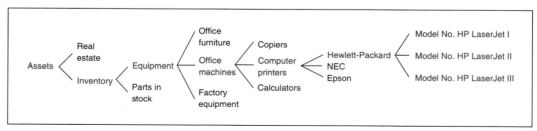

Figure 4–1   Example of Increasing Specificity

manufacturers, printers would have to be listed by brand name: Hewlett-Packard, NEC, and Epson. The Hewlett-Packard technician who performs the maintenance must go one step further and identify each Hewlett-Packard printer by model number. As Figure 4–1 shows, a term may be sufficiently specific at one of the seven levels—but at the next level it becomes too broad.

Your purpose and audience may sometimes require a general rather than a specific term. To include printer model numbers in a company's annual report, a detailed parts list in a sales brochure, or highly technical language in a memo to the accounting department would, of course, be inappropriate. In all the writing you do, you must decide what your purpose is and who your audience will be, and then select a term that is neither too general nor too specific for the context.

Defining Terms

Remember that you must sometimes define terms for your audience. Suppose you are making a proposal to your boss, who must pass your proposal along to his or her boss for final approval. You may be using terms that your boss's superior will not recognize because you work with details that will be unfamiliar to someone interested in only the big picture. If you want your proposal to be approved, you should do everything you can to make your ideas readily understandable. In some cases, you may define specific terms; in others, you may prefer to omit specialized terms and write at a more general level.

How you define the terms that need explanation depends on the context. It may often be sufficient to give a brief explanation, in everyday language, of a technical or specialized term.

■   Concerns that a *hacker* (malicious computer user) may steal and misuse biometric templates used to verify personal identity are as yet unfounded.

Or you may find it easiest to provide an extended definition to familiarize an audience new to a specialized term.

■   Our new search engine will permit Boolean searching capabilities. That is, it will permit **and** searches for two or more keywords, **or** searches when something is referred to in more than one way, **not** searches to exclude certain terms, and **proximity** searches of terms near other terms in a string of text, like a sentence or title.

Sometimes it may be necessary to provide a formal definition of a word. (See Chapter 3 for a complete discussion of formal definitions.) To write such a definition, place the term in a category and show how the term differs from other members of that category.

■   A lease [*term*] is a contract [*category*] that conveys real estate for a specified period of time at a specified rent [*how a lease differs from other contracts*].

■ Conciseness

Conciseness is freedom from unnecessary words. Wordiness, as well as stilted or pretentious language, can place a barrier between you and your audience by making your ideas difficult to understand. As you revise your writing, be particularly alert for two types of wordiness: redundancy and padded phrases.

Redundancy

Redundancy is the use of words—especially modifiers—that merely repeat the meaning of something already stated. *Round circles* is an example of redundancy (*round* is not needed to modify *circles,* which are always round). When selected carefully, modifiers—whether adjectives, adverbs, prepositional phrases, or subordinate clauses—can make the words they describe vivid and specific (for example, a *frosty* night). However, avoid modifiers that simply repeat the idea contained in the word they modify, such as the expressions in the following list.

blue ~~in color~~	to plan ~~ahead~~
to resume ~~again~~	basic ~~essentials~~
square ~~in shape~~	to attach ~~together~~
brief ~~in duration~~	visible ~~to the eye~~

Padded Phrases

A *padded phrase* is a phrase that expresses in several words an idea that could easily be expressed in a word. *Due to the fact that* is a padded phrase—a better choice is the word *because.* Examine your work for padded language, often composed of the following words: *case, fact, field, factor, manner,* and *nature.*

There are times, however, when longer wording or phrasing clarifies meaning.

■ *In terms of* gross sales, the year has been successful; *in terms of* net income, however, it has been discouraging.

Instead of being redundant, the phrase *in terms of* balances the sentence and highlights the contrast in meaning. Expressions such as these must be evaluated individually. If the expression does not contribute to the meaning of the sentence, use its simpler substitute.

■ Biased Language

Biased language refers to words and expressions that offend because they make inappropriate assumptions or stereotypes about gender, ethnicity, physical or mental disability, age, or sexual orientation. The easiest way to avoid bias is simply not to mention differences among people unless the differences are relevant to the discussion. Keep current with accepted usage, and, if you are unsure of the appropriateness of an expression or the tone of a passage, have several colleagues review the material and give you their honest assessment.

Sexist Language

Sexist language can be an outgrowth of sexism, the arbitrary stereotyping of men and women in their roles in life. Sexism, a form of biased language, can breed and reinforce inequality. To avoid sexism in your writing, treat men and women equally, and do not make assumptions about traditional or occupational roles. Accordingly, use nonsexist occupational descriptions in your writing.

Instead of	*Use*
chairman	chair, chairperson
foreman	supervisor
manpower	staff, personnel, workers
policeman/policewoman	police officer
salesman	salesperson

Use parallel terms to describe men and women.

Instead of	*Use*
man and wife	husband and wife
Ms. Jones and Bernard Weiss	Ms. Jones and Mr. Weiss;
	Mary Jones and Bernard Weiss
ladies and men	ladies and gentlemen;
	women and men

Sexism can creep into your writing by the unthinking use of male pronouns where a reference could apply equally to a man and a woman. One way to avoid such usage is to rewrite the sentence in the plural.

■ ~~Every~~ *All* employ~~ee~~*ees* will have ~~his~~ *their* manager~~s~~ sign ~~his travel voucher.~~ *their travel vouchers.*

Other possible solutions are to use *his or her* instead of *his* alone or to omit the pronoun completely if it is not essential to the meaning of the sentence.

■ Everyone must submit ~~his~~ *an* expense report by Monday.

He or she can become monotonous when repeated constantly, and a pronoun cannot always be omitted without changing the meaning of a sentence. Another solution is to omit troublesome pronouns by using the imperative mood whenever possible.

■ ~~Everyone must submit his or her~~ *Submit all* expense ~~report~~ *reports* by Monday.

Other Types of Biased Language

Identifying people by racial, ethnic, or religious categories is simply not relevant in most workplace writing. Telling readers that an engineer is Native American or that a professor is African American almost never conveys useful information. It also reinforces stereotypes, implying that it is rare for a person of a certain background to have achieved such a position. It also is inappropriate stereotyping to link a profession or some characteristic to race or ethnicity: a Jewish lawyer, an African-American jazz musician, an Asian-American mathematics prodigy.

Consider how you refer to people with disabilities. If you refer to "a disabled employee," you imply that the part (*disabled*) is as significant as the whole (*employee*). Use "an employee with a disability" instead. Similarly, the preferred usage is "a person who uses a wheelchair" rather than "a wheelchair-bound person"; the latter expression inappropriately equates the wheelchair with the person. Generally, however, you should refer to a disability only if it is necessary to your meaning.

Terms that refer to a person's age are also open to inappropriate stereotyping. Referring to older colleagues as "geezers" and to younger colleagues as "kids" is derogatory, at the least.

In most workplace writing, such issues are simply not relevant. Of course, there are contexts in which race, ethnicity, or religion should be identified. For example, if you are writing an Equal Employment Opportunity Commission report about your firm's hiring practices, the racial composition of the workforce is relevant. In such cases, you need to present the issues in ways that respect and do not demean the individuals or groups to which you refer.

■ Point of View

Some writers feel that, especially in job-related writing, it is immodest or inappropriate to use the first-person point of view—that is, to speak of themselves as *I* or *me*. However, in most cases, your message will be clearer and easier to follow if you speak of yourself in the first person.

■ ~~The technician~~ *I* will complete the wiring and test the system at the end of June.

■ ~~The~~ *I performed all the* tests described in the attached report ~~were all performed by writers~~.

Avoid the use of *one* as a pronoun because it is inexact, indirect, and pretentious.

■ ~~One~~ *I* can only conclude that the new valves are not effective on the old fire trucks.

Avoid the impersonal *it is,* which suggests that the writer is trying to avoid responsibility.

■ ~~It is regrettable that~~ *I regret that we cannot accept* the material shipped on the 12th ~~is unacceptable~~.

Some writers, looking for ways to make their work sound more authoritative or more serious, introduce expressions such as *It should be noted that* or *I am inclined to think that* in their writing. Such expressions only add wordiness.

■ ~~It should be noted that the~~ *The* gaskets tend to turn brittle after six months in the warehouse.

The more natural your writing sounds, the more effectively it will communicate.

■ Plain Language

In recent years, consumer interest groups, lawmakers, and businesses have become concerned about the problem of affectation and legal-sounding language in insurance policies, contracts, government regulations, and other writing. As a result, many states have created "plain-language laws," which require that documents be written in clear, understandable language. The federal government also now requires that all its new regulations be written in plain language.

Plain-language guidelines stress that writers communicate with their audiences in language that is both uncomplicated and accurate. The guidelines are especially useful for communications intended for audiences unfamiliar with the specialized vocabulary of the writer's occupation or profession. However, even with the best of intentions, you cannot always avoid using specialized terms and concepts. This discussion will help you sort out the difference between writing that is plain and accurate on the one hand and writing that is either too complicated or too simplistic on the other hand.

How to Avoid Affectation

Affectation is the use of language that is more technical or showy than it needs to be to convey meaning. Such inflated language creates a smoke screen that the audience must penetrate to discover the writer's meaning. The following example, in which a company needs to tell employees about its policy for personal phone calls, is all too common in job-related writing.

INFLATED	It is the policy of the company to provide the proper telephonic apparatus to enable each employee to conduct the interoffice and intrabusiness communication necessary to discharge his or her responsibilities; however, it is contrary to company practice to permit telephones to be utilized for personal employee communications. Coin-operated apparatus in the building lobby may be used for personal communications.
PLAIN	Your telephone is provided for company business; do not use it for personal calls. Instead, please use the pay phones in the lobby for personal calls.

Most people would have to read the first version of the policy several times before deciphering its message. The meaning of the revised version, which uses direct, simple, and precise language, is evident at a glance. The following passages show how "legalese" can be converted into plain language.

INFLATED	I hereby authorize the above repair work to be done along with the necessary material, and hereby grant you and/or your employees permission to operate the car or truck herein described on streets, highways, or elsewhere for the purpose of testing and/or inspection.
PLAIN	You have my permission to make repairs listed on this work order and to use the necessary materials. You or your employees may drive my car or truck to test its performance.

In the revised version, notice the absence of the legal-sounding phrases: *I hereby authorize, hereby grant, herein described, the above repair work,* and a*nd/or.* Notice that when it is translated into straightforward English, the statement gains in clarity what it loses in pomposity. Consider the following example:

INFLATED	The Model 3211 is a solution that provides the capability of performing the printing and binding functions to produce documents on demand in one effortless, seamless process.
PLAIN	The Model 3211 can print and bind documents in one integrated process.

The first sentence reads like an important pronouncement. Stripped of its pretentious phrases, however, it is actually a simple statement.

You can also help your audience by eliminating strings of nouns used as modifiers.

INFLATED	Your staffing level authorization reassessment plan should result in a more efficient process for hiring new employees.
PLAIN	Your plan to reassess authorizations for staffing levels should result in a more efficient process for hiring new employees.

In the first example, the noun *plan* is preceded by four modifiers. Such strings, known as *jammed modifiers,* impede the audience, who must wonder when the noun being modified will appear.

Another type of indefensible affectation is the useless elongation of standard words. Frequently, one hears *analyzation, summarization,* and *notation;* the correct words are *analysis, summary,* and *note.* The additions to such words do not make them mean anything more precise; they make them both incorrect and long-winded.

If you know the possible reasons for affectation, you will be taking the first step toward avoiding it. The following list addresses the most common reasons for affected writing. Review and revise your writing if you recognize any of these tendencies. As with other writing tasks, if you cannot be detached or objective enough to evaluate your writing for affectation, have a trusted fellow student or coworker do so and revise accordingly.

- *Impression.* Pretentious language is sometimes used to impress others. Do not attempt to make a favorable impression with showy language while failing to recognize that evidence and logic will create a much more positive impression, whether you are a student trying to impress a teacher or an employee trying to impress a superior or customer.

- *Insecurity.* If you are insecure in your facts, conclusions, or arguments, don't try to cover these gaps with a smoke screen of pretentious language. Continue to research the topic until you are certain of what to say.

- *Imprecision.* Try to be as precise as possible rather than filling in for missing information with vague language. Don't say "the policy will have a positive impact upon the department" unless you can describe precisely how the policy will in fact positively affect the department.

- *Imitation.* Avoid the tendency to imitate the poor writing you see around you. For example, maybe everyone in your company refers to themselves as *the writer* rather than *I* in letters and memos. These practices are frequently simply bad habits thoughtlessly repeated rather than formal company policy. At least find out before falling into the habit with everyone else.

- *Initiation.* If you just completed your education or training for an occupation, it's natural to feel that one way to prove your professional standing is to use technical terminology and jargon as much as possible. Although this impulse usually passes with time, be especially careful to avoid it in your writing for senior officials and customers. These readers are much less likely to be as technically knowledgeable as you.

Avoiding Affectation

WRITER'S CHECKLIST

- ☐ Write in the first person (*I*); avoid *the writer* and *one*.
- ☐ Choose simple words that say exactly what you mean — do not substitute big, imprecise words for well-thought-out, precise language.
- ☐ Avoid trying to impress your reader with pretentious language — such as *discharge responsibilities, aforesaid, hereto* — or with vague or trendy language — such as *factoid, infomercial, right-sizing, solution* (used to mean a product or service).
- ☐ Be certain of your facts, conclusions, and arguments. Insecurity in these areas can lead to inflated language.
- ☐ Revise your writing, identifying wording that should be replaced with clearer, shorter, common words and phrases.

When and How to Use Technical Terminology

Technical terms are standard, universally recognized words used in a particular field to refer to specific principles, processes, or devices. Unlike the legalese and inflated language discussed in the previous section, technical terms are useful and often essential in communicating accurately and concisely. For example, the term *divestiture* has a specific meaning for audiences familiar with management strategies. Similarly, the term *logic gate* would be understood by an audience who studied computer science or electrical engineering. If you are certain that your audience (and potential audience) will understand a technical term, use it to ensure precision. If you are at all uncertain, however, define the term in plain language when you first use it. If your audience is likely to be confused by a concept, explain it, perhaps including an easy-to-understand example. Digressing into an explanation, though less efficient than using a technical term, is sometimes required to make your writing easily understandable—your ultimate goal. (See Defining Terms and Concepts (pages 84–87) in Chapter 3 for guidance on how to define terms accurately and incorporate them smoothly into your writing.)

When and How to Use Jargon

Jargon is highly specialized technical slang that is unique to an occupational group. If you are addressing a particular occupational group, jargon (like technical terminology) may provide a timesaving and efficient means of communicating with them. For example, software developers understand the term *interface*—a boundary across which data or information flows (such as a computer screen) or software that links a computer with the commands or images that allow communication between the computer and its user.

Jargon enters the language for a variety of reasons. Common words that already have established meanings in everyday speech are sometimes applied to new concepts and devices. For example, *access*—a noun meaning the ability to enter, approach, communicate with, or pass to or from—has always been part of our language. However, *access* as a transitive verb means *to get at something,* such as a computer file, and should be used only in the context of the technology field. (Although you can access a computer file, you cannot access a novel.) Technical shorthand is not a satisfactory substitute for everyday language outside the field in which it is standard.

Another type of jargon is used to define occupations euphemistically. Tactfulness dictates that if you are writing to an undertaker and must refer to his occupation, you should use the term *funeral director.* For similar reasons, a garbage collector is frequently called a *sanitation worker.*

When jargon becomes so specialized that it applies only to one company or subgroup of an occupation, it is referred to as "shop talk." For example, an automobile manufacturer might produce a "pollution-control valve—Model LV-20." In the department where the device is built, it may be referred to as an "LV-20." Obviously, shop talk is appropriate only for those familiar with its special vocabulary and should be reserved for speech, informal memos, and e-mail messages within a company.

■ Two Revised Drafts

Figures 4–2 and 4–3 show two drafts of the sales brochure that was outlined and drafted in Chapters 2 and 3. In Figure 4–2, the writer has taken her second draft and, after allowing for a cooling-off period, critiqued her work, using the main points covered in this chapter as her guide. Figure 4–3 shows a revised version of the draft. Notice that the writer has not simply made mechanical, sentence-level corrections to her work. Instead, she used her marginal comments to revise the structure and organization as well as its sentences.

The Lifemaker System 40
The Compact, Affordable Home Gym
Designed for Maximum Fitness Conditioning

DRAFT

Home gyms were designed to eliminate the hassle and expense of going to a health club to work out, but most of them are too bulky and awkward to fit either your budget or your wallet. The Lifemaker System 40 is designed for (limped) living space, a modest budget, and maximum fitness needs.
sp

Compact Design

too much jargon
The Lifemaker's multiple stations provide a technologically sophisticated strength training program, (and is) architecturally configured for minimal space and maximal efficiency. (At 4 (fett) wide and 7 feet long,) your living room can (easily) accommodate the Lifemaker with more (ease) than other home systems. At the same time, the Lifemaker offers more stations and more exercises. ——— *faulty comparison*

missing pronoun

misplaced modifier

sp

redundant

Point of view

Move this ¶ to introduction
(One) need not compromise (your) exercise needs with an (overside) or ineffective system. Our home gym lets you integrate a complete home exercise system into your available space and your budget.
sp

Cast-Iron Weight Stack

need direct object "of plates"

agreement
The dual cast-iron weight <u>stacks totals</u> 200 lbs. Which can be arranged to offer a resistance range of 10 to 150 pounds. In addition, Lifemaker offers <u>the only weight system</u> on the market that can be adjusted in (multiplied) increments.
sp

not true!!

too vague "can be adjusted in 5, 10, 15 pound increments"

Adjustable Cables

missing subject-verb agreement

The Lifemaker's unique cable system (allows) quick (reconfiguring) of the weight stacks without taking apart the entire system. <u>Just pulling</u> the center rod and <u>one can</u> add or remove as many plates as you need. The cable tension can also be adjusted to make sure your muscles are working against all the possible resistance in each exercise to increase reflexor capacity and resistance ability.

too much jargon; too vague

verb agreement; point of view

Figure 4–2   Draft Sales Brochure (Marked for Revision) (continued)

page 2

Easy Assembly and Maintenance

sounds
awkward
redundant

You can assemble the Lifemaker yourself in under an hour; we even include all the tools needed for assembly. The system requires little maintenance and upkeep; simply check all parts each time you exercise and
tighten cable tensions. You can clean the system by wiping all parts with a
damp cloth; unlike most other systems, no special cleaning fluids or oiling
is necessary.   *not true!! most systems don't*
                                 require special treatment

make
more
personal
"is
pleased
to offer
you ..."

Affordable

Lifemaker, Inc. is offering this state-of-the-art, compact home gym at only
$999.99. All parts carry a two-year guarantee, and replacement parts can
be shipped to you in under 24 hours by calling our 800 number.

For a limited time, you can also purchase the Lifemaker System 40 on a no-
interest monthly payment plan, because at Lifemaker, Inc., we believe that
add bit   an exercise system should strengthen your back, not flatten your wallet.
about talking
to service rep
                                 dangling modifier and
                                 sounds wrong — "within 24
                                 hours of placing an order"

Figure 4–2   Draft Sales Brochure (Marked for Revision) (continued)

The Lifemaker System 40
The Compact, Affordable Home Gym
Designed for Maximum Fitness Conditioning

Home gym systems are designed to eliminate the hassle and expense of working out at a health club, but most systems take up too much space and can injure both your budget and your back. The Lifemaker System 40 offers a solution to the problem of oversized, overpriced, and ineffective home gyms, because Lifemaker is designed to fit a limited living space, a modest budget, and maximum fitness requirements. Purchasing a Lifemaker System 40 will let you integrate a complete weight and cable exercise system into your living space and your budget.

Compact Design

The Lifemaker's comprehensive strength-training program is designed to occupy minimal space. The system offers more than 40 exercise combinations, but because it measures only 4 feet wide and 7 feet long, Lifemaker will fit easily into almost any room.

Multiple Stations

Three workout stations let you move through your conditioning program as efficiently as if you owned a roomful of weight and cable machines. In addition, the multiple stations are designed so that two people can work out at the same time.

Cast-Iron Weights

The Lifemaker features dual weight stacks totaling more than 200 pounds of cast-iron plates. The dual stacks offer a resistance range of 10 to 150 pounds; resistance can be adjusted in 5-, 10-, or 15-pound increments.

Adjustable Cables

A unique cable system allows you to reconfigure the dual weight stacks without taking apart the entire system. Simply pull the rod located between the stacks and you can add or remove as many plates as you need for a particular exercise. The cable tension can also be adjusted to increase or decrease the amount of resistance within exercise sets.

Easy Assembly, Easy Maintenance

The Lifemaker System 40 can be assembled in less than an hour; no special tools are needed for assembly. You can maintain the Lifemaker in good condition simply by wiping down the system with a damp cloth; no oiling or scrubbing of parts is ever necessary. All parts carry a two-year guarantee and can be shipped to you within 24 hours of your placing an order.

Affordable

Lifemaker, Inc., is pleased to offer you this state-of-the-art, compact home gym for only $999.99. You can also purchase the Lifemaker on a low-interest monthly payment plan. Call (800) 554-1234 and we will be happy to arrange a plan that works with your financial needs. At Lifemaker, Inc., we believe that owning a home gym system should strengthen your back, not flatten your wallet.

Introduces major benefits from Figure 2–2

Headings and white space makes brochure inviting to readers

Expands equipment fitness, maintenance, and affordability benefits from introductory paragraph

Figure 4–3   Final Sales Brochure

CHAPTER 4 SUMMARY: Revising for Essentials

Use the following checklist to help you remember the various aspects of revision that this chapter has covered. Refer to this list both before and after you write the final draft of any document; fix any problems before your reader sees them.

☐ Have I allowed a cooling period?

☐ Is my content complete and accurate?

☐ Does the subject of each sentence accurately identify the doer of the action expressed in the verb?

☐ Are all nominalizations eliminated?

☐ Do all subjects and verbs agree in number?

☐ Do all pronouns and their antecedents agree in number and in gender?

☐ Are verb tenses accurate and consistent?

☐ Have I eliminated any dangling or misplaced modifiers?

☐ Are all sentences complete and properly punctuated?

☐ Have I eliminated all comma errors?

☐ Are all the words spelled correctly?

☐ Is the language precise; unambiguous; and free of jargon, biased language, and ethnic stereotyping?

☐ Have I removed all redundancy, padding, and affectation?

☐ Is the point of view appropriate and consistent?

■ Exercises

Exercises followed by the symbol 🆆 are continued at **bedfordstmartins.com/ writingthatworks**, Chapter 4.

1. Each of the following sentences contains a faulty comparison. Rewrite each sentence to eliminate the error.

   a. The copier equipment in the direct-mail department operates more efficiently than the customer-relations department.
   b. The production manager expressed greater appreciation for the temporary help than the sales manager.
   c. Julia Valenti, the Human Resources Manager, felt that the applicant was better qualified than Charles Crane, the Director of Administrative Services.

2. Each of the following sentences contains a modifier that may qualify either of two elements within the sentence. Locate the squinting modifier and rewrite the sentence in two ways.

   a. The transformer that was sparking violently shocked the line operator.
   b. The accountant who was making budget calculations hastily rose from the desk and left the room.
   c. After the committee decided that the work must be completed by Monday, in spite of other commitments, it adjourned immediately.
   d. He planned after the convention to take a short vacation.

3. Each of the following sentences contains an unclear pronoun reference. Rewrite the sentences as necessary to eliminate the errors.

a. Many members complained that their representatives made decisions secretly without considering them.
b. The crane operator did not file a safety grievance and does not plan it.
c. Our company decided to relocate in Grandview Hills, after rejecting Westville and Dale City, which was a difficult decision to make.
d. Anita has held positions in two insurance companies and in an auto-rental firm, and it should help her in finding a new job.
e. Ms. Jardina wanted to meet with her assistant, Ms. Sanfredini, but she was unable to do so until after lunch. W

4. Each of the following sentences contains a faulty pronoun-antecedent agreement. Rewrite each sentence to eliminate the error.

a. Everyone did their own work.
b. Either the president or the managers will do their best to help you.
c. Any customer who writes to us should have their letter answered promptly.
d. Either of the companies has the right to exercise their option to sell stock.
e. The engineering staff is moving their facilities on Friday. W

5. Each of the following sentences contains at least one padded phrase. Rewrite each sentence to eliminate such phrases.

a. We began the project in the month of April.
b. He opened the conversation with a reference to the subject of inflation.
c. The field of engineering is a profession that offers great opportunities.
d. The process was delayed because of the fact that the chemicals were impure.
e. The human resources manager spoke to the printing-plant supervisor with regard to the scheduling of employee vacations. W

6. In each of the following sentences, select the correct word or words from the two items in parentheses. In some sentences, the choice involves the correct pronoun; in other sentences, it involves the correct verb. After adjusting for agreement, you may need to revise several sentences further to avoid sexism.

a. The supervisor asked each employee to decide whether (he/they) wanted to work overtime to finish the project.
b. Her job during the negotiations (was/were) to observe and then report her observations to the manager.
c. Our line of products (is/are) sold in the West and in the Midwest.
d. Neither John nor Peter remembered to submit (his/their) work on time.
e. The Association of Corporate Attorneys failed because (they/it) never received full support from the member companies. W

7. Revise the following sentences to correct any errors in agreement. The errors may be in subject-verb agreement or in pronoun-antecedent agreement.

a. A survey of residents in the selected communities show a large potential market for our product.
b. After each of the passages are translated, the report is given to the Office of Policy Analysis.
c. The committee is planning to submit their recommendations before the end of the week.
d. The course instructs students in the basics of the subject and provides him with hands-on time.

W On the Web
For online quizzes on grammar, style, punctuation, mechanics, word choice, and composing and revising, go to Chapter 4, bedfordstmartins.com/writingthatworks

W On the Web
For online quizzes for ESL students on grammar and punctuation, go to Chapter 4, bedfordstmartins.com/writingthatworks

      e. A project engineer must be able to justify the changes they make in a technician's drawing. **W**

8. Each of the following sentences contains either a dangling modifier or a misplaced modifier. Locate the errors and correct them. Add any necessary words.

    a. An experienced technician, the company was anxious to hire her.

    b. Before taking the training course, it is recommended that each operator read the Safe Operation Manual.

    c. After evaluating the 38 answers, the test was found by the production manager to reveal a serious deficiency.

    d. Hoping to be promoted for her contribution to the project, the vice president's report represents three months of work.

    e. We purchased the store's inventory that was going out of business. **W**

9. Correct any sentence fragments or run-on sentences in this exercise. Add words and punctuation as necessary.

    a. Judge Ernest Owen rejected the appeal. Eight days after it was made.

    b. You may attend the conference. After you submit your request to the section supervisor.

    c. Nice to have talked to you.

    d. Have a profitable meeting.

    e. You can take the Universal Remote with you. Anywhere you need a remote control! **W**

■ Collaborative Classroom Projects

1. During the next 15 minutes, correct the comma faults in the following sentences by adding, changing, or deleting words and punctuation as needed. Your instructor may ask you not to use your text or other materials to help you with this exercise. When finished, you may be asked to exchange papers to evaluate the results.

    a. The electric voltage in the line was too high, he dared not risk touching it.

    b. An emergency occurs, another committee is born.

    c. Members may pay their dues immediately, they may choose to have a statement mailed to their homes or offices.

    d. The computer printer has separate drawers for paper, and the toner cartridge.

    e. One should never be ashamed to be somewhat sentimental, for, a certain amount of sentimentality makes a person human.

    f. The new law did not put all computer hackers behind bars, it did make some fearful, though.

    g. The engine overheated, the operator turned it off.

    h. A letter of transmittal for a report may include background information supplementary information or confidential information.

    i. If becoming a supervisor sounds interesting to you you should start to prepare now.

    j. My sister's friend manages a small elegant specialty shop in Hartford.

    k. Whenever you can take some management courses do so.

    l. Should you move to a supervisory job from a technical one you must quickly become people-oriented.

m. On January 3, 2004, we shall meet at Mystic Seaport to discuss the future of fishing in the waters off Cape Cod Massachusetts.

n. Norma who is the president's assistant is located in room ES 12.

o. All children especially those aged 6 to 12 fascinate me.

p. We need two printers for our office in Vance Canada and in Calgary.

2. Each of the following sentences contains a redundant word, phrase, or clause. During the next 15 minutes, rewrite the sentences to eliminate the redundant elements. Your instructor may ask you not to use your text or other materials to help you with this exercise. When finished, you may be asked to exchange papers to evaluate the results.

   a. Our experienced salespeople, who have many years of work behind them, will plan an aggressive advertising campaign to sell the new product.

   b. Any two raceway assemblies can be connected together with the plate as shown.

   c. The radio announcer kept repeatedly saying, "Buy PDQ brand pretzels!"

   d. Dissatisfied employees should give their complaints to the manager who is in charge as supervisor.

   e. If you are interested in economics, do not neglect to read the above-mentioned book, which was discussed previously.

3. Let's have some fun with affectation. During the next 15 minutes, try to figure out common proverbs buried in these overwritten substitutes. When finished, you may be asked to exchange papers to evaluate the results.

   EXAMPLE   Everything that coruscates with effulgence is not ipso facto aureous.

   TRANSLATION   Everything that glitters is not gold.

   a. Never calculate the possible number of juvenile poultry until the usual period of incubation has been accomplished.

   b. People who reside in transparent domiciles should not cast geological specimens.

   c. The warm-blooded, feathered, egg-laying vertebrate animal that is among the first invariably comes in the possession of a small, legless, crawling invertebrate animal.

   d. Where there is gaseous evidence of flammable matter, there is an indicated insinuation of incendiary pyrotechnic.

   e. Ornithological specimens of identical plumage tend to congregate in close proximity.

   f. Do not utter loud or passionate vocal expressions because of the accidental overturning of a receptacle containing a whitish nutritive liquid.

   g. Do not traverse a structure erected to afford passage over a waterway prior to the time of drawing nigh to the same.

   h. Hemoglobin is incapable of being extracted from the edible root of *brassica rapa*.

   i. Deviation from the ordinary or common routine is that which gives zest to the cycle of existence.

   j. A donee would be wise to abolish the habitual casting of glances into the oral cavity of equestrian specimens.

4. Each of the following passages contains unnecessary jargon, padded phrases, and affectation. During the next 20 minutes, revise the passages. Your instructor may

ask you not to use your text or other materials to help you with this exercise. When finished, you may be asked to exchange papers to evaluate the results.

  a. With reference to the matter that management has declared to be in the best interest of the furtherance of company-employee relations, the president has been authorized and empowered to grant each and every employee, upon the attainment of 30 years of continued and uninterrupted service to the company, an additional period of vacation that shall be of one week's duration.
  b. I hereby designate Mr. Samson, who has been holding the position and serving in the capacity of assistant technical supervisor, to be named and appointed to the position and function of deputy director of customer relations. In his newly elevated position Mr. Samson will report, in the first instance, directly to the department director—that is, to me.
  c. Purchasers of the enclosed substance should carefully and thoroughly follow the instructions provided herein for the use of the substance, and should in no case whatsoever consume, or otherwise partake of, said substance without proceeding in the manner set forth on the accompanying circular of instructions.

5. During the next 15 minutes, examine each italicized word in the following sentences. If the word is incorrect, rewrite the sentence using the correct word. Otherwise, make no changes. Your instructor may ask you not to use your text or other materials to help you with this exercise. When finished, you may be asked to exchange papers to evaluate the results.

  a. His appearance won't have an *affect* on his ability.
  b. The *principle* problem is lack of funds.
  c. Buy your envelopes at the *stationery* store.
  d. The highest achievers are more likely *then* the others to believe they're responsible for what is good and not good in their lives.
  e. Did the loss *effect* you personally?
  f. The Miami City *Counsel* meets Fridays.
  g. I would like to go to *they're* concert.
  h. *Its* been a long time since we met as a committee.
  i. We will work on the project *thru* next Thursday.
  j. He plans to attend *irregardless* of the consequences.

6. Find a study partner in the class and exchange copies of the rough drafts of an upcoming assignment well in advance of the deadline. Using the revision checklist on page 130, identify specific areas for improvement or correction in order to help your partner receive a better grade. Return the draft to your partner ahead of the due date so that he or she can incorporate your suggestions.

■ Research Projects

1. Research Project 1 in Chapter 3 asked that you write a rough draft about a business or technological field that, until now, you knew nothing about. Continue to revise the draft, using the suggestions on page 106. When revising, remember to

  a. Allow a cooling period.
  b. Pretend a stranger has written your draft.

    c. Revise in passes.

    d. Be alert to your most frequent problems.

    e. Read your draft aloud.

    f. Ask someone else to read and criticize your draft.

    You may also want to keep a journal of your revisions, noting what was easy and what was difficult for you. Your instructor may ask you to submit your journal when you submit your report.

2. Locate at least three of your past academic research papers that have already been evaluated by another instructor for another class. Now review each paper for organization and content, accuracy and completeness, and effective sentences with correct basic construction. Review the material in this chapter to guide you through your revision process. Using a red pencil, mark all changes you would now suggest in your papers.

3. Interview any instructor whom you admire and respect. Ask the instructor what revision process he or she uses when preparing work for class or when writing his or her own correspondence, papers, or proposals. Write a draft of the information gathered in the interview. Include any new information you gained about good writing habits.

4. Write a letter to your state representative asking that attention be given to a matter of concern to you. Use at least three outside sources to supply evidence that a problem exists. Put your letter aside for at least three days, then revise it. Put your letter aside for another three days, then revise it again. Note the changes you have made. Be ready to submit all drafts when you submit your letter.

5. Collect at least six articles on the same current event from as many different newspapers as possible. The articles may present different aspects of the same event. Using Chapter 4 as your guide, check the articles for subject-verb agreement, pronoun-antecedent number agreement, pronoun-antecedent gender agreement, consistency of tense and person, dangling modifiers, misplaced modifiers, and sentence problems such as fragments and run-on sentences. Also check for preciseness, including faulty comparisons, unclear pronoun reference, and imprecise word choice. Finally, review style looking for incorrect spelling, redundancy, padded phrases, affectation, technical terminology, and jargon. Make a list of the errors you found. Be ready to share your list and sources with your classmates.

6. Choose a controversial topic in your field of study. Topics might relate to engineering (legislation and ethics), computer science (laws governing the Internet; censorship), or environmental sciences (environmentally conscious legislation). Once you have selected a topic, research it to discover your own point of view on the subject. Then, using as much evidence as possible, write a memo to your boss (or instructor) stating why your company or organization (or university) should take a stand in support of your view.

■ Web Projects

Projects followed by the symbol W are continued at **bedfordstmartins.com/ writingthatworks**, Chapter 4.

1. The Internet has many sites offering English grammar help, rules, and advice. Formulate a question about grammar, and locate three sites that offer grammar advice. Which site is most helpful to you? Write a brief paragraph explaining why. W

2. Explore the Web to find at least one example of good writing and one of poor writing on the same subject. Using Chapter 4 as your guide, critique the examples. Edit the poor examples.

3. Locate a company on the Web that you are interested in learning more about, and write an inquiry letter and e-mail. Compare the replies you receive in terms of style, tone, and level of detail. W

4. Find three corporations or professional organizations on the Web and check their Web sites for biased language. Print out examples and edit them to eliminate bias. W

5 Revising for Coherence, Emphasis, and Ethics

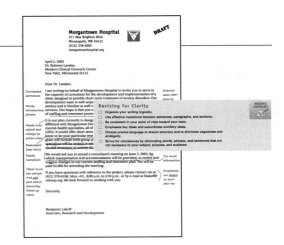

If you have followed the revision cycle outlined in Chapter 4, you should have a draft that is accurate, logically organized, grammatically correct, and free of all nonessential information. One last revision cycle remains. This time, your goal is to link, unify, and highlight ideas so that your readers can grasp them with a minimum of time and effort.

The basic building blocks of the draft are paragraphs. Effective paragraphs must be unified around a central idea so that every sentence is related to the idea stated in the topic sentence. Paragraphs must be the appropriate length—long enough to develop a central idea but not so long that they overwhelm the audience with too many details. Paragraphs must also be coherent, with all ideas arranged in a logical order, with transitional devices linking sentences and paragraphs throughout the draft so that the audience can follow your reasoning from sentence to sentence and from paragraph to paragraph.

Writers can make their material more accessible to their audience by revising to achieve emphasis. Effective writing highlights the facts and ideas that the writer considers most important and subordinates those that the writer considers less important. This chapter provides you with a number of devices that you can use to achieve emphasis using the active and passive voices, highlighting primary while subordinating secondary ideas, taking advantage of introductory words and phrases, using parallel structure and lists to present ideas that are equal in importance, and using a number of other highlighting techniques. The combined aim of these revision techniques is clarity: writing that is direct, orderly, and precise.

This chapter will also help you consider the possible ethical implications of these revisions and earlier ones, making sure that you do not use language in ways that could mislead readers or suppress important information that readers should know.

Finally, because it is important to consider the physical appearance of your writing when you submit the finished version, this chapter ends with a set of guidelines (page 157) to ensure that the appearance of your document reflects the effort that you have put into creating its contents.

W On the Web
For online resources for revising for coherence, emphasis, and ethics, go to Chapter 5, bedfordstmartins.com/ writingthatworks

■ Paragraph Unity

Suppose you were responsible for writing the report of a committee examining possible locations for your company's new distribution center in the United States. The committee narrowed thirty possible locations to three. The beginning of your outline might look like this:

■   I. Method committee used to narrow locations
   A. Considered 30 locations
   B. Eliminated 20 locations because of problems with labor supply, tax structure, and so forth
   C. Narrowed selection to three cities
   D. Visited Chicago, Minneapolis, and Philadelphia
   E. Observations follow in the report

From this group of items, you could write the following paragraph:

Topic sentence

Specific example of how locations were narrowed

Another specific example of how the committee decided on the three cities

Concluding thought and transition to the next idea, which will follow in a new paragraph

■   The committee narrowed 30 possible locations for the new distribution center to three. From the original 30, 20 possibilities were eliminated almost immediately for reasons ranging from unfavorable tax structures to inadequate labor supplies. Of the remaining ten locations, the committee selected for intensive study the three cities that seemed to offer the best transportation and support facilities: Chicago, Minneapolis, and Philadelphia. The committee then visited these three cities, and its observations on each follow.

Because the sentences in the paragraph evolved from the items listed in the outline, every sentence is directly related to one central idea—narrowing the selection of possible locations for the distribution center to three cities. Notice that the paragraph does not contain the committee's final recommendation or the specific advantages of each of the three cities. Those details will follow later in the report. To include such details in this paragraph would make the paragraph stray from its one central idea. In fact, the function of any paragraph is to develop a single thought or idea within a larger piece of writing.

When every sentence in a paragraph contributes to developing one central idea, the paragraph has unity. If a paragraph contains sentences that do not develop the central idea, it lacks unity. The following is a later paragraph from the report in which possible locations for the new distribution center are evaluated. Does this paragraph have unity?

■ Probably the greatest advantage of Chicago as the location for our new distribution center is its excellent transportation facilities. The city is served by three major railroads. *In fact, Chicago was at one time the hub of cross-country rail transportation.* Chicago is also a major center of the trucking industry, and most of the nation's large freight carriers have terminals there. *We are concerned, however, about the delivery problems that we've had with several truck carriers. We've had far fewer problems with air freight.* Both domestic and international air cargo services are available at O'Hare International Airport. Finally, except in the winter months when the Great Lakes are frozen, Chicago is a seaport, accessible through the St. Lawrence Seaway.

Voices from the Workplace

Larrell Walters, Edison Material Technology Center

Larrell Walters is the Vice President of Product Development at the Edison Material Technology Center in Ohio, where he oversees the work of a team of engineers. Providing clear instructions to Edison's engineers is one of Larrell's responsibilities. When he revises his instructions, he makes sure that they are written in the active voice.

"I learned early that using the active voice is key for effective business communication. If I said, 'A and B should be done,' it somehow never seemed to get done, but if I said, 'Engineering should do A and B,' it never failed to happen." He also makes sure that he presents information clearly and in a format that highlights key points. "I learned that the use of lists is very important in business communication. A paragraph of sentences is much more dense and difficult to grasp than a succinct list, so your odds of communicating successfully are much better with a list."

Kezia Scales, Communities in Schools

Kezia Scales works for Communities in Schools, a nonprofit organization that assists schools whose students are at risk of academic failure, by connecting them with local community resources. Kezia is responsible for identifying schools that CIS might benefit, securing funds for new school programs, and promoting the organization.

To fulfill these responsibilities, Kezia composes a variety of documents — from informal memos to formal reports and grant proposals. The success of her writing depends on her careful revisions and understanding of her readers. "The people that I write to are generally too busy to read through a dense, long-winded document; therefore, I edit down to the bare essentials. They are also too busy to read between the lines to discover my true meaning, so I edit for absolute clarity. Above all, they're certainly too busy to sift through typos, spelling mistakes, and grammatical inconsistencies. I edit everything I write in order to discover and correct mistakes and to produce clean, clear, readable pieces of writing."

Every sentence in this paragraph should have been about the advantages of Chicago's transportation facilities, as presented in the topic sentence. The three italicized sentences, however, do not develop that central idea. The sentence about Chicago as the former hub of rail transportation, although historically accurate, is not relevant to the company's assessment. The two sentences about the relative merits of truck and air carrier delivery are not relevant here. Stripped of these sentences, the paragraph is unified because each of the remaining sentences is directly related to the central idea.

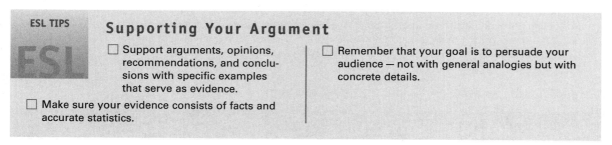

ESL TIPS

Supporting Your Argument

☐ Support arguments, opinions, recommendations, and conclusions with specific examples that serve as evidence.

☐ Make sure your evidence consists of facts and accurate statistics.

☐ Remember that your goal is to persuade your audience — not with general analogies but with concrete details.

One way to make sure that your paragraph has unity is to provide a topic sentence that clearly states the central idea of that paragraph. In the previous paragraph the topic sentence opens the paragraph:

■ Probably the greatest advantage of Chicago as the location for our new distribution center is its excellent transportation facilities.

For workplace writing, it's best to begin a paragraph with the topic sentence — this placement benefits both the writer and the reader. The writer has no difficulty constructing a unified paragraph because every sentence supports the topic sentence and the central idea it expresses. The reader knows immediately what the paragraph is about because the opening sentence states the central idea.

Occasionally, however, a topic sentence may be placed somewhere other than at the beginning of a paragraph. Placing the topic sentence at the end of a paragraph emphasizes the central idea because all the sentences build up to that idea. Notice how the sentences in the following paragraph lead up to the topic sentence:

■ A study by the Department of Agriculture revealed that insect damage in our region increased from 15 percent to 23 percent between 1999 and 2001. During this past year, many farmers reported a 30-percent increase in insect damage over the previous year. Furthermore, another recent study found that certain destructive insects are migrating north into our area. *Clearly, we should prepare for increased insect damage in the coming year.*

Although a topic sentence placed at the end of a paragraph provides a forceful conclusion, it also makes reading the paragraph more difficult — for this reason it should be done only occasionally in workplace writing.

Writing Your Topic Sentence

☐ Make sure your topic sentence contains (1) a subject and (2) a claim about the subject that will be supported in the paragraph.

The project | will benefit the employees.

subject + claim to be supported by in the paragraph

☐ Place your topic sentence at or near the beginning of your paragraph.

☐ Support your topic sentence in the body of the paragraph with specific examples.

■ Paragraph Length

Paragraph length should be tailored to the needs of your audience. A new paragraph provides your reader with a physical break and signals a new idea. Long paragraphs can intimidate your reader by failing to provide manageable subdivisions of thought. Overly short paragraphs have a disadvantage, too: They may make it difficult for your reader to see the logical relationships between your ideas. A series of short paragraphs can also sacrifice unity by breaking a single idea into several pieces.

Although there are no fixed rules for paragraph length, paragraphs in on-the-job writing average about 100 words each, with two or three paragraphs to a double-spaced, printed page. Paragraphs in letters tend to be shorter; two- or even one-sentence paragraphs are not unusual in letters. The best advice is that a paragraph should be just long enough to deal adequately with the central idea stated in its topic sentence. A new paragraph should begin whenever the subject changes significantly.

■ Paragraph Coherence

An effective paragraph has not only unity but coherence; that is, it takes the reader logically and smoothly from one sentence or idea to the next. Consider the following paragraph from a set of instructions. Does each sentence or idea lead logically and clearly to the one that follows?

■   The Lifemaker's cables can be adjusted for too much slack. To adjust the cable attached to the weight stack next to the weight upright, find the end of the 125″ cable. Turn the end of the cable clockwise. Thread the cable farther into the weight tube. Turn the cable about an inch counterclockwise.

Because each sentence in the paragraph says something about how to adjust cables on the Lifemaker home-fitness machine, the paragraph has unity. Yet the paragraph does not move as smoothly from one sentence to the next as it could. Nor does the paragraph make clear how each idea relates to the others. Transitional devices will achieve both these goals.

Transitions between Sentences

Transitional devices are words and phrases that help the reader to move smoothly from one sentence to the next and to see the logical relationships between the sentences. Notice how the simple technique of putting the steps in sequence (see the italicized words and phrases) provides effective transitions between ideas in the sample paragraph:

■ The Lifemaker's cables can be adjusted for too much slack. To adjust the cable attached to the weight stack next to the weight upright, *first* find the end of the 125″ cable. *Then* turn the end of the cable clockwise *in order to* thread it farther into the weight tube. *When you have finished,* turn the cable about an inch counterclockwise.

Now, because the transitional devices provide coherence, the reader can follow the writer's step-by-step instructions easily.

The following list includes other words and phrases that commonly function as transitional devices:

To express	*Use*
Result	*therefore, as a result, consequently, thus, hence*
Example	*for example, for instance, specifically, as an illustration*
Comparison	*similarly, likewise*
Contrast	*but, yet, still, however, nevertheless, on the other hand*
Addition	*moreover, furthermore, also, too, besides, in addition*
Time	*now, later, meanwhile, since then, after that, before that time*
Sequence	*first, second, third, then, next, finally*

Some of the words and phrases in this list are nearly synonymous but imply somewhat different logical connections. Be sure that the transitional words and phrases you choose convey the precise meaning you intend. For a more complete list of common transitions, see Table A–5 in the Handbook, page 691.

The use of pronouns, such as *he, she, they,* and *it,* is another transitional device. Because pronouns refer to a person or thing mentioned in a previous sen-

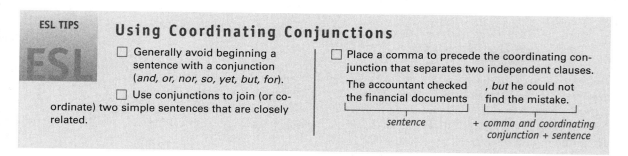

ESL TIPS   **Using Coordinating Conjunctions**

☐ Generally avoid beginning a sentence with a conjunction (*and, or, nor, so, yet, but, for*).

☐ Use conjunctions to join (or coordinate) two simple sentences that are closely related.

☐ Place a comma to precede the coordinating conjunction that separates two independent clauses.

The accountant checked the financial documents ⎿_____sentence_____⏌ , *but* he could not find the mistake. ⎿_+ comma and coordinating conjunction + sentence_⏌

tence, they bind sentences and ideas together. Notice the use of pronouns as transitional devices in the following paragraph:

■ We have recently discovered a problem with the new billing software. *It* consistently fails to note reimbursement amounts when *it* generates invoices. The billing staff is concerned that the software poses an administrative nightmare. *They* believe that the software could generate a complete billing cycle without noting any reimbursements that are due to clients. *Bill Mendena,* the billing supervisor, reports that the computer services department does not consider the problem an administrative hazard. *He* has pointed out to me, however, that when the software does not note reimbursements, the billing employees must do a computer search for every client in our current account base. *He* believes that this fact warrants a thorough analysis of the problem.

It refers to the billing software.

They refers to the billing staff.

He refers to Bill Mendena.

Another transitional device is the repetition of key words and phrases that link sentences and ideas. Notice how repetition of the key words and phrases in the following paragraph moves the paragraph forward:

■ Over the past several months, I have heard complaints about the Merit Award *Program.* Specifically, many employees feel that this *program* should be linked to annual *salary increases.* They believe that *salary increases* would provide a much better incentive than the current $1,000 and $1,500 *cash awards* for exceptional service. In addition, these *employees* believe that their supervisors consider the *cash awards* a satisfactory alternative to *salary increases.* Although I don't think this practice is widespread, the fact that the *employees* believe that it is justifies a reevaluation of the Merit Award *Program.*

ESL TIPS

Using Transitions

☐ Use transitions to help your reader understand the flow of your writing and the relationships between your ideas.

☐ Use transitions to connect your ideas between the main sections of the body of your text and between sentences within paragraphs.

☐ Avoid overusing transitions — do not begin each sentence with a transition.

Transitions between Paragraphs

Transitional devices used to link sentences can also be effective for transitions between paragraphs. The repetition of a key phrase, for example, connects the first paragraph in the following example with the second.

■ Consumers spend more money for plumbing repairs than for any other home repair service. The most common repair that plumbers make is the clearing of drains. Because the kitchen *sink drain* is used more often than any other drain in the home, that is the drain that is most often clogged.

   Clearing the *sink drain* yourself is easier than you might expect. You probably have all the tools you need. . . .

144 Chapter 5 ◆ Revising for Coherence, Emphasis, and Ethics

Another transitional device for linking paragraphs is to begin a paragraph with a sentence that summarizes the preceding paragraph. In the following excerpt from a report, notice how the first sentence in the second paragraph summarizes the ideas presented in the first paragraph:

■ Each year, forest fires in our region cause untold destruction. For example, wood ashes washed into streams after a fire often kill large numbers of fish. In addition, the destruction of the vegetation along stream banks causes water temperatures to rise, making the streams unfit for several varieties of cold-water fish. Forest fires, moreover, hurt the tourist and recreation business because vacationers are not likely to visit flame-blackened areas.

Opening sentence summarizes examples from preceding paragraph —————— *These losses, and many other indirect losses caused by forest fires, damage not only the quality of life but also the economy of our region.* They also represent a huge drain on the resources and personnel of the Department of Natural Resources. For example, our financial investment last year in fighting forest fires . . .

If used sparingly, another effective transitional device between paragraphs is to ask a question at the end of one paragraph and answer it at the beginning of the next. This device works well in the following example:

■ Robotics has become an ugly word for many people because it has sometimes meant the displacement of employees from their jobs. The fact is, however, that robotics creates many more jobs than it eliminates. The vast number of people employed in the automobile industry, compared with the number of people who had been employed in the harness-and-carriage-making business, is a classic example. Almost always, the jobs that have been eliminated by robotics have been menial, unskilled jobs, and the people who have been displaced have been forced to increase their skills. The result has been better and higher-paying jobs for many workers. *In view of these facts, is robotics really bad?*

Transition using a question and answer —————— *There is no question that robotics has freed many people from boring and repetitive work. . . .*

When you use this transitional device, make sure that the second paragraph does, in fact, answer the question posed in the first. Again, do not use this device too often. Your reader may find it monotonous and gimmicky if it is overdone.

WRITER'S CHECKLIST

Creating Effective Paragraphs

- ☐ Unify the paragraph around a central idea.
- ☐ Ensure that every sentence relates to the topic sentence.
- ☐ Arrange ideas (and sentences) in a logical order.
- ☐ Use transitional words, phrases, and clauses so readers can follow the logic of your paragraph.
- ☐ Keep paragraphs to an appropriate length:
  - ■ Long enough to develop your central idea
  - ■ Short enough not to overwhelm your reader with unnecessary details

Achieving Emphasis

Effective writing is also emphatic writing—it highlights the facts and ideas that the writer considers most important and subordinates those of less importance. By focusing the reader's attention on the key elements in a sentence, emphatic writing enables the reader to determine how one fact or idea in a sentence is related to another. Emphatic writing, then, offers you a powerful means for making your material more accessible to your audience. You can achieve emphasis through a number of techniques: using the active voice, highlighting primary and subordinating secondary ideas, taking advantage of introductory words and phrases, and creating patterns for ideas that are equal in importance through parallel structure and lists. Other highlighting techniques include arranging ideas in climactic order, varying sentence length, labeling ideas, and using mechanical devices such as dashes and italics.

Active and Passive Voice

If you were going to relate the information contained in the following two sentences to someone in conversation, which version would you use?

1. The committee members were introduced by David Cohen.
2. David Cohen introduced the committee members.

You would probably choose the second sentence because it conveys its message more directly than the first. By making David Cohen the *actor* (or *doer*), sentence 2 readily communicates the fact that he performed the activity described. Sentence 1, in contrast, subordinates his role; the focus of the sentence is on the committee members as the *receivers* of the action ("members were introduced"). David Cohen, though still the performer of the action, appears in a *by* phrase at the end of the sentence, rather than as the subject of the sentence. What accounts for the difference in "feel" between the two sentences is that sentence 2 is in the active voice, while sentence 1 is in the passive. A sentence is in the active voice if the subject of the sentence acts; it is in the passive voice if the subject is acted upon.

Use the active voice to achieve emphasis in your writing—it allows your audience to move quickly and easily from the actor (the subject) to the action performed (the verb) to the receiver of the action (direct object). In passive-voice sentences, which tend to be longer than active-voice sentences, the reader often has to reach the end of the sentence to find out who (or what) performed the action that the subject received.

ACTIVE   Rajesh Patel prepared the layout design for the new pump. [The subject—*Rajesh Patel*—acts on *the layout design*—the direct object.]

PASSIVE   The layout design for the new pump was prepared by Rajesh Patel.
                       [The subject—*the layout design*—receives the action.]

When writing instructions, use the active voice to convey your message. Compare the following two versions of a paragraph giving Emergency Medical Technicians (EMTs) directions for treating a serious burn. The first version is written entirely in the passive voice; the second uses the active. If you were the EMT who had to follow these instructions, which version would you find easier to read and understand?

PASSIVE   The following action must be taken when a serious burn is treated. Any loose clothing on or near the burn is removed. The injury is covered with a clean dressing, and the area around the burn is washed. Then the dressing is secured with tape. Burned fingers or toes are separated with gauze or cloth so that they are prevented from sticking together. Medication is not applied unless it is prescribed by a doctor.

ACTIVE   Take the following action when treating a serious burn. Remove any loose clothing on or near the burn. Cover the injury with a clean dressing and wash the area around the burn. Then secure the dressing with tape. Separate burned fingers or toes with gauze or cloth to prevent them from sticking together. Do not apply medication unless a doctor prescribes it.

Occasionally, of course, the passive voice can be useful. For example, when the doer of the action is less important than the receiver of the action, the writer can emphasize the receiver by making it the subject of the sentence.

EFFECTIVE   The new medical secretary was recommended for the position by sev-
PASSIVE   eral staff doctors.

The important person in this sentence is the medical secretary, not the doctors who made the recommendation. To give the secretary—the receiver of the action—the needed emphasis, the sentence makes sense in the passive voice.

The same principle holds true in the sciences for situations where the data are more important than the scientist collecting that data. Laboratory or test reports are good examples of the proper use of the passive voice.

EFFECTIVE   The test was conducted to identify the soil pH levels at the site.
PASSIVE

The passive voice is also useful when the performer of the action either is not known or is not important.

EFFECTIVE   The wheel was invented thousands of years ago. [Who invented it is
PASSIVE   not known.]

As you write—and revise—select the voice, active (usually) or passive (occasionally), that is appropriate to your purpose. However, be careful to maintain consistency of voice. Avoid making an awkward switch from active to passive (or vice versa), either within a sentence or between sentences.

■   *ten applicants took the*
After the test for admission to the training program, ~~had been taken by ten applicants~~
each one wrote a brief essay on his or her career plans.

Subordination

Read the following passage.

■   The computer is a calculating device. It was once known as a mechanical brain. It has revolutionized society.

Reading the passage—a group of three short, staccato sentences—is like listening to a series of drumbeats of identical tone. The writing, like the music, is monotonous because every sentence has the same subject-verb structure. Further, the writing is unemphatic because every idea is given equal weight. The passage can be revised to eliminate the monotonous sentence structure and to stress the most important idea: The computer has revolutionized society.

■   The computer, *a calculating device once known as a mechanical brain,* has revolutionized society.

The key to transforming a series of repetitive, unemphatic sentences is *subordination,* a technique in which a fact or an idea is shown to be secondary in importance to another fact or idea in the same sentence. You can subordinate an element in a sentence in the following three ways:

- Make it a dependent clause.
- Make it a phrase.
- Make it a single modifier.

With all three methods, the less-important element can be combined with the more-important element to form one unified sentence.

Ways of Subordinating

Create a dependent clause.   A dependent clause (also called a *subordinate clause*) has a subject and a predicate but by itself is not a sentence. You must join a dependent clause to a sentence (called an *independent clause*) with a connecting word. When you join two sentences by subordination, one sentence becomes the independent clause, and the other sentence, introduced by a connecting word, becomes the dependent clause. The words most commonly used to introduce dependent clauses are *who, that, which, whom, whose* (relative pronouns) and *after, although, because, before, if, unless, until, when, where, while* (subordinating conjunctions). A few word groups are also used to introduce dependent clauses—*as soon as, even though, in order that, so that.*

In the following example, two sentences are turned into one sentence that contains a subordinate clause.

WITHOUT SUBORDINATE CLAUSE	Their credit union has a lower interest rate on auto loans. Our credit union provides a fuller range of services.
WITH SUBORDINATE CLAUSE	*Although their credit union has a lower interest rate on auto loans,* our credit union provides a fuller range of services.

Create a phrase.   A *phrase* is a group of related words that does not have a subject and predicate and that acts as a modifier. In the following two-sentence passage, one sentence is turned into a subordinate phrase that modifies an element in the other sentence.

WITHOUT SUBORDINATE PHRASE	The Beta Corporation now employs 500 people. It was founded ten years ago.
WITH SUBORDINATE PHRASE	The Beta Corporation, *founded ten years ago,* now employs 500 people.

Use a single modifier.   A single modifier may be either a one-word modifier:

■ The file is ~~obsolete. It is~~ taking up valuable storage space.
   ^obsolete

or a compound modifier:

■ The police radio was ~~out of date. It was~~ auctioned to the highest bidder.
   ^out-of-date

Depending on the context of your writing—your subject, your purpose, and your audience—you may find that one way of subordinating is more effective than another in a specific sentence. In general, the degree of subordination becomes more emphatic as the writer moves from using a single modifier to a subordinate phrase to a subordinate clause. In the following example, the same idea has been subordinated in each of these three ways.

WITHOUT SUBORDINATION	The landscape designer's report was extensively illustrated. It covered ten pages.
SINGLE MODIFIER	The landscape designer's *ten-page* report was extensively illustrated.
SUBORDINATE PHRASE	The landscape designer's report, *covering ten pages,* was extensively illustrated.
SUBORDINATE CLAUSE	The landscape designer's report, *which covered ten pages,* was extensively illustrated.

Subordinating to Achieve Emphasis

Just as you can determine the kind of subordinate element that you think is most appropriate in a given sentence, so you can decide, according to the context in which you are writing, which ideas you should emphasize and which you should subordinate. In the following sets of examples, two sentences have been combined into one, in two different ways. Notice how the emphasis varies in each set.

WITHOUT SUBORDINATION	Blast furnaces are used mainly in the smelting of iron. They are used all over the world.
EMPHASIZES PURPOSE	Blast furnaces, *in use all over the world,* are used mainly in the smelting of iron.
EMPHASIZES EXTENT	Blast furnaces, *used mainly in the smelting of iron,* are used all over the world.

If you wish to emphasize an item in a sentence, place it either at the beginning or at the end of the sentence; if you wish to subordinate an item, place it in the middle of the sentence.

Avoiding Overloaded Sentences

Subordination is a technique that can help you to write clear and readable sentences, but like many useful devices, it can be overdone. Be especially careful not to pile one subordinating clause on top of another—doing so will force your reader to work harder than necessary to understand what you are saying. The following sentence is hard to read because the bottleneck of subordinate clauses prevents the reader from moving easily from one idea to the next.

TOO MUCH SUBORDINATION	When the two technicians, who had been trained to repair Maurita printers, explained to Erin that the new Maurita 5090 printer, which she had told them was not working properly, needed a new part, she decided that until the part arrived the department would have its sales letters reproduced by an independent printing supplier.
EFFECTIVE SUBORDINATION	Erin told the two Maurita technicians that the new Maurita 5090 printer was not working properly. The technicians examined the printer and explained to her that it needed a new part. She decided that until the part arrived, the department would have its sales letters reproduced by an independent printing supplier.

Subordinating everything is as bad as subordinating nothing. For example, study the next three sample paragraphs of a letter from a garage owner to a parts supplier.

TOO LITTLE SUBORDINATION	I am returning the parts you sent me, and I am enclosing the invoice that came with them. You must have confused my order with someone else's. I ordered spark plugs, condensers, and points, and I received bearings, piston rings, head gaskets, and valve-grinding compound. I don't need these parts, but I need the parts I ordered. Please send them as soon as possible.
TOO MUCH SUBORDINATION	You must have confused my order with someone else's, because although I ordered spark plugs, condensers, and points, I received bearings, piston rings, head gaskets, and valve-grinding compound; therefore, I am returning the parts you sent me, along with the invoice that came with them, in the hope that you will send me the parts that I need as quickly as possible because this delay has already put me behind schedule.

EFFECTIVE
SUBORDINATION

I am returning the parts you sent me, along with the invoice that came with them, because you must have confused my order with someone else's. Although I ordered spark plugs, condensers, and points, I received bearings, piston rings, head gaskets, and valve-grinding compound. Because I need the parts that I ordered and this mix-up is causing an unexpected delay, please send me the parts that I ordered as quickly as possible.

Introductory Words and Phrases

Another way to achieve emphasis is to begin a sentence with an introductory element—a modifying word or phrase that contains the idea you wish to stress. Such a modifier would normally occur later in the sentence.

■   Sales have been good recently.

■   *Recently,* sales have been good. [Emphasizes the recentness of good sales]

When you use introductory words and phrases, though, keep in mind the following. First, beginning a sentence with a modifying word or phrase may lead you to leave a dangling modifier. The first sentence in the following example contains a dangling modifier because the phrase *to advance* cannot logically modify *a commitment to lifetime learning.* The second sentence corrects the error by making it clear that *to advance* modifies the pronoun *you.*

INCORRECT   To advance, a commitment to lifetime learning is required.

CORRECT   To advance, you must commit yourself to lifetime learning.

Second, beginning a sentence with a modifying word or phrase may accidentally change the meaning of the sentence. The first of the following sentences instructs the reader to measure the volume of serum that drips over a period of 15 seconds. The second sentence instructs the reader to wait 15 seconds before making the measurement—a completely different thought.

■   Measure the volume of serum that drips into the graduated cylinder in 15 seconds. [Emphasizes measurement over a period of 15 seconds]

■   In 15 seconds, measure the volume of serum that drips into the graduated cylinder. [Emphasizes the time until measurement begins]

Once again, make sure that your sentences say exactly what you intend them to say.

Parallel Structure

Parallel structure requires that sentence elements—words, phrases, and clauses—that are alike in function be alike in structure as well. In the following example, the three locations in which a cable is laid are all expressed as prepositional phrases.

■ The cable was laid *behind the embankment, under the street,* and *around the building.*

Parallel structure can produce an economy of language, clarify meaning, indicate the equality of related ideas, and, frequently, achieve emphasis. Parallel structure allows your audience to anticipate a series of units within a sentence. The reader realizes, for instance, that the relationship between the second unit (*under the street,* in the example) and the subject (*cable*) is the same as that between the first unit (*behind the embankment*) and the subject. A reader who has sensed the pattern of a sentence can go from one idea to another more quickly and confidently.

Parallel structure can be achieved with words, with phrases, and with clauses. Whichever you use to make a sentence parallel depends, as it does with subordination, on the degree of emphasis you wish to create. In general, words in parallel structure produce some emphasis, phrases produce more emphasis, and clauses produce the most emphasis of all.

PARALLEL WORDS	If you want to earn a satisfactory grade in the receptionist training program, you must be *punctual, courteous,* and *conscientious.*
PARALLEL PHRASES	If you want to earn a satisfactory grade in the receptionist training program, you must recognize the importance *of punctuality, of courtesy,* and *of conscientiousness.*
PARALLEL CLAUSES	If you want to earn a satisfactory grade in the receptionist training program, *you must arrive punctually, you must behave courteously,* and *you must study conscientiously.*

To make the relationship among parallel units clear, repeat the word (or words) that introduces the first unit.

■ The advantage is not in the pay but ˄the greater opportunity.
　　　　　　　　　　　　　　　in

■ The study of electronics is a necessity and ˄challenge to the trainees.
　　　　　　　　　　　　　　　　　　　a

Sentences containing parallel structure contribute to the clarity of your writing—those with faulty parallel structure are often awkward and difficult to read.

■ Adina Wilson was happy about her assignment and ˄getting ˄a pay raise.
　　　　　　　　　　　　　　　　　　　about   her

■ Jason advises his employees to work hard and ˄against relying on luck.
　　　　　　　　　　　　　　　　　　not to rely

Lists

You can also use lists to achieve emphasis. Lists break up blocks of dense text and complex sentences, allow key ideas to stand out, and show the relationship of parallel or sequential ideas. Be aware, however, that lists must be grammatically parallel. When you use a list of phrases or short sentences, begin each with the same part of speech.

NOT PARALLEL   Please note the following policy changes:
- Employees can no longer use company telephones for long-distance personal calls.
- For any written copy that is not to go out of the office, use low-grade yellow paper rather than bond.
- Make double-sided copies rather than one-sided photocopies of all internal correspondence.

PARALLEL   Please note the following policy changes:
- Do not use company phones for personal long-distance calls any longer.
- Use low-grade yellow paper rather than bond for any written copy that is not to go out of the office.
- Make double-sided copies rather than one-sided photocopies of all internal correspondence.

Notice how much more smoothly the revised version reads when all items begin with imperative verbs.

Lists help focus your audience's attention because they stand out from the text around them. Be mindful, however, not to overuse lists in an attempt to avoid writing paragraphs. When a document consists almost entirely of lists, the audience is unable to distinguish important from unimportant ideas. Further, the information lacks coherence because the audience is forced to connect strings of separate items without the help of transitional ideas. To make sure a list fits with the surrounding sentences, provide adequate transition before and after the list.

For lists that indicate the rank or sequence of items, number them; for lists that do not show items by rank or sequence, use bullets, as shown in the previous example and in the Writer's Checklist below.

WRITER'S CHECKLIST

Using Lists

- [ ] List only comparable items.
- [ ] Use parallel structure throughout.
- [ ] Use only words, phrases, or short sentences.
- [ ] Provide adequate transitions before and after lists.
- [ ] Use numbers when rank or sequence is important.
- [ ] Use bullets when rank or sequence is not important.
- [ ] Do not overuse lists.

■ Other Ways to Achieve Emphasis

You can create a feeling of anticipation in your audience by arranging a series of facts or ideas in climactic order. Begin such a series with the least-important or lowest-impact idea and end it with the most-important or highest-impact one.

CLIMACTIC   The hostile takeover of the company will result in some employees
ORDER   being relocated to different cities, some being downgraded, and some
                being let go.

The writer leads the audience step by step from the lowest potential impact on employees to the highest: (1) the disruption caused by employee relocation, (2) the more serious problem of downgrading jobs, and (3) finally, the most devastating impact, the loss of jobs.

An abrupt change in sentence length can also achieve effective emphasis.

■   We have already reviewed the problems that the accounting department identified during the past year. We could continue to examine the causes of our problems and point an accusing finger at all the culprits beyond our control, but in the end it all leads to one simple conclusion: *We must cut costs.*

Sometimes, simply labeling ideas as important creates emphasis.

■   We can do a number of things that will help us to achieve our goal. We can conduct sales contests in the field; in the past, such contests have been quite successful. We can increase our advertising budget and hope for a proportionate increase in sales. We can be prepared to step up production when the increase in sales makes it necessary. *But most important,* we can do everything in our power to make sure that we are producing the best communication equipment on the market.

If you don't overuse them, direct statements such as *most important* should make your audience take particular notice of what follows.

Another kind of direct statement is the warning to your audience that something dangerous is about to follow. Warnings most often appear in instructions, where they may be brought to the audience's attention by a special format—the material may be boxed off, for instance—or by attention-getting devices such as ALL-CAPITAL letters, <u>underlined words</u>, or a distinctive typeface, such as **boldface**

WARNING
DO NOT proceed to the next instruction until you have unplugged the equipment. The electrical power generated by this equipment can kill!

---

or *italic* type. These features can be used to emphasize important words and phrases in warnings.

Other typographical devices can be used to highlight key information. A dash within a sentence, for example, can alert the audience to what follows it.

■   We will begin work on the project—as soon as the contract is signed.

Italics can be used occasionally to emphasize a word or phrase.

■   Sales have *not* improved since we started the new incentive program.

The problem with devices such as italics and the dash is that they are so easy to use that we tend to rely on them too readily, as in the following examples.

OVERUSE OF ITALICS	Sales have *not* improved since we started the new incentive program and are not likely to improve unless we initiate a more *aggressive* advertising campaign.
OVERUSE OF DASHES	The rating panel—John Burton, Carol Ramirez, and Pat Nelson— evaluated the three job applicants—Mary Fontana, David Moschella, and Tyrone Braxton—and found them well qualified.

Overuse of such typographical devices may cancel their effectiveness. The reader quickly learns that the writer is using the signals to point out subordinate as well as truly important material.

WRITER'S CHECKLIST

Achieving Emphasis

- ☐ Use the active voice.
- ☐ Subordinate secondary ideas.
- ☐ Use introductory words and phrases to stress key ideas.
- ☐ Use parallel structure to focus attention on how ideas are related.
- ☐ Use lists (such as this one) to highlight ideas by setting them apart from surrounding text.
- ☐ Arrange ideas in least-important to most-important order.
- ☐ Use typographical devices selectively, such as ALL CAPITAL LETTERS or *italic,* **boldface,** or <u>underlined</u> text.
- ☐ Label key ideas as important.

■ Clarity

Clear writing is direct, precise, and concise. These are the goals of all job-related writing. Many writing elements described in this text contribute to clarity, beginning with the overall structure and organization of your writing. A method of development and an outline that organizes your thoughts in a logical, meaningful sequence bring coherence as well as unity to your writing. Clear transitions contribute to clarity by providing the smooth flow that enables the audience to connect your thoughts with one another.

Proper emphasis and subordination will help your readers to sort out which ideas are most important, which are least important, and which will fall somewhere in between. Careful pacing, adjusted to your topic and audience, will prevent you from overwhelming your readers or bogging them down with unnecessary information.

Likewise, a consistent point of view is essential to clarity; if you switch from the first person to the third person in mid-sentence or mid-paragraph, you are certain to confuse your reader.

Precise word choice contributes to clarity by eliminating ambiguity and vagueness. Vague words, clichés, careless use of idioms (especially for readers for whom English is a second language), and inappropriate usage all detract from clarity.

That conciseness is a requirement of clearly written communications should be evident to anyone who has ever attempted to decipher an insurance policy or legal contract. Too many words can impede clear communication, just as too many cars on a highway can impede traffic. Critically evaluate your draft to remove unnecessary words, phrases, and sentences — those that do not directly contribute to your meaning.

Revising for Clarity

WRITER'S CHECKLIST

- [ ] Organize your writing logically.
- [ ] Use effective transitions between sentences, paragraphs, and sections.
- [ ] Be consistent in your point of view toward your topic.
- [ ] Emphasize key ideas and subordinate ancillary ideas.
- [ ] Choose precise language to ensure accuracy and to eliminate vagueness and ambiguity.
- [ ] Strive for conciseness by eliminating words, phrases, and sentences that are not necessary to your subject, purpose, and audience.

■ Ethical Issues and Revision

When you make the revision choices discussed in this chapter and in Chapter 4, you should be aware of the potential ethical choices involved in some of those decisions. Consider, for example, the discussion in the previous section about how warnings can be emphasized with all-capital letters, boldface, italics, and boxed sections. Using language and design to appropriately emphasize a clear danger to the reader is a positive ethical choice — and a relatively uncomplicated one.

However, not all choices may be so easy or so clear-cut. You may struggle, for example, over how to present potential dangers, disadvantages, or limitations while trying to achieve the objective of promoting a product, an idea, or even yourself (as in a letter of application or a résumé). Many choices you make depend on your own ethical standards and on the specific work circumstances surrounding these choices. Obviously, no textbook can tell you how to act ethically in every situation; however, be aware that the way you express ideas can affect the audience's perceptions of your ethical stance. Following are some typical ethical dilemmas to watch for and avoid as you revise.[1]

- *Using language that attempts to evade responsibility.* Do not inappropriately use the passive voice (discussed earlier in this chapter) to avoid responsibility for an action or to obscure an issue, as in the following examples: "several mistakes were made in the processing of your claim" (who made them?) and "it has been decided that annual bonuses will be discontinued this year" (who has decided?). Although writers sometimes use the passive voice and vague language unintentionally, attempts to evade responsibility for a problem or future commitment clearly involve an ethical choice.

- *Using language that attempts to mislead the audience.* As discussed in Chapter 4, label information correctly and appropriately. Consider the company document that stated, "A *nominal* charge will be assessed for using our facilities." When clients objected that the charge was very large, the writer pointed out that the word *nominal* means "the named amount" as well as "very small." In this situation, the audience had a strong case in charging that the company was attempting to be deceptive. In other circumstances, various abstract words, technical or legal jargon, and euphemisms—when used to mislead an audience or to hide a serious or dangerous situation—are unethical, even though technical or legal experts could interpret them as accurate.

- *Deemphasizing or suppressing important information.* A writer using a very small typeface or a footnote to deemphasize a negative feature of a product or service could be perceived as suppressing important information. Likewise, failing to mention disadvantages could easily mislead the audience. Even making a list of advantages, where they stand out, and then burying a disadvantage in the middle of a paragraph could unfairly mislead the target audience. Use document design to emphasize information important for the audience. See Chapter 8 for document design techniques.

- *Emphasizing misleading or incorrect information.* In a technique similar to hiding negative information, a writer might be tempted to dramatically highlight a feature or service that the audience would find attractive—but

---

[1] Based on and adapted from "Linking Ethics and Language in the Technical Communications Classroom" by Brenda R. Sims, *Technical Communication Quarterly* 2.3 (Summer 1993): 285–299.

the feature or service may be available only with some models of a product or at extra cost. In that case, the audience could justifiably object that the writer has given them a false impression in order to sell a product or service, especially if the extra cost was also deemphasized.

On the job, such ethical dilemmas do not always present themselves as clear-cut choices. To help avoid the ethical problems described here as well as others, ask the following questions as you complete your revision:

- Is the communication honest and truthful?
- Am I ethically consistent in my communication?
- Am I acting in my employer's best interest? the public's? my own?
- What would happen if everybody acted or communicated in this way?
- Does the action or communication violate anyone's rights?
- Am I willing to take responsibility for the communication, publicly and privately?

Above all, keep in mind that your language choices and their ethical implications are important—they influence how the audience perceives your ethical stance *and* that of your employer.

■ Physical Appearance

The most thoughtfully prepared, carefully written, and conscientiously revised writing will quickly lose its effect if it has a poor physical appearance. In the classroom or on the job, a sloppy document will invariably lead your reader to assume that the work that went into preparing it was also sloppy. In the classroom, that carelessness will reflect on you; on the job, it can reflect on your employer as well.

Unless your instructor provides other specific instructions, use the following guidelines for preparing your document:

- Use good-quality, white paper.
- Make sure your printer produces a clear, dark image.
- Use at least one-inch margins on all sides of the page.
- Make sure that the text is not crowded and that ample white space separates sections.

The appropriate physical format of specific types of writing such as letters or formal reports is discussed elsewhere in this book. Format guidance for letters and memos appears in Chapter 9, and guidance for formal reports is discussed in Chapter 12. Also review Digital Shortcuts: Laying Out the Page, on page 158.

Laying Out the Page

You can use a variety of word-processing features to improve the layout and other elements affecting the appearance of your text on the page.

■ *Page margins.* Page margins, usually preset at one inch on all sides of a page, can be changed for an entire page or for blocks of text within a page.

■ *Columns.* Lines of text can be arranged to run across the page from left to right or arranged in two or more columns. The columns feature can also be used for data in tables, membership lists, financial statements, rosters, and the like.

■ *Margin alignment.* Text columns can be perfectly aligned in the right margin as well as the left margin.

■ *Centering.* Words, lines of text, and blocks of text can be centered between the right and left margins, a feature useful for creating titles, letterheads on stationery, and captions for tables and figures.

■ *Line, word, and letter spacing.* The space between lines of text can be adjusted (single-, double-, triple-spaced, etc.), and unnecessary space between words and letters on a line can be eliminated.

■ *Headers and footers.* Headers (titles at the top of a page) and footers (titles at the bottom of a page) can be inserted automatically on each page.

■ *Type fonts.* The text for letters, reports, manuals, and other types of documents can be printed with a variety of type fonts that you deem appropriate to your purpose and readers. (A *font* is a complete set of letters, numbers, and other type characters with a distinctive and uniform design.)

■ *Type style.* The text may also be printed using a variety of type styles with the basic font chosen. Type-style options include boldface, italic, and underlining to highlight or otherwise create distinctive text.

■ *Preview mode.* Preview mode allows you to view a full page of your document on-screen exactly as it will look when it is printed. Evaluate the overall look of a page and correct it if necessary before it is printed to save time and paper.

■ *Style sheets and templates.* The format specifications for recurrent documents with a uniform look can be created and saved as a separate file. The file can be called up and automatically applied over and over for subsequent versions of the same kind of document.

CONSIDERING
AUDIENCE
AND PURPOSE

Presenting Your Ideas

☐ Write paragraphs that are long enough to develop a central idea but not so long that they overwhelm readers with too many details or unrelated information.

☐ Link your ideas in logical order and tie them together with transitional devices.

☐ Highlight key ideas and subordinate secondary and supporting ideas.

☐ Don't suppress or obscure information important to your readers.

☐ Strive for writing that is direct, orderly, and precise through logical organization, effective transitions, consistent point of view, proper emphasis and subordination, and language that is precise and economical.

☐ Create final drafts that look crisp, uncluttered, and professional.

■ A Rough and Revised Draft

Figures 5–1 and 5–2 show rough and revised versions of a letter written to persuade a well-known health specialist to serve as a consultant for a hospital's new outpatient clinic. As you compare the two drafts, note that the writer has not only corrected problems of coherence, clarity, and emphasis, but has also rephrased and shifted sentences so that the persuasive purpose comes through more clearly. Note also that the writer does not spell out the abbreviation LSW (Licensed Social Worker) because the recipient would be familiar with the abbreviation.

Morgantown Hospital

211 New Brighton Blvd.
Minneapolis, MN 55413
(612) 378-4000
morgantownhospital.org

DRAFT

April 2, 2003
Dr. Roberta Landau
Menken Clinical Outreach Center
New Paltz, Minnesota 55112

Dear Dr. Landau:

Overloaded sentences

Wordy introductory phrase

I am writing on behalf of Morgantown Hospital to invite you to serve in the capacity of consultant for the development and implementation of a clinic designed to provide short-term treatment of anxiety disorders. Our development team is well-acquainted with your clinical experience with anxiety and is familiar as well with your expertise in the area of outpatient services. Our hope is that you will advise our development team on issues of staffing and treatment protocols for the new clinic.

Subordinate reference to experience; distracts from main point

— *Not parallel*

Needs transition! and change to active voice

Redundant (see intro)

It is our plan currently to design the clinic as a small outpatient division affiliated with Morgantown Hospital. The clinic would be staffed by ten mental-health specialists, all of them board-certified psychologists and LSWs. It would offer short-term treatment for anxiety disorders, which we know to be your particular research and clinical interest. The clinical program will include both group and individual therapy. On a monthly basis, specialists will be invited to address the general public about the diagnosis and treatment of anxiety disorders.

Transitions within sentences

No — she's not involved in this part

Needs transition

We would ask you to attend a consultant's meeting on June 5, 2003, for which transportation and accommodation will be provided, to review and suggest changes to our current staffing and treatment plan. You will be paid $2,000 for attending the meeting.

Too much information

Yikes! much too abrupt. And add part about bimonthly follow-up visits

If you have questions with reference to the project, please contact me at (612) 378-6168, Mon.–Fri., 8:00 a.m. to 4:30 p.m., or by e-mail at blakoff@ mhosp.org. We look forward to working with you.

Emphasize our desire to work with her

Sincerely,

Benjamin Lakoff
Associate, Research and Development

Figure 5–1   Draft of a Persuasive Letter (with Writer's Notes)

Morgantown Hospital

211 New Brighton Blvd.
Minneapolis, MN 55413
(612) 378-4000
morgantownhospital.org

April 3, 2003
Dr. Roberta Landau
Menken Clinical Outreach Center
New Paltz, Minnesota 55112

Dear Dr. Landau:

Shorter, more focused introduction

Over the past year, Morgantown Hospital has been planning a new outpatient clinic devoted to the diagnosis and treatment of anxiety disorders. *Currently,* our development team is seeking expert advice about optimal ways to organize staff and implement treatment protocols. *Because* your name was recommended to us as a leading authority on staffing and treatment issues, we would like to invite you to serve as consultant to our anxiety clinic project.

Transitions link sentences

A brief description of the project may help to clarify our invitation. The anxiety clinic, which is scheduled to open in January 2004, will function as a small outpatient division of Morgantown Hospital and maintain a permanent staff of seven to ten board-certified psychologists and LSWs. Treatment programs will emphasize short-term individual and group therapies for a wide range of anxiety disorders.

Transitions link paragraphs

Your advice on selecting the clinic's staff and organizing its range of treatments would be of great value to our development team. If you agree to work with us on the project, we would ask you to attend a consultant's meeting, scheduled for June 5, 2003, to review and suggest revisions to our current plans for staff and treatments. Following the meeting on June 5, we would ask you to visit the clinic and review its status on a bimonthly basis.

If you decide to work with us on the clinic project, Morgantown Hospital will be happy to pay for your hotel and travel expenses. The hospital also will provide you with a $2,000 honorarium for attending the initial meeting and an annual honorarium of $5,000 for as long as you continue to visit and evaluate the clinic.

We look forward to hearing from you soon. If you have any questions about the clinic and your role in helping us plan it, please contact me at (612) 378-6168 or by e-mail at blakoff@mhosp.org.

Sincerely,

Benjamin Lakoff
Associate, Research and Development

Figure 5–2   Revised Draft of a Persuasive Letter

CHAPTER 5 SUMMARY: Revising for Coherence, Emphasis, and Ethics

When reviewing your draft, ask the following questions to verify that you have used crucial style devices to help readers focus on and grasp your central points and examples.

☐ Does each paragraph develop a single thought or idea within the larger piece of writing?

☐ Does each paragraph have a topic sentence?

☐ Are the sentences in each paragraph related to the paragraph's central idea?

☐ Are paragraphs long enough to adequately explain the paragraph's central idea but not so long as to burden readers with more details than necessary?

☐ Do the sentences in each paragraph contain enough transitional words and phrases so that readers can follow the logical relationship among ideas?

☐ Are sentences in the active voice when the doer of the action should be highlighted?

☐ Are sentences in the passive voice when the doer of the action is unimportant or unknown?

☐ Are secondary ideas subordinated to primary ideas?

☐ Are introductory words and phrases used to achieve emphasis?

☐ Are ideas of equal importance written in parallel structure using words, phrases, clauses, or lists?

☐ Are lists grammatically parallel in structure?

☐ Are other highlighting devices used appropriately?

☐ Does the writing achieve clarity through its logical organization, effective transitions, consistent point of view, precise word choice, and meaningful conciseness?

☐ Do any potential ethical problems need to be resolved?

☐ Is the physical appearance of the final document neat and clean?

W On the Web
For online quizzes on grammar, style, punctuation, mechanics, word choice, and composing and revising, go to Chapter 5, bedfordstmartins .com/writingthatworks

---

■ Exercises

Exercises followed by the symbol W are continued at bedfordstmartins.com/ writingthatworks, Chapter 5.

1. Read the following paragraph and then (a) underline the topic sentence of the paragraph, and (b) cross out any sentences that do not contribute to paragraph unity.

   Frequently, department managers and supervisors recruit applicants without working through our corporate human resources office. Our human resources departments at all of our locations across the country have experienced this problem. Recently, the manager of our tool-design department met with a graduate of MIT to discuss an opening for a tool designer. The graduate was sent to the human resources department, where she was told that no such position existed. When the tool-design manager asked the director of human resources about the matter, the manager learned that the company president had ordered a hiring freeze for two months. I'm sure that our general employment situation will get better. As a result of the manager's failure to work through proper channels, the applicant was not only disappointed but bitter.

W̲ On the Web
For online quizzes for ESL students on grammar and punctuation, go to Chapter 5, bedfordstmartins.com/ writingthatworks

2. The sentences in the following paragraphs have been purposely placed in the wrong order. Rearrange the sentences in each paragraph so that the paragraphs move smoothly and logically from one sentence to the next. Indicate the correct order of the sentences by placing the sentence numbers in the order in which the sentences should appear.

   a. (1) If such improvements could be achieved, the consequences would be significant for many different applications. (2) However, the most challenging technical problem is to achieve substantial increases in the quantities of electrical energy that can be stored per unit weight of the battery. (3) The overall process yields about 70 percent of the electricity originally put into the battery. (4) A storage battery is a relatively efficient way of storing energy.

   b. (1) Each atrium is connected to the ventricle below by a valve that allows blood to flow in only one direction. (2) The two upper chambers are called atria, and the two lower chambers are called ventricles. (3) The ventricles are also connected by one-way valves to the main outgoing blood vessels. (4) The organ is divided into four chambers. (5) The heart is a fist-sized, heavily muscled organ located approximately in the center of the chest.

   c. (1) It merely shrank the public's wealth and eventually created even more unemployment. (2) So Pericles, who was the boss man of the city-state, took action. (3) However, it was also having a recession. (4) Finally, in order to combat unemployment and the increasing recession, Pericles decided to go to war with Sparta. (5) But all this public spending didn't produce any goods. (6) As part of it, he built some of the greatest architectural wonders of the world. (7) About 500 years before the birth of Christ, Athens was the world center of democratic civilization. (8) For these artistic achievements, the people elected him to the top spot three times. (9) He started a tremendous public-works program.

3. Underline the topic sentence in each of the following paragraphs.

   a. Whether you use a hand mower, a power reel mower, or a rotary power mower to cut your lawn, the blades should be sharp enough to trim the grass cleanly without bruising or tearing the leaves. Both the cutting edge of the bedknife or reel-type mower and the reel blades should be sharp, and the reel should be set firmly against the bedknife. Make any necessary adjustments of the bedknife or of the roller (which determines the height of cut) on a flat surface, such as a concrete walk. Rotary mower blades in particular require frequent sharpening. On most rotary mowers, height of cut is fixed by adjusting the wheels in holes or slots on the mower frame.

   b. One property of material considered for manufacturing processes is hardness. Hardness is the internal resistance of the material to the forcing apart or closing together of its molecules. Another property is ductility, the characteristic of material that permits it to be drawn into a wire. The smaller the diameter of the wire into which the material can be drawn, the greater the ductility. Material may also possess malleability, the property that makes it capable of being rolled or hammered into thin sheets of various shapes. Engineers, in selecting materials to use in manufacturing, must consider the materials' properties before deciding which ones are most desirable for use in production.

c. People who raise houseplants must periodically replace the soil that serves as the growing medium for most indoor plants. When the soil of plants housed in small pots needs to be replaced, the plant is usually potted up—that is, transplanted to a pot of the next larger size. The plant, with its root ball intact, is removed from the small pot, and fresh dirt is piled into the larger container, with space allowed for the root ball. The plant is then carefully inserted into the new soil. For plants already in the largest-sized pots, the indoor gardener may take the plant, along with its root ball, out of the pot, discard the remaining earth, put in a similar amount of fresh dirt, and then return the plant to its original container.

d. Scientists disagree on what memory is and even on how to describe it. Sometimes it is defined by its duration. Primary memory, the portion of active consciousness that lets you repeat a sentence you just heard, rarely declines with age. Secondary memory, which lasts from a few seconds to a few days and includes things like who borrowed your pen, erodes as we get older. Alternatively, memory can be divided by function: implicit, involving learned skills, such as swinging a tennis racquet or speaking French, that become automatic; semantic, comprising objective facts, such as the date of the Battle of Hastings, general knowledge, and information independent of context; and episodic, concerning specific events defined by time, place, and personal history. Only the last of these three degenerates dramatically over time.

4. Each of the following pairs of sentences lacks a transition from the first sentence to the second. From the list of transitional devices on page 142, select the most appropriate one for each sentence pair. Then rewrite the sentences as necessary.

a. Ms. Silvenski arrived at the post office just before closing time. She was not able to mail her package because it had not been wrapped according to post office specifications.

b. An improperly cut garment will not hang attractively on the wearer. When you sew, you should be sure to lay out and cut your pattern accurately and carefully.

c. The Doctors Clinic was able to attain its fund-raising goal on time this year. Mercer Street Hospital was forced to extend its fund-raising deadline for three months.

d. When instructing the new tellers, the branch manager explained how to deal with impatient customers. The personal-banking assistant told the new employees that they should consult her if they had difficulty handling those customers.

e. There are several reasons why a car may skid on ice. The driver may be going faster than road conditions warrant.

5. Underline the transitional words and phrases in the following paragraphs.

a. Homeowners should know where the gutters on their houses are located and should be sure to keep them in good repair, because gutters are vulnerable to various weather conditions. On many houses, gutters are tucked up under or into the eaves, so that they appear as little more than another line or two of trim. As a result, many homeowners are not even aware that their houses have gutters. Unless the gutters are well maintained, however, the thousands of gallons of water that may fall onto the roof of the average house each year can easily damage or weaken the gutters. During the winter months, the weight of snow and ice may pull gutters away from the house or loosen the downspout straps. Clogged and frozen downspouts may also develop seam cracks. When spring comes, these seam cracks sometimes create leaks that may allow heavy rains to flood the yard or the house instead of draining properly into the sewer system. In addition, melting snow that flows freely off the roof may go down the house wall, wetting it sufficiently to cause interior wall damage.

b. The causes of global climate change remain in dispute. Existing theories of climate, atmospheric models, and statistical data are inadequate to provide planners with information on future weather patterns. In the long run, research may lead to more reliable forecasts of climate. For the present, however, planners have no choice but to heed expert judgments about the world's future climate and its effect on agriculture and other sectors of the economy.

6. Bring to class a document that you have written either in this (or another) class or at your job. Under the direction of your instructor, take the following steps:

   a. Circle all the words or phrases that provide transition between sentences.
   b. If you find two sentences that do not have adequate transition, place an X in the space between them.
   c. For sentences that seem not to have adequate transition, insert a word, phrase, or clause that will improve the transition.

7. Write an opening paragraph for two of the following topics. The audience for each topic is specified in parentheses.

   a. My favorite instructor (to someone nominating him or her for a teaching award)
   b. Ways to improve employee motivation (to the president or head of the organization that employs you)
   c. Ways to improve student advising at your school (to the dean of students or someone in an equivalent position)
   d. What to look for in a first apartment (to a friend who's looking)
   e. The advantages of budgeting (to a spendthrift friend)

8. Business writing is more forceful if it uses active-voice verbs. Revise the following sentences so that verbs are in the active voice. Add subjects if necessary.

   a. The computers were powered up each day at 7:00 a.m.
   b. Initial figures for the bid were submitted before the June 1 deadline.
   c. A separate bill from AT&T will be sent to customers who continue to use AT&T as their long-distance carrier.
   d. Substantial sums of money were saved by customers who enrolled early in our stock-option plan.
   e. A significant financial commitment has been made by us to ensure that our customers will be able to take advantage of our discount pricing.
   f. Smaller-sized automated equipment was ordered so that each manager could have an individual computer.

9. Rewrite the following sentences to eliminate excessive subordination.

   a. The duty officer who was on duty at 3:30 a.m. was the one who took the call that there was a malfunction in the Number 3 generator that had been repaired at approximately 9:00 a.m. the previous morning.

b. I have referred your letter that you wrote to us on June 20 to our staff attorney who reviewed it in the light of corporate policy that is pertinent to the issue that you raise.

c. Will your presentation that is scheduled for the 12th of next May and that will answer questions submitted in advance be circulated before the 12th to those who will be attending the workshop?

10. Some of the following sentences violate the principle of parallel structure. Identify the incorrect sentences and revise to make them parallel. The sentences may be correctly changed in more than one way. ☒

   a. We expected to be disappointed and that we would reject the proposal.
   b. Etiquette is important in social life, and you need it in business too.
   c. To type fast is one thing, but typing accurately is another.
   d. Do you prefer filing, typing, or balancing the budget?
   e. Is your home well heated and with adequate ventilation?
   f. The mailing notation should not only appear on the original but also on the copies.

■ Collaborative Classroom Projects

Projects followed by the symbol ☒ are continued at **bedfordstmartins.com/writingthatworks**, Chapter 5.

1. Choose a topic sentence from the following list and, using the guidelines offered in this chapter, write a unified and coherent paragraph that develops that sentence. Then, in groups, evaluate each paragraph. Using the Writer's Checklist on page 144 as your evaluation guide, in group discussion decide which tips are most difficult to follow and why.

   a. I chose [name your major] because I am interested in [name one skill or task such as "working with numbers" or "helping people"].
   b. On-the-job writing courses show why the principles of good writing are important.
   c. Working at a part-time [or full-time] job has helped me appreciate my education in three specific ways.
   d. Business ethics today is simply good business.
   e. Job opportunities for employees are created by company growth.
   f. Good management-labor relations and higher productivity are mandatory for the creation of new jobs.
   g. Every successful industrial corporation has at least one bread-and-butter product that sells well every year.
   h. Labor unions are no longer the powerful monoliths they were 50 years ago.

2. Rewrite each of the following sentences so that the verb is in the active voice. Whenever a potential subject is not given in a sentence, supply one as you write. When you have finished your sentences, divide into groups to share and discuss them. Is there much variation in the wording of your sentences? Is the meaning of the sentence affected by the differences in wording? Is a different tone implied?

   a. The entire building was spray-painted by Charles and his brother.
   b. It was assumed by the superintendent that the trip was postponed until next Tuesday.

    c. The completed form should be submitted to Tim Hagen by the 15th of every month.

    d. The fluid should be applied sparingly and should be allowed to dry for eight to ten seconds.

    e. The metropolitan area was defined as groups of counties related by commuting patterns by the researchers. **W**

3. Combine each of the following series of short sentences into one unified sentence. Use subordination to indicate how the ideas expressed in the sentence relate to each other and to emphasize the most important idea or ideas. When you have completed the sentences, exchange papers with a classmate. Mark each subordinate clause and underline the most important idea in your classmate's sentences. Then compare your paper to the one you evaluated.

    a. I recorded my speech on a videotape. The videotape can be recorded over. It does not need to be erased.

    b. It rained this morning. The construction crew stayed indoors. Members played a game of hearts. Valdez won.

    c. It had snowed for a week. I like to ski. I was delighted.

    d. He studied autoCAD at a technical school. He joined his brother's firm as a CAD specialist in 2001.

    e. Thomas Edison was one of America's greatest inventors. Teddy Roosevelt was the twenty-sixth president of the United States. Edison and Roosevelt were friends. **W**

4. Rewrite the following lists to make them parallel. The first three writers to finish the assignment will write their sentences on the board or on a transparency for the overhead projector so that the class can discuss and approve the revisions.

    a. Carry this emergency equipment in your car during long winter trips:
- Chains for tires and towing
- Snow shovel
- Scraper
- Sand or salt
- A cell phone
- For minor repairs, a car tool kit
- Flashlight—be sure to check for fresh batteries
- Flares, reflectors
- First-aid kit
- Blankets
- A bottle of water
- Jumper cables are also a good idea

    b. Keep these safety tips in mind as you work on your car:
- Wear safety goggles when working under the hood, especially when dealing with the battery.
- The engine should be operated only in a well-ventilated area.
- Fans and belts are dangerous when moving—you or your clothing could get caught in them.
- Avoid contact with hot metal parts, such as the radiator and the exhaust manifold.

5. Divide into small groups to write as many variations as possible for the following sentences, making the elements within them parallel in each construction. When your group is finished, share your results with the rest of the class. **W**

    a. The system is large and convenient, and it does not cost very much.

    b. The processor sends either a ready function code or transmits a standby function code.

    c. The log is a record of the problems that have occurred and of the services performed.

    d. The committee feels that the present system has three disadvantages: It causes delay in the distribution of incoming mail, duplicates work, and unnecessary delays are created in the work of several other departments.

    e. In our first list, we inadvertently omitted the seven lathes in room B-101, the four milling machines in room B-117, and from the next room, B-118, we also forgot to include 16 shapers.

    f. This product offers ease of operation, economy, and it is easily available.

■ Research Projects

1. Find a document (instructions, direct-mail advertising, or other sample) that you believe demonstrates one or more of the four ethical problems discussed in this chapter: using language that attempts to evade responsibility, to mislead the audience, to deemphasize or suppress important information, or to emphasize misleading or incorrect information. As your instructor directs, (1) report what ethical problems you see and describe how the document might be revised to eliminate those problems, and (2) rewrite the samples to eliminate the ethical problems.

2. Find a study partner in the class and, with the approval of your instructor, exchange copies of the rough drafts of an upcoming assignment well in advance of the deadline. Using the chapter summary at the end of this chapter, identify specific areas for improvement in order to help your partner receive a better grade. Return the draft to your partner ahead of the due date so that he or she can incorporate your suggestions.

3. Find at least three news articles on the same current event. Underline and identify examples of subordinate clauses used to achieve emphasis. Write a brief summary of how this method in news reporting has affected the outcome of the news articles. Include whether you think the subordination used was effective or overused. Select examples from the articles to explain and support your conclusions.

4. Gather at least six samples of business writing: three from printed sources that use lists to convey information in a paragraph and three from printed sources that use conventional sentences to convey information in a paragraph. Compare the samples and evaluate whether lists or sentences work better. Revise at least two of your samples from lists to sentences or from sentences to lists and compare the results to the original. Which works better — the original or your revision? Support your conclusion with examples from the sample texts.

5. Find at least three newspaper articles that use climactic order to achieve emphasis. Create a list of facts or ideas from each article, beginning with the least important idea and ending with the most important idea. Explain why you think the author of each article chose this method of organization.

■ Web Projects

Projects followed by the symbol 🅦 are continued at **bedfordstmartins.com/ writingthatworks**, Chapter 5.

1. Locate at least three ".com" sites where you can purchase a product online that contain examples of writing that seeks to persuade. Write a brief analysis of the language, noting voice, overloaded sentences, and the use of subordination. Is the writing persuasive? Support your conclusions using examples from the texts at the sites. 🅦

2. Internet sites often use lists to convey information in a quickly readable format. Find samples of text from at least five Web sites related to your field of occupational interest that contain lists. Print out the lists and note the order of arrangement. Rank the items in the lists by order of importance. How accurately and effectively are the lists used to provide information?

3. Many Web sites, especially ".com" sites, include disclaimers meant to alleviate the site's responsibility for potential ethical dilemmas. Find at least three sites that offer disclaimers. What content at each site do you believe initiated the disclaimer? Write a brief narrative summarizing your findings and citing examples from the text at the sites.

4. The language of advertising can be used to deemphasize or suppress information, or to emphasize misleading or incorrect information. Suppose you have been asked to research and recommend a new scanner or another piece of office equipment for your company. As you look for the best piece of equipment to purchase, preview several different Web sites offering similar products. Because you will want to act in your employer's best interest, at each site (1) make a list of statements that you believe make that site and its product trustworthy and reliable, and (2) list statements that you believe may misrepresent information. Write a brief summary of your findings and recommend the site you feel is the best place to make your online purchase.

5. Your company needs to hire several more employees in the coming months, and you are part of a committee that is working with the human resources director to find the best candidates. You have been asked to review three online employment agencies as your company looks for the one to best represent its hiring needs. Select three online employment agencies, make notes about each one, and compare them to one another. Then, in a memo to your boss, recommend one of the employment agencies and explain why you think this agency is the right one for your company. As you prepare your recommendation, refer to the chapter summary on page 162.

PART TWO

Essential Skills: Collaboration, Research, and Design

While Part One discussed the principles of effective writing that apply to all on-the-job writing, Part Two focuses on skills that you will need to approach more complex projects requiring collaboration, research, and design. The following chapters will help you prepare for the specific writing and communicating presented in Part Three — such as writing correspondence, reports, and proposals, and developing presentations.

◆ **Collaboration.** Chapter 6 discusses the importance of the writing strategies learned in Chapters 1 through 5 to collaborative writing projects on the job, whether you are a member of a collaborative writing team or the team leader.

◆ **Research.** Chapter 7 provides extensive treatment to researching your subject, including using the library and Internet, interviewing, using questionnaires, and making firsthand observations. You will also find advice for using the APA (American Psychological Association) and MLA (Modern Language Association) styles of documenting your research.

◆ **Design.** Chapter 8 gives detailed advice on formatting effective documents; developing illustrations, charts, and graphs; and successfully integrating them with your text. Attention to format and design is key to your success in creating instructions, reports, proposals, presentations, and other communications that will appeal to your audience.

6 Collaborative Writing

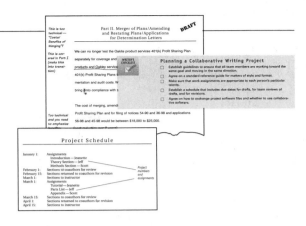

O n the job or in the classroom, no one works in a vacuum. To some degree, everyone must rely on the help of others to do their jobs. No matter what you write or how often you write, you will likely have to collaborate with other people. *Collaborative writing* involves working with other people as a team to produce a single document, with each member of the team contributing equally to the planning, designing, and writing. It also involves sharing equal responsibility for the end product.

Collaborative writing is generally done for one of three reasons:

1. The project requires expertise or specialization in more than one subject area.

2. The project benefits from the merging of different perspectives.

3. The size of the project, the time constraints imposed on it, or the importance of the project to your organization requires a team effort.

The larger and more important the document, the more likely it is to be produced collaboratively. Sales proposals, for example, often require contributions from many different types of experts (engineers, systems analysts, scientists, financial specialists, sales managers, etc.). Formal reports and specifications are among other documents that are commonly written collaboratively. For collaborative writing projects, the writing process varies only by the addition of a reviewing step; otherwise, the process itself is no different, consisting of planning, researching, writing, reviewing, and revising. Typically, one person then edits the draft to unify the writing style and manages the reproduction and distribution of the finished document.

⬜ On the Web
For online resources
for writing collabora-
tively, see Chapter 6,
bedfordstmartins.com/
writingthatworks

⬛ Advantages and Disadvantages of Collaborative Writing

Collaborative writing offers many benefits.

- *Many minds are better than one.* Collaborative teams usually produce work considerably better than the work produced by any one of its members. Team members stimulate each other to consider ideas and perspectives different from those they would have explored individually.

- *Team members provide immediate feedback*—even if it is sometimes con- tested and debated—which is one of the great advantages of collaborative writing. Fellow team members may detect problems with organization, clarity, logic, and substance—and point them out during reviews. The fact that you may receive multiple responses also makes criticism easier to ac- cept; if three out of three team members offer the same criticism, you can more readily accept it. It's like having your own personal set of critics—but critics who have a personal stake in helping you do a good job.

- *Team members play devil's advocate for each other;* that is, they take con- trary points of view to try to make certain that all important points are cov- ered and that all potential problems have been exposed and resolved.

- *Team members help each other past the frustrations and stress of writing.* When one team member needs to make a decision, there is always some- one to talk it over with.

- *Team members write more confidently knowing that their peers will offer constructive criticism*—not to find fault but to make the end product better.

- *Team members develop a greater tolerance of and respect for the opinions of others.* Team members become more aware of and involved in the plan- ning of a document than if they were working alone because of the team discussion that takes place during the planning stage. The same is true of reviews and revisions.

The primary disadvantage of collaborative writing is the demand it can place on your time, energy, and ego as a writer. Collaborative writing takes more time and energy than writing alone and exposes your writing to criticism.

⬛ Functions of the Collaborative Writing Team

Writing teams collaborate on every facet of the writing process: (1) planning the document, (2) researching the subject and writing the draft, (3) reviewing the drafts of other team members, and (4) revising the draft on the basis of comments from all team members. (Read the section Conducting Productive Meetings in Chapter 15 before calling your first meeting.)

Voices from the Workplace

Joseph G. Rappaport, Transport Workers Union

As a policy adviser at Transport Workers Union Local 100, a union representing New York City's 34,000 subway and bus workers, Joseph Rappaport produces fact sheets, leaflets, and legislative testimony, and edits the union's Web site and advertising. Many of the documents that Joseph and his colleagues create are written collaboratively.

"One person usually takes the lead in getting a letter or leaflet out the door. I try hard to respond quickly to drafts composed by that person. I always make a concrete suggestion if I don't think a word, a phrase, or a sentence works. There is nothing less helpful than getting a letter marked up with notes that say 'This doesn't work' and no ideas on what might work better. Quick turnaround and detailed suggestions for revision help the collaborative writing process work smoothly."

Claire Zulkey, Ebel Dunnell Merrick, Inc.

Claire Zulkey is a copywriter at Ebel Dunnell Merrick, Inc., an advertising company in Chicago. On the job, Claire collaborates with her coworkers on everything from print campaigns to television commercials — a process that begins with creative brainstorming.

"Sometimes you have a spectacular idea and you get cheered on and supported by your coworkers. Sometimes you have a seed of something, maybe just a line or an image, and it's gratifying to work with others to build it into something complete." Although collaborating isn't always easy, Claire says, "If you didn't collaborate, you could miss out on ideas for improving your writing, and making your projects the best they can be."

Planning

The team collectively identifies the readers, purpose, and scope of the project. The team conceptualizes the document to be produced, creates a broad outline of the document, divides the document into segments, and assigns each segment to individual team members, often on the basis of team-member expertise.

In the planning stage, the team develops a schedule and sets any writing style standards that the team is expected to follow. The schedule includes due dates for drafts, reviews of the drafts, revisions, and the final document. Milestone deadlines must be met, even if the drafts are not as polished as the individual writers would like. One missed deadline can delay the entire project.

The team plans, as a group, as much of the document as is practical. Beyond a certain level, however, the team does not have sufficient command of details to plan realistically at this preliminary stage and must assign detailed planning to individual team members. During the planning stage, the team also produces a schedule for each stage of the project. The agreed-upon schedule should include the due dates for drafts, for team reviews of the drafts, and for revisions. It is important that each team member meet these deadlines, even if the draft submitted is sketchy or not quite as good as desired. The other team members will have the opportunity to comment on the draft and suggest improvements. A deadline missed by one team member may hold up the work of the entire team, so all team members should be familiar with the schedule and submit their drafts and revisions on time.

As part of the planning process, the team should agree on a standard reference guide for style and format that all team members will follow in writing their drafts. The guidelines should provide for uniformity and consistency in the writing, which is especially important because different team members are writing separate sections of the same document. Lacking a standard guide, the team should establish project style guidelines that address the following issues:

- Levels of headings and their style: all-capital letters, all underlined, first letter capitalized, or some combination of these
- Spacing and margin guidelines
- Distinction between research sources that must be cited and those that need not be cited
- Use of the active voice, the present tense, and the imperative mood
- Reference or Works Cited format (if they are used)
- Capitalization of words in the text
- Abbreviations, acronyms, and symbols
- Standards for terms that should be written as one word, two words, or hyphenated (*on site/onsite, e-mail/email, on-line/online*)
- Format and wording of disclaimers (to satisfy legal or policy requirements)

In addition, the team must agree on the format and handling of project software files. The most efficient means of sharing drafts electronically is for everyone to

WRITER'S CHECKLIST

Planning a Collaborative Writing Project

- ☐ Establish guidelines to ensure that all team members are working toward the same goal and moving in the same direction.
- ☐ Agree on a standard reference guide for matters of style and format.
- ☐ Make sure that work assignments are appropriate to each person's particular talents.
- ☐ Establish a schedule that includes due dates for drafts, for team reviews of drafts, and for revisions.
- ☐ Agree on how to exchange project software files and whether to use collaborative software.

use the same operating system and word-processing, graphics, and spreadsheet software. If that's not possible, the team must decide on an effective alternative. For guidelines on using software specifically designed for collaborative writing, see Digital Shortcuts: Sharing Files Online on page 178.

Research and Writing

The planning stage is followed by the research and writing stages. These are periods of intense independent activity by the individual team members. At this point, you gather information for your assigned segment of the document, create a master outline of the segment, flesh out the outline by providing the necessary details, and produce a first draft, using the guidelines discussed in Chapters 2 and 3. Collaboration requires flexibility: The team should not insist that individual team members slavishly follow the agreed-upon outline if it proves to be inadequate or faulty in one or more areas. When a writer pursues a specific assignment in detail, he or she may find that the general outline for that segment was based on insufficient knowledge and is not desirable, or even possible, as written. Or perhaps during the research process, a writer may discover highly relevant information that is not covered in the team's working outline. In such cases, the writer must have the freedom to alter the outline. If the deviation is great enough, the writer should consult with the other team members before proceeding.

Revise your draft until it is as good as you can make it, following the guidelines in Chapters 4 and 5. Then, by the deadline established for submitting drafts, send copies of the draft to all other team members for their review. You may circulate the draft by distributing hard copy, by sending e-mail (as described in Digital Shortcuts: Advantages of Using E-mail for Collaborative Writing), or by sharing files online (as described in Digital Shortcuts: Sharing Files Online on page 178). To set up a document for electronic review, see Digital Shortcuts: Setting Up a Document for Electronic Review and Revision on page 181.

DIGITAL SHORTCUTS

Advantages of Using E-mail for Collaborative Writing

- E-mail encourages members of a collaborative team to communicate more readily with each other, share information, ask questions, and solve problems.

- E-mail also reduces the likelihood of miscommunication because comments are written.

- E-mail can reduce the frequency of face-to-face communication, but it does not eliminate the need for a group to meet in person.

- A draft sent as an attachment enables collaborative team members to solicit feedback electronically and revise the original draft based on the comments received. This process can be repeated for each team member until all sections are in final form and ready for consolidation into the master copy maintained by the team leader.

Reviewing

During the review stage, team members assume the role of target readers in order to clear up in advance any problems that might arise for that reader—a customer, a senior official in the organization, or the board of directors, for example. Each team member reviews the work of the other team members carefully and critically (but also with sensitivity to the person whose work is being reviewed), checking for problems in content, organization, and style.

Figures 6–1 and 6–2 represent one section of a proposal that was written to persuade a company president to merge the company's profit-sharing plans. The proposal describes the merger process and shows its associated costs. Two collaborative-writing team members have worked together to prepare the document. Figure 6–1 shows the second member's initial draft, which describes the merger's benefits and costs, with the first team member's comments on the draft. Because the entire report will be sent to the client company's president, whose time is limited and who has only a general knowledge of profit-sharing plans and mergers, the reviews must carefully note any parts of the proposal that are not appropriate for a nonexpert reader.

As Figure 6–1 shows, reviewing a colleague's draft is similar to reviewing your own work: A good reviewer evaluates a document in terms of audience and purpose, coherence, emphasis, and correctness. For this reason, the revision strategies you studied in Chapters 4 and 5 will serve as your foundation for collaborative work. Revising collaborative writing is much like revising any other type of writing: The writer mulls over the suggested changes, checks questionable facts, and then reworks the draft. Figure 6–2 shows the same section of the proposal, revised in response to the team member's comments.

The review stage may lead to additional planning. If, for example, a review of the first draft reveals that the original organization for a section was not adequate or correct, or if new information becomes available, the team must return to the planning stage for that segment of the document to incorporate the newer knowledge and understanding.

 On the Web
For more on this topic, see Chapter 6, bedfordstmartins .com/writingthatworks

---

DIGITAL SHORTCUTS

Sharing Files Online

- Use collaborative software such as the instant-messaging software from Yahoo!, AOL, and Jabber, and Microsoft's Messenger and NetMeeting:
  - To exchange instant messages
  - To share files online
  - To conduct live text, audio, or video chats
  - To jointly compose on a virtual whiteboard or an application window
- Use groupware such as Lotus Notes or Groove:
  - To create and manage group schedules
  - To organize and file materials in secure, accessible databases

Title is too technical— "Costs/ Benefits of Merging"?

This is covered in Part I (make this into transition)

Part II. Merger of Plans/Amending and Restating Plans/Applications for Determination Letters

DRAFT

Attempts to state problem and offer a solution

We can no longer test the Oakite product services 401(k) Profit Sharing Plan separately for coverage and nondiscrimination because combined, <u>Oakite products and Oakley services have fewer than 50 employees</u>. The merger of the 401(k) Profit Sharing Plans takes care of this problem while reducing the implementation and audit costs. We (wil) need to amend and restate the new plan to *sp* bring it into compliance with tax law 409921-65.

Too technical and you need to emphasize <u>benefits</u>.

The cost of merging, amending, restating, and redesigning the surviving 401(k) Profit Sharing Plan and for filing of notices 54-90 and 36-98 and applications 56-98 and 45-98 would be between $18,000 to $25,000.

(cost <u>reduction</u> over 2 years)

Provides costs but no incentives

Additional Comments: Team Member #2 (B. Reisner, Sales Development)

Information sounds correct, but the prospective client will need definitions and explanations for many terms and names (notices 54-90 and 36-98). Also note in your opening that Part I explains the problems associated with maintaining separate plans. Doing so will give you a better lead into your section than you've got at this point.

Further, break down specific financial costs and benefits that will result from the merger. Don't go into detail here; remember, Part III describes the details of the merger process. Simply note specific costs for specific services in a table, and give an estimate of the client's projected financial gain. NOTE: The range for costs is $19,000 to $26,000, not $18,000 to $25,000. CHECK: Can client deduct merger costs from gross profit?

Finally, promote our services with more vigor. You're not simply reporting information so that Mr. B. can phone up another company to do the merger—you're talking him into working with Brady Associates.

Figure 6–1   Draft Section of a Proposal with Comments of a Team Member

---

Part II. Benefits and Costs of Merging Current Profit-Sharing Plans

Statement of problem and offer of solution

As Part I of this report explains, the separate profit-sharing plans for your two companies, Oakite Products and Oakley Services, can no longer ensure that each employee is assigned the correct number of shares and the correct employer contribution. In addition, administrative costs for maintaining separate plans are high. If you commissioned Brady Associates to merge the plans, however, adequate tests could be performed to ensure accuracy, and administrative costs would be greatly reduced.

Further, although a merger would require you to make certain changes to your current profit-sharing procedures, Brady Associates would help you amend and restate the new plan so that it complies with the most recent tax legislation. Brady Associates will also prepare and file necessary merger documents with the Departments of Taxation and Labor.

Incentives for selecting proposed solution

The estimated cost for merging, amending, and refiling the profit-sharing plans would be between $19,000 and $26,000. Please see Table 1 for a breakdown of specific costs.

In reality, you would incur no cost if Brady Associates merged your profit-sharing plans because of reduced administrative costs. According to our estimates, the merger would give you a yearly net reduction of $36,000 in administrative costs. Thus, you would save approximately $11,000 during the first year of administering the plan and at least $36,000 annually after the first year. See Table 2 for a breakdown of net reductions in administrative costs.

Figure 6–2   Revised Section of Draft Proposal in Figure 6–1

■ Revising

Each team member now evaluates the reviews of other team members and accepts or rejects the suggested revisions. At this point, you, as a writer, must be careful not to let your ego get in the way of good judgment. You must consider each suggestion objectively on the basis of its merit, rather than simply reacting negatively to criti-

WRITER'S CHECKLIST

Reviewing Drafts by Other Writers

- ☐ Does the draft meet the established purpose of the document?
- ☐ Does the draft meet the needs of the identified reader?
- ☐ Does the material fall within the predetermined scope of coverage?
- ☐ Does the draft generally follow the agreed-upon outline?
- ☐ Is the content complete?
- ☐ Are there technical errors or anything that seems technically questionable?
- ☐ Do details and examples support the main points?

Setting Up a Document for Electronic Review and Revision

- Let your reviewers know which of the following methods you would like them to use.
  - Tracked changes on a *single draft* — multiple reviewer edits are highlighted on your draft for you to accept or reject.
  - Tracked changes on *multiple drafts* — reviewers' comments are made directly to their drafts, which are automatically saved along with your original draft, all in one document.
- You can revise the document by accepting or rejecting reviewer edits (using the tracked-changes method on a single draft) or by merging the reviewers' versions (using the multiple-versions method).

Inserting and Reviewing Comments

- To insert their comments, reviewers highlight the text or graphic for comment, click on the Insert Comment button on the tool bar, and type comments in a window at the bottom of the screen — material commented on is highlighted in color, numbered, and marked with the reviewer's initials.
- To view their comments, click on the highlighted text or on the reviewer's initials — when you move your cursor over the text or initials, the comments pop up — or read the comments at the bottom of your screen.
- To add changes reviewers make in the Comments area, manually copy and paste them into your draft.

Making Tracked Changes to a Single Draft

- This option highlights reviewer edits on one draft so that they can be individually accepted or rejected.
  - You can also protect the draft by assigning a password that will prevent any changes except for tracked changes and comments.
  - To do so, specify password access before e-mailing or posting your draft online.
- Reviewers may add, delete, or move text or graphics and even reformat the document.
- The software automatically highlights the changes (usually by underlining text changes and permitting you to specify different formatting for other changes) so that you can easily locate reviewer changes when accepting or rejecting them.
- Reviewers may also insert comments in the Comments area.

Making Tracked Changes to Multiple Drafts

- This option highlights reviewer edits on their copies of the draft.
- To use this option, set up your document so that it automatically saves the original draft and each succeeding reviewer version. (See the Help menu for details about how to enable this feature.)
- This option shows all versions of the draft within one consolidated document and includes the name of each reviewer and the date changes were made.
- Reviewers can edit the document as if it were their own — adding, deleting, reformatting, moving text or graphics, or adding comments in the Comments area.
- You compare each version and merge edits as needed to the master draft.

cism of your writing. Writers who are able to accept criticism and use it to produce a better product participate in the most fruitful kind of collaboration.

■ The Role of Conflict in Collaborative Writing

It is critically important to the quality of the document being produced that the viewpoints of all team members be considered. However, when writers collaborate, conflicts occur. They may range from a relatively minor difference over a grammatical point (whether to split an infinitive) to a major conflict over the basic approach to the document being written (whether there is too little or too much detail for the intended reader). Regardless of the severity of the conflict, it must be worked through to a conclusion or compromise that all team members can accept, even though all might not entirely agree. When the group can tolerate some disharmony and work through conflicting opinions to reach a consensus, its work is enhanced.

Although mutual respect among team members is necessary, too much deference can inhibit challenges—and that reduces the team's creativity. You have to be willing to challenge another team member's work, while still being sensitive to that person's ego. The same rule applies to collaborative writing that applies whenever critical give-and-take occurs: Focus on the problem and how to solve it rather than on the person.

Conflicts over valid issues almost always generate more innovative and creative work than does passive acceptance. However, even though the result of conflict in a peer writing team is usually positive, it can sometimes produce self-doubt or doubt about your fellow team members. Remember that conflict is a natural part of group work. Learn to harness it and turn it into a positive force.

To maximize the benefits and minimize the negative effects of conflict, emphasize areas of agreement. Then identify differences of opinion and ask why they exist. If differences occur over facts, simply determine which are or are not correct. If it is a problem of differing goals, encourage each team member to look at the problem from the other person's perspective in the light of the project's purpose statement. When conflict arises for other reasons, define the problem, describe or brainstorm alternate solutions, and select the one solution—or compromise—that best satisfies the views of each team member and of the overall team.

The following suggestions can help you manage conflict:

- Avoid taking a win-or-lose stand if you are personally involved in the conflict. If you use a win-or-lose approach, your victory will be at the other person's expense. This approach is not constructive because, by definition, there must be a loser. Most conflicts don't start out this way, but when one team member regards a compromise as a personal defeat, a conflict can lead to nonproductive results.

- Avoid accusations, threats, or disparaging comments. Instead, try to emphasize common interests and mutual goals, bearing in mind that conciliation fosters cooperation. Expressing a desire for harmonious relations can have a very disarming effect on an aggressive personality in the group.

Working in a Collaborative Group

- ☐ Know the people on your team and establish a good working rapport with them.
- ☐ Put the interests of your team ahead of your own.
- ☐ Think collectively, as a group. Do not regard one person's opinion as more or less important than another's.
- ☐ Participate constructively in group meetings.
- ☐ Be an effective listener (see Listening in Chapter 15, page 540).
- ☐ Be receptive to constructive criticism.
- ☐ Provide constructive feedback to your team members.
- ☐ Meet your established deadlines.

- Support your position with facts. Point out the ways that your position could benefit the team's ultimate goal. Show how your position is consistent with precedent, prevailing norms, or accepted standards (if true, of course). Tactfully point out any overlooked disadvantages or logic errors in the other person's point of view. Again, focus on the problem and the solution, not the person.

- Use bargaining strategies to arrive at an exchange of concessions until a compromise is reached. Both parties win through a compromise. Even if you settle for less than you initially wanted, you don't risk losing out altogether as in a win-or-lose struggle. A successful compromise satisfies each participant's minimum needs.

- Use collaboration to resolve conflict. This means each team member accepts the others' goals and all members work to achieve the best outcome for the team. A flexible, exploratory attitude is a prerequisite for collaboration; each team member must understand the others' points of view and determine the group's needs for it to be successful.

Sharing Boilerplate Material

- ■ If boilerplate material (policy statements, instructions, procedures, correspondence, or reports created by colleagues) that meets your needs exists in other company documents, copy and paste the information into your document. Don't redo work that has already been done.

- ■ Discuss sources of boilerplate material in team planning meetings and store them in electronic folders or on shared network drives or internal Web sites for sharing with other team members.

- ■ Be sure to edit the material to make it an exact fit.

- ■ There is no need to acknowledge such sources. Borrowing these passages is neither plagiarism nor a violation of copyright because the information is simply being used in a different setting by the organization to which it already belongs.

■ Leading a Collaborative Writing Team

Although the team may designate one person as its leader, that person shares decision-making authority with the other team members while assuming the additional responsibility of coordinating the team's activities, organizing the project, and producing the final product. Leadership can be granted by mutual agreement among team members to one team member or it can be rotated among members if the team produces many documents over time. The teams that collaborate best are composed of members who are professionally competent, who have mutual respect for the abilities of the other members, and who are compatible enough to work together harmoniously toward a common goal.

On a practical level, the team leader's responsibilities will include scheduling and leading meetings, writing and distributing minutes of meetings, and maintaining the master copy of the document during all stages of its development. To make these activities as efficient as possible, the leader should prepare and distribute forms to track the project's status. These forms should include style guidelines mutually agreed to in the project planning meeting, a project schedule, and transmittal sheets to record the status of reviews.

Schedule

All team members must know not only what is expected of them but when it is expected. The schedule provides this information. Schedules come in different formats. Figure 6–3, for example, shows a schedule used for a team project for a business writing class. Figure 6–4 shows a bar-chart schedule for the production of a software user's manual that required coordination among the writing, review, and

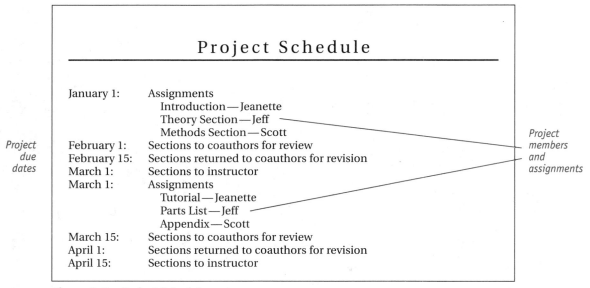

Figure 6–3   Project Schedule

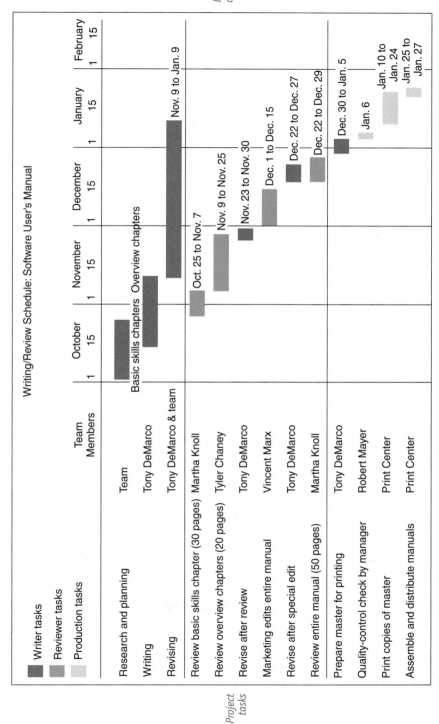

Figure 6–4 Project Schedule Presented as a Bar Chart

185

production staffs over a five-month period. Regardless of the format, the schedule must state explicitly who is responsible for what, and when the draft of each section is due.

Review Transmittal Sheet

The team leader should provide review transmittal sheets for drafts circulated on paper instead of by e-mail. Writers attach the sheets to their drafts for each reviewer to sign off as having reviewed the draft. The review transmittal sheet shows at a glance the status of the project during the review cycle. It also lists in order those who must review the draft, as shown in Figure 6–5. (Remember that as part of a collaborative writing team, you will act as both writer and reviewer.)

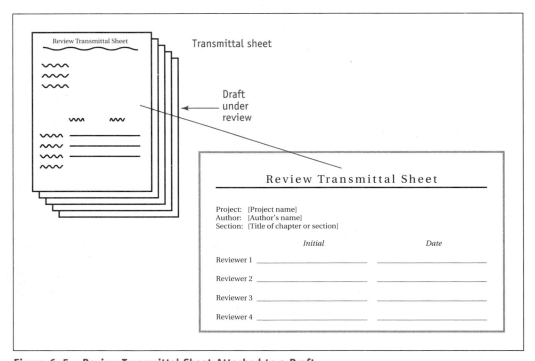

Figure 6–5   Review Transmittal Sheet Attached to a Draft

■ Collaborating with Other Departments

In some work settings, writing-team leaders arrange for the cooperation of different departments within the organization. For example, the team leader may need to meet with the art or media production staff to:

- Plan for the creation of graphs, charts, drawings, maps, etc.
- Plan for the document's cover.
- Arrange for photographs to be taken or scanned.

The team leader may meet with the print production staff to:

- Inform them of when to expect the manuscript.
- Discuss any special printing requirements, such as color, special bindings, document size, foldout pages, etc.

In addition, the team leader may need to obtain reviews and approval from other organizations, such as the sales and legal departments.

CHAPTER 6 SUMMARY: Collaborative Writing

Form a collaborative writing team when:

- ☐ Your project requires specialists in more than one subject area.
- ☐ Your project would benefit from the merging of different perspectives.
- ☐ Your project's size, importance, or deadline requires a team effort.

As a member of a collaborative writing team, you are expected to:

- ☐ Work with others as a team of peers to plan, design, and write a single document.
- ☐ Ensure that all important points are discussed and all problems addressed.
- ☐ Learn tolerance and respect for the opinions of others.
- ☐ Research the topics of your assigned section.
- ☐ Write your draft.
- ☐ Review the work of other team members.
- ☐ Revise your draft based on comments from other team members.
- ☐ Maintain the project schedule.
- ☐ Share equal responsibility for the end product.

As a team leader, you are expected to:

- ☐ Share decision-making authority with other team members.
- ☐ Coordinate the activity of team members.
- ☐ Maintain the project schedule.
- ☐ Coordinate the production of the final product.

■ Exercises

Exercises followed by the symbol Ⓦ are continued at **bedfordstmartins .com/writingthatworks**, Chapter 6.

1. a. Draft a 300-word summary of a news article, then exchange it with a study partner by e-mail. Review each other's work, make suggestions for revision, and return the file by e-mail. Refer to Digital Shortcuts on pages 177, 178, and 181. Together decide which method you will use to mark the files. Also review the Writer's Checklist: Reviewing Drafts by Other Writers on page 180.

    b. Bring a hard-copy draft of your writing assignment to class and exchange it with another student. Each student makes comments and suggestions for revision and returns the draft for rewriting.

2. Schedule a telephone, e-mail, or personal interview with a health-care, business, technology, or industry representative who is part of a collaborative writing team. Before the interview, review this chapter to help you prepare a list of questions to ask about details of the collaborative writing style used by his or her group or company. Keep your interview to no more than 20 to 30 minutes. Consider asking about planning meetings and how they are conducted, collaboration with other specialists or peer reviews, drafts of documents and how they are circulated and commented on for revision, and any positive or negative experiences your interviewee found most helpful during the collaborative writing process. After the interview, prepare an outline, a draft, and a final report on your findings. Be ready to share your interview report with your classmates, and send the person you interviewed a thank-you letter.

3. Assume that your collaborative writing team of three or four students has been hired by a restaurant's national headquarters to conduct an evaluation of a local restaurant. Appoint a team leader who will assign specific items for each group member to observe while in the restaurant—for example, the cleanliness of the silverware and rest rooms, the attentiveness of the waitstaff, the quality of the food, and so on. As a group, summarize your findings in an outline and then create a draft letter addressed to the person who hired your team.

4. Assume that there has been an increased dropout rate at your school recently. Form a collaborative writing team with at least two other classmates to prepare a 300-word report listing the possible causes and solutions to the problem.

5. Form a collaborative writing team with two or three classmates and choose a product or service, then create a company name. Decide on the nature of your business (service, manufacturing, etc.), the scope and size of your business (international, many branches), and the audience of your business (client, consumer group) for your company's product or service. Develop and design a logo, letterhead, and business card appropriate to your company and clients. Submit your finished products to your instructor.

6. Form a collaborative writing team with your classmates based on common occupational interests, such as agriculture, communications, computer science, or engineering. Assume that you have been asked by your university's freshman recruiting staff to create a document based on your experience as a student, explaining why your campus is a great place to prepare for the occupational interest you and your team have chosen. In your group, appoint a team leader and a team recorder, and decide how to organize and write this assignment so that recruiters can use your material to persuade high school students to attend your university.

7. Form a collaborative writing group that will meet weekly for the rest of the semester to discuss and write about the new material you learned in class and the assigned reading that you did that week. Your group will submit a brief, informal memo to your instructor each week that summarizes your group's discussion. Individually, you will also keep a weekly journal that records the group's interactions, activities, conflicts, and progress throughout the semester. In your final journal entry, comment on whether you think your writing group functioned as a productive writing team and analyze why or why not.

8. Choose three classmates with whom you share similar interests to help you work on one of the following collaborative writing assignments. With instructor approval, your group may substitute another topic as long as each member of the group is familiar with the topic.

   a. Write a report on an extracurricular activity listed in the campus catalog that you and your teammates participate in. Explain the activity and why it is worthwhile. Support your report with details.
   b. Write a report on careers related to your and your teammates' fields of study. Explain the jobs available, the industries they are related to, locations, rate of pay, etc. What is the outlook overall?
   c. Write a report summarizing the computer lab facility your university offers students. As lab users, do you feel that the facility is adequate or in need of improvement? Support your report with details.
   d. Write a report explaining how to operate a piece of equipment that everyone in your group uses at least weekly, such as a microwave, a CD or DVD player, or some other more sophisticated item. Evaluate the effectiveness of the equipment and make any suggestions you may have for improving it.

9. Collaborate with a classmate to develop a process that your class can follow to review and comment on each other's written work. Before you begin, review this chapter. Then create an outline and a rough draft for a plan that facilitates peer feedback. Highlight the specific benefits of your plan and be ready to share your plan with the rest of the class.

10. Form a collaborative group of no more than six members in which both genders are represented equally. Appoint a group leader and a group recorder. Based on your personal experiences, brainstorm as a group to create a list of gender-related issues that you have encountered as college students such as the stereotyping of women and men with regard to verbal or mathematical abilities or technological skills, for example. Use your collaborative lists to generate a brief narrative about these campus gender issues that includes the ideas of each group member. Be ready to share your report with the rest of the class or write an individual report summarizing the personal interactions of your group during your meetings. W

■ Collaborative Classroom Projects

Projects followed by the symbol W are continued at **bedfordstmartins.com/ writingthatworks**, Chapter 6.

1. a. An important stage of the collaborative writing process is the planning stage, during which time all members of the team need to work toward the same goal, select a reference guide, set up a schedule, and agree on how to enforce the standards that have been established. Assume that your boss has given you a collaborative writing assignment on a topic specific to the company's main product. In groups of five or fewer, take the next 30 minutes to:
   (1) Become acquainted with one another's expertise by asking each person to talk about his or her background for two minutes or less.
   (2) Select a team leader.

(3) Decide the time schedule for making initial assignments and submitting drafts, coauthor reviews, and revisions.

(4) Decide what method you will use to enforce the timeline.

(5) Decide what other guidelines are necessary to ensure the group's success.

Keep in mind that unstated policies can lead to confusion about responsibilities. Therefore, when your group has discussed project guidelines, the team leader will summarize these policies in a list.

b. During the next 15 minutes, make a list of the duties that a collaborative team leader would be responsible for during a collaborative writing project, and brainstorm a list of qualities needed to lead a collaborative writing team. When you have completed your lists, refer to Leading a Collaborative Writing Team (pages 184–186). In ten minutes or less, decide if your group's list is similar or dissimilar to the suggestions stated in this chapter, and which of your ideas to share with your class.

c. Using the same group and leader, experiment with positive conflict, which almost always generates more innovative and creative work than does passive acceptance. Assuming that half of the members of your team are smokers and half are nonsmokers, as a team write a recommendation on whether your company should provide a smokers' lounge. The smokers on the team claim that the existing nonsmoking lounge is large enough to be divided into two separate areas, while the nonsmokers feel smoking in the building should not be permitted. As a team, spend 45 minutes developing an outline of the pros and cons for both sides of the issue.

(1) Quickly establish who is a nonsmoker and who is a smoker.

(2) Appoint a team leader.

(3) Brainstorm your list of pros and cons for first one side of the issue and then the other.

During the next 15 minutes, quickly draft your collaborative outline and be ready to share it with the class.

2. Divide into groups of five or fewer members. Assume that your class will be featured in an upcoming brochure focusing on diverse and talented students who are attracted to your campus. As a team, you have been asked to submit a one-page summary of the individual strengths of your team members. Begin by taking 30 minutes to:

a. Write a one-page statement about yourself. Think about the special awards or honors you have received and the details of your life that helped to shape you into the college student you are today. Explain what influences directed you toward your chosen field of study and how long you have known that this was the right choice for you. Describe the mentors who have been important in your life. Talk about your employment experiences and how they fit into your course of study and plans for a career. Focus on any leadership or managerial experiences that have contributed to your personal growth.

b. After all personal statements have been completed, spend the next several minutes reading the statements as a means of peer reviewing and introducing yourselves to each other.

c. Appoint a team leader who will coordinate your group as you select and edit a paragraph or two from each paper to complete a collaborative report titled "[your university/college] Attracts Diverse and Talented Students." Be prepared to share your group's report with the class. ⓦ

Research Projects

1. Form a collaborative team to research and write an owner's manual for a cellular or wireless telephone, a DVD player, a personal digital assistant, or another item of your choice. Your manual should have four distinct sections: Physical Description, Theory of Operation, Operating Instructions, and Maintenance Instructions. Each section should be fully developed, which means your group will need to research the broad subject as well as the subject of each individual section of the manual.

2. Meet with your instructor and your collaborative writing team to select a research and writing project. Potential projects might include a pamphlet or brochure describing what every freshman student should know about basic services available on your campus; a document explaining how to use a research facility, media resource center, or resources at the library; or a pamphlet or brochure describing the job-search information and job-placement centers on your campus.

   Once your group has set up specific project guidelines, divide tasks by assigning the research and writing of report segments either to separate members of the group or to two-person teams. Make certain that every member of the group reads and comments on the first draft of every other member's segment and all of the group composes the brief introduction and conclusion of the report.

3. Form a collaborative writing team to research and write a major report for the head of the department responsible for this course, recommending the purchase of laptop computers for students to borrow for class projects. In your proposal, identify the type and brand of computer you will be evaluating, as well as how and where you will gather information on the product (in person at a retail location, on the Internet, etc.).

   a. Decide on a team leader and an evaluation board, then:
      - Write a memo requesting your instructor's approval for your team to undertake the project and to evaluate specific computer brands and models.
      - Create biweekly progress reports, to start as soon as your team has received project approval and to continue for the duration of the project.
   b. Have the team leader delegate research responsibilities so that members are able to collect information that answers why the computers are needed and how many are needed; describe the specific features the portable computers should have (such as memory size, operating speed, and compatibility with personal computers already installed at the college); describe the types of software that should be installed; define what the total cost will be and whether an educational discount or quantity discount is available; and answer how the computers should be kept secure and how borrowing them would be controlled.
   c. Decide collaboratively on dates for submission of the proposal, progress reports (every two weeks from project approval), the final report, and the final presentation.
   d. Present an oral description of your research to the other team members, as well as a report on the results of your preliminary evaluation. Each team member should do the same.
   e. Have the team leader present the final results of the project and the recommendations to an evaluation board.

f. Finally, (1) prepare and submit a joint (single) copy of the proposal, progress reports, and formal report, and (2) make group oral presentations. Provide handouts of any printed information you have obtained or of any important text from your proposal (see Using Handouts in Chapter 15). As a team, consider how much the visual appearance of your report will influence whether your recommendations receive approval. If the department head likes what he or she reads, your report may be attached to his or her budget request to demonstrate why the computers are needed (this is commonly known as "the justification"). Consequently, the quality of your report, both in appearance and in content, can help convince those readers who will approve the expenditure for your request. Your instructor will award a group mark for each assignment, which all team members will receive.[1]

■ Web Projects

1. Several of today's successful companies encourage collaborative writing on the job. Search the Web to learn how such companies advertise their team approach when hiring. Sample sites include those for companies such as Saturn and the Kimberly-Clark Corporation. Prepare an outline listing the kinds of collaborative writing assignments that a writer at a particular company might encounter. Your outline should cover areas such as product information, warranty information, employment training, management styles, and so on.

2. You are part of a collaborative team at your company that has been asked to write a recommendation for health-care insurance alternatives for employees. Visit the Web sites of at least three companies to research available options. Sample sites of major U.S. health-insurance companies include Aetna, Blue Cross, and Humana.

3. You are part of a collaborative team at your company that has been asked to write a recommendation to purchase wireless telephones and services for field representatives. Visit the Web sites of three companies to research available options. Sample sites of major wireless telephone companies include Telephone Support Systems, Bell Atlantic Mobile, and AT&T Wireless Services.

---

[1] This exercise is adapted, with permission, from "An Integrated Collaborative Writing Project" by Ron S. Blicq, in *Collaborative Technical Writing: Theory and Practice*, ed. Richard Louth and Martin Scott (Hammond, LA: Association of Teachers and Technical Writing, n.d.), pp. 57–60.

7 Researching Your Subject

T om Cabines, Production Manager of Nebel Desktop Publishers, received a
memo from Alice Enklend, Purchasing Director, asking him how many copies
of an employee manual a corporate customer had commissioned the firm to print.
Tom probably had the answer at his fingertips or was able to find it after a quick look
at his computer's production-scheduling spreadsheet. Tom's *research*—or tracking
down of information on the topic—would be minimal.

Suppose, instead, that Tom were asked to write a market-research report for
the president of Nebel Desktop Publishers about developing a Web publishing
division. How would he go about obtaining the necessary information? For this
task he would have to do some extensive work, which could involve primary
research—conducting interviews or collecting questionnaire responses on the
topic—or secondary research—gathering information from the library, the
Internet, or both.

This chapter discusses tools, strategies, and resources for researchers of various levels of expertise. You will find the following sections:

W On the Web
For online resources
for conducting re-
search, see Chapter 7,
bedfordstmartins.com/
writingthatworks

- **Conducting Primary Research,** covers the use of experience, interviews,
  observations, and questionnaires to collect information (page 194).

- **Conducting Secondary Research,** covers the use of the library and the
  Internet to collect information (page 202).

- **Evaluating Print and Online Sources,** Recording Information, and
  Avoiding Plagiarism, provides advice for selecting sources, taking notes,
  quoting, paraphrasing, and summarizing (page 213).

- **Documenting Sources,** offers guidelines and examples for using the
  American Psychological Association (APA) and the Modern Language
  Association (MLA) styles of documentation (page 222).

■ Conducting Primary Research: Experience, Interviews, Observations, and Questionnaires

Primary research is the gathering of raw data from such sources as first-hand experience, interviews, direct observations, and questionnaires. In fact, direct observation and interaction are the only ways to obtain certain kinds of information, about behavior, natural phenomena, and the operation of systems and equipment. For example, you might use primary research to test the usability of instructions you have created.

In an academic setting, you may talk about resources with your peers, your instructors, and especially a research librarian. On the job, you may rely on your own knowledge and experience and that of your colleagues. In this setting, begin by brainstorming with colleagues about what sources will be most useful for your project and how you can track them down.

Beginning with Experience

If your research topic deals with something familiar (a hobby or an area of interest, for example) or relates to an occupation you are in or hope to be in, you may already know enough information to get started. In addition, you can check your home or office for any materials you have acquired on the subject. Based on this background, make a rough outline — it will tell you how much you know about the topic. Your own experience is a starting point from which you can expand your knowledge by finding and using other sources discussed in this chapter.

Interviewing for Information

To learn from the experience of others, you may be able to do some of your research by *interviewing* someone who is an expert on the subject. This process includes determining the proper person to interview, preparing for the interview, conducting the interview, and expanding your notes immediately after the interview.

Determining Whom to Interview

Many times, your subject or purpose logically points to the proper person to interview for information. If, for instance, you were writing about how to use the Web to market a software development business, the logical experts to interview would include someone with extensive experience in Web marketing and someone who has built a successful business developing software. The following sources can help you identify an appropriate person to interview: (1) workplace colleagues or faculty in relevant academic departments, (2) a local firm or organization whose staff includes experts on your subject, (3) information from Internet research, (4) local chapters or Web pages of professional societies, and (5) yellow or business pages of the telephone directory.

Voices from the Workplace

Susan U. Ladwig, Reinhart Boerner Van Deuren

Susan U. Ladwig is an associate attorney in the Employee Benefits Department at Reinhart Boerner Van Deuren in Milwaukee, Wisconsin. Among her responsibilities is researching legal issues and developing legal memoranda and legal documents reflecting her research. A significant part of Susan's work involves researching on the Internet.

Susan describes the Internet as a powerful tool and resource in her business: "The Internet has become a basic research tool for attorneys who must quickly access the most up-to-date information on law changes, corporations, court decisions, and various legal subjects. Learning how to critically evaluate and efficiently gather key data from the Internet is an important skill for students."

Liz Goodwin, Melrose Public Library

As a librarian's assistant, Liz Goodwin works at the circulation desk, where she helps patrons find books and conduct research on specific subjects.

"Sometimes, patrons come to the circulation desk with only the author's name or a partial title for a book. Other times, they are interested in a subject but don't know much about it. In these cases, I have found the Internet to be a very useful resource. Our library has moved all of our data online. We no longer have a traditional card catalog. This makes it very easy to search for books by subject. Sometimes I will consult Web sites like <booksinprint.com>, which offers a comprehensive list of titles. I also rely on other Internet sites for research purposes. Many times, a patron will come to the library wanting a book he or she saw on a morning talk show. When this happens, I go online to find the show's Web site for more information. <amazon.com> and <bn.com> are also sites that I frequently use.

"A few months ago, I was given the task of finding out what were the most popular books of 2002. We wanted to know how often these books were checked out of the library so we could petition for more funding to buy more books. I consulted a few Internet resources, like the *New York Times* best-seller list and <amazon.com>. Because I knew these sites were reputable, I could base my research on their findings."

Preparing for the Interview

Once you have selected the person or persons you would like to interview, learn as much as possible about each person and the organization for which he or she works. When you contact the prospective interviewee, explain who you are, why you would like to interview him or her, the subject and purpose of the interview, and how much time it will take. Also let your interviewee know that you will allow him or her to review your draft.

After you have made the appointment, prepare a list of questions to ask your interviewee. Avoid vague, general questions such as "What do you think of the Internet?" Instead, ask specific but open-ended questions such as "How do you use the Internet to help clients?" and "How has use of the Internet helped your organization?" Such questions prompt interviewees to provide specific information. Organize your questions so that you begin with the least complex aspects of the topic, then move to the more complex aspects.

Conducting the Interview

Arrive for your interview on time. Once you've introduced yourself, take a few minutes to chat informally—this will help both you and your interviewee to relax. During the interview, follow the guidelines listed in Writer's Checklist: Interviewing for Information.

WRITER'S CHECKLIST

Interviewing for Information

- ☐ Be pleasant but purposeful. Feel free to ask leading questions on the subject. Use your prepared list of questions as your guide.
- ☐ Stay on track. If the interviewee strays too far from the subject, ask a specific question to redirect the conversation.
- ☐ Be flexible. If a prepared question is no longer suitable, move to the next question.
- ☐ Some answers prompt additional questions; ask them as they arise.
- ☐ Let your interviewee do most of the talking. Remember that the interviewee is the expert.
- ☐ Take only memory-jogging notes that will help you recall the conversation later. Concentrate on key facts and figures.
- ☐ Use a tape recorder if both you and your interviewee are comfortable with it.
- ☐ As the interview comes to a close, take a few minutes to skim your notes. If time allows, ask the interviewee to clarify anything that is ambiguous.
- ☐ After thanking the interviewee, ask permission to telephone to clarify a point or two as you complete your interview notes.

Expanding Your Notes after the Interview

As soon as possible after the interview, review your notes, fill in any material that is obviously missing, and summarize the speaker's remarks. Then convert the notes to complete sentences. Select the important information you need and transfer it to your outline or working draft.

A day or two after the interview, thank the interviewee in a brief letter or e-mail.

Observing Firsthand

Visiting a location and conducting firsthand observations may provide valuable information about how a process or procedure works or how a group interacts. If you are planning research that involves observation, choose your sites and times carefully, and be sure to obtain permission in advance. During your observations, remain as unobtrusive as possible and keep accurate, complete records that indicate date, time of day, duration of the observation, and so on. Save interpretations of your observations for future analysis.

Using a Questionnaire

Consider expanding the number of people you gather information from beyond those you've interviewed by using a questionnaire. A *questionnaire*—a series of questions on a particular topic, sent out to a number of people—is an interview on paper. It has several advantages over the personal interview, and several disadvantages.

Advantages

- A questionnaire allows you to gather information from more people more quickly than you could through personal interviews.
- It enables you to obtain responses from people who are difficult to reach or who are in scattered geographical locations.
- Respondents have more time to think through their answers than they would under the pressure of composing thoughtful and complete answers to an interviewer.
- The questionnaire may yield more objective data because it reduces the possibility that the interviewer's tone of voice or facial expressions might influence an answer.
- The cost of distributing and tabulating a questionnaire is lower than the cost of conducting numerous personal interviews.

Disadvantages

- The results of a questionnaire may be slanted in favor of those people who have strong opinions on a subject because they are more likely to respond than those with only moderate views.
- Even if a questionnaire is designed to let one question lead logically to another, the questionnaire does not allow specific follow-up to answers.
- Distributing questionnaires and waiting for replies may take considerably longer than conducting a personal interview.

Selecting Questionnaire Recipients

Selecting the proper recipients for your questionnaire is crucial if you are to gather representative and usable data. If you wanted to survey the opinions of large groups in the general population—for example, all medical technologists working in private laboratories or all independent garage owners—your task would not be easy. Because you cannot include everybody in your survey, you need to choose a representative cross section—for example, include enough people from around the country, of both genders, and with varied educational training. Only then could you make a generalized statement based on your findings from the sample. (The best sources of information on sampling techniques are marketing-research and statistics texts.)

Preparing and Designing Your Questionnaire

A key goal in designing a questionnaire is to keep it as brief as possible. The longer it is, the less likely the recipient will be to complete and return it. Next, the questions should be easy to understand. A confusing question will yield confusing results, whereas a carefully worded question will be easy to answer. Ideally, recipients should be able to answer most questions with a "yes" or "no" or by checking or circling a choice among several options. Such answers are easy to tabulate and require minimum effort on the part of the respondent, thus increasing your chances of obtaining a response. (See also Creating Print Forms, page 261.)

■ Do you recommend that the flextime program be made permanent?

☐ Yes   ☐ No   ☐ No opinion

If you need more information than such questions produce, provide an appropriate range of answers, as in the following example.

■ How many hours of overtime would you be willing to work each week?

☐ 4 hours   ☐ 8 hours   ☐ Over 10 hours
☐ 6 hours   ☐ 10 hours   ☐ No overtime

WRITER'S CHECKLIST ✓

Creating a Questionnaire

☐ Prepare a cover letter, a memo (if the questionnaire is to be circulated within an organization), or an e-mail explaining who you are, the questionnaire's purpose, the date by which you need a response, and how and where to send the completed questionnaire. Include your contact information (mailing address, phone number, and e-mail address).

☐ Include a stamped, self-addressed envelope if you are using regular mail.

☐ Construct as many questions as possible that can be quickly answered with "yes," "no," or a check mark.

☐ Include a section for additional comments, where respondents may clarify their overall attitude toward the subject.

☐ State whether the information provided and the respondent's identity will be kept confidential.

☐ Include questions about the respondent's age, gender, education, occupation, and so on, only if such information will be of value in interpreting the answers.

☐ Consider offering some tangible appreciation to those who answer the questionnaire by a specific date, such as a copy of the results or, for a marketing questionnaire, a gift certificate.

Questions should be neutral; their wording should not lead respondents to give a particular answer, which can result in inaccurate or skewed data.

SLANTED   Would you prefer the freedom of a four-day workweek?

NEUTRAL   Would you choose to work a four-day workweek, ten hours a day, with
                     every Friday off?

The sample cover memo and questionnaire in Figures 7–1 and 7–2 were sent to employees who had participated in a large organization's six-month program of flexible working hours.

Luxwear Products Corporation
Memo

To: All Company Employees
From: Nelson Barrett, Human Resources Director   *NB*
Date: October 17, 2003
Subject: Review of Flexible Working Hours Program

Please complete and return the questionnaire enclosed regarding Luxwear's trial program of flexible working hours. Your answers will help us decide whether we should make the program permanent.

Return the completed questionnaire to Ken Rose, Mail Code 12B (fax 212- 936-8358), by October 27. Your signature on the questionnaire is not necessary. All responses will be confidential and given serious consideration. Feel free to raise additional issues pertaining to the program.

If you want to discuss any item in the questionnaire, call Pam Peters in the Human Resources Department at extension 8812, or send her an e-mail at pp1@lpc.com.

Enclosure: Questionnaire

Figure 7–1   Questionnaire Cover Memo

Flexible Working Hours Program
Questionnaire

1. What kind of position do you occupy?

    ☐ Supervisory
    ☐ Nonsupervisory

2. Indicate to the nearest quarter of an hour when you begin work under flextime.

    ☐ 7:00 a.m.   ☐ 8:15 a.m.
    ☐ 7:15 a.m.   ☐ 8:30 a.m.
    ☐ 7:30 a.m.   ☐ 8:45 a.m.
    ☐ 7:45 a.m.   ☐ 9:00 a.m.
    ☐ 8:00 a.m.   ☐ Other (specify) _____

3. Where do you live?

    ☐ Talbot County   ☐ Greene County
    ☐ Montgomery County ☐ Other (specify) _____

4. How do you usually travel to work?

    ☐ Drive alone   ☐ Walk
    ☐ Bus   ☐ Car pool
    ☐ Train   ☐ Motorcycle
    ☐ Bicycle   ☐ Other (specify) _____

5. Has flextime affected your commuting time?

    ☐ Increase: Approximate number of minutes _____
    ☐ Decrease: Approximate number of minutes _____
    ☐ No change

6. If you drive alone or in a car pool, has flextime increased or decreased the amount of time it takes you to find a parking space?

        ☐ Increased   ☐ Decreased   ☐ No change

7. Has flextime had an effect on your productivity?

    a. Quality of work
        ☐ Increased   ☐ Decreased   ☐ No change

    b. Accuracy of work
        ☐ Increased   ☐ Decreased   ☐ No change

    c. Quiet time for uninterrupted work
        ☐ Increased   ☐ Decreased   ☐ No change

8. Have you had difficulty getting in touch with coworkers who are on different work schedules from yours?

    ☐ Yes   ☐ No

Figure 7–2   Questionnaire (continued)

9. Have you had trouble scheduling meetings within flexible starting and quitting times?

    ☐ Yes   ☐ No

10. Has flextime affected the way you feel about your job?

    ☐ Yes   ☐ No

    If yes, please answer (a) or (b):

    a. Feel better about job
        ☐ Slightly   ☐ Considerably

    b. Feel worse about job
        ☐ Slightly   ☐ Considerably

11. How important is it for you to have flexibility in your working hours?

    ☐ Very   ☐ Not very   ☐ Somewhat   ☐ Not at all

12. Has flextime allowed you more time to be with your family?

    ☐ Yes   ☐ No

13. If you are responsible for the care of a young child or children, has flextime made it easier or more difficult for you to arrange baby-sitting or day-care services?

    ☐ Easier   ☐ More difficult   ☐ No change

14. Do you recommend that the flextime program be made permanent?

    ☐ Yes   ☐ No

15. Please describe below or on a separate page any major changes you recommend for the program.

Thank you for your assistance.

Figure 7–2   Questionnaire (continued)

■ Conducting Secondary Research: The Library and Internet

Secondary research is the gathering of information that has been analyzed, assessed, evaluated, compiled, or otherwise organized into accessible form. Sources include books and articles, as well as reports, Web documents, e-mail discussions, audio and video recordings, business letters, minutes of meetings, operating manuals, brochures, and so forth. To find these materials, you will need to conduct research using your library and the Internet.

As you look for sources, keep in mind that in most cases the more recent the information, the better. Articles in periodicals and newspapers are current sources because they are published frequently. Academic (.edu), organizational (.org), and government (.gov) Web sites can include recent research, works in progress, interviews, articles, papers, and conference proceedings.

When a resource seems useful, consider its authorship and other aspects of a text or document as outlined in Evaluating Print Sources (page 213) and Evaluating Online Sources (page 215). Then read the material carefully and take notes that include any additional questions about your topic. Some of your questions may eventually be answered in other sources; questions that remain unanswered can guide you to further research.

Library Research

Libraries offer organized paths to the world of scholarship and information and to the Internet. Library resources include online catalogs for locating books, online databases and indexes for locating and retrieving articles, specialized tools, and subject directories for using the Web.

You may want to begin your library research by meeting with a research librarian. Research librarians are information specialists who can help you quickly find the best print or online resources for your topic—a brief conversation can focus your research and save you time. In addition, use your library's homepage to access its catalog, article databases, Web directories, and more. A sample of a college library's homepage is shown in Figure 7–3. A sample of a library's online catalog page is shown in Figure 7–5, article database page in Figure 7–7, and a Web subject directory page in Figure 7–4.

Your search strategy depends on the kind of information you are seeking. For example, if you need the latest data offered by government research or information about a specific company, check the Web. To save time, begin by searching your library's online subject directory to the Web, as shown in Figure 7–4. Likewise, if you need a current article on a topic, you might search an online database—such as InfoTrac—subscribed to by your library, as shown in Figure 7–8. For an overview of a subject, check your library's reference materials (as shown in Figure 7–3). For historical background, your best resources are books, periodicals, and primary historical documents.

W On the Web
For resources for finding libraries in your area or online, see Chapter 7, bedfordstmartins.com/ writingthatworks

W On the Web
For glossaries of common library and Internet research terms, see Chapter 7, bedfordstmartins.com/ writingthatworks

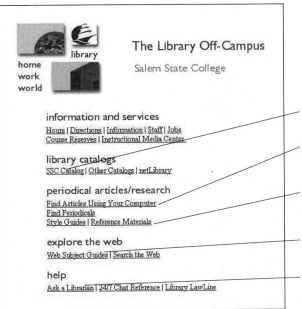
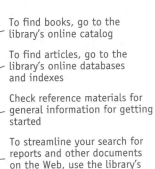

To find books, go to the library's online catalog

To find articles, go to the library's online databases and indexes

Check reference materials for general information for getting started

To streamline your search for reports and other documents on the Web, use the library's Web directory

Take advantage of a librarian's help, online or in person

Figure 7–3   College Library Homepage

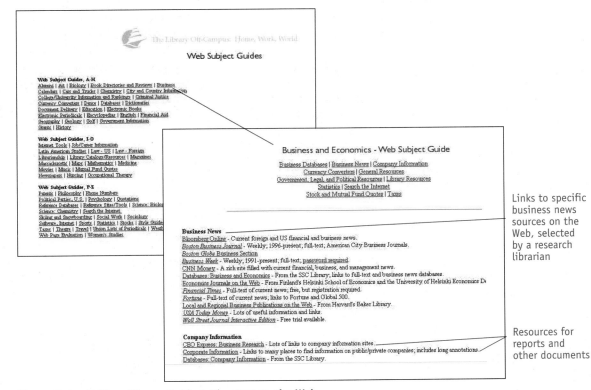

Links to specific business news sources on the Web, selected by a research librarian

Resources for reports and other documents

Figure 7–4   College Library Subject Directory to the Web

Using Online Catalogs (Locating Books)

A library's online catalog—accessed through a library terminal or the Internet—allows you to search a library's holdings, indicates an item's location and availability, and may allow you to arrange an interlibrary loan.

You can search a library's online catalog by author, title, subject, or keyword. The most typical ways of searching the catalog are to search by subject or keyword.

Methods for searching online catalogs vary. If you are at the library, ask a reference librarian to give you a brief tour of the online catalog; otherwise, check the library's homepage or catalog page for guidelines or FAQs (Frequently Asked Questions) on using the catalog. Information on a few basic steps and some directions for locating materials will prepare you to start your research.

Follow these basic steps to search an online catalog:

- *Start with a question or a thesis statement.* If your topic is unfamiliar, try to find a background article on it. Is there a specialized encyclopedia, reference book, or summary that brings some of the research and history of the topic together in one location? Talk to a reference librarian about good starting points.

- *Limit the scope of your search.* Do you need to describe why the topic is important? Will the chronology of changes in the topic strengthen your argument? The catalog may provide a shortcut to the library's online reference section.

- *Become familiar with the way the online catalog works.* What advice is available from a librarian or from help screens on the library's homepage or catalog page? What search options are available? Look for the best strategies for locating appropriate materials.

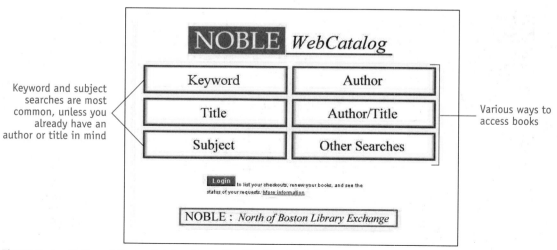

Keyword and subject searches are most common, unless you already have an author or title in mind

NOBLE *WebCatalog*

Keyword	Author
Title	Author/Title
Subject	Other Searches

Various ways to access books

Login to list your checkouts, renew your books, and see the status of your requests. More information

NOBLE : *North of Boston Library Exchange*

Figure 7–5 College Library Catalog Page (for Finding Books)

- *Sum up your thesis in two or three key terms.* What words might you use to conduct keyword or key subject searches? Consider checking the subject headings issued by the Library of Congress <loc.gov> for categories relevant to your topic. Academic and public libraries organize their resources and subject searches according to standard Library of Congress topic areas.

If your search turns up too many results, narrow your search by using the "limit search" or "advanced search" option offered by many catalogs. An example of an advanced search by keyword is shown in Figure 7–6.

Using Databases and Indexes (Locating Articles)

Most libraries subscribe to online databases, also known as periodical indexes, that provide access to collections of online articles, among other resources. Figure 7–7 is an example of a page that provides access to articles. Available through a library's Web site, these databases and indexes typically include the following:

- *InfoTrac*—a collection of databases of articles (many in full text) with specialized databases in business, health, and other fields
- *ProQuest*—a database of articles (many in full text) with specialized databases for nursing, biology, and psychology
- *EBSCOhost*—a database of articles (many in full text) with specialized databases in a range of subjects
- *FirstSearch*—a collection of specialized databases such as WorldCat (library collections) and ArticleFirst (articles; some in full text)
- *Lexis/Nexis Universe*—a collection of databases containing news, business, legal, and congressional information (most articles in full text)

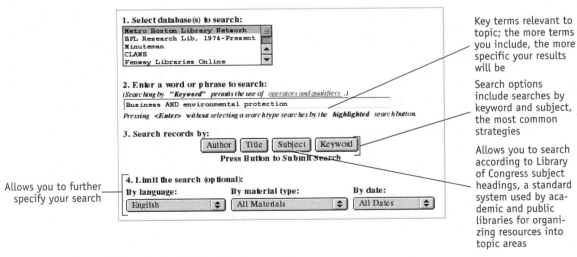

Figure 7–6   Advanced Search of a Catalog (by Keyword)

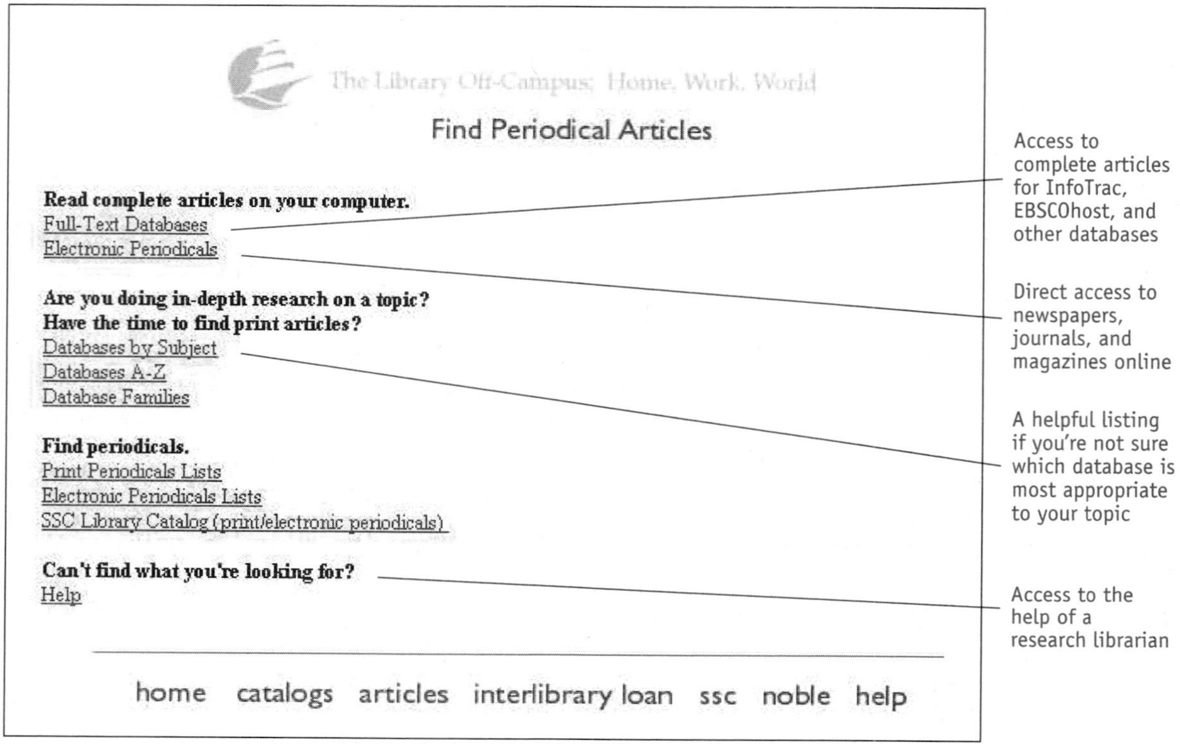

The Library Off-Campus: Home, Work, World

Find Periodical Articles

Read complete articles on your computer.
Full-Text Databases
Electronic Periodicals

Are you doing in-depth research on a topic?
Have the time to find print articles?
Databases by Subject
Databases A-Z
Database Families

Find periodicals.
Print Periodicals Lists
Electronic Periodicals Lists
SSC Library Catalog (print/electronic periodicals)

Can't find what you're looking for?
Help

Access to complete articles for InfoTrac, EBSCOhost, and other databases

Direct access to newspapers, journals, and magazines online

A helpful listing if you're not sure which database is most appropriate to your topic

Access to the help of a research librarian

home   catalogs   articles   interlibrary loan   ssc   noble   help

Figure 7–7   College Library Article Database Page

W On the Web
For access to online library catalogs, see Chapter 7, bedfordstmartins.com/ writingthatworks

These databases are excellent resources for articles published within the last ten to twenty years. Some include descriptive abstracts and full texts of articles. To find older articles, you may need to consult a print index, such as the *Readers' Guide to Periodical Literature* and the *New York Times Index,* or a reference librarian. (For more information on print indexes, see Locating Reference Works below.)

To locate articles in a database, conduct a keyword search, as shown in Figure 7–6. If your search turns up too many results, narrow your search by connecting two search terms with *AND*—"business writing AND employment"—or use other options offered by the database, such as a limited, modified, or advanced search.

Locating Reference Works

In addition to articles and books, you may want to consult reference works such as encyclopedias, dictionaries, and atlases for a brief overview of your subject. *Bibliographies,* which are lists of works written about a topic, can direct you to more specialized sources. Ask your reference librarian to recommend reference works and bibliographies that are most relevant to your topic—many are located online and can be accessed through your library's homepage.

Encyclopedias.   Encyclopedias are comprehensive, multivolume collections of articles arranged alphabetically. Some, such as the *Encarta Encyclopedia*

Detailed search
guidelines

Brief keyword search
instructions

Most recent articles
will appear first in
your results

More options for
focusing your search;
results will include
only 2002 articles
available in full text

Search
options

Search results provide
access to the articles
themselves

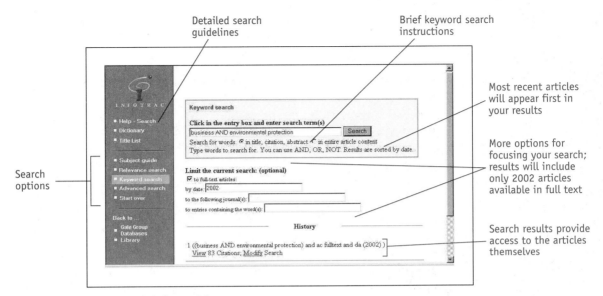

Figure 7–8   InfoTrac Search for Articles

<encarta@msn.com>, cover a wide range of subjects, while others, such as *The Encyclopedia of Careers and Vocational Guidance,* 11th ed., edited by William Hopke (Chicago: Ferguson, 1999), and the *McGraw-Hill Encyclopedia of Science and Technology,* 8th ed., edited by Sybil P. Parker (New York: McGraw-Hill, 1997), focus on specific areas.

Dictionaries.   General and specialized dictionaries are available in print, on CD-ROM, and on the Web. General dictionaries can be compact or comprehensive, unabridged publications. Specialized dictionaries define terms used in a particular field, such as engineering, computers, architecture, or consumer affairs, and offer detailed definitions of field-specific terms, usually written in straightforward language.

Handbooks and Manuals.   Handbooks and manuals are typically one-volume compilations of frequently used information in a particular field. They offer brief definitions of terms or concepts, standards for presenting information, procedures for documenting sources, and visuals such as graphs and tables.

Bibliographies.   Bibliographies list books, periodicals, and other research materials published in areas such as engineering, medicine, the humanities, and the social sciences. One example is *The St. Martin's Bibliography of Business and Technical Communication* by Gerald J. Alred (New York: St. Martin's, 1997).

General Guides.   The annotated *Guide to Reference Books,* 11th ed., by Robert Balay (Chicago: American Library Association, 1996). This book can help you locate reference books, indexes, and other research materials. Check your library's homepage or ask your reference librarian to find out if your library subscribes to specialized indexes such as the following:

Business Periodicals Index, 1958–. Alphabetical subject listing; issued monthly.

Government Reports Announcements and Index, 1965–. Semimonthly index of reports, arranged by subject, author, and report number.

Index to the Times (London), 1790–. Monthly.

Monthly Catalog of U.S. Government Publications, 1895–. Unclassified publications of all federal agencies, listed by subject, author, and report number; issued monthly.

New York Times Index, 1851–. Alphabetical list of subjects covered in *New York Times* articles; issued bimonthly.

Readers' Guide to Periodical Literature, 1900–. Monthly index of about 200 general U.S. periodicals, arranged alphabetically by subject.

Wall Street Journal Index, 1958–. Monthly index of business and financial news covered in the *Wall Street Journal.*

WRITER'S CHECKLIST

Using Common Library Terms

☐ *Abstract:* a shortened version of a long document that gives the reader the important points

☐ *Bibliographic information:* the author and publication information needed to locate an item in a library

☐ *Bibliography:* (1) a listing of sources used in the writing of a document; (2) in the MLA format, it is called a Works Cited page; in the APA format, it is called the References page

☐ *Bound periodical:* several issues of a journal or magazine that are secured together in book form

☐ *Call number:* the number assigned to every item in the library to help locate the item

☐ *Circulation desk:* the desk where a patron can check out, return, and renew library materials

☐ *Interlibrary loan:* material requested from another library and sent to the patron's library for use

☐ *Journal:* a periodical containing scholarly articles written by experts in a particular subject area

☐ *Magazine:* a periodical meant for the general public

☐ *Microform:* books or articles on film that must be viewed on a particular machine

☐ *Periodical:* a publication issued regularly, such as a newspaper, magazine, or journal

Atlases and Statistical Sources.   *Atlases* provide representations of the physical and political boundaries of countries, climate, population, or natural resources. *Statistical sources* are collections of numerical data. They are the best source for such information as the U.S. gross domestic product, the consumer price index, or the demographic breakdown of the general population.

Atlas

> *Microsoft® Encarta® World Atlas 2001.* CD-ROM for Windows®. Microsoft Corporation, 2001.

Statistical Sources

> *American Statistics Index.* Washington: Congressional Information Service, 1978–. Monthly, quarterly, and annual supplements.

> U.S. Bureau of the Census. *Statistical Abstract of the United States.* Washington: Government Printing Office, 1879–. Annual. <census.gov>

Internet Research

Anyone with Internet access can search through the staggering amount of information that it offers (including access to many public university library catalogs and databases, as noted earlier in this chapter). Although the Internet contains a wealth of information, unlike a library, it has no one indexing scheme, no single catalog that brings the information together for browsing or easy access. However, search engines such as Google—and the Web directories provided by such engines and by your library's homepage—can streamline your search process.

Using Search Engines and Web Subject Directories

To locate specific subjects, you can use two types of search tools: a subject directory and a search engine. A *subject directory* (also known as an index) organizes information by broad subject categories (business, entertainment, health, sports) and related subtopics (marketing, finance, investing). (See Figure 7–9, and also Figure 7–4, which shows a college library's Web subject guide.) A subject-directory search eventually produces a list of specific sites that contain information about the topics you request. Once you locate a site of interest that you want to revisit, you can bookmark it.

A *search engine* locates information based on words or combinations of words that you specify. The software engine then lists for you the documents or files that contain one or more of these words in their titles, descriptions, or text. Also available are *meta-search engines*—tools that do not maintain an internal database but instead launch your query to multiple databases of various Web-based resources (other search engines or subject directories). The following subject directories, search engines, and meta-search engines are among the most widely used on the Web.

Main directory provides broad topic areas

Business subdirectory provides specific resources selected by Google editors

Figure 7–9   Google's Main Subject Directory with Business Subdirectory

Web Subject Directories

Galaxy. <einet.net/galaxy.html>. The Internet's oldest searchable directory, Galaxy categorizes Web resources by type, such as commercial organization, collection, article, or directory.

Infomine. <lib-www.ucr.edu/>. Infomine is a Web directory specializing in Web resources of interest to academics and scholars.

Internet Public Library. <ipl.org>. The IPL's own collections of over 40,000 Internet resources, hand picked, organized, and described by librarians and library students.

Librarians' Index to the Internet. <lii.org>. Geared toward librarians and nonlibrarians, the Librarians' Index to the Internet is a searchable, annotated directory of more than 6,500 Internet resources that are evaluated and described by research librarians.

Scout Report Archives. <scout.cs.wisc.edu/archives>. Librarians and educators at the University of Wisconsin-Madison have selected and annotated more than 10,000 academically-useful Web sites.

Yahoo! <yahoo.com>. The popular Yahoo! directory is the most detailed subject directory available.

WWW Virtual Library. <lib.org/Home.html>. The Virtual Library is a noncommercial catalog of the Web started by the creator of HTML and the World Wide Web itself.

Search Engines

AltaVista. <altavista.com>. AltaVista is one of the largest, most comprehensive search engines, with a strong advanced query option. This engine also allows you to search for sites by their modification dates.

FastSearch. <alltheweb.com>. FastSearch may be the biggest and fastest search engine, searching 300 million Web pages in under half a second.

Google. <google.com>. Google is a fast and easy-to-use search engine that provides a relevancy ranking for all sites. You can opt to use the "I'm Feeling Lucky™" button, which takes you directly to the Web site of the first search result.

InfoSeek. <infoseek.go.com>. Though smaller than other search engines, InfoSeek offers excellent content and allows you to conduct a search based on the results of a previous search.

Northern Light.<northernlight.com>. Northern Light is a search engine that helps you narrow your search by organizing the results into separate folders; it also includes a for-a-fee section.

Yahoo. <yahoo.com>. Perhaps the easiest search engine for the new researcher, Yahoo also features a helpful subject directory.

Meta-Search Engines

Dogpile. <dogpile.com>. Dogpile searches other search engines for responses to your query and reports what each one found.

Inference Find. <infind.com>. Infind searches a select group of search engines for responses to your query, merges the results, removes redundancies, and presents the results in concise clusters.

Metacrawler. <metacrawler.com>. Also accessible at <metafind.com>. Metacrawler searches other engines for responses to your query, lists the search engines where relevant sites were found, and allows you to e-mail the results.

Combining Search Engines and Directories.   Increasingly, search sites are using a hybrid approach. For example, some search engines, such as Northern Light <northernlight.com>, search not only the Web but also their own database of articles—content that is edited and compiled by staff librarians and not available elsewhere on the Web. Other sites combine search engines with directories; for example, Google offers a standard search engine and directory as well as a special contributor-generated directory referred to as an "Open Directory" <dmoz.org>.

Improving Your Search Results.   As comprehensive as search engines and directories may seem, none is complete or objective. Most search sites are incomplete, carrying only a preselected range of content. Many, for example, do not index Adobe Portable Document Files (PDF) files or Usenet Newsgroups and many

W On the Web
For information on
evaluating search en-
gines, see Chapter 7,
bedfordstmartins.com/
writingthatworks

cannot index databases and other non-HTML-based content. Further, a search engine's ranking of the sites recommended as relevant to your topic is based on a number of different strategies. Some sites base relevance on how high on the given page your search term appears, on the number of appearances of your term, or on the number of other sites that link to the page. Almost all major search sites now sell high rankings to the highest bidders, so your results may not highlight the pages most relevant to your search.

Your best strategy is to investigate how your favorite search engines work; nearly all provide detailed instructions on their help pages. Many search engines also give you the option of conducting an advanced search, which provides you with a number of ways to obtain more selective results. Figure 7–10 shows an

**DIGITAL
SHORTCUTS**

Searching the Web

■ Enter words and phrases that are as specific to your topic as possible. For example, if you are looking for information about *nuclear power* and enter only the term *nuclear,* the search will also yield listings for *nuclear family, nuclear medicine,* and *nuclear winter.*

■ Use Boolean operators (AND, OR, NOT) to narrow your search. For example, if you're searching for information on breast cancer and are finding references to nothing but prostate cancer, try "breast AND cancer NOT prostate."

■ Consider conducting an advanced search (see Figure 7–10) to further narrow your search.

■ Check any search tips available at the engine you use. For example, some engines allow you to narrow your search by combining phrases with double quotation marks: "usability testing" will return only pages that have the full compound phrase.

■ Try out a variety of search engines and consider how well they provide information relevant to your search. You may want to stick to using your favorite engine, but you will get more varied results if you use more than one.

■ If you are interested in obtaining as many hits as possible, consider using a meta-search engine such as Dogpile <dogpile.com> and Metacrawler <metacrawler.com>.

*Specify key terms
and number
of results desired*

*Limit your search
to a specific
domain (.org,
.edu, .com, etc.)*

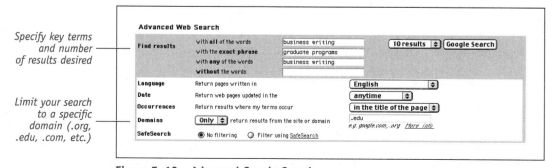

Figure 7–10   Advanced Google Search

advanced search conducted on Google for business writing programs—a search limited to results in English and to sites within the ".edu" domain. This particular advanced search resulted in ten selective hits.

Although search engines vary in what and how they search, you can use some of the basic strategies in Digital Shortcuts: Searching the Web (page 212).

Locating Business and Government Sites.   The Web includes numerous sites devoted to specific subject areas. Following are some suggested resources for researching a business topic.

Business Resources

Business Resources on the Web <webbusiness.cio.com>

Business Internet Resources <pace.edu/library/links/links.html>

Inc. Business Resources on the Web <inc.com/ibr>

Yahoo!'s Business Resources <dir.yahoo.com/Business_and_Economy>

Government Resources

Federal Government Agencies Directory <lib.lsu.edu/gov/fedgov.html>

FedStats <fedstats.gov>

■ Evaluating Print and Online Sources, Recording Information, and Avoiding Plagiarism

As you research your topic, consider your sources carefully. As you interview for information or work with print or online material, evaluate each source by asking yourself the following questions: Is the information accurate and up-to-date? Is the speaker or author reputable and qualified? Is the publisher or sponsoring organization well-established and respected in the field?

Once you've decided which materials to use, you will need to record information from each source so that you can accurately quote, paraphrase, and summarize it in your paper or report, as is explained on pages 217–221.

Evaluating Print Sources

After you have located a number of books and articles, you need to decide which ones to continue to use in your research. A factor to consider is the author's reputation: Is the writer an authority in the field? Has he or she written other, highly regarded books or articles in the field? You might begin by asking a librarian, an instructor, or an expert who is familiar with the subject area, whether the author has an established reputation in the field. Also consider the points in Writer's Checklist: Evaluating Print Resources (page 214).

Evaluating Print Resources

For a Book

☐   Is the text recent enough and relevant to your topic? Is it readily available?

☐   Who is the author? Does the preface or introduction indicate the author's purpose?

☐   Does the author present information in an unbiased way? Are the language, tone, and style inviting?

☐   Does the table of contents relate to your topic? Does the index contain terms related to your topic? Does the text contain a bibliography, reference list, or footnotes?

☐   Are the chapters useful? (Skim through one that seems related to your topic — notice especially the introduction, headings, and closing.)

☐   Does the book contain informative diagrams or other visuals?

For an Article

☐   Is the article recent enough and relevant to your topic? Is it readily available?

☐   Is the publisher of the magazine or other periodical well known? Who is the publication's main audience? (The mainstream public? A small group of professionals?) Does the publication target or show bias toward a particular audience?

☐   What is the article's purpose? (For a journal article, read the abstract; for a newspaper article, read the headline and the lead sentences.)

☐   Does the article contain informative diagrams or other visuals that indicate its scope?

Document the following information about any book that you decide to include in your research:

Call number

Author (if the author is an organization, indicate that fact)

Title

City of publication

Publisher's name

Year of publication

For an article, record the following information:

Author

Title of the article

Name of the journal in which the article appears

Journal volume and issue numbers

Date of publication

Page numbers of the article

When you are ready to prepare a bibliography for your research report, you can do so easily using this information. To document sources, you can use the Print Screen key to print out the search screen containing the full bibliographic citation. You can also download the bibliographic citation from an online database to your hard drive, or you can e-mail the citation to yourself. You can do the same for the texts of articles you retrieve.

If you make a habit of sending your search results and articles to your e-mail address, you will have a record of your research—and the sources themselves—ready for your use when you begin to draft your paper or presentation.

Evaluating Online Sources

Evaluate the usefulness of information on the Internet with the same standards that you use to evaluate information from other sources. Is it accurate? Is it up-to-date? Is the author qualified and reputable? Is the sponsor of the site or journal reputable? These standards apply for printed material, for people you interview, or for any other source. (For detailed criteria for evaluating authors, see below.)

The easiest way to ensure that information is valid is to obtain it from a reputable source. For example, data from the Bureau of Labor Statistics, the Securities and Exchange Commission, and the Bureau of the Census are widely used by U.S. businesses. Likewise, online versions of established, reputable journals in medicine, engineering, computer software, and other fields merit the same level of trust as the printed versions. However, as you move away from established, reputable sites, exercise more caution. Be especially wary of unmoderated discussion groups on Usenet and other public bulletin-board systems. Remember that anyone with access can place information on the Internet, so for many sources there are no editorial checks and balances in place. Treat information obtained from these sources cautiously.

Keep in mind the following four criteria when evaluating Internet sources: authority, accuracy, bias, and currency.[1]

Authority

Because anyone can publish on the Web, it is sometimes difficult to determine authorship of a document, and frequently a person's qualifications for speaking on a topic are absent or questionable. If you do not recognize the author or the organization sponsoring the site as well known and respected in the field, check the site's "about us" page or mission statement if available. This information should give you a sense of the site's purpose and perspective. Ask the following questions to help you determine the authority of a site or document.

- Is the author's document listed or linked from a reliable source or document?

---

[1] From Leigh Ryan, *The Bedford Guide for Writing Tutors*, 3rd ed. (Boston: Bedford/St. Martin's, 2002).

- Is the author referenced or mentioned positively by another author or organization whose authority you trust?
- Does the document give ample biographical information about the author so you can evaluate his or her credentials, or can you get this information by linking to another document?

If the publisher or sponsor is an organization, you may generally assume that the document meets the standards and aims of the group. Consider also:

- The suitability of the organization to address this topic.
- Whether this organization or agency is recognized and respected in the field.
- The relationship of the author to the publisher or sponsor. (Does the document tell you something about the author's expertise or qualifications?)

Accuracy

Criteria for evaluating accuracy might include the following:

- Other sources that the document relies on are linked or are included in a bibliography.
- Background information can be verified.
- Methodology is appropriate for the topic.
- With a research project, data that was gathered includes explanations of research methods and interpretations.
- The graphs and visuals are free of distortion.
- The site is modified or updated regularly.

Bias

To determine bias, consider how the context reveals the author's knowledge of the subject and his or her stance on the topic. Check the site for the following:

- The site identifies in some form the audience it targets.
- The site was developed by a recognized academic institution; government agency; or national, international, or commercial organization with an established reputation in the subject area.
- The author shows knowledge of theories, techniques, or schools of thought usually related to the topic.
- The author shows knowledge of related sources and attributes them properly.
- The author discusses the value and limitations of the approach, if it is new.
- The author acknowledges that the subject itself or his or her treatment of it is controversial, if you know that to be the case.

Currency

If currency is important, consider whether the document has a publication or "last updated" date or includes date of copyright, gives dates showing when information was gathered, or gives information about new material when appropriate.

W On the Web
For more resources for evaluating Web content, see Chapter 7, **bedfordstmartins.com/ writingthatworks**

Evaluating Online Resources

WRITER'S CHECKLIST

- [ ] *Who* is the author? Why should that author be trusted?
- [ ] *What* is the main focus of the page? Does it make sense?
- [ ] *Where* does the site originate? Is it put out by an organization, an individual, or an institution?
- [ ] *When* was the site put online? Is it updated regularly?
- [ ] *Why* does that page exist? Can you find a purpose statement or an "about us" page? Is there a particular bias?
- [ ] *Does* the information available compare favorably with at least two other reputable online sources?

Taking Notes

The purpose of taking notes is to condense and record information from the books, articles, Web sites, and other sources used for your research. The notes you take will furnish much of the material for your outline and final written work.

When working with paper sources (books and journals), you can photocopy material and highlight important passages with a highlighter, jot notes on index cards, or keyboard them into your laptop or desktop computer. If you are using Internet sources, you can highlight passages and cut and paste them into a word-processing file, in addition to taking notes. When you cut and paste information from the Internet, always include the source to provide proper credit in your final work. Otherwise, you will be plagiarizing from the source. If the source is copyrighted, you may also be guilty of copyright infringement. (See Avoiding Plagiarism on page 221.)

Whichever method you use, identify the source of the information and include the author's last name (also include first name or initials if you have two authors with the same last name) and the page number or numbers on which the material appears in the original source. If you have consulted more than one book or article by an author, include the title as well; for long titles, you may use a shortened form.

As you take notes, make a list of the topics you will cover in your research (as Christine Thomas did in Chapter 1). Identify your notes as appropriate with these topics (sometimes called *slugs*). When you arrange the cards or word-processing notes by topic in preparation for creating an outline, you can use the slugs as a guide in organizing your material.

For the sake of accuracy and correctness, be careful to distinguish whether you are *quoting directly* from your source, *paraphrasing* (restating the text you're using in your own words), or *summarizing* (writing down a highly condensed version of the text). If you are a beginning researcher, you should probably stick to writing down direct quotations. Then, when you turn to actually writing your research paper, you can decide whether you want to quote directly, paraphrase, or summarize.

Quoting from Your Sources

Direct Quotations

A *direct quotation* is a word-for-word copy of the text of an original source. Choose direct quotations (which can be of a word, a phrase, a sentence, or, occasionally, a paragraph) carefully and use them sparingly. Enclose direct quotations in quotation marks and separate them from the rest of the sentence by a comma or colon. The initial capital letter of a quotation is retained if the quoted material originally began with a capital letter.

■ The economist stated, "Regulation cannot supply the dynamic stimulus that in other industries is supplied by competition."

When a quotation is divided, the material that interrupts the quotation is set off, before and after, by commas, and quotation marks are used around each part of the quotation.

■ "Regulation," he said in a recent interview, "cannot supply the dynamic stimulus that in other industries is supplied by competition."

Indirect Quotations

An *indirect quotation* is a paraphrased version of an original text. It is usually introduced by the word *that* and is not set off from the rest of the sentence by punctuation marks.

■ In a recent interview he said that regulation does not stimulate the industry as well as competition does.

Deletions or Omissions

Deletions or omissions from quoted material are indicated by three ellipsis points (. . .) within a sentence and a period plus three ellipsis points (. . . .) at the end of a sentence.

■ "If monopolies could be made to respond . . . we would be able to enjoy the benefits of . . . large-scale efficiency. . . ."

If you are following the MLA guidelines, enclose the ellipsis points in brackets.

■ "If monopolies could be made to respond [. . .] we would be able to enjoy the benefits of [. . .] large-scale efficiency [. . .]."

When a quoted passage begins in the middle of a sentence rather than at the beginning, ellipsis points are not necessary; the fact that the first letter of the quoted material is not capitalized tells the reader that the quotation begins in mid-sentence.

- Rivero goes on to conclude that "coordination may lessen competition within a region."

Inserting Material into Quotations

When it is necessary to insert a clarifying comment within quoted material, use brackets.

- "The industry is an integrated system that serves an extensive [geographic] area, with divisions existing as islands within the larger system's sphere of influence."

When quoted material contains an obvious error or might be questioned in some other way, the expression *sic* (Latin for "thus"), in italic type and enclosed in brackets, follows the questionable material to indicate that the writer has quoted the material exactly as it appeared in the original.

- The company considers the Baker Foundation to be a "guilt-edged [*sic*] investment."

Incorporating Quotations into Text

Quote word-for-word only when your source concisely sums up a great deal of information or reinforces a point you are making. Quotations must also relate logically, grammatically, and syntactically to the rest of the sentence and surrounding text.

Depending on the length, there are two methods of handling quotations in your text. For MLA style, a quotation of three or fewer lines is incorporated into the text and enclosed in quotation marks. For APA style, a quotation of fewer than 40 words is incorporated into the text and enclosed in quotation marks.

Material that runs four lines or longer (MLA style) or at least 40 words (APA style) is usually set off from the body of the text by being indented from the left margin ten spaces (MLA style) or five to seven spaces (APA style). The quoted passage is spaced the same as the surrounding text and is not enclosed in quotation marks, as shown in the following example, which uses MLA style. If you are not following a specific style manual, you may block indent ten spaces from both the left and right margins for reports and other documents.

- After reviewing a large number of works in business and technical communication, Alred sees an inevitable connection between theory, practice, and pedagogy:

  > Therefore, theory is necessary to prevent us from being overwhelmed by what is local, particular, and temporal. In turn, pedagogy both mediates practice and transforms our theory. Indeed, one reason I find this work rewarding is that I sense it puts me at the intersection of theory, practice, and pedagogy as they are involved with writing in the workplace. (ix–x)

  The use of the Web today has reinforced this connection because it calls on the Web-page designer to engage in a teaching function as well as reflect on the practice of Web design. For example, the widespread use of . . .

Notice that the quotation blends with the content of the surrounding text, which uses transitions to introduce and comment on the quotation. At the end of the document, the following entry appears in the MLA-style list of works cited as the source of the quotation in the example.

■ Alred, Gerald J., Charles T. Brusaw, and Walter E. Oliu. The Business Writer's Handbook. 7th ed. Boston: Bedford, 2003.

Do not rely too heavily on the use of quotations in the final version of your document. Generally, avoid quoting anything that is more than one paragraph.

Paraphrasing

Paraphrasing is restating or rewriting in your own words the essential ideas of another writer. Because the paraphrase does not quote the source word for word, quotation marks are not necessary. However, paraphrased material should be credited because the *ideas* are taken from someone else. The following example is an original passage explaining the concept of object blur. The paraphrased version restates the essential information of the passage in a form appropriate for a report.

ORIGINAL	One of the major visual cues used by pilots in maintaining precision ground reference during low-level flight is that of object blur. We are acquainted with the object-blur phenomenon experienced when driving an automobile. Objects in the foreground appear to be rushing toward us, while objects in the background appear to recede slightly.
PARAPHRASED	Object blur refers to the phenomenon by which observers in a moving vehicle report that foreground objects appear to rush at them, while background objects appear to recede slightly.

Strive to put the original ideas into your words without distorting them.

Summarizing

A *summary* is a highly condensed version, in the researcher's own words, of an original passage. Summary notes present only the essential ideas or conclusions of the original and are considerably shorter than paraphrases of the same passage. As with directly quoted and paraphrased material, the source of summarized information must be credited in a footnote.

Following this passage is a brief summary of its content.

ORIGINAL	Now that we have learned something about the nature of elements and molecules, what are fuels? Fuels are those substances that will burn when heat is applied to them. Some elements, in themselves, are fuels. Carbon, hydrogen, sulfur, magnesium, titanium and some other metals are examples of elements that can burn. Coal, charcoal and coke, for

example, are almost pure carbon; hydrogen, another element, is a highly flammable gas. But the most familiar combustible materials are not pure elements; they are compounds and mixtures.

Wood, paper and grass are principally composed of molecules of cellulose, a flammable substance. If we examine the chemical makeup of this compound, we will discover what elements form the basic fuels in most solid materials. The cellulose molecule contains twenty-one atoms: six carbons, ten hydrogens and five oxygen atoms: $C_6H_{10}O_5$. Since oxygen is not flammable . . . , it follows that the carbon and hydrogen found in most common combustible solids are the elements that burn. This conclusion becomes even stronger when we look at common flammable liquids. Gasoline, kerosene, fuel oils and other petroleum compounds are composed of only carbon and hydrogen atoms, in varying amounts. These compounds, called hydrocarbons (hydrogen + carbon), will all burn.[2]

SUMMARIZED   The chemical makeup of a substance determines whether it's flammable. Carbon and hydrogen are highly flammable elements, so material made up largely of these elements, called hydrocarbons, are good fuels.

Take summary notes to remind yourself of the substance of a research source. Summarized information can also be useful to your reader because it condenses passages that give more details than the reader needs.

Avoiding Plagiarism

Plagiarism is the use of someone else's unique ideas without acknowledgment, or the use of someone else's exact words without quotation marks and appropriate credit. Plagiarism is considered to be the theft of someone else's creative and intellectual property and is not accepted in business, science, journalism, academia, and other fields.

You may, however, quote or paraphrase the words and ideas of another if you document your source. Although you do not enclose paraphrased ideas or materials in quotation marks, you must document their sources. Paraphrasing a passage without citing the source is permissible only when the information paraphrased is common knowledge in a field. *Common knowledge* refers to information on a topic widely known and readily available in handbooks, manuals, atlases, and other references. If you intend to publish, reproduce, or distribute material that includes quotations from published works, you may need to obtain written permission from the copyright holder to do so.

In the workplace, employees often borrow from in-house manuals, reports, and other company documents. Using such boilerplate information is neither plagiarism nor a violation of copyright.

---

[2]James H. Meidl, *Flammable Hazardous Materials* (Beverly Hills, CA: Glencoe Press, 1970), pp. 8–9.

■ Documenting Sources

As a writer, by documenting your sources, you identify where you obtained the facts, ideas, quotations, and paraphrases you used in preparing a written report. This information can come from books; newspaper, magazine, or trade journal articles; manuals; proposals; investigative reports; interviews; e-mail; the Internet; and other sources. Documenting sources achieves three important purposes:

- It allows readers to locate and consult the sources used and to find further information on the subject.
- It enables writers to support their assertions and arguments in such documents as proposals, reports, and trade journal articles.
- It helps writers to give proper credit to others and thus avoid plagiarism by identifying the sources of facts, ideas, quotations, and paraphrases.

This section shows citation models and sample pages for two principal documentation systems: APA and MLA.

> American Psychological Association. *Publication Manual of the American Psychological Association.* 5th ed. Washington, D.C.: American Psychological Association, 2001. See also <apastyle.org>.

- The APA system of citation is often used in the social sciences. It is referred to as an author/date method of documentation because parenthetical in-text citations and a reference list (at the end of the paper) emphasize the author(s) and date of publication so that the currency of the research is clear.

> *MLA Handbook for Writers of Research Papers.* 6th ed. New York: Modern Language Association of America, 2003. See also <mla.org>.

- The MLA system is used in the humanities. MLA style uses parenthetical citations and a list of works cited (at the end of the paper), and places greater importance on the pages on which cited information can be found than on the publication date.

APA Style

APA In-Text Citations

To document direct quotations in text, give the author's last name, the year of publication, and the page number in parentheses.

■ The "first electronic war" (Butrica, 1996, p. 2) was fought as much in the research laboratory as on the battlefield.

The page number is optional for paraphrased information and ideas.

■ World War II was the occasion of radar's first application in warfare, and Great Britain led the way in radar research (Butrica, 1996).

If the author's name is mentioned in the text, give only the year of publication and the page number in parentheses.

■ According to Butrica (1996), the use of radar as an offensive and defensive warfare agent made World War II "the first electronic war" (p. 2).

Include no more information than is necessary to enable readers to find the corresponding entry in the reference list. If the author's name and the year of publication are mentioned in the text, give only the page number for direct quotations.

■ As Butrica pointed out in his 1996 research, "technology forever changed the way we make war" (p. 196).

Omit parenthetical information for paraphrased material.

■ In his 1996 research, Butrica pointed out the impact of technology on warfare.

If the citation follows a block quotation, place the citation after the final punctuation mark, as shown in Figure 7–11 on page 231. Use the spacing shown in the examples. Within the citation itself, separate the name, date, and page number with commas. Allow one space after each comma. Use the abbreviation *p.* or *pp.* before page numbers.

If your reference list includes more than one work by the same author published in the same year, add the lowercase letters *a, b, c,* and so forth, to the year in both the reference list entries and the text citations: (Ostro, 1993b, p. 347). When a work has two authors, cite both names joined by an ampersand: (Hey & Walters, 1997). For the first citation of a work with three, four, or five authors, include all names.

■ As Burns, Brooks, and MacNeil (1999) argued . . .

For subsequent citations, include only the name of the first author followed by *et al.* (not italicized).

■ Burns et al. (1999) put forth the alternate theory . . .

For a work with six or more authors, use the name of the first author followed by *et al.* in all citations.

■ Their findings led to a radical change in the way the metals were processed (Hargrove et al., 2000, p. 21).

When two or more works by different authors are cited in the same parentheses, list the citations alphabetically and use semicolons to separate the citations: (Hey & Walters, 1997; Knapp, 1996; Ostro, 1993a). The works cited in the examples would be listed alphabetically, as follows, in a reference list.

Burns, S., Brooks, J., & MacNeil, W. (1999). *Science in the mirror: A retrospective look at physics.* Cambridge, MA: Harvard University Press.

Butrica, A. J. (1996). *To see the unseen: A history of planetary radar astronomy.* The NASA History Series. Washington, DC: U.S. Government Printing Office.

Hey, T., & Walters, P. (1997). *Einstein's mirror.* Cambridge, England: Cambridge University Press.

Knapp, B. (1996). *Grolier educational elements series: Vol. 6 Silicon.* Danbury, CT: Grolier Educational.

Ostro, S. J. (1993a). Planetary radar astronomy. *Reviews of Modern Physics, 65,* 1235–1279.

Ostro, S. J. (1993b). Radar astronomy. In S. P. Parker & J. M. Pasachoff (Eds.), *McGraw-Hill encyclopedia of astronomy* (pp. 347–348). New York: McGraw-Hill.

If you are citing a source created by a corporation or an organization, use its name as the author.

■ However, high employment rates in the Midwest affected this trend considerably (U.S. Department of Labor, 1999).

If you are quoting a source by an unknown author, use a brief version of the title in your citation.

■ Textile manufacture had replaced the local maritime trade well before the mid-nineteenth century ("A Short History," p. 19).

If two or more sources have authors with the same last name, use first initials in your citation (J. Kellogg, p. 414). When citing e-mail, phone calls, or personal interviews, use the words *personal communication* in your parenthetical citation.

■ Linda Waters (personal communication, November 28, 2000), an executive at CorTex, stated the case succinctly. . . .

To refer to an entire Web site (not just to a particular article or document at that site), include the URL in your parenthetical citation.

■ The U.S. Department of Commerce provides current statistics on international trade at the Bureau of Economic Analysis Web site http://www.bea.doc.gov/bea/rels.htm.

However, you should not include the Web site in your reference list, if you are citing the entire site. If you are citing a specific document from a Web site, you should follow the format that you would for a print document (citing the author, year, and page or paragraph number). If there are no page or paragraph numbers in the online document, include just the author and the year in your parenthetical citation (you will provide further details in the reference list).

■ In his previous address to the group, he expressed his belief in the value of using technology in the classroom (Maxwell, 2002).

APA Citation Format for Reference List

The reference list should begin on the first new page following the end of the text. Begin each new entry at the left margin, and indent the second and subsequent lines five spaces or one-half inch from the left margin. (Your instructor may require you to use a paragraph indent instead. If so, begin at a paragraph indent, with subsequent lines continuing at the left margin.) Double-space within and between entries.

Include full page numbers when citing a range of pages for articles (119–124, not 119–24) and indicate with a comma if the page flow of an article is interrupted (119–124, 128–132). Use the abbreviation *p.* or *pp.* only with articles in newspapers (not in magazines or other sources), chapters in edited books, or proceedings.

Include only sources that were essential to the preparation of your document; do not include background reading. Do not include forms of personal communication, such as letters, e-mail, messages from electronic bulletin boards, and telephone conversations. Cite these sources only in the text.

The following listing specifies the APA format and order of elements in a reference list.

Author

- Alphabetize the list by author's last name and initials.
- List multiple works by the same author in publication date order, from earliest to latest.
- For works by corporations or government agencies, alphabetize by organizational name.
- When no author is given, alphabetize by the first significant word in the title.

Publication Date

- Enclose in parentheses.
- For journals and books, give only the year.
- For periodicals other than journals, give the year, comma, and month or day.

Title

- Capitalize the first word of the title and subtitle of books, articles, or chapters.
- Lowercase all other words except proper nouns.
- Italicize the titles of books.
- Do not use quotation marks or italics for titles of articles or chapters from books.
- End titles with a period.

Multiple Volume or Series Publications

- List the series number following the title.
- List the volume number following the title.
- List the edition number following the title, if it is not the first.

Publishing Information

- List the publishing information last for citations to books, pamphlets, and conference proceedings.
- Show a shortened form of the publisher's name.
- Include the publisher's city and state.
- Abbreviate the state name using the postal code.
- If the publisher's city is well known (e.g., New York), omit the state name.
- Omit terms like *Publisher, Co.,* and *Inc.*
- Do not abbreviate the words *Books* and *Press.*

Periodicals

- Show the title of a journal, magazine, or newspaper in upper- and lower-case letters.
- List the volume and page numbers after the title.
- Italicize the title and volume numbers.
- Separate elements with commas and end with a period.

Online Sources

- Review the guidelines for citing electronic sources on page 228.

APA Documentation Models

Books

Single Author

Hassab, J. C. (1997). *Systems management: People, computers, machines, materials.* New York: CRC Press.

Multiple Authors

Testerman, J. O., Kuegler, T. J., Jr., & Dowling, P. J., Jr. (1998). *Web advertising and marketing* (2nd ed.). Rocklin, CA: Prima.

Corporate Author

Ernst and Young. (1999). *Ernst and Young's retirement planning guide.* New York: Wiley.

Edition Other Than First

Estes, J. C., & Kelley, D. R. (1998). *McGraw-Hill's interest amortization tables* (3rd ed.). New York: McGraw-Hill.

Multivolume Work

Standard and Poor. (1998). *Standard and Poor's register of corporations, directors and executives* (Vols. 1–3). New York: McGraw-Hill.

Work in an Edited Collection

Thorne, K. S. (1997). Do the laws of physics permit wormholes for interstellar travel and machines for time travel? In Y. Terzian & E. Bilson (Eds.), *Carl Sagan's universe* (pp. 121–134). Cambridge, England: Cambridge University Press.

Encyclopedia or Dictionary Entry

Gibbard, B. G. (1997). Particle detector. In *World Book encyclopedia* (Vol. 15, pp. 186–187). Chicago: World Book.

*Articles in Periodicals (*See also *Electronic Sources)*
Magazine Article

Coley, D. (1997, June). Compliance for the right reasons. *Business Geographics, 12,* 30–32.

Journal Article

Rossouw, G. J. (1997). Business ethics in South Africa. *Journal of Business Ethics, 16,* 1539–1547.

Newspaper Article

Mathews, A. W. (1997, October 1). The Internet generation taps into Morse code. *Wall Street Journal,* pp. B1, B7.

Article with Unknown Author

American City adds Nashville, Memphis. (1997, September 26). *The Business Journal,* p. 16.

Electronic Sources

An Entire Web Site

The APA recommends that, at minimum, a reference to a Web source should provide a document title or description, a date (of the publication or retrieval of the document), an address (URL) that links directly to the document or section, and an individual or corporate author, whenever possible. On the rare occasion that you need to cite multiple pages of a Web site (or the entire site), provide a URL that links to the site's homepage.

Association for Business Communication. (2002). Retrieved April 20, 2002, from http://www
.theabc.org

A Document on a Web Site, with an Author

Locker, K. O. (1995). *The history of the association for business communication.* Retrieved April 20,
2001, from the Association for Business Communication Web site: http://www.theabc.org/
history.html

A Document on a Web Site, with a Corporate or Organizational Author

General Motors. (2001). *Company profile.* Retrieved April 20, 2001, from http://www.gm.com/
company/corp_info/profiles/

Article or Other Work from a Database

Goldbort, R. C. (2001, March). Scientific writing as an art and as a science. *Journal of
Environmental Health, 63*(7). Retrieved April 19, 2001, from Expanded Academic ASAP
database.

Article in an Online Periodical

Tiernen, R. (2001, April 18). Waiting for wireless. *SmartMoney.com.* Retrieved April 19, 2001, from
http://www.smartmoney.com/techmarket/index.cfm?story=20010418

E-mail

Personal communications (including e-mail and messages from discussion groups and electronic bulletin boards) are not cited in an APA reference list. They can be cited in the text as follows: "According to J. D. Kahl (personal communication, October 2, 2001), Web pages need to reflect. . . ."

Publication on CD-ROM

Money 99. (1997). [CD-ROM]. Redmond, WA: Microsoft.

Multimedia Sources (Print and Electronic)
Map or Chart

Asia. (2001). [Map]. Maps.com. Retrieved April 20, 2001, from http://www.maps.com/explore/atlas/
political/asia.html

Wisconsin. (2000). [Map]. Chicago: Rand.

Film or Video

Lawrence, D. (Director), & Christopher, J. (Editor). (2001). *Emergency film group video* [Video].
Retrieved April 20, 2001, from http://www.efilmgroup.com/video1.rm

Massingham, G. (Director), & Christopher, J. (Editor). (1998). *Introduction to hazardous chemicals*
[Motion picture]. Edgartown, MA: Emergency Film Group.

Radio or Television Program

Norris, R. (Host). (2001, April 3). Energy supplies. *All things considered* [Radio broadcast]. Boston:
WGBH. Retrieved April 20, 2001, from http://www.npr.org/programs/atc

Novak, R. (Host). (2001, April 16). Do Americans really want a tax cut? *CNN: Crossfire* [Television
broadcast]. Washington, DC: CNN.

Other Sources
Published Interview

Gates, B. (2000, April 17). The view from the very top [Interview]. *Newsweek, 135,* 36–39.

Personal Interview and Letters

Personal communications (including telephone conversations) are not cited in a
reference list. They can be cited in the text as follows: "According to J. D. Kahl (personal communication, October 2, 2001), Web pages need to reflect. . . ."

Brochure or Pamphlet

Library of Congress. U.S. Copyright Office. (1999). *Copyright registration for online works* [Brochure].
Washington, DC: U.S. Government Printing Office.

Government Document

U.S. Department of Energy. (1998). *The energy situation in the next decade* (Technical Publication
No. 11346-53). Washington, DC: U.S. Government Printing Office.

Report

Bertot, J. C., McClure, C. R., & Zweizig, D. L. (1996). *The 1996 national survey of public libraries and the Internet: Progress and issues: Final report.* Washington, DC: U.S. Government Printing Office.

Unpublished Data

Wisniewski, K., & Hussar, D. (2002). [Oregon small business statistics by county]. Unpublished raw data.

APA Sample Pages

This report examines the nature and disposition of the 3,458 ethics cases handled company-wide by CGF's ethics officers and managers during 2002. The purpose of such reports is to provide the Ethics and Business Conduct Committee with the information necessary for assessing the effectiveness of the first year of CGF's Ethics Program (Davis, Roland, & Tegge, 2001). According to Matthias Jonas (1999), recommendations are given for consideration "in planning for the second year of the Ethics Program" (p. 152).

The Office of Ethics and Business Conduct was created to administer the Ethics Program. The director of the Office of Ethics and Business Conduct, along with seven ethics officers throughout CGF, was given the responsibility for the following objectives, as described by Rossouw (1997):

> Communicate the values, standards, and goals of CGF's Program to employees. Provide company-wide channels for employee education and guidance in resolving ethics concerns. Implement company-wide programs in ethics awareness and recognition. Employee accessibility to ethics information and guidance is the immediate goal of the Office of Business Conduct in its first year. (p. 1543)

The purpose of the Ethics Program, established by the Committee, is to "promote ethical business conduct through open communication and compliance with company ethics standards" (Jonas, 2001, p. 89). This report examines the nature and disposition of the 3,458 ethics cases handled company-wide by CGF's ethics officers and

Shortened title and page number

One-inch margins; text double-spaced

Long quote indented five to seven spaces, double-spaced, without quotation marks

In-text citation gives name, date, and page number

Figure 7–11   APA Sample Page

Heading centered

List alphabetized by authors' last names and double-spaced

Hanging-indent style used for entries

References

Davis, W. C, Roland, M., & Tegge, D. (2001). *Working in the system: Five new management principles.* New York: St. Martin's Press.

Hassab, J. C. (1997). *Systems management: People, computers, machines, materials.* New York: CRC Press.

Jonas, M. (1999). The Internet and ethical communication: Toward a new paradigm. *Journal of Ethics and Communication, 27,* 147–177.

Jonas, M. (2001). Ethics in organizational communication: A review of the literature. *Journal of Ethics and Communication, 29,* 79–99.

Library of Congress. U.S. Copyright Office. (1999). *Copyright registration for online works* [Brochure]. Washington, DC: U.S. Government Printing Office.

The one-minute manager. (1998). [CD-ROM]. Boston: Bedford/ St. Martin's.

Rossouw, G. J. (1997). Business ethics in South Africa. *Journal of Business Ethics, 16,* 1539–1547.

Figure 7–12   APA Sample List of References

MLA Style

MLA In-Text Citations

When you cite a source in text, give only the author's last name and the page number or numbers in parentheses.

- Preparing a videotape of measurement methods is cost-effective and can expedite training (Peterson 151).

If the author's name is mentioned in the text, give only the page number of the source in parentheses.

- Peterson summarized the results of these measurements in a series of tables (183–91).

If two or more sources have authors with the same last name, include their initials (or first names if their names begin with the same letter) to avoid confusion.

- These results were summarized 40 years ago (R. Peterson 183–91). S. Peterson has recently suggested the reevaluation of these findings (29).

Include no more information than is necessary to enable readers to find the corresponding entry in the list of works cited. To cite an entire work rather than a particular page in a work, mention the author's name in the text and omit the parenthetical citation.

Place a parenthetical citation in text between the closing quotation mark or the last word of the sentence (or clause) and the end punctuation mark (usually a period). Use the spacing shown in the examples. If the parenthetical citation refers to an indented quotation, however, place it outside the last sentence of the quotation, as shown.

- . . . a close collaboration with the physics and technology staffs is essential. (Minsky 42)

If you are citing a page or pages of a multivolume work, give the volume number, followed by a colon, a space, and the page number(s): (Jones 2: 53–56). If the entire volume is being cited, identify the author and the volume: (Smith, vol. 3).

For more than one work by the same author, give the title of the work (or a shortened version if the title is long) in the parenthetical citation, unless you mention it in the text. If, for example, your Works Cited include more than one work by Thomas J. Peters, the citation for his book *The Pursuit of Wow: Every Person's Guide to Topsy-Turvy Times* would appear as (Peters, *Pursuit* 93). Use only one space between the title and the page number.

To cite a source written by two or three authors, include all of the names in your parenthetical citation: (Rotherson and Peters 467–75); for a source written by four or more authors, include the first author's name followed by the phrase *et al.* (and others, not italicized) or give all the authors' last names (depending on the style used in the works-cited list). To cite a source in which a separate work is quoted, provide the name of the person being quoted.

■ According to Billings, there is a greater potential for a small business to succeed in an urban area (qtd. in Kooper et al. 421).

To quote a source written by a corporation or an organization, use that name as the author.

■ However, many declining industries that fueled the economy of the 1950s are now being faced with a government mandate to clean up and preserve the environment (Environmental Protection Agency 16–17).

To quote a source by an unknown author, use a brief version of the title in your citation.

■ The benefits of this treatment have been known since the early 1980s ("Audio Therapy" 56).

For a sentence that refers to two separate sources, include both in your parenthetical citation, separating them with a semicolon.

■ Some analysts believe that the impact of electronic commerce caused the extreme market fluctuations of the late 1990s (Jones 174; Dragonetti 267).

To cite electronic sources, follow the same rules that you would for print sources, including as much identifying information as available (names and page numbers).

■ As pointed out in a recent Slate.com article, America's poor are more numerous, but less visible than ever (Connors).

If no names are indicated in the electronic source, use the title (full or shortened) in your citation; if no page numbers are indicated, do not cite any numbers, unless there are paragraph or section numbers. In this case, use the abbreviation *par.* or *sec.* in your citation. Do not include URLs in your parenthetical citations, but do include them in your works-cited list.

■ According to one online article, the organization's stated mission is to connect North American exporters with appropriate markets in Eastern Europe ("Business to Go" par. 18).

MLA Citation Format for a List of Works Cited

Begin the list of works cited on the first new page following the end of the text. Each new entry should begin at the left margin, with the second and subsequent lines within an entry indented five spaces or one-half inch. Double-space within and between entries.

The following listing specifies the format and order of elements in a list of works cited.

Author

- Alphabetize the list by the author's last name for a single author and by the last name of the first author for works with more than one author.
- List multiple works by the same author in alphabetical order by first significant word in the title. Put three hyphens and a period in place of the author's name for the second and subsequent titles.
- When a corporation or government agency is the author, alphabetize by organizational name, followed by a period.
- When no author is given, alphabetize by the first significant word in the title.
- For edited works, follow the editor's name with *ed.* or *eds.* (for more than one editor).

Title

- Capitalize the first word in the title and subtitle and all significant words thereafter.
- Underline the title of a book or pamphlet.
- Put quotation marks around the titles of articles in periodicals, essays in collections, or papers in proceedings.
- End titles with a period.

Multiple Volume or Series Publications

- Give the name of the series and series number of volumes after the title.
- Specify the edition if not the first.

Publication Information

- List the place of publication, publisher's name, and date of publication.
- Use a shortened form of the publisher's name.
- When publication information cannot be found, use *n.p.* (no publication place), *n.p.* (no publisher), and *n.d.* (no date).
- For familiar reference works, list only the edition and year of publication.

Periodicals

- For journal articles, list the volume number, date, and page numbers after the title of the periodical.
- For an article in a magazine or newspaper, omit the volume number.
- For a newspaper, give the edition and page number(s).

Online Sources

- Review the following guidelines for citing online sources below.

Online Sources.   Citations for online sources are similar to citations for printed sources. To cite an online source, begin with the author, title, and, if the information is included in a printed version, publication information. Indicate the date the document was created or updated and the date the information was retrieved and include in angle brackets the Web address (the URL) or enough address information to allow the reader to retrieve the source. Titles of entire Web sites should be underlined. Treat any articles or graphics included at the site as you would those from print sources. Personal communications, such as e-mail messages and bulletin-board postings, follow the format for letters and interviews.

Standards continue to evolve for citations of online and electronic sources. When citing online information, the two primary goals are to give credit to the author and to enable readers to retrieve the source.

Indenting.   Use a hanging indent, with second and additional lines indented five spaces or one-half inch from the left margin.

Spacing.   Double-space within and between the entries of the works-cited list.

Dates.   The correct format for dates is as follows: day, month, year, with no commas (19 Jan. 2003). Abbreviate all months except May, June, and July.

MLA Documentation Models
Books
Single Author

Hassab, Joseph C. Systems Management: People, Computers, Machines, Materials. New York: CRC, 1997.

Multiple Authors

Testerman, Joshua O., Thomas J. Kuegler, Jr., and Paul J. Dowling, Jr. Web Advertising and Marketing. 2nd ed. Roseville, CA: Prima, 1998.

Corporate Author

Ernst and Young. Ernst and Young's Retirement Planning Guide. New York: Wiley, 1999.

Edition Other Than First

Estes, Jack C., and Dennis R. Kelley. McGraw-Hill's Interest Amortization Tables. 3rd ed. New York: McGraw, 1998.

Multivolume Work

Standard and Poor. <u>Standard and Poor's Register of Corporations, Directors and Executives</u>. 3 vols.
New York: McGraw, 1998.

Work in an Edited Collection

Gueron, Judith M. "Welfare and Poverty: Strategies to Increase Work." <u>Reducing Poverty in America:
Views and Approaches</u>. Ed. Michael R. Darby. Thousand Oaks: Sage, 1996. 237–55.

Encyclopedia or Dictionary Entry

Gibbard, Bruce G. "Particle Detector." <u>World Book Encyclopedia</u>. 1999 ed.

Articles in Periodicals (See also *Electronic Sources*)
Magazine Article

Coley, Don. "Compliance for the Right Reasons." <u>Business Geographics</u> June 1997: 30–32.

Journal Article

Rossouw, George J. "Business Ethics in South Africa." <u>Journal of Business Ethics</u> 16 (1997):
1539–47.

Newspaper Article

Mathews, Anna Wilde. "The Internet Generation Taps Into Morse Code." <u>Wall Street Journal</u> 1 Oct.
1997, natl. ed.: B1+.

Article with Unknown Author

"American City Adds Nashville, Memphis." <u>Business Journal</u> 26 Sept. 1997: 16.

Electronic Sources
An Entire Web Site

<u>Association for Business Communication</u>. Aug. 1999. Assn. for Business Communication. 20 Apr.
2001 <http://www.theabc.org/>.

A Document from a Web Site, with an Author

Locker, Kitty O. "The History of the Association for Business Communication." <u>Association for
Business Communication</u>. 25 Oct. 1995. Assn. for Business Communication. 20 Apr. 2001
<http://www.theabc.org/history.htm>.

A Document from a Web Site, with a Corporate Author

General Motors. "Company Profile." <u>General Motors</u>. 2001. 19 Apr. 2001 <http://www.gm.com/
company/corp_info/profiles/>.

A Document from a Web Site, with an Unknown Author

"Forgotten Inventors." Forgotten Inventors. PBS Online. 2001. 19 Apr. 2001 <http://www.pbs.org/
wgbh/amex/telephone/sfeature/index.htm>.

Article from a Database (Subscription)

Goldbort, Robert C. "Scientific Writing as an Art and as a Science." Journal of Environmental Health
63.7 (2001): 22. Expanded Academic ASAP. InfoTrac. Salem State Coll. Lib., Salem, MA.
19 Apr. 2001.

Article in an Online Periodical

Ray, Tiernan. "Waiting for Wireless." SmartMoney.com 18 Apr. 2001. 19 Apr. 2001 <http://www
.smartmoney.com/techmarket/index.cfm?story=20010418>.

Publication on CD-ROM

Money 99. CD-ROM. Redmond: Microsoft, 1998.

E-mail Message

Kahl, Jonathan D. "Re: Web page." E-mail to the author. 2 Oct. 2001.

Multimedia Sources (Print and Electronic)
Map or Chart

Wisconsin. Map. Chicago: Rand, 2000.

"Asia." Map. Maps.com. 2000. 20 Apr. 2001 <http://www.maps.com/explore/atlas/political/asia.html>.

Film or Video

Massingham, Gordon, dir., and Jane Christopher, ed. Introduction to Hazardous Chemicals.
Videocassette. Edgartown, MA: Emergency Film Group, 1998.

Lawrence, Detrick, dir. Emergency Film Group: Homepage Web Video. 2001. 20 Apr. 2001 <http://
www.efilmgroup.com/video1.rm>.

Radio or Television Program

"Do Americans Really Want a Tax Cut?" CNN: Crossfire. Host Robert Novak. CNN. 16 Apr. 2001.

"Energy Supplies." Host Emily Harris. All Things Considered. Natl. Public Radio. WGBH, Boston.
3 Apr. 2001. 20 Apr. 2001 <http://www.npr.org/programs/atc/>.

Other Sources
Published Interview

Gates, Bill. "The View from the Very Top." Interview. Newsweek 17 Apr. 2000: 36–39.

Personal Interview

Sariolgholam, Mahmood. Personal interview. 29 Nov. 2000.

Personal Letter

Viets, Hermann. Letter to all students, fac., and staff. 1 Sept. 1998. University of Wisconsin, Milwaukee.

Brochure or Pamphlet

Library of Congress. US Copyright Office. Copyright Registration for Online Works. Washington: GPO, 1999.

Government Document

United States. Dept. of Energy. The Energy Situation in the Next Decade. Technical Pub. 11346-53. Washington: GPO, 1998.

Report

Bertot, John Carlo, Charles R. McClure, and Douglas L. Zweizig. The 1996 National Survey of Public Libraries and the Internet: Progress and Issues: Final Report. Washington: GPO, 1996.

Lecture or Speech

McKinney, Scott. Lecture. Demarest Hall, Hobart and William Smith Colls., Geneva, NY. 3 May 2002.

Krug, Steve. "Don't Make Me Think: The Art of Designing User-Friendly Websites." New England School of Art & Design at Suffolk U. Boston Public Lib. 3 Apr. 2001.

MLA Sample Pages

Author's last name and page number

Marks 14

This report examines the nature and disposition of the 3,458 ethics cases handled company-wide by CGF's ethics officers and managers during 2002. The purpose of such reports is to provide the Ethics and Business Conduct Committee with the information necessary for as-

One-inch margins; text double-spaced

sessing the effectiveness of the first year of CGF's Ethics Program (Davis 142). According to Matthias Jonas, recommendations are given for consideration "in planning for the second year of the Ethics Program" ("Internet" 152).

The Office of Ethics and Business Conduct was created to administer the Ethics Program. The director of the Office of Ethics and Business Conduct, along with seven ethics officers throughout CGF, was given the responsibility for the following objectives, as described by Rossouw:

Long quote indented one inch (or ten spaces), double-spaced, without quotation marks

> Communicate the values, standards, and goals of CGF's Program to employees. Provide company-wide channels for employee education and guidance in resolving ethics concerns. Implement company-wide programs in ethics awareness and recognition. Employee accessibility to ethics information and guidance is the immediate goal of the Office of Business Conduct in its first year. (1543)

In-text citations give author and page number; title used when multiple works by same author(s) cited

The purpose of the Ethics Program, according to Jonas, established by the Committee, is to "promote ethical business conduct through open communication and compliance with company ethics standards" ("Ethics" 89). This report examines the nature and the

Figure 7–13   MLA Sample Page

Works Cited

Association for Business Communication. Aug. 1999. Assn. for Business
　　Communication. 20 Apr. 2001 <http://www.theabc.org/>.

Davis, W. C., Roland Marks, and Diane Tegge. Working in the System: Five
　　New Management Principles. New York: St. Martin's, 2001.

Hassab, Joseph C. Systems Management: People, Computers, Machines,
　　Materials. New York: CRC, 1997.

Jonas, Matthias. "Ethics in Organizational Communication: A Review of the
　　Literature." Journal of Ethics and Communication 29 (2001): 79–99.

---. "The Internet and Ethical Communication: Toward a New Paradigm."
　　Journal of Ethics and Communication 27 (1999): 147–77.

Library of Congress. US Copyright Office. Copyright Registration for Online
　　Works. Washington: GPO, 1999.

The One-Minute Manager. CD-ROM. Boston: Bedford, 1998.

Rossouw, George J. "Business Ethics in South Africa." Journal of Business
　　Ethics 16 (1997): 1539–47.

Sariolgholam, Mahmood. Personal interview. 29 Nov. 2000.

Heading centered

List alphabetized by authors' last names or titles and double-spaced

Hanging-indent style used for entries

Figure 7–14　MLA Sample List of Works Cited

Other Style Manuals

Many professional societies, publishing companies, and other organizations publish manuals that prescribe bibliographic reference formats for their publications or for publications in their fields. In addition, several general style manuals are well known and widely used.

Biology

Council of Science Editors. *Scientific Style and Format: The CBE Manual for Authors, Editors, and Publishers.* 6th ed. New York: Cambridge University Press, 1994. See also <councilscienceeditors.org>.

Chemistry

American Chemical Society. *ACS Style Guide: A Manual for Authors and Editors.* 2nd ed. Washington, D.C.: American Chemical Society, 1998. See also <acs.org>.

Government Documents

United States Government Printing Office. *Style Manual.* Washington, D.C.: U.S. Government Printing Office, 2000. See also <gpo.gov>.

Journalism

Goldstein, Norm, ed. *Associated Press Stylebook and Briefing on Media Law.* New York: Associated Press, 2002. See also <ap.org>.

Law

Harvard Law Review et al. *The Bluebook: A Uniform System of Citation.* 17th ed. Cambridge: Harvard Law Review Association, 2000. See also <legalbluebook.com>.

Medicine

American Medical Association. *American Medical Association Manual of Style.* 9th ed. Baltimore: Williams, 1998. See also <ama-assn.org>.

Political Science

American Political Science Association. *Style Manual for Political Science.* Rev. ed. Washington, D.C.: APSA, 2001. See also <apsanet.org>.

Social Work

National Association of Social Workers. *An Author's Guide to Social Work Journals.* 4th ed. Washington, D.C.: National Association of Social Workers Press, 1997. See also <naswpress.org>.

CHAPTER 7 SUMMARY: Researching Your Subject (continued)

Information sources available to you as you research job-related topics include the record of firsthand observations that you gather directly and the results of research published by others that is available in print or online.

- ☐ Firsthand observations and experiments are essential to gather information about behavior, natural phenomena, and the functions of processes or equipment. To gather observational information:
    - Choose sites and times carefully and, as necessary, request permission in advance.
    - Keep complete, accurate records and note dates, times, durations, and other details.
    - Remain as unobtrusive as possible to not interfere with the process under observation.
- ☐ Interview yourself. Your own knowledge, training, and experience may provide essential information.
- ☐ Personal interviews with subject-matter experts can provide up-to-date information not readily available elsewhere, but interviews require thoughtful preparation.
    - Select the subject-matter expert most likely to be helpful.
    - Prepare specific questions before the interview.
    - Take careful notes during the interview.
    - Review and summarize your notes immediately after the interview.
- ☐ Questionnaires permit you to obtain the views of groups of people without the time and expense necessary for conducting numerous personal interviews.
    - Design the questionnaire to gather as much information as you need with as little effort as possible on those answering the questions.
    - Formulate questions so that the answers can be readily tabulated.
    - Carefully select respondents to ensure that their responses represent a cross section of the population to which you wish to generalize your results.
- ☐ Libraries provide organized access to a wealth of information in their print, audiovisual, and digitized collections. Researchers can acces the information through:
    - Online catalogs.
    - Databases and indexes.
    - Reference works.
- ☐ The Internet provides online access to immense amounts of information, although its lack of a coherent organization makes locating salient information a challenge. To increase the odds of locating what you need, use:
    - Subject directories of sites.
    - Search engines.
    - Meta-search engines.
- ☐ Evaluate print and online sources of information for their relevance, timeliness, and accuracy.
    - Review the information source for its depth and breadth of coverage of your topic.

> **CHAPTER 7 SUMMARY: Researching Your Subject** *(continued)*
>
> - ■ Ensure that the source is reputable.
> - ■ Evaluate the information for any evidence of bias.
> - ■ Keep detailed records of these sources for your bibliography.
> - ☐ Take notes that accurately summarize the information relevant to your topic.
> - ☐ Avoid plagiarism by giving complete and accurate credit to all your information sources, which will:
>   - ■ Allow readers to locate the source of the information given.
>   - ■ Establish your credibility by supporting your work with information from existing sources.
>   - ■ Give proper credit to your sources.
> - ☐ Document the information that you quote, paraphrase, or summarize in your text:
>   - ■ In brief *parenthetical citations* in text, with full information in an alphabetical list of works cited.
>   - ■ In *numbered references* in text that refer to full information in a reference section, where citations are listed numerically in the order of their first citation in text.
>   - ■ In *notes* that appear either at the bottoms of text pages (footnotes) or in a separate section at the end of a chapter or section (endnotes).

■ Exercises

1. Prepare an MLA-style works-cited page using the following list of sources:
   - John O'Connor, Exploring American History. Globe Book Company, New York, 1994
   - Randy W. Roberts and James Stuart Olson, Editors. American Experiences: Readings in American History, Volume one. Fifth edition. Longman, New York, 2001
   - Helen Jackson. A Century of Dishonor: A Sketch of the United States Government's Dealings with Some of the Indian Tribes. Corner House, Williamstown, MA, 1973
   - Paul Rubenstein, Writing for the Media. Prentice Hall, Englewood Cliffs, NJ, 1988
   - Highsmith's Complete School & Library Catalog. Highsmith Inc., Fort Atkinson, WI, 1998
   - Lee Hopkins, Do You Know What Day Tomorrow Is? Scholastic Inc., New York, 1989
   - Anthony Burgess, Ernest Hemingway and His World. Charles Scribner and Sons, New York, 1985

- Charles Elster, Tooth and Nail: a Novel Approach to the New SAT. Harcourt Brace & Company, San Diego, 1994
- James Miller, Jr., Russian and Eastern European Literature. Scott, Foresman and Company, Glenview, IL, 1976
- Kenneth Koch, Sleeping on the Wing; An Anthology of Modern Essays on Reading and Writing. Random House, New York, 1973

2. Prepare an APA-style reference page using the following list of sources:

- Donald Bolander, Instant Synonyms and Antonyms. Career Institute, Mundelein, IL, 1970
- Anthony Burgess, Ernest Hemingway and His World. Charles Scribner and Sons, New York, 1985
- George Clare, Last Waltz in Vienna: The Rise and Destruction of a Family, 1842–1942. Henry Holt and Company, New York, 1989
- Andrew Roberts, The Concise Columbia Dictionary of Quotations. Avon Books, New York, 1990
- Highsmith's Complete School and Library Catalog. Highsmith Inc, Fort Atkinson, WI, 1998
- Lee Hopkins, Do You Know What Day Tomorrow Is? Scholastic Inc, New York, 1989
- Andrew Hurley, Against All Hope: The Prison Memoirs of Armand Valladores. Alfred A. Knopf Inc., New York, 1987
- Randy W. Roberts and James Stuart Olson, Editors. American Experiences: Readings in American History, Volume one. 5th Edition. Longman New York, 2001

3. Practice inserting MLA- and APA-style parenthetical citations into the text of a research paper.

   a. Begin by imagining that you are writing a paper that includes a discussion about the importance of organizing space. Here is an excerpt from that paper:

   ■ Organizing your home and work space can be one of life's greatest problems for some people. Having your spaces organized can make the difference between a peaceful existence and misery! To conquer this problem, you must first analyze your own organizational level. We each have a different way of organizing and also a different concept of what organized means in terms of our own homes and work spaces. Do you consider yourself "organized"? Are your drawers and closets as neat as you would like them? Or, are your rooms a mess, but you know exactly where to find any item that is missing? The first step to becoming organized is to define what the term means to you and to decide what degree of organization would bring peace to your life.

   b. Now incorporate into the above paragraph three direct quotations or three sentences of paraphrased content from the following excerpts from a book titled *A New Way of Looking at Organizing,* by Judy Morgenstern. The material is all from page 1 of the text, published in 1999 by Anchor Books in New York. You may insert the three sentences (quotations or paraphrased text) anywhere you wish in the paragraph as long as the context makes sense and as long as Morgenstern's three excerpts are not included consecutively within your paragraph. Following is the text from Judy Morgenstern's book to be incorporated into and cited in your paper:

If I asked you to describe an organized space, what would you say? From most people, I hear things like "neat and tidy," "spare," "minimalist," and "boring." But an organized space has nothing to do with these traits. There are people whose homes and offices appear neat as a pin on the surface. Yet, inside their desk drawers and kitchen cabinets, there is no real system, and things are terribly out of control. By contrast, there are many people who live or work in a physical mess, yet feel very comfortable in this environment and can always put their hands on whatever they need in a second. Could they be considered organized? Absolutely.

Being organized has less to do with the way an environment *looks* than how effectively it *functions*. If a person can find what she needs when she needs it, feels unencumbered in achieving her goals, and is happy in her space, then that person is well organized.

I'd like to propose a new definition of organization: Organizing is the process by which we create environments that enable us to live, work, and relax exactly as we want to. When we are organized, our homes, offices, and schedules reflect and encourage who we are, what we want, and where we are going.

Misconceptions affect the way you think about any process, poisoning your attitude toward it and eroding even your best efforts to succeed by convincing you before you start that you're bound to fail. Following is one of the most common beliefs about organizing, and the debunking facts that will change your thinking.

> Misconception: Organizing is a mysterious talent. Some lucky people are born with it, while others, like you, are left to suffer.
> Fact: Organizing is a skill. In fact, it's a remarkably simple skill that anyone can learn.

c. Create parenthetical documentation for this material first in MLA style and then in APA style. Refer to the text of this chapter for guidelines and examples for both styles of parenthetical citation.

■ Collaborative Classroom Projects

1. *Paraphrase* the following passage. Then *summarize* the information. Identify your notes by stating the topic of the passage.

   To keep pipes from freezing, wrap the pipes in insulation made especially for water pipes, or in layers of old newspaper, lapping the ends and tying them around the pipes. Cover the newspaper with plastic to keep out moisture. When it is extremely cold and there is real danger of freezing, let the faucets drip a little. Although this wastes water, it may prevent freezing damage. Know where the valve for shutting off the water coming into the house or apartment is located. You may as a last resort have to shut off this main valve and drain all the pipes to keep them from freezing and bursting.

2. Prepare a brief parenthetical citation in MLA style and in APA style for each of the following reference items and then create an MLA-style works-cited page and an APA-style Reference page containing full information about each citation.

a. A magazine article beginning on page 24 and ending on page 32 of the June 2000 issue of Electronic Publishing, by Sterling Ledet, titled "Reaching Customers on the Web." Your reference is on page 26.

b. An unsigned article, "Power Play: Will Electricity Deregulation Jolt Consumers?" in the June 2000 issue of Consumer Reports, volume 62, number 6. The article appears in its entirety on page 60.

c. Roger M. Schwarz's book titled The Skilled Facilitator: Practical Wisdom for Developing Effective Groups, published by Jossey-Bass Publishers of San Francisco in 1994. Your reference is on page 149.

d. An article in the Washington Post titled "Pension Errors May Be Rising, But Finding Them Is Up to You," by Albert Crenshaw. The article begins on page 1 and ends on page 4 of Section H of the June 22, 2000, issue. Your citation is on page H4.

e. A Web site titled "The Trade Development Homepage" at <http://ita.doc.gov/td/td_home/tdhome.html>, hosted by the International Trade Administration and the U.S. Department of Commerce. The site has no copyright date, but you accessed it on September 13, 2003.

f. An online article from the New York Times Magazine, "The Way We Live Now: Competitive States of America," by Mark Kingwell. The article was published on June 25, 2003, and you accessed it on July 10, 2003, at <http://nytimes.com/library/magazine/home/20000625mag-waywelivenow.html>.

g. An online book titled Hal's Legacy: 2001's Computer as Dream and Reality, edited by David G. Stork. The book was published by the MIT Press in Cambridge, Massachusetts, in January 1997, and you accessed it online on August 1, 2003, at <http://mitpress.mit.edu/e-books/Hal/>.

h. An online government publication titled The United States Government Manual, published by the National Archives and Records Administration and found at <http://access.gpo.gov/nara/nara001.html>. The page is dated January 7, 2002, and you accessed it on August 19, 2003.

i. A booklet titled "Security in the Workplace: Improving the Safety of Federal Employees," by the Department of Justice, U.S. Marshal's Service and published in Washington, D.C., by the Government Printing Office in 2002. Your reference is on page 12.

j. Your interview of the City Manager of Plainview, Texas, on March 1, 2003. Her name is Annette Diggs.

k. An article titled "Creating electronic documents that interact with diagnostic software for onsite service," by Mark Harmison that appears on pages 92 through 101 of the journal IEEE Transactions on Professional Communication. It appears in the June 2002 issue of the journal, volume 40, number 21. You cite information on pages 95 and 99.

l. Computer software called Microsoft Money 2003: Business and Personal issued by Microsoft Press in 2003. The software is available on disk or CD-ROM.

m. The sixth edition of the Dictionary of Computer and Internet Terms by Douglas Downing, Michael Covington, and Melody M. Covington. The dictionary was published in Hauppauge, New York, in 1998. You cite material from the section "To the reader" on page ix.

n. An article from the 1998 (4th) edition of the McGraw-Hill Concise Encyclopedia of Science and Technology titled "Virology."

3. Bring to class information related to your area of study from three Web sites. Print out relevant pages from each site and draft a brief synopsis of the resources provided there. Form groups with three to five students who share your major. Review the guidelines in this chapter for evaluating a Web site and draft a list of questions to consider when evaluating a Web site as a research resource specific to your field. Evaluate and compare each of the sites that your group members have found and decide which sites would be the most valuable for your research. Write a brief group summary of your findings to share with the class.

4. Using the online sources that you brought to class for Collaborative Classroom Project 3, work in a group of three to five students to create an MLA-style list of Works Cited and an APA-style Reference list from your collective online sources. (Refer to the Documenting Sources section of this chapter as needed.)

■ Research Projects

Note: The research projects in this chapter may be used as the basis for the preparation of a formal report according to the guidelines presented in Chapter 12.

1. Select a topic from your career field or another area of interest. Using the online catalog in your library, locate five books on your topic. Document your sources according to the MLA or APA guidelines in this chapter.

2. Using a periodical database that your college library has access to, locate five articles—from magazines, newspapers, or journals—on the topic you chose for Research Project 1. Document your sources according to the MLA or APA guidelines in this chapter.

3. Choose a topic related to your area of study and interview someone knowledgeable about your subject. Incorporate the information that you gathered at your interview in a research paper and document the interview according to MLA or APA style. Submit to your instructor your organized notes of the interview and the letter or e-mail that you sent to request the interview.

4. Your campus has recently been in the news because of its lack of international students; you have been asked to serve on a student committee charged with the task of finding out why. Your committee has decided to develop a questionnaire to distribute to the international students on campus asking for their feedback concerning this issue. In preparing your questionnaire you will want to keep in mind the guidelines in this chapter for preparing a questionnaire, and also the guidelines for working with an international audience in Chapters 8 and 9. Submit your questionnaire to your instructor.

■ Web Projects

Projects followed by the symbol Ⓦ are continued at **bedfordstmartins.com/ writingthatworks**, Chapter 7.

1. Prepare an APA-style Reference list or MLA-style list of Works Cited using the annotated list of online sources provided at the *Writing That Works* Web site. Ⓦ

2. Using Google (<google.com>) or another reliable search engine, locate three to five Web sites that feature information relevant to a topic that interests you. Evaluate these sites according to the guidelines in this chapter and write a brief explanation of what makes these sites potentially valuable to your topic. Document these sites (either the whole site or specific pages or documents within the site) according to MLA or APA documentation guidelines.

3. Review the online catalog search in this chapter (illustrated in Figures 7–5 and 7–6). Choose a topic related to your area of study and conduct a step-by-step on-line catalog search by keyword. What three to five books would you consider using, and why?

4. Use one of your library's online periodical databases (such as InfoTrac) to find articles related to a recent discovery or an important trend in your field. Write a three-page report of your findings, using the APA or MLA style of documentation. Cite your sources within your text and include an APA-style reference list or an MLA-style list of works cited.

5. Assume you are a manager at a small manufacturing firm (you choose the product that your company produces). Because of a rising national concern about the environment and land use, the board of directors has asked your department to develop a policy statement outlining your corporation's views on the conservation of natural resources. Use your library's Web subject directory to locate information about how government environmental policy affects your business. Submit your list of at least five sites with your notes, describing the information contained at each site and giving reasons why you chose these sites. Include with your notes an APA-style reference list or an MLA-style list of works cited.

8 Designing Effective Documents and Visuals

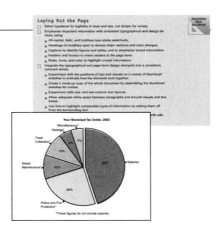

This chapter is divided into three main parts: Designing Documents, and Creating Printed Forms—two sections that offer detailed information for document layout and design and for the creation of printed forms—and Creating Visuals—a section that provides guidelines and models for designing illustrations and integrating them with text, and for using graphics to communicate with an international audience. (See Chapter 15, pages 527–531, for guidance on preparing presentation graphics.)

Clarity and consistency are important not only for good writing but also for the design and layout of any document—especially one that includes visuals—and to the creation and use of the visuals themselves. Effectively designed documents help readers locate the information they need and grasp how the parts fit together. The Designing Documents section describes how to achieve these goals by providing your readers with carefully selected visual cues. Whether you are creating a memo, a report, or a newsletter, everything from your choice of type size and style to the arrangement of text and visuals on each page contributes to your reader's experience of your document. The Creating Printed Forms section covers the printed form, a document that may include a minimum amount of text but that can sometimes be the most effective and efficient way to communicate.

The Creating Visuals section of this chapter focuses on how to use visual aids to increase your reader's understanding of your topic. Tables, graphs, drawings, charts, maps, and photographs—often collectively called *visuals*—can express ideas or convey information that words alone cannot. Clear, concise visuals support your text and help your readers focus on key points. By allowing readers to understand and interpret data at a glance, visuals can encourage faster decision-making and be used to persuade your audience.

■ Designing Documents

Most memos, letters, meeting minutes, progress reports, and other routine communications are formatted according to a predetermined set of standards. Business-correspondence formats, for example, are discussed in Chapter 9; formal-report formats are discussed in Chapter 12. However, certain high-visibility, complex, or special-purpose documents, such as those aimed at customers, stockholders, or clients, require special layout and design consideration. This section introduces you to the document layout-and-design principles for such nonroutine materials. Thoughtfully applied, these principles will make even the most complex information look accessible and give readers a favorable impression of the writer and the organization that produced it. To accomplish these goals, a design should (1) offer a simple and uncluttered presentation of the topic; (2) highlight structure, hierarchy, and order; (3) help readers find information easily; and (4) reinforce an organization's image.

Effective design is based on visual simplicity and harmony, such as using compatible fonts and the same highlighting device for similar items. Design should reveal hierarchy by signaling the difference between topics and subtopics, between primary and secondary information, and between general points and examples. Writers can achieve effective layout and design through their selection of fonts, their choice of devices to highlight information, and their arrangement of text and visual components on a page. Such visual cues make information easy to find. Finally, the design of a document should project the appropriate image of an organization. For example, if clients are paying a high price for consulting services, they may expect a sophisticated, polished design; if employees inside an organization expect management to be frugal, they may accept — even expect — economical and standard company design.

Typography

Typography refers to the style and arrangement of type on a printed page. A complete set of all the letters, numbers, and symbols available in one typeface (or style) is called a *font*. The letters in a typeface have a number of distinctive characteristics, some of which are shown in Figure 8–1.

Typeface

For most on-the-job writing, select a typeface primarily for its simplicity and legibility. Avoid typefaces that may distract readers with contrasts in thickness or with odd-looking features, as is often the case with script and cursive typefaces. Choose popular typefaces with which readers are familiar, such as Times Roman, or any of the following:

- Baskerville
- Bodoni
- Century
- Garamond
- Gill Sans
- Helvetica
- Palatino
- Univers

W On the Web
For more information on designing effective documents and visuals, see Chapter 8, **bedfordstmartins.com/ writingthatworks**

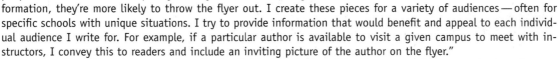

Voices from the Workplace

Alvin Blunt, Nuclear Regulatory Commission

Alvin Blunt has worked in the field of graphic design for more than 30 years. As chief of the Graphics Section at the Nuclear Regulatory Commission, he produces a variety of documents and art, including brochures and posters, and designs the agency's Web graphics and pages.

When designing a document, says Alvin, "the first thing to consider is your audience, and how and where your document will be viewed." Alvin explains his process: "I visualize the end product before I design it." He and his team carefully consider "the most important components of the document and build designs around them . . . taking a little idea and embellishing it."

Alvin's advice to writers as they design their documents is: "Use no more than three typefaces. Use a proper amount of distance between lines and margins so that your document looks professional." He encourages writers to be selective when incorporating photos and drawings, and to consider format and visuals carefully: "Keep a consistent theme throughout the document." Finally, he urges writers to "remember copyright restrictions," requesting permission as needed and giving credit to original sources.

Emily Rankin, Bedford/St. Martin's

As a marketing associate at Bedford/St. Martin's, Emily Rankin's responsibilities include assisting the head of the marketing division, creating marketing copy for book covers, and producing flyers that advertise Bedford's new products and special offers.

Emily describes the objectives of the flyers that she writes and designs: "A flyer must highlight our company name and our products and be as straightforward as possible. A flyer must describe specific packaging offers simply and provide appealing cover shots of the books that we're promoting options for. A flyer must also provide correct information for contacting the local sales representative and marketing manager."

Because flyers are important marketing documents, Emily considers specific guidelines when creating and designing them. "Flyers should be clean and uncluttered so that people can find information quickly. If they have to sift through too much irrelevant information, they're more likely to throw the flyer out. I create these pieces for a variety of audiences—often for specific schools with unique situations. I try to provide information that would benefit and appeal to each individual audience I write for. For example, if a particular author is available to visit a given campus to meet with instructors, I convey this to readers and include an inviting picture of the author on the flyer."

Emily offers this advice to writers in the field of marketing: "For flyers or really any marketing pieces—whether for a general reader or a reader with very specific concerns—the most important thing to remember is: Keep your audience in mind!"

Do not use more than two or three typefaces—using multiple typefaces will create disharmony in your document. To create a dramatic contrast between headings and text, as in a newsletter, use a typeface for the heading that is distinctively different from that of the text. You can also use a noticeably different typeface within a graphic element. In any case, experiment before making your final decision. (Keep in mind that not all fonts have the same assortment of symbols and other characters that you may need for your graphics.)

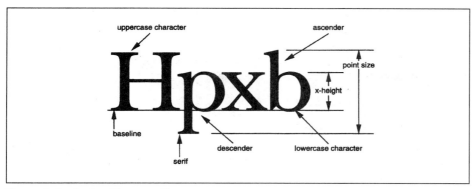

Figure 8–1   Letter Character Features

One major distinction among typefaces is the presence or absence of serifs. Serifs, shown in Figure 8–1, are the small projections at the end of each stroke in a letter. The text of this book is set in Utopia, a serif typeface. Serif type is easier to read, especially in the smaller sizes, and it works best for main text. Sans serif (without serif) type, however, works best for headings.

Type Size

Ensure that your font size is easily readable. Small fonts can cause eyestrain and make the text look crammed and intimidating. Six-point type, for example, is too small for almost anything other than footnotes and classified ads. Likewise, type that is too large makes reading difficult and is inefficient. Ideal point sizes for text in paper documents range from 8 to 13 points, with 10- or 12-point type most commonly used. For documents that will be read from a distance or that are geared toward visually impaired readers, use large type sizes. Figure 8–2 illustrates a range of type sizes.

Highlighting Devices

Highlighting devices can give a document a visual logic and organization. For example, rules and boxes can set off steps and illustrations from surrounding explanations. Consistency is important: Use the same technique to highlight a particular

6 pt.   This size might be used for dating a source.
8 pt.   This size might be used for footnotes.
10 pt.   This size might be used for figure captions.
12 pt.   This size might be used for main text.
14 pt.   This size might be used for headings.

Figure 8–2   Samples of 6- to 14-Point Type

feature throughout your document. However, be selective about how you use typographical devices and special graphics; too many design devices clutter a page and interfere with comprehension.

Writers use a number of methods to emphasize important words, passages, and sections within documents:

- Typographical devices
- Headings and captions
- Headers and footers
- Rules, icons, and color

Typographical Devices

When used sparingly, **boldface** type, *italics,* and ALL CAPITAL LETTERS can help you achieve emphasis.

- Use **boldface** type for headings or short passages of text that you wish to draw attention to.
- Use *italics* to highlight a key term or phrase, or if you wish to slow readers, as in cautions or warnings.
- Use ALL CAPITAL LETTERS for headings (if you don't use boldface) or to alert readers to crucial steps in a process, as in instructions, or to indicate danger, such as in a caution or warning message.

Headings and Captions

Headings—titles and subtitles within the body of a document—divide material into comprehensible segments by highlighting the main topics and signaling topic changes. They indicate the hierarchy within a document and help readers decide which sections they need to read. *Captions* are titles that highlight or describe illustrations or blocks of text. Captions often appear below figures, above tables, and in the left or right margins next to blocks of text.

Headings appear in many typeface variations (boldface being most common) and often use sans serif typefaces. The most common positions for headings and subheadings are centered, flush left, indented, or by themselves in a wide left margin. Insert an additional line of space above a heading to emphasize the division on the page. Major section or chapter headings normally appear at the top of a new page. Never leave a heading as the final line on a page—the heading is disconnected from its text and thus ineffective. Instead, move the heading to the start of the next page.

Headers and Footers

A *header* is identifying information carried at the top of each page; a *footer* contains similar information at the bottom of each page. (The header at the top of this page reads "Chapter 8 ◆ Designing Effective Documents and Visuals," and includes the page number.) Document pages may have headers or footers or both. They carry such information as the topic or subtopic of a section, the section numbers, the date the document was written, page numbers, the document name, or the section title. Although headers and footers are important reference devices, do not include too much information in them to avoid visual clutter. Headers and footers are usually in a smaller font size than the main text.

Rules, Icons, and Color

Rules are vertical or horizontal lines used to divide one area of the page from another or to create boxes; used in moderation, rules isolate and highlight important information for ease of reading. See Figure 8–3 for a sample page from a report illustrating a variety of highlighting devices.

An *icon* is a pictorial representation of an idea; it can be used to identify specific actions, objects, or sections of a document. Commonly used icons include the small envelopes on Web pages to symbolize e-mail links and national flags to symbolize different language versions of a document. To be effective, icons must be simple and easily recognizable to your reader.

Color and screening (or shading) can distinguish one part of a document from another or unify a series of documents. Color and screening can set off sections within a document, highlight examples, or emphasize warnings. They are especially useful in graphs, maps, and drawings to differentiate boundaries and to depict the actual colors of geological and biological samples. In tables, you can use screening to highlight column titles or sets of data to which you want to draw the reader's attention.

Page Design

Page design is the process of combining the various design elements on a page to make a coherent whole. The flexibility of your design is based on the capabilities of your software, how the document will be reproduced, and your budget. (High-quality offset color printing, for example, is far more expensive and time consuming to reproduce than black-and-white printing.)

Thumbnail Sketches

Before you spend time positioning text and visuals on a page, you may want to create a thumbnail sketch, in which blocks indicate the placement of elements. The thumbnails are usually sketched by hand on lined tablet or graph paper. They need not be formal or even neat. They are simply a way to brainstorm design options before you begin the actual layout of the report, newsletter, brochure, or other document. Figure 8–4 shows thumbnail sketches of designs for an 8½-by-11-inch report with two columns per page and for an 8½-by-11-inch newsletter with three columns per page. You can go further by roughly assembling all the thumbnail pages, showing size, shape, form, and general style of a large document. Such a mock-up, called a *dummy,* allows you to see how a finished document will look. As you work with elements on the page, experiment with different layouts to make sure that your ideas work in practice.

Page heading with report title →

Chapter title with boldface →

Optical and Handwritten Character Recognition Software: Recent Developments

Since the inception of computers, programmers have been teaching them to mimic humans. One such task that humans often take for granted is literacy. The process of reading printed text with a computer is called Optical Character Recognition (OCR). This method is optical because it uses a scanner to measure the reflected light off a piece of paper much like a copy machine does (Srihari and Lam 1–4). Along with OCR technology came handwriting recognition. Handwriting recognition occurs when the computer identifies each character the user writes with an electronic pen. Both OCR and handwriting recognition currently allow the computer almost 100 percent accuracy in understanding the writing of its human counterpart ("Looking Forward" 213).

Boldface headings →

What Are the Practical Applications?

OCR and handwriting recognition are used daily for such tasks as reading your tax forms and checking your passport at customs. The IRS, for example, receives about 200 million tax forms every year. So OCR is an important technology in processing tax forms because of OCR's speed and accuracy compared with manual interpretation. Another useful application of OCR technology is in delivering the mail on time. The United States Postal Service (USPS), as well as many parcel delivery services worldwide, use OCR to process mail. The USPS uses an OCR system to scan each mail piece to find the printed ZIP code within the delivery address. If the four additional numbers, called ZIP+4TM, are not at the end of the ZIP code, then the computer reads the entire address and looks it up in a database to find its ZIP+4TM number. This ZIP code is then converted to a bar code, which is printed on the bottom of the envelope for sorting. This system can process up to 45,000 pieces of mail an hour (Srihari and Lam 12). . . .

How Does Scanning Work?

When the computer scans a page of text it does so graphically. All the computer sees at first is a grid of many small dots where each dot is either black or white. A typical scanner reads 300 of these dots per square inch.

Boxed figure with caption →

In the first step of processing a page of text, the computer looks at the whole document and decides which regions contain text, and within those regions it searches for individual letters and numbers. The software then scans in dots that make up each character and compares them with the shapes of letters used in English or other Roman-character-based languages. After comparing the dots, the software picks the letter or number that looks the most similar. After every character

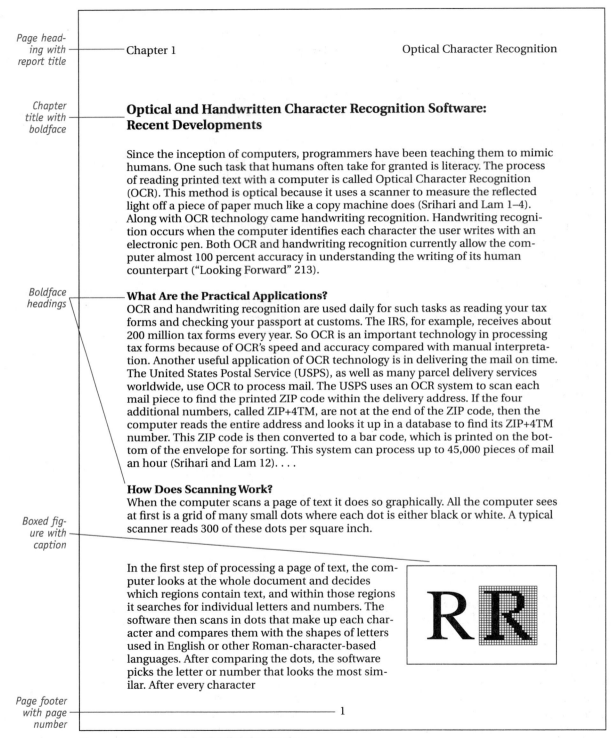

Page footer with page number →

Figure 8–3   Page with Highlighting Devices

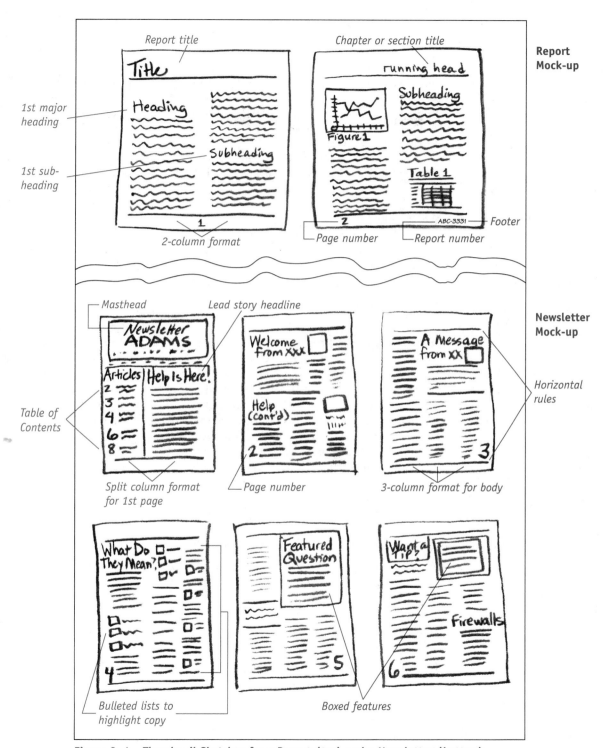

Figure 8–4 Thumbnail Sketches for a Report (*top*) and a Newsletter (*bottom*)

Columns

As you design pages, consider the size and number of columns. A single-column format works well with larger typefaces, double-spacing, and left-justified margins. For smaller typefaces and single-spaced lines, the two-column structure enhances legibility by keeping text columns narrow enough so readers need not scan back and forth across the width of the entire page for every line. Check your document for single words or parts of words that appear alone as first or last lines of your columns. Figure 8–5 shows the report in Figure 8–3 formatted in two columns.

White Space

White space visually frames information and breaks it into manageable chunks. For example, white space between paragraphs helps readers see the information in the paragraphs as units. Use extra white space between sections as a visual cue that one section is ending and another is beginning. You need not have access to sophisticated equipment to make good use of white space.

Left- or Full-Justified Margins

Left-justified margins are generally easier to read than full-justified margins because the uneven contour of the right margin (or "ragged" right) allows the spacing within and between words to be more uniform. Full justification causes your word-processing software to insert irregular-sized spaces between words, producing unwanted white space or unevenness in blocks of text, often making your document more difficult to read. Full-justified text is more appropriate for publications such as corporate annual reports, consumer booklets, sales brochures, and other documents aimed at a broad readership that expects a more formal, polished appearance. Full justification is often useful with multiple-column formats because the spaces between the columns (alleys) need the definition that full justification provides. Figure 8–6 shows left-justified (top) and full-justified (bottom) text columns.

W **On the Web**
For advice on using word-processing software to lay out your document, see Chapter 8, bedfordstmartins.com/writingthatworks

Lists

Lists are an effective way to highlight words, phrases, and short sentences. Further, they are easy to read. Lists are particularly useful for certain types of information:

- Steps in sequence
- Materials or parts needed
- Items to remember
- Criteria for evaluation
- Concluding points
- Recommendations

Avoid both too many lists and too many items in lists. See Chapter 5, pages 151–152, for more information about using lists effectively.

Optical and Handwritten Character Recognition Software: Recent Developments

Since the inception of computers, programmers have been teaching them to mimic humans. One such task that humans often take for granted is literacy. The process of reading printed text with a computer is called Optical Character Recognition (OCR). This method is optical because it uses a scanner to measure the reflected light off a piece of paper much like a copy machine does (Srihari and Lam 1–4). Along with OCR technology came handwriting recognition. Handwriting recognition occurs when the computer identifies each character the user writes with an electronic pen. Both OCR and handwriting recognition currently allow the computer almost 100 percent accuracy in understanding the writing of its human counterpart ("Looking Forward" 213).

What Are the Practical Applications?

OCR and handwriting recognition are used daily for such tasks as reading your tax forms and checking your passport at customs. The IRS, for example, receives about 200 million tax forms every year. So OCR is an important technology in processing tax forms because of OCR's

to 45,000 pieces of mail an hour (Srihari and Lam 12). . . .

How Does Scanning Work?

When the computer scans a page of text it does so graphically. All the computer sees at first is a grid of many small dots where each dot is either black or white. A typical scanner reads 300 of these dots per square inch.

The Letter R as printed (*left*) and as scanned into a matrix of dots (*right*).

In the first step of processing a page of text, the computer looks at the whole document and decides which regions contain text, and within those regions it searches for individual letters and numbers. The software then scans in dots

Figure 8–5   Page Formatted in Two Columns with Left-Justified Text

Illustrations

Readers notice illustrations, especially large ones, before they notice text. Therefore, choose the size of an illustration according to its relative importance within your document. For newsletter articles and publications aimed at wide audiences, consider especially the proportion of the illustration to the text. For magazine designers, for example, page layout is more dramatic and appealing when the major illustration (photograph, drawing, and so on) occupies three-fifths rather than half the available space. The same principle can be used to enhance the visual appeal of a report.

While aesthetic considerations are important, it's most important that your document is clear and useful. For example, it may be aesthetically pleasing to gather

Left-justified columns

Optical and Handwritten Character Recognition Software: Recent Developments

Since the inception of computers, programmers have been teaching them to mimic humans. One such task that humans often take for granted is literacy. The process of reading printed text with a computer is called Optical Character Recognition (OCR). This method is optical because it uses a scanner to measure the reflected light off a piece of paper much like a copy machine does (Srihari and Lam 1–4). Along with OCR technology came handwriting recognition. Handwriting recognition occurs when the computer identifies each character the user writes with an electronic pen. Both OCR and handwriting recognition currently allow the computer almost 100 percent accuracy in understanding the writing of its human counterpart ("Looking Forward" 213).

What Are the Practical Applications?
OCR and handwriting recognition are used daily for such tasks as reading your tax forms and checking your passport at customs. The IRS, for example, receives about 200 million tax forms every year. So OCR is an important technology in processing tax forms because of OCR's speed and accuracy combined with manual interpreta

to 45,000 pieces of mail an hour (Srihari and Lam 12). . . .

How Does Scanning Work?
When the computer scans a page of text it does so graphically. All the computer sees at first is a grid of many small dots where each dot is either black or white. A typical scanner reads 300 of these dots per square inch.

The Letter R as printed (*left*) and as scanned into a matrix of dots (*right*).

In the first step of processing a page of text, the computer looks at the whole document and decides which regions contain text, and within regions it searches for individual le

---

Full-justified columns

Optical and Handwritten Character Recognition Software: Recent Developments

Since the inception of computers, programmers have been teaching them to mimic humans. One such task that humans often take for granted is literacy. The process of reading printed text with a computer is called Optical Character Recognition (OCR). This method is optical because it uses a scanner to measure the reflected light off a piece of paper much like a copy machine does (Srihari and Lam 1–4). Along with OCR technology came handwriting recognition. Handwriting recognition occurs when the computer identifies each character the user writes with an electronic pen. Both OCR and handwriting recognition currently allow the computer almost 100 percent accuracy in understanding the writing of its human counterpart ("Looking Forward" 213).

What Are the Practical Applications?
OCR and handwriting recognition are used daily for such tasks as reading your tax forms and checking your passport at customs. The IRS, for example, receives about 200 million tax forms every year. So OCR is an important technology in processing tax forms because of OCR's speed and accuracy combined with manual interpretation

to 45,000 pieces of mail an hour (Srihari and Lam 12). . . .

How Does Scanning Work?
When the computer scans a page of text it does so graphically. All the computer sees at first is a grid of many small dots where each dot is either black or white. A typical scanner reads 300 of these dots per square inch.

The Letter R as printed (*left*) and as scanned into a matrix of dots (*right*).

In the first step of processing a page of text, the computer looks at the whole document and decides which regions contain text, and within regions it searches for individual le

Figure 8–6 Left-Justified (*top*) and Full-Justified (*bottom*) Text Columns

illustrations in one place (such as at the end of a report), but placing them in the text closer to their accompanying explanations makes them more effective and provides visual breaks from blocks of text. (Creating visuals and integrating them with text are discussed later in this chapter, beginning on page 267.)

Laying Out the Page

☐ Select typefaces for legibility in style and size, not simply for variety.

☐ Emphasize important information with consistent typographical and design devices, using:

- All-capital, italic, and boldface type styles selectively.
- Headings (in boldface type) to denote major sections and topic changes.
- Captions to identify figures and tables, and to emphasize boxed information.
- Headers and footers to orient readers at the page level.
- Rules, icons, and color to highlight crucial information.

☐ Integrate the typographical and page-level design elements into a consistent, coherent whole.

- Experiment with the positions of text and visuals on a variety of thumbnail sketches to evaluate how the elements look together.
- Create a mock-up copy of the whole document by assembling the thumbnail sketches for review.
- Experiment with one- and two-column text layouts.
- Allow adequate white space between paragraphs and around visuals and text boxes.
- Use lists to highlight comparable types of information by setting them off from the surrounding text.
- Position visuals in proportion to their importance and set them off with adequate white space.

■ Creating Printed Forms

Because they provide a timesaving, efficient, and uniform way to supply and record data, business forms are used for countless purposes in almost all occupations. A well-designed form saves time and effort for both the person filling it out and the person retrieving and evaluating the data. It is easier and quicker to supply information by filling out a well-designed form than by writing a memo, letter, or report. For the person gathering and interpreting data, the form provides each piece of information in the same place on every copy of a form—an important advantage to those gathering questionnaire responses or similar types of information from many people. Without a form, every sheet of paper submitted would be different and would require time-consuming reading and interpretation.

To create an effective form, first determine what kind of information you seek;

then make a pencil-and-paper draft of the form, putting in all the fields for information you've decided to include, arranged in the order you consider the most logical. The form should be logical from the point of view of the person supplying the data and the person receiving it, and, ideally, the form should be self-explanatory. (See Sequencing Data, page 263.)

If any coworkers will use the form, show the draft to them—you'll be rewarded for the extra time this step takes by the helpful criticism and suggestions they will likely provide. Once you're satisfied with the draft, prepare a final copy of the form using a forms-design software package, such as Omniform, Smartdraw, or PathMaker, to produce it.

Instructions and Captions

You've probably had the experience, at some time or another, of starting to fill out a form only to realize too late that you've put your name on the line intended for your street address. To prevent such confusion for your readers, provide clear instructions in the proper place.

Place instructions at the beginning of long or complicated forms.

INSTRUCTIONS FOR COMPLETING THIS FORM

1. Complete the applicable blue-shaded portions on the front of pages 1, 2, and 3.
2. Mail page 1 to the Securi-Med Insurance Company at the address shown above.
3. Give page 2 to your doctor.
4. If services were rendered in a hospital, give page 3 to the hospital.
5. Use the back of page 1 to itemize bills that are to go toward your major medical deduction.

Instructions for distributing the various copies of multiple-copy paper forms are normally placed at the bottom of the form. These instructions are repeated on every page of the form.

On the form itself, keep your requests for information brief and to the point; avoid repetition by combining requests for related pieces of information under an explanatory heading, such as the "Vehicle Information" heading in the second example that follows, and by simplifying requests to as few words as possible (such as "make" and "model") in the concise version of the following.

REPETITIOUS   What make of car do you drive? _____

What year was it manufactured? _____

What model is it? _____

What is the body style? _____

CONCISE   **Vehicle Information**

Make _____ Year _____

Model _____ Body style _____

Planning for Responses

Word questions in ways best suited to the types of data you hope to collect. In general, there are two types of questions: closed-ended questions and open-ended questions.

- *Closed-ended questions* provide a list of answers from which the respondent can select, limiting the range of possible responses. These questions are best used when you want to make sure you receive a standardized, easy-to-tabulate response. Some types of closed-ended questions are the following:
  - Multiple choice: Choose one (or sometimes more than one) from a list of options.
  - Ranked choice: Rank items in a list from best to worst, sweet to sour, and so on.
  - Forced choice: Choose true or false, good or bad, strong or weak, and so on.
- *Open-ended questions* allow respondents to answer in their own words. Such questions are most appropriate if you wish to elicit answers you may not have anticipated (as in a complaint form) or if there are too many possible answers to use a multiple-choice format. However, the responses to open-ended questions are difficult to tabulate and analyze.

Closed-ended questions permit readers to make check marks or circles or to underline their responses; next best, they allow readers to write numbers, single words, or brief phrases. Sentence responses, although necessary for open-ended questions, are the least effective because they take the most time to write and to read, and they can be difficult to analyze.

Make captions as specific as possible. For example, if the due date for the form is other than the date on which the form is being filled out, make the caption read "Effective date," "Date due," or whatever it may be, rather than simply "Date." As in all job-related writing, put yourself in your reader's place and try to imagine the sorts of requests that would be clear to you.

Sequencing Data

Try to arrange your requests for information in an order that will be most helpful to your reader. At the top of the form, include the title and any preliminary information, such as the name of the organization, the title of your form, a file number or reference number, and a privacy or confidentiality statement, if necessary. The title of the form should be concise, and it should describe the form's use and application, such as that in Figure 8–7. If space is critical, place the title in the top

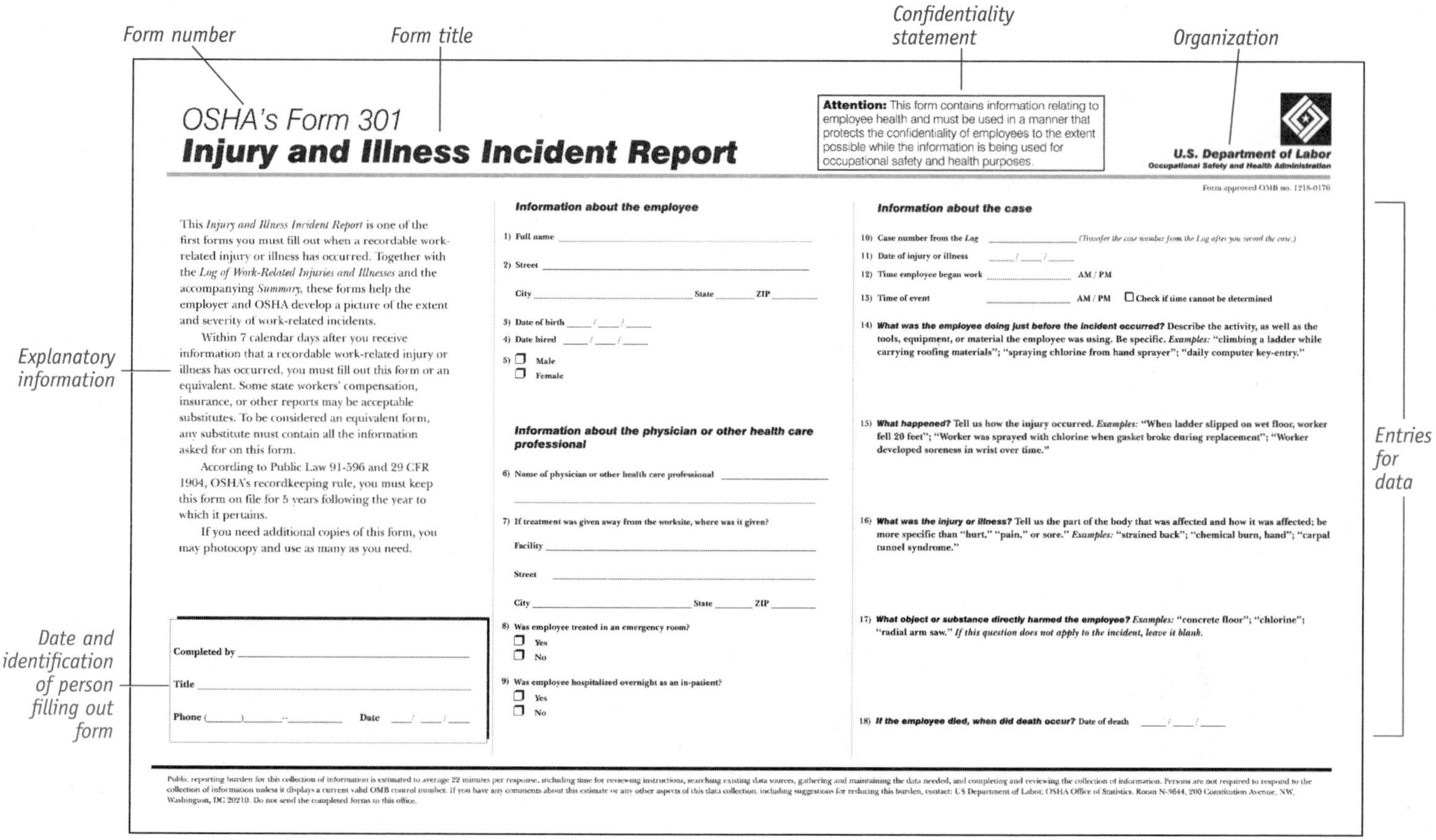

OSHA's Form 301
Injury and Illness Incident Report

Attention: This form contains information relating to employee health and must be used in a manner that protects the confidentiality of employees to the extent possible while the information is being used for occupational safety and health purposes.

U.S. Department of Labor
Occupational Safety and Health Administration

Form approved OMB no. 1218-0176

This *Injury and Illness Incident Report* is one of the first forms you must fill out when a recordable work-related injury or illness has occurred. Together with the *Log of Work-Related Injuries and Illnesses* and the accompanying *Summary*, these forms help the employer and OSHA develop a picture of the extent and severity of work-related incidents.

Within 7 calendar days after you receive information that a recordable work-related injury or illness has occurred, you must fill out this form or an equivalent. Some state workers' compensation, insurance, or other reports may be acceptable substitutes. To be considered an equivalent form, any substitute must contain all the information asked for on this form.

According to Public Law 91-596 and 29 CFR 1904, OSHA's recordkeeping rule, you must keep this form on file for 5 years following the year to which it pertains.

If you need additional copies of this form, you may photocopy and use as many as you need.

Completed by ______
Title ______
Phone (___)___-___ Date ___/___/___

Information about the employee

1) Full name ______
2) Street ______
City ______ State ______ ZIP ______
3) Date of birth ___/___/___
4) Date hired ___/___/___
5) ☐ Male
☐ Female

Information about the physician or other health care professional

6) Name of physician or other health care professional ______
7) If treatment was given away from the worksite, where was it given?
Facility ______
Street ______
City ______ State ______ ZIP ______
8) Was employee treated in an emergency room?
☐ Yes
☐ No
9) Was employee hospitalized overnight as an in-patient?
☐ Yes
☐ No

Information about the case

10) Case number from the *Log* ______ (*Transfer the case number from the Log after you record the case.*)
11) Date of injury or illness ___/___/___
12) Time employee began work ______ AM / PM
13) Time of event ______ AM / PM ☐ Check if time cannot be determined
14) ***What was the employee doing just before the incident occurred?*** Describe the activity, as well as the tools, equipment, or material the employee was using. Be specific. *Examples:* "climbing a ladder while carrying roofing materials"; "spraying chlorine from hand sprayer"; "daily computer key-entry."
15) ***What happened?*** Tell us how the injury occurred. *Examples:* "When ladder slipped on wet floor, worker fell 20 feet"; "Worker was sprayed with chlorine when gasket broke during replacement"; "Worker developed soreness in wrist over time."
16) ***What was the injury or illness?*** Tell us the part of the body that was affected and how it was affected; be more specific than "hurt," "pain," or sore." *Examples:* "strained back"; "chemical burn, hand"; "carpal tunnel syndrome."
17) ***What object or substance directly harmed the employee?*** *Examples:* "concrete floor"; "chlorine"; "radial arm saw." *If this question does not apply to the incident, leave it blank.*
18) ***If the employee died, when did death occur?*** Date of death ___/___/___

Public reporting burden for this collection of information is estimated to average 22 minutes per response, including time for reviewing instructions, searching existing data sources, gathering and maintaining the data needed, and completing and reviewing the collection of information. Persons are not required to respond to the collection of information unless it displays a current valid OMB control number. If you have any comments about this estimate or any other aspects of this data collection, including suggestions for reducing this burden, contact: US Department of Labor, OSHA Office of Statistics, Room N-3644, 200 Constitution Avenue, NW, Washington, DC 20210. Do not send the completed forms to this office.

Figure 8–7 Form with Sequence Helpful to Reader *Source:* Occupational Safety and Health Administration.

left-hand corner of the form. In the main portion of the form, include the entries you need to obtain the necessary data. At the end of the form, include space for the signature of the person filling out the form and the date if they are necessary.

Within the main portion of your form, the arrangement of the entries will depend on several factors. The subject matter of the entries will frequently determine the most logical order. A form requesting reimbursement for travel expenses, for instance, would logically begin with the first day of the week (or month) and end with the last day of the appropriate period. If the response to one item is based on the response to another item, be sure that the items appear in the correct order. Whenever possible, group requests for related information together. If a form is to move from one individual or one department to another, to be partly filled out by each in turn, put the data to be supplied by the first individual or department at the top of the form, the data to be supplied by the second next, and so on. Regardless of the sequence, arrange each section of the form in the manner that we read—from left to right and from top to bottom.

Entry Lines

When you prepare a form to be filled out manually in pen or pencil, pay particular attention to the arrangement of the entry lines on which the responses will be filled in. The form can be laid out so that the person completing it supplies information on a writing line, in a writing block, or in square boxes. The writing line is simply a rule with a caption:

❑   **Name:** _____

The writing block is essentially the same as a writing line except that each entry is enclosed in a ruled block, making it easy for the person filling out the form to associate a caption with the correct line, as follows.

NAME		TELEPHONE
STREET ADDRESS		
CITY	STATE	ZIP CODE

On some forms, the captions are arranged horizontally, as in the previous example. On other forms, they are listed vertically, as follows.

DESTINATION	
SOURCE	
SUPPLIER	
METHOD OF SHIPMENT	

When all possible responses to questions can be anticipated, such as for closed-ended questions, you can save your reader time and effort by supplying a labeled check box for each possible answer. Such a design will also save you time and effort in retrieving the data.

EXAMPLE   Would you buy another Matrix computer?   ☐ Yes   ☐ No

The boxes may either precede or follow the question. Be sure, however, that the boxes and their labels are spaced so that the boxes will not be mistakenly associated with the wrong labels.

Spacing

Be sure to provide enough space for the person filling out the form to enter the data. Everyone has filled out a form on which the address, signature, or other information could not possibly fit in the space allowed for it. Such forms frustrate the user, make the information supplied hard to read, and increase the possibility of introducing errors as you retrieve the data.

DESIGNING YOUR DOCUMENT

Creating Forms

☐ Organize the questions in a logical order.

☐ Reduce repetition by grouping related requests under a common heading.

☐ Arrange the form so that it can be read and filled out from top to bottom and left to right.

☐ Word closed-ended questions with options that can be answered with check marks, circles, or underlining; minimize the use of open-ended questions, which require a narrative response.

☐ Design information entry lines or boxes with sufficient space.

☐ Ensure that the form is self-explanatory.

☐ Use the top of the form for the title, explanatory information, and instructions for filling out and submitting the form.

☐ If necessary, include a privacy or confidentiality statement to inform users of whether their responses are protected from disclosure.

☐ Circulate a draft of the form for review before printing and distributing it.

CONSIDERING AUDIENCE AND PURPOSE

Evaluating Form Design

☐ Who is the audience for your form?

☐ Can your audience understand the purpose of the form from the title? from the instructions?

☐ Are the questions sequenced logically for your audience?

☐ Do the instructions explain where your audience should submit the completed form?

☐ Does a confidentiality or privacy statement inform your audience that their information is protected from improper disclosure?

■ Creating Visuals

Designing and Integrating Visuals with Text

Tables allow the easy comparison of large numbers of statistics that would be difficult to understand if they appeared in sentence form. Graphs make trends and mathematical relationships immediately evident. Drawings, photographs, charts, and maps render shapes and spatial relationships more concisely and efficiently than text can. By allowing the reader to interpret data at a glance, visuals not only encourage faster decision-making but may add to the persuasiveness of your document or Web site.

When using tables and illustrations, consider your purpose and your reader carefully. For example, a drawing of the major regions of the brain for a high school science class would be different from an illustration provided for research scientists studying brain abnormalities. Be aware, though, that even the best visual only enhances, or supports, the text. It is your writing that must carry the burden of providing context for the visual and pointing out its significance.

To make the most effective use of visuals and to integrate them smoothly with the text of your document, consider your graphics requirements even before you begin to write. Plan your visuals—tables, graphs, drawings, charts, maps, or photographs—when you're planning the scope and organization of your final work, whether it's a report, newsletter, brochure, presentation, or Web site. Make graphics an integral part of your outline, noting approximately where each should appear throughout the text. At each place where you plan to include a visual, either make a rough sketch of the visual or write "illustration of . . ." and enclose each suggestion in a box in your outline. If you are working on your computer, you can copy and paste graphics directly into your outline at the appropriate places using your computer's clipboard feature. As noted in Chapter 2, outlines are a means to an end, not an end in themselves, so like other information in an outline, these boxes and sketches can be moved, revised, or deleted as required.

Plan your graphics from the beginning stages of your outline so that they will be integrated throughout all versions of the draft to the finished work. The following guidelines, which apply to most visual materials you might use to supplement or clarify the information in your text, will help you create and incorporate your visual materials within your documents effectively.

1. **Why include your visual?** Make clear in the text why you've included the illustration. The amount of description each visual requires will vary with its complexity and its importance to your document. Consider your readers' backgrounds: nonexperts require lengthier explanations than experts do, as a rule.

2. **Is the information in your visual accurate?** Be sure to gather the information in your visual from reliable sources. Review the guidance in Chapter 7 on evaluating Internet and library sources, pages 213–217.

3. **Is your visual focused?** To keep your illustration to the point, include only information necessary to the discussion in the text and eliminate unnecessary labels, arrows, boxes, and lines.

4. **Are terms and symbols in your visual defined and consistent?** Keep terminology consistent. Do not refer to something as a "proportion" in the text and as a "percentage" in the illustration. Define all acronyms in the text, figure, or table. If any symbols are not self-explanatory, include a listing (known as a *key*) that defines them.

5. **Does your visual specify measurements and distances?** Specify the units of measurement used or include a scale of relative distances, when appropriate. Ensure that relative sizes are clear or indicate distance by a scale, as on a map.

6. **Is the lettering readable?** Position the lettering of any explanatory text or labels horizontally for ease of reading, if possible.

7. **Is the title clear?** Give each illustration a concise title that clearly describes its contents.

8. **Is there a figure or table number?** Assign a figure or table number, if your final product is a document containing five or more illustrations. The figure or table number precedes the title:

   ■ Figure 1. Projected sales for 2004–2005

   Note that graphics (photographs, drawings, maps, etc.) are generically labeled "figures," while tables are labeled "tables."

9. **Is a list of figures or tables needed?** In documents with more than five illustrations, list the illustrations by title, together with figure and page numbers, or table and page numbers, following the table of contents. The figures so listed should be titled "List of Figures." The tables so listed should be titled "List of Tables."

10. **Are figure or table numbers referred to in your text?** Refer to each illustration by its figure or table number in the text of documents.

11. **Are visuals appropriately placed in your text?** If an illustration is central to a discussion, place it as close as possible to the text where it is discussed. However, no illustration should appear before it is mentioned in your text. If an illustration is lengthy and detailed, place it in an appendix and be sure to refer to the illustration in the text of your document.

12. **Do visuals stand out from surrounding text?** Allow adequate white space on the page around and within each illustration.

13. **Are sources for your visuals acknowledged?** If you wish to use an illustration that is copyrighted, first obtain written permission from the copyright holder. Acknowledge such borrowings in a source or credit line below the caption for a figure and below any footnotes at the bottom of a table. Information that is not copyrighted (that is in the public domain) can be used without obtaining written permission to reproduce it. Publications of the federal government, for example, are not copyrighted, but you should acknowledge their source in a credit line. (Such a credit line appears in Figure 8–7.)

A discussion of visuals commonly used in on-the-job writing follows. Your topic will ordinarily determine the best type of visual to use.

(If you have an international audience, be sure to read Using Graphics to Communicate Internationally, beginning on page 295, as well as Writer's Checklist: Using International Graphics on page 297.)

Tables

A table is useful for showing large numbers of specific, related data in a brief space. The data may be numerical, as in Figure 8–8, or verbal, as in Table 8–1 (on page 296). Because a table displays information in rows and columns, your readers can easily compare data and see its significance more clearly than if it were presented in the text.

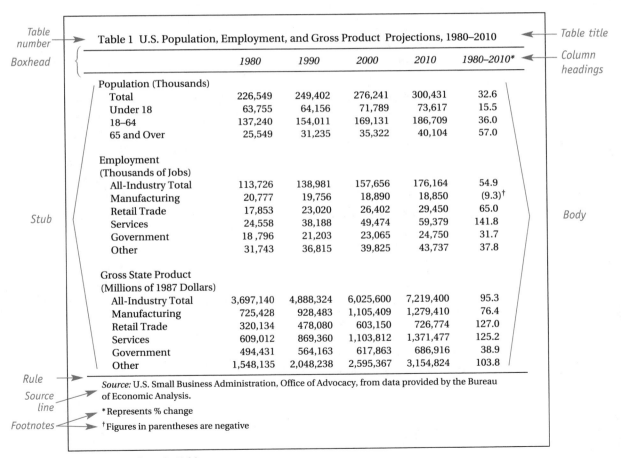

Table 1 U.S. Population, Employment, and Gross Product Projections, 1980–2010

	1980	1990	2000	2010	1980–2010*
Population (Thousands)					
Total	226,549	249,402	276,241	300,431	32.6
Under 18	63,755	64,156	71,789	73,617	15.5
18–64	137,240	154,011	169,131	186,709	36.0
65 and Over	25,549	31,235	35,322	40,104	57.0
Employment (Thousands of Jobs)					
All-Industry Total	113,726	138,981	157,656	176,164	54.9
Manufacturing	20,777	19,756	18,890	18,850	(9.3)†
Retail Trade	17,853	23,020	26,402	29,450	65.0
Services	24,558	38,188	49,474	59,379	141.8
Government	18,796	21,203	23,065	24,750	31.7
Other	31,743	36,815	39,825	43,737	37.8
Gross State Product (Millions of 1987 Dollars)					
All-Industry Total	3,697,140	4,888,324	6,025,600	7,219,400	95.3
Manufacturing	725,428	928,483	1,105,409	1,279,410	76.4
Retail Trade	320,134	478,080	603,150	726,774	127.0
Services	609,012	869,360	1,103,812	1,371,477	125.2
Government	494,431	564,163	617,863	686,916	38.9
Other	1,548,135	2,048,238	2,595,367	3,154,824	103.8

Source: U.S. Small Business Administration, Office of Advocacy, from data provided by the Bureau of Economic Analysis.

*Represents % change

†Figures in parentheses are negative

Labels (left side): Table number, Boxhead, Stub, Rule, Source line, Footnotes

Labels (right side): Table title, Column headings, Body

Figure 8–8   Sample Table

Following are the elements of a typical table, as shown in Figure 8–8, with guidelines.

- *Table number.* Number each table sequentially throughout the text.
- *Table title.* Create a title that describes concisely what the table represents; place it above the table.
- *Boxhead.* In the boxhead (beneath the title) provide column headings that are brief but descriptive. Include units of measurement either as part of the heading or enclosed in parentheses beneath it. Standard abbreviations and symbols are acceptable. Avoid vertical or diagonal lettering.
- *Stub.* In the left-hand vertical column of a table, called the stub, list all the items to be shown in the body of the table.
- *Body.* Provide data in the body of your table below the column headings and to the right of the stub. (Each datum element is located in a *cell.*) Within the body, arrange columns so that the terms to be compared appear in adjacent rows and columns. Where no information exists for a specific cell, substitute a row of dots or a dash to acknowledge the gap. If you substitute the abbreviation "N/A" for missing data in a cell, add a footnote to clarify whether it means "not available" or "not applicable."
- *Rules.* Use rules (lines) to separate your table into its various parts. Include horizontal rules below the title, below the body of the table, and between the column headings and the body of the table. You may include vertical rules to separate the columns, but do not use rules to enclose the sides of the table.
- *Source line.* Below the table, include a source line to identify where you obtained the data (when appropriate). Many organizations place the source line below the footnotes.
- *Footnotes.* Include a footnote when you need to explain an item in the table. Use symbols (*, †) or lowercase letters (sometimes in parentheses) rather than numbers to make it clear that the notes are not part of the data or the main text.
- *Continuing tables.* When you must divide your table to continue it on another page, repeat the column headings and give the table number at the head of each new page with a "continued" label ("Table 3, continued"), as shown in Figure 8–9.

To list relatively few items that would be easier for the reader to grasp in tabular form, use an informal table.

■ The sound-intensity levels (decibels) for the three frequency bands (in hertz) were determined to be:

Frequency Band (Hz)	Decibels
600–1200	68
1200–2400	62
2400–4800	53

Table 4

Assessment of Electronic Media and Format Standards in Federal Agencies: Number, Percent, and Basis for Use by Agency

Format	Standard for each format used							
	Agency mandated		Common agency practice		Other		None	
	Number	Percent	Number	Percent	Number	Percent	Number	Percent
Database								
Oracle	7	38.9	8	44.4	1	5.6	1	5.6
WAIS	1	4.3	21	91.3	0	0.0	0	0.0
MARC	1	33.3	1	33.3	0	0.0	0	0.0
Sybase	0	0.0	4	80.0	0	0.0	0	0.0
dBase	0	0.0	8	80.0	0	0.0	0	0.0
Other	2	4.4	21	46.7	12	26.7	9	20.0
Spreadsheet								
Lotus 1-2-3	6	25.0	9	37.5	3	12.5	5	20.8
Excel	4	11.8	24	70.6	0	0.0	4	11.8
Other	0	0.0	0	0.0	0	0.0	2	50.0
Tagged markup								
HTML	21	13.3	114	72.2	6	3.8	15	9.5
SGML	2	13.3	9	60.0	2	13.3	1	6.7
XML	0	0.0	1	33.3	0	0.0	1	33.3
Other	0	0.0	7	53.8	1	7.7	4	30.8
Image								

Table 4, continued

Assessment of Electronic Media and Format Standards in Federal Agencies: Number, Percent, and Basis for Use by Agency

Format	Standard for each format used							
	Agency mandated		Common agency practice		Other		None	
	Number	Percent	Number	Percent	Number	Percent	Number	Percent
Audio								
WAV	2	15.4	8	61.5	0	0.0	2	15.4
AU	4	66.7	0	0.0	0	0.0	1	16.7
AIFF	1	50.0	0	0.0	0	0.0	0	0.0
Other	0	0.0	1	20.0	2	40.0	1	20.0
Video								
MOV	0	0.0	5	62.5	0	0.0	2	25.0
MPEG	1	10.0	5	50.0	1	10.0	2	20.0
AVI	1	20.0	3	60.0	0	0.0	0	0.0
Other	0	0.0	0	0.0	1	50.0	0	0.0
Text								
ASCII	21	13.3	87	70.7	6	4.9	15	9.5

Figure 8–9   Divided Table (Continued on a Second Page)

Although you need not include titles or table numbers to identify informal tables, you do need to include headings that describe the information provided and columns and rows that are properly aligned.

DESIGNING
YOUR
DOCUMENT

Creating Tables

☐ Use tables to present data that you want readers to quickly evaluate and compare, and that would be difficult or tedious to present in your main text.

☐ Identify each table with a concise, descriptive title and a unique table number.

☐ Use horizontal lettering, if possible.

☐ Do not enclose the left and right sides with vertical rules.

☐ Include a source line when necessary to identify where you obtained your data.

☐ For tables continued on another page, repeat the table number (followed by "continued"), title, and column headings.

☐ Use informal tables — those without a title or number — when there are only a few items to categorize.

Graphs

Graphs, also called *charts,* present numerical data in visual form, showing trends, movements, distributions, and cycles more readily than tables do. Although graphs present statistics in a format that is easy to understand, they are less accurate than tables. For this reason, they are often accompanied by tables that give exact numbers. (Note the difference between the graph and table showing the same data in Figure 8–10.) To solve the problem of showing only approximate data in graphs, you can include the exact data for each column—if this will not clutter your graph—giving the reader both a quick overview of the data and accurate numbers. (See Figures 8–11 and 8–15.) The most commonly used graphs are line graphs, bar graphs, pie graphs, and picture graphs, all of which you can easily render on your computer once you have entered your data into a spreadsheet or database application.

Line Graphs

The line graph shows the relationship between two or more sets of figures. The graph is composed of a vertical axis and a horizontal axis that intersect at right angles, each representing one set of data. The relationship between the two sets is readily indicated by points plotted along appropriate intersections of the two axes that are then connected to form a continuous line.

The line graph's vertical axis usually represents amounts, and its horizontal axis usually represents increments of time (Figure 8–11).

Line graphs with more than one plotted line allow for comparisons between two sets of data. In creating such graphs, label each plotted line, as shown in Figure 8–12. You can emphasize the difference between the two lines by

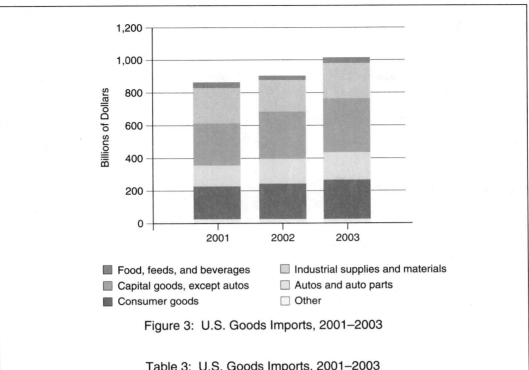

Figure 3: U.S. Goods Imports, 2001–2003

Table 3: U.S. Goods Imports, 2001–2003

Imports	2001	2002	2003	02–03	98–03	96–03
	Billions of Dollars			*Percent Change*		
Total (BOP Basis)*	876.4	917.2	1,030.2	12.3	54.1	92.0
Food, feeds, and beverages	39.7	41.2	43.6	5.7	40.6	57.9
Industrial supplies and materials	213.8	200.1	222.6	10.7	36.7	59.9
Capital goods, except autos	253.3	269.6	296.9	10.1	61.0	121.0
Autos and auto parts	139.8	149.1	179.5	20.4	51.7	95.6
Consumer goods	193.8	216.5	239.6	10.7	63.8	95.3
Other	29.3	35.4	43.9	24.1	106.1	148.0

Source: U.S. Department of Commerce.
*Balance of Payment Basis for Total. Census Basis for Sectors.

Figure 8–10   Graph and Table Showing the Same Data

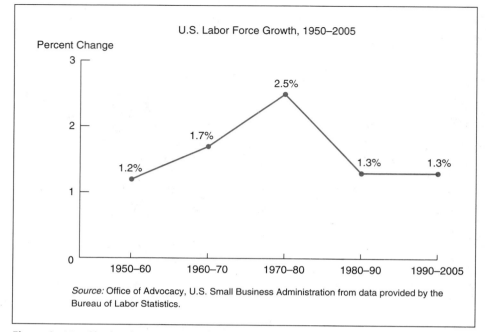

*Vertical axis shows
quantity, and
horizontal axis
shows time
increments*

Figure 8–11   Single-Line Graph

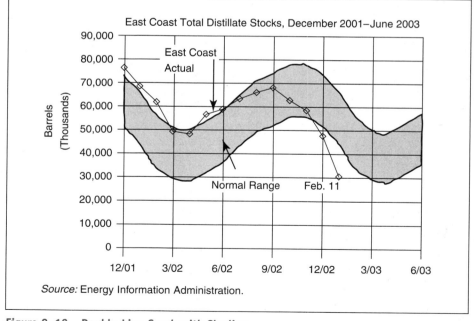

*Actual data plotted
with normal range
shaded to highlight
difference*

Figure 8–12   Double-Line Graph with Shading

shading the space that separates them. The following guidelines apply to most line graphs:

1. Give your graph a title that describes the data clearly and concisely.

2. Indicate the zero point of the graph (the point where the two axes meet). If the range of data makes it inconvenient to begin at zero, insert a break in the scale, as in Figure 8–13; otherwise, the graph would show a large area with no data.

3. Divide the vertical axis into equal portions, from the least amount at the bottom to the greatest amount at the top. The caption for this scale may be placed at the upper left (as in Figure 8–11), or, as is more often the case, vertically along the vertical axis (as in Figure 8–12).

4. Divide the horizontal axis into equal units from left to right, and label them to show what values each represents.

5. Include enough points to plot—accurately depict—the data; too few data points will distort depiction of the trends (Figure 8–14).

6. Keep grid lines to a minimum so that the curved lines stand out. Detailed grid lines are unnecessary because precise values are usually shown either on the graph or in an accompanying table.

7. Include a label or a key when necessary to define symbols or visual cues to the data, such as in the box below the data in Figure 8–16.

8. Include a source line under the graph at the lower left, indicating where you obtained the data (Figures 8–8 and 8–10 through 8–12).

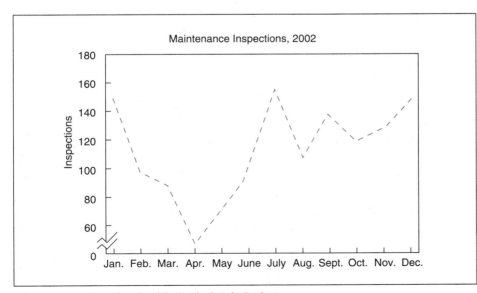

Break in vertical scale to emphasize the zero point

Figure 8–13   Line Graph with Vertical Axis Broken

9. Present all type horizontally if possible, although the type for the vertical-axis caption is usually presented vertically (Figure 8–12).

Be sure to proportion the vertical and horizontal scales so they present data precisely and without visual distortion — to do otherwise is inaccurate and potentially unethical. (See also Ethical Issues and Revision in Chapter 5, pages 155–157.) In Figure 8–14, the graph on the left gives the appearance of a dramatic decrease in the number and rate of accidents because the scale is compressed and some of the data are omitted. The graph on the right, which includes more data, more accurately represents the information.

Time increments (right) expanded to render data free of distortion

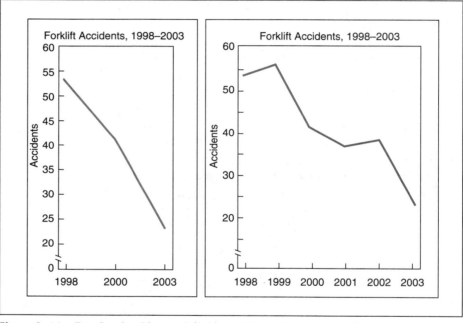

Figure 8–14 Two Graphs: Distorted (*left*) and Distortion-Free (*right*)

Bar Graphs

Bar graphs consist of horizontal or vertical bars of equal width but scaled in length or height to represent some quantity. They are commonly used to show the following proportional relations:

- Different types of information during different periods of time (Figure 8–15)
- Quantities of the same kind of information at different points in time (Figure 8–16)
- Quantities of different information during a fixed period of time (Figure 8–17)
- Quantities of the different parts that make up a whole (Figure 8–18)

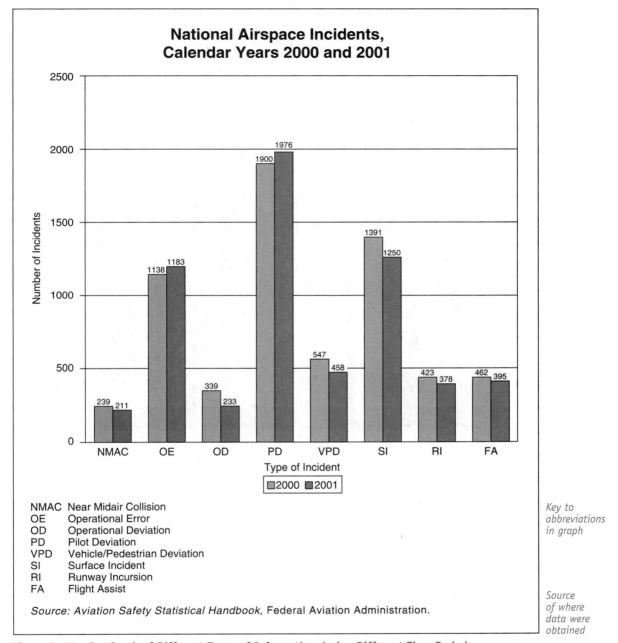

**National Airspace Incidents,
Calendar Years 2000 and 2001**

NMAC Near Midair Collision
OE   Operational Error
OD   Operational Deviation
PD   Pilot Deviation
VPD   Vehicle/Pedestrian Deviation
SI   Surface Incident
RI   Runway Incursion
FA   Flight Assist

*Key to
abbreviations
in graph*

Source: Aviation Safety Statistical Handbook, Federal Aviation Administration.

*Source
of where
data were
obtained*

Figure 8–15   Bar Graph of Different Types of Information during Different Time Periods

Bar graph with table of specific data for each month

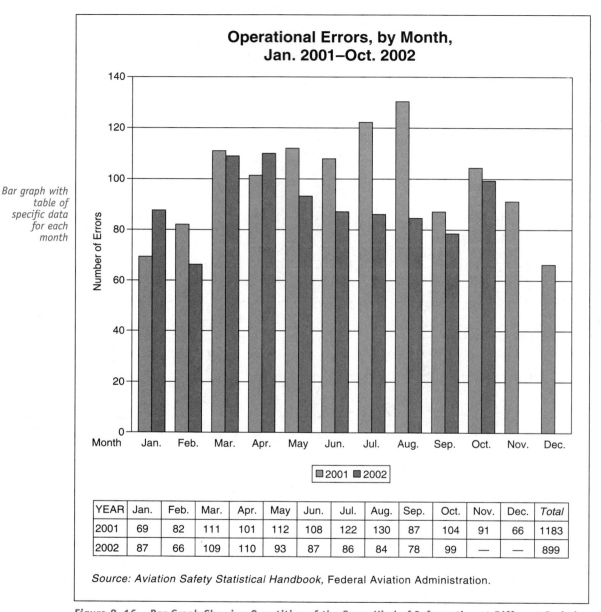

Operational Errors, by Month, Jan. 2001–Oct. 2002

YEAR	Jan.	Feb.	Mar.	Apr.	May	Jun.	Jul.	Aug.	Sep.	Oct.	Nov.	Dec.	*Total*
2001	69	82	111	101	112	108	122	130	87	104	91	66	1183
2002	87	66	109	110	93	87	86	84	78	99	—	—	899

Source: Aviation Safety Statistical Handbook, Federal Aviation Administration.

Figure 8–16   Bar Graph Showing Quantities of the Same Kind of Information at Different Periods of Time

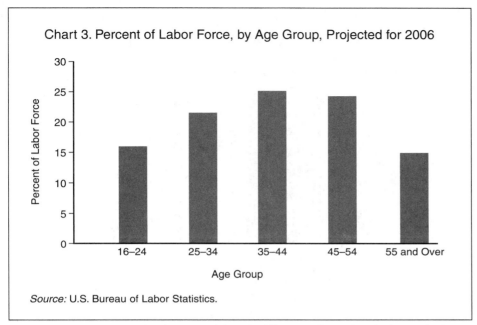

Chart 3. Percent of Labor Force, by Age Group, Projected for 2006

Source: U.S. Bureau of Labor Statistics.

Figure 8–17   Bar Graph Showing Quantities of Different Information during a Fixed Period of Time

Bar graphs can also indicate what proportion of a whole the various component parts represent. In such a graph, the bar, which is theoretically equivalent to 100 percent, is divided according to the proportion of the whole that each item sampled represents. (Compare the displays of the same data in Figures 8–18 and 8–20.) In some bar graphs, the completed bar does not represent 100 percent because not all parts of the whole have been included or not all are pertinent in the sample (Figure 8–19). Bar graphs are also used to track project schedules, where each bar represents the time allotted for each task of a project. A project-tracking bar graph, also called a *timeline graph,* is shown in Figure 6–4, page 185.

Note that in Figure 8–21, a type of bar graph showing travel frequency, the exact quantities appear at the end of each picture column, eliminating the need to have an accompanying table giving the percentages. If the bars are not labeled, as in Figures 8–16 and 8–19, the different portions must be clearly indicated by shading, cross-hatching, or other devices. Include a key that represents the various subdivisions.

Pie Graphs

A pie graph presents data as wedge-shaped sections of a circle. The circle equals 100 percent, or the whole, of some quantity (a tax dollar, a bus fare, the hours of a working day), with the wedges representing the various parts into which the whole is divided. In Figure 8–20, for example, the circle stands for a city tax dollar and is divided into units equivalent to the percentages of the tax dollar spent on various city services. Note that the slice representing salaries is slightly offset

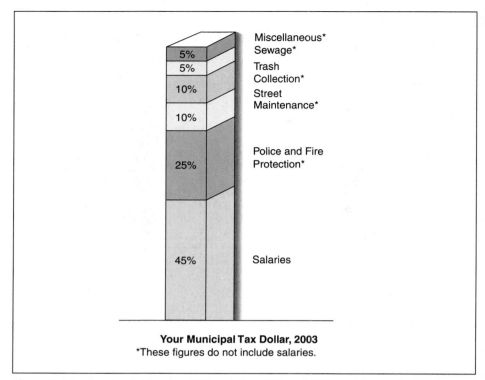

Explanatory note clarifies data

Figure 8–18 Bar Graph Showing Different Quantities of Different Parts of a Whole

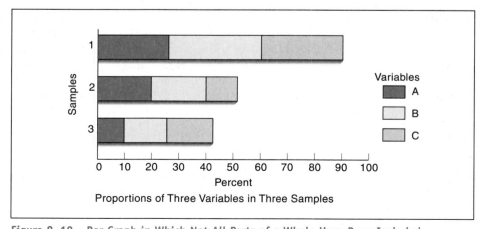

Figure 8–19 Bar Graph in Which Not All Parts of a Whole Have Been Included

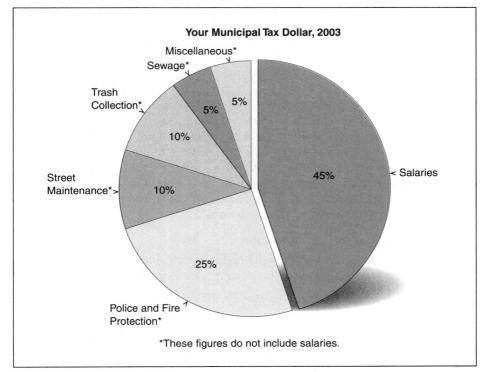

Figure 8-20   Exploded Pie Graph (Same Data as Figure 8-18)

(exploded) from the others to emphasize that data. This feature is commonly available on computer software that produces pie graphs.

The relationships among the various statistics presented in a pie graph are easy to grasp, but the information is often general. For this reason, a pie graph is often accompanied by a table that presents the actual figures on which the percentages in the graph are based.

Following are guidelines for constructing pie graphs:

1. Keep in mind that the complete 360° circle is equivalent to 100 percent.
2. When possible, begin at the 12 o'clock position and sequence the wedges clockwise, from largest to smallest. (This is not always possible because the default setting for some charting software sequences the data counterclockwise.)
3. Apply a distinctive pattern or various shades of gray for each wedge.
4. Keep all labels horizontal and, most important, provide the percentage value of each wedge.
5. Check to see that all wedges and their respective percentages add up to 100 percent.

Although pie graphs have a strong visual impact, they also have drawbacks. If more than five or six items of information are presented, the graph looks cluttered and, unless percentages are labeled on each section, the reader cannot compare the values of the sections as accurately as on a bar graph.

Picture Graphs

Picture graphs (also called *pictograms*) are modified bar graphs that use picture symbols to represent the item for which data are presented. Each symbol corresponds to a specified quantity of the item, as shown in Figure 8–21. Note that exact percentages are also included because the picture symbol can indicate only approximate figures. Pictograms usually work well for nonexpert audiences because they make the data more vivid and easier to remember. They are also popular in presentations because they add an element of entertainment to the data. Here are some tips on preparing picture graphs:

1. Use symbols that are self-explanatory.
2. Have each symbol represent a specific number of units and be sure to include accurate numerical quantities for each row of data.
3. Show larger quantities by increasing the number of symbols rather than by creating a larger symbol.

Quantity increases represented by increased number of symbols

Quantity for each symbol specified

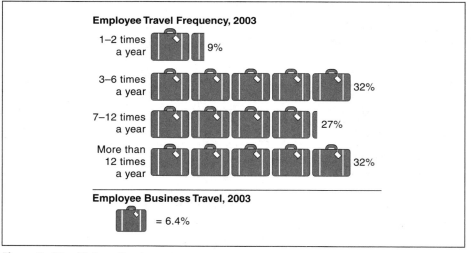

Figure 8–21   Picture Graph

Dimensional-Column Graphs

Consider a common on-the-job reporting requirement—tracking a series of expenses over a given period of time. Assume that you wish to show your company's expenses over a three-month period for security, courier, mail, and custodial services. Once you enter the data for these services into a spreadsheet program, you can display them in a variety of graph styles. As you select from among the options

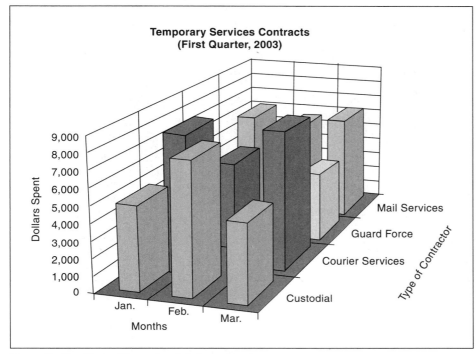

Three-dimensional columns obscure data for February and March

Figure 8–22   Three-Dimensional Column Graph

available, keep in mind your reader's need to interpret the data accurately and quickly, so keep the graph style as simple as possible for the information shown.

Graphs that depict columns as three-dimensional pillars are popular—they give the data a solid, three-dimensional, building-block appearance. They can, however, obscure rather than clarify the information, depending on how they are displayed. Consider the graph in Figure 8–22. Although the data are accurate, they cannot be interpreted as shown. The axis showing expenditures cannot be correlated with most columns representing the various services. The graph also obscures the columns for courier and guard-force services. Finally, this graph style does not allow readers to spot trends for expenditures over the three-month period, which is key information to decision-makers.

The graph in Figure 8–23 presents more clearly the same data as that shown in Figure 8–22. The trends of expenditures are easy to spot, and all the data are at least visible. Yet this graph is not ideal. To interpret the information, the reader would need to put a ruler on the page and align the tops of the columns with the axis showing expenditures.

The three-dimensional appearance can also cause confusion: Is the front or back of each column the correct data point? Also somewhat confusing is that, at first glance, the reader is tricked into interpreting the spaces between the column clusters as columns because they are of equal width.

The graphs in Figures 8–24 and 8–25 would best represent the data, depending on your intent. Figure 8–24 avoids the ambiguity of the graph in Figure 8–23 by

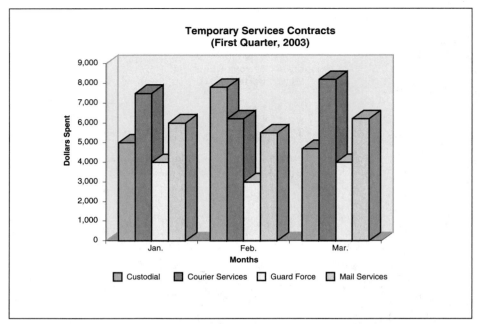

Tops of three-dimensional columns cannot be interpreted without a ruler

Figure 8–23   Three-Dimensional Column Graph (Same Data as in Figure 8–22)

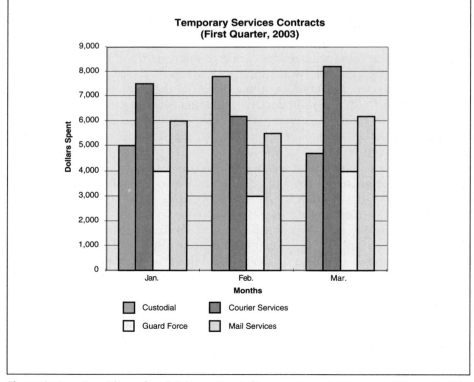

Two-dimensional columns make data easy to interpret at a glance

Figure 8–24   Two-Dimensional Column Graph (Same Data as in Figures 8–22 and 8–23)

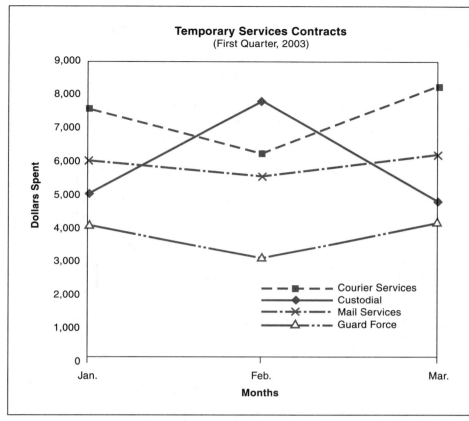

Line graph makes data trends easy to interpret at a glance

Figure 8–25   Line Graph (Same Data as in Figures 8–22 through 8–24)

showing the data in two dimensions. It also displays the horizontal lines for expenditures on the vertical axis, thus making the data for each column easier to interpret. If you wished to show relative expenses among the four variables for a given quarter, this graph would be ideal. However, if you wished to show trends for the entire three-month period in contract expenditures at a glance, the graph in Figure 8–25 is preferable.

When precise dollar amounts for each service are equally important, you can provide a table showing that information.

As Figures 8–22 through 8–25 show, the more complicated a graph looks, the harder it is to interpret. On balance, simpler is better for the reader. Use this principle when you review your computer graphics on-screen in several styles and consider your reader's needs before deciding which style to use.

Drawings

A drawing is useful when your reader needs an impression of an object's general appearance or an overview of a series of steps or directions. Note, for example, the sequence of drawings in Chapter 13 that show the steps used to install a waste

W **On the Web**
For access to image libraries on the Web, see Chapter 8, bedfordstmartins.com/ writingthatworks

disposer (Figure 13–2). Drawings are the best choice when you need to focus on details or relationships that a photograph cannot capture. A drawing can emphasize the significant piece of a mechanism, or its function, and omit what is not significant—for example, a cutaway drawing can show the internal parts of a piece of equipment in such a way that their relationship to the overall equipment is clear (Figure 8–26). An exploded-view drawing can show the proper sequence in which parts fit together or the details of each individual part (Figure 8–27).

Drawings are also the best option for illustrating simple objects or tasks that do not require photography (Figure 8–28). However, if the actual appearance of an object (a dented fender) or a phenomenon (an aircraft wind-tunnel experiment) is necessary to your document, a photograph is essential.

For drawings that require a high degree of accuracy and precision, seek the help of a graphics specialist. For general-interest images needed to illustrate newsletters and brochures, search the clip-art libraries provided with word-processing programs, graphics programs, and the numerous image libraries available on the Web. These sources contain thousands of noncopyrighted symbols, shapes, and images of people, equipment, furniture, buildings, and the like.

Many organizations have their own format specifications for drawings. In the absence of such specifications, the following guidelines should be helpful:

1. Show the equipment from the point of view of the person who will use it.

2. When illustrating part of a system, show its relationship to the larger system of which it is a part.

Cutaway shows internal structure of a device (hard disk drive)

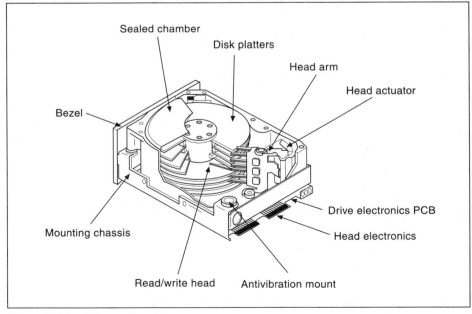

Figure 8–26 Cutaway Drawing

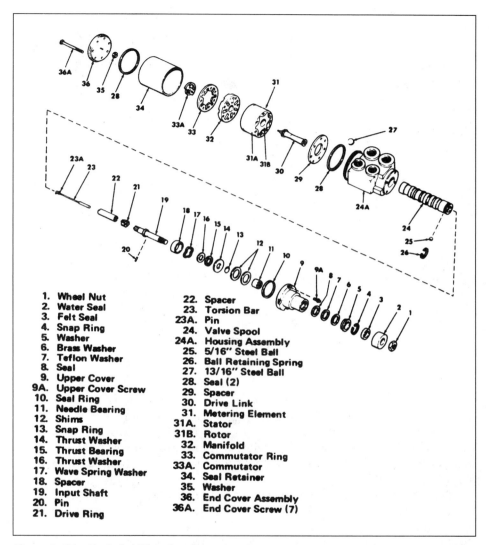

Exploded view shows all parts of a mechanism (power-steering valve), the sequence of their alignment, and part names

1. Wheel Nut
2. Water Seal
3. Felt Seal
4. Snap Ring
5. Washer
6. Brass Washer
7. Teflon Washer
8. Seal
9. Upper Cover
9A. Upper Cover Screw
10. Seal Ring
11. Needle Bearing
12. Shims
13. Snap Ring
14. Thrust Washer
15. Thrust Bearing
16. Thrust Washer
17. Wave Spring Washer
18. Spacer
19. Input Shaft
20. Pin
21. Drive Ring

22. Spacer
23. Torsion Bar
23A. Pin
24. Valve Spool
24A. Housing Assembly
25. 5/16" Steel Ball
26. Ball Retaining Spring
27. 13/16" Steel Ball
28. Seal (2)
29. Spacer
30. Drive Link
31. Metering Element
31A. Stator
31B. Rotor
32. Manifold
33. Commutator Ring
33A. Commutator
34. Seal Retainer
35. Washer
36. End Cover Assembly
36A. End Cover Screw (7)

Figure 8–27   Exploded-View Drawing   *Source:* Courtesy of the Harnischfeger Corporation.

3. Draw the different parts of an object in proportion to one another, unless you indicate that certain parts are enlarged.

4. For drawings used to illustrate a process, arrange them from left to right and from top to bottom.

5. Label important parts of each drawing so that text references to them are clear and consistent.

6. Depending on the complexity of what is shown, label the parts themselves, or use a letter or number key. (See Figure 8–27.)

Prevent Repetitive-Motion Injuries

Before beginning keying and during breaks throughout the day, take time to do the stretches as shown.

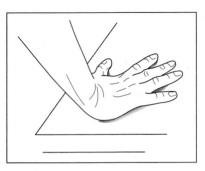 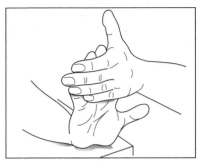

Gently press the hand against a firm flat surface, stretching the fingers and wrist. Hold for five seconds.

Rest the forearm on the edge of a table. Grasp the fingers of one hand and gently bend back the wrist, stretching the hands and wrist. Hold for five seconds.

Figure 8–28   Drawing

Flowcharts

A *flowchart* is a diagram that shows the stages of a process from beginning to end; it presents an overview that allows readers to grasp essential steps quickly and easily. Flowcharts can illustrate a variety of processes ranging from the stages required to refine bauxite ore into aluminum to the steps required to prepare a manuscript for publication.

Flowcharts can take several forms to represent the steps in a process: labeled blocks (Figure 8–29), pictorial representations (Figure 8–30), or standardized symbols (Figure 8–31). The items in any flowchart are always connected according to the sequence in which the steps occur and flow left to right or top to bottom. When the flow is otherwise, indicate it with arrows.

Flowcharts that document computer programs and other information-processing procedures use standardized symbols set forth in *Information Pro-*

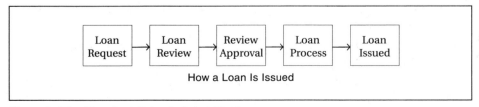

Figure 8–29   Flowchart Using Labeled Blocks

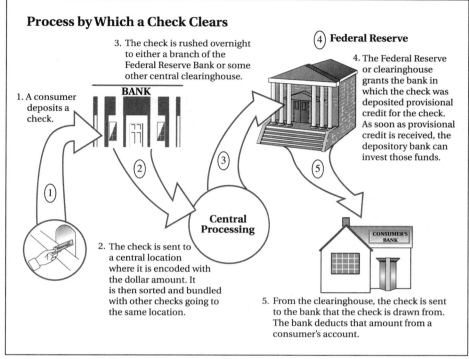

Process by Which a Check Clears

3. The check is rushed overnight to either a branch of the Federal Reserve Bank or some other central clearinghouse.

④ **Federal Reserve**

4. The Federal Reserve or clearinghouse grants the bank in which the check was deposited provisional credit for the check. As soon as provisional credit is received, the depository bank can invest those funds.

1. A consumer deposits a check.

BANK

Central Processing

2. The check is sent to a central location where it is encoded with the dollar amount. It is then sorted and bundled with other checks going to the same location.

CONSUMER'S BANK

5. From the clearinghouse, the check is sent to the bank that the check is drawn from. The bank deducts that amount from a consumer's account.

Pictorial flowchart with numbered steps and directional arrows

Figure 8–30   Flowchart Using Pictorial Symbols

cessing—*Documentation Symbols and Conventions for Data, Program, and System Flowcharts, Program Network Charts, and System Resources Charts,* ISO publication 1985 (E).

Follow these guidelines when creating a flowchart:

1. With labeled blocks and standardized symbols, use arrows to show the direction of flow, especially if the flow is opposite to the normal direction. With pictorial representations, use arrows to show the direction of all flow.

2. Label each step in the process, or identify it with a conventional symbol. Steps can also be represented pictorially or by captioned blocks.

3. Include a key if the flowchart contains symbols that your audience may not understand.

4. Leave adequate white space on the page. Do not crowd the steps and directional arrows too closely together.

Organizational Charts

An organizational chart shows how the various parts of an organization are related to each other. Such illustrations give readers an overview of an organization or indicate the lines of authority within an organization (Figure 8–32).

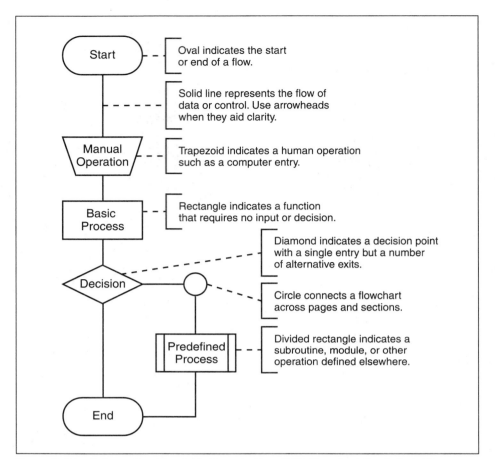

Standardized symbols for information-processing flowcharts

Oval indicates the start or end of a flow.

Solid line represents the flow of data or control. Use arrowheads when they aid clarity.

Trapezoid indicates a human operation such as a computer entry.

Rectangle indicates a function that requires no input or decision.

Diamond indicates a decision point with a single entry but a number of alternative exits.

Circle connects a flowchart across pages and sections.

Divided rectangle indicates a subroutine, module, or other operation defined elsewhere.

Figure 8–31   Information Standards Organization (ISO) Flowchart Symbols (with Annotations)

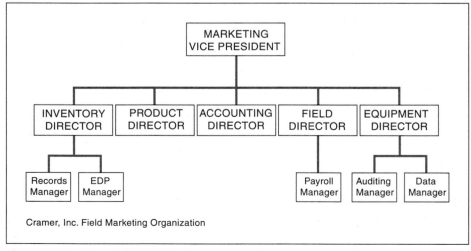

Boxes are linked to show hierarchy of and relationships among units in an organization

Cramer, Inc. Field Marketing Organization

Figure 8–32   Organizational Chart

290

The title of each organizational part (office, section, division) is placed in a separate box. These boxes are then linked to a central authority. If useful to your readers, include the name of the person occupying the position identified in each box. As with all illustrations, place the organizational chart as close as possible following the text that refers to it.

Maps

Maps can be used to show the specific geographic features of an area (roads, mountains, rivers) or to show information according to geographic distribution (population, housing, manufacturing centers, and so forth) (Figure 8–33).

Keep in mind the following points as you create maps for use with your text:

1. Clearly identify all boundaries within your map. Eliminate those that are unnecessary to the area you want to show.
2. Eliminate unnecessary information. For example, if population is the focal point, do not include mountains, roads, rivers, and so on.
3. Include a scale of miles or feet, or kilometers or meters, to give your reader an indication of the map's proportions.
4. Indicate which direction is north.

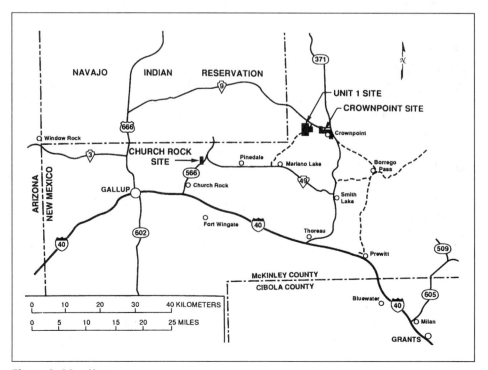

Focus of map is location of three sites (highlighted with call-outs and arrows)

Note state, reservation, and county boundaries; highways; and scales of distance

Figure 8–33   Map

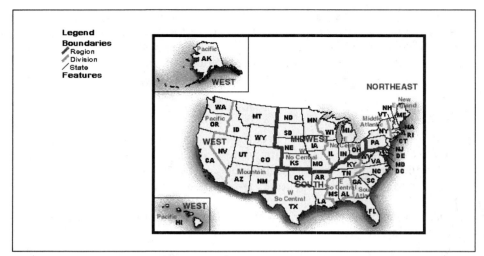

Figure 8–34 Map Showing Legend and Shading to Depict Data
Source: U.S. Census Bureau.

5. Emphasize key features by using shading, dots, crosshatching, or appropriate symbols, and include a key telling what the different colors, shadings, or symbols represent (Figure 8–34).

Photographs

Photographs are vital to show the surface appearance of an object or to record an event or the development of a phenomenon over a period of time. Not all representations, however, call for photographs. They cannot depict the internal workings of a mechanism or below-the-surface details of objects or structures. Such details are better shown in drawings or diagrams.

Highlighting Photographic Objects

If you are taking the photo, stand close enough to the object so that it fills your picture frame. A camera will photograph only what it is aimed at; accordingly, select important details and the camera angles that will record these details. To show the relative size of an unfamiliar object, place a familiar object—such as a ruler, a book, a tool, or a person—near the object that is to be photographed, as shown in Figure 8–35.

Ask the printer reproducing your publication for special handling requirements if you use glossy photographs. If you use digitized photos, ask about the preferred resolution of the images. The higher the resolution, the better the quality. You can create digitized photos using scanners and digital cameras, so ensure that the equipment has the necessary memory for the resolution required by the printer.

DIGITAL
SHORTCUTS

Using Graphics Software[1]

- *Vector graphics* packages allow you to manipulate predefined shapes (boxes, circles, arcs, lines, letters) that you then combine to produce images. Vector packages render crisp, high-resolution images that are ideal for producing complex technical graphics (isometric drawings, exploded views, and detailed line drawings), as well as basic images (flowcharts and organizational charts). These images — lines, shapes, letters — retain high-quality resolution regardless of the size at which they are produced.

- *Bitmapped* (or *raster*) programs allow you to manipulate individual pixels (picture elements or dots) to produce lines, shapes, and patterns. These programs — also called *paint programs* — work best with images that have broad variations in colors, shapes, or hues, such as photos and detailed drawings. Use these programs to edit photos, create Web graphics, or modify screen shots for use in print and online publications. You can alter these images by manipulating the color and intensity of the dots. The resolution quality of the images is affected by the number of dots they contain — more dots equal higher quality. At lower resolution, the images have a fuzzy or jagged appearance.

Which program should you use? Select the program based on the type of image you will produce.

Use a vector program for:

- Line drawings.
- Blueprints.
- Flow and organizational charts.
- Isometric drawings.
- Network and process diagrams.

Use a bitmapped program for:

- Photographs.
- Computer screen shots.
- Web graphics.
- Special effects.

Note that most vector programs can convert vector images to dots to create bitmap images for editing with a bitmap image editor.

[1]Based on "An Introduction to Illustration Software" by Bryan J. Follas, *Intercom,* September/October 2001: 6–8.

Using Color

Color is in many cases the only way to communicate crucial information—in medical, chemical, geological, and botanical publications, for example, readers often need to know exactly what an object or phenomenon looks like to accurately interpret it. In these circumstances, color reproduction is the only legitimate option available.

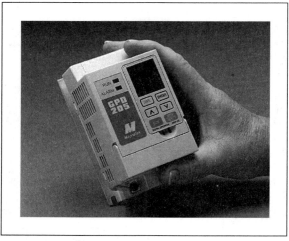

Device being held by a human hand to illustrate its relative size

Figure 8–35 Photo of Control Device
Source: Photo courtesy of Ken Cook Company.

 On the Web
For information on locating photographs and other images for your documents, see Chapter 8, bedfordstmartins.com/ writingthatworks

Posting color images at a Web site is no more complicated or expensive than posting black-and-white images. For publications, however, preparing and printing color photographs are complex technical tasks performed by graphics and printing professionals. If you are planning to use color photographs in your publication, discuss with these professionals the type, quality, and number of photographs required.

Be mindful that color reproduction is significantly more expensive than black-and-white reproduction. Color can also be tricky to reproduce accurately without losing contrast and vividness. For this reason, the original photographs must be sharply focused and rich in contrast.

DIGITAL SHORTCUTS

Computer Graphics

Creating computer graphics allows you to:

- Save images for future use and update them as necessary.
- Print images on paper for use in reports, other documents, and Web sites.
- Send images to presentation software programs to produce transparencies and 35-mm slides for meetings.
- Communicate image files to others electronically via e-mail.
- Automate sharing and updating data in images created and maintained in different applications — spreadsheet, database, graphics, word-processing, and presentation programs.

Using Graphics to Communicate Internationally

More than ever, business and technical communicators use graphics to communicate with international audiences. As companies expand their markets in Saudi Arabia, China, South America, the countries of the former Soviet Union, and dozens of other places, the marketplace becomes more global, a trend marked by the prevalence of multinational corporations, the international subsidiaries of many companies, multinational trade agreements, the increasing diversity of the U.S. workforce, and even increases in immigration. The audiences for these communications include clients, business partners, colleagues, and current and potential employees and customers. Even though English is rapidly becoming the global language of business and science, many people speak it as a second or third language. For this reason, graphics offer distinct advantages for communicating in a global business climate.

- Graphics can communicate a message more effectively than text, particularly in the context of safety warnings or cautions.
- Graphics can sometimes replace technical terms that are difficult to translate.

Despite their unquestionable value in communicating with international readers, symbols, images, and even colors are not free from cultural associations: How they are perceived depends on many factors—including the values and norms of a given culture. Thus, there are no universally accepted graphics standards, with the exception of the symbols used in mathematics and certain scientific and engineering disciplines (e.g., the voltage symbol used in electrical engineering).

Writers who create documents for an international audience can avoid confusing and possibly offending their readers by understanding the following cultural differences in connotation.

Punctuation Marks

Punctuation marks, like words, are language specific. For example, in North America the question mark generally represents the need for information or the Help function in a computer manual or program. In many countries, this symbol is not understood at all. To avoid confusion, when possible include a key that associates the English-language question mark with the local language's equivalent mark.

Religious Symbols

Religious symbols that carry simultaneous religious and nonreligious meanings have long been used in North America, where it is common to use the cross as a symbol for first aid or a hospital. In Muslim countries, a cross represents Christianity; a crescent (usually green) is a symbol for first aid.

Colors

The use of a particular color can distort or even change the meaning of graphics symbols. Red commonly indicates warning or danger in North America, Europe, and Japan. In China, however, red symbolizes joy. In Europe and North America, blue generally has a positive connotation; in Japan, the color represents villainy. In Europe and North America, yellow represents caution or cowardice; in Arab countries, yellow generally means fertility or strength.

People, Parts of the Body, and Gestures

Depicting people and parts of the body in graphics can be problematic (Table 8–1). If your graphics will reach an international audience, it is better to avoid depictions of people eating or representations of bare arms and feet. Nudity in advertising, for example, generally is acceptable in Europe but not in North America or in predominantly Muslim countries. Even showing isolated body parts could lead to communication difficulties. For example, some Middle Eastern cultures regard the display of the soles of one's shoes to be disrespectful and offensive. Therefore, a technical manual that attempts to demonstrate the ease of running a software program by showing a user with his or her feet up on a desk could be considered offensive to that audience.

Communicators producing instructions often use hand gestures such as the victory sign ( ) or the "OK" sign ( ) as positive motivators. However, the meaning of each of these gestures varies by culture. In Australia, for example, the victory sign conveys the same meaning as holding up the middle finger in North America. Similarly, the gesture that means "OK" in North America can mean "worthless" in France, can mean "money" in Japan, and is a sexual insult in many other parts of the world. Even a smile may have different connotations. In Japan, smiling can be a sign of joy or can be used to hide displeasure; in some Asian cultures, smiling may be considered a sign of weakness.

Further, a manual that contains a pointed finger to indicate "turn the page" might offend someone in Venezuela. A writer preparing a manual for export to Honduras could indicate "caution" by using a picture of a person touching a finger below the eye.

Table 8–1 International Implications of Gestures and Body Language

Body Part	Gesture	Country	Interpretation
Head nodding	Up and down	Bulgaria	No
Left hand	Showing palm	Muslim countries	Dirty, unclean
Index finger	Pointing to others	Venezuela, Sri Lanka	Rude
Index-to-thumb circle	Circular OK	Germany, Netherlands	Rude
Ankle and leg	Crossing over knee	Indonesia, Syria	Rude
Eye	Touching finger below eye	Honduras	Caution

Cultural Symbols

W **On the Web**
For links to intercul-
tural resources for
business writers,
see Chapter 8,
bedfordstmartins.com/
writingthatworks

Signs and symbols are so culturally rooted that we often lose sight of the fact that they may be understood only in our culture. A Michigan manufacturer of window fans wanted to use easily understood symbols to represent the two speeds of its product: fast and slow. The technical communicators selected a rabbit and a turtle. However, recognition of these animals as symbols of speed and slowness requires familiarity with Aesop's fables—a Western tradition.

Technology Symbols

The symbols or icons we create to represent technology are laden with cultural assumptions. If users do not have regular contact with fax machines, photocopiers, computers, or cellular phones, technical and business communicators cannot predict how users will interpret representations of these devices.

Using International Graphics

CONSIDERING
AUDIENCE
AND PURPOSE

☐ Consult with someone from your intended audience's country who will be able to recognize and explain the effects of subtle visual elements on your intended readers.

☐ Acknowledge diversity within your company and recognize that not everyone interprets visual information in the same way.

☐ Learn about the use of gestures in other cultures as a first step to learning about cultural context, because the interpretation of gestures differs widely.

☐ Invite international and intercultural communication experts to speak to your colleagues and contact companies in your area that may have employees who could be resources for cultural discussions.

☐ Be sure that the graphics you use have no unintended religious or symbolic implications.

☐ Use few colors in your graphics. Generally, black-and-white or gray-and-white illustrations are less problematic.

☐ Create simple visuals. Simple shapes with few elements are easier to read in most cultures.

☐ Use outlines or neutral abstractions to represent human beings. For example, use stick figures for bodies or a circle for a head.

☐ Be consistent in labeling elements. Use simple, consistent signs for all visual items.

☐ Explain the meaning of icons or symbols. Include a glossary to explain technical symbols that cannot be changed (e.g., company logos).

☐ Test icons and symbols in context with members of your target audience. Usability testing with cultural experts is critical.

☐ Organize visual information for intended audiences. North American readers tend to read visuals from left to right in clockwise rotation. Middle Eastern cultures read visuals from right to left in counterclockwise rotation.

Reading Practices

Whether text is read right to left or left to right influences how graphics are sequenced. In the Middle East and in many parts of Asia, for example, text is read from right to left. For these audiences, you will need to alter the design and sequencing of text and graphics.

Directional Signs

The signs we use to represent direction or time are open to misinterpretation. For example, the arrow sign on shipping cartons can be interpreted to mean either that the carton should be placed with the arrow pointing up to the top of the carton, or pointing down to the carton's most stable position. Western cultures tend to indicate the future (or something positive) by pointing to the right (→) and the past (or something negative) by pointing to the left (←); in the Chinese culture, left represents honor and right self-destruction.

Careful attention to the different connotations visual elements may have for an international audience makes translations easier, saves a company from potential embarrassment, and, over time, earns respect for the company and its products and services.

CHAPTER 8 SUMMARY: Designing Effective Documents and Visuals

Integrating Visuals and Text

☐ Have you noted in your document planning outline the approximate location of your graphics?

☐ Does the text preceding a table or figure make clear why the visual is there and what it shows?

☐ Is the language in the text describing the graphic consistent with the language in the graphic?

☐ Do all graphics have clear, concise captions?

☐ Is the graphic located as close as possible to — but following — the text describing it?

☐ Have you allowed adequate white space around and within the graphics in your documents?

☐ Have you obtained permission to reproduce copyrighted graphics in your document?

☐ Do the layout and design of your finished document highlight the organization and hierarchy of your information?

Designing Forms

☐ Are your forms organized in a logical order for those filling them out and for those interpreting the information they contain?

☐ Did your coworkers review the draft form before you printed it?

☐ Have you designed questions that can be answered simply and briefly and that provide the information that you need?

Exercises

1. Create a table that shows the tasks involved in seasonal maintenance (like lawn or automobile care) that you perform over the period of one year.

2. Assume that a survey of 100 companies resulted in the following distribution percentages by type of industry: computer-related, 32 percent; industrial equipment, 7 percent; business services, 8 percent; telecommunications, 10 percent; media and publications, 10 percent; consumer goods, 10 percent; medical and pharmaceutical, 14 percent; other, 9 percent. Prepare a pie graph showing the distribution.

3. Create a line or bar graph that compares sales in thousands of dollars among the various truck-parts divisions of the ABC Corporation for 2000, 2001, and 2002. Sales for each division are as follows:
   - axles: 2000 ($225), 2001 ($200), 2002 ($75)
   - universal joints: 2000 ($125), 2001 ($100), 2002 ($35)
   - frames: 2000 ($125), 2001 ($100), 2002 ($50)
   - transmissions: 2000 ($75), 2001 ($65), 2002 ($50)
   - clutches: 2000 ($35), 2001 ($30), 2002 ($15)
   - gaskets and seals: 2000 ($28), 2001 ($25), 2002 ($20)

4. Briefly explain whether a photograph or a line drawing would better illustrate features of the following subjects: a dry-cell battery (for an article in a general encyclopedia), a flower arrangement (in a florist's brochure), an electrical-outlet box (in a wiring instructions booklet), or the procedure for wrapping a sprained ankle (for a first-aid handbook).

5. Create a flowchart for a process or procedure important to your field of study or to the topic of your current writing project. Introduce and explain the flowchart, relating it to your topic and explaining discrete actions, decisions, or repetitions of specific procedures that occur in the process that the flowchart depicts.

6. Beginning at the main entrance and ending at the checkout desk, draw a flowchart that traces the path you follow in the process of locating and obtaining books from your library (as outlined in Chapter 7).

7. Create an organizational chart for a club or group to which you belong or for the department in your area of study.

8. Design a weekly time card for factory employees at United Agricultural Products. Employees work Mondays through Fridays, 8:00 a.m. to noon, 12:30 p.m. to 3:30 p.m., and have a half hour for lunch. Include on the time card a column listing the days of the week (vertical column) and columns labeled "Time In," "Time Out" (morning), "Lunch," "Time In," "Time Out" (afternoon), and "Overtime" (horizontal columns). Supervisors are to fill in the times that employees actually arrive at work, the times they leave for the day, the times of their lunch breaks, and the overtime hours (if any) that employees work each day. Include columns for the total hours worked each day and a final box or space for total hours worked for the week. Be sure to leave spaces for the dates that the time card covers and for the signatures of both the employee and the supervisor.

9. Design a printed form to be used by the medical staff administrative assistant of a hospital. The form is for the reappointment of staff physicians for the coming year.

It should be designed to obtain the following information: the physician's name, office address, and office telephone number; the physician's status on the hospital staff (temporary or permanent); the hospital department in which the physician wishes to admit patients (medicine or surgery); the number of the physician's state license; and the physician's birth date. It should also provide for "yes" and "no" answers about whether the physician in question has attended a satisfactory number of committee meetings, whether the physician has satisfactorily completed all of his or her medical records, and whether the hospital has taken any disciplinary action against the physician during the past year. Finally, the form should provide for the signature of the hospital's chief of staff and the date of that signature.

10. Design a printed form for recording your monthly budget, including housing, food, utilities, transportation (car, bus, subway), insurance (car, life, property, medical), school, clothing, entertainment, and the like. Include columns that show the amount you budgeted for each item, the amount actually spent, and the difference. Finally, include space for totaling expenses for each column.

■ Collaborative Classroom Projects

1. Divide into groups of three and create an outline for a major class writing project. In the outline, indicate each place in which you plan to include a graphic, and describe the type of graphic you are including. Describe in your outline how the graphic will benefit your document (be as specific as possible) and how it will be helpful to readers. Write a detailed description of the data it will present and how you plan to prepare it or otherwise obtain it.

2. Divide into teams of five or fewer students who share a similar major area of study and design a form that would be commonly used in your field. Refer to this chapter for examples of forms.

3. Bring to class a printed form (such as a college application form or government form) that you believe could be designed more effectively. As your instructor directs:

   a. Critique the form and create a list of what could be improved.
   b. Recommend specific steps for improving the form.
   c. Create a new form either yourself or in a group.

4. Divide into teams with classmates who share a similar major area of study. Using thumbnail sketches, design a brochure advertising a new student association for students majoring in your field. Include the following information: the date, time, and place of your call-out meeting; your new association's purpose on campus; and a description of who is eligible to belong. Your brochure plan must include columns and visuals and be at least two 8½-by-11-inch pages.

5. Bring to class an example of a newsletter from a source on campus, such as a campus group or department, or from a source outside campus, such as a community-service group or business. Divide into groups of five or fewer. For the next forty-five minutes, rank your samples by order of their effectiveness. Which samples best accomplish their purpose? Why? Refer to this chapter for guidelines on page design. Be prepared to defend your choices to your classmates.

■ Research Projects

1. Interview someone from another country or culture about a specific aspect of business (or an aspect of another field). Write a report of 500 to 700 words on two cultural differences between ideas held in that country or culture and ideas broadly held in the United States. Consider punctuation marks, religious symbols, colors, body parts and gestures, directional signals, or technology symbols. Do not use any specific examples already discussed in this chapter.

2. Select five drawings from reports, articles, or textbooks. Explain how effectively each illustration makes the text more meaningful or easier to follow, supports the ideas presented in the text, and has been correctly placed in relation to the text.

3. Using magazines, journal articles, and other printed sources, gather information about how visuals are used in your field. In a brief narrative, show examples of visuals used in marketing, engineering, continuing education, job recruitment, health-care sciences, and other areas relevant to your field. Document all sources correctly. Refer to this chapter for guidelines on the placement of visuals.

4. Graphics are such a vital part of doing business today that many places hire professionals to assist with their graphic and visual advertising. Visit an advertising agency or marketing firm in your area and review the kinds of work that they do for other businesses. Ask to see a copy of their price list and samples of their work, and ask what kinds of businesses use their services. Write a brief narrative summarizing the information you gathered on your visit and include your opinion of how a business in your field would use the services of an advertising agency or a marketing firm.

■ Web Projects

Projects followed by the symbol W are continued at **bedfordstmartins.com/ writing that works**, Chapter 8.

1. Create a bar graph showing the median sales price of new single-family homes in the United States for 1975 and at five-year intervals through the most current data available at the Web site of the U.S. Census Bureau at <census.gov>.

2. Using the Web to gather your data, create a line graph that plots home-mortgage interest rates or the population in any U.S. metropolitan area currently over 1 million over the past 20 years. Present the same information in a table. Access a list of federal agency Internet sites at the *Writing That Works* Web site. W

3. On the Web you can find PDF versions of corporate annual reports. One excellent resource is the Library of Annual reports at <reportgallery.com>, which posts more than 2,000 reports and covers most of the Fortune 500 companies. After reviewing the guidelines in this chapter for creating documents and integrating visuals:

   a. Choose a report (available in a PDF version) that is well-designed, poorly-designed, or some combination. Print out the report and evaluate it according to its:

- Use of typography
  - type face
  - type size
- Use of highlighting devices
  - boldface, italics, and capital letters
  - headings and captions
  - headers and footers
  - rules, icons, and color
- Use of page design
  - overall layout
  - columns
  - white space
  - margins
  - lists
  - illustrations

b. Mark the pages of the report, indicating any changes you would make to improve its design. You may focus on one aspect of the report, such as its use of headings or illustrations. Feel free to sketch out your ideas.

c. Write a memo to your instructor in which you explain what does and does not work about the report's original design, supporting your ideas with information in this chapter. Specify how your changes would improve the document's design. Attach to your memo the marked up printout of the report and any sketches you've created.

While Parts One and Two discussed the principles of effective writing that apply to all on-the-job writing tasks, Part Three focuses on the practical applications of these principles. Chapters 9 through 17 provide explicit guidelines for writing — with plenty of examples — the most common types of work-related communications: memos, business letters, e-mail messages, instructions, proposals, forms, and a variety of formal and informal reports. A new chapter (16) provides advice for writing for the Web. Finally, this part ends with a chapter that puts everything you learned earlier in the text to its first practical test: finding a job appropriate to your education and abilities.

9 Understanding the Principles of Business Correspondence

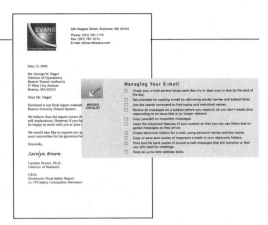

B usiness correspondence, the communication among people within organizations or between those people and their clients or customers, is essential to the success of individuals and businesses. Because of their importance, such communications should be well written; those that are not waste considerable time and money. For example, the poorly written letter shown in Figure 9–1 was actually sent to a law firm (the actual names have been changed). The staff at the law firm could not understand it, even though a number of attorneys, paralegal assistants, and secretaries were familiar with the case. Staff members exchanged e-mails and phone calls with Ralph Madison and others at his company without success. Finally the law firm had to send someone to the company to identify the specific services the company wanted its legal counsel to perform.

This letter wasted the time of a highly paid staff—and caused a delay in legal services to Ralph Madison's company. Further, carelessly written letters or e-mails project a poor image of the writer that can result in other kinds of losses. A reader's negative reaction to an unclear or unprofessional message, for example, can cost a firm its reputation and future business—and can even cost an employee his or her job.

This chapter covers the following skills essential to successful business correspondence:

- Selecting the appropriate medium for your message (page 306)
- Writing business messages (page 311)
- Formating business letters (page 319)
- Writing and formatting memos (page 325)
- Meeting deadlines (page 332)
- Sending e-mail: protocol and strategies (page 334)
- Writing international correspondence (page 341)

W On the Web
For more advice on writing and formatting business correspondence, see Chapter 9, bedfordstmartins.com/writingthatworks

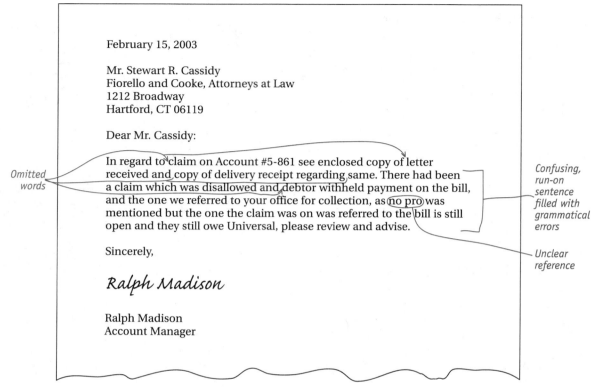

Omitted words

Confusing, run-on sentence filled with grammatical errors

Unclear reference

February 15, 2003

Mr. Stewart R. Cassidy
Fiorello and Cooke, Attorneys at Law
1212 Broadway
Hartford, CT 06119

Dear Mr. Cassidy:

In regard to claim on Account #5-861 see enclosed copy of letter received and copy of delivery receipt regarding same. There had been a claim which was disallowed and debtor withheld payment on the bill, and the one we referred to your office for collection, as no pro was mentioned but the one the claim was on was referred to the bill is still open and they still owe Universal, please review and advise.

Sincerely,

Ralph Madison

Ralph Madison
Account Manager

Figure 9–1   Poorly Written Letter

■ Selecting the Appropriate Medium

Important as they are, letters and e-mail are not the only means of communication available to businesspeople. The law firm, for example, eventually had to meet with Ralph Madison to accurately interpret his request to "review and advise." You can choose from a wide array of possibilities, from relatively recent technologies such as e-mail, fax, voice mail, and videoconferencing to more traditional means of communication such as letters and memos, telephone calls, and face-to-face meetings. With so many means of communication available, how do organizations and individuals decide which is preferable in a given situation?

Basic considerations in selecting the appropriate medium are the audience and the objective of the communication. For example, when you need to solve a problem, a written message (even one by e-mail) can take too long or create more confusion. A telephone call is then the more efficient choice. When you need precise wording and you and your reader need a permanent record of the information exchanged, a written message (letter, memo, or e-mail) will be the best

Voices from the Workplace

Kate Bishop, Blackboard, Inc.

Kate Bishop is the manager of the Learning Services Department at Blackboard, Inc., a leading provider of Internet infrastructure software for e-Education. She and her team travel to colleges and other education providers around the world, teaching faculty how to use Blackboard software to put course work online. Because members of the Learning Services Department are so rarely in the same place at the same time, e-mail is their primary mode of communication.

Kate offers the following tips for using e-mail: "Although the ease of e-mail invites informality, be careful. Sarcasm and humor are often misunderstood when they are used in e-mails, because there are no voice or facial cues to imply a humorous intent. As a rule of thumb, if you think the recipient could possibly misinterpret the tone of a statement, find another way to say it. In a business environment, it is also crucial that you maintain standard rules of capitalization, sentence structure, spelling, and punctuation. Stick to proper grammatical and editorial style. And always carefully reread your message at least twice before you hit Send. Check for the following common mistakes: typographical/spelling errors, incorrect or unnecessary recipient(s), remarks that could be misinterpreted based on tone, inappropriate or offhand comments."

Mark Lin, GlaxoSmithKline Pharmaceuticals

As a senior pharmaceutical representative, Mark Lin spends much of his time communicating face-to-face with doctors, nurses, and other health-care professionals in his sales territory. Because he doesn't work in an office, Mark relies on written communication to convey information to his colleagues and superiors — mainly through memos and reports that he sends as e-mail attachments.

Mark's most common written communications are memos to his managers that report on items such as his success in his territory and his approach to individual clients. At Mark's company, these memos are known as business plans. "In a business-plan memo," Mark explains, "I include an analysis of the business in my sales territory for the past and present and a statement of my business goals for the future. I also provide specific 'attack' details on how I will achieve my sales goals. In the business analysis section of the memo, I provide specific market share data points and a detailed written explanation of this numerical data — this ensures that my manager does not misinterpret any of the information included in my plan."

Mark comments on the role of the business-plan memo. "The tone of my business plans is more formal and straightforward than the other reports and e-mails that I write on a more regular basis. For one thing, my business plans clearly state the strategies that will guide both my work and my results for an entire quarter — which is very important. Also, because much of the content of a business plan is based on hard data — sales numbers and market-share percentages — there is little room for my own opinions and other more informal "chitchatty" embellishments — my manager doesn't have time for all of that! I know my business plan will be reviewed closely by all of my immediate superiors, so it is important that even my writing style conveys my professionalism."

option. When you wish to establish a close rapport with someone in the interest of a long-term working relationship, a face-to-face meeting is indispensable.

Following is a description of the primary methods of communicating and some of their salient characteristics. All are currently in use because each communicates certain kinds of information better than the others, even though the advantages overlap in some cases.

Letters on Organizational Stationery

Letters are most appropriate for first contacts with new business associates or customers as well as for other official business communications. Stationery with an organization's printed letterhead and the writer's handwritten signature communicates formality, respect, and authority. A written promise, conveyed above the signature of an employee who has the authority to act on behalf of an organization, ensures that the information is accurate and that the sender will honor it. For example, a formal letter is often used to summarize the terms and conditions of a proposed business relationship. If you use express or overnight deliveries for letters and other documents, phone or send an e-mail or fax message ahead to alert the recipient that the material has been sent. If speed is essential and you need to send a signed letter, you can fax it and follow up by mailing the original letter.

Memos: Printed and Electronic

Printed and electronic memos are one of the most frequently used forms of communication among members of the same organization, even when offices are geographically separated. These in-house communications have many of the same characteristics of letters, but memos are convenient for a wider variety of functions—from announcements of organizational policy to short reports.

Memo formats in most organizations are standardized. These formats eliminate the need for a letterhead, an inside address, a salutation, goodwill paragraphs, and formal closing elements. As discussed later in this chapter, memo writers must follow their organization's protocol and traditional forms. This includes whether to use a "MEMO" header; what order to use for "To:," "From:," "cc:," "Date:," and "Subject:"; and where to place your initials or signature, if required. (See pages 330–332 for memo formats.)

E-mail Messages

E-mail (electronic mail) is used to send information, maintain professional relationships, elicit discussions, collect opinions, and transmit many other kinds of messages. E-mail can be a less formal means of communication than either letters or memos; however, e-mail provides the advantage that the same information can be sent simultaneously at great speed to many recipients. For groups that may often exchange e-mail, creating a discussion group (or listserv) is convenient.

Because e-mail recipients can print copies of messages they receive or easily forward them to others, business messages should always be written with care and reviewed for accuracy before being sent. Note that e-mail is a less private form of communication than the other types described here. For guidance about writing e-mail messages and ensuring their confidentiality, see pages 334–341.

Faxes

A fax (facsimile transmission) is most useful when speed is essential and when the information—a drawing or contract, for example—must be viewed in its original form. Faxes are also useful when the recipient does not have access to e-mail or the programs to view e-mail attachments or when the material has not yet been converted into electronic form. Note that faxed correspondence may seem less official than a traditional letter, in part because the recipient does not receive the original stationery. However, faxes are growing in acceptance even in legal correspondence (some courts now allow filing of official documents by fax). Of course, if an original is also important, the paper copy can be sent separately by overnight or regular mail. Faxed letters should be sent with a fax cover sheet (available as a word-processing template) or a commercially prepared fax stick-on label.

Telephone Calls and Conferences

One of the advantages of phone calls is that they enable participants to interpret tone of voice, so they are often helpful in resolving misunderstandings or clarifying information. Of course, a phone call does not provide the visual and other physical cues possible during face-to-face meetings.

Conference calls take place among three or more participants. They are a less expensive alternative to a face-to-face meeting that would require the participants to travel to a central meeting place. They also provide a setting for the immediate resolution of issues. Conference calls are more efficient if the person setting up the call works from an agenda shared by all the participants. That person must be prepared to direct the discussion as though he or she were leading a meeting. Of course, the call must be planned to ensure that everyone is available at the same time. Timing is especially important when participants are located in different time zones—especially for international calls. The participants should also take notes on any key points or decisions made during the call. (For further information on such conferences, see the discussion of meetings in Chapter 15, pages 544–554.)

Voice-Mail Messages

Voice-mail systems allow callers to record messages when the person called is not available. Anticipate your response if you receive a voice-mail recording instead of the person you've called. When leaving a voice-mail message, enunciate clearly and leave your name, phone number, and the date and time of the call. Leave a succinct message ("Call me about the deadline for the new project" or "I got the package from RTL, so you don't need to call the distributor"). Speak as if you were actually talking to the person rather than simply recording a message. If the message is complicated or contains numerous details, use another medium, such as an e-mail message or a letter, to ensure that the information is communicated accurately. If you want to discuss a subject, let the recipient know the subject so he or she can prepare a response when returning your call.

Face-to-Face Meetings

Face-to-face meetings are most appropriate for initial or early contacts with business associates and customers with whom you intend to develop an important long-term relationship. Meetings are also the best medium for exchanges in which you need to solve a serious problem. The most productive meetings occur when all participants come prepared to contribute to a collective effort toward a well-defined objective. (See Conducting a Productive Meeting in Chapter 15 for a more detailed discussion of how to conduct effective meetings and record the meeting discussions and decisions.)

Videoconferencing

Videoconferences are particularly useful for meetings where travel is impractical or too expensive. Unlike telephone conference calls, videoconferences have the advantage of allowing participants to see as well as to hear one another. Videoconferences work best with participants who are at ease in front of a camera.

■ Writing Business Messages

This chapter focuses on three of the most common forms of written correspondence: business letters, memos, and e-mail messages. It also covers the increasingly important subject of international correspondence. Further, the process of writing business correspondence involves many of the steps that go into most other on-the-job writing, as described in Chapter 1, as well as some special considerations.

1. Establish your purpose, your reader's needs, and your scope.
2. Outline key points. For a short letter, memo, or e-mail, jot down the points you wish to make and the order in which you wish to make them (see Chapter 2).
3. Write a rough draft from the outline.
4. Allow for a cooling period (see Chapter 4), especially when a letter or an e-mail responds to a problem. Don't vent emotions, as illustrated in the

Selecting the Medium

- ☐ Consider your audience, purpose, and what is typical or expected in your organization as you select the medium for communicating.

- ☐ Generally, use written forms and messages for precise wording; use telephone, videoconference, and in-person communication when you need, for example, to resolve a misunderstanding.

- ☐ Use letters on organizational stationery for first contacts; printed letterhead on quality paper communicates formality, respect, and authority.

- ☐ Use memos (printed and electronic) for in-house business communications — from policy announcements to short reports.

- ☐ Use e-mail to send messages and electronic documents, maintain professional relationships, elicit discussions, and collect opinions from distant as well as wide audiences.

- ☐ Use faxes when the exact image of nondigital documents must be viewed and when speed matters.

- ☐ Use telephone calls and conferences when give-and-take or tone of voice is important; conference calls, when carefully planned, are often a less expensive alternative to a face-to-face meeting for participants in distant locations.

- ☐ Use voice mail for short, uncomplicated messages.

- ☐ Use face-to-face meetings for early contacts with business associates and customers or solving problems.

- ☐ Use videoconferencing as a substitute for face-to-face meetings when travel is impractical; participants need to be at ease in front of a camera.

cartoon on page 335. Even a lunch-hour cooling period can give you a chance to remove any hasty and inappropriate statements made in the heat of the situation.

5. Revise the rough draft, checking for sense as well as for grammar, spelling, and punctuation.

6. Adjust the format, especially the arrangement and spacing of letter parts (see pages 319–325), and print a copy for review before signing it.

7. Assume final responsibility: Even if a secretary or an assistant does your word processing, check his or her work; when you sign a letter or a memo, you are responsible for its appearance and accuracy.

Letter Writing: Goodwill and the "You" Viewpoint

As a writer of a business letter, you have an opportunity that a report writer doesn't have: You are addressing the reader directly, and therefore you are in a very good position to take your reader's needs into account and build goodwill for yourself and for your company. If you ask yourself, "How might I feel if I were the recipient of such a letter?" you can gain insight into the needs and feelings of your reader—

and then tailor your message to fit those needs and feelings. Remember that you have a chance to build goodwill for your business or organization. Many companies spend millions of dollars to create a favorable public image. A letter to a client that sounds impersonal and unfriendly can quickly tarnish that image; a thoughtful letter that communicates sincerity can greatly enhance it.

Suppose, for example, you are a store manager who receives a request for a refund from a customer who forgot to enclose the receipt with the request. In a letter to the customer, you might write:

- The sales receipt must be enclosed with the merchandise before we can process the refund.

However, if you consider how you might keep the goodwill of the customer, you might word that request this way:

- Please enclose the sales receipt with the merchandise so that we can send your refund promptly.

Notice that this version uses the word *please* and the active voice, while the first version uses only the passive voice. In general, the active voice creates a friendlier, more courteous tone than the passive, which can sound impersonal and unfriendly. (For a discussion of the active and passive voices, see Chapter 5.) Polite wording, such as the use of *please,* also helps to create goodwill.

However, you can go one step further. You can put the reader's needs and interests first by writing from the reader's point of view. Often, but not always, doing so means using the words *you* and *your* rather than the words *we, our, I,* and *mine.* That is why the technique has been referred to as using the "you" viewpoint or "you" attitude. For example, consider the point of view of the original sentence in the example just given:

- The sales receipt must be enclosed with the merchandise before *we can process* the refund.

The italicized words focus on the writer's need to process the refund. Even the second version, although its tone is more polite and friendly, emphasizes the writer's need to get the receipt "so that we can send your refund promptly." (The writer, of course, may want to get rid of the problem quickly.)

What is the reader's interest? The reader is not interested in helping the business process its accounts. He or she simply wants the refund—and by emphasizing that need, the writer encourages the reader to act quickly. Consider the following revision written from the "you" viewpoint:

- So you can receive your refund promptly, please enclose the sales receipt with the merchandise.

This sentence stresses that it is to the reader's benefit to act on this matter.

Be aware, however, that both goodwill and the "you" viewpoint can be over-done. Used thoughtlessly, both techniques can produce a fawning, insincere tone—what might be called *plastic goodwill*. Avoid language full of false praise and sicken-ingly sweet phrases. Any attempt at goodwill that is insincere will be recognized by your reader and thus will be counterproductive. Consider the opening of the letter that follows from a writer who has corresponded only once with the recipient:

PLASTIC   You are just the kind of customer that deserves the finest service that anyone can offer—and you deserve our best deal. Knowing how careful you are at making decisions, I know you'll think about the advantages of using our consulting service.

In this example, the writer barely knows the customer yet makes an assumption about what "kind of customer" the recipient may be. Further, the writer charac-terizes the customer as careful "at making decisions." The sentence sounds phony. A far better approach is to make goodwill reasonable for the circumstances and provide specifics that are appropriate to your knowledge of the reader.

APPROPRIATE   From our earlier correspondence, I can understand your need for reli-able service—we strive to give all our priority clients our full attention. After you have reviewed our proposal, I am confident you will appreci-ate our "Five-Star" consulting option.

Using Tone to Build Goodwill

WRITER'S CHECKLIST

☐ *Be respectful,* not demanding.

DEMANDING   Submit your answer in one week.

RESPECTFUL   I would appreciate your answer within one week.

☐ *Be modest,* not arrogant.

ARROGANT   My report is thorough, and I'm sure that you won't be able to con-tinue without it.

MODEST   This report contains a detailed description of the refinancing options, and I hope you find it useful.

☐ *Be polite,* not sarcastic.

SARCASTIC   I just received the shipment we ordered six months ago. I'm sending it back — we can't use it now. Thanks!

POLITE   I am returning the shipment we ordered on March 12, 2003. Unfortunately, it arrived too late for us to be able to use it.

☐ *Be positive and tactful,* not negative and condescending.

NEGATIVE   Your complaint about our prices is way off target. Our prices are definitely not any higher than those of our competitors.

TACTFUL   Thank you for your suggestion concerning our prices. We have found, however, that our prices are competitive with those of our competitors.

Organize reader-focused correspondence to achieve goodwill by presenting the main point or good news early—at the outset, if at all possible. The pattern for neutral or good news should be as follows:

1. Main point or good news
2. Explanation of details or facts
3. Goodwill

By presenting the main point or good news first, you increase the likelihood that the reader will pay careful attention to details, and you achieve goodwill from the start. Figure 9–2 shows an example of a good-news letter.

November 11, 2003

Ms. Barbara L. Mauer
157 Beach Drive
San Diego, CA 92113

Dear Ms. Mauer:

Good-news opening

Please accept our offer of the position of records administrator at Southtown Dental Center.

Explanation

If the terms we discussed in the interview are acceptable to you, please come in at 9:30 a.m. on November 15. At that time, we will ask you to complete our personnel form, in addition to . . .

Goodwill closing

I, as well as the others in the office, look forward to working with you. Everyone was favorably impressed with you during your interview.

Sincerely,

Mary Hernandez

Mary Hernandez
Office Manager

Figure 9–2   Good-News Letter

Negative Messages and the Indirect Pattern

Communicating bad news is sometimes necessary in the workplace. When you must do so, presenting bad news or refusals indirectly is often more effective than presenting them directly. Research has shown that people form their impressions and attitudes very early when reading letters. Consider this example. A college student who had applied for a scholarship received a letter explaining that he had not won it. The letter began: "I'm sorry, but you were not a recipient of this year's Smith Scholarship." In disappointment, the student threw the letter on his desk and left his apartment. Three days later, he picked up the letter and read further. It went on to say that the committee thought his record was so strong that he should call immediately if he were interested in another, but lesser-known, scholarship. The student called but was told that the other scholarship had been awarded to someone else. Because the student had not called immediately, he lost an important opportunity.

Although the relative directness of business messages may vary, it is generally more effective to present bad news indirectly, especially if the stakes are high for a reader.[1] This principle is based on two related facts: (1) readers form their impressions and attitudes very early in correspondence, and (2) you as a writer may wish to subordinate the bad news to reasons that make the bad news understandable. Further, in international correspondence, far more cultures are generally indirect in their business communication than they are direct.

Consider the thoughtlessness in the job rejection that follows.

■ Dear Ms. Mauer:

Your application for the position of records administrator at Southtown Dental Center has been rejected. We have found someone more qualified than you.

Sincerely,

Although the letter is concise and uses the pronouns *you* and *your,* the writer has not considered how the recipient will feel as she reads the letter. The letter is, in short, rude. The pattern of this letter is (1) bad news, (2) curt explanation, (3) close. A better general pattern for bad-news correspondence is the following:

1. Context (or "buffer")
2. Explanation
3. Bad news
4. Goodwill

The opening (often called a "buffer") should provide a context for the subject and establish a professional tone. Then the body should provide an explanation by reviewing the details or facts that lead, for example, to a negative decision or refusal. Give the negative message simply, based on the facts, but do not belabor the bad news or provide an inappropriate apology. Neither the details nor an overdone apology can turn bad news into something positive. Your goal should be to

---

[1] Gerald J. Alred, "'We Regret to Inform You': Toward a New Theory of Negative Messages," in *Studies in Technical Communication,* ed. Brenda R. Sims (Denton, TX: University of North Texas and NCTE, 1993), pp. 17–36.

establish for the reader that the writer or organization has been *reasonable* given the circumstances. To accomplish this goal, you need to organize the explanation carefully and logically, as discussed in Chapter 2.

The closing should establish or reestablish a positive relationship through goodwill or helpful information. Consider, for example, the revised rejection letter shown in Figure 9–3. This letter carries the same disappointing news as the first one, but the writer begins by not only introducing the subject but also thanking the reader for her time and effort. Then the writer explains why Ms. Mauer was not accepted for the job and offers her encouragement in finding a position in another office. Bad news is never pleasant; however, information that either puts the bad news in perspective or makes the bad news seem reasonable maintains respect between the writer and the reader. The goodwill closing is intended to reestablish an amicable business relationship. (See Sensitive and Negative Messages on pages 367–381 in Chapter 10 and Persuading Your Audience on pages 72–76 in Chapter 3 for more examples.)

November 11, 2003

Ms. Barbara L. Mauer
157 Beach Drive
San Diego, CA 92113

Dear Ms. Mauer:

Context (or "buffer") opening

Thank you for your time and effort in applying for the position of records administrator at Southtown Dental Center.

Explanation leading to bad news

Because we need someone who can assume the duties here with a minimum of training, we have selected an applicant with over ten years of experience.

Goodwill closing

I am sure that with your excellent college record you will find a position in another office.

Sincerely,

Mary Hernandez

Mary Hernandez
Office Manager

Figure 9–3 Courteous Bad-News Letter

Openings and Closings

Most other business messages should follow the patterns for openings and closings discussed in Chapter 3, pages 91–95. Openings, for example, must identify the subject and its interest or relevance to your readers.

■ Yesterday, I received your letter and the pager, number AJ 50172. I sent the pager to our quality-control department for tests.

   Carol Moore, our lead technician, reports that preliminary tests indicate . . .

Because business letters are often more personal than reports and other forms, an opening must also establish a tone that is appropriate and achieves your purpose.

■ I'm seeking advice about organizational communication, and several people have suggested that you are an authority on the subject.

The tone of respect in this opening is not only appropriate but also persuasive, because it appeals to the reader's pride. Other openings might appeal to the reader's curiosity or personal interests, as in the following:

■ I have a problem you may be willing to help solve.

■ Mr. Walter Jenkens has given us your name as a reference for his company's services. I hope you'll be willing to help us by answering some specific questions about his company.

   Closings for correspondence, in addition to following the principles illustrated in Chapter 3, can also provide an incentive for the reader to act, as in the following:

■ Please sign the forms today, mark the changes you want made, and return the material to me in the preaddressed envelope. If you can approve everything for me within two days, I should have the amended contract in your hands by the end of the week.

For more examples of openings and closings in various types of correspondence, review the examples in Chapter 10.

Writing Style and Accuracy

Business messages may legitimately vary from informal, in an e-mail to a close business associate, to formal (or restrained), in a letter to someone you do not know. (Even if you are writing to a close associate, you should always follow the rules of standard grammar, spelling, and punctuation.)

INFORMAL   It worked! The new process is better than we had dreamed.

RESTRAINED   You will be pleased to know that the new process is more effective than we had expected.

You will normally use the restrained style more frequently than the informal one. Remember that an overdone attempt to sound casual or friendly, like overdone goodwill, can sound insincere. However, do not adopt a style so formal that your letters or memos read like legal contracts; that type of writing appears wordy, pompous, and affected—and may well irritate your reader.

AFFECTED   Please be advised that we no longer possess an original copy of the brochure requested. Herewith enclosed is a photographic copy for your use. Address any further query to this office for assistance as required.

IMPROVED   We are currently out of original copies of our brochure, so I am sending you a photocopy. If I can help further, please let me know.

The excessively formal writing style of the affected version is full of out-of-date business jargon; expressions such as *query* (for request or question), *be advised that,* and *herewith* are old-fashioned and pretentious. Good business letters have a more conversational style, as the improved version illustrates. The improved version is not only less stuffy but also more concise.

Being concise in writing is important, but don't be so concise that you become blunt. Responding to a written request that is vague with "Your request was unclear" or "I don't understand," could easily offend your reader. Instead, ask for more information and establish goodwill to encourage your reader to provide the information.

■   I will need more information before I can answer your request. Specifically, can you give me the title and the date of the report you are looking for?

Although this version is longer, it promotes goodwill and will elicit a faster, more helpful response.

A letter, a memo, or an e-mail (as described later) is a written record, so it must be accurate. Facts, figures, and dates that are incorrect or misleading can cost time, money, and goodwill. Remember that when you sign a letter or initial a memo, you are responsible for it. Therefore, allow yourself time to review any correspondence carefully before sending it. Whenever possible, ask someone who is familiar with the situation to review an important letter or other message. Listen with an open mind to any criticisms of what you have written. Make whatever changes you believe are necessary. Review Accuracy and Completeness on page 106 in Chapter 4.

Also review your message for punctuation, grammar, and spelling. In business as elsewhere, accuracy and attention to detail are equated with carefulness and reliability. The kindest conclusion a reader can come to about a letter containing mechanical errors is that the writer was careless. Do not give your reader cause to form such a conclusion.

Formatting Business Letters

As described earlier in this chapter, letters communicate formality, respect, and authority. So, just as the clothes you wear to job interviews play a part in the first impression you make on potential employers, the appearance of a business letter may be crucial in influencing a recipient who has never seen you. A neat appearance alone will not improve a poorly written letter, but a sloppy appearance will detract from a well-written one.

Although word-processing software provides templates for correspondence, it may not provide specific dimensions and spacing. To achieve a professional appearance, center the letter on the page vertically and horizontally. Although one-inch margins are the default standard in many word-processing programs, it is more important to establish a picture frame of blank space surrounding the page of text. When you use organizational letterhead stationery, consider the bottom of the letterhead as the top edge of the paper. The right margin should be approximately as wide as the left margin. To give a fuller appearance to very short letters, increase both margins to about an inch and a half. Use your computer's full-page or print-preview feature to check for proportion.

The two most common formats for business letters are the full-block style shown in Figure 9–4 and the modified-block style shown in Figure 9–5. In the *full-block style*, which should be used only with letterhead, the entire letter is aligned at the left margin. In the *modified-block style*, the return address, date, and complimentary close begin at the center of the page and the other elements are aligned at the left margin. All other letter styles are variations of the full-block and modified-block styles.

If your employer requires a particular format, use it. Otherwise, follow the guidelines provided here, and review the examples shown in Figures 9–4 and 9–5.

Heading

The heading is the writer's full return address—street or post-office box, city and state, postal code—or printed letterhead and the date. The writer's name is not included in the heading (unless it is part of a printed letterhead) because it appears at the end of the letter. In giving your address, do not use abbreviations for words such as Street, Avenue, First, or West (as part of a street or city name). You may either spell out the name of the state in full or use the standard Postal Service abbreviations. The date usually goes directly beneath the last line of the address. Do not abbreviate the name of the month.

■   1638 Parkhill Drive East
Great Falls, MT 59407
April 8, 2004

Begin the heading about two inches from the top of the page. If you are using company letterhead that gives the address, enter only the date three lines below the last line of printed copy.

Letterhead
(with address)

520 Niagara Street, Braintree, MA 02184

Phone: (781) 787-1175
Fax: (781) 787-1213
E-mail: cbrown@evans.com

Date

May 15, 2003

Inside
address

Mr. George W. Nagel
Director of Operations
Boston Transit Authority
57 West City Avenue
Boston, MA 02210

Salutation

Dear Mr. Nagel:

Enclosed is our final report evaluating the safety measures for the
Boston Intercity Transit System.

Body

We believe that the report covers the issues you raised and that it is
self-explanatory. However, if you have any further questions, we would
be happy to meet with you at your convenience.

We would also like to express our appreciation to Mr. L. K. Sullivan of
your committee for his generous help during our trips to Boston.

Complimentary
close

Sincerely,

Signature

Carolyn Brown

Typed name
Title

Carolyn Brown, Ph.D.
Director of Research

Additional
information

CB/ls
Enclosure: Final Safety Report
cc: ITS Safety Committee Members

Figure 9–4   Full-Block-Style Letter (with Letterhead)

Center

3814 Oak Lane
Dedham, MA 02180
December 8, 2003

*Heading from
center to right*

Dr. Carolyn Brown
Director of Research
Evans and Associates
Transportation Engineers
520 Niagara Street
Braintree, MA 02184

Inside address

Dear Dr. Brown:

Salutation

Thank you very much for allowing me to tour your testing facilities.
The information I gained from the tour will be of great help to me in
preparing the report for my class at Marshall Institute. The tour has
also given me some insight into the work I may eventually do as a laboratory technician.

Body

I especially appreciated the time and effort Vikram Singh spent in
showing me your facilities. His comments and advice were most
helpful.

Again, thank you.

Sincerely,

*Complimentary
close aligned
with heading*

Leslie Warden

Signature

Leslie Warden

Typed name

Center

Figure 9–5   Modified-Block-Style Letter (without Letterhead)

Inside Address

The inside address is the recipient's full name, title, and address.

■ Ms. Gail Smith
Production Manager
Docuform Printing Company
14 President Street
Sarasota, FL 33546

Place the inside address two to six lines below the date, depending on the length of the letter. The inside address should be flush with (or aligned with) the left margin, which should be at least one inch wide.

Salutation

Place the salutation (or greeting) two lines below the inside address, also flush with the left margin. In most business letters, the salutation contains the recipient's title (Mr., Ms., Dr., etc.) and last name, followed by a colon. If you are on a first-name basis with the recipient, you would include his or her title and full name in the inside address but use only the first name in the salutation.

■ Dear Ms. Smith:

■ Dear Dr. Smith:

■ Dear Captain Smith:

■ Dear Professor Smith: [Note that titles such as Captain and Professor are not abbreviated.]

■ Dear Gail: [if you are on a first-name basis]

For women who do not have a professional title, use Ms. (for either a married or an unmarried woman). If the woman has expressed a preference for Miss or Mrs., honor her preference. When you do not know whether the recipient is a man or a woman, you may use a title appropriate to the context of the letter. The following are examples of titles you may find suitable:

■ Dear Customer:

■ Dear Homeowner:

■ Dear Service Manager:

When a person's name could be either feminine or masculine, one solution is to use both first and last names in the salutation.

■ Dear Pat Smith:

In the past, writers to large companies or organizations customarily addressed their letters to "Gentlemen." Today, however, this is inappropriate. Writers who do not know the name or the title of the recipient often address the letter to an appropriate department in the attention line or identify the subject in a subject line in place of a salutation.

■ National Business Systems
501 West National Avenue
Minneapolis, MN 55107-5011

Attention: Customer Relations Department

I am returning three pagers that failed to operate. . . .

■ National Business Systems
501 West National Avenue
Minneapolis, MN 55107-5011

Subject: Defective Parts for SL-100 Pagers

I am returning three pagers that failed to operate. . . .

Body

The body of the letter should begin two lines below the salutation (or below the inside address if no salutation appears). Single-space within paragraphs and double-space between paragraphs with the first line of each new paragraph at the left margin or indented five spaces from the left margin. The right margin should be approximately as wide as the left margin. (In very short letters, you may increase both margins to about an inch and a half.)

Complimentary Close

Start the complimentary close or conventional "good-bye" two lines below the body. Use a standard expression such as *Sincerely yours, Yours truly,* or *Respectfully yours.* (If the recipient is a friend as well as a business associate, you can use a friendly, less formal close: *Best wishes, Cordially, Sincerely, Best regards.*) Only the first word of the complimentary close is capitalized, and the expression is followed by a comma. Four lines below the complimentary close, and aligned at the left with the close, type your full name. On the next line, place your business title if it is appropriate to do so. Then sign your name in the space between the complimentary close and your typed name. If you are writing to someone with whom you are on a first-name basis, it is acceptable to sign only your given name; otherwise, sign your full name, as shown in Figures 9–4 and 9–5.

Second Page

If a letter requires a second page, always carry at least two lines of the body over to page two. The second page also should have a heading containing the recipient's name, the page number, and the date. (Never use letterhead for a second page.) The heading starts one inch from the top edge of the page and may go in the upper-left-hand corner or across the page, as shown in Figure 9–6.

End Notations

Business letters sometimes require additional information—the initials of the typist (if other than the writer), an enclosure notation, or a notation that a copy of the letter is being sent to one or more named people. Place any such information flush left with the margin, two lines below the last line of the complimentary close in a long letter, four lines below in a short letter.

Initials are not used when the writer is also the person typing the letter, as is common. If an assistant has typed the letter, however, that person's initials should appear (all lowercase) two lines below the last line of the complimentary-close block either by themselves or following the author's initials (all uppercase and followed by a slash), as shown in Figure 9–7.

Enclosure notations, which indicate that the letter writer is sending material along with the letter (an invoice, an article, and so on), may take several forms.

- Enclosure [for a single item]

- Enclosures (2)

Even though you use an enclosure notation, make a reference in the body of the letter to the enclosed material. Enclosures are described briefly if the letter is long and formal, as shown in Figure 9–4, or if the nature of the enclosed items is not ob-

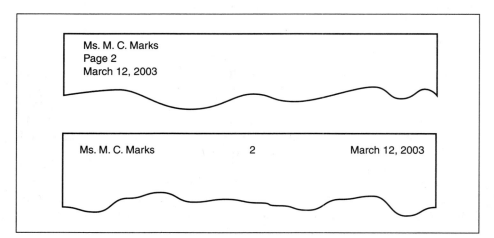

Figure 9–6 Headers for the Second Page of a Letter

vious. Enclosures are not described if the letter is short and the enclosures are obvious to the reader.

Copy notations (cc:) tell the reader that a copy of the letter is being sent to one or more named individuals.

- cc: Ms. Marlene Brier
  Mr. David Williams

  [Brier and Williams receive only the letter.]

- cc/enc: Mr. Tom Lee

  [Lee receives both the letter and the enclosure.]

A *blind-copy notation (bcc:)* is used when the sender does not want the addressee to know that a copy is being sent to one or more other recipients. That means the blind-copy notation must not appear on the original letter, only on the letter to the blind-copy recipient, as shown in Figure 9–7.

A business letter may, of course, contain all the end notations described in this section (see Figure 9–7).[2]

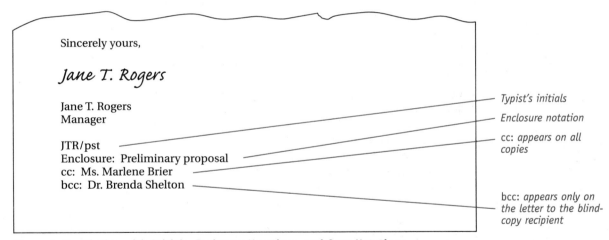

Figure 9–7   Closing with Initials, Enclosure Notations, and Copy Notations

Writing and Formatting Memos

Much of the general advice on business correspondence given earlier in this chapter applies to memos. However, the memo—printed or electronic—is routinely used for a wide range of internal communications—from short notes to one-page reports and internal proposals. Among their other uses, memos:

---

[2] For more detailed guidance on business-letter format, see William A. Sabin, *The Gregg Reference Manual*, 9th ed. (New York: Glencoe, 2000).

- Announce policies.
- Confirm conversations.
- Exchange information.
- Delegate responsibilities.

- Request information.
- Transmit documents.
- Instruct employees.
- Report results.

As this partial list illustrates, memos provide a record of the decisions made and many actions taken in an organization. For this reason, clear and effective memos are essential to the success of any organization. A poorly written memo sends a garbled message that could baffle readers, cause a loss of time, produce costly errors, or even offend.

Memo Protocol and Strategy

The decision to send memos on paper, attached to an e-mail message, or delivered as an e-mail depends on the organizational practice and the purpose of the communication, as discussed earlier in Selecting the Appropriate Medium (pages 306 and 311). Some organizations may prefer the printed memo for announcements and other official messages while reserving e-mail for informal communications. Others may use e-mail almost exclusively not only because of its speed but also because it fosters the easy exchange of information. Even when e-mail substitutes for printed memos, some recipients print copies of important e-mails to highlight sections or to save a hard copy for their records.

Although such practices vary, be alert to the protocol of sending memos in your organization. For example, consider who should receive a memo and in what order—senior managers, for example, take precedence over junior managers. Failure to observe rank in the "To" line is a strategic mistake that can undermine the effectiveness of any memo, no matter how well written. Observing rank reflects well on the writer because it demonstrates his or her understanding of the organizational structure of the department or company.

Managers who write clear and accurate memos gain respect and credibility. Consider the unintended secondary messages the following notice conveys:

POOR   It has been decided that the office will be open the day after Thanksgiving.

The first part of the sentence ("It has been decided") not only sounds impersonal but also communicates an authoritarian, management-versus-employee tone: Somebody "decides" you work. The passive voice also suggests that the decision-maker does not want to say "I have decided" and thus be identified (in any case, the office staff would undoubtedly know). One solution, of course, is to remove the first part of the sentence.

BETTER   The office will be open the day after Thanksgiving.

Even this statement sounds impersonal. The best solution would be to suggest both that the decision is good for the company and that employees should be privy to (if not a part of) the decision-making process.

BEST   Because we must meet the December 15 deadline for submitting the
                        Bradley proposal, the office will be open the day after Thanksgiving.

By subordinating the bad news (the need to work on that day), the writer focuses
on the reasoning behind the decision to work. Employees may not necessarily like
the message, but they at least understand that the decision is not arbitrary because it is tied to an important deadline. As this example illustrates, much of the
strategy for business letters discussed earlier in this chapter, such as in Negative
Messages and the Indirect Pattern (page 314), applies to memos as well.

Memo Style and Tone

To produce a memo that is both effective and efficiently written, outline your
memo, even if you simply jot down points to be covered and then order them logically. (To review this process, see Chapter 2.) With careful preparation, your
memos will be both concise and adequately developed. Adequate development of
your thoughts is crucial to the memo's clarity, as the following example indicates.

INCOMPLETE   Be more careful on the loading dock.

DEVELOPED   To prevent accidents on the loading dock, follow these procedures:
                        1. Check to make sure . . .
                        2. Load only items that are rated . . .
                        3. Replace any defective parts . . .

Although the original version is concise, it is not as clear and specific as the revision. Don't assume your reader will know what you mean. State what you mean
explicitly. Readers may be pressed for time and misinterpret your memo if it is
vague.

Each memo should address only one subject, as the memo in Figure 9–8 illustrates. If you need to cover two subjects, write two memos. Multisubject
memos are not only difficult to file (thus easily lost) but also confusing to a hur-
ried reader.

Whether your memo is formal or informal depends entirely on your reader
and your objective. Is your reader a coworker, superior, or subordinate? A memo
to a coworker who is also a friend is likely to be informal, while an internal proposal to several readers or to someone two or three levels higher in your organization is likely to be more formal. Consider the following versions of a statement:

TO AN EQUAL   I can't go along with the plan because I think it poses serious logistical
                        problems. First, . . . [informal, casual, and forceful response written to
                        an equal]

TO A SUPERIOR   The logistics of moving the department may pose serious problems.
                        First, . . . [formal, impersonal, and cautious response to a superior]

A memo giving instructions to a subordinate should also be relatively formal and
impersonal but more direct — unless you are trying to reassure or praise. Using an

overly chatty, casual style in memos to your subordinates may confuse them about the relationship and make you seem either insincere or ineffectual. However, if you become too formal, sprinkling your writing with fancy words, you may seem stuffy and pompous. You may also be regarded as rigid and incapable of moving the organization ahead. When writing to subordinates, remember that *managing* does not mean *dictating*. An imperious tone—like false informality—will not make a memo an effective management tool. When you write a memo to a subordinate, adopt a positive yet reasonable tone, as in the following example.

■ Because we must meet the December 15 deadline for submitting the Bradley proposal, the office will be open the day after Thanksgiving. I am also temporarily reassigning several members of the office staff as shown below. . . .

Memo Openings

Memo openings are crucial because readers in the workplace are busy meeting deadlines and coping with dozens of messages every day. Although methods of development vary, a memo should begin with a statement of the main idea that the subject line announces.

MAIN IDEA   Because the e-mail addresses of individuals make the site vulnerable to hacker attacks, I recommend that we no longer post the e-mail addresses of our laboratory employees on our Web site.

Even if your opening gives the essential background of a problem, state the main point early in the first paragraph.

BACKGROUND   Last year we did not hire new staff because of the freeze on hiring. As a result of the increased workload described in this memo, we need to hire two additional application support specialists this year.

When the reader is not familiar with the subject or with the background of a problem, provide an introductory background paragraph before stating the main point (shown in *italics* below) of the memo. Doing so is especially important in memos that serve as records for crucial information months or years later.

MAIN IDEA   ACM Electronics has asked us to prepare a comprehensive brochure for its Milwaukee office by August 9, 2005. We have worked with electronics firms in the past, so this job should not cause significant problems. I estimate that it will take two months to complete. Ted Harris has requested time and cost estimates for the project, Fred Moore in production will prepare the cost estimates, and *I would like you to prepare a tentative schedule for the project.*

Generally, longer memos or those dealing with complex subjects benefit most from more thorough introductions. However, even when writing a short memo about a familiar subject, remind readers of the context. In the following examples, words that provide context are shown in *italics*.

■ *As we discussed after yesterday's meeting,* we need to set new guidelines for . . .

■ *As Maria recommended,* I reviewed the office reorganization plan. I like most of the features; however, the location of the receptionist and administrative assistant . . .

Do not state the main point first when (1) the reader is likely to be highly skeptical or (2) you are disagreeing with a person in a position of higher authority. In such cases, a more persuasive tactic is to state the problem first, then present the specific points supporting your final recommendation. For more information on openings and closings, see pages 91–95 in Chapter 3.

Memo Lists and Headings

Using lists is an effective strategy to give your points impact in a memo. Lists can be read and their meaning grasped more quickly than a paragraph that says the same thing. Be careful, however, not to overuse lists. A memo that consists almost entirely of lists is difficult for the reader to understand because he or she must mentally connect the separate and disjointed terms on the page. Further, lists lose their impact when they are overused. A particularly useful type of list is one for messages sent to numerous readers whose responses you need to tabulate.

■ I can meet at 1 p.m. _____
                2 p.m. _____
                3 p.m. _____

Another attention-getting device, particularly in long memos, is the use of headings. Headings have a number of advantages:

1. They divide material into manageable segments.
2. They call attention to main topics.
3. They signal a shift in topic.

Especially for memos to several readers, headings allow each reader to scan them and read only the section or sections appropriate to his or her needs. Notice the use of both a list and headings in Figure 9–8.

Memo Closings

A memo closing can accomplish many important tasks, such as building positive relationships with readers, encouraging colleagues and employees, and letting recipients know what you will do or what you expect of them.

■ I will discuss the problem with the marketing consultant and let you know by Monday what we are able to change.

Although routine statements are sometimes unavoidable ("Thanks again for your help"), make your closing work for you by providing specific prompts to which the reader can respond.

■ If you would like further information, such as a copy of the questionnaire we used, please e-mail me at delgado@prn.com

Memo Formats and Parts

Memo formats vary from organization to organization. Although there is no single, standard form, Figure 9–8 shows a typical 8½-by-11-inch format with a company name.

Regardless of the parts of the memo included, an element requiring careful preparation is the subject-line title (such as "Schedule for ACM Electronics Brochure" in Figure 9–8). Subject-line titles in both memos and e-mail messages function much like the titles of reports: They announce the topic. They are also an important aid to filing and later retrieval. Therefore, they must be accurate. The memo should deal only with the single subject announced in the subject line, and the title should be complete. However, the title should not substitute for an opening that provides a context for the message.

VAGUE	Subject: Tuition Reimbursement
VAGUE	Subject: Time-Management Seminar
SPECIFIC	Subject: Tuition Reimbursement for Time-Management Seminar

CONSIDERING AUDIENCE AND PURPOSE

Writing Memos and Other Correspondence

☐ Determine the most appropriate medium for your message based on your audience and your purpose. What would be most appropriate and best achieve your purpose? A letter? A memo? An e-mail? A fax?

☐ Keep your readers' needs in mind as you write a letter, a memo, an e-mail, or a fax.

☐ Bring your reader more directly into the communication by appropriately using the "you" viewpoint.

☐ Consider whether a formal (somewhat restrained) or informal writing style would be more appropriate for your purpose and your audience. Remember that an attempt to sound casual or friendly can instead seem insincere.

☐ Even when writing to a close associate, be considerate of your reader and use appropriate grammar, spelling, and punctuation.

☐ For international correspondence, review the tips on communicating with those in other cultures in Writing International Correspondence (page 341).

PROFESSIONAL PUBLISHING SERVICES MEMO

TO: Barbara Smith, Publications Manager
FROM: Hannah Kaufman, Vice President   *HK*
DATE: April 14, 2003
SUBJECT: Schedule for ACM Electronics Brochure

ACM Electronics has asked us to prepare a comprehensive brochure for its Milwaukee office by August 9, 2003. We have worked with electronics firms in the past, so this job should be relatively easy to prepare. My guess is that the job will take nearly two months. Ted Harris has requested time and cost estimates for the project. Fred Moore in production will prepare the cost estimates, and I would like you to prepare a tentative schedule for the project.

Additional Personnel

In preparing the schedule, check the availability of the following:

1. Production schedule for all staff writers
2. Available freelance writers
3. Dependable graphic designers

Ordinarily, we would not need to depend on outside personnel; however, because our bid for the *Wall Street Journal* special project is still under consideration, we could be short of staff in June and July. Further, we have to consider vacations that have already been approved.

Time Estimates

Please give me the time estimates by April 19. A successful job done on time will give us a good chance to obtain the contract to do ACM Electronics' annual report for its stockholders' meeting this fall.

I know your staff can do the job.

cc: Ted Harris, President
     Fred Moore, Production Editor

Standard memo title
Memo heading

Introduction

Headings signal shifts in topics

Closing

Additional recipients

Figure 9–8   Typical Memo Format

Capitalize the first letter of all major words in a title. Do not capitalize articles, prepositions, or conjunctions of fewer than four letters unless they are the first or last words of the title.

If you are sending a printed memo, the final step is signing or initialing a memo, a practice that lets readers know that you have approved its contents. Where you sign or initial the memo depends on the practice of your organization: Some writers sign their name at the end of a memo, others sign their initials next to their typed name. Follow the practice of your employer. Figure 9–8 shows a typical placement of initials.

■ MEETING THE DEADLINE: The Time-Sensitive Memo

Deadlines are a part of every job. More than once in your career you will be asked to do a seemingly impossible task—write an important one-page memo that requires some information gathering in less than an hour.

Assignments such as these are generally given to you by your supervisor, often at the last minute, to meet a time-sensitive deadline. These memos are often written for the signature of someone else who is higher up in the organization. When you get such an assignment, do not panic. Instead, use the following straightforward principles drawn from this book to focus all your mental energies on the task at hand.

Understand the Assignment

Make sure that you understand the assignment. Nothing could be worse than to waste time under a short deadline by misunderstanding the purpose or intended reader of the memo. Ask the person giving you the assignment to be as explicit as possible about:

- The topic.
- The reader and the reader's background.
- The purpose and intended outcome.
- The key points that must be covered.
- The person in the organization who will sign the memo.

Gather Information

Gather the information that will help you write the memo. This essential background information can almost always be located within your company or organization. Sources include previous letters and memos, press releases, contracts, budget data, handbooks, speeches by senior officials, legal opinions, and the like. Be careful to gather *only* the information pertinent to the memo. The person asking for the memo will usually provide essential background information or tell you where to find it. If the information is not forthcoming, be sure to ask for it.

As long as the information originated in your organization, fits your context, and is accurate and well written, use as much of it as you need. If necessary, revise such material for consistency of content, style, and format as you draft the memo. When using information from other sources, make sure you avoid plagiarism and any violation of copyright (see page 221). However, works published by U.S. government agencies are in the public domain—that is, they are not copyrighted—and can be used without prior approval.

On the job, you will have another source of information that you may not always have in the classroom—your experience. In fact, one reason you may receive such an assignment is your knowledge of the subject, reader, organization, or professional area. Practicing the techniques of brainstorming, discussed on pages 8–9, will prepare you to draw the most benefit from your experience when you are under pressure.

Organize Your Thoughts

Do not overlook this important step. Your memo should have an opening, a middle, and a closing. Organizing the information into this structure does not have to be a formal process—you won't have time to create a full-blown outline, nor will one be necessary. Jot down the points you need to make in a sequence that makes sense. Keep it simple. In some cases, you will organize by classifying and dividing your subject matter, presenting the information on one subject before going on to another subject. Sometimes a problem-and-solution order makes sense. At other times, a chronological, sequential, or general-to-specific order will be appropriate.

Write the Draft

With the right information and a structure for organizing it, the writing will not be difficult. Stick to your plan—your rough outline—and begin. Make the structure easy for you and your reader to follow. Cover only one subject in each paragraph. After a topic sentence, provide essential supporting information—facts, examples, policy, procedures, guidelines.

Write a quick draft first; you can polish it later. Put your ideas down as quickly as you can. Write without worrying about grammar, sentence structure, or spelling. Given the limited time available, your main focus should be on getting your ideas down.

Polish the Draft

Turn to your written draft as a critic would to someone else's work. You will not have much time left, but discipline yourself to read the draft several times, concentrating on different elements each time.

First, concentrate on larger issues. Is the information accurate? Is it complete? Have you made all your points? Are they organized in the right sequence? Have you provided too much information? Revise accordingly.

Next, focus on polishing at the sentence and word level. Aim for simple sentences in the active voice. Don't use only short sentences, however. Longer sentences break the monotony of too many simple sentences strung together. Structure longer sentences so that subjects and verbs agree and primary ideas are distinct from subordinate ideas. Use parallel structure to convey matching ideas. Use lists where possible to ensure that each item is given equal weight and is expressed in the same grammatical form. Don't forget to review punctuation. A misplaced comma or semicolon can change the meaning of a sentence. Remember, in this situation you do not have time for a cooling period, so watch for any emotionally charged language.

As a final review, use your spell checker, but don't rely solely on the spell checker to catch all of your spelling errors. Make sure you read through a paper version of the memo at least once to catch any remaining errors. If you have time, ask a second reader to help you.

Take a Well-Deserved Break

After your draft is written, you may e-mail it to a superior for review before you prepare the final form for signature and distribution.

Now sit back and enjoy the sense of professional pride you have earned from a job well done under pressure!

■ Sending E-mail: Protocol and Strategies

E-mail (or *email*) can function in the workplace as a medium to send information, elicit discussions, collect opinions, and transmit documents and files of all types. Correspondence, reports, meeting notices, questionnaires, and digital files of all kinds are routinely sent to colleagues throughout an organization and to others worldwide through e-mail. As described in Selecting the Appropriate Medium (page 306), e-mail is particularly useful for facilitating discussions and collecting opinions. E-mail enables a collaborative writing team, for example, to exchange multiple drafts of a document to produce the final document. (See Chapter 6.) When used for exchanging ideas rapidly, e-mail is often conversational in tone and can become something between a telephone conversation and a memo. Even in these informal exchanges, you need to think carefully about your reader and the accuracy and appropriate level of detail of the information you send.

The writing advice given earlier in this chapter also applies to e-mail messages, especially when they replace memos inside an organization or when they replace business letters for communications to those outside an organization. Be aware, however, that recipients outside an organization may consider e-mail to be less appropriate than business letters on printed organizational stationery. Moreover, some customers, clients, and others may have limited access to e-mail or may check their e-mail infrequently.

Review and Confidentiality Implications

E-mail is a quick and easy way to communicate, but avoid the temptation to dash off a first draft and send it as is. Be careful to follow the rules of netiquette, discussed in the section that follows. As with other workplace correspondence, maintain a high level of professionalism when you send an e-mail: The message should be grammatically and factually correct, with no ambiguities or unintended implications. It should include all crucial details. When you send an informal message to a colleague, you can correct misunderstandings relatively easily—but at the expense of wasted time. Take even more care when sending messages to superiors in your organization or to people outside the organization. Time spent reviewing your e-mail can save a great deal of time and embarrassment sorting out misunderstandings resulting from sending a careless message.

Confidentiality is another issue to keep in mind when you are sending e-mail. All messages sent by e-mail, no matter how personal, sensitive, or proprietary, can be intercepted by someone other than the intended recipient. Remember, e-mail messages are never truly deleted, even when you think you've removed them from your computer. Not only can the information be printed, circulated, and forwarded, but most companies back up and save all company e-mail on computer tape. Employers can legally monitor e-mail communications. Some companies make this policy known, but others do not. Companies can also be legally compelled to provide e-mail messages to a third party, such as a court of law. Consider the content of all your messages given these possibilities. The potential for the unintended release of inappropriate information makes the need for a careful review of your text before you click Send all the more important.

Dilbert

Observing Netiquette

To maintain a high level of professionalism in workplace e-mail, observe the rules of netiquette (*Internet + etiquette*).

- Use company e-mail only for appropriate business.
  - Do not send or forward jokes or humorous stories, use biased language, or discuss office gossip.
  - Do not send *flames* (e-mails that contain abusive, obscene, or derogatory language) to attack someone.
  - Do not send *spams* (mass-distributed e-mails that often promote personal projects and interests).
- Respond to incoming e-mail promptly. If you receive an assignment by e-mail that will take a few days or longer to complete, send a response saying so.
- Be scrupulous about typing e-mail addresses and otherwise ensuring that the intended recipient receives the message.
- Send an attachment only after verifying that your recipient wants or needs the file and that your recipient's software will accept it. Be aware that attachments can consume download time and disk space.
- Consider posting a large file at an Internet server and supplying the file's address so that your recipient may download the file at his or her convenience.
- Do not write in all-uppercase letters; such a message is difficult to read and is considered the equivalent of shouting. Likewise, do not write in all-lowercase letters; it is considered lazy and too informal for professional work.
- Avoid e-mail abbreviations used in personal e-mail and chat rooms (*BTW* for *by the way,* for example).
- Do not use emoticons (keyboard characters used to create sideways faces conveying emotions) for business and professional e-mail. For advice on providing typographic emphasis, review the next section on design considerations.

DIGITAL SHORTCUTS

Sending an E-Mail Attachment

Sending attachments to your e-mail messages is a quick, convenient alternative to sending paper copies or disks through the regular mail. However, large files, like graphics, slow transmission speed. In addition, the recipient's software or Internet provider may not be able to accept large files. Consider using a compression software utility like WinZip, which typically reduces the file size by 80 percent or more.

A word of caution: Viruses can be embedded in e-mail attachments, so make sure you regularly update your virus-scanning software.

Design Considerations

W On the Web
For more advice on sending e-mail attachments, see Chapter 9, bedfordstmartins.com/ writingthatworks

The dynamics of a computer screen and the limitations of some Internet service providers require that you keep in mind some special design considerations when you are sending e-mail. The following are especially important:

- Break the text into brief paragraphs. No one wants to read long, dense blocks of text on a computer screen.

- Do not overwhelm your reader with lengthy passages. If your message runs much longer than a screen of text, consider sending it as an attached file along with a brief e-mail message that functions as a cover memo for the longer attachment.

- If you must send a document with tables and bulleted lists, do so in an attachment, making sure that the recipient has compatible software to view and save the attachment, as tables and lists do not always transmit well.

- Be considerate of the technical capabilities of your recipient. Check before sending memory-hungry attachments that may not be accepted by your recipient's software or Internet service provider or that may download very slowly.

- Put your response to someone else's e-mail message at the beginning (or top) of the e-mail window. Don't make the recipient scroll down to the end of the original message to find your response.

- In quoting the message you're replying to, include only those parts relevant to your reply. Clearly indicate the difference between your response and the text quoted in the incoming e-mail by marking the beginning of the quoted text with a greater-than symbol (>).

- Always fill in the subject line with a concise phrase that describes the topic of your message. The recipient can then decide at a glance when he or she needs to read it. Subject lines also help your reader organize and file incoming messages.

Many e-mail systems do not offer the array of typographical cues that most word-processing programs provide or may not be compatible with the system you are using. For that reason, avoid using boldface, italics, and a variety of fonts because your recipient's e-mail system may not be able to read them. Instead, use a variety of alternative highlighting devices, but be consistent. For example, capital letters or asterisks, used sparingly, can substitute for boldface, italics, and underlines as emphasis:

- Dr. Wilhoit's suggestions benefit doctors AND patients.

- Although the proposal is sound in *theory,* it will never work in *practice.*

Intermittent underlining can replace solid underlining or italics when referring to published works in an e-mail message:

- My report follows the format outlined in _The Business Writer's Handbook_.

Salutations, Closings, and Signature Blocks

Because e-mail can function as a letter, memo, or personal note, finding a suitable greeting and a complimentary closing can be difficult. If your employer follows a certain form, adopt that practice. Otherwise, use the following guidelines:

- When e-mail functions as a personal note to a friend, you can vary informal salutations (*Hi Mike,* or *Hello Jenny,*) and closings (*Take care,* or *Cheers,*).

- When e-mail goes outside an organization to someone with whom you have not yet corresponded, you can use the standard letter salutation (*Dear Professor Tucker:* or *Dear Docuform Customer:*) and a slightly informal closing (*Best wishes,* or *Sincerely,*).

- When e-mail functions as a memo, you may omit the salutation and closing because both your name and the name(s) of the recipient(s) appear in the "To" and "From" sections of the message. However, some e-mail users adopt a slightly more personal greeting, especially if the distribution list is relatively small or a single individual (*Project colleagues* or *Andreas* [recipient's first name]).

Of course, you may wish to use some combination of these approaches, depending on your relationship with the recipients and the practice among those with whom you exchange e-mail. Be aware that in some cultures, business correspon-

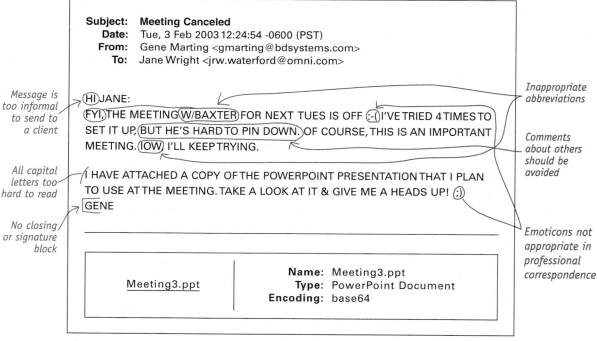

Figure 9–9   Inappropriate E-mail (with Attachment)

dents do not use first names as quickly as in U.S. correspondence (page 342). See examples of inappropriate and appropriate e-mail messages in Figures 9–9 and 9–10, respectively.

Because e-mail does not provide letterhead with standard addresses and contact information, many companies and individual writers include *signature blocks* (called *signatures* for short) at the bottom of their messages. Signatures, usually preprogrammed to appear on every e-mail sent, supply information that company letterhead usually provides in other correspondence. Some e-mail signature blocks can include automated links that connect a Web site or blank e-mail message already addressed. If your organization recommends a certain format or restricts the content of signatures, adhere to that standard. Otherwise, choose a signature that lets your reader know your full name, official title, department or

```
Subject:   Baxter Meeting Canceled
   Date:   Tue, 3 Feb 2003 12:24:54 -0600 (PST)
   From:   Gene Marting <gmarting@bdsystems.com>
     To:   Jane Wright <jrw.waterford@omni.com>

Jane:

I need to cancel the meeting with Thomas Baxter for next Tuesday (Feb 10).
I will work to schedule another meeting because we need to meet with him.

I have attached a copy of the PowerPoint presentation that I'd like to use at the meet-
ing. Let me know if you see possible improvements.

Thanks,

Gene


================================
Gene Marting, Manager
Sales Division, Building Systems, Inc.
3555 South 47th Street, Boise, ID 83703
Off: 208-719-6620 Fax: 208-719-5500
http://www.building/sys/com
e-mail: gmarting@bdsystems.com
================================
```

Signature block separated from message

| Meeting3.ppt | **Name:** Meeting3.ppt
Type: PowerPoint Document
Encoding: base64 |

Figure 9–10   Revised, Appropriate E-mail (with Attachment)

division, and the organization for which you work. Other items often included in a signature are telephone and fax numbers, and mailing and Internet addresses. Many e-mail programs allow you to create multiple signature blocks, so you can have one for professional and one for personal use.

When you use a signature block at the bottom of an e-mail message, separate the signature from the message by two or three spaces. Other cues can highlight the signature: A line of hyphens (-), underlines (_), equals signs (=), tildes (~), or asterisks (*) can effectively separate a signature from the e-mail message. Usually, typographical highlights begin at the left margin and continue until the end of the signature's longest line, as shown in Figure 9–10.

Avoid using quotations, aphorisms, and other messages ("May the Force be with you") in professional signatures. As with all design features, use signature blocks appropriate for the tone of your correspondence and the professional image of you and your organization.

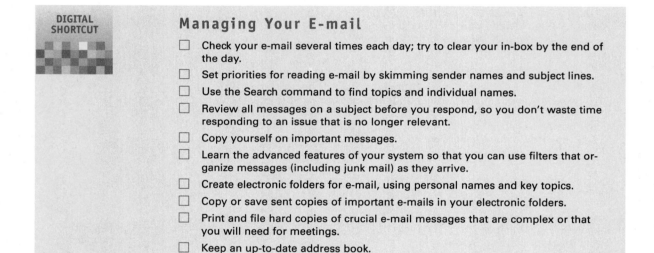

DIGITAL SHORTCUT

Managing Your E-mail

- ☐ Check your e-mail several times each day; try to clear your in-box by the end of the day.
- ☐ Set priorities for reading e-mail by skimming sender names and subject lines.
- ☐ Use the Search command to find topics and individual names.
- ☐ Review all messages on a subject before you respond, so you don't waste time responding to an issue that is no longer relevant.
- ☐ Copy yourself on important messages.
- ☐ Learn the advanced features of your system so that you can use filters that organize messages (including junk mail) as they arrive.
- ☐ Create electronic folders for e-mail, using personal names and key topics.
- ☐ Copy or save sent copies of important e-mails in your electronic folders.
- ☐ Print and file hard copies of crucial e-mail messages that are complex or that you will need for meetings.
- ☐ Keep an up-to-date address book.

Formatting Correspondence

For Letters

- ☐ Use good quality white paper and envelopes of standard size.
- ☐ Center the letter on the page, framing it with white space.
- ☐ Place the inside address of a letter two to six lines below the printed letterhead, aligned with the left margin, which should be at least one inch wide.
- ☐ Place the salutation two lines below the inside address, also aligned with the left margin.
- ☐ Begin the body of the letter two lines below the salutation.
- ☐ Single-space within paragraphs and double-space between paragraphs.
- ☐ Start the complimentary close two lines below the body of your letter.
- ☐ If a letter requires a second page, always carry at least two lines of the body over to page two.
- ☐ After you have finished writing a letter, check the arrangement and spacing of its parts.

For Memos

- ☐ Use your organization's protocol in formatting a memo, such as deciding whether to use "MEMO" as a header and what order to use for "To:", "From:", "cc:", "Date:", and "Subject:".
- ☐ Check your use of headings and the general professional look before you initial or sign your memo, depending on your organization's practice.

For E-mails

- ☐ Break the text into brief paragraphs for easy reading on the screen.
- ☐ If you must include tables or other graphic elements, attach them to your message as an accompanying file.

■ Writing International Correspondence

With organizations participating in the increasingly global marketplace, you may need to write letters, memos, or e-mail messages to readers whose native language is not English. Because English is widely taught and used in international business, you will be able to send most international correspondence in English. If you must use a translator, however, be sure that the translator understands the purpose of your correspondence. It is also prudent to let your reader know (in the letter itself or in a postscript) that a translator helped write the letter. For first-time contacts, consider sending both the English version and a translation in the reader's native language.

Culture and Business Writing Style

Just as U.S. business writing style has changed over time, ideas about appropriate business writing style vary from culture to culture. You must be alert to the needs and expectations of readers from different cultural and linguistic backgrounds.

For example, in the United States, direct, concise writing demonstrates courtesy by not wasting another person's time; in other cultures (in countries such as Spain and India), such directness and brevity suggests that the writer dislikes the reader so much that he or she wishes to make the communication as brief as possible. Whereas a U.S. business writer might consider one brief letter sufficient to communicate a request, a writer in another culture may expect an exchange of three or four longer letters to pave the way for action.

Japanese business writers, as another example, often use traditional openings that reflect on the season, compliment the reader's success, and offer hopes for the reader's continued prosperity. These traditional openings may strike some U.S. readers as being overly elaborate, literary, or even insincere. Likewise, Japanese business writers express negative messages and refusal letters indirectly to avoid embarrassing the recipient or causing a loss of face.

In U.S. business correspondence, traditional salutations such as *Dear* and complimentary closings such as *Yours truly* have, through custom and long use, acquired meanings quite distinct from their dictionary definitions. Understanding the unspoken meanings of these forms and using them naturally is routine for those who are a part of U.S. business culture. Likewise, people in many cultures are slower to use an individual's first name in communications than are most Americans. In fact, in some cultures, first names are never used in business settings — even if the individuals have worked together for years. Such customs vary from culture to culture and even within cultures. Therefore, when you read correspondence from businesspeople in other cultures or countries, be alert to these differences and consider how you should address them and your own colleagues in correspondence.

As suggested earlier, the first step in avoiding misunderstandings is to be aware that differences exist and to learn how they affect communication. To learn more about this subject, use the term *intercultural communication* to search library and reliable Internet sources.

ⓦ On the Web
For information on international business standards, customs, and communication, see Chapter 9, **bedfordstmartins.com/ writingthatworks**

Language and Usage

Take special care in international correspondence to avoid American idioms ("it's a slam dunk," "give a heads up," and the like), unusual figures of speech, and allusions to events or attitudes particular to American life. Such expressions could easily confuse your reader. Avoid humor, irony, and sarcasm because they are easily misunderstood outside their cultural context.

Pretentious or overly ornate writing (as in affectation, which is discussed in Chapter 4) will also impede the reader's understanding. Moreover, if you plan to use jargon or technical terminology, ask yourself whether the words you choose might be found in the abbreviated English-language dictionary that your reader would likely be using.

Write clear and complete sentences, as discussed in Chapters 4 and 5. Unusual word order or rambling sentences will frustrate and confuse a non-native reader of English. Read your writing aloud to identify overly long sentences and to eliminate any misplaced modifiers or awkwardness. Long sentences that contain more information than the reader can comfortably absorb should be divided into two or more sentences. Also avoid using an overly simplified storybook style. A reader who has studied English as a second language might be insulted by a condescending tone and childish language.

Finally, proofread your correspondence carefully; a misspelled word such as *there* for *their* or *discreet* for *discrete* will be particularly troublesome for a nonnative reader of English—especially if that reader turns to a dictionary for help and cannot find the word because it is misspelled.

Dates, Time, and Measurement

Countries differ in their use of formats to represent dates, time, and other kinds of measurement. To represent dates, most countries typically write the day before the month and year. For example, 1/11/04 means 1 November 2004 in most parts of the world; in the United States, it means January 11, 2004. To avoid uncertainty, write out the name of the month to make the entire date immediately clear to all international readers. Time poses similar problems, so you may need to specify time zones or refer to international standards, such as Greenwich Mean Time (GMT) or Universal Coordinated Time (UCT), for clarity.

Use of other international standards, such as commas for decimal points and the metric system (standard in most countries except the United States and the United Kingdom), will also help your reader. For up-to-date information about accepted conventions for numbers and symbols in chemical, electrical, data-processing, pharmaceutical, and other fields, consult guides and manuals specific to the subject matter.

Cross-Cultural Examples

Figures 9–11 and 9–12 are two versions of a letter written by a U.S. businessman to a Japanese businessman. The letter in Figure 9–11 does not respect the politeness norms important to Japanese readers in the opening and closing, including the salutation (*Dear Ichiro*). The letter contains affectation (*limited capacity*) and is filled with slang (*heads up, powers that be*), idioms (*fruits of your labor, burning the midnight oil*), jargon (*temp*), and inappropriately informal language (*stuff, lots of folks*).

Compare that letter to the one in Figure 9–12, which is written in language that is literal and specific. The letter opens by expressing concern about the recipient's family and prosperity because that type of expression honors Japanese traditional patterns in business correspondence. The letter is also free of American slang, idioms, and jargon. The sentences are shorter, bulleted lists are used to break up the paragraphs, contractions are not used, and months are spelled out.

When you write for international readers, rethink the ingrained habits that define how you express yourself, learn as much as you can about the cultural expectations of others, and focus on politeness strategies that demonstrate your respect for your readers. Doing so will help you achieve clarity and mutual understanding.

Sun West Corporation, Inc.

2565 North Armadillo
Tucson, AZ 85719
Phone: (602) 555-6677
Fax: (602) 555-6678   sunwest@aol.com

February 27, 2004

Ichiro Katsumi, Investment Director
Toshiba Investment Company
1-29-10 Ichiban-cho
Tokyo 105, Japan

Abrupt opening: add personal greeting

Informal

Dear Ichiro:

Avoid contractions

Slang

I've just received a heads up that you'll be coming to visit us in Tucson next month. That's great, we've been looking forward to seeing you for some time now, especially since we heard you're interested in investing in our company because, as you know, cash flow is very important to any company, especially a small one like ours.

Weak strategy

Slang

Jargon

U.S. date format

Jargon

I've been asked by the powers that be here to confirm your flight reservations. A temp took the original information, but because of his limited capacity, I need to confirm it again. You'll be coming in on 3/20/04 on Delta, flight 435 at 2:00 p.m. And we'll send someone to pick you up at the airport. I'm sure you'll be tired, you'll probably have some computer equipment with you and lots of luggage, so be sure to tell the skycap to help you and we'll reimburse you for that and anything else you spend money on. When you get off the plane, just go to the baggage claim, then get your stuff then go outside to the limo area and our driver will be there with a sign with your name on it.

Affectation

Informal slang

Contraction

Now, to the important stuff. In all honesty, we are very excited that you are coming to invest in our company. I think this will provide us with a much-needed infusion of funds with which to not only stabilize but spur growth of our little company. Our products are unique and we could never expand without your help since Tucson's a growing place with lots of folks moving here. And, of course, you'd end up being the recipients of the fruits of your labor, too. So if all works out well, we should realize immense profits in two years or so. And despite what other people around the world say about Americans, we really are hard workers, especially my boss who heads up the company—nose to the grindstone every day and burning the midnight oil every night!

Informal

Idioms

Figure 9–11   Inappropriate International Correspondence (Marked for Revision)
(continued)

Ichiro Katsumi   2   February 27, 2004

Informal — (Anyway,) I've enclosed a guidebook and map of Tucson and material on our company. If you see anything you'd like to do in town, let me know, and if you have any questions about the company before we see you, just drop us a quick e-mail or fax (I don't think (snail mail) will get to us in time).

Jargon ——

Have a safe trip, ——— *Abrupt: add more goodwill*

Ty Smith

Ty Smith
————————— *Position title needed*

Figure 9–11   Inappropriate International Correspondence (Marked for Revision) (continued)

Sun West Corporation, Inc.

2565 North Armadillo
Tucson, AZ 85719
Phone: (602) 555-6677
Fax: (602) 555-6678   sunwest@aol.com

February 27, 2004

Ichiro Katsumi
Investment Director
Toshiba Investment Company
1-29-10 Ichiban-cho
Tokyo 105, Japan

Formal salutation ——— Dear Mr. Katsumi:

Polite opening acknowledges recipient and his family ——— I hope that you and your family are well and prospering in the new year. We at Sun West Corporation are very pleased that you will be coming to visit us in Tucson this month. It will be a pleasure to meet you, and we are very gratified and honored that you are interested in investing in our company.

So that we can ensure that your stay will be pleasurable, we have taken care of all of your travel arrangements. You will:

- Leave Narita–New Tokyo International Airport on Delta Airlines flight #75 at 5:00 p.m. on March 20, 2004.
- Arrive at Los Angeles International Airport at 10:50 a.m. local time and depart for Tucson on Delta flight #186 at 12:05 p.m.
- Arrive at Tucson International Airport at 1:30 p.m. local time on March 20.

Checklist-style schedule with times and dates spelled out ———
- Depart Tucson International Airport on Delta flight #123 at 6:45 a.m. on March 27.
- Arrive in Salt Lake City, Utah, at 10:40 a.m. and depart at 11:15 a.m. on Delta flight #34 and arrive in Portland, Oregon, at 12:10 p.m. local time.
- Depart Portland, Oregon, on Delta flight #254 at 1:05 p.m. and arrive in Tokyo at 3:05 p.m. local time on March 28.

Courteous and helpful contact information ——— If this information is not accurate or if you need additional information about your travel plans or information on Sun West Corporation, please call, fax, or e-mail me directly. That way, we will receive your message in time to make the appropriate changes or additions.

Figure 9–12 Appropriate International Correspondence (continued)

Mr. Ichiro Katsumi   2   February 27, 2004

After you arrive in Tucson, a chauffeur from Skyline Limousines will be waiting for you at Gate 12. He or she will be carrying a card with your name, will help you collect your luggage from the baggage claim area, and will then drive you to the Loews Ventana Canyon Resort. This resort is one of the most prestigious in Tucson, with spectacular desert views, high-quality amenities, and one of the best golf courses in the city. The next day, the chauffeur will be back at the Ventana at 9:00 a.m. to drive you to Sun West Corporation.   — *Specific arrival plans*

We at Sun West Corporation are very excited to meet you and introduce you to all the members of our hardworking and growing company family. After you meet everyone, you will enjoy a catered breakfast in our conference room. At that time, you will receive a schedule of events planned for the remainder of your trip. Events include presentations from the president of the company and from departmental directors on:

- The history of Sun West Corporation.
- The uniqueness of our products and current success in the marketplace.   *Specific trip event*
- Demographic information and benefits of being located in Tucson.   *plans*
- The potential for considerable profits for both our companies with your company's investment.

We encourage you to read through the enclosed guidebook and map of Tucson. In addition to events planned at Sun West Corporation, you will find many natural wonders and historical sites to see in Tucson and in Arizona in general. If you see any particular event or place that you would like to visit, please let us know. We will be happy to show you our city and all it has to offer.

Again, we are very honored that you will be visiting us, and we look forward to a successful business relationship between our two companies.   — *Polite closing*

Sincerely,

Ty Smith

Ty Smith
Vice President

Enclosures (2)

Figure 9–12   Appropriate International Correspondence (continued)

CHAPTER 9 SUMMARY: Understanding the Principles of Business Correspondence

Selecting the Appropriate Medium

☐ Letters on your organization's stationery
- ■ To represent a commitment to the recipient
- ■ To formalize a business relationship

☐ Memos: printed and electronic
- ■ To communicate and circulate information within your organization

☐ E-mail messages
- ■ To communicate quickly within your organization and with customers and others outside your organization
- ■ To transmit text and graphics files electronically

☐ Faxes
- ■ To transmit a document that is not available in electronic format
- ■ To transmit a document that must be viewed in its original form (for instance, a letter with a signature or official seal)

☐ Telephone calls and conferences
- ■ To provide a setting for clarifying information and resolving issues
- ■ To provide an alternative to a face-to-face meeting
- ■ To enable participants to hear each other's voices

☐ Voice-mail messages
- ■ To communicate brief messages

☐ Face-to-face meetings
- ■ To make initial or early contacts with associates and customers with whom you wish to build a relationship
- ■ To plan a project, to make group decisions around specific objectives, or to solve a serious problem

☐ Videoconferencing
- ■ To provide an alternative to a face-to-face meeting
- ■ To enable participants to hear and see one another

Writing Business Messages

☐ Follow the writing process.

☐ Use goodwill and the "you" viewpoint.

☐ Use the direct pattern for good news:
1. Main point or good news
2. Explanation of facts
3. Goodwill close

☐ Use the indirect pattern for some negative messages:
1. Context (or "buffer")
2. Explanation
3. Bad news
4. Goodwill close

☐ Review letter opening and closing.

☐ Consider writing style and accuracy.

Formatting Business Letters

☐ Prepare a heading or use printed letterhead.

☐ Provide an inside address.

☐ Create an appropriate salutation, body, and complimentary close.

☐ Design a second page correctly, if needed.

☐ Add end notations as required.

Writing and Formatting Memos

☐ Follow memo protocol and strategy.

☐ Organize your ideas.

☐ Adjust the style and tone.

☐ Prepare an opening.

☐ Use lists and headings strategically.

☐ Prepare a closing.

☐ Use appropriate memo format.

☐ Prepare the subject-line title.

Meeting the Deadline: The Time-Sensitive Memo

☐ Make sure that you understand the assignment.

☐ Gather pertinent background information.

☐ Organize your major points into a sequence that makes sense.

☐ Write the draft quickly, including only one subject in each paragraph.

☐ Polish the draft, focusing on content and organization before revising at the sentence level.

Sending E-mail: Protocol and Strategies

☐ Consider appropriate use of e-mail.

☐ Review all e-mail messages for accuracy and readability before sending them.

☐ Recognize that all e-mail messages are subject to interception by someone other than the person or persons for whom the message is intended; write them accordingly.

☐ Observe the rules of netiquette.

☐ Consider the design needs of e-mail messages.

☐ Create an appropriate salutation, closing, and signature block.

Writing International Correspondence

☐ Use words likely to appear in your reader's English-language dictionary.

☐ Adjust for cultural preferences in the organization of ideas.

☐ Consider the decision-making style of your recipient's culture.

☐ Avoid using humor and slang.

☐ Read the letter aloud for ambiguity and confusing sentence structure.

☐ Check for appropriate forms of dates, times, and measurements.

■ Exercises

1. You are the manager of accounting for a company that sells computer-software packages. You have just received word from the comptroller that there has been a change in the expense allowances for employees using their own cars on business. Previously, one rate was applied to all employees, but now there will be different allowance rates for regular and nonregular drivers.

   Regular drivers are those who use their own cars frequently on the job to drive to their sales territories. Nonregular drivers are those employees—such as home-office personnel—who only occasionally use their cars on business.

   Prepare a memo or an e-mail to communicate the following information to all employees: The revised allowance is effective immediately. Drivers will be reimbursed according to the following formulas: Regular drivers will receive 30¢ per mile for the first 650 miles driven per month, and 10¢ for each additional mile. Nonregular drivers will receive 30¢ per mile for the first 150 miles per month, and 10¢ for each additional mile.

2. Explore the templates offered by your word-processing software. Most word-processing packages offer several styles of business-document templates, both contemporary and traditional. (This feature is included in Microsoft Word in the pull-down menu under Tools.) Use a template for letters offered by your software to format a letter you have composed. Print out the letter and submit it to your instructor with a memo that addresses the following questions:

   a. Why did you choose this particular template?
   b. Did the template make writing your letter easier? Why or why not?
   c. Why do businesses request that their employees use a template when formatting business letters?

3. Complete this assignment either on your own or as part of a collaborative team.

   a. You are director of corporate communications for a nationwide insurance company called The Provider Group. Management has asked you to design a letterhead that reflects a "modern, yet responsible image." For this project, collect as many samples of letterheads as you can. Then, using word-processing software with graphics capability, design a letterhead for The Provider Group (using a local address, phone number, and any other appropriate details). As you design, consider the image and personality your design will project as well as the amount of information you should provide.
   b. Survey three or four organizations in your area (including your college) to determine the standard letter formats they use (full block, modified block, etc.). Evaluate the formats using the guidelines provided in this chapter and in Chapter 8.
   c. Using the results in parts a and b, determine the best format for letters sent to clients by The Provider Group. Answer the questions in Exercise 2a through 2c.

4. Write a brief narrative describing how you plan to use or have used e-mail to collaborate on a writing assignment with fellow students or with colleagues at your job.

5. Write a brief narrative describing an on-the-job e-mail message you have received that was inappropriate or that communicated information so poorly that you had to ask for a clarification.

6. Prepare an e-mail to inform a group of international customers of the following: Your company's newsletter will now be delivered electronically, by e-mail, and will be updated monthly instead of bimonthly. Customers who wish to receive the print version of the newsletter will be charged an annual handling fee of $30. New items listed in the newsletter can be ordered at your company's Web site at a 10 percent discount. Customers need to inform the company if they wish to cancel their subscriptions to the newsletter. Be sure to present these changes positively—with your customers' point of view in mind. Refer to the following sections of this chapter: Sending E-mail: Protocol and Strategies (page 334) and Writing International Correspondence (page 341).

7. Rewrite the following statements, improving them as indicated.

   a. Rewrite the following statement to make it more positive and less blunt:

      ■ I will not pay you because you have not sent the final software upgrade. If you do not send the right one immediately, I will not pay you at all.

   b. Rewrite the following passage to make it more friendly:

      ■ I wrote for the Music Collection you advertised on TV, and, not only did it take six weeks to get here, but it was the wrong set of CDs. Can't you get anything right? I'm canceling payment on my check and sending this set of CDs back!

   c. Rewrite the following passage to make it clear and unpretentious:

      ■ With reference to your recent automobile accident, I have been unable to contact you due to the fact that I have been in Chicago working day and night on a proposal—a biggie. I should be back in the office in the neighborhood of the 15th or so. In the unforeseen and unlikely event that I should be delayed, you can utilize Mr. Strawman, of my office, who will also endeavor in your behalf.

   d. Rewrite the following statements so they reflect the "you" viewpoint:
      (1) I want you to buy this "Handy-Fone" so that I can win the sales award for this month.
      (2) We must receive a copy of your W-4 form to complete our files.
      (3) Our business is built on our commitment to quality that we pass on to our customers.
      (4) I can't finish your income-tax calculations until I receive your December receipts. Then I'll be able to file for the expected refund.

   e. Improve the business-letter style or memo-writing strategy of the following statements:
      (1) Pursuant to V. B. Lanham's instructions, I have prepared a thorough analysis that your department should have prepared last year.
      (2) Records of all long-distance telephonic communications should be submitted prior to the penultimate day of the subsequent month.
      (3) You are hereby notified that your vacation schedule must be submitted to my office two months prior to the dates so that I may avoid disruptive interferences. It is hoped this practice will find the acceptance of all staff members. If you have any questions, please feel free to call me. Thanks.

8. Draft an inquiry letter to Mr. José Espinosa of the Spanish Tourist Bureau in Madrid, Spain, asking for information about work opportunities in Spain. Explain that you are interested in relocating to Spain after you graduate. To draft the letter,

first gather information about both the proper protocol and the format of the letter. With the approval of your instructor, ask a faculty member at your college who teaches Spanish (and would understand the form and protocol of such a letter) to comment on the appropriateness of the letter you have drafted.

9. Based on your own experience as a student, write a memo to your instructor on one of the following topics in no more than 30 minutes:

   a. Should student tickets to athletic events on campus be included with the price of tuition?
   b. Should smoking be permitted in campus facilities?
   c. Should students be allowed to bring laptop computers to class for taking notes?

   Be sure to cover the points you feel must be included to support your conclusion.

10. You work for Smith Consultants, and your boss has asked you to draft a complaint letter to your software-supply company—the level of service and technical support to date has not met your boss's expectations. Include the following points:

    a. Telephone calls from your employees to the software help department are often not returned in a timely fashion. Sometimes they are not returned at all.
    b. Software assistance personnel often blame your hardware for the problem; however, when consulted, the hardware representative reports that the problem is with the software.
    c. Promised monthly four-hour in-service training sessions have not been scheduled for the past three months.

    You must also mention that your company is considering not paying the software provider the remaining 30 percent of the purchase amount. However, this is a very delicate matter because Smith Consultants has already invested thousands of dollars in the software system and would like to resolve the problem without losing the investment. Following the principles of business correspondence offered in this chapter, submit your draft in correct business-letter format to your instructor.

■ Collaborative Classroom Projects

1. Divide into small groups (three or four students) and elect a group leader. As a writing team, draft a letter explaining the changes in shipping charges to customers of your wholesale office-supply company.

   For more than five years, your company has been able to charge mail-order customers a flat shipping rate of $5.95 for any order under $300. This has been a strong advertising point for the company. However, profits have fallen steadily in the past two years, so the president of your company has announced that shipping charges will increase in two months. Shipping will be $5.95 for orders under $100 and will increase by $3 for each additional $1 to $100 worth of product.

   Your writing team must inform your existing customers of the change—a difficult task because the customers have been conditioned by your marketing representatives to expect "the industry's most reasonable" shipping charges. The letter should provide the context and explanation of the charges, the bad news, and a goodwill close. Follow the guidelines in this chapter for reference.

2. Divide into two groups of equal numbers. One group represents the local electric company's consumers, and the other group represents the company's marketing representatives. If you are the consumer group, write a letter as a team to the

utility commissioner asking that the rate increase requested by the electric company not be granted. If you are in the marketing group, write a letter as a team asking the utility commissioner to grant your rate-increase request. Each group has 30 minutes to write the letter, which should address the following issues:

a. Dependability of service of the utility
b. Need for a rate increase
c. Ability of customers to pay for the increase

Trade letters, and during the next 30 minutes, work as a group to write bad-news response letters from the utility commissioner's office. If you are writing to the consumers, break the bad news that the rate increase will be necessary. If you are writing to the electric company's representatives, break the bad news that a rate increase will not be granted. Remember to provide a context, an explanation, the bad news, and a goodwill close when drafting your replies.

3. Divide into small groups and appoint a group leader to facilitate a 45-minute discussion of e-mail. What are its benefits? For example, how can it save a company time and money? What are its drawbacks? For example, how can e-mail cause problems at work when misused? Ask each member of your group to explain how he or she has handled inappropriate e-mail at work in the past and to suggest ways to discourage inappropriate e-mail at work. During the last 15 minutes of your session, create an outline of your discussion and share it with the rest of the class.

4. In small groups, explore the different media used for communicating on the job. For each medium that follows, list situations in which you would use each. Draw on your varied experiences to provide a wide range of situations. Be ready to share your list with the rest of the class.

a. A Letter on organizational stationery
b. A Memo
c. An E-mail
d. A Fax
e. A Phone call
f. Voice mail
g. A Face-to-face meeting
h. A Videoconference

5. In a small group, team-write a 30-minute memo on one of the following topics, and format it according to the guidelines in this chapter.

a. Describe to a visiting professor your last three class assignments. Include what you learned.
b. Describe to a visiting student the food services available on campus.
c. Describe to an incoming freshman the campus policy on computer use by students. If possible, describe the location of the computer labs and their availability to students.

■ Research Projects

1. Locate a poorly written business letter. Sources can include correspondence that you receive in the mail (or by e-mail) at home or at work. Rewrite the letter to make it more professional. Submit both letters to your instructor, with a cover memo explaining what you revised and why.

2. Find a letter containing bad news that you believe is unnecessarily blunt. Rewrite the letter to protect the goodwill of the organization that sent it. Attach your revision to the original, and submit both to your instructor.
3. Locate a letter containing exaggerated, overdone goodwill. Sources to consider are mass-produced sales letters. Rewrite the letter, retaining goodwill while eliminating poor style.
4. Interview an employee at a local corporation. Determine generally how many different forms of communications media (letters, memos, e-mail, etc.) the interviewee uses and which medium he or she uses most often. Ask an interviewer to discuss the challenges and successes experienced as a writer on the job.
5. You work for a company that is expanding to include several international branches. Research and write an informal investigative report on cultural differences in business communication: slang expressions and technical jargon, methods of addressing people, punctuation marks, colors, references to body parts, physical gestures, technology symbols, cultural symbols, or other aspects of written communication.

   You may choose one culture to compare to the United States in great detail or more than one culture to compare on differing points. Before beginning your research and writing, determine your audience, purpose, and the scope of your report.

Web Projects

Projects followed by the symbol W are continued at **bedfordstmartins.com/writingthatworks**, Chapter 9.

1. Search the Web for sites dedicated to the subject of e-mail etiquette and choose one to review in detail. In a brief narrative, analyze the advice given at the site, discussing the points that you agree or disagree with. Explain why you agree or disagree. W
2. Search the Web for three articles about e-mail etiquette. Write a brief analysis in which you compare and contrast the content of the articles. E-mail your analysis to your instructor and include links to the articles analyzed.
3. Search online to find articles in online business magazines on appropriate style and tone for business correspondence. Select one article to summarize in 150 to 250 words. Be ready to prepare an oral summary for class discussion. W
4. Search the Web to find three or more sites dedicated to writing and formatting business correspondence. Write a memo in which you review the sites, and recommend those with the best advice and examples. Send your memo to your instructor as an e-mail attachment. Be sure to include links to the sites reviewed. W

10 Writing Business Correspondence

There are almost as many types of workplace correspondence as there are reasons for writing. This chapter discusses some of the most common types.

- Routine and Positive Messages
  - Acknowledgments
  - Covers (or Transmittals)
  - Inquiries and Responses
  - Responding to Inquiries
  - Sales and Promotions
  - Recommendations
- Sensitive and Negative Messages
  - Refusals
  - Complaints
  - Adjustments
  - Collections

For each of these types, you must also determine what format—such as letter, memo, or e-mail—is best. Keep in mind any company or organizational protocol for the form or medium for specific types of messages. (See pages 306–311 for advice on selecting the medium most appropriate for your purpose and audience.)

Because of their importance to breaking into a profession as well as for career advancement, job-application letters and résumés are discussed separately in Chapter 17, along with other job-seeking strategies.

■ Routine and Positive Messages

The types of correspondence discussed in this section provide the opportunity to build goodwill with readers and create a positive image of your organization.

Acknowledgments

One way to build goodwill with colleagues and clients is to let them know that you have received something they sent and to express thanks. A letter, an e-mail, or a memo that serves these functions is usually a short, polite note. The example shown in Figure 10–1 is typical and could be sent as a letter or an e-mail.

Dear Mr. Evans:

Acknowledgment   I received your comprehensive report today. When I finish studying it in detail, I'll send you our cost estimate for the installation of the Mark II Energy Saving System.

Thanks to writer   Again, thanks for preparing such a thorough analysis.

Regards,

Roger

Figure 10–1   Acknowledgment by Letter or E-mail

Covers (or Transmittals)

When you send a formal report, proposal, brochure, or similar material, you should include a short message, often called a *cover* (or *transmittal*) *letter,* that identifies what you are sending. An e-mail message that is used to send an electronic attachment also serves this purpose, as does a memo sent within an organization. The cover message also provides you with a record of when and to whom you sent the material.

Keep your remarks brief. Your opening should explain what is being sent and why. A cover letter that accompanies a report, for example, may identify its title, briefly describe its contents, state its purpose, and note who requested the report. In an optional second paragraph, you might summarize the information or point out any sections of particular interest to the reader. This paragraph could mention the conditions under which the material was prepared, such as limitations of time or budget. Your closing paragraph should contain acknowledgments, offer more assistance, or express the hope that the material will fulfill its purpose. If your letter accompanies a proposal, you could mention a key point or two as to why your firm is the best one to do the job. For advice on proposal cover letters, see Chapter 14, page 494.

Figure 10–2 is an example of a cover letter that is brief and to the point. Figure 10–3 is a bit more detailed, touching on the manner in which the information was gathered. (See also Figure 14–7 for a longer cover letter for a sales proposal.)

Inquiries and Responses

An inquiry letter or e-mail can be as simple as a request for a free brochure or as complex as asking a consultant to define specific requirements for a usability testing lab. (For job applications, another type of inquiry letter, see Chapter 17.)

Voices from the Workplace

Anna Rose Eckenrode, Charter Communications

Anna Rose Eckenrode is a human resources data supervisor at Charter Communications, a provider of broadband services that include high-speed Internet access and interactive television. On the job, Anna is in frequent contact with the company's 280 stores, company personnel and upper-level management, and outside vendors and consultants "by e-mail, written correspondence, and telephone."

"In my correspondence with store managers," she explains, "I convey information about corporate policies and procedures and provide instructions on how to implement corporate changes. In my correspondence to supervisors, managers, vice presidents, and the president of our company, I convey business procedures. When I write to personnel, I often need to explain policy changes in detail." Much of Anna's correspondence provides instructions. "Letters that I write that provide instructions, especially detailed ones, need to be very clear and concise. My readers need to be able to understand my message completely."

Anna also writes letters of recommendation for employees who have done well in the evaluation process. "I write to our Plant Manager about promoting outstanding employees. My letters explain and highlight an employee's strengths and are important in ensuring that he or she receives the appropriate salary increase."

Tobin H. Van Pelt, Icosystem Corporation

As a complexity scientist at Icosystem Corporation, Tobin Van Pelt works with collaborative teams of scientists, engineers, and software developers to create models for successful business environments. "A typical project requires a great deal of routine correspondence between team members and clients, such as data requests and frequent project update summaries. Almost all of this correspondence takes place through e-mail. As a result of experiencing many of the pitfalls that can occur when using e-mail, I have adopted some general guiding principles for composing these correspondences."

Tobin emphasizes the importance of being careful with sensitive information. "It is far too easy to mistakenly send e-mails containing sensitive information to the wrong people — it only involves the click of a mouse as opposed to the actual addressing of an envelope." He is also careful with the tone of his e-mails. "When writing a formal e-mail, I force myself to step into a different style of writing than I would otherwise typically use while writing an informal message." Tobin urges writers to state their purposes and messages effectively. "If the purpose of an e-mail is to request information, then state this succinctly in the e-mail header, and repeat this request more formally in the first line of the message." He also recommends that writers edit e-mail messages with the same care that is paid to print letters and memos. "One of the most common habits is the tendency to misspell words, not use proper grammar, and use other constructions that closely mimic the way we speak. I'm careful not to allow these habits to enter my professional e-mails. And I always use my spell checker before sending a formal message."

There are two broad categories of inquiries: those that benefit the recipient and those that benefit the writer. Inquiries of obvious benefit to the recipient include requests for information about a recently advertised product. Inquiries that primarily benefit the writer include, for example, a request to a professional association to send demographic information about its members. If your inquiry is of the second kind, be particularly considerate of your reader's needs. Your objective

ECOLOGY SYSTEMS AND SERVICES

39 Beacon Street, Boston, Massachusetts 02106
(617) 351-1223 • Fax: (617) 351-2121
ecologysystems.com

May 24, 2004

Mario Espinoza, Chief Engineer
Louisiana Chemical Products
3452 River View Road
Baton Rouge, LA 70893

Dear Mr. Espinoza:

Identification of enclosure ——— Enclosed is the final report on our installation of pollution-control
equipment at Eastern Chemical Company, which we send with
Eastern's permission. Please call me collect (ext. 1206) or e-mail me
Offer of assistance ——— at the address below if I can answer any questions.

Sincerely,

Susan Wong

Susan Wong, Ph.D.
Technical Services Manager
swong@ecologysystems.com

SW/ls
Enclosure: Report

Figure 10–2 Brief Cover Letter (for a Report)

will probably be to obtain, within a reasonable time, answers to specific questions. You will be more likely to receive a prompt, helpful reply if you follow the guidelines listed in Considering Your Audience and Purpose: Writing Inquiries (page 361) and illustrated in Figure 10–4.

Responding to Inquiries

When you receive an inquiry, read it quickly to determine whether you have both the information and the authority to respond. If you do, reply as promptly as you can, answering every question asked. Adjust the length of your response to the questions and the information provided by the writer. Even if the writer has asked

WATERFORD PAPER PRODUCTS
P.O. Box 413
WATERFORD, WI 53474

Phone: (414) 738-2191 • Fax: (414) 738-9122
waterfordpaper.com

January 16, 2004

Mr. Roger Hammersmith
Ecology Systems, Inc.
1015 Clarke Street
Chicago, IL 60615

Dear Mr. Hammersmith:

Enclosed is the report estimating our power consumption for the year as requested by John Brenan, Vice President, on September 4.

Identification of enclosure

The report is a result of several meetings with the Manager of Plant Operations and her staff and an extensive survey of all our employees, delayed by the transfer of key staff in Building A. We believe, however, that the report will provide the information you need in order to furnish us with a cost estimate for the installation of your Mark II Energy Saving System.

Background and purpose of report

We would like to thank Diana Biel of ESI for her assistance in preparing the survey. If you need any more information, please let me know.

Acknowledgment of help

Sincerely,

James G. Evans

James G. Evans
New Projects Office
jge@waterfordpaper.com

Enclosure

Figure 10–3   Long Cover Letter (for a Report)

P.O. Box 113
Dayton, OH 45409
March 11, 2004

Jane E. Metcalf
Engineering Services
Miami Valley Power Company
P.O. Box 1444
Miamitown, OH 45733

Dear Ms. Metcalf:

Reason for request

Could you please send me some information on heating systems for a computerized, energy-efficient house that a team of engineering students at the University of Dayton is designing?

The house, which contains 2,000 square feet of living space (17,600 cubic feet), meets all the requirements in your brochure "Insulating for Efficiency." We need the following information, based on the southern Ohio climate:

List of questions

1. The proper-size heat pump for such a home.
2. The wattage of the supplemental electrical heating units required.
3. The estimated power consumption and rates for those units for one year.

Offer to share results and contact information

We will be happy to send you our preliminary design report and any other information about the project that may interest you. If you have questions or suggestions, please contact me at kjparsons@udayton.edu or call 513-229-4598.

Thank you for your help.

Sincerely,

Kathryn J. Parsons

Kathryn J. Parsons
Engineering Student
University of Dayton

Figure 10–4   Inquiry Letter

Writing Inquiries

- ☐ Make your questions specific, clear, and concise.
- ☐ Phrase your questions so that the reader will know immediately the type of information you are seeking, why you need it, and how you will use it.
- ☐ If possible, present your questions in a numbered list to make it easy for your reader to address them.
- ☐ Keep the number of questions to a minimum.
- ☐ Offer some inducement for the reader to respond, such as promising to share the results of what you are doing.
- ☐ Promise to keep responses confidential, if appropriate.
- ☐ Close by thanking the reader for taking the time to respond. Provide contact information, such as a phone number or an e-mail address, to simplify a reply.

a question that seems silly or has what you feel is an obvious answer, respond courteously and as completely as you can. You may tactfully point out that the writer has omitted or misunderstood something.

If you feel you cannot answer an inquiry, find out who can and forward the inquiry to that person. Notify the writer that you have forwarded the inquiry, as shown in Figure 10–5. If you reply to a forwarded inquiry, state in the first paragraph why someone else is answering, as shown in Figure 10–6.

Subject: **Report Received**
    Date: Fri, 19 March 2004 11:42:25 -0500 (EST)
    From: Jane E. Metcalf <metcalf@mvpc.org>
      To: Kathryn J. Parsons <kjparsons@udayton.edu>

Dear Kathryn Parsons:

Thank you for inquiring about the heating system we recommend for homes designed according to the specifications in our brochure "Insulating for Efficiency."

Acknowledgment of inquiry

Because I cannot answer your specific questions, I have forwarded your inquiry to Michael Wang, Engineering Assistant in our Development Group. He should be able to answer your questions, and you should hear from him shortly.

Notification of forwarding

Best wishes,

Jane E. Metcalf

```
===============================
```
Jane E. Metcalf, Director of Public Information
Miami Valley Power Company
P.O. Box 1444 ~ Miamitown, OH 45733
Office 513-264-4800 ~ Fax 513-264-4889
Web ~ mvpc.org
```
===============================
```

Figure 10–5   **Response to an Inquiry (Indicating That the Request Has Been Forwarded)**

MIAMI VALLEY POWER COMPANY
P.O. BOX 1444
MIAMITOWN, OH 45733
(513) 264-4800 · mvpc.org

March 24, 2004

Ms. Kathryn J. Parsons
P.O. Box 113
Dayton, OH 45409

Dear Ms. Parsons:

Acknowledgment of inquiry

Jane Metcalf forwarded to me your inquiry of March 11 about the house that your engineering team is designing. I can estimate the heating requirements of a typical home of 17,600 cubic feet as follows:

Responses to list of questions

1. For such a home, we would generally recommend a heat pump capable of delivering 40,000 Btus, such as our model AL-42 (17 kilowatts).
2. With the AL-42 efficiency, you don't need supplemental heating units.
3. Depending on usage, the AL-42 unit averages between 1,000 and 1,500 kilowatt-hours from December through March. To determine the current rate for such usage, check with Dayton Power and Light Company.

Offer of further help

I can give you an answer that would apply specifically to your house based on its design (such as number of stories, windows, and entrances). If you send me those details, I will be happy to provide more precise figures for your interesting project.

Sincerely,

Michael Wang

Michael Wang
Engineering Assistant
mwang@mvpc.org

Figure 10–6   Response to an Inquiry (Letter)

Sales and Promotions

A sales letter or promotional message requires a thorough understanding of both the product, service, or business and the potential customer's needs. For this reason, many businesses (such as major retailers) employ specialists to compose their sales letters and other promotional material. However, if you work in a small business or are self-employed, you may need to write sales letters yourself. An effective sales message accomplishes the goals described in Writer's Checklist: Writing Effective Sales Letters below.

Your first task is to determine your audience: those who should receive your letter or other material. You may address former customers, people who have purchased a product or service from you and may do so again. You also might want to seek new customers interested in certain products or services. Companies that specialize in marketing techniques compile and sell such lists of members of professional, fraternal, and religious organizations, trade-show attendees, and the like. Because these lists tend to be expensive, select them with care.

Once you decide who should receive your sales letter, learn as much as you can about their age, sex, vocation, geographical location, educational level, financial status, and interests. You must be aware of your readers' needs so you can effectively tell them how your product or service will satisfy those needs.

Analyze your product or service carefully to determine your strongest psychological sales points—the product's intangible benefits rather than its physical features—and build your sales letter around those points. Begin by identifying how your product or service will make your reader's job easier, status higher, personal life more pleasant, and so on. Then in the body of the letter, show how your

---

Writing Effective Sales Letters

- ☐ Develop your letter to accomplish three basic goals.
  - ■ Open by attracting your reader's attention and arousing his or her interest.
  - ■ Describe features of the product or service that would appeal strongly to your reader's wants or needs.
  - ■ Suggest ways that the reader can immediately use the product or service.
- ☐ Be certain that any claim you make in a sales letter is truthful, not an overstatement. Mail fraud carries heavy legal penalties. If you say that a product is safe, you could be guaranteeing its absolute safety. Therefore, say that the product is safe *provided that normal safety precautions are taken.*
- ☐ Present evidence to convince your reader that your product or service is everything you claim it to be. Don't exaggerate, make unreasonable claims, speak negatively of a competitor, or use other unfair tactics. You can build confidence with a money-back guarantee, a free trial offer, testimonials, or case histories.
- ☐ Make the customer's response easy and worthwhile. You might include a map to your store, a discount coupon, instructions for phone-in orders and free delivery, or a Web address for more information, special discounts, and online orders.

product or service can satisfy the need or desire identified in your opening. Describe the physical features of your product in terms of their benefit to your reader. Help your reader imagine using your product or service—and enjoying its benefits.

Minimize the negative effect price can have on your reader. You might mention the price along with a reminder of the benefits; state it in terms of a unit rather than a set ($20 per item instead of $600 per set); identify the daily, monthly, or even the yearly cost based on the estimated life of the product; suggest a series of payments rather than the total; or compare the cost with that of something the reader accepts readily ("costs the same as a movie and a dinner out").

Figure 10–7 shows a typical sales letter. Notice its light, friendly tone—an ap-

---

Janice's Cycle Shop
775 First Avenue, Ottumwa, IA 52501
(515) 273-5111 • fax (515) 273-5511

janicecycle.com

April 5, 2003

Mr. Raymond Sommers
350 College Place
Sharpsville, IA 52156

Dear Mr. Sommers:

Needs of reader — Are you ready to go bike riding this spring—but your bike isn't?

Benefits of service — Janice's Cycle Shop will get your bike in shape for the beautiful days ahead. We will lubricate all moving parts; check the tires, brakes, chain, lights, horn, and other accessories; and make any minor repairs—all for only $29.95 with the coupon enclosed with this letter.

Convenience of service — Just stop in any day, Monday through Saturday, between 8:00 a.m. and 9:00 p.m. We are conveniently located at the corner of First and Walker. If you bring your bike in before 10:00 a.m., you can enjoy a spring bike ride that evening.

Happy riding!

Janice's Cycle Shop

Figure 10–7   Sales Letter

proach frequently used by small, local businesses to make the reader feel comfortable about coming to them. The signature line of sales letters often show the name of the company rather than the name of an individual, as is the case in this example. The e-mailed sales message in Figure 10–8 also uses an informal but professional tone, appealing to the readers' interests while instilling confidence in the company's ability to provide timely information.

From:	contact_us@cartoonbank.com
Sent:	Wednesday, April 02, 2003 3:27 PM
To:	Mary Hughes
Subject:	A Gift for Registering

Welcome Mary Hughes!

Thanks for registering at Cartoonbank.com, your premier source for New Yorker cartoons and cover prints.

As a special gift for becoming a member we want to give you an exclusive coupon. Use the coupon code "WELCOME1" on your next purchase of $100 or more and receive 10% off.

Incentive for customer to return

Almost every cartoon that has ever appeared in The New Yorker is available from The Cartoon Bank as a framed or matted print or a T-shirt or sweatshirt.

http://www.cartoonbank.com

Links for easy response

New Yorker cartoons are also a great way to get your message across in a Power Point presentation or lighten up your company newsletter or corporate annual report. Learn more about our licensing benefits by going here:

http://www.cartoonbank.com/licensing.asp

Benefits of product described with a business audience in mind

The Cartoon Bank is also home to The New Yorker's Vintage Cover Collection (1925–1992). Over 60 years of illustrated cover art available as large museum-quality prints.

http://www.cartoonbank.com/covers.asp

Description of other products written to a general audience

Find all this and more at Cartoonbank.com, including Limited-Edition Signed Cover Lithographs, New Yorker Desk Diaries, cartoon books, and more!

And remember use "WELCOME1" and save 10% on your next purchase!

If you need any help at all, please don't hesitate to contact us by e-mail (mailto:toon@cartoonbank.com) or phone (1-800-897-TOON). You can also chat online with a live customer service representative by clicking on the green button located on the upper left of every page in Cartoonbank.com.

Customer service contact information and friendly close

Yours in good humor,

Bob Mankoff
President

Figure 10–8   Sales E-mail

Recommendations

A recommendation can range from a statement on a form provided by a prospective employer to a detailed reference letter evaluating the professional accomplishments and personal characteristics of someone seeking employment.

To write an effective recommendation or reference letter, you must be familiar enough with the applicant's abilities or actual performance to make an evaluation and then communicate it truthfully and without embellishment. For a reference letter to achieve its purpose, you must specifically link the applicant's skills, abilities, knowledge, and characteristics to the position requirements.

In a recommendation solicited by a prospective employer, always respond directly to the inquiry carefully, addressing any specific questions. For the record, you must identify yourself: name, title or position, employer, and address. You could begin by explaining the circumstances and time period of your acquaintance with the person you are recommending. You should mention, with as many supporting details as possible, one or two outstanding characteristics of the applicant. Organize the details in your letter in decreasing order of importance. Conclude with a brief summary of the applicant's qualifications and a clear statement of recommendation. Figure 10–9 is a typical recommendation letter.

When you serve as a reference or supply a letter of reference, be aware that applicants have a legal right to examine the materials in an organization's files that concern them, unless they sign a waiver of their right to do so. For guidance on the job search, including resignation letters, see pages 625–627.

■ Sensitive and Negative Messages

Writing sensitive or negative messages requires careful thought. You must decide, for example, how direct or indirect your message should be and then choose words that maintain a professional relationship with a correspondent despite any difficult circumstances. Refer also to Negative Messages and the Indirect Pattern on pages 314–316 as well as Tone: Goodwill and the "You" Viewpoint on pages 311–314. See Chapter 17, pages 625–627, for resignation letters.

Refusals

When you receive a request to which you must give a negative reply, you may need to write a refusal message containing bad news—something that a reader does not want to receive. Unless the stakes are very low, opening with the bad news can affect your reader negatively. The ideal refusal says *no* in such a way that you avoid antagonizing your reader while managing to maintain goodwill. To do so, you must convince your reader that the reasons for refusing are logical or understandable before you present the bad news. The following pattern effectively deals with this problem:

1. *Context.* In the opening (often called a "buffer"), introduce the subject and establish a professional tone.

IVY COLLEGE

DEPARTMENT OF BUSINESS
WEST LAFAYETTE, IN 47906
(691) 423-1719

(691) 423-2239 (FAX)
IVCO@IVY.EDU (E-MAIL)

January 14, 2004

Mr. Phillip Lester
Director of Human Resources
Thompson Enterprises
201 State Street
Springfield, IL 62705

Dear Mr. Lester:

As her employer and her former professor, I am pleased to recommend
Kerry Hawkins. I've known Kerry for the last four years, first as a student in my class and for the last year as a research assistant.

Circumstances and time writer has known applicant

Kerry is an excellent student, with above-average grades in our program. On the basis of a GPA of 3.6 (A = 4.0), Kerry was offered a
research assistantship to work on a grant under my supervision. In
every instance, Kerry completed her library search assignments on
time, and her reports were always well written. The material they provided met the requirements for my work and more. While working
15 hours a week on this project, Kerry has maintained a class load of
12 hours per semester.

Outstanding characteristics of applicant

I strongly recommend Kerry for her ability to work independently, to
organize her time efficiently, and to write clearly and articulately. If you
would like more information about why I believe Kerry is so outstanding, please e-mail me at mpaul@ivy.edu or call (691) 423-4326.

Recommendation and summary of qualifications

Sincerely yours,

Michael Paul

Michael Paul
Professor of Business

Visit Ivy at ivy.edu

Figure 10–9   Recommendation Letter

2. *Explanation.* Review the facts that lead logically to the bad news, but try to see things from your reader's point of view.

3. *Bad news.* State your refusal, based on the facts, concisely and without apology.

4. *Goodwill.* In the closing, establish or reestablish a positive relationship by providing an option, assure the reader of your high opinion of his or her product or service, offer a friendly remark, or merely wish the reader success.

In the case of a rejected proposal, as in Figure 10–10, the writer expresses appropriate and genuine appreciation for the reader's time, effort, and interest.

Memo

To: Darrell Munro
From: Amelia Jackson, Screening Procedures Committee *AJ*
Date: May 17, 2004
Subject: Response to Proposed Security-Clearance Procedures

Context and thanks

The Screening Procedures Committee appreciates the time and effort you spent on your proposal for a new security-clearance procedure.

Figure 10–10 Memo Rejecting an Internal Proposal *(continues through page 369)*

Notice in the continuation of Figure 10–10 that the writer thoroughly details the reasons for the refusal with the goal of convincing the reader that the conclusion is reasonable.

Explanation with logical reasons

We reviewed the potential effects of implementing your proposed security-clearance procedure on a company-wide basis. We asked the Systems and Procedures Department to review the data, survey industry practices, seek the views of senior management and department heads, and submit the idea to our legal staff. As a result of this process, we have reached the following conclusions:

- The cost savings you project are correct only if the procedure could be universally required.
- The components of your procedure are legal, but most are not widely accepted by our industry.
- Based on our survey, some components could alienate employees who would perceive them as violating an individual's rights.
- Enforcing company-wide use would prove costly and impractical.

Figure 10–10 Memo Rejecting an Internal Proposal (continued)

The writer states the negative message concisely, clearly, and as positively as possible.

> For these reasons, the committee recommends that divisions continue their current security screening procedures.

Refusal

Figure 10–10   Memo Rejecting an Internal Proposal (continued)

The writer closes by working to reestablish goodwill and avoids rehashing the bad news (not writing "Again, we're sorry we can't use your idea").

> Because some components of your procedure may apply in certain circumstances, we would like to feature your ideas in the next issue of *The Guardian*. I have asked the editor to contact you next week. On behalf of the committee, thank you for the thoughtful proposal.

Goodwill closing with option

Figure 10–10   Memo Rejecting an Internal Proposal (continued)

Refusals often vary with what is at stake for the writer or reader. The refusal in Figure 10–11 declines an invitation to speak, and the stakes for the writer are relatively low; however, the writer wishes to acknowledge the honor of being asked. Figure 10–12 shows a letter rejecting a job applicant in which the stakes are higher. Finally, Figure 10–13 shows a refusal sent to a supplier whose product was not selected, yet the writer wishes to maintain a harmonious relationship. For advice about writing resignation and job refusal letters, see Chapter 17, pages 625–627.

Complaints

By the time you need to write a complaint letter (sometimes called a "claim letter"), you may be irritated and angry. If you write a letter that reflects only your annoyance and anger, you may simply seem petty and irrational. As a result, the best complaint letters—the ones taken seriously—do not sound complaining.

Remember, too, that the person who receives your complaint may not be the one who was directly responsible for the situation. An effective letter should assume that the recipient will conscientiously correct the problem.

Although the circumstances and severity of the problem may vary, effective complaint letters (or e-mails) should generally follow this pattern.

1. Identify the problem or faulty item(s) and include relevant information such as invoice numbers, part names, and dates, as well as a copy of the receipt, bill, or contract.

WATASHAW ENGINEERING COMPANY

301 Industrial Lane
Decatur, IL 62525
Phone: (708) 222-3700
Fax: (708) 222-3707
wec.com

March 29, 2004

Javier A. Lopez, President
TNCO Engineering Consultants
9001 Cummings Drive
St. Louis, MO 63129

Dear Mr. Lopez:

Positive context

I am honored to have been invited to address your regional meeting in St. Louis on May 17. That you would consider me as a potential contributor to such a gathering of experts is indeed flattering.

Review of facts and refusal

On checking my schedule, I find that I will be attending the annual meeting of our parent corporation's Board of Directors on that date. Therefore, as much as I would enjoy addressing your members, I must decline.

Goodwill closing with option

I have been very favorably impressed over the years with your organization's contributions to the engineering profession, and I would welcome the opportunity to participate in a future meeting.

Sincerely,

Ralph P. Morgan

Ralph P. Morgan
Research Director
rpm@wec.com

RPM/lcs

Figure 10–11   Letter Refusing a Speaking Invitation

Liberty Associates
3553 West Marshall Road
San Diego, California 92101

Phone: (619) 555-1001
Fax: (619) 555-0110
libertyassociates.com

January 19, 2004

Ms. Sonja Yadgar
2289 South 63rd Street
Hartford, CT 06101

Dear Ms. Yadgar:

Thank you for your interest in financial counseling at Liberty
Associates. I respect your investment experience and professionalism,
and I enjoyed our conversation.

Shortly after our meeting, an especially appropriate, well-qualified internal candidate applied for the position, and we have decided to offer
the job to that individual. I say in all honesty that the decision was very
difficult. Both Nancy Linh and I were impressed with your qualifications and believe that you have a great deal to offer our profession.

Please do stay in touch. Best wishes for the future.

Sincerely,

Meike Künkel

Meike Künkel
Vice President
Director of Development

*Positive
context*

*Review of
facts and
refusal*

Goodwill closing

Figure 10–12   Letter Rejecting a Job Applicant

2. Explain logically, clearly, and specifically what went wrong—especially for a
   problem with a service. (Avoid speculating about why you think a problem
   occurred.)

3. State what you expect the reader to do to solve the problem to your
   satisfaction.

MARTINI BANKING AND DATA SYSTEMS

251 West 57th Street
New York, New York 10019
Phone: (212) 555-1221   Fax: (212) 555-2112
martinisystems.com

February 11, 2004

Mr. Henry Coleman
Abbott Office Products, Inc.
P.O. Box 544
Detroit, MI 48206

Dear Mr. Coleman:

Positive context

Thank you for your cooperation and your patience with us as we struggled to reach a decision. We believe our long involvement with your company indicates our confidence in your products.

Review of facts and refusal

Based on our research, we found that the Winton Check Sorter has all the features that your sorter offers and, in fact, has two additional features that your sorter does not. The more important one is a backup feature that retains totals in its memory, even if the power fails. The second additional feature is stacked pockets, which are less space-consuming than the linear pockets on your sorter. After much deliberation, therefore, we have decided to purchase the Winton Check Sorter.

Goodwill closing

Although we did not select your sorter, we were very favorably impressed with your system and your people. Perhaps we will be able to use other Abbott products in the future.

Sincerely,

Muriel Johansen

Muriel Johansen
Business Manager

Figure 10–13   Letter Rejecting a Sales Proposal

To reach someone who can help you in a large organization, first check its Web site or call its main office so you can address your letter to the appropriate department (often Customer Service, Consumer Affairs, or Adjustments). In smaller organizations, you might write to a vice president in charge of sales or service. For very small businesses, write directly to the owner. As a last resort, you may find that sending copies of a complaint letter to more than one person in the company will get fast results. Each employee who receives the letter will know (because of the notation at the bottom of the page) that others, possibly higher in the organization, have received the letter and will take note of whether the problem is solved. Figure 10–14 shows a typical complaint letter.

Adjustments

An adjustment letter responds to a complaint and tells the customer what your company intends to do about the problem. You should settle such matters quickly and courteously, always trying to satisfy the customer at a reasonable cost to your company. An effective adjustment letter actually builds goodwill as it both repairs any damage that has been done and restores the customer's confidence in your company.

Open your letter with what the reader will consider good news.

- Grant the adjustment, if appropriate, for uncomplicated situations ("Enclosed is a replacement for the damaged part").

- Reveal that you intend to grant the adjustment by admitting that the customer was right ("Yes, you were incorrectly billed for the delivery"). Then explain the specific details of the adjustment. This method is good for adjustments that require detailed explanations.

- Apologize for the error ("Please accept our apologies for not acting sooner to correct your account"). This method is effective when the customer's inconvenience is as much an issue as money.

- Use a combination of these techniques. Often, situations that require an adjustment also require flexibility.

The tone of your correspondence is critical. Grant adjustments graciously; a settlement made grudgingly will do more harm than good. No matter how unreasonable the complaint, your response should be positive and respectful, focusing not on the unfortunate situation but on what you are doing to correct it. Not only must you be gracious, you must also acknowledge the error in such a way that the customer or client will not lose confidence in your organization.

Before granting an adjustment to a claim for which your company is at fault, as illustrated in Figure 10–15, you must determine what happened and what you can do to satisfy the customer. Be certain that you are familiar with your company's adjustment policy. In addition, be careful about your wording; for example, "we have just received your letter of May 7 about our defective product" could be

BAKER MEMORIAL HOSPITAL

Diagnostic Services Department
501 Main Street, Springfield, OH 45321
(513) 683-8100 • Fax (513) 683-8000
bakermemorial.org

September 23, 2004

Manager, Customer Relations
Computer Solutions, Inc.
521 West 23rd Street
New York, NY 10011

Subject: HV3 Monitors

On July 9, I ordered nine HV3 monitors for your model MX-15 diagnostic scanner. The monitors were ordered from your Web site.

Explanation of error

On August 2, I received from your Newark, New Jersey, parts warehouse seven HL monitors. I immediately returned those monitors with a note indicating the mistake that had been made. However, not only have I failed to receive the HV3 monitors I ordered, but I have also been billed repeatedly.

Enclosures substantiating complaint

I have enclosed a copy of my confirmation e-mail, the shipping form, and the most recent bill. If you cannot send me the monitors I ordered by November 1, please cancel my order.

Request for solution

Sincerely,

Paul Denlinger

Paul Denlinger
Manager

pld@bakermemorial.org

Enclosures

Figure 10–14   Complaint Letter

International Hotels

EXECUTIVE OFFICE

September 26, 2003

Ms. Elizabeth Shapiro
2374 N. Kenwood Ave.
Fresno, CA 93650

Dear Ms. Shapiro:

We are sorry that you and your husband's stay with us did not go
smoothly. Providing dependable service is what's expected of us—and
when our staff doesn't provide high-quality service, it's easy to understand our guests' disappointment. I truly wish we had performed better
and that your vacation plans had not been disrupted.

Gracious tone

We are eager to restore your confidence in our ability to provide dependable, high-quality service. Please accept the enclosed certificate
for one weekend's stay at any of our 500 hotels worldwide. I hope we
will have the pleasure of welcoming you and your husband again soon.

Adjustment

Ms. Shapiro, in addition, we appreciate your taking the time to write. It
helps to receive comments such as yours, and we conscientiously follow through to be sure proper procedures are met. I assure you your
letter is being put to good use.

Positive closing

Yours truly,

Ms. M. J. Matthews

Ms. M. J. Matthews
Executive Office

Enclosure: Certificate

**10113 Executive Drive/Chicago, Illinois 60601
800-964-9400   interhotel.com**

Figure 10–15   Adjustment Letter (Company Takes Responsibility)

ruled in a court of law as an admission that the product is, in fact, defective. Treat every claim individually, and lean toward giving the customer the benefit of the doubt.

Sometimes you may decide to grant a partial adjustment to regain the customer's lost goodwill, even though the claim is not really justified, as in Figure 10–16.

You also might need to educate your reader about the use of your product or service. Customers sometimes submit unjustified claims honestly believing them to be fair (for example, a problem resulting from a customer not following maintenance instructions properly). You would grant such a claim only to build goodwill. When you write a letter of adjustment in such a situation, give the explanation before granting the claim—otherwise, your reader may never get to the explanation. If your explanation establishes customer responsibility, do so tactfully, as Figure 10–17 illustrates.

Writing Tactful Adjustment Letters

☐ Address your reader respectfully, whether you apologize, explain, educate, or offer an adjustment.

☐ Explain what caused the problem if such an explanation will help restore your reader's confidence or goodwill.

☐ Explain specifically how you intend to make the adjustment if it is not obvious in your opening.

☐ Express appreciation to the customer for calling your attention to the situation, explaining that this helps your firm keep the quality of its product or service high.

☐ Point out any steps you may be taking to prevent a recurrence of whatever went wrong, giving the customer as much credit as the facts allow.

☐ Avoid recalling the problem in your closing ("Again, we apologize . . ."). Close positively, looking forward, not back.

Collections

Collection letters serve two purposes: (1) to collect the overdue bill and (2) to preserve the customer relationship. In some states, collection letters should be prepared by attorneys because certain language and requirements must be followed to demand payment. However, even if you never need to write a collection letter, understanding the collection-letter series offers important insights into the strategies of sensitive correspondence.

Most companies use a series of collection letters in which the letters become increasingly demanding and urgent. The series usually proceeds in three stages, each of which may include several letters as well as follow-up phone calls. All letters should be courteous and show a genuine interest in the customer and whatever problems may be preventing prompt payment.

The first stage consists of reminders stamped on the invoice ("overdue"), form

Computer Solutions, Inc.
521 West 23rd Street
New York, NY 10011

Customer Relations
Phone: (212) 574-3894
Fax: (212) 574-3899
ssiegel@compsol.com

September 28, 2003

Mr. Fred J. Swesky
7811 Ranchero Drive
Tucson, AZ 85761

Dear Mr. Swesky:

Thank you for your letter regarding the replacement of your CS5
Notebook Computer.

You said in your letter that you used the unit on an open deck. As our
service representative pointed out, this model is not designed to operate in extreme heat. As the instruction manual accompanying your
new CS5 states, such exposure can produce irreparable damage.
Because your unit was used in such extreme heat conditions, we
cannot honor the warranty.

Explanation of customer responsibility

However, we are enclosing a certificate entitling you to a trade-in
allowance equal to your local CSI dealer's markup for the unit. This
means you can purchase a new unit at wholesale, provided you return
your original unit to your local dealer.

Partial adjustment

Sincerely yours,

Susan Siegel

Susan Siegel
Assistant Director

SS/mr
Enclosure

Figure 10–16   Adjustment Letter (Customer Is Responsible)

SWELCO Coffeemaker, Inc.

9025 North Main Street   Phone: (800) 233-5656
Butte, MT 59702   Fax: (800) 233-3010

August 26, 2003

Mr. Carlos Ortiz
638 McSwaney Drive
Butte, MT 59702

Dear Mr. Ortiz:

Enclosed is your SWELCO Coffeemaker, which you sent to us on August 17.

Education of customer

In various parts of the country, tap water may have a high mineral content. If you fill your SWELCO Coffeemaker with water for breakfast coffee before going to bed, a mineral scale will build up on the inner wall of the water tube—as explained on page 2 of your SWELCO Instruction Booklet.

Adjustment and instruction

We have removed the mineral scale from the water tube of your coffee-maker and thoroughly cleaned the entire unit. To ensure the best service from your coffeemaker in the future, clean it once a month by operating it with four ounces of white vinegar and eight cups of water. To rinse out the vinegar taste, operate the unit twice with clear water.

Positive closing

With proper care, your SWELCO Coffeemaker will serve you faithfully and well for many years to come.

Sincerely,

Helen Upham

Helen Upham
Customer Services

HU/mo
Enclosure

swelco.com

Figure 10–17   Educational Adjustment Letter (Accompanying a Product)

letters, or brief personal notes. These early reminders should maintain a friendly tone that emphasizes the customer's good credit record. They should remind the customer of the debt and may even solicit more business by including promotional material for new items. As in the example in Figure 10–18, you might suggest that nonpayment may be a result of a simple error or oversight.

In the second stage, the collection letters are more than just reminders. You now assume that some circumstances are preventing payment. Ask directly for

ABBOTT OFFICE PRODUCTS, INC.

P.O. Box 544
Detroit, MI 48206
Phone: (313) 567-1221
Fax: (313) 567-2112
abbott.com

August 30, 2004

Mr. Thomas Holland
Walk Softly Shoes
1661 East Madison Boulevard
Garfield, AL 36613

Dear Mr. Holland:

With the new school year about to begin, your shoe store must be busier than ever as students purchase their back-to-school footwear. Perhaps in the rush of business you've overlooked paying your account of $1,200 which is now 60 days overdue.

Tactful reminder

Enclosed is our fall sales list. When you send in your check for your outstanding account, why not send in your next order and take advantage of these special prices.

Enclosure seeks future business

Sincerely,

Henry Bliss

Henry Bliss
Sales Manager
hb@abbott.com

Figure 10–18 First-Stage Collection Letter

payment, and inquire about possible problems, perhaps inviting the customer to discuss the matter with you. You might suggest an optional installment payment plan if you are able to offer one. Mention the importance of good credit, appealing to the customer's pride, self-esteem, and sense of fairness. Remind the customer that he or she has always received good value from you. Make it easy to respond with a return envelope, a toll-free telephone or fax number, or a Web address where the payment can be made. At this stage, your tone should be firmer and more direct than in the early stage, but never rude, sarcastic, or threatening. Notice how the second-stage letter shown in Figure 10–19 is more direct than the first-stage letter but no less polite.

Third-stage collection letters reflect a sense of urgency, for the customer has not responded to your previous letters. Although your tone should remain courteous, make your demand for payment explicit. Point out how reasonable you have been, and urge the customer to pay at once to avoid legal action. Again, make it easy to respond by providing a return envelope, a toll-free telephone or fax number, or a Web address, as shown in Figure 10–20.

Dear Mr. Holland:

Inquiry about problems

We are concerned that we have not heard from you about your overdue account of $1,200 even though we have written three times in the past 90 days. Because you have always been one of our best customers, we have to wonder if some special circumstances have caused the delay. If so, please feel free to discuss the matter with us.

Direct request

By sending us a check today, you can preserve your excellent credit record. Because you have always paid your account promptly in the past, we are sure that you will want to settle this balance now. If your balance is more than you can pay at present, we will be happy to work out mutually satisfactory payment arrangements.

Options for response

Please use the enclosed envelope to send in your check, or call (800) 526-1945, toll-free, to discuss your account.

Sincerely,

Henry Bliss

Henry Bliss
Sales Manager
hb@abbott.com

Figure 10–19   Second-Stage Collection Letter

Dear Mr. Holland:

Your account in the amount of $1,200 is now 180 days overdue. You have already received a generous extension of time and, in fairness to our other customers, we cannot permit a further delay in payment.

Urgent request

Because you have not responded to any of our letters, we will be forced to turn your account over to our attorney for collection if we do not receive payment immediately. Such action, of course, will damage your previously fine credit rating.

Explicit demand

Why not avoid this unpleasant situation by sending your check in the enclosed return envelope within 10 days or by calling (800) 526–1945 to discuss payment.

Options for response

Sincerely,

Henry Bliss

Henry Bliss
Sales Manager
hb@abbott.com

Figure 10–20   Third-Stage Collection Letter

CHAPTER 10 SUMMARY: Writing Business Correspondence

Routine and Positive Messages

☐ *Acknowledgments* build goodwill with colleagues and clients by confirming the arrival of something they sent and expressing thanks.

☐ *Cover* (or *transmittal*) messages accompany material sent to a recipient, identify what is being sent, and explain why it is being sent.

☐ *Inquiries and responses* state clearly the information wanted, who wants it, and why. Answer inquiries by responding to all the questions or forwarding the inquiry to someone who can.

☐ *Sales and promotions* attract the reader's attention to a product, service, or business by arousing interest, emphasizing benefits, and inviting a response.

☐ *Recommendations* evaluate the professional accomplishments and personal characteristics of someone seeking employment.

Sensitive and Negative Messages

☐ *Refusals* deny requests or give negative replies while working to maintain goodwill.

☐ *Complaints* use a professional tone to describe a problem and how you expect it to be corrected to your satisfaction.

☐ *Adjustments* tell customers how your company intends to redress a complaint and apologize if the company is at fault.

☐ *Collections* work to preserve the customer relationship while collecting payment on an overdue account.

■ Exercises

1. Write a cover letter for a report or a term paper that you are preparing for another course. Address your letter to the appropriate instructor.

2. The following situations require different types of correspondence. Read *a* through *e*, and then write the letters, memos, or e-mails assigned by your instructor, using the proper format for each.

    a. You are writing a letter requesting a free booklet that explains how college students can apply for scholarships to study abroad. Address a letter to Nancy Reibold, the executive director of the Global Initiative Center at 1012 Third Avenue, New York, NY 10021. You learned about this booklet when you were surfing the Web and came upon the Global Initiative Center Web site.

    b. Assume that you are Nancy Reibold and you received the request for the booklet. You are out of copies at the moment, however, because you have received more requests than anticipated. You expect to receive more copies within two weeks. Write a response to the inquiry explaining these circumstances. Tell the reader that you will send the booklet, titled "Study Abroad," as soon as you can—and offer the alternative of downloading a document that you will make available at your Web site.

    c. You are Nancy Reibold's assistant at the Global Initiative Center, and you are both angry. You have just received 10,000 copies of the booklet from the Jones Printing Company, 105 East Summit Street, New Brunswick, NJ 08910. When you opened the carton, you discovered each booklet is missing several pages. This is the second printing mistake made by Jones Printing, and the shipment is late as well, even though Robert Mason, the sales representative, had promised that you would have no problems this time. Nancy Reibold wants to "get this problem corrected immediately." Write a complaint letter to Robert Mason for Ms. Reibold to sign.

   d. Assume that you are Robert Mason. You have received the complaint letter about the printing mistake. After checking, you discover that the booklets sent to the Global Initiative Center had been subcontracted to another printing firm (ILM Printing Company) because of the backlog at Jones. You know that Jones Printing will not be billed for the booklets if you return them to ILM Printing within five working days. You decide that you must write an adjustment letter to Ms. Reibold quickly, asking her to return the booklets.

   e. Assume that you are Robert Mason. Send a convincing, detailed memo to J. R. Jones, your boss and President of Jones Printing, recommending that ILM Printing Company not be used for future subcontracting work.

3. You manage Sunny River Resort. Charles James, director of the Sunny River Business League, has requested the free use of your lodge for a two-day staff meeting. You'd like the business league to use your meeting room, but you have a problem: You charge any group $250 per day to use the room. You can't afford to give it away. The room has a number of fixed and variable costs required to clean, pay for lighting and air-conditioning, and supply and repair equipment. Also, what might happen if others knew you had provided the room at no cost? Write a letter to Mr. James selling him on the idea of using your lodge while holding to the $250 fee. Use tact, a positive tone, and persuasive details.

4. You are the manager of Hamon's Fine Clothing. Dr. Klaus Müller, a busy cardiac surgeon, has purchased two suits (total $1,275) from you—and is six months overdue in paying for them despite several standard-form notices. You'll now need to start a series of collection letters, but you want to make the pace slow. Dr. Müller is highly respected in the community. Write a series of collection letters, spacing them appropriately (date the first letter January 2).

5. You manage BT Discount Auto Parts. Jeff Price, a 23-year-old friend of your nephew, owes $325 for parts. You allowed him to charge his purchase two months ago because your nephew said Jeff was reliable and promised to cover the bill if he didn't pay. Your nephew has offered to give you a check, but you prefer to collect from Jeff. Write a collection-letter series to Jeff Price starting on July 1.

6. You are Mr. Henry Coleman of Abbott Office Products, who received the letter in Figure 10–13. Write a memo to R. P. McMurphy, Vice President of Engineering (with a copy to Pat Smith, Director of Marketing), recommending improvements in the check sorter (or another office system of your choice). Collect facts by visiting a local office-systems store or examining its catalog.

7. You have recently purchased a local high-end camera store and wish to build your business. You have a mailing list of former customers, but many of them were unhappy with the previous owner's products and service. You would like to win them back. You specialize in the highest-quality digital and SLR cameras as well as accessories. The shop is also an authorized repair service for Nikon and Sony cameras and lenses. Your partner is highly qualified as both a photographer and an expert in digital imaging for commercial and Web applications.

The community you serve is relatively affluent, but the former owner's reputation included overcharging customers and refusing to service what he sold. Your store is located on East Capitol Drive near a variety of appliance stores and restaurants, and a chain electronics store that sells cameras but is not known for quality service. You believe that satisfied customers will improve your business.

Write a sales letter, addressed to former customers, effectively promoting your services. Plan this letter as the basis for other promotional materials.

8. Eight years ago, you opened Tiny Tots Day Care with six children, and it has grown to a capacity of 65 children. Its reputation is so high that there is a waiting list of 78 children. As the director and owner of the center, you now face a problem that you have never before encountered. You must expel a child from the center.

You need to write a letter to Mr. and Mrs. Brady telling them that their four-year-old son, Brett, is being expelled from Tiny Tots. Since Brett entered your center, things haven't been the same. This child is not able to get along with other children. In his two months at Tiny Tots, he has bitten six children (causing one child to require stitches); kicked a teacher; and regularly scratched, hit, and pulled hair. Several parents have threatened to pull their children out of your center if Brett does not leave. Despite several conferences with Brett's parents, who seem reasonable and concerned about their son, you have observed no changes in his behavior. Write the letter to the Bradys following the pointers for a refusal letter. Remember that this is the Bradys' only child, and choose your words carefully.

9. As your instructor directs, write a 300- to 500-word analysis of one of the sample refusal letters in this chapter. Evaluate the letter, describing how each sentence contributes to the refusal-letter strategy.

10. The word-processing program of your office software most likely offers templates for formatting various styles of business letters. Click to open a new file, and then click on letters and faxes to explore the options available. Common styles include classic, contemporary, and block. Select a style to compose a brief letter to your instructor evaluating the course. When you have completed your letter, choose another style for a second version of your letter. To transfer the text of your letter, you may use shortcuts, such as copy and paste. Submit both copies of your letter to your instructor.

11. In a brief essay, discuss why you think e-mail will or will not replace the traditional paper business letter. Relate your essay to your field of study or occupational interest, and give examples of changes you expect in the workplace of the future. Consider all areas relevant to your field, such as customers, clients, suppliers, competitors, technology, and so forth.

■ Collaborative Classroom Projects

1. Choose a partner in class. For the next 45 minutes, write a one-page recommendation for your partner as part of an application for an upcoming leadership retreat. The retreat, sponsored by an industrial consortium, is being facilitated by faculty from your university's Organizational Leadership Center. Include in your letter:

   a. How you know the applicant.
   b. Specific leadership skills of this person that you have noticed.

    c. Why you think he or she is a good candidate for the retreat.

    d. What you think the applicant will learn from the retreat.

        To get started on this project, you and your partner should agree on the best system for exchanging information about each other's skills, abilities, knowledge, and personal characteristics in relation to leadership training.

        When you have completed your recommendations, exchange letters with another pair of students. In the time allotted by your instructor, evaluate with your partner the two letters you receive. Review them as if you were on the selection committee choosing retreat participants. Decide whether each recommendation is helpful, and write any comments or questions on the letters before you return them to their writers or your instructor.

2. Form groups of five or fewer members. Your company, an office-supply business, has just mistakenly sent a letter to all your customers offering a 20 percent discount off the total of their next order. The letter was supposed to have offered a 20 percent discount off the most expensive item in their next order. After receiving input from all appropriate departments, the company president has decided the business cannot afford to grant the overall 20 percent discount. You have been instructed to draft a letter to your customers explaining the mistake and clarifying that they will be allowed to take 20 percent off of only the most expensive item, not the entire order. Your company president asks that you appeal to your customers' vested interest in your company's ability to keep prices competitive and advises you to ask for their understanding of the error. Appoint a team leader, and as a group, take no more than 20 minutes to brainstorm the points you want to include in the letter. During the next 20 minutes, draft your letters individually. As a group, select one letter that best represents your group's ideas.

3. Form into small groups of classmates who are majoring in the same area. Appoint a team leader. Assume that you belong to an academic or professional organization in need of funds for a project or trip. Come up with a fund-raising event that your organization will sponsor by brainstorming a list of services related to your major and expertise that your group could offer. Then take 20 minutes to draft a letter to prospective contributors that does the following:

- Describes your group and its objectives
- Explains why your group is raising money (perhaps for a trip to observe a facility or to attend a conference related to your area of study, requiring money for travel, accommodations, meals, and registration fees)
- Explains why your group has sent the letter to its recipient (perhaps as an alumnus of your organization or a supporter of your university)
- Explains what your group hopes to learn or gain from the trip or project. (For example, students of management may visit a successful company to observe its management methods and training system as part of a research project.)
- Makes clear the benefits of contributing both in terms of the services received and the good done by supporting your trip or project
- Provides specific details about the fund-raising services available
- Inspires the reader to contribute and explains how to do so

Overall, your letter should catch the attention of your readers, arouse their interest, and convince them that your fund-raiser provides a valuable service while raising money for a worthwhile cause.

4. Your class has been asked to organize a three-hour workshop on business writing for your university's continuing education department. As a class, you have

discussed this with your instructor and decided that because of your course loads, your jobs, and other outside responsibilities you are unable to volunteer to conduct a successful workshop at this time. Appoint a class leader or facilitator and a class recorder. As a group, draft a letter to the Department of Continuing Education explaining why your class cannot help. Brainstorm to develop a list of points to include in your letter. Open the letter with an explanation of the context, introducing the subject and establishing the tone. Then explain the facts, lead logically to your refusal, and conclude with goodwill in order to retain a positive relationship with the department. (Keep in mind that your class's refusal creates a sensitive situation for your instructor who will be working again with the Department of Continuing Education.) After you have completed your letter, your instructor may want to give the class feedback.

■ Research Projects

1. Find an actual letter refusing a request or delivering bad news (job-application refusal, denial of credit, and so on) that you believe is unnecessarily blunt. Rewrite the letter using the refusal strategy discussed in this chapter. Submit to your instructor a copy of the original letter and your revision.

2. Write a 300- to 500-word report on how correspondence fosters positive customer relations in business and industry. Your research may include books, journals, and other printed material. You may even want to research one or more companies, in terms of their use of correspondence to attract and keep customers. You might discuss styles or techniques that companies use when writing to customers, factors companies consider when replying to complaints, or reasons for answering customers' letters. Conclude with your own observations.

3. Conduct a personal or telephone interview with someone in business who uses letters or e-mail to contact customers. Real-estate agents, self-employed service businesses, product representatives, politicians, medical caseworkers, and government employees are examples of candidates for an interview. Prepare a list of questions before the interview, and plan on taking no more than 30 minutes of your interviewee's time. Possible questions include the following: Why do you write letters or e-mail messages to your customers or clients? What results do you expect? What writing styles do you find to be most successful? Can you describe a specific scenario in which a letter or an e-mail helped to solve a difficult problem? Develop similar questions of your own. After the interview, summarize your findings in a brief narrative.

4. Choose one of the following topics:
   a. How to write effective sales letters (or, generally, how to write persuasively)
   b. How to write recommendation letters
   c. How to respond to complaint letters
   d. How to write effective complaint letters

   Research printed material to learn what experts have written about your topic. Write a brief critical analysis of at least three articles on your topic. Compare and contrast the articles and, in conclusion, give your opinion on the article with the most helpful advice. Support your analysis with examples from the articles.

5. You are an employee of a large company that is considering in-house day care. As a member of the research committee exploring this option, you have been asked

to identify three companies that already offer this service to their employees. You are to write to each of the three companies and ask for a description of their service and day-care center. Include questions such as the following:

a. How many employees use the day-care service?
b. How many children on average use the center daily?
c. How many hours a day or night is the center open?
d. How many staff persons are employed at the center?
e. What is the salary of the director of the center?
f. How large is the center in square feet?
g. Is the center new construction or a remodeled part of the company's facility?
h. Are the company and employees pleased with the day-care center?
i. How are the center's operating costs covered?

You may include any additional relevant questions or choose to substitute an alternative topic such as job-sharing, flextime, or a company menu of benefits that allows employees to select their own benefits.

■ Web Projects

Projects followed by the symbol W are continued at **bedfordstmartins.com/ writingthatworks**, Chapter 10.

1. a. Write a brief report on how online companies use e-mail to solicit business and maintain good customer relations. Focus on three or four specific companies that have a significant presence on the Web — perhaps companies with which you have done business, such as an online bookstore or newspaper. Gather as many examples of e-mail from these companies as possible and write a brief critical analysis of each. Include any information about styles or techniques used and the effectiveness of these e-mails as sales tools. Support your views with examples from the texts, and include printouts of the e-mails with your report.

   b. Write a brief report on how online companies reply to e-mails from customers. Research the Web, focusing on three or four specific companies that have a significant presence on the Web, and research any printed materials available on this subject. You may even wish to contact the department or individuals responsible for replying to customer correspondence. Include in your report any information you discover about styles or techniques that companies use in replies, factors companies consider when replying to complaints, or efforts to answer every customer's e-mail. Be sure that your report includes any necessary documentation.

2. You work for a small, budget-conscious company of fewer than 50 employees. Your boss has asked you to investigate one of the items listed below for possible purchase by your company. Your boss's primary consideration is cost. Using the Web, review information provided by at least three online vendors about the product or service you are interested in. E-mail the vendors to obtain any further information you may need. Which vendor offers the best value? Write a persuasive memo to your boss that explains your recommendation for the product or service. Include key points from your research, and support your recommendation with specific details. Possible products and services to investigate include the following:

- A wireless communication system
- A company vehicle (for purchase or lease)
- A computer software package
- A security system
- An accounting or other business-related service

3. Select an issue relevant to your area of study and professional interest that you feel requires new or different legislation. Begin by searching federal, state, or local government Web sites for information on this topic. Evaluate the issue and possible solutions, then write a persuasive letter using good sales-letter techniques to your state senator or representative (or other appropriate official) with your suggestions for legislative changes or new legislation on the issue. Include a brief summary of the problem, your solution, and the benefits and practical application of your solution. Be specific and concise. [W]

4. Search the Web to find sites offering examples of business letters.

   a. Print out three to five letters and write a brief analysis of their style, tone, language, and concerns. Do they follow the principles of good correspondence outlined in this chapter? Are they effective? Why or why not? How are they different from or similar to contemporary business sales correspondence in style, tone, language, and audience? Be specific.

   b. Print out three to five letters that seem to you to be particularly dated. Rewrite them so that they are contemporary in style, tone, and language and geared toward present-day readers. When you hand in your assignment, include printouts of the original letters with your revised versions. [W]

5. Review at least three online companies that specialize in e-mail marketing. Begin by entering the key search terms "e-mail marketing," "online marketing," "Internet marketing," or "Internet e-mail marketing," using at least three different search engines, such as InfoSeek, Lycos, Yahoo!, AltaVista, or other browsing tools. In your review, explore what these companies promise to provide the customer, what are the differences or similarities among these companies are in terms of their goals and business styles, and why these companies hire professional writers to develop their sales-oriented e-mail correspondence. Then consider how the sales e-mail is different from or similar to the traditional sales letter.

11 Writing Informal Reports

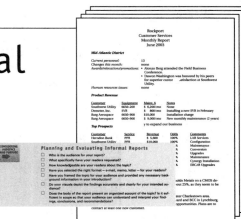

The successful operation of many organizations depends on reports that are either circulated within the organization or submitted to customers, clients, and others. What is a report? Although the term is used to refer to hundreds of different types of written communications, it can be defined as a document that provides requested or needed information in an organized format to a specific audience.

Reports fall into two broad categories: formal and informal. *Formal reports*, explained in detail in Chapter 12, generally grow out of projects that require many months of work, large sums of money, and the collaboration of many people. They may run several hundred pages and usually include a table of contents and other devices to aid the reader because of their length and scope of coverage. *Informal reports*, however, generally run from a few paragraphs to a few pages and provide information on projects that typically take a few hours or days to complete. They include only the essential elements of a report: an introduction, a body, conclusions, and, when appropriate, recommendations. Because of their brevity and limited scope, informal reports are customarily written as letters (for recipients outside a company) or as memos (for recipients within a firm). (See Chapters 9 and 10 for guidance on writing and formatting letters and memos.) This chapter discusses report-writing strategies and the most common types of informal reports:

W **On the Web**
For more help with writing informal reports, see Chapter 11, bedfordstmartins.com/ writingthatworks

- Trouble Reports (page 392)
- Investigative Reports (page 396)
- Progress and Periodic Reports (page 396)
- Trip Reports (page 404)
- Test Reports (page 404)

■ Planning and Writing Informal Reports

Taking Notes

For a report to be successful, you need to include all the information that will meet the objective of your report (such as information that will persuade your audience to adopt a plan of action) and the needs of your readers (information that will enable your readers to understand your proposal and see its logic and benefits). To achieve these goals, collect information and keep notes as the activity progresses. Otherwise, you may have trouble obtaining or trying to remember the information you need later to write the report. The purpose of taking notes is to record, in an abbreviated form, the background information that will go into your report. Be careful, however, not to make your notes so brief that you forget what you intended when you wrote them. (See Chapter 7 for more on note-taking.) Once you have prepared your notes, organize them into a sequence that makes sense from the perspective of your objective and audience, as explained in Chapter 2. If you are working with an outline, add your notes to the appropriate places to flesh it out.

Considering Audience

An informal report is almost always written for a specific small group of readers (or a single reader)—usually at their request. As a result, readers will likely be familiar with the subject of the report, making it easier for you to determine how much background information to provide and how much specialized or technical language to use. Note, for example, that the writer of the test report in Figure 11–7 (last paragraph) assumes that her reader is familiar with Occupational Safety and Health Administration (OSHA) standards. Without such knowledge, the reader would be unable to interpret the test findings. (See Determine Your Audience's Needs in Chapter 1 for additional guidance on audience analysis.)

■ The Parts of the Informal Report

Most informal reports that you will be called on to write will have three or four main parts: the introduction, the body, conclusions, and recommendations.

1. The *introduction* announces the subject of the report, gives its purpose, and, when appropriate, provides background on who assisted with or provided information for the report. The introduction should also concisely summarize any conclusions, findings, or recommendations made in the report. A concise summary is useful to your readers because it provides essential information at a glance and helps them focus their thinking.

Voices from the Workplace

David Noyes, Neumann Monson Wictor Architects

For David Noyes, project architect with Neumann Monson Wictor, writing informal reports is a frequent and an essential part of his job. The most common reports that he writes are summaries of the regular progress meetings that take place among the architects, contractors, and clients involved in the design and building process.

David explains: "These reports summarize any problems discussed, questions asked, and decisions agreed upon at each meeting. They are important primarily because they can be considered legal documents — if a legal issue ever arose or an injury ever occurred on the site of a building project, these notes can be used to determine responsibility for the problem." David's most crucial summaries are those that record meetings with clients that take place before the construction begins. "My design concept is usually directly based upon this initial input. After developing an initial plan, I usually return to the clients and ask them to critique it. We repeat this process until the design is refined and finalized."

When writing summaries, David keeps the following strategies in mind. "First, I include the title of the project; the date; and the names, titles, and contact information of all participants. Next, I summarize the information as clearly and concisely as possible — if my reports were to be misunderstood, they could lead to potentially expensive and even dangerous mistakes. I also make sure that my technical points are absolutely accurate. Finally, I edit my reports so that they are never longer than two or three pages — otherwise, people won't take the time to read them!"

Hélène Ducros, University of North Carolina

Hélène Ducros, a native of France, studied at the School of Law at the University of North Carolina, where she now works as an administrator of international programs. At her job, Hélène communicates with students, administrators, and faculty members, and writes international correspondence and informal reports.

When writing the brief, periodic reports required by the university — in which she provides updates on her projects and on specific aspects of her job — Hélène keeps her objectives in mind. "I focus on the purpose of my writing, my content, and my readers. My goal is to convey information clearly and concisely, not to impress my readers with my stylistic effects." When a specific format is not required by university administrators, Hélène chooses to write her informal reports as brief memos: "I find the memo to be the clearest and most direct format to get across some basic facts in an organized manner. The reader can access information in one glance."

Hélène describes her writing process: "It always includes a preparatory phase in which I jot down a few ideas, organizing what I want to say. I refer to this outline while writing the text of my document." Hélène also carefully revises her informal reports and other communications: "I want people to have a good professional impression of me no matter what. Once I have typed my report, I review it carefully. I try to be very attentive to spelling mistakes and faulty grammar, especially because I am not a native English speaker. I try to use clear and direct language, so there are no ambiguities as to what I mean."

2. The *body* presents a clearly organized account of the report's subject — the results of a market survey, the findings of a test carried out, or the status of a construction project, and so on. The amount of detail you include in the body depends on your objective, the complexity of your subject, and your readers' familiarity with the subject.

3. The *conclusion* summarizes your findings and tells readers what you think the significance of those findings may be.

4. *Recommendations* — which are included in some reports — are sometimes combined with conclusions in one section at the end of the report. In this section, you recommend a course of action that you believe is warranted by your findings. Recommendations can range from suggestions for instituting new work procedures, for developing new products or marketing campaigns, for setting up new departmental responsibilities, or for hiring new employees.

■ Types of Informal Reports

Because there are so many different types of informal reports, and because the categories sometimes overlap (a trip report, for example, might also be a progress report), it would be unrealistic to attempt to study or try to itemize every type. However, it is possible to become familiar with report writing in general and to examine some of the most frequently written kinds of informal reports in the workplace. This chapter looks at trouble reports, investigative reports, progress reports, periodic reports, trip reports, and test reports.

Trouble Reports

Accidents involving personal injuries, equipment failures, and work stoppages (those caused by equipment failures, worker illnesses, etc.) occur in many industrial and construction settings. Every such incident must be reported so that management can determine its cause and take any necessary steps to prevent a recurrence. A *trouble report* — also called an *accident report* or an *incident report*, depending on the situation — is the record of an accident or breakdown that may even be used by the police or by a court of law in establishing guilt or liability. Because trouble reports can help prevent further injury or disruption in service and serve as legal evidence, they should be prepared as accurately, objectively, and promptly as possible.

The trouble report is usually a memo written by the person in charge of the site where the incident occurred, addressed to his or her superior. (Although some companies have printed forms for specific types of trouble reports, even they include a section in which the writer must explain in detail what happened.)

Figure 11–1 shows a trouble report written by a safety officer after interviewing all the people involved in the accident.

Consolidated Energy, Inc.

To: Marvin Lundquist, Vice President
        Administrative Services
From: Kalo Katarlan, Safety Officer   *KK*
        Field Service Operations
Date: August 19, 2004
Subject: Field Service Employee Accident on August 7, 2004

An Accident Review was conducted on Friday, August 16, 2004, at the
Reed Service Center. The attendees were as follows:

Injured Representative:	John Markley
Union Representative:	Harry Hartsock
Employee's Supervisor:	Carl Timmerinski
Safety Officer:	Kalo Katarlan
Safety Officer, Field Service Operations:	Marie Sonora
Date of Accident:	August 7, 2004
Days of Lost Time:	2

How accident was evaluated — employee interviews

Accident Summary

John Markley visited the site of a rewiring job on German Road. Chico
Ruiz was working there, stringing new wire, and John was checking
with Chico about the materials he wanted for framing a pole. Some
trees had been trimmed in the area, and John offered to help remove
some of the debris by loading it into his pickup truck. While John
loaded branches into the bed of the truck, a piece broke off in his right
hand and struck his right eye.

What happened, who was involved, what injury resulted

Accident Details

1. John's right eye was struck by a piece of tree branch. John had just
   undergone laser surgery on his right eye on Monday, August 5, to
   reattach his cornea. At the time of the accident, he was not wearing
   protective eyeware.
2. John immediately covered his right eye with his hand, and Chico
   Ruiz gave him a paper towel with ice to cover his eye and help ease
   the pain.
3. After the initial pain subsided, John got into his truck and began to
   back up to return to the Service Center. Chico reminded John about

Events are listed in order of occurence

Figure 11–1   **Trouble Report (Memo with Recommendations)** (continued)

Lundquist   2   August 19, 2004

the pole trailer parked behind his truck and then returned to the crews he was supervising. John continued backing up, but did not see the tree behind him because his visibility was blocked by the tree debris in his truck bed.

4. When John struck the tree, his head struck the back window of the truck, shattering the glass. He was not wearing a safety helmet.

5. John returned to the Service Center to report the accident to his supervisor. However, because he had pieces of glass inside his clothes and on his neck, he decided to go home to shower and change clothes. He also used eyedrops prescribed to him after his surgery to thoroughly wash his injured right eye.

6. The next day, August 8, John went to Downtown Worker's Care because he was experiencing headaches. He was diagnosed with a bruised eyeball and eyelid. The headaches were caused by the impact to his head when it hit the rear window of his truck.

7. On Monday, August 12, John returned to his eye surgeon. Although bruised, his eye was not damaged, and the surgically implanted lens was still in place.

To prevent a recurrence of such an accident, the Safety Department will require the following actions in the future:

List of corrective actions

• When working around and moving debris such as tree limbs or branches, all service-crew employees must wear helmets and safety eyewear with side shields.

• Service-crew employees must always consider the possibility of shock for an injured employee. If crew members cannot leave the job site to care for the injured employee, someone on the crew must call for assistance from the Service Center. An injured employee should never be allowed to drive immediately after an accident. The Service Center phone number is printed in each service-crew member's handbook.

• All service-crew employees must conduct a "circle of safety" check around any vehicle before moving it.

Figure 11–1 Trouble Report (Memo with Recommendations) (continued)

Writing a Trouble Report

☐ On the *subject line* of your memo, state what you are reporting:
SUBJECT: Personal-Injury Accident in Section A-40.

☐ Write a brief *introductory summary* of the incident.

☐ In the *body* of your memo:

■ State exactly when and where the accident or breakdown took place.

■ Describe any physical injury or any property damage that occurred.

■ Itemize any expenses that resulted from the incident (for example, an injured employee may have missed a number of workdays, or an equip-ment failure may have caused a disruption in service to the company's customers).

■ Include precise data on times, dates, location, treatment of injuries, names of any witnesses, and any other crucial information. Insurance claims, workers' compensation awards, and lawsuits may hinge on the information in a trouble report.

☐ In your *conclusion,* provide a detailed analysis of what you believe caused the trouble.

■ Avoid condemnation or blame; be thorough, exact, and objective, and support any opinion you offer with facts.

■ Mention what was or will be done to correct the conditions that may have led to the incident.

☐ Include your *recommendations* for preventing further incidents (such as in-creased safety precautions, improved equipment, or the establishment of training programs). If you are speculating on the cause of the accident, make sure that this is clear to the reader.

Customizing Templates for Your Documents

Save time by customizing templates in your word-processing software for routine doc-uments — including letters, faxes, reports, and more.

■ Click on File and New for an options menu of dozens of standard-format tem-plates.

■ Select a template and enter the customized information requested (names, headings, headers and footers, page numbers; recipient in the "To" line and sender in the "From" line; routine salutations and closings for correspondence; clip-art images; and the like).

■ Save your customized information as a "document" template; your saved tem-plate will have its own icon for easy retrieval.

■ The same format and customized information will appear each time you open the template to create a new document.

Investigative Reports

Investigative reports are most often written in response to a request for information. You might be asked, for instance, to check the range of prices that companies charge for a particular item or service, to conduct an opinion survey among customers, to study alternative procedures for performing a specific operation, to review business trends in your line of work, and so on. You would then present your findings in an investigative report.

Investigative reports are usually prepared as memos if written within an organization and as letters if written by an outside consultant. The results of long, complex investigations are usually written as formal reports. (See Chapter 12.) For memo and letter reports, open with a brief introductory summary that includes a statement of the information you were seeking and any relevant background as to why the investigation was necessary and who requested it. Then, in the body of the memo or letter, describe the extent of or method used for your investigation. Finally, state your findings and any recommendations based on the findings.

In the example shown in Figure 11–2, a store manager has investigated three alternative ways of reducing shoplifting in his store and recommended the one most suitable for the store's size and budget.

Progress and Periodic Reports

Progress reports and *periodic reports* both describe the status of work performed over the course of an ongoing project. The chief difference between them is how often they are written. The progress report is issued at certain stages or milestones during a project. The periodic report, sometimes called a status report, details the status of an ongoing project at regular intervals—weekly, monthly, quarterly. Both types of reports may be required for work being performed within an organization or by an outside consultant.

Green Department Stores
Memo

To: William Bernardi, Regional Manager
From: Julius Chernoff, Department Manager *JC*
Date: September 23, 2003
Subject: Shoplifting at Store E-5150

As we have discussed over the last several months, shoplifting at Store E-5150 has increased since the store opened one year ago this month. Although we have budgeted $10,000 a year for shoplifting losses, our monthly inventory check shows that we have lost $11,800 in merchandise this year. The loss was especially evident during the summer months. It is time to take action to reverse this trend.

Proposed Solutions

My staff and I have researched several different options for minimizing shoplifting in our store. They include hiring security guards, using strategically placed security cameras in the store, and using undercover employees. In investigating options available to us, we considered effectiveness, convenience, and price.

Security Guards

We first considered hiring security guards. I met with the president of Hall Security on July 25. Hall Security is a local company that has been in business ten years. I also talked to other store managers in the area who have contracts with Hall Security—all are very pleased with the service and its effectiveness. They believe that the presence of uniformed security guards in their stores discourages theft. The managers surveyed report shoplifting reduction rates of from 50 to 70 percent. I can provide you with detailed data from these interviews at your request.

If we decide to have one security guard on duty during all store hours, we would pay a flat monthly rate of $1,900. One guard on duty from 4 p.m. until 10 p.m. daily, our busiest hours, would cost $1,000 a month. We are not considering the option of a night guard because we have not had any problems with break-in burglaries after hours.

Security Cameras

We next considered the use of security cameras. The cameras provide a record of thefts in progress and make prosecuting shoplifters much easier once they're caught. The technicians from TSC Inc., a camera service company, visited our store on August 5. They studied the floor plan to determine the most effective placement of cameras throughout the store. They recommend six cameras placed so that we have a view of the whole store at all times. We would need to purchase a single

Introduction and background

Section heading and overview of options

First option investigated, with findings

Recommendation

Second option investigated, with findings

Figure 11–2   Investigative Report (Memo with Recommendations) (continued)

William Bernardi   2   September 23, 2003

monitor that would display each camera's view on a rotational basis every ten seconds. The monitor would be located in the store manager's office where I or, in my absence, someone I designate, can observe activity throughout the store's retail space. The videotapes can be kept for a week and then recorded over.

Impressions of service

TSC Inc. would install the system and train our employees to operate it. TSC Inc. also provides a five-year on-site service warranty for the cameras and monitor. They make service calls to the store during business hours within four hours of being called. Total cost, including installation, will be $3,000. We were impressed with the knowledge, experience, and professionalism of the TSC representatives. They provided data for stores comparable to ours that showed an average 60 to 75 percent drop in the incidence of shoplifting. I called several store managers where the cameras are in use, and they verified these results.

Third option investigated, with findings

Undercover Employees

The third option examined is the use of undercover employees. This option involves having store employees who pose as customers as they stroll through the store monitoring customers for shoplifting. We estimate that this option would require two employees each shift. They would alternate between their regular duties, such as stocking shelves, and performing inventory-control tasks. If we also employ security guards, these two units could work in conjunction to help discourage theft.

Risks associated with option

However, the option has some risks associated with it. It would require that our employees receive training in the legal rights of customers and could potentially put our employees at risk in encounters with criminals. Hall Security Services can provide training over a one-week period at a cost of $1,200 per employee.

Recommendations

Section heading and recommendations based on findings

After completing our research on these possibilities for theft prevention, my staff and I believe that the best option is the installation of security cameras. After comparing the cost of the system with the amount of merchandise we are losing, we believe that the expense is worth the investment. Once the system is installed, there will be negligible expense in its use and maintenance. Our research shows that theft has declined in more than 90 percent of the stores that have security cameras. Pending our approval, TSC Inc. can install the system in four days. Once it is installed, we would evaluate the effectiveness of the system on a monthly basis and I would provide you with a monthly status report. I look forward to your assessment of this recommendation.

Figure 11–2   Investigative Report (Memo with Recommendations) (continued)

Progress Reports

The purpose of a progress report is to keep others—usually management—informed of the status of a project. In answering various questions (Is the project on schedule? running smoothly? within its budget?), the report lets readers know precisely what work has been completed, what work remains to be done, and the reasons for any possible delays. Often the report will include recommendations for changes in procedure or will propose new courses of action. Progress reports are generally prepared when a particular stage of a project is reached.

The projects most likely to generate progress reports are long-term and fairly complex. The construction of a building, the development of a new product, the opening of a branch office in another part of town, and a major reorganization of an organization's Web site are examples of such projects. Progress reports are frequently required in the contract for a project that will take weeks, months, or longer to complete.

Progress reports allow managers to keep track of the project and to make any necessary adjustments in assignments, schedules, and budget allocations while the project is under way. Progress reports can make it easier for management to schedule the arrival of equipment and supplies so that they will be available when needed. Such reports can, on occasion, avert crises. If a hospital had planned to open a new wing in February, for instance, but a shortage of wallboard caused a two-month lag in construction, a progress report would alert hospital managers to the delay—in time for them to prepare alternative plans.

Many projects, of course, require more than one progress report. In general, the more complicated the project, the more frequently management will want to review it. All reports issued during the life of a project should be submitted in the same format to make it easier for readers to recognize at a glance where they need to focus their attention. Progress reports sent outside the company are normally prepared as letters (see Figure 11–3); those circulated within a company can be written as memos. The first in a series of reports should identify the project in detail and specify what materials will be used and what procedures will be followed throughout the project. Later reports in the series contain only a transitional introduction that briefly reviews the work discussed in the previous reports. The body of the reports should describe in detail the current status of the project. Every report should end with any conclusions or recommendations—for instance, alterations in schedule, materials, or procedures.

In the example shown in Figure 11–3, a contractor reports to the city manager on his progress in renovating the county courthouse. Notice that the emphasis is on meeting specified costs and schedules.

Periodic Reports

Periodic reports are issued at regular intervals—daily, weekly, monthly, quarterly, annually—rather than at particular stages in a project. Employees routinely submit status reports to their supervisors about their ongoing projects.

Quarterly and annual reports, because of their scope, are usually presented as formal reports. (See Chapter 12 for a discussion of the scope and format of formal

August 15, 2003

Walter M. Wazuski
County Administrator
109 Grand Avenue
Manchester, NH 03103

Subject line identifies topic and number in series —— Subject: Progress Report 8 for July 1–31, 2003

Dear Mr. Wazuski:

Project status summary —— The renovation of the County Courthouse is progressing on schedule and within budget. Although the cost of certain materials is higher than our original bid indicated, we expect to complete the project without exceeding the estimated costs because the speed with which the project is being completed will reduce overall labor expenses.

Costs

Materials used to date have cost $78,600, and labor costs have been $193,000 (including some subcontracted plumbing). Our estimate for the remainder of the materials is $59,000; remaining labor costs should not exceed $100,000.

Detailed status of project —— *Work Completed*

As of July 31, we finished installation of the circuit-breaker panels and meters, of level-one service outlets, and of all subfloor wiring. The upgrading of the courtroom, the upgrading of the records-storage room, and the replacement of the air-conditioning units are in the preliminary stages.

Work Schedule

We have scheduled the upgrading of the courtroom to take place from August 25 to October 5, the upgrading of the records-storage room from October 6 to November 12, and the replacement of the air-conditioning units from November 15 to December 17. We see no difficulty in having the job finished by the scheduled date of December 23.

Sincerely yours,

Tran Nuguélen

Tran Nuguélen, Project Engineer
ntran@hobardcc.com

Figure 11–3   Progress Report (Letter to Client)

reports). Most other kinds of periodic reports seldom run longer than a page or two. Like progress reports, these shorter reports are most often written as memos or e-mails within an organization and as letters when sent to clients and customers outside an organization.

Many kinds of routine information that must be reported periodically—and that do not require a narrative explanation—can be either recorded on forms or entered into computer databases or spreadsheets. Examples include human resources, accounting, and inventory records; production and distribution figures; and travel and task logs.

Preprinted forms have established formats (see Chapter 8), as do formal reports. One- and two-page periodic reports, however, can be organized in a variety of ways. The standard format of introduction, body, and conclusions and recommendations may serve your needs. Otherwise, modify the organizational pattern to suit your reader's reporting requirements.

The sample periodic report shown in Figure 11–4 is sent monthly from a company's district sales manager to the regional sales manager. This periodic report would be sent to the regional sales manager either with a brief cover memo or as an attachment to a brief e-mail. Notice that there is no traditional opening and closing, which are superfluous because the report is routine; that is, it goes to the

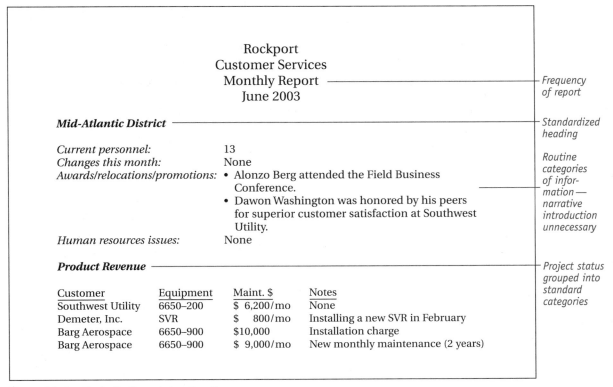

Figure 11–4   Periodic Report (continued)

Monthly Report, Mid-Atlantic District   June 2003

Project status grouped into standard categories

Top Prospects

Customer	Service	Revenue	Odds	Comments
Herndon Bank	PPR	$ 5,600	100%	LAR Services
Southwest Utility	PPR	$10,000	100%	Configuration
MacDonalds	PPR	$10,000	100%	Maintenance
MacDonalds	PPR	$ 6,900	100%	Conversion
Reece Corp.	PPR	$13,000	100%	Upgrades
Reece Corp.	PPR	$ 2,300	100%	Maintenance
Gabbard Mfg.	PPR	$25,000	80%	Cynergy Installation
Gabbard Mfg.	ERCAR	$95,000	50%	ERCAR Upgrades

Competitive Customer or Marketplace News

Charlestown Marketing is still waiting to hear from Bitnolds Metals on a CMOS decision. The odds of our getting this new business are about 25%, as they seem to be happy with Cynergy.

Charlestown Marketing is starting to go outside the greater Charlestown area. Meetings are scheduled with Sailco at the Norfolk Shipyard and BCC in Lynchburg, VA. We will explore potential CMOS or used 6650-2903 opportunities. Plans are to contact at least one new customer a week to try to expand our business.

Cynergy, Inc.'s new maintenance offering is not going over well with some customers. We should be able to take advantage of this.

Watsorg's decision will be announced on July 24–28. This is for $18 to $20 million, going either to us or to Cynergy. The problem is that we finished our "best and final" presentation in the first week of February, and Watsorg gave Cynergy an extension to the end of the month. Dragging this out increases Cynergy's odds of winning. However, the last word is that the negotiations are not going well with Cynergy, so we are keeping our fingers crossed.

AREDOT is installing the largest Saki tape library system in the world. The salesman said that Saki had been working with a company to develop a "virtual tape system" when Embry was sold to Jordan. This caused Jordan to not get the contract. We have a question as to why Rockport didn't pursue this business. Saki is supposed to be our partner and Customer Services could use the business.

Charlestown Marketing is bidding on some LIPSUM directors at AREDOT after some persuasion from Charlestown Marketing Services. This bid has no service attached and lowest price will most likely win.

2

Figure 11–4   Periodic Report (continued)

Monthly Report, Mid-Atlantic District   June 2003

Charlestown Customer Services met with a CARL Team Director from Columbus, Ohio, to discuss future services with CARL. He is considering Rockport as the prime contractor for all necessary services in Charlestown. He will base his decision on the cost analysis.

Significant Wins/Accomplishments

Hector Martinez convinced Barg Aerospace to acquire two additional 6650A-900s from us on a rental basis with a two-year maintenance contract worth $9,000 per month per machine. The installation team has installed the second 900 and will install the third in coming weeks.

Charlestown Customer Services completed installation of a Cynergy 2063 and a Rockport 1006 at Ft. Lee, VA. We partnered with Rathbone Corporation to win the business.

Product Issues

Lareneg's short-link dual copy was attempted again and failed, with catastrophic results. The software support center has spent a great deal of time on this problem with no support from the Lareneg customer. Their management is escalating this issue to Isotoru Nagabishi and Will Reynolds. The local Customer Services team is being unduly burdened with costs associated with what seems to be a product problem. The cost of mileage, conference calls, and expenses is significant.

Secard performance issues have continued from last month. We applied new code with high hopes, but no improvement was noted by the customer. Currently, ERT traces are running to gather more information. The customer is getting very concerned with this issue, and they are our only Secard customer in Charlestown.

Project status grouped into standard categories

3

Figure 11–4   Periodic Report (continued)

same person every month and covers the same topics. For this reason, the format and headings do not change from month to month. It also goes to a high-level manager who receives many such reports each month, so he does not have time to read unnecessary narrative. Because it is written to someone completely familiar with the background details of the projects discussed, the district sales manager can write a spare narrative with many shorthand references to equipment, customers, and project status. For example, he mentions a "best and final" presentation to Watsorg rather than writing that Rockport, his company, has presented its final sales proposal to Watsorg, Inc., for equipment and services. He need not spell out the details of the project because the regional sales manager is already familiar with them. Such an abbreviated narrative is appropriate for the intended reader.

Trip Reports

Many companies require or encourage employees to prepare reports on their business trips. A trip report not only provides a permanent record of a business trip and its accomplishments but also enables many employees to benefit from the information that one employee has gained.

A trip report can be a memo or an e-mail addressed to your immediate superior. On the subject line, give the destination (or purpose) and dates of the trip. Explain the purpose of the trip in a brief introductory summary and note whom or where you visited and what you accomplished. The report should devote a brief section to each major event and may include a heading for each section (you needn't give equal space to each event, instead elaborating on the more important events). End the report with any appropriate conclusions and recommendations. See Figure 11–5 for a sample trip report.

CONSIDERING AUDIENCE AND PURPOSE

Planning and Evaluating Informal Reports

- ☐ Who is the audience for your report?
- ☐ What specifically have your readers requested?
- ☐ How knowledgeable are your readers about the topic?
- ☐ Have you selected the right format — e-mail, memo, letter — for your readers?
- ☐ Have you framed the topic for your audience and provided any necessary background information in your introduction?
- ☐ Do your visuals depict the findings accurately and clearly for your intended audience?
- ☐ Does the body of the report present an organized account of the topic? Is it sufficient in scope so that your audience can understand and interpret your findings, conclusions, and recommendations?

Test Reports

Test reports, also called *laboratory reports* when tests are performed in laboratories, record the results of tests and experiments. Normally, those who write test reports do so as a routine part of their work. Tests that form the basis of reports are not limited to any particular occupation; they commonly occur in many fields, from chemistry to fire science, from metallurgy to medical technology, and include studies on cars, blood, mercury thermometers, pudding mixes, smoke detectors—the list is endless. Information collected in testing may be used to upgrade or abandon products or to streamline testing or manufacturing procedures.

Because accuracy is the essential goal of a test report, be sure to take careful notes while you are performing the test. Then state your findings in clear, straightforward language. Use tables, graphs, or illustrations if they will help your readers interpret the findings. (See Chapter 8 for guidance in preparing visuals.) Because a test report should be objective, it is one of the few writing formats in which the passive voice is usually more suitable than the active voice (see Chapter 5). The

MEMO

70th Transportation Battalion   Summerhill Air Force Base

DATE: 20 March 2004
TO: Captain Robert T. Havens, Flight Operations Officer
FROM: Sergeant Caroline J. Barstow, Flight Operations Specialist
SUBJECT: Aviation Life Support Equipment Course,   *CJB*
             Fort Eustis, Virginia, 15 February to 15 March 2004

Introduction

I attended the Aviation Life Support Equipment (ALSE) Course at Fort
Eustis, Virginia, to become the qualified ALSE technician for the 70th
Transportation Battalion. The four-week course covered the inspection,
maintenance, and repair of aviation life-support equipment. These
skills will enable me to run an efficient ALSE organization, to teach my
subordinates about ALSE, and to instruct pilots and their crews on
equipment safety measures.

Week One

The first week opened with training on the proper methods to assemble
and disassemble the LPU-2/P, 3/P, and I O/P life preservers. We learned
to inspect and perform leakage tests on each type of preserver, and to
repair a faulty life preserver. Finally we practiced folding and packing
each type of preserver for readiness. . . .

Week Two

The second week began with instructions on inspecting and stocking
medical items for first-aid kits. ALSE technicians are required to inspect
and keep a bench stock of all medical items used in first-aid kits. We
learned where to locate information on the storage, shelf life, and destruction of medical supplies. We then inspected a general-purpose
first-aid kit, an airman's individual first-aid kit, and an aircraft first-
aid kit.

Week Three

The third week was devoted solely to flight helmets, beginning with the
SPH-4 helmet. Although it will soon be phased out, it is still in use. We
were shown how to properly fit a pilot or crew member using a thermo-

Memo format

*Subject line with
dates and purpose
of trip*

*Headings separate
sections of report*

*Introductory summary
of purpose, location,
and usefulness of trip*

*Week-by-week
summary of activities*

Figure 11–5   Trip Report (Memo) (continued)
This report was adapted from the original version by Shana L Richardson of Pennsylvania State
University, Altoona Branch, and was submitted by her instructor, Dr. Sandra Petrulionis.

Trip Report   page 2

plastic liner (TPL) inside the helmet. These liners mold to the head and prevent hot spots. We also went over troubleshooting procedures, in case something wasn't working properly, and learned how to assemble, disassemble, inspect, and repair this helmet in less than one hour. . . .

Week-by-week summary of activities

Week Four

The fourth week began with guidance on the proper procurement, handling, and storage of oxygen cylinders. We learned how to fill the cylinders and test them for the correct volume of oxygen. Safety requirements were also discussed in regard to the room design and floors for cylinder storage.

We next learned to use the PRC-1/12 and the PRC-90 handheld radios. We performed a maintenance check to ensure that the radios were operational and learned how to test the batteries using an AN/PRM-32 tester. . . .

Conclusions and Recommendations

Value of trip, follow-up activities, and recommendations for future activity

I believe that the course will help me organize and operate an efficient ALSE shop for the 70th Transportation Battalion. The course emphasized how important it is for all aviators and aviation personnel to learn the basics about ALSE equipment and safety. Our current ALSE shop would benefit from several points covered in the training, and I plan to proceed with the following improvements:

- Conduct an inventory on all equipment in the shop
- Turn in all excess equipment
- Inspect all first-aid and survival kits
- Redo all equipment files kept on pilots and crew chiefs
- Install personal lockers for each pilot/crew chief

Bulleted list highlights information

- Destroy expired medical items
- Order a new bench stock of parts
- Acquire a sewing machine for repairing equipment
- Develop new inventory sheets for all equipment sets

In the future, I recommend that our battalion incorporate ALSE classes into our monthly training regimen. Thank you for giving me the opportunity to attend this course.

Figure 11–5 Trip Report (Memo) (continued)

format in which test reports are prepared depends on the intended audience: letters for customers outside your organization and memos for employees within your organization.

On the subject line, identify the test you are reporting. If the purpose of the test is not obvious to your reader, explain it in the body of the report. Then, if it is helpful to your reader, outline the testing procedures. You need not give a detailed explanation of how the test was performed; rather, provide just enough information for your reader to have a general idea of the testing methods. Next, present the data—the results of the test. If an interpretation of the results would be useful to your reader, furnish such an analysis in your conclusion. Close the report with any recommendations you are making as a result of the test.

Figure 11–6 shows a test report that notes briefly how the test was conducted. Figure 11–7 shows a test report that explains in detail how the tests were performed and describes the federal standards upon which the testing was based.

BIOSPHERICS Inc.

4928 Wyaconda Road
Rockville, MD 20852
(301) 492-3331
Fax: (301) 492-1832
biosphericsinc.com

March 14, 2004

Mr. Luigi Sebastiani, General Manager
Midtown Development Corporation
114 West Jefferson Street
Milwaukee, WI 53201

SUBJECT: Results of Analysis of Soil Samples for Arsenic

Dear Mr. Sebastiani:

The results of our analysis of your soil samples for arsenic showed considerable variation; a high iron content in some of the samples may account for these differences.

Following are the results of the analysis of eight soil samples. The arsenic values listed are based on a wet-weight determination. The moisture content of the soil is also given to allow conversion of the results to a dry-weight basis if desired.

Hole	Depth	Moisture (%)	Arsenic Total (ppm)
1	12"	19.0	312.0
2	Surface	11.2	737.0
3	12"	12.7	9.5
4	12"	10.8	865.0
5	12"	17.1	4.1
6	12"	14.2	6.1
7	12"	24.2	2,540.0
8	Surface	13.6	460.0

I noticed that some of the samples contained large amounts of metallic iron coated with rust. Arsenic tends to be absorbed into soils high in iron, aluminum, and calcium oxides. The large amount of iron present in some of these soil samples is probably responsible for retaining high levels of arsenic. The soils highest in iron, aluminum, and calcium oxides should also show the highest levels of arsenic, provided the soils have had approximately equal levels of arsenic exposure.

If I can be of further assistance, please do not hesitate to contact me.

Yours truly,

Gunther Gottfried

Gunther Gottfried, Chemist
ggottfried@biosphericsinc.com

Report in letter format for customer

Test identified in subject line

Testing methodology

Table of areas tested and findings

Interpretation of test findings

Figure 11–6   Test Report (Letter to Customer)

BIOSPHERICS
Inc.

4928 Wyaconda Road
Rockville, MD 20852
(301) 492-3331
Fax: (301) 492-1832
biosphericsinc.com

April 4, 2004

Mr. Leon Hite, Administrator
The Angle Company, Inc.
1869 Slauson Boulevard
Waynesville, VA 23927

*Report
in letter
format for
customer*

Dear Mr. Hite:

On August 30, Biospherics Inc. performed asbestos-in-air monitoring at your Route
66 construction site, near Front Royal, Virginia. Six persons and three construction
areas were monitored.

*Scope
of test*

All monitoring and analyses were performed in accordance with "Occupational
Exposure to Asbestos," U.S. Department of Health and Human Services, Public
Health Service, National Institute for Occupational Safety and Health, 1995. Each
worker or area was fitted with a battery-powered personal sampler pump operating
at a flow rate of approximately two liters per minute. The airborne asbestos was collected on a 37-mm Millipore-type AA filter mounted in an open-face filter holder.
Samples were collected over an eight-hour period.

*Testing
methodology*

In all cases, the workers and areas monitored were exposed to levels of asbestos
fibers well below the standard set by the Occupational Safety and Health
Administration. The highest exposure found was that of a driller exposed to 0.21
fibers per cubic centimeter. The driller's samples were analyzed by scanning elec-
tron microscopy followed by energy-dispersive X-ray techniques that identify the
chemical nature of each fiber, to identify the fibers as asbestos or other fiber types.
Results from these analyses show that the fibers present are tremolite asbestos. No
nonasbestos fibers were found.

Test findings

Yours truly,

Allison Jones

Allison Jones, Chemist
AJ/jrm

Figure 11–7   Test Report with Methodology Explained (Letter to Customer)

CHAPTER 11 SUMMARY: Writing Informal Reports

Check informal reports to make sure that:

☐ The *introduction* states the subject and purpose and summarizes your conclusions and recommendations.

☐ The *body* presents a detailed account of the work reported on.

☐ The *conclusion* summarizes findings and indicates their significance.

☐ The *recommendations* of actions you believe should be taken are based on the conclusions.

The following types of informal reports are typical:

☐ Trouble reports

- Identify the precise details, such as time and place of an accident or other incident.
- Indicate any injuries or property damage.
- State a likely cause of the accident or incident.
- Specify what is being done to prevent a recurrence, if that's possible.

☐ Investigative reports

- Open with a statement of the information the writer has sought.
- Define the extent of the investigation.
- Present the findings, interpretations, conclusions, and, when appropriate, recommendations.

☐ Progress and periodic reports

- Inform the reader of the status of an ongoing project either at certain stages (progress) or at regular intervals (periodic).
- Alert readers to any necessary adjustments in scheduling, budgeting, and work assignments.

☐ Trip reports

- Include the destination and dates of the trip.
- Explain why the trip was made, who was visited, and what was accomplished.
- State any findings or recommendations based on the purpose of the trip.

☐ Test reports

- State the purpose of the test and indicate the procedures used to conduct the test.
- Indicate the results of the test or experiment and any interpretations helpful to the reader.

■ Exercises

1. Write one of the following trouble reports in the form of a memo.

   a. You are the traffic manager of a trucking company that has had four highway accidents within a one-week period. Using the following facts, write a trouble report to your company president, Michael Spangler.

- Your company operates in your state.
- The four accidents occurred in different parts of the state and on different dates (specify the date and location of each).
- Each accident resulted in damage not only to the truck (specify the dollar amount of the damage) but to the cargo (specify the type of cargo and the dollar amount of the damage).
- Only one of the accidents involved another vehicle (a company truck swerved into a parked car when a tire blew out). Give the make and year of the damaged car and its owner's name.
- Only one of the accidents involved injury to a company driver (give the name).
- Your maintenance division traced all four of the accidents to faulty tires, all the same brand (identify the brand), and all purchased at the same time and place (identify the place and date).
- The tires have now been replaced, and your insurance company, Acme Underwriters, has brought suit against the tire manufacturer to recover damages, including lost business while the four trucks were being repaired (specify the dollar amount of the lost business).

b. You are the dietitian at a hospital. A fire has occurred in the cafeteria, which is under your supervision. Using the following information, write a trouble report to the hospital's administrator, Megan Garnett.

- The chief cook, Pincus Berkowitz, came to work at 5:30 a.m. (specify the date).
- He turned on the gas jets under the grill. The pilot light had gone out, and the jets did not light.
- The cook went to find a match, neglecting to turn off the gas jets.
- He found matches, returned, and lit a match, thus igniting the accumulated gas under the grill.
- The resulting explosion destroyed the grill (estimate the damage) and injured the cook.
- The fire was put out by the security force, but the fire department was called as a precaution.
- The cook was treated by the emergency-room physician, then admitted to the hospital's burn unit as a patient, with second-degree burns on his hands, face, and neck.
- He was hospitalized for three days and will be away from work for four weeks.

2. You are a human resources specialist assigned to investigate why your company is not finding enough qualified candidates to fill its need for electronics technicians and to recommend a solution to the problem. You have conducted your investigation and determined the following:

- In the past, you recruited heavily from among military veterans, but the reduction of active military personnel has all but eliminated this source. Want ads are not producing adequate numbers of veterans.
- The in-house apprentice program, which recruits graduating high school students, has produced a declining number of candidates in recent years because more students are going to college.
- Several regional technical schools are producing very well trained and highly motivated graduates. Competition for them is keen, but you believe that an aggressive recruiting campaign will solve your problem.

Write an investigative report to your boss, Cynthia Mitchum, Director of Human Resources, explaining the causes of the problem and offering your recommended solution.

3. As the medical staff administrative assistant at a hospital, write a progress report to the director of the hospital outlining the current status of the annual reappointment of committees. Use the following facts to write the report:

   - A total of ten committees must be staffed.
   - The chief of staff has telephoned each person selected to chair a committee, and you have sent each of them a follow-up letter of thanks from the chief.
   - You have written letters to all physicians who are currently on committees but are not being reappointed, informing them of the fact.
   - You have written letters to all physicians being asked to serve on committees.
   - You expect to receive replies from those physicians declining the appointment by the 15th of the following month.
   - Once committee assignments have been completed, you will type the membership lists of all committees and distribute them to the complete medical staff.

4. You are a field-service engineer for a company that markets diesel-powered emergency generators. Based on the following information, write a trip report:

   You have just visited five cities to inspect the installation of your company's auxiliary power units in hospals, and you need to report to your manager about your findings. You visited the following hospitals and cities:

   > May 26 — New Orleans General Hospital in New Orleans
   > May 27 — Our Lady of Mercy Hospital in San Antonio
   > May 28 — Dallas Presbyterian Hospital in Dallas
   > May 29 — St. Elizabeth Hospital in Oklahoma City
   > May 30 — Jefferson Davis Memorial Hospital in Atlanta

   You found that each installation was properly done. With the cooperation of the administrators, you switched each hospital to auxiliary power for a one-hour trial run. All went well. You held a brief training session for the maintenance staff at each hospital, teaching them how to start the engine and how to regulate its speed to produce 220 volts of electricity from the generator at 60 hertz. You want to commend your company's sales staff and field personnel for creating a positive image of your company in the minds of all five customers you visited.

5. a. Locate a test report that you wrote for a laboratory class that you are taking or have taken. Rewrite the report according to the guidelines in this chapter, and submit it in memo form to your instructor.

   b. Submit a trouble or investigative report explaining any processes or projects that you are working on for school, for work, or for your home. (Specify the type of report.) Review this chapter for guidelines for writing such reports.

6. Each of the following topics presents a situation in which a company plans a significant change that could threaten its existing customer base. Select one of the following topics (or create your own topic based on your area of study and professional interest) and write a memo in which you offer your recommendations for ensuring that the change that your company proposes will not jeopardize its existing customer base. With your customers in mind, make specific suggestions for facilitating as smooth and positive a transition as possible.

   a. Assume that you are part of the management team of a fast-food restaurant with a "burgers only" identity—and a loyal customer base—that wants to add distinctive and healthful menu items.

   b. Assume that you are part of the management team for an apparel manufacturing firm known for its conservative fashions. Your firm is about to introduce a new line of clothing with a distinctly contemporary appeal.

c. Assume that you work for a medical insurance company concerned with the rising number of medical claims being submitted by your customers. To combat this, your company has initiated a campaign designed to entice your customers to adopt healthier lifestyles, and has begun sending brochures and personalized letters to customers with particular medical histories. Many customers have expressed concern that this is an indication that the company will become more reluctant to pay their claims.

7. Try a new or better method to accomplish a task and document the steps and results. For example, try balancing your checkbook using the computer or try a different system for doing the week's laundry or grocery shopping. Then write a test report in the form of a memo to your instructor. Include each step of the process or the procedures you used and the results of your test. If appropriate, compare the test process to your old way of accomplishing the task. Include in your memo any observations that would be helpful in interpreting your test report.

8. Write a trip report to your boss, Monica Jenkins, CEO of Jenkins Marketing Specialists, Inc. Your goal in writing a trip report is to inform management about new procedures, equipment, or laws, or to supply information affecting products, operations, and services. Ms. Jenkins supported your request to attend the Business Etiquette Conference, sponsored by the Business Management Association and held at Delta State University in Cleveland, Mississippi, at Broom Hall, College of Business. The six-day conference was held April 18–23, 2004.

   Your goal is to let Ms. Jenkins know that you gathered valuable information that will benefit the company.

   a. Begin by writing an introductory paragraph in which you identify the event (exact date, sponsor name, conference theme/name, and location) and preview the topics to be discussed in your report.

   b. Next, in the body, summarize three to five main points from one presentation you attended each day at the conference. State how you benefited from the conference and how what you learned will also benefit the reader and Jenkins Marketing Specialists, Inc.

   c. In the closing, express appreciation, suggest action to be taken, or synthesize the value of the trip or conference.

   In your report, highlight interesting and important facts using typographical tools such as boldface, headings, and bullets. Itemize your expenses on a separate page as an attachment to your report.

Collaborative Classroom Projects

1. In small groups, collaborate to write a trouble report about a problem on campus. Choose a topic that has a simple solution, like a busy campus intersection that needs a traffic signal or a parking problem that could be relieved by providing students with incentives to use the bus system. Other topics might address overly complicated procedures for dropping or adding a class or using online resources at the library. Submit your report to your instructor in memo form.

2. Contact a friend or an individual who works in a field related to your professional area of interest. Ask him or her to provide you with a copy of one of the types of reports discussed in this chapter. (Because many reports in organizations are confidential, you may wish to ask for a report that is several years old on an issue that

is no longer current.) Bring the report to class and be prepared to discuss the report's effectiveness in terms of the writer's purpose, audience, and specific organizational or corporate practices.

3. Form groups of five members or fewer. Your group is part of a public relations (PR) and design firm. Your client is an old and well-established company (like Coca-Cola or Procter & Gamble) and is well known by an established logo. The company, however, is not realizing its desired growth because its image is considered by the youngest generation of new consumers to be flat and uninspiring. Your PR firm has been hired to develop a new upscale logo and promote a fresh company image. Your group will have approximately 30 minutes to brainstorm a strategy and then 15 minutes to develop an outline of your collective instructions or suggestions. Be ready to share your outline with the rest of the class.

4. As a class, plan to visit a lab or learning center on campus, preferably one outside your department. Determine as a group which lab you would like to visit and the specific purposes of your visit. The lab may be a science lab, a computer lab, an engineering lab, or a writing center. After an explanation of the lab's procedures and a tour of the lab or center, your class will reconvene in your own classroom and write a trip report about the visit. Include the date of the visit, your destination, the purpose of your trip, and an explanation of what you learned during the visit.

■ Research Projects

1. Gather information pertinent to one of the following topics and present the information in a two- to three-page investigative report.
   a. Your energy-consumption habits at home
   b. Your recommendations on the best hotel or motel in your area for out-of-town guests
   c. Which of two local garages that have serviced your car you would recommend to a friend
   d. Which Internet-access provider you would recommend to a colleague and why

2. You want to volunteer 10 to 12 hours a week for a local community organization.
   a. Begin by investigating at least three such organizations that accept volunteers, such as nursing homes, hospitals, political and civic groups, or schools. Detail the type of volunteer help needed, the hours and days when the help is needed, whether any training is required, and whom you'll report to. Also be sure to find out if volunteers do hands-on work with people—such as playing games with children or adults or bathing, lifting, or turning those who aren't mobile—or if volunteers work behind the scenes, making solicitation calls, addressing envelopes, stocking supplies, etc.
   b. Then write an eight- to ten-page investigative report in which you evaluate each of the three organizations in light of the above criteria, as well as from the point of view of your own background, experience, and future vocational goals.
   c. Finish by selecting the one that is most suitable for you and explain the reasons for your selection.

3. Choose one of the types of informal reports discussed in this chapter—trouble, investigative, progress, periodic, trip, or test—and create a report based on an article that you find in the Business Day section of the *New York Times*. The report should be a minimum of 1,000 words (approximately four pages) but no longer than 1,500 words.

   a. Begin by submitting a memo to your instructor, detailing the type of report you will write and providing a brief outline that details your role as the writer of the report, your title, and the company you work for, as well as your reader, his or her title, and the company he or she works for. Clearly explain the purpose of the report and why you are writing it. State how you expect the reader to use the information provided in this report or what you would like to have happen as a result of your report.

   b. Then write your report, using any visual aids you think necessary for your reader to understand the report. Turn in the article with your report.

4. Write an informal two- to three-page investigative report on workplace safety, standard business practices or important trends in your field, or another topic. Read a minimum of three articles from newspapers, journals, books, or other printed sources to gather information about your subject.

5. With your instructor's approval, choose an ongoing current issue that has been in the news for at least one month. Topics might include political campaigns, tax issues, unsolved crimes of major importance, international crises, finance issues (including the stock market or economic policy), and educational issues (such as safety in schools or the ability of schools to prepare students for the workplace). Over the next six weeks, submit to your instructor a regular progress report. Include in each report any change in the status of the issue that you have chosen. Document your media sources. In your final report, suggest what you think could be done to solve the problem. Be as specific as possible.

■ Web Projects

Projects followed by the symbol **W** are continued at **bedfordstmartins.com/ writingthatworks**, Chapter 11.

1. Search the Internet to find the site of a well-established organization or company and assume that you are responsible for its Web site. Write a progress report on the current status and future plans for your organization's Web site. In your report, discuss the elements that you plan to keep, those that you will cut, and those that need to be refined. Explain why and how you plan to carry out these tasks.

2. Research online a business, organization, or government agency and write a 300- to 500-word investigative informal report. Your report should focus on one specific function or feature of the organization. Define the function or feature, investigate its effectiveness, evaluate its effectiveness, and make specific recommendations for improving the function or feature. **W**

3. Assume that your boss, the president of a small business, has asked you to gather information from the Small Business Administration (SBA) that will benefit your company, such as opportunities for government contracts, or special programs or

training available through the SBA. Prepare an investigative report of 300 to 500 words and submit it to your instructor. **W**

4. The Government Printing Office (GPO) produces and distributes federal government information and publications to the public and to the U.S. Congress and U.S. federal agencies. Visit the GPO's Web site (<access.gpo.gov/>), and focus on a topic area that relates to your professional interests. Prepare an informal report that summarizes the information you've gathered. **W**

Topics to consider include the following:

- Industrial trends in the United States
- Government reports or special programs related to your field
- Legislation that impacts your field
- Business, contracting, or employment opportunities

12 Writing Formal Reports

Formal reports are written accounts of major projects. Such projects include research into new developments in a field, explorations of the feasibility of a new product or a new service, or an end-of-year review of developments within an organization. Because of the variety of purposes they serve, formal reports can be called by many different names: feasibility study, annual report, investigative report, research report, analytical report, and the like. Regardless of their purpose, formal reports contain various components that make up the parts of the report. The purpose, scope, and complexity of the project will determine which components will be included and how they are organized. Most formal reports—certainly those that are long and complex—require a carefully planned structure and signposts that provide readers with an easy-to-recognize guide to the material in the report. Such aids as a table of contents, a list of figures, and an abstract (a brief summary of the report) make the information in the report more easily accessible. Making a formal topic outline, which lists the report's major facts and ideas and indicates their relationship to one another, should help you to write a well-organized report.

Formal reports are organized to address the needs of more than one audience. These audiences will occupy a variety of positions in the organization receiving the report, have different levels of knowledge about your topic, and be responsible for reading and responding to different parts of the report. Although everybody will skim the table of contents, managers and other decision-makers will focus on the executive summary because it concisely summarizes the report in full. These readers need to know the "bottom line" quickly for its potential impact on their staffing, organizational, and budget decisions. They may also need to refer to the glossary for definitions of special terms. Technical experts, however, will be responsible for implementing the report's recommendations, so they need

W On the Web
For more help with writing formal reports, see Chapter 12, bedfordstmartins.com/writingthatworks

417

to understand in detail how the conclusions and recommendations were reached. General readers whose needs are less immediate may read only the abstract to decide on whether to read the whole report. Few in your audience will read the entire report, so an executive summary and abstract must be written to make sense independently of the rest of the report. Likewise, overlapping content is appropriate in the introduction, executive summary, abstract, and conclusions and recommendations.

This chapter discusses the parts of formal reports, the information they should include, and how best to organize them into an effective final product. As you read the chapter, keep in mind all that you've learned about the process of drafting and revising on-the-job writing tasks, because careful planning, drafting, and revising, as much as using the organizational frameworks covered in this chapter, form the basis for a successful formal report. Formal-report preparation involves researching and generating a substantial amount of information, which you will need to evaluate, select, and organize before you begin the drafting process. The research required for a formal report can be extensive, so brainstorming and refining the scope of the topic are essential. (See Chapter 1 to review information-gathering and brainstorming strategies.)

In addition, plan to write several outlines for your report: one as an overview of the whole project and smaller, more specific outlines for individual sections. Breaking the work into parts can make the daunting task of pulling together a long report more manageable. (Chapter 2 discusses a variety of outlining and organizational strategies.)

Finally, you will need to write multiple drafts of the report, evaluating and revising them for coherence, clarity, and correctness. You will also need to review the drafts to see whether the individual sections of the report connect smoothly and logically, whether sources are used correctly and consistently, and whether visuals—drawings, tables, graphs, charts, photographs, and maps—are well designed and correctly positioned. Because of the extensive revisions required for a long report, collaborative reviews of your work will help you immensely; colleagues, fellow students, or instructors can offer revision suggestions to supplement your own evaluations of the report. (For a review of revising strategies, see Chapters 4 and 5. Chapter 6 describes the collaborative reviewing process.)

■ Order of Elements in a Formal Report

Most formal reports are divided into three major parts—front matter, body, and back matter—each of which, in turn, contains a number of elements. The number of elements needed and the order in which they are presented depends on the subject, the objective for writing the report, the length of the report, the kinds of material covered, and the standard practice of the organization for which the report is prepared. Many companies and governmental and other institutions have a preferred style for formal reports and furnish guidelines that staff

Voices from the Workplace

Judy Prono, Los Alamos National Laboratory

At Los Alamos, one of the national laboratories of the U.S. Department of Energy, Judy Prono leads a team of writers and editors. She and her staff of 21 are responsible for writing almost all of the documents produced at the lab — from flyers to 100-page formal reports.

Judy carefully plans the formal reports she produces. "First, I identify the purpose of the report in terms of its audience. For example, our Technical Divisions publish annual reports aimed at the various funding organizations of the Department of Energy. In these reports, it's important to highlight the Technical Divisions' accomplishments." Judy then plans the content and scope, keeping in mind the report's multiple audiences. "I have to think about what kind of information to convey and how to organize that information. I have to decide how technical I want the material to be. After all, you are only writing one report, and you want to reach all audiences. I tend to write more summaries and overviews and allow the sections of the body of the report to address the more technical side. In general, you want to start with the big picture and get more specific as the report continues."

Because formal reports are often collaborative and complex documents, Judy stresses the importance of managing the details of each project. "When writing large reports, you have to be very organized and have to keep track of all the pieces. It is essential to keep tabs on what is coming in, and to gently prod people who still owe material. I use all manner of friendly coercion to get a report out on time. Sometimes you have to be a taskmaster!"

Ted Kalo, Congressional Staff Member

Ted Kalo is Minority Deputy Chief General Counsel for the office of Representative John Conyers Jr. On the job, Ted prepares memos for hearings and writes statements for Representative Conyers. Following the 2000 presidential election, Ted researched and wrote a report detailing voting irregularities and possible civil-rights violations, state by state, across the country.

Ted describes his initial approach to researching and organizing the election report. "Based on the little knowledge I began with on the subject, I came up with a few categories that the research might fall under, such as spoiled ballots from voting machines and voter intimidation. After I did some more research, I came up with new categories that I hadn't thought of before, and made an outline for each state. Then I began to fill in the outlines with data."

As he drafted and revised his report, Ted was careful to provide his readers with accessible information and clear conclusions. "After I organized the report, I converted the information to paragraph form and tried to put it into more elegant prose. Once the report was finished, I took a few days to think about what the larger lessons were. Was what happened in the Florida election rare — or was this a countrywide problem? My report indicated that voting irregularities were indeed a widespread problem. I wrote an introduction to the report that identified what these greater problems were. I knew my introduction had to be compelling, so I used less clinical language and tried to guide the reader through all of the data."

members must follow. If your employer has prepared a set of style guidelines, follow it; if not, use the format recommended in this chapter. Most formal reports are delivered with a transmittal letter or memo that presents the document to the reader. The following list includes most of the elements a formal report might contain:

- Transmittal Letter or Memo (precedes front matter; page 421)
- Front Matter
  - Title Page (page 422)
  - Abstract (page 423)
  - Table of Contents (page 427)
  - List of Figures (page 427)
  - List of Tables (page 427)
  - Foreword (page 427)
  - Preface (page 428)
  - List of Abbreviations and Symbols (page 430)
- Body
  - Executive Summary (page 431)
  - Introduction (page 433)
  - Text (including headings) (page 436)
  - Conclusions (page 443)
  - Recommendations (page 443)
  - Explanatory Footnotes (page 443)
  - Works Cited (or References) (page 445)
- Back matter
  - Appendixes (page 446)
  - Bibliography (page 448)
  - Glossary (page 448)
  - Index (page 448)

DIGITAL SHORTCUTS

Automating Report Formatting

Use your word-processing software to create templates that permit you to customize the format of your report. Save your template to ensure consistency each time you create a formal report. *Note:* If you are using Microsoft Word, click on Format in the tool bar to find the Style Gallery option — this allows you to implement an existing report template. If you prefer to create a new style sheet, select the Style option. Creating a template allows you to automate:

- Fonts and font sizes for text, headings, titles, footnotes, headers, and footers
- Paragraphs, including indentation and margins
- Lists, including indentation from the margin and spacing
- Number of columns
- The table of contents based on a report's headings and subheadings

Transmittal Letter or Memo

When you submit a formal report, you should include with it a brief transmittal (or cover) letter or memo that identifies the topic the formal report addresses and why the report was prepared. Written in the form of a standard business letter or memo, the transmittal most often opens with a brief paragraph (one or two sentences) explaining what is being sent and why. The next paragraph contains a brief summary of the report's contents or stresses some feature that would be important to the audience. This section may also mention any special conditions under which the material was prepared (limitations of time or money, for instance). The closing paragraph may acknowledge any help received in preparing the report, or express the hope that the information fulfills its purpose.

Typically, most transmittal letters and memos are composed of these elements. In any case, they should be brief—usually one page. Figure 12–1 shows a sample transmittal memo. Examples of short and long transmittal letters are also shown in Figures 10–2 and 10–3.

CGF Aircraft Corporation
Memo

To: Members of the Ethics and Business Conduct Committee
From: Merlin Mendez, Director of Ethics and Business Conduct *MM*
Date: March 1, 2004
Subject: Reported Ethics Cases 2003

Addressed to recipients designated by the program

Enclosed is the annual Ethics and Business Conduct Report, as required by CGF Policy NB-AAG-200, for your evaluation. This report covers the first year of our Ethics Program and contains a review of the ethics cases handled by CGF ethics officers and managers during 2003.

Brief opening describes the enclosure

The ethics cases reported are analyzed according to two categories: (1) major ethics cases, or those potentially involving serious violations of company policy and/or illegal conduct, and (2) minor ethics cases, or those that do not involve serious policy violations and/or illegal conduct. The report also examines how all the reported cases were learned of and how the substantiated major ethics cases were resolved.

Brief summary of report contents

It is my hope that this report will provide the Committee with the information needed to assess the effectiveness of the first year of CGF's Ethics Program and to plan for the coming year. Please let me know if you have any questions about this report or if you need any further information. I may be reached at (860) 212-2121 and at e-mail address <mxm@cgf.com>.

Closing with offer of additional support

Enclosure: Ethics and Business Conduct Report

Enclosure notation

Figure 12–1   Transmittal Memo for a Formal Report   *Source:* The report in this chapter is adapted from a report prepared by Susan Litzinger, a student at Pennsylvania State University.

■ Front Matter

The front matter, which includes all the elements that precede the body of the report, serves several purposes: (1) It gives the audience a general idea of the author's purpose in writing the report; (2) it indicates whether the report contains the kind of information that the audience is looking for; and (3) it lists where in the report the audience can find specific chapters, headings, illustrations, and tables. Not all formal reports require every one of these elements. A title page and table of contents are usually mandatory, but whether an abstract, a list of figures, a list of tables, a foreword, a preface, and a list of abbreviations and symbols are included will depend on the scope of the report and its intended audience. Scientific and technical reports, for example, often include a separate listing of abbreviations and symbols, while in most business reports, such lists are unnecessary. The front-matter pages are numbered with lowercase Roman numerals. Throughout the report, page numbers are often centered either near the bottom or near the top of each page.

Title Page

Although the formats of title pages vary, the page should include the following information: (1) the full title of the report; (2) the name(s) of the writers, principal investigators, or compilers that prepared it; (3) the date the report was issued; (4) the name of the organization for which the writer(s) works; and (5) the name of the organization or person to which the report is submitted.

1. *Full title of the report.* The title should reflect the topic as well as the scope and objective of the report. Titles often provide the only basis on which audiences can decide whether to read a report. Aim for accuracy and conciseness: titles too vague or too long not only hinder the audience but can prevent efficient filing and later retrieval. Follow these guidelines when creating the title:
   - Focus on the subject matter of the report. Avoid titles that begin "Notes on," "Studies on," "A Report on," or "Observations on." These phrases are often redundant and state the obvious. However, phrases such as "Annual Report" or "Feasibility Study" should be used in a title or subtitle because they help define the purpose and scope of the document.
   - Avoid using abbreviations in the title. Use them only when the report is intended for an audience familiar enough with the topic that the abbreviation will be understood.
   - Do not include the period covered by a report in the title; include that information in a subtitle:

EFFECTS OF PROPOSED HIGHWAY CONSTRUCTION ON PROPERTY VALUES
Tri-State Regional District
Annual Report, 2003

2. *Names of the writers, principal investigators, or compilers.* Frequently, contrib-utors simply list their names. Sometimes they identify themselves by their job title in the organization (Jane R. Lihn, Cost Analyst; Rodrigo Sánchez, Head, Research and Development). They also identify themselves by their tasks in contributing to the report (Antoine Baume, Compiler; Wanda Landowska, Principal Investigator).

3. *Date or dates of the report.* For one-time reports, list the date when the report is to be distributed. For periodic reports, which may be issued monthly or quarterly, list the period that the present report covers in a subtitle, as well as the date when the report is to be distributed.

4. *Name of the organization for which the writer works.*

5. *Name of the organization or individual to which the report is being submitted,* if the work is being done for an organization other than your own.

These categories are standard on most title pages. Some organizations may require additional information. A sample title page appears in Figure 12–2.

The title page, although unnumbered, is considered page i (small Roman numeral one). The back of the title page, which is blank and unnumbered, is considered page ii, and the abstract then falls on page iii so that it appears on a right-hand (i.e., odd-numbered) page. For reports with printing on both sides of each sheet of paper, it is a long-standing printer's convention that right-hand pages are always odd-numbered and left-hand pages are always even-numbered. (Note the pagination in this book.) New sections and chapters of reports typically begin on a new right-hand page. Reports with printing on only one side of each sheet can be numbered consecutively regardless of where new sections begin.

W On the Web
For more examples of formal reports, see Chapter 12, bedfordstmartins.com/ writingthatworks

Abstracts

An *abstract* is a condensed version of a longer work that summarizes and highlights the major points. One of its main purposes is to enable your prospective reader to decide whether to read the whole work. Usually 200 to 250 words long, an abstract must make sense independently of the work it summarizes. Depending on the kind of information they contain, abstracts are usually classified as either descriptive or informative.

A *descriptive abstract* includes information about the purpose, scope, and methods used to arrive at the findings contained in the report. It is thus a slightly expanded table of contents in paragraph form. Provided that it adequately summarizes the information, a descriptive abstract need not be longer than several sentences. (See Figure 12–3.)

An *informative abstract* is an expanded version of the descriptive abstract. In addition to information about the purpose, scope, and methods of the original report, the informative abstract includes the results, conclusions, and recommendations, if any. The informative abstract thus retains the tone and essential scope of the report while omitting its details.

Report title and subtitle

REPORTED ETHICS CASES
Annual Report, 2003

Report author

Prepared by Susan Litzinger
Director of Ethics and Business Conduct

Date report issued

Report Distributed March 1, 2004

Report recipient

Prepared for
The Ethics and Business Conduct Committee
CGF Aircraft Corporation

Figure 12-2   Title Page of a Formal Report

Page header provides flush right report title

ABSTRACT ——————————————————————— *Section heading*

This report examines the nature and disposition of 3,458 ethics cases handled company-wide by CGF Aircraft Corporation's ethics officers and managers during 2003. The purpose of this annual report is to provide the Ethics and Business Conduct Committee with the information necessary for assessing the effectiveness of the Ethics Program's first year of operation. Records maintained by ethics officers and managers of all contacts were compiled and categorized into two main types: (1) major ethics cases, or cases involving serious violations of company policies and/or illegal conduct, and (2) minor ethics cases, or cases not involving serious policy violations and/or illegal conduct. This report provides examples of the types of cases handled in each category and analyzes the disposition of 30 substantiated major ethics cases. All cases are analyzed according to the mode of contact used in reporting. Recommendations are offered for planning for the second year of the Ethics Program.

Purpose, scope, and period covered

Methodology

Detailed scope of material covered

iii

Page footer provides page number

Figure 12–3   Descriptive Abstract of a Formal Report

Writing Abstracts

WRITER'S CHECKLIST

Include the following information:

- ☐ The subject
- ☐ The scope
- ☐ The purpose
- ☐ The methods used
- ☐ The results obtained (informative abstract only)
- ☐ The recommendations made, if any (informative abstract only)

Do not include the following kinds of information:

- ☐ A detailed discussion or explanation of the methods used
- ☐ Administrative details about how the research was undertaken, who funded it, who worked on it, and the like, unless such details have a bearing on the document's purpose
- ☐ Illustrations, tables, charts, maps, and bibliographic references
- ☐ Any information that does not appear in the original document

Which of the two types of abstract should you write? The answer depends on your employer. If it has a policy, comply with it. Otherwise, aim to satisfy the needs of the principal readers of your report. Informative abstracts satisfy the needs of the widest possible audience, but descriptive abstracts are preferable for information surveys, progress reports that combine information from more than one project, and any report that compiles a variety of information. For these types of reports, conclusions and recommendations either do not exist in the original or are too numerous to include in an abstract. Typically, an abstract follows the title page and is numbered page iii. Figure 12–4 shows an informative abstract, which is an expanded version of the descriptive abstract shown in Figure 12–3.

Write the abstract after finishing your report. Otherwise, your abstract may not accurately reflect the final product. Begin with a topic sentence that announces

Page header provides report title

Reported Ethics Cases — 2003

Section heading

ABSTRACT

Purpose and scope

This report examines the nature and disposition of 3,458 ethics cases handled company-wide by CGF Aircraft Corporation's ethics officers and managers during 2003. The purpose of this annual report is to provide the Ethics and Business Conduct Committee with the information necessary for assessing the effectiveness of the Ethics Program's first year of operation. Records maintained by ethics officers and managers of all contacts were compiled and categorized into two main types:

Methodology

(1) major ethics cases, or cases involving serious violations of company policies and/or illegal conduct, and (2) minor ethics cases, or cases not involving serious policy violations and/or illegal conduct. This report provides examples of the types of cases handled in each category and analyzes the disposition of 30 substantiated major ethics cases. All cases are analyzed according to the mode of contact used in reporting.

Conclusions

The effectiveness of CGF's Ethics Program during the first year of implementation is most evidenced by (1) the active participation of employees in the program and the 3,458 contacts employees made regarding ethics concerns through the various channels available to them, and (2) the action taken in the cases reported by employees, particularly the disposition of the 30 substantiated major ethics cases. Disseminating information about the disposition of ethics cases, particularly information about the severe disciplinary actions taken in major ethics violations, sends a message to employees that unethical and/or illegal conduct will not be tolerated.

Recommendations

Recommendations for planning for the second year of the Ethics Program are (1) continuing the channels of communication now available in the Ethics Program, (2) increasing financial and technical support for the Ethics Hotline, (3) disseminating the annual ethics report in some form to employees to ensure employees' awareness of CGF's commitment to uphold its Ethics Policy and Procedures, and (4) implementing some measure of recognition for ethical behavior to promote and reward ethical conduct.

Page footer provides page number

iii

Figure 12–4 Informative Abstract of a Formal Report

at least the subject and scope of the report. Then, using the major and minor heads of your table of contents to distinguish primary from secondary ideas, decide what material is relevant to your abstract. Write clearly and concisely, eliminating unnecessary words and ideas, but do not omit articles (*a, an, the*) and important transitional words and phrases (*however, therefore, but, in summary*). Write complete sentences, but avoid stringing a group of short sentences end to end; instead, combine ideas by using subordination and parallel structure. As a rule, spell out most acronyms and all but the most common abbreviations (°C, °F, mph). Finally, as you summarize, keep the tone and emphasis consistent with the original report. (For additional advice, review Summarizing in Chapter 7, page 220.)

Table of Contents

A *table of contents* lists all the headings of the report in their order of appearance, along with their page numbers. It includes a listing of all front matter and back matter except the title page and the table of contents itself. The table of contents begins on a new right-hand page. Note that in Figure 12–5 the table of contents is numbered page v because it follows the abstract (page iii), and because page iv is blank.

Along with the abstract, a table of contents enables your audience to preview the information covered in a report and decide whether to read further. It also aids a reader who may want to look only at certain sections of the report. For this reason, the wording of chapter and section titles in the table of contents should always be identical to those in the text.

Sometimes, the table of contents is followed by lists of figures and tables contained in the report. These lists should always be presented separately, and a page number should be given for each item listed.

List of Figures

When a report contains more than five figures, list them by title, along with their page numbers, in a separate section beginning on a new page and immediately following the table of contents. Number figures consecutively with Arabic numbers. Figures include all illustrations—drawings, photographs, maps, charts, and graphs—contained in the report.

List of Tables

When a report contains more than five tables, list them, along with their titles and page numbers, in a separate section immediately following the list of figures (if there is one). Number tables consecutively with Arabic numbers.

Foreword

A *foreword* is an optional introductory statement written by someone other than the author. It generally provides background information about the publication's significance and places it in the context of other works in the field. The author of

Page header provides report title

Major and subordinate headings differentiated by typeface and indentations

Page footer provides page number

v

Figure 12–5   Table of Contents of a Formal Report

the foreword is usually an authority in the field or an executive of the company. The author's name and affiliation and the date the foreword was written appear on a separate line below the foreword.

Preface

A *preface* is an optional introductory statement used to announce the purpose, background, or scope of the report. Sometimes a preface specifies the audience for whom the report is intended, and it may also highlight the relationship of the report to a given project or program. A preface may contain acknowledgments of help received during the course of the project or in the preparation of the report, and, finally, it may cite permission obtained for the use of copyrighted works. If a preface is not included, place this type of information, if it is essential, in the introduction (discussed later in this chapter). Figure 12–6 shows a sample preface.

The preface follows the table of contents (and the lists of figures and tables and the foreword, if these are present). It begins on a separate page and is titled "Preface."

Reported Ethics Cases—2003 *Page header provides report title*

PREFACE *Section heading*

The CGF Aircraft Corporation takes its commitment to an ethical work environment seriously. Throughout its 64-year history, CGF has fostered high ethical standards in its relations with its customers, suppliers, and employees. The size, diversity, and decentralized locations of our workforce make it imperative that CGF's ethical commitment—both in principle and in practice—be formalized. To this end, the CGF Aircraft Corporation established a corporation-wide ethics program in August 2002. The goal of the program is to "promote a positive work environment that encourages open communication regarding ethics and compliance issues and concerns." *Background and purpose of program*

The Office of Ethics and Business Conduct (OEBC) was created to implement and administer the program. The director of the OEBC and seven ethics officers from throughout the corporation are responsible for the following program objectives: *Program background*

- Communicate the values and standards for CGF's Ethics Program to employees.
- Inform employees about company policies regarding ethical business conduct.
- Establish company-wide channels for employees to obtain information and guidance in resolving ethics concerns.
- Implement company-wide ethics-awareness and education programs.

Bulleted list makes objectives easy to read

This report examines the nature and disposition of the ethics cases handled by the OEBC in 2003, the first year of operation. The report was compiled to provide the corporation's Ethics and Business Committee of the OEBC with the information necessary to assess the effectiveness of the first year of CGF's ethics program. *Purpose and scope of report* — *Audience for report*

This report represents the efforts of the dedicated staff of the OEBC, the ethics officers, and the many managers and employees throughout CGF. We wish to acknowledge their active support and contributions to this report and to the program. *Acknowledgment of help in preparation of report*

vii *Page footer provides page number*

Figure 12–6   Preface of a Formal Report

List of Abbreviations and Symbols

When the abbreviations and symbols used in a report are numerous, and when there is a chance that the audience will not be able to interpret them, the front matter should include a list of all abbreviations and symbols and what they stand for in the report. Such a list, which follows the preface, is particularly appropriate for technical reports whose audience is not restricted to technical specialists.

Figure 12–7 shows an example of a list of symbols that appear in a report as part of equations that calculate the transfer of heat and water vapor from the surface of cooling ponds at industrial sites. The list is made up of special symbols used in this report. The author assumes that the report readers have a technical education, however, because Btu (British thermal unit), Hg (chemical symbol for mercury), and similar terms are not identified.

Symbols arranged in alphabetical order

SYMBOLS

A	Pond surface area, ft^2 or acres
A_0	One-half the daily insulation, Btu/ft^2
A_n	Surface area of nth segment of the plugflow model, ft^2
C	Cloud cover in tenths of the total sky obscured
C_1	Bowen's ratio, 0.26 mmHg/°F
C_P	Heat capacity of water, Btu/lb/°F
E_1, E_2	Estimation of equilibrium temperatures using data from off-site and on-site records, respectively, °F
$E(x)$	Estimation of equilibrium temperature using monthly average meteorologic data, °F
e_a	Saturation pressure of air above pond surface, mmHg
e_s	Saturation pressure of air at surface temperature, T_s, mmHg
g	Skew coefficient
H	Heat content, Btu

Figure 12–7   List of Symbols

■ Body

The body—the main part of a formal report—includes the following:

- An executive summary
- An introduction
- The text (including headings, tables, illustrations, and references)
- Conclusions and recommendations

Number the first page of the body page 1 in Arabic rather than Roman numerals. For guidance about page-level layout-and-design elements—typography, margins, columns, headers and footers, and the like—see Chapter 8, pages 251–261.

Executive Summary

The body begins with an executive summary that provides a more complete overview of the report than the abstract does. It enables readers to quickly scan the report's primary points. The summary states the purpose of the investigation and gives major findings, provides background, states the scope, provides conclusions, and, if any are made, gives recommendations. It also describes the procedures used to conduct the study. Although more complete than an abstract, the executive summary should not contain a detailed description of the work on which the findings, conclusions, and recommendations were based. The length of the summary is proportional to the length of the report; typically, the summary should be approximately 10 percent of the length of the report.

Some executive summaries follow the organization of the report. Others highlight the findings, conclusions, and recommendations by summarizing them first, before going on to discuss procedures or methodology.

Like the abstract, the executive summary should be written so that it can be read independently of the report. It must not refer by number to figures, tables, or references contained elsewhere in the report. Because executive summaries are frequently read in place of the full report, all uncommon symbols, abbreviations, and acronyms must be spelled out.

Figure 12–8 shows an executive summary of the report on the Ethics Program at CGF Aircraft Corporation.

Writing Executive Summaries

WRITER'S CHECKLIST

☐ Write the executive summary after you have completed the original document.

☐ Avoid using terminology that may not be familiar to your readers.

☐ Spell out all uncommon symbols, abbreviations, and acronyms.

☐ Do not refer by number to figures, tables, or references contained elsewhere in the report.

☐ Make the summary concise, but do not omit transitional words and phrases (such as *however, moreover, therefore, for example,* and *in summary*).

☐ Include only information discussed in the original document.

EXECUTIVE SUMMARY

Page header provides report title

Purpose

This report examines the nature and disposition of the 3,458 ethics cases handled by the CGF Aircraft Corporation's ethics officers and managers during 2003. The purpose of this report is to provide CGF's Ethics and Business Conduct Committee with the information necessary for assessing the effectiveness of the first year of the company's Ethics Program.

Background

Effective January 1, 2003, the Ethics and Business Conduct Committee (the Committee) implemented a policy and procedures for the administration of CGF's new Ethics Program. The purpose of the Ethics Program, established by the Committee, is to "promote a positive work environment that encourages open communication regarding ethics and compliance issues and concerns." The Office of Ethics and Business Conduct was created to administer the Ethics Program. The director of the Office of Ethics and Business Conduct, along with seven ethics officers throughout the corporation, was given the responsibility for the following objectives:

Bulleted list highlights objectives

- Communicate the values and standards for CGF's Ethics Program to employees.
- Inform employees about company policies regarding ethical business conduct.
- Establish company-wide channels for employees to obtain information and guidance in resolving ethics concerns.
- Implement company-wide ethics-awareness and education programs.

Employee accessibility to ethics information and guidance was available through managers, ethics officers, and an ethics hotline.

Scope

Major ethics cases were defined as those situations potentially involving serious violations of company policies and/or illegal conduct. Examples of major ethics cases included cover-up of defective workmanship or use of defective parts in products; discrimination in hiring and promotion; involvement in monetary or other kickbacks; sexual harassment; disclosure of proprietary or company information; theft; and use of corporate Internet resources for inappropriate purposes, such as conducting personal business, gambling, or access to pornography.

Scope

Minor ethics cases were defined as including all reported concerns not classified as major ethics cases. Minor ethics cases were classified as informational queries from employees, situations involving coworkers, and situations involving management.

Page footer provides page number

Figure 12–8   Executive Summary of a Formal Report (continued)

Reported Ethics Cases—2003

The effectiveness of CGF's Ethics Program during the first year of implementation is most evidenced by (1) the active participation of employees in the program and the 3,458 contacts employees made regarding ethics concerns through the various channels available to them, and (2) the action taken in the cases reported by employees, particularly the disposition of the 30 substantiated major ethics cases. Disseminating information about the disposition of ethics cases, particularly information about the severe disciplinary actions taken in major ethics violations, sends a message to employees that unethical or illegal conduct will not be tolerated.

Conclusions

Based on these conclusions, recommendations for planning the second year of the Ethics Program are (1) continuing the channels of communication now available in the Ethics Program, (2) increasing financial and technical support for the Ethics Hotline, the most highly utilized mode of contact in the ethics cases reported in 2003, (3) disseminating this report in some form to employees to ensure their awareness of CGF's commitment to uphold its Ethics Policy and Procedures, and (4) implementing some measure of recognition for ethical behavior, such as an "Ethics Employee of the Month" award to promote and reward ethical conduct.

Recommendations

2

*Page footer provides
page number*

Figure 12–8   Executive Summary of a Formal Report (continued)

Introduction

The *introduction* provides your audience with any general information—such as why the report has been written—required to understand the details of the rest of the report. State the subject, the purpose, the scope, and the way you plan to develop the topic. You may also describe how the report will be organized, but, as with the descriptive abstract, exclude specific findings, conclusions, and recommendations. Figure 12–9 shows the introduction to the report on the CGF Ethics Program. Note that the contents of the introduction and the contents of the preface may overlap in some cases.

Introducing the Subject

The introduction should state the subject of the report. However, it should also include any necessary background information on the definition, history, or theory of the subject that provides context for the audience.

Stating the Purpose

The statement of purpose in your introduction should function as a topic sentence does in a paragraph. It should make your audience aware of your goal as they read your supporting statements and examples and tell them whether your material provides a new perspective or clarifies an existing perspective.

Page header provides report title

Purpose

Subheading signals shift in topic

Background

Bulleted list makes information easy to read

Background

Heading signals shift in topic

Page footer provides page number

Reported Ethics Cases — 2003

INTRODUCTION

This report examines the nature and disposition of the 3,458 ethics cases handled company-wide by CGF's ethics officers and managers during 2003. The purpose of this report is to provide the Ethics and Business Conduct Committee (the Committee) with the information necessary for assessing the effectiveness of the first year of CGF's Ethics Program. Recommendations are given for the Committee's consideration in planning for the second year of the Ethics Program.

Ethics and Business Conduct Policy and Procedures

Effective January 1, 2003, the Committee implemented Policy NB-AAG-200 and Procedure NB-ACG-202 for the administration of CGF's new Ethics Program. The purpose of the Ethics Program, established by the Committee, is to "promote a positive work environment that encourages open communication regarding ethics and compliance issues and concerns" (CGF's "Ethical Business Conduct").

The Office of Ethics and Business Conduct (OEBC) was created to administer the Ethics Program. The director of the OEBC, along with seven ethics officers throughout CGF, was given the responsibility for the following objectives:

- Communicate the values and standards for CGF's Ethics Program to employees.
- Inform employees about company policies regarding ethical business conduct.
- Establish company-wide channels for employees to obtain information and guidance in resolving ethics concerns.
- Implement company-wide ethics-awareness and education programs.

Employee accessibility to ethics information and guidance became the immediate and key goal of the OEBC in its first year of operation. The following channels for contact were set in motion during 2003:

- Managers throughout CGF received intensive ethics training; in all ethics situations employees were encouraged to go to their managers as the first point of contact.
- Ethics officers were available directly to employees through face-to-face or telephone contact, to managers, to callers using the Ethics Hotline, and by e-mail.
- The Ethics Hotline was available to all employees, 24 hours a day, 7 days a week, to anonymously report ethics concerns.

Confidentiality Issues

CGF's Ethics Policy ensures confidentiality and anonymity for employees who raise genuine ethics concerns. Procedure NB-ACG-202 guarantees appropriate discipline, up to and including dismissal, for retaliation or retribution against any employee who properly reports any genuine ethics concern.

3

Figure 12–9 Introduction to a Formal Report (continued)

Documentation of Ethics Cases

The following requirements were established by the director of the OEBC as uniform guidelines for the documentation by managers and ethics officers of all reported ethics cases:

- Name, position, and department of individual initiating contact, if available
- Date and time of contact
- Name, position, and department of contact person
- Category of ethics case
- Mode of contact
- Resolution

Managers and ethics officers entered the required information in each reported ethics case into an ACCESS database file, enabling efficient retrieval and analysis of the data.

Major/Minor Category Definition and Examples

Major ethics cases were defined as those situations potentially involving serious violations of company policies and/or illegal conduct. Procedure NB-ACG-202 requires notification of the Internal Audit and the Law Departments in serious ethics cases. The staffs of the Internal Audit and the Law Departments assume primary responsibility for managing major ethics cases and for working with the employees, ethics officers, and managers involved in each case.

Examples of situations categorized as major ethics cases:

- Cover-up of defective workmanship or use of defective parts in products
- Discrimination in hiring and promotion
- Involvement in monetary or other kickbacks from customers for preferred orders
- Sexual harassment
- Disclosure of proprietary customer or company information
- Theft
- Use of corporate Internet resources for inappropriate purposes, such as conducting private business, gambling, or access to pornography

Minor ethics cases were defined as including all reported concerns not classified as major ethics cases. Minor ethics cases were classified as follows:

- Informational queries from employees
- Situations involving coworkers
- Situations involving management

Page header provides report title

Subheading

Methodology

Bulleted list highlights guidelines

Subheading

Methodology

Bulleted lists high-lights examples

Page footer provides page number

Figure 12–9   Introduction to a Formal Report (continued)

Stating the Scope

The statement of scope tells the audience how much or how little detail to expect. Does your report present a broad survey of the topic, or does it concentrate on one part of the topic? Once you state your scope broadly, stop. Save the details for the main body of the report.

Previewing How the Topic Will Be Developed

In a long report, state how you plan to develop or organize your topic. Is the report an analysis of the component parts of some whole? Is it an analysis of selected parts (or samples) of a whole? Is the material presented in chronological order? Does it move from details to general conclusions, or from a general statement to the details that verify the statement? Does it set out to show whether a hypothesis is correct or incorrect? Stating your topic allows your audience to anticipate how the subject will be presented and gives them a basis for evaluating how you arrived at your conclusions or recommendations.

Text (Body)

Generally the longest section of the report, the text (or body) presents the details of how the topic was investigated, how the problem was solved, how the best choice from among alternatives was selected, or whatever else the report covers. This information is often clarified and further developed by the use of illustrations and tables and may be supported by references to other studies.

Most formal reports have no single best organization—it will depend on the topic and on how you have investigated it. The text is ordinarily divided into several major sections, comparable to the chapters in a book. These sections are then subdivided to reflect logical divisions in your main sections. See the sample table of contents (Figure 12–5) for an example of how the text for the report on the Ethics Program at the CGF Aircraft Corporation was organized. Figure 12–10 shows the body of the same report.

Headings

The use of headings (or heads) in the body of formal reports is important. Headings make the report more accessible to the audience by (1) dividing the body into manageable segments, (2) calling attention to the main topics, and (3) signaling changes of topics. Especially for long and complicated reports, you may need several levels of headings to indicate major divisions and subdivisions of the topic. Make headings most effective by following these guidelines:

- Use headings to signal a new topic or, if it is a lower-level heading, a new subtopic within the larger topic.
- Avoid too many or too few headings or levels of headings; too many clutter a document and too few fail to provide recognizable structure.

ANALYSIS OF REPORTED ETHICS CASES

Reported Ethics Cases by Major/Minor Category

CGF ethics officers and managers company-wide handled a total of 3,458 ethics situations during 2003. Of these cases, only 172, or 5 percent, involved reported concerns of a serious enough nature to be classified as major ethics cases (see Figure 1). Major ethics cases were defined as those situations potentially involving serious violations of company policy and/or illegal conduct.

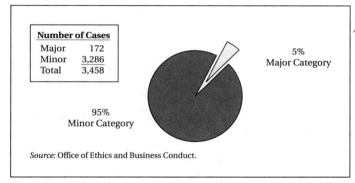

Number of Cases	
Major	172
Minor	3,286
Total	3,458

5%
Major Category

95%
Minor Category

Source: Office of Ethics and Business Conduct.

Figure 1.   Reported ethics cases by major/minor category in 2003.

Major Ethics Cases

Of the 172 major ethics cases reported during 2003, 57 percent, upon investigation, were found to involve unsubstantiated concerns. Incomplete information or misinformation most frequently was discovered to be the cause of the unfounded concerns of misconduct in 98 cases. Forty-four cases, or 26 percent of the total cases reported, involved incidents partly substantiated by ethics officers as serious misconduct; however, these cases were discovered to also involve inaccurate information or unfounded issues of misconduct. Only 17 percent of the total number of major ethics cases, or 30 cases, were substantiated as major ethics situations involving serious ethical misconduct and/or illegal conduct (CGF "2003 Ethics Hotline Results") (see Figure 2).

Page header provides report title

New section heading

Figure labeled and cross-referenced in text (cross-reference precedes figure)

Figure boxed and set off by white space above and below

Heading signals shift in topic

Cross-reference precedes figure

Page footer provides page number

Figure 12–10   Body of a Formal Report (continued)

Page header provides report title

Reported Ethics Cases—2003

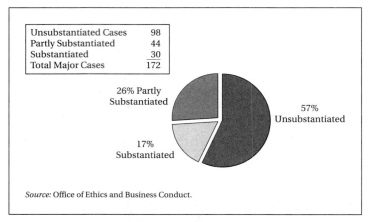

Unsubstantiated Cases	98
Partly Substantiated	44
Substantiated	30
Total Major Cases	172

26% Partly Substantiated

57% Unsubstantiated

17% Substantiated

Source: Office of Ethics and Business Conduct.

Pie chart showing percentages and augmented with specific values

Figure 2.   Major ethics cases in 2003.

White space above and below figure boxes

Of the 30 substantiated major ethics cases, seven remain under investigation at this time, and two cases are currently in litigation. Disposition of the remainder of the 30 substantiated reported ethics cases included severe disciplinary action in five cases: the dismissal of two employees and the demotion of three employees. Seven employees were given written warnings, and nine employees received verbal warnings (see Figure 3).

■ Employee Dismissal
■ Employee Demotion
■ Employee Written Warning
☐ Employee Verbal Warning
▨ Case Pending
▨ Case Currently in Litigation

Total Substantiated Cases = 30

Source: Office of Ethics and Business Conduct.

Figure with key to shading of values on pie chart

Figure 3.   Disposition of substantiated major ethics cases in 2003.

Page footer provides page number

Figure 12–10   Body of a Formal Report (continued)

Reported Ethics Cases—2003

Minor Ethics Cases

Subheading

Minor ethics cases included those that did not involve serious violations of company policy and/or illegal conduct. During 2003, ethics officers and company managers handled 3,286 such cases. Minor ethics cases were further classified as follows:

- Informational queries from employees
- Situations involving coworkers
- Situations involving management

Bulleted list highlights information

As might be expected during the initial year of the Ethics Program implementation, the majority of contacts made by employees were informational, involving questions about the new policies and procedures. These informational contacts comprised 55 percent of all contacts of a minor nature and numbered 2,148. Employees made 989 contacts regarding ethics concerns involving coworkers and 149 contacts regarding ethics concerns involving management (see Figure 4).

Cross-reference precedes figure

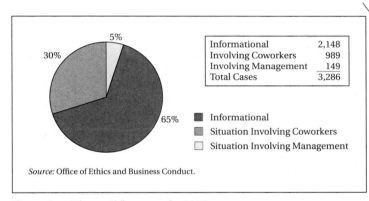

Figure 4.   Minor ethics cases in 2003.

White space above and below figure box

Mode of Contact

The effectiveness of the Ethics Program rested on the dissemination of information to employees and the provision of accessible channels through which employees could gain information, report concerns, and obtain guidance. Employees were encouraged to first go to their managers with any ethical concerns, because those managers would have the most direct knowledge of the immediate circumstances and individuals involved.

Figure 12–10   Body of a Formal Report (continued)

Page header provides report title

Reported Ethics Cases—2003

Other channels were put into operation, however, for any instance in which an employee did not feel able to go to his or her manager. The ethics officers company-wide were available to employees through telephone conversations, face-to-face meetings, and e-mail contact. Ethics officers also served as contact points for managers in need of support and assistance in handling the ethics concerns reported to them by their subordinates.

The Ethics Hotline became operational in mid-January 2003 and offered employees assurance of anonymity and confidentiality. The Ethics Hotline was accessible to all employees on a 24-hour, 7-day basis. Ethics officers company-wide took responsibility on a rotational basis for handling calls reported through the hotline.

In summary, ethics information and guidance was available to all employees during 2003 through the following channels:

Bulleted lists summarize parallel information in parallel form

- Employee to manager
- Employee telephone, face-to-face, and e-mail contact with ethics officer
- Manager to ethics officer
- Ethics Hotline

Cross-reference precedes figure

The mode of contact in the 3,458 reported ethics cases was as follows (see Figure 5):

- In 19 percent of the reported cases, or 657, employees went to managers with concerns.
- In 9 percent of the reported cases, or 311, employees contacted an ethics officer.
- In 5 percent of the reported cases, or 173, managers sought assistance from ethics officers.
- In 67 percent of the reported cases, or 2,317, contacts were made through the Ethics Hotline.

White space above and below figure

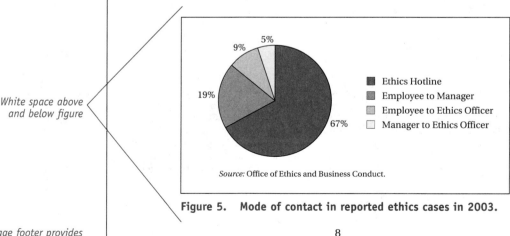

Figure 5.   Mode of contact in reported ethics cases in 2003.

Page footer provides page number

8

Figure 12–10   Body of a Formal Report (continued)

- Ensure that headings at the same level are of relatively equal importance and follow parallel structure.
- Subdivide sections only as needed; not every section requires lower-level headings.
- Subdivide higher-level headings into two or more lower-level headings whenever possible.
- Do not allow a heading to substitute for discussion; the text should read as if the heading were not there.
- Do not leave a heading as the final line of a page. If two lines of text cannot fit below a heading, start the section at the top of the next page.

Although various systems exist, the following style guidelines for up to five levels of headings are common:

First-Level Head

- All capital letters underlined or in 18-point boldface type
- Centered or flush left on the line by itself
- Two spaces above and one below

Second-Level Head

- All capital letters or in 14-point boldface type
- Flush left on a line by itself
- One space above and one space below

Third-Level Head

- Capital and lowercase letters underlined or in boldface type
- Flush left on a line by itself
- One space above and one space below

Fourth-Level Head

- Capital and lowercase letters *not* underlined or in boldface type
- One space above and one space below

Fifth-Level Head

- Indented as a paragraph on the same line as the first line of material it introduces
- Underlined or in italic typeface
- First letter capitalized; all others lowercase except proper nouns
- Ends with a period
- One space above the heading

The following example demonstrates these guidelines:

FIRST-LEVEL HEADING

The text of the document begins here.

SECOND-LEVEL HEADING

The text of the document begins here.

Third-Level Heading

The text of the document begins here.

Fourth-Level Heading

The text of the document begins here.

Fifth-level heading. The text of the document begins here and continues normally to the next line of the page.

The decimal numbering system uses a combination of numbers and decimal points to subordinate levels of headings in a report. The system is used primarily for scientific and technical reports. The following outline shows the correspondence between different levels of headings and the decimal numbers used:

---

1. MAJOR IDEA
1.1 Supporting idea for 1
1.2 Supporting idea for 1
1.2.1 Example or illustration of 1.2
1.2.2 Example or illustration of 1.2
1.2.2.1 Detail for 1.2.1
1.2.2.2 Detail for 1.2.1
1.3 Supporting idea for 1
2. MAJOR IDEA

Although the second-, third-, and fourth-level headings are indented in an outline or table of contents, as headings they are flush with the left margin in the body of the report.

Conclusions

The *conclusions* section of a report pulls together the results or findings presented in the report and interprets them in the light of its purpose and methods. Consequently, this section is the focal point of the work, the reason for the report in the first place. The conclusions must grow out of the findings discussed in the body of the report; moreover, they must be consistent with what the introduction states as the purpose of the report and the report's methodology. For instance, if the introduction states that the report's objective is to assess the market for a new product, then the conclusion should focus on the requirements of the market examined and on how appropriate the new product is for that market.

Recommendations

Recommendations, which are sometimes combined with the conclusions, state a course of action that should be taken based on the results of the study. (Whether or not the report should make recommendations is determined when the report is being planned.) What consulting group should the firm hire for a special project? Which Web-page designer should the company sign a contract with? What new and emerging markets should the firm target? Which make of delivery van should the company purchase to replace the existing fleet? The recommendations section says, in effect, "I think we should purchase this, or do that, or hire them."

The emphasis here is on the verb *should*. Recommendations advise the audience on the best course of action based on the researcher's findings. Generally, a decision-maker in the organization, or a customer or client, makes the final decision about whether to accept the recommendations.

Figure 12–11 shows the conclusions and recommendations from the report on the CGF Ethics Program.

Explanatory Footnotes

Occasionally, you will need to offer an explanation of an idea mentioned in the main body of the text. This type of footnote is generally placed at the foot of the page on which the idea appears.

> A description of the 76 variables identified for inclusion in the regression equations, together with their method of construction, data, source, means, and ranges, is given in Appendix A. The following discussion elaborates on those variables that proved most important in explaining housing-price variations.[1]
>
> [1] The number in parentheses in the following discussion refers to the variable number as used in regression equations.

(See Chapter 7 for additional guidance on the purpose of these notes.)

Page header
provides
report title

CONCLUSIONS AND RECOMMENDATIONS

Conclusions

The effectiveness of CGF's Ethics Program during the first year of implementation is most evidenced by (1) the active participation of employees in the program and the 3,458 contacts employees made regarding ethics concerns through the various channels available to them, and (2) the action taken in the cases reported by employees, particularly the disposition of the 30 substantiated major ethics cases.

One of the 12 steps to building a successful Ethics Program identified by Frank Navran in *Workforce* magazine is an ethics communication strategy. Navran explains that such a strategy is crucial in ensuring

> that employees have the information they need in a timely and usable fashion and that the organization is encouraging employee communication regarding the values, standards and the conduct of the organization and its members (Navran 119).

Indented quotations
set off for emphasis

The 3,458 contacts by employees during 2003 attest to the accessibility and effectiveness of the communication channels that exist in CGF's Ethics Program.

An equally important step in building a successful ethics program is listed by Navran as "Measurements and Rewards," which he explains as follows:

> In most organizations, employees know what's important by virtue of what the organization measures and rewards. If ethical conduct is assessed and rewarded, and if unethical conduct is identified and dissuaded, employees will believe that the organization's principals mean it when they say the values and code of ethics are important (Navran 121).

MLA-style in-text
citation

Disseminating information about the disposition of ethics cases, particularly information about the severe disciplinary actions taken in major ethics violations, sends a message to employees that unethical and/or illegal conduct will not be tolerated. Making public the tough-minded actions taken in cases of ethical misconduct provides "a golden opportunity to make other employees aware that the behavior is unacceptable and why" (Ferrell and Gardiner 129).

MLA-style in-text
citation

Recommendations

With these two points in mind, I offer the following recommendations for consideration for plans for the Ethics Program's second year:

Bulleted list highlights
information

- Continuation of the channels of communication now available in the Ethics Program
- Increased financial and technical support for the Ethics Hotline, the most highly used mode of contact in the reported ethics cases in 2003

Page footer provides
page number

Figure 12–11   Conclusions and Recommendations of a Formal Report (continued)

Reported Ethics Cases — 2003
_____

- Dissemination of this report in some form to employees to ensure employees' awareness of CGF's commitment to uphold its Ethics Policy and Procedures
- Implementation of some measure of recognition for ethical behavior, such as an "Ethics Employee of the Month," to promote and reward ethical conduct

To ensure that employees see the value of their continued participation in the Ethics Program, feedback is essential. The information in this annual review, in some form, should be provided to employees. Knowing that the concerns they reported were taken seriously and resulted in appropriate action by Ethics Program administrators would reinforce employee involvement in the program. While the negative consequences of ethical misconduct contained in this report send a powerful message, a means of communicating the *positive* rewards of ethical conduct at CGF should be implemented. Various options for recognition of employees exemplifying ethical conduct should be considered and approved.

Continuation of the Ethics Program's successful 2003 operations, with the implementation of the above recommendations, should ensure the continued pursuit of the Ethics Program's purpose: "to promote a positive work environment that encourages open communication regarding ethics and compliance issues and concerns."

10

Page header provides report title

Recommendations

Page footer provides page number

Figure 12–11   Conclusions and Recommendations of a Formal Report (continued)

Works Cited (or References)

If you refer to material in or quote directly from a published work or other research source, you must provide a list of references in a separate section called Works Cited. If your instructor or employer has a preferred reference style, follow it; otherwise, use the MLA or APA documentation guidelines provided in Chapter 7. (*Note:* If you use the APA style, your list of works cited is titled "References.")

For a relatively short report, the works-cited section should appear at the end of the report. See Figure 12–12 for the works-cited section of the CGF Ethics Program report. For a report with a number of sections or chapters, the works-cited section should fall at the end of each major section or chapter. In either case, every works-cited section should be labeled as such and should start on a new page. If a particular reference appears in more than one section or chapter, it should be repeated in full in each appropriate works-cited section. In MLA style, parenthetical references within the text of a document refer readers to sources cited in the works-cited section. The ethics report in this chapter uses in-text citations in MLA style throughout. Two of the references cited in Figure 12–11, for example, are as follows: (Navran 121) and (Ferrell and Gardiner 129). Chapter 7, pages 222–242, provides detailed guidance for creating in-text citations.

Header provides report title

Works-cited listing follows MLA format

Page footer provides page number

Reported Ethics Cases — 2003

WORKS CITED

CGF. "Ethical Business Conduct Program." 5 April 2003. <http://www.CGF .com/companyoffices/aboutus/ethics/nbacg2.htm>.

CGF. "2003 Ethics Hotline Investigation Results." 5 April 2004. <http://www .CGF.com/companyoffices/aboutus/funfacts/html/ethics.html>.

Ferrell, O. C., and Gareth Gardiner. In Pursuit of Ethics: Tough Choices in the World of Work. Springfield: Smith Collins, 1991.

Kelley, Tina. "Corporate Prophets, Charting a Course to Ethical Profits." New York Times 8 Feb. 1998: BU12.

Navran, Frank. "12 Steps to Building a Best-Practices Ethics Program." Workforce Sept. 1997: 117–22.

11

Figure 12–12   Works-Cited Section of a Formal Report

Using footnotes and citing works in reports helps you avoid plagiarism. Plagiarism in a college course may result in formal academic misconduct charges; on the job it can get you fired. Plagiarism in some cases is illegal; at the very least, it is unethical. For detailed information about documenting sources and avoiding plagiarism, see Chapter 7.

■ Back Matter

The *back matter* of a formal report contains supplemental information, such as one or more appendixes that include ancillary information that is necessary for a full understanding of the report, a bibliography that lists the location of additional information about the topic, and a glossary of terms.

Appendixes

An *appendix* contains information that clarifies or supplements the text — long charts and supplementary graphs or tables, copies of questionnaires and other material used in gathering information, texts of interviews, pertinent correspondence, and explanations too long for explanatory footnotes but helpful to the reader who is seeking further assistance or clarification.

The report may have one or more appendixes; generally, each appendix contains one type of material. For example, a report may have one appendix presenting a questionnaire and a second appendix presenting a detailed computer printout tabulating questionnaire results.

Evaluating Formal Reports

CONSIDERING AUDIENCE AND PURPOSE

☐ Who is the principal audience for the report?

☐ Who is the secondary audience?

☐ Is the transmittal letter or memo necessary and addressed to the principal audience?

☐ What is the order of elements that make up the front matter, body, and back matter of the report?

☐ Does the title page include the report title, preparer, and recipient?

☐ Does the abstract highlight the report's *major* points for the principal and secondary audiences?

☐ Does the table of contents list section titles exactly as they appear throughout the report?

☐ Does the body of the report sufficiently explain the topic so that the principal audience can interpret the significance of the findings, conclusions, and recommendations?

☐ Does the executive summary describe the purpose, *major* findings and conclusions, recommendations, and methodology used to reach the findings?

☐ Can the executive summary be read independently of the report?

☐ Does the introduction state the purpose of the report, the scope of material it covers, how you plan to develop the topic, and how the report will be organized?

☐ Is the body of the report divided into sections that best represent how the topic was developed to reach its findings, conclusions, and recommendations?

■ Are sections logically subdivided?

■ Are major and subordinate headings parallel in structure, and do they signal the logic of these subdivisions?

☐ Do the conclusions grow logically from the report's findings?

☐ Do the recommendations advise the audience on the appropriate course of action to take based on the findings?

☐ Do the works cited or references provide enough information to permit a reader to locate a source of interest?

☐ Is the material in the appendixes of sufficient importance to be included but so voluminous or ancillary that its presence in the body of the report would impede the reader?

Place the first appendix on a new page directly after the bibliography. Each additional appendix also begins on a new page. Identify each appendix with a title and a heading. Appendixes are ordinarily labeled Appendix A, Appendix B, and so on. If your report has only one appendix, label it "Appendix," followed by the title. To call it Appendix A implies that an Appendix B will follow.

If there is only one appendix, the pages are generally numbered 1, 2, 3, and so forth. If there is more than one appendix, the pages are double-numbered according to the letter of each appendix (for example, the first page of Appendix B would be numbered B-1).

Bibliography

The bibliography is the alphabetical listing of all the information sources you consulted to prepare the report—not just the ones you cite specifically in citations and endnotes or footnotes. Accordingly, the bibliography may be longer than the works-cited section. Further, because it is arranged alphabetically, it enables a reader interested in seeing whether you consulted a particular source to locate it quickly. Like other elements in the front and back matter, the bibliography starts on a new page and is labeled by name.

Glossary

A *glossary* lists and defines selected terms found in the report. Include a glossary only if the report contains many words and expressions that will be unfamiliar to your intended audience. Arrange the terms alphabetically, with each entry beginning on a new line. Then give the definition after each term. Even though the report may contain a glossary, the terms that appear in it should be defined when they are first mentioned in the text.

The glossary, labeled as such, appears directly after the appendix and begins on a new page.

Index

On the Web
For more advice on creating an index, see Chapter 12, bedfordstmartins.com/ writingthatworks

An *index* is an optional alphabetical list of all the major topics and their subcategories discussed in the report. It cites the page numbers where discussion of each topic can be found and allows the audience to find information on topics quickly and easily. The index is always the final section of a report.

DIGITAL SHORTCUTS

Creating an Index

Word-processing software can help you save time when creating an index for your report.

- Review the document to identify entries (the words, phrases, figure captions, or symbols that you wish to index).
- Following your software's instructions, highlight and code these entries. (In Microsoft Word, for example, you can mark a keyword, and the software can automatically mark all other instances of the word.)
- Following your coding, the software sorts the entries, eliminates duplications, and arranges the entries alphabetically with their page numbers in a separate section at the end of the document.
- If you wish, create headings for each alphabetical grouping of the index (A, B, C, etc.).
- Carefully review and revise your draft index.

◼ Graphic and Tabular Matter

Formal reports often contain illustrations and tables that clarify and support the text. These materials may be numbered and sequenced in varying ways. The following guidelines show one conventional system for numbering and smoothly integrating such materials into the text. For a full discussion of the creation and use of illustrations, see Chapter 8.

Identify each figure with a title and a number, in Arabic numerals, above or below the figure. For fairly short reports, number figures sequentially throughout the report (Figure 1, Figure 2, and so forth). For long reports, number figures by chapter or by section. According to this system, the first figure in Chapter 1 would be Figure 1.1 (or Figure 1–1), and the second figure would be Figure 1.2 (or Figure 1–2). In Chapter 2, the first figure would be Figure 2.1 (or Figure 2–1), and so on.

In the text, refer to figures by number rather than by location ("Figure 2.1" rather than "the figure below"). When the report is typed, the figures may not fall exactly where you originally expected.

Identify each table with a title and a number, centering both of these lines above the table. For fairly short reports, number the tables sequentially throughout the report (Table 1, Table 2, and so on). For long reports, number tables by chapter or by section, according to the system described for figure numbering. As with figures, refer to tables in the text by number rather than by location ("Table 4.1" [or "Table 4–1"] rather than "the above table").

CHAPTER 12 SUMMARY: Writing Formal Reports

Formal reports are written accounts of major projects. Following a transmittal letter or memo, they ordinarily contain three parts: front matter, body, and back matter.

The front matter consists of:

- ☐ Abstract
- ☐ Table of Contents
- ☐ List of Figures
- ☐ List of Tables
- ☐ Foreword
- ☐ Preface
- ☐ List of Abbreviations and Symbols

The body includes:

- ☐ Executive Summary
- ☐ Introduction
- ☐ Text (including headings, figures, tables, and explanatory footnotes)
- ☐ Conclusions
- ☐ Recommendations
- ☐ Explanatory Footnotes
- ☐ Works Cited (or References)

The back matter consists of:

- ☐ Appendixes
- ☐ Bibliography
- ☐ Glossary
- ☐ Index

■ Exercises

1. Complete the following audience-profile questionnaire for a hypothetical research, investigative, or annual report that you have been asked to prepare. Briefly explain the topic of your formal report and then answer the following questions:

    a. Who is your audience? (Write a 75- to 100-word description.)
    b. What does your audience already know about the subject?
    c. What do you want your audience to know?
    d. What might be your readers' attitude toward the topic? (Explore several alternatives.)
    e. Why will your audience be reading the report?
    f. How will your readers' perception of the report affect the project?

2. Write a brief narrative identifying different types of formal reports and list different situations in which each might be used.

3. Prepare a statement that defines the scope of a formal report covering the benefits, risks, and costs of establishing an on-site fitness center at a local business with more than 200 employees.

4. Keeping in mind that presentation is an important part of a formal report, prepare a title page for a hypothetical formal report and bring it to class. Refer to pages 422–423 for guidelines as you design your title page.

5. Using a sample report (or a recent formal report you have written), prepare a transmittal letter addressed to your instructor explaining what the report concerns. Include with your letter the title page and table of contents for the report.

6. Write a brief narrative explaining why you think either the executive summary or the abstract is the most important single piece of a formal report. Refer to the report included in this chapter, or another sample report, to support your conclusions.

7. Assume you are starting a business of your own. Based on what you know about your business, write a formal report that explains what your business will be, and what city would be the best location for your business and why. Assume that you are preparing this report to attach to your request for funding from the Small Business Administration. Submit an outline to your instructor before you begin your draft.

8. Write a formal report based on information you already know about a business, an organization, a sports team, or a government agency that suggests ways to cut costs or improve its financial earnings. Submit an outline to your instructor before you begin your draft.

Collaborative Classroom Projects

1. In groups of three or four members, consider the following questions:
   a. Why should a formal report contain a table of contents?
   b. When is a descriptive abstract more appropriate than an informative abstract?
   c. What types of information should not appear in an abstract?
   d. What is the function of a preface in a formal report?
   e. What function do heads perform in a formal report?
   f. What is the difference between conclusions and recommendations?
   g. What is the difference between a works-cited section and a bibliography section?
   h. What types of material should appear in an appendix?
   i. What is the function of a glossary in a formal report?

   Choose a group recorder to submit your answers to your instructor.

2. Bring to class a sample abstract for a journal article related to your major field of study. Divide into teams with classmates who share a similar major area of study. Appoint a group leader and recorder. As a group, review the abstracts and answer the following questions about each:
   a. How many words are in the abstract?
   b. Is the abstract descriptive or informative? How do you know?
   c. What is the abstract's purpose? What is its scope?

      d. Is the abstract clear and concise?

      e. Does the abstract encourage you to read the rest of the report?

      f. How would you improve the abstract?

3. Your campus is considering purchasing new computers for each classroom. Divide into groups of five or six members and for the next 45 minutes develop a formal-report outline for an investigative report on the topic. Brainstorm areas such as the value of computerized classrooms and their effect on teaching and learning, and the costs—the sources for funding and fees for students. Be ready to share your group's outline with your classmates when completed.

4. As a class, discuss the executive summary shown in Figure 12–8. Assume that the audience is, for example, the board of directors of CGF Aircraft Corporation. Consider these questions:

      a. How does the executive summary introduce the report? Does it include the appropriate information?

      b. Is the background information sufficient?

      c. What is the purpose of the report?

      d. What is the scope of the report?

      e. Are costs an important concern of this report?

      f. Are the conclusions effective?

      g. How long would you expect the report to be?

5. Bring to class an example of a formal report that you find at a government, nonprofit, or corporate organization, or on the Web. Photocopy the report, then cut the photocopied report into its separate sections—headings, subheadings, tables, graphs, text, scope, topic sentences, paragraphs, and so on—and place the pieces in an envelope. Form groups of three or four members, exchange envelopes, and reassemble the reports as quickly as possible. Compare the reassembled versions with the originals.

■ Research Projects

1. Write a formal report on a topic from your career field or other area of interest. You may want to use the topic you selected and the information you gathered in doing the research projects for Chapter 7. Prepare a topic outline for the report, including a title page, descriptive abstract, table of contents, preface, executive summary, heads, conclusions and/or recommendations, works-cited or references section, and any additional elements your report may require. Create a transmittal letter for the report addressed to your instructor and submit both for your instructor's review.

2. Use the following topics for brainstorming a subject for your own formal report or develop your own topic. (Determine a hypothetical audience and organizational setting before creating the report.)

   • A comparative analysis of the most desirable place in the country to relocate an actual business (compare at least two locations).

   • An analysis of the value of establishing a day-care facility for working parents at a local company.

   • An analysis of campus cultural and entertainment activities, showing that some should be eliminated, added, or both.

- An analysis of the job opportunities in a specific field (for example, law, finance, accounting). Use at least six authoritative (government, academic, etc.) sources in your analysis.
- A report recommending the most useful personal computer or network for an actual local small business.
- An analysis of technical training facilities (colleges, trade schools, private agencies, etc.) in the area that would support a high-tech company planning to relocate here.

3. Conduct research to prepare an analytical formal report that compares two possible courses of action. Imagine you work for a small company that has revenues of about $100 million in sales (and profits of about $4 million a year). Your company's sales force numbers 20 members who collectively travel approximately 1,000 miles a week. Your company now needs a new fleet of cars, all the same make and model for the sales force. The cars should be economical, but large enough to accommodate the samples (of equipment, books, etc.). You have been asked to determine whether the fleet should be purchased or leased.

   Begin by developing a profile of your company so that you understand its needs and resources. Next, select three or four makes and models of cars. Choose specific features of the cars that you can compare. Analyze these features to determine (1) which car is the most cost-effective and the most suitable choice for your company and (2) whether to purchase or lease a fleet of these cars. In your report, clearly define, justify, and explain your findings:

- State the purpose of your report and your findings.
- Inform readers of how and where you gathered information.
- Define the criteria on which you based your research, given your company and its needs.
- Compare and contrast available options.
- Explain your conclusion and recommendations.

4. Select a topic that is relevant to your major area of study or your life. For example, you may want to conduct research for an investigative report or feasibility study you've been assigned at work, or for a personal issue such as finding the right graduate school or dealing with an issue in your community. Explain to your instructor in a cover memo whether this document is part of a longer document, whether its format or organization was predetermined, and whether it incorporates sections prepared by others. Explain how and where you gathered your information. Refer to this chapter to make certain that you include all necessary front matter, body, and back matter, as well as all appropriate optional sections in your formal report. Your instructor may advise you on specific sections to include.

■ Web Projects

Projects followed by the symbol Ⓦ are continued at **bedfordstmartins.com/ writingthatworks**, Chapter 12.

1. Using the *Occupational Outlook Handbook* at the Bureau of Labor Statistics Web site, write a formal report in which you analyze two different job positions in your major area of study. Include in your report the required background, working conditions, pay scale, geographic expectations, and job outlook. Prepare your

report as if you are trying to decide objectively between two occupations, and include a conclusion and recommendations section. W

2. Using the Bureau of Economic Analysis Web site, select the Overview of the Economy section and write a report explaining the last three years of economic data for the United States, covering production, purchases, prices, and personal income. Assume the report is for your area's Business and Industry Council conference that you will be attending in the future. W

3. You are a company manager in a small manufacturing firm (100 employees) and are part of a team assigned to gather information about retirement funding programs. Using the Web, find at least three different programs to compare. After reviewing the three different sites, make a list of all components that should be considered when your team makes a recommendation to your company president. For this report, you will be concerned more with programs available than with individual companies. W

4. Write a brief narrative describing how you think the Internet has changed formal-report writing. Begin by searching the Web to discover formal reports available online. List examples and provide a brief comparative analysis of each. Note whether Web sites are referenced in formal reports. Include a discussion of how you think the Internet has changed formal-report writing in business and industry.

13 Writing Instructions

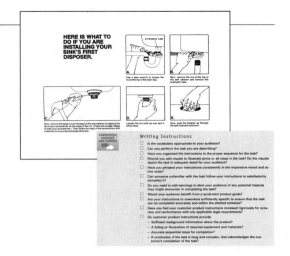

When you tell someone how to perform a specific procedure or task, you are giving instructions. Instructions may describe how to carry out a particular task in the workplace (send a file to a digital copier); perform a procedure (process a Medicare form); operate equipment (use a spray-paint gun); or assemble, repair, or maintain equipment (replace a seal on a high-pressure pump).

How many times have you heard people complain about instructions being unclear, inaccurate, or poorly illustrated? Poor instructions can cause miscommunications and delays in an important project or, worse, be directly responsible for an injury, which could result in damage claims and lawsuits. If your instructions are based on clear thinking and careful planning, they should enable your audience to carry out the procedure or task successfully. Clear, easy-to-follow instructions can also build goodwill for your company. This chapter will provide guidance for:

- Planning and writing instructions (page 455).
- Creating instructions for coworkers (page 467).
- Creating instructions for products (page 470).

Planning and Writing Instructions

To write effective instructions, you must assess the needs of your audience, learn how to perform the operation yourself, organize the instructions in the proper sequence, use illustrations when they would be helpful, write directly to your reader, test the instructions when you have finished them, include necessary warnings and cautions, and even designs for users averse to reading instructions.

On the Web For more help with writing instructions, see Chapter 13, bedfordstmartins.com/writingthatworks

Assess Your Audience's Needs

Learn your audience's level of knowledge and experience, and try to put yourself in their position. Are they skilled in the kind of task for which you are writing instructions? If they are knowledgeable about the subject, use the specialized vocabulary appropriate to the subject. If they have little or no knowledge of the subject, use plain language or include a glossary for specialized terms.

Learn to Perform the Operation Yourself

To write accurate and easily understood instructions, you must thoroughly understand the task you are describing. Otherwise, your instructions could prove embarrassing or even dangerous. For example, the container of a brand-name drain cleaner carries the following warning:

- Use only as directed.

Then the instructions direct the user to do the following:

- Fill sink with 1 to 2 inches of water, then close off drain opening.

Users would find it difficult to raise the water level in the sink *before* closing the drain! The writer of these instructions did not carefully observe the actual sequence of steps required to use the product, or he or she would have written the instructions accurately. In this case, users simply ignored the instructions and performed the task according to common sense, so no harm was done. Suppose such confusing instructions were given for administering an intravenous fluid or for assembling high-voltage electrical equipment. The results of such inaccurate advice could be both dangerous and costly.

The writer of the drain-cleaning instructions undoubtedly knew better and was just careless. Sometimes, though, a writer may attempt to write instructions for a procedure that he or she does not understand adequately. Don't let that happen to you. As you watch, ask questions about any step that is not clear to you. Direct observation should enable you to write instructions that are exact, complete, and clear. Also make certain that you know the reason for the procedure, the materials and tools required, and the end result of the task.

Once you understand the procedure yourself, you must determine the most effective way to present it to your audience.

Organize the Instructions

To make your instructions easy to follow, divide them into short, simple steps, and arrange the steps in the correct sequence (review the information on sequential organization in Chapter 2). The steps can be given in either of two ways. You can label each step with a sequential number, as follows:

Voices from the Workplace

James Bates, U.S. Department of Housing and Urban Development

As a community builder with the U.S. Department of Housing and Urban Development (HUD), James Bates works to connect the agency's constituency—which includes home buyers, community organizations, banks and developers, the media, legislators, and mayors in upstate New York—with HUD's community development programs. James leads projects that help communities develop and carry out strategies for reducing homelessness, increasing homeownership, financing shopping centers in low-income neighborhoods, and responding to natural disasters.

Whether he's reporting on a project or providing instructions to technical staff, James keeps in mind some basic communication principles. "Tell people only what is most relevant for them to know given their position and level of interest. Technical staff want to know about resources, timetables, and the processes they need to follow. Clients want to know what they are going to get and when they will get it. Managers want to know the bottom line—solutions, recommendations, and actions."

Considering his varied audiences and presenting information clearly by using straightforward language are essential to James's work. "When I communicate with higher-ups, I make sure that my words aren't adulterated with 'tech speak.'" When working with clients in the community, James says, "it's easy to lapse into 'government speak' and lose a genuine opportunity to connect with the public and to get community buy-in on what we are trying to accomplish. I make sure that our mission and message are always conveyed in an audience-sensitive manner. I let people know we are about partnerships and collaboration."

Visit the HUD Web site at <hud.gov>.

Beth Blazon, St. Joseph's Hospital

Beth Blazon is an occupational therapist at St. Joseph's Hospital in Nashua, New Hampshire, where she specializes in acute inpatient, outpatient, and pediatric therapies. At the hospital, Beth develops rehabilitation plans and works one-on-one with her patients to help them perform occupational exercises. Before her patients are discharged, Beth equips each with written instructions for exercises to be completed at home—exercises that are crucial for patients' full recovery.

"I make my instructions simple, taking into account any language or cognitive barriers the patient may have. I also tailor the instructions to each person, keeping in mind the person's daily activities. For example, if a person doesn't cook, there is no point teaching that person how to conserve energy while cooking."

Beth's strategy for writing instructions is to keep them focused, brief, and visual. "I don't want my readers to have to sift through paragraphs of information they will not need. I keep my instructions as basic as possible, using as few words as possible. I've found that the use of pictures helps a lot, especially when demonstrating exercises."

■ 1. Connect each black cable wire to a brass terminal.

2. Attach one 4-inch green jumper wire to the back.

3. Connect both jumper wires to the bare cable wires.

Or you can use words that indicate time or sequence, as follows:

■ *First*, assess the problem that the customer reports to you. *Next*, observe and test the system in operation. *At that time*, question the customer until you understand the problem completely. *Then*, test the following. . . .

When two operations must be performed at the same time, include both operations in the same step.

WRONG   1. Hold the Control key down.
               2. Press the Bell key before releasing the Control key.

RIGHT   1. While holding the Control key down, press the Bell key.

Use Visuals Where Needed

Well-thought-out illustrations can make even the most complex instructions easier to understand. In addition to demonstrating the steps of your instructions, drawings, photographs, and diagrams can help your audience identify parts and the relationships between them. The value of illustrations will depend on your audience's needs and on the nature of the project. Generally, instructions for inexperienced readers should be more thoroughly illustrated than those for experienced readers. Do not, however, rely on an illustration alone to carry the meaning of a set of instructions. Refer to the illustration in the instructions to explain what it shows, and use labels on the illustration to further clarify its purpose.

Ensure that step-by-step instructions are placed next to the steps illustrated so that the audience immediately recognizes the connection between the two. Figure 13–1 shows instructions that guide a medical lab technician through the steps of streaking a saucer-sized disk of material (called agar) used to grow bacterial colonies for laboratory examination. The streaking is done by hand with a thin wire, looped at one end for holding a sample of the inoculum. When necessary or advisable, illustrate each step in your instructions (Figure 13–2), making certain that the illustration represents the current model of the equipment.

A technique especially useful for inexperienced readers is to show a close-up of a portion of a larger image, as in Figure 13–3, which illustrates installation of a shower floor drain. The "magnified" image can show essential details impossible to see in a larger picture. Linking the two images visually puts the close-up in context for the reader. See Design for Users Averse to Reading Instructions on page 465, for additional suggestions for designing visuals for instructions. (For a complete discussion of how to create and use effective illustrations, see Chapter 8.)

STREAKING AN AGAR PLATE

Distribute the inoculum over the surface of the agar in the following manner:

Step 1. After sterilizing the loop in an open flame, beginning at one edge of the saucer, thin the inoculum by streaking back and forth over the same area several times, sweeping across the agar surface until approximately one-quarter of the surface has been covered. *Sterilize the loop.*

Step 2. Streak at right angles to the originally inoculated area, carrying the inoculum out from the streaked areas onto the sterile surface with only the first stroke of the wire. Cover half of the remaining sterile agar surface. *Sterilize the loop.*

Step 3. Repeat as described in Step 2, covering the remaining sterile agar surface.

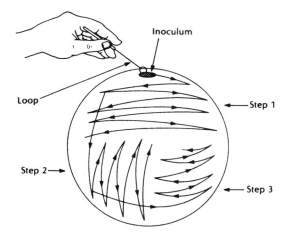

Single illustration shows a three-step process

Labels on the illustration link it to the steps in the instructions

Plate enlarged to emphasize the pattern and sequence of strokes

Figure 13–1   Step-by-Step Instructions with Illustration

Write Directly to Your Reader

The clearest and simplest instructions are written as commands. Addressing each sentence directly to your audience in the imperative mood and the active voice makes your instructions easier to follow and less wordy than if written in the passive voice.

PASSIVE   The access lid should be closed by the operator.

ACTIVE/IMPERATIVE   Close the access lid.

Although instructions should be concise, do not try to achieve conciseness by leaving out needed words such as articles (*a, an, the*), pronouns (*you, this, these*), and verbs. Doing so will certainly shorten sentences, but sentences shortened this

Each step of a process illustrated separately

Instructions written in the imperative mood

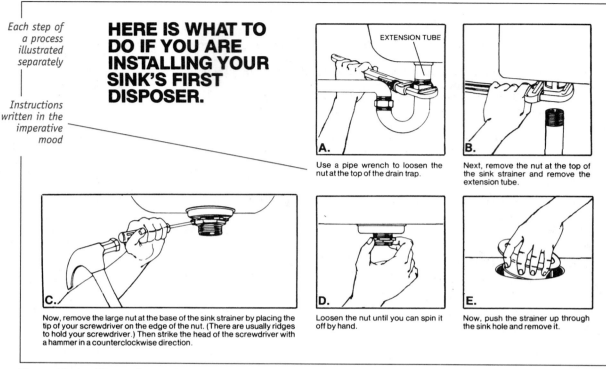

HERE IS WHAT TO DO IF YOU ARE INSTALLING YOUR SINK'S FIRST DISPOSER.

A. Use a pipe wrench to loosen the nut at the top of the drain trap.

B. Next, remove the nut at the top of the sink strainer and remove the extension tube.

EXTENSION TUBE

C. Now, remove the large nut at the base of the sink strainer by placing the tip of your screwdriver on the edge of the nut. (There are usually ridges to hold your screwdriver.) Then strike the head of the screwdriver with a hammer in a counterclockwise direction.

D. Loosen the nut until you can spin it off by hand.

E. Now, push the strainer up through the sink hole and remove it.

Figure 13–2   Illustrating Each Step in a Set of Instructions   *Source:* "Installation of Kenmore Waste Disposers," Courtesy of Sears, Roebuck and Company, 1997, Hoffman Estates, IL.

way usually have to be read more than once to be understood—actually defeating the purpose of short sentences. The following instruction for cleaning a power punch press assembly (a machine that punches holes and other patterns into materials), for example, is not easily understood at first reading.

UNCLEAR   Pass brush through punch area for debris.

The meaning of the phrase *for debris* needs to be made clearer. Revised, the instruction is readily understandable.

CLEAR   Pass a brush through the punch area to clear away any debris.

In any operation, certain steps must be performed with more exactness than others. Anyone who has boiled a three-minute egg for four minutes understands this all too well. Alert your audience to the steps that require exact timing or measurement.

VAGUE   Let the liquid cool.

PRECISE   Let the liquid cool for 30 minutes.

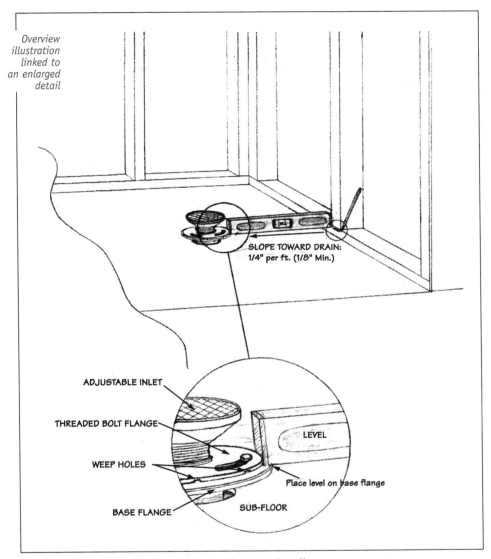

Overview illustration linked to an enlarged detail

SLOPE TOWARD DRAIN: 1/4" per ft. (1/8" Min.)

ADJUSTABLE INLET

THREADED BOLT FLANGE

WEEP HOLES

BASE FLANGE

SUB-FLOOR

LEVEL

Place level on base flange

Figure 13–3   Close-up of an Image to Illustrate Details

Test Your Instructions

To test the accuracy and clarity of your instructions, ask someone who is not familiar with the operation to use the instructions you have written to perform the task or procedure. A first-time user of your instructions can spot missing steps or point out passages that should be worded more clearly. As you watch your tester follow your instructions, note any steps that seem especially puzzling or confusing and revise them for clarity.

Writing Instructions in Plain Language

- ☐ Identify and write to your average reader.
- ☐ Keep in mind your average reader's level of technical knowledge.
- ☐ Avoid unnecessary jargon.
- ☐ Avoid confusing terms and constructions, such as:
  - ■ Including undefined abbreviations and acronyms.
  - ■ Using two different words for the same thing.
  - ■ Giving an obscure meaning to a word.
- ☐ Write in the imperative mood.
- ☐ Use the active voice.
  - ■ It makes clear who is supposed to do what.
  - ■ It uses fewer words.
- ☐ Use *you* and other pronouns.
  - ■ They allow you to write directly to the reader rather than to a group.
  - ■ They pull the reader into the writing and make it relevant to the reader.
- ☐ Write short sentences.
  - ■ Aim for one message in each sentence.
  - ■ Break up information into smaller, easier-to-understand units.
- ☐ Use simple tenses; use the present tense as much as possible.
- ☐ Select word placement carefully.
  - ■ Keep subjects and objects close to their verbs.
  - ■ Put *only, always,* and other conditional words next to the words they modify.
  - ■ Put *if* phrases after the main clauses to which they apply, not before.

Include Warnings and Cautions

Warnings and cautions are essential to instructions involving potentially hazardous equipment or materials. In fact, product liability laws require a manufacturer to warn potential users of (1) dangers in the *normal use* of the product and (2) dangers in the *foreseeable misuse* of the product. A manufacturer, however, need not warn of *open and obvious* dangers. Hence, instructions for an electric knife need not warn the user not to use the knife for shaving a beard—an obvious danger that is also neither "normal use" nor "foreseeable" by the manufacturer. Instructions for an electric knife would need to warn users to take care when holding food to be sliced, because a slip of the hand could result in injury—a danger in normal use.

Even if the danger is open and obvious, the manufacturer may have a duty to warn users who may not be aware of the extent or degree of danger. If the likelihood of injury is serious, the manufacturer is also required to display a warning on the product itself.

Language of Warnings

In general, all instructions for the proper use of a product should be *clear, readable,* and *understandable.* However, readers must also be warned specifically of dangers that they might expect and dangers that they might not. Remember, a danger that is obvious to you as the writer of the instructions may not be obvious to the user. Instructions not only must warn of all risks and hazards but also must warn *adequately.* An adequate warning must do three things:

- Identify the hazard and the potential seriousness of the risk.
- Give the likely results of ignoring the warning.
- Describe how to avoid the hazard and thus the injury.

To ensure that a warning is adequate, the language in it must be clear and explicit.

VAGUE   Failure to disengage the blades may result in bodily harm.

EXPLICIT   If you do not disengage the blades, they can amputate your fingers.

Avoid words that are open to interpretation or need further defining: *proper, excessive, frequently, often, seldom, may, might, could, recommended, occasionally.* If potential users comprise a diverse group, consider their familiarity (if any) with the product, level of literacy, and nationality.

Visual Symbols and Signal Words

Position warnings to potential hazards *before* the equipment is used or the material is handled. Make sure that they stand out from the text and are easily readable—use an open, uncrowded format so that they do not blend in with the instructions. A clear border of heavy lines or white space adds visual emphasis to warnings. Use symbols and icons in the text to reinforce warnings, as illustrated in Figure 13–4. Use line drawings of products that depict the physical sources of

READ SAFETY SIGNS CAREFULLY AND FOLLOW THEIR INSTRUCTIONS

Danger signs identify the most serious hazards and are attached to machines near specific hazard areas.

Keep safety signs in good condition. Replace any missing or damaged safety signs.

Icons depict types of hazards

Figure 13–4   Typical Warning Icons with Text

hazards and, if possible, the nature of the hazard. Don't show a picture of what *not* to do unless you put a slash (/) through the image. And don't use cartoons for safety warnings because they dilute warnings, trivialize the hazard, may imply that you are "talking down" to readers, and are difficult to design simply.

Warning words, symbols, icons, and labels are increasingly standardized, although industry practices do vary. Certain signal words in boldface and their corresponding colors are becoming standards:

DANGER (red) = hazard or unsafe practice that *will* result in severe injury or death.

WARNING (orange) = *could* result in severe injury or death

CAUTION (yellow) = could result in *minor* injury or property damage

NOTICE (blue) = information unrelated to safety

The hazard-alert symbol—an international standard—should appear with the signal word.

Hazard-Alert Symbol and Signal Word

Use cautions and warnings only when absolutely necessary, however. Too many may cause your audience to ignore those that are essential.

Design for Users Averse to Reading Instructions

Even clear, well-illustrated instructions are of no value if no one reads them. How can you reach an instruction-averse audience? Customers want to use a new device as soon as they receive it. However, if the product comes with a thick user's manual of dense, legalistic text, they will avoid it. This attitude can lead to accidents, increased calls to help lines, dissatisfied customers, and lost time and productivity.

To address this problem, many firms have adopted a two-tier approach in their instructions. In addition to a full-scale user's manual, essential for products such as automobiles, cell phones, washers, dryers, or ovens, they produce a quick-start guide with color pictures, easy-to-follow-diagrams, and minimal text. When users are given a choice between a 200-page owner's manual and an 8-page glossy color booklet, they opt for the booklet. In another approach, many computer companies now provide quick-setup posters with few words and large photographs that are color coded to parts on the equipment, as shown in Figure 13–5. Other firms produce laminated cards and booklets with indexed tabs that permit readers to find at a glance what they're looking for—the correct air pressure for tires, how to set an oven timer, and the like, as shown in Figure 13–6. To create

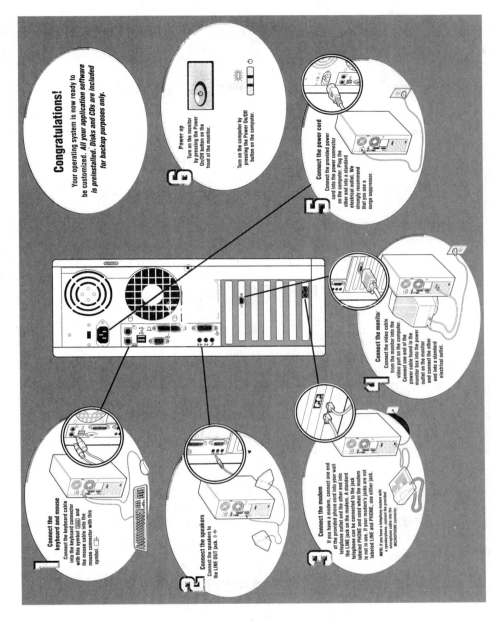

Figure 13–5 Poster of Illustrated Instructions

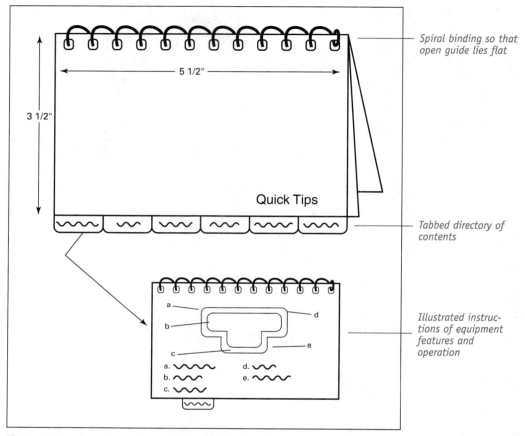

Figure 13–6 **Laminated Pocket-Sized Owner's Guide**

instructions for complex procedures, consider using the two-tier approach. Although many other options exist for providing customers with product help, such as CD-ROMs, Web sites, help lines, and instructor-led classes, they are outside the scope of this text.

■ Creating Instructions for Coworkers

Employees write many kinds of informal, nontechnical instructions to coworkers every day. They are frequently sent by e-mail. In the e-mail instructions in Figure 13–7, for example, a budget analyst requests data about an office's copier program from the manager of that program to plan for the upcoming fiscal year's budget.

Other informal instructions to coworkers may describe how to perform routine workplace activities. The instructions in Figure 13–8 lay out the steps necessary to process a company's consumer correspondence, from intake to response.

Subject: Planning Call for FY 2005 Budget
Date: March 1, 2003
From: Carol Quenten
To: Gene Carruthers

Gene,

We are planning the 2005 budget cycle, and I'll need the following information about the copier program.

- Current and projected monthly maintenance charges for each copier and the totals
- Any indication of projected maintenance increases from our vendors
- The number of copiers we lease and the number we own
- The number of copiers we need to replace based on a seven-year life cycle per machine
- The projected costs for replacing our current copiers with networked copiers

Do not include projected toner and paper costs at this time.

Fill in the data on the budget form located on the shared S:\ drive at S:\OCIOO\IMD\copiers. The information is due for my review on 3/15/2003. Thanks.

================================
Carol Quenten, Budget Analyst
TechQuest Inc.
119 Trowbridge Rd., Minneapolis, MN 55401
(507) 333-3333 Fax: (507) 333-3334
cquenten@techquest.com
techquest.com
================================

Bulleted questions for ease of reading and response

Qualifying guidance

Details on submitting answers

Figure 13–7   Informal Employee-to-Employee Instructions

Note the use of headings, the organization of the required tasks, and the straight-forward language of the memo.

Organizing and Highlighting Instructions

DIGITAL
SHORTCUTS

When writing instructions, use the following features of your word-processing software to organize and highlight information:

- Font size and boldface
- Outlining feature
- Numbered-list feature
- Bulleted-list feature
- Clip-art icons and symbols

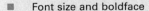

Instructions arranged in sequential order

Boldface headings identify major steps

Bullets identify tasks within each major step

XYZ Corporation

Consumer Response Department
Procedures for Handling Correspondence

1. Intake
When the Customer Response Department receives a written consumer query or comment, the Department Assistant:
- Logs in the correspondence in the electronic tracking system.
- Makes a paper copy.
- Gives the copy to the Section Analyst for review.
- Retains the original in the Section Tracking Folder.

2. Content Review
The Department Analyst:
- Reviews the content.
- Meets with the Department Chief to discuss response strategy, staff assigned to respond, and date due to the Department Supervisor.

The due date is two working days before the response is due to the Vice President for Consumer Affairs.

3. Staff Assignment
The Department Analyst:
- Informs the Department Assistant of who will respond and the due date.
- Meets with the assistant and provides any necessary background for the reply.

4. Staff Response
- The respondent e-mails the draft reply to the Department Assistant on or before the due date.
- The Department Assistant logs the draft into the database and forwards it to the Department Analyst for review.

5. Response Review
The Department Chief and Department Analyst meet to:
- Make any necessary revisions to the draft.
- Forward the draft to the Department Assistant for incorporation into the final draft.

The Department Assistant:
- Enters the final draft into the company electronic document database.
- Maintains a record of concurrences on the final draft.
- Prepares a paper correspondence package for signature.

6. Approval
- The Department Supervisor approves the correspondence package.
- The Department Assistant forwards it to the Vice President for Consumer Affairs for review and signature.

Figure 13–8 Coworker Instructions for Processing Correspondence

Creating Instructions for Products

Some instructions are intended to help customers assemble and maintain products. These instructions tend to be formally written and carefully reviewed for accuracy and for their adherence to policy and legal requirements before they are used. Figures 13–9 and 13–10 show two sets of relatively simple technical instructions, one without and one with an illustration.

Organizing Instructions for Products

Many instructions for product assembly are organized into four parts: (1) Introduction, (2) Required Equipment and Materials, (3) Procedural Steps, and (4) Conclusion.

Introduction

Use an introduction to provide any needed background information, to state the purpose of the procedure, or to offer a theory of operation to help your audience understand why the product works the way it does. Figure 13–11 includes an introduction that explains the purpose of the instructions.

Required Equipment and Materials

If special tools, materials, or equipment are needed to complete your instructions, inform your audience at the outset—don't let them get well into the procedure and then learn about such requirements. Provide a well-labeled section that tells them clearly what they need before they begin the procedure.

Procedural Steps

The procedural steps are the sequential steps required to complete the instructions. Review the section on sequential organization in Chapter 2 (pages 34–38) for a full discussion of this method of development.

Cleaning the Inside of the Grill

1. Disconnect the igniter wire from the igniter before cleaning the grill. Do not mistake the brown and black accumulation of grease and smoke for paint. The interiors of gas grills are not painted at the factory (and should never be painted).
2. Remove the grill lid, cooking grate, grease cup, and Drip VapoRISER Bar. Discard old lava rock or briquets. Attach the grease cup to the grease hanger and empty it after each use.
3. Using a scrub brush, apply a strong solution of detergent and water or grill cleaner to the insides of the grill lid and the bottom. Rinse and allow the equipment to air dry completely.

Instructions written in imperative mood

Figure 13–9   Product-Maintenance Instructions

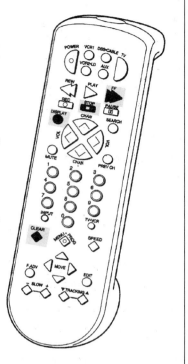

Time Counter

Purpose of product

The time counter shows the actual time it takes to record a program or play back a segment of a prerecorded tape. It helps locate the beginning or end of programs you taped. The time counter resets to 0:00:00 whenever the tape is ejected from the VCR.

For example, if a 30-minute program was recorded at the beginning of the tape, you would:

1. Insert the prerecorded tape. Press STOP. Make sure the tape is rewound.

2. Press DISPLAY twice to display only the time counter on the TV screen.

3. Press CLEAR to reset the time counter to 0:00:00.

4. Press FF on remote or turn the shuttle on the VCR clockwise to fast forward the tape until the time counter reads 0:30:00. Press STOP.

   This is the approximate end of the program and you can begin recording at this spot.

5. Press DISPLAY twice to remove the time counter from the screen and return to the normal displays.

Purpose of product

Step-by-step instructions keyed to the illustration

Figure 13–10 **Instructions with an Illustration** *Source:* "VR542 User's Guide," Courtesy of Thompson Consumer Electronics, Inc., 1995, Indianapolis, IN.

Purpose of product

When you are using one of the basic hookups, the TV•VCR button lets you switch between the picture coming from the VCR or the picture from the TV channel. This button lets you record a program on the VCR while watching another channel on the TV.

Step-by-step instructions to be performed sequentially

A. Press VCR1 to set the remote to control the VCR.
B. Press TV•VCR to see the picture from the VCR. The VCR indicator lights in the display panel.
C. Press CHANNEL up or down on the VCR or CHAN on the VCR's remote to change channels on the VCR. The channel number changes in the display panel.
D. Press TV•VCR to see the TV channels. The VCR indicator does not light in the display panel. Change channels using the TV's remote.
E. Return the TV to the VCR viewing channel—CH3 or CH4.
F. Press VCR1, then TV•VCR to switch back to the picture from the VCR.

Figure 13–11 **Introduction for Instructions** *Source:* "VR542 User's Guide," Courtesy of Thompson Consumer Electronics, Inc., 1995, Indianapolis, IN.

Conclusion

Brief instructions can simply end with the last step in the procedure. For longer and more complex instructions, add a conclusion section that satisfies your audience's sense of confidence about completing the job successfully.

- Congratulations on successfully assembling your gas grill. With proper care, it will serve you well for many years to come.

Writing Instructions

CONSIDERING AUDIENCE AND PURPOSE

- ☐ Is the vocabulary appropriate to your audience?
- ☐ Can you perform the task you are describing?
- ☐ Have you organized the instructions in the proper sequence for the task?
- ☐ Should you add visuals to illustrate some or all steps in the task? Do the visuals depict the task in adequate detail for your audience?
- ☐ Have you phrased your instructions consistently in the imperative mood and active voice?
- ☐ Can someone unfamiliar with the task follow your instructions to satisfactorily complete it?
- ☐ Do you need to add warnings to alert your audience of any potential hazards they might encounter in completing the task?
- ☐ Would your audience benefit from a quick-start product guide?
- ☐ Are your instructions to coworkers sufficiently specific to ensure that the task can be completed accurately and within the allotted schedule?
- ☐ Have you had your customer product instructions reviewed rigorously for accuracy and conformance with any applicable legal requirements?
- ☐ Do customer product instructions provide:
  - Sufficient background information about the product?
  - A listing or illustration of required equipment and materials?
  - Accurate sequential steps for completion?
  - A conclusion, if the task is long and complex, that acknowledges the customer's completion of the task?

CHAPTER 13 SUMMARY: Writing Instructions

Planning and Writing Instructions

- ☐ Begin by learning the needs and experience level of your audience.
- ☐ Make sure that you understand the task thoroughly (for technical instructions to accompany products, learn to perform the operation yourself).
- ☐ Organize the task into short, simple steps.
- ☐ Present each step in the correct sequence.
- ☐ Use visuals to illustrate steps and procedures where needed
- ☐ Write directly to your readers, using the active, imperative voice.
- ☐ Write clearly and concisely — short sentences are best.
- ☐ Use plain language (avoid technical jargon).
- ☐ Test your instructions and revise as needed.

Creating Instructions to Accompany Products:

In addition to steps for Planning and Writing instructions listed above:

- ☐ At the beginning of your instructions, include an introduction that:
  - ■ mentions any necessary details, background information, and preparation
  - ■ lists all required equipment and materials
- ☐ Within procedural steps, include necessary warnings and cautions.
- ☐ When reviewing your instructions:
  - ■ verify that measurements, times, and relationships are precise and accurate
  - ■ have someone else test your instructions while you observe
- ☐ If you are creating instructions for users averse to reading manuals, consider creating a quick-start guide with images, easy-to-follow diagrams, and minimal text.

Creating Instructions for Coworkers:

In addition to step for Planning and Writing instructions listed above:

- ☐ Use the e-mail or memo formats to provide instructions to coworkers.
- ☐ Within instructional e-mails and memos, organize and highlight information by using headings; numbered lists for major steps; and bullet points for tasks within each major step.

Exercises

1. Write a set of instructions for one of the following topics. Assume that your audience has no knowledge of the subject. Use illustrations where they would be helpful to your audience.

    a. How to program your VCR/DVD to record a television show that will be broadcast in several hours from the time you programmed your machine
    b. How to use a particular type of software to create a document
    c. How to introduce a new pet into the home
    d. How to prepare a room, an apartment, or a house for a tornado or another type of storm

2. Collect examples of instructions written in the passive voice and rewrite them using the active voice.

3. Locate two sets of assembly, how-to-use, or cleaning instructions from products that you have recently purchased. Key the instructions on your word processor. Using the insert-comment technique you learned in Chapter 6 (Digital Shortcuts, page 181), critique the instructions you have copied, and compare the two using the Writer's Checklist on page 462. Discuss ways that the instructions could have been improved and comment on what is well written.

4. Write two sets of instructions on how to get from the closest airport to your school's student center. Assume your audience is made up of two groups of potential students: native speakers of English and non-native speakers of English (see Chapter 9 for helpful information on international communication strategies).

5. Collect examples of instructions that are written using ambiguous words like "might" or "may" and write them using explicit words.

Collaborative Classroom Projects

1. In groups of four to six, appoint a recorder to take notes, then for 20 minutes brainstorm as a group a list of short, common, yet specific action verbs that would be useful in writing directions for using everyday household or office items. Examples include words like *turn, screw, hammer,* and *rinse.* Remember to include terms for electronic items. When you have finished, read your list to the rest of the class. As a class, discuss why directions written for the consumer use short, common action verbs.

2. Bring to class at least one example of confusing assembly (or other how-to) instructions. Then, in groups of five or fewer members, for 10 minutes read all of the samples and choose one sample to revise. In no more than 20 minutes, revise the instructions, using this chapter as your reference. Be ready to share the revisions with the rest of the class.

3. In groups of four to six, go to your school's computer lab and explore the types of color photocopiers, scanners, and other kinds of technology available to students. Determine if instructions on how to use the equipment are available to students;

if they are already available, improve them. Begin by determining whom the audience is for these instructions and their technological skills and aptitudes. Then brainstorm all of the steps necessary to use the equipment (go to the Web site of the respective equipment companies for details, if necessary). Write the instructions and include as many visuals as necessary to help your users. Be ready to present your group's instructions to the class.

4. In groups of four to six, write assembly instructions for a product in the classroom. For example, assume that the instructor's desk needs to be assembled. Write an introduction, a required equipment and materials section, a procedural-steps section, and conclusion. Share your instructions with the class.

5. Bring different eating utensils to class, such as forks, spoons, and chopsticks. Write directions on how to use each utensil, then create packaging for each utensil upon which the instructions could be placed (for example, some types of chopsticks come enclosed in long, narrow sleeves with sparse visual instructions on them). Remember to consider space constraints and cultural issues in your designs.

■ Research Projects

1. Using your library's databases, find at least five journal articles on product safety and writing instructions, warnings, and so on. Summarize the information in each article, paying special attention to information on warnings and cautions. Present your information to the class.

2. Using your library's online and printed material resources, research articles and books on creating effective instructions. Use words like "technical writing" and "instructions" in your search. Then present your findings to the class.

3. Locate someone in your area involved in professional or technical writing. Schedule a 20-minute telephone or in-person interview. Make a list of questions regarding writing instructions, such as:
   a. How do you assess your audience's needs?
   b. Where and when did you learn how to perform the tasks for which you wrote instructions?
   c. How do you organize instructions and choose visuals?
   d. How are your instructions tested?

   Write a brief narrative summarizing the interview.

4. Numerous chemicals are used in the cleaning of educational institutions' bathrooms, offices, carpeting, and so on. For this assignment, write a formal report on the types of cleaning products used by your institution's cleaning or maintenance crews and the training of employees in the use of these products.

   Begin by interviewing the director of maintenance (or the person in a similar position at your institution) about the kinds of cleansers and chemicals used for specific types of cleaning. Ask about the precautions needed and specific instructions given to those who work with these chemicals. Ask about the amount and cost of these products on a monthly or yearly basis.

   Next, inquire about training given to employees in the use of these chemicals (your Human Resources Department may conduct these). Ask how much training and instruction is offered and what subjects are covered. Ask if there are any special sessions offered to non-native speakers or readers of English.

For this report, make recommendations on product safety and worker training and instruction based on your findings. Include a graph or chart with your report.

5. Write a formal report based on information gathered for Research Project 4. Research "green," or environmentally friendly, products that can be used in place of more toxic cleansers. Be sure to address the ability of such cleansers to clean heavily populated environments, the potential cost of such products, and the training or instruction needed for their use. Then recommend a course of action to the head of maintenance regarding the use of traditional cleansers, environmentally friendly cleansers, or a combination of both. Include a graph or chart with your report.

■ Web Projects

Projects followed by the symbol Ⓦ are continued at **bedfordstmartins.com/ writingthatworks**, Chapter 13.

1. Explore the following two Web sites to discover how they use illustrations to help convey their messages to the consumer: SafetyStore, an online catalog of safety and preparedness products, and the U. S. Coast Guard, Office of Boating Safety. Make a list of the variety of illustrations used and their individual purposes. Analyze the style of text that accompanies the illustrations. Determine the goals of these sites and whether these sites accomplish their goals. Support your conclusions with examples. Ⓦ

2. In groups of four to six, go to Yahoo!, Hotmail, and a third e-mail provider of your choice and determine which service is more appropriate for (a) e-mail users over the age of 65 with six months or less experience with computers, and (b) e-mail users under the age of 8 with six months or less experience with computers. Begin by determining the technological skills and the e-mailing needs and wants of the users in the respective groups. Then review the three sites and provide a comparative analysis of each. Make a recommendation to the class.

3. You are a student worker in your school's library who has been asked to create instructions to help new students research journals online. Assume your audience knows very little about virtual libraries, databases, journals, or interlibrary loan. Create a set of instructions. Be sure to include an introduction and define terms new students may not know.

4. Create instructions for the e-mail service(s) you chose in Web Project 2 for e-mail users over age 65 and for e-mail users under age 8. If you chose the same service for both groups, write the instructions for each group specifically; that is, remember to take into consideration the age, e-mail needs and wants, and computer experience of each group. Consider that some members of each group may be averse to reading instructions.

5. Imagine that you are designing the Web site for your own online store. In a letter directed to your instructor, describe the store and the products you would sell.

Then go to major online retailers and analyze how these sites lead the online shopper to their respective "checkouts." Make a list of the variety of graphics used in these processes. Then, in your letter, describe what you think are the most effective strategies and graphics (remember to consider your audience), and describe the ones you would use for your site and explain why. **W**

14 Writing Proposals

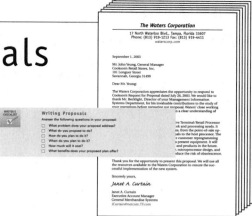

A *proposal* is a document written to persuade readers to adopt a plan or course of action. Your readers may be colleagues within your organization or potential customers outside the organization. If your objective is to persuade your organization's management to make a change or an improvement or perhaps to fund a project you would like to launch, you would write an *internal proposal*. If your objective is to persuade someone outside of your company to agree to a plan or take a course of action, you would write an *external proposal,* such as a sales proposal. A *sales proposal,* which may be either solicited or unsolicited, seeks to persuade a potential customer to purchase your products or services. This chapter discusses the audience for, the organization of, and the writing strategies used to develop these proposals in the following sections:

- Persuasive Writing (page 480)
- Internal Proposals (page 481)
- Sales Proposals (page 489)
- Meeting the Deadline: The Time-Sensitive Proposal

Because a proposal offers a plan to fill a need, readers will evaluate your plan based on how well you answer the following questions: *What* is the existing problem that the proposal addresses? *What* do you propose to do? *What* are the benefits of what you propose? *How* do you plan to do it? *When* do you plan to do it? *How much* will it cost?

To answer these questions effectively, make certain that your proposal is organized and written to address the needs of your entire audience. You will likely have more than one reader because proposals often require more than one level of approval. As you assess your readers, take into account their role in the organization.

W On the Web
For more help with writing proposals, see Chapter 14, bedfordstmartins.com/ writingthatworks

- *Executives* and other high-level decision-makers, for example, will want to know the long-term benefits of what you propose, as well as the amount of money and the number of personnel that your plan requires.
- *Managers* will need to evaluate your credibility and consider how your plan addresses their problem. They will also need to know how they would put your plan into action. They would be responsible for site preparation, staff training and motivation, and the schedule.
- *Technical staff* will need even more information on how to put your plan to work and will focus on the sections in your proposal that cover your previous experience and the proposed detailed solution, including the work plan, schedule, blueprints, and diagrams.

For example, if your primary reader is an expert on your subject, but his or her supervisor is not, you would provide an executive summary for the supervisor, summarizing the goal of the project and its budget, schedule, and personnel estimates in nontechnical language. (For advice on writing executive summaries, see Chapter 12, pages 431–433.) To further address the needs of nontechnical readers, consider including a glossary of specialized terms used throughout the proposal, or an appendix that explains highly detailed information in nontechnical language. Also consider adding a list of acronyms and other abbreviations as appropriate, especially for nontechnical readers. Detailed examples of the parts of proposals that address the requirements of various readers appear in Writing a Long Sales Proposal, pages 494–506.

Any proposal—whether it is an internal proposal or an external (sales) proposal, or whether it is short and uncomplicated or long and complex—should be planned and organized carefully. A short or medium-length proposal consists at least of an introduction, a body, and a conclusion. A long proposal, as will be discussed, generally contains more parts to accommodate the increased variety of information it represents.

In the *introduction* of your proposal, state your purpose and scope; state the problem you propose to solve and your solution to it. Indicate in your introduction the dates on which you propose to begin and complete work on the project, any special benefits of your proposed approach, and the total cost of the project. If you are writing a sales proposal, you could also refer to any previous positive association your company may have had with the potential customer.

In the *body* of your proposal, explain in detail (1) what products and services you are offering (if you are writing a sales proposal), (2) how the job will be done, (3) the procedures you will use to perform the work and the materials you will use (if applicable), (4) a schedule indicating when each stage of the project will be completed, and (5) a breakdown of the costs of the project.

In the *conclusion* of your proposal, emphasize the benefits of your solution, products, or services, and persuade the reader to take action. Use an encouraging and confident tone. If you are concluding a sales proposal, express your appreciation for the opportunity to submit the proposal and your confidence in your company's ability to do the job. You might add that you look forward to establish-

Voices from the Workplace

Susan McLaughlin, Paragon Alliance

As a partner at Paragon Alliance, Susan McLaughlin supervises market research, teaches seminars on communication, meets with clients, and writes sales proposals to persuade potential clients to do business with Paragon.

"At first, I really sweat blood writing proposals," Susan explains, "but I learned that simple logic is the answer. In the opening, I state the problem the client needs help with, as I understand it. Then, in the body of the proposal, I explain how I propose to solve the client's problem and what it will cost. Finally, in closing, I offer to provide anything else that might be needed and thank the client for the opportunity to bid for the job."

Susan emphasizes that a successful proposal is persuasive on multiple levels. "The really important thing about a proposal is its tone. Both the content and the tone must be persuasive, convincing the client not only that you have the solution to the problem but that you are capable of doing the job. The way you present your ideas is as important as the ideas themselves. You must support your appeal with logic, facts, statistics, and examples wherever possible."

Terry Kalna, International Speedway Corporation

Terry Kalna is director of Marketing Partnerships for the International Speedway Corporation (ISC). Terry's job is to generate the millions of dollars in sponsorship revenue that fund the corporation's annual IndyCar races. When he's not on the phone or in meetings with current and prospective clients, Terry writes brief sales proposals to persuade companies to partner with ISC.

"Proposals are one of the most important facets of the sales process," Terry explains. Because many of the companies he approaches receive up to 30 proposals a day, Terry strives to attract his readers' attention. "The marketing or advertising executives reading your proposal have little time, so you must condense your thoughts into a short and easily readable piece. A proposal that is concise, unique, and exciting may be your only ticket in their door. Typically, I try to draw upon my audience's emotions by highlighting the glamour and passion of our sport."

Terry explains that understanding his audience is crucial. "It is important to know the needs of the company that you are approaching and to highlight the elements you have that can help them meet their goals. You must choose your wording carefully, so as to position yourself as a consultant. This will help you to build trust with the client and take the proposal to the next level. That level is a face-to-face meeting, which I always request in the closing of my proposal. Last, it is important to be proactive and let them know that you will follow up."

ing good working relations with the customer and that you would be glad to provide any additional information that might be needed. Your conclusion could also review any advantages your company may have over its competitors. It should specify the time period during which your proposal can be considered a valid offer. If any supplemental material (such as blueprints or price sheets) accompany the proposal, include a list of them at the end of the proposal.

■ Persuasive Writing

A proposal, by definition, is persuasive writing because you are attempting to convince your readers to do something. Your goal is to prove to your readers that they need what you are proposing to do, and that it is practical and appropriate. For an unsolicited proposal, you may even need to convince your readers that they have a problem serious enough to require a solution. You would then offer your solution by first building a convincing case demonstrating the validity of your approach.

In persuasive writing, how you present your ideas is as important as the ideas themselves. Support your appeal with relevant facts, statistics, and examples. Your supporting evidence must lead logically, even inevitably, to your conclusions and your proposed solution—that is, begin with the most important evidence and end with valid but secondary evidence. Avoid ambiguity; do not wander from your main point; and, above all, never make false claims. Also, acknowledge any real or potentially conflicting opinions; doing so allows you to anticipate and overcome objections to your proposal and even helps support your argument. By acknowledging negative details or opposing views, you not only gain credibility but also demonstrate good ethics.

The tone of your proposal should be positive, confident, and tactful. The following example, addressed to the Qualtron Corporation, is inappropriate because of its arrogant and condescending tone:

■   The Qualtron Corporation has obviously not considered the potential problem of not having backup equipment available when a commercial power failure occurs. The corporation would also be wise indeed to give a great deal more consideration to the volume of output expected per machine.

The following version of the same passage is positive, confident, and tactful:

■   The system should be redesigned so that it can provide backup equipment in the event of a commercial power failure. The system should also be based on realistic expectations of the output of each machine. For example, . . .

WRITER'S CHECKLIST

Writing Proposals

Answer the following questions in your proposal:

- ☐ What problem does your proposal address?
- ☐ What do you propose to do?
- ☐ How do you plan to do it?
- ☐ When do you plan to do it?
- ☐ How much will it cost?
- ☐ What benefits does your proposed plan offer?

Internal Proposals

The purpose of an internal proposal is to suggest a change or an improvement within an organization. For example, an internal proposal can recommend one of the following:

1. A change in the way something is being done
2. That something new be done
3. That funding be authorized for a large purchase

The first kind of proposal might recommend that the management of multiple manufacturing operations be decentralized. The second kind might be a proposal to initiate a telecommuting program (as Christine Thomas did in Chapter 1). The third kind might propose upgrading a computer network operating system.

An internal proposal, often in memo format, is sent to a superior within the organization who has the authority to accept or reject the proposal. Internal proposals generally follow a three-part organization:

- Introduction
- Body
- Conclusion

Writing the Introduction

The introduction of your internal proposal should establish that a problem exists and needs a solution. This section is sometimes called a "problem statement." (Internal proposals are sometimes referred to as problem-solution memos.) If the audience is not convinced that there is a problem, your proposal will not succeed.

After you identify the problem, summarize your proposed solution and indicate its benefits and estimated total cost. Notice how the introduction in Figure 14–1 states the problem directly and then summarizes the writer's proposed solution.

Writing the Body

The body of your internal proposal should offer a practical solution to the problem and provide the details necessary to inform and persuade your readers. In this section, put yourself in your readers' position—ask what information would convince you to make the decision you are asking them to make. Then, being as specific as possible, provide the following information:

1. Sufficient background information to describe the extent of the problem
2. The methods to be used in achieving the proposed solution

Acme, Inc.
Memo

To: Joan Marlow, Director, Human Resources
From: Leslie Galusha, Chief, Employee Benefits *LG*
Date: June 12, 2003
Subject: Employee Fitness and Health-Care Costs

Health-care and worker's compensation insurance costs at Acme, Inc., have risen 200 percent over the last five years. In 1998, costs were $600 per employee per year; in 2003, they have reached $1,200 per employee per year. This doubling of costs mirrors a national trend in which health-care costs are anticipated to rise at the same rate for the next 10 years. It is essential that we control these escalating expenses. They are eating into Acme's profit margin because Acme pays 80 percent of the costs for employee coverage.

Healthy employees bring direct financial benefits to companies in the form of lower employee insurance costs, lower absenteeism rates, and reduced turnover. Regular physical exercise promotes fit, healthy people by reducing the risk of coronary heart disease, diabetes, osteoporosis, hypertension, and stress-related problems. I propose that to promote regular, vigorous physical exercise for our employees, Acme implement a health-care program that focuses on employee fitness.

Attachment: Employee Fitness Proposal

Introduction clearly states problem

Introduction summarizes proposal solution

Figure 14–1 Introduction of an Internal Proposal (transmittal memo)

3. Information about equipment, materials, and staff requirements

4. A breakdown of costs

5. A schedule for completing the project, possibly broken down into separate tasks

The sample body shown in Figure 14–2 is an attachment to the transmittal of an internal proposal begun in Figure 14–1.

Writing the Conclusion

The conclusion of your internal proposal should tie everything together, restate your recommendation, and close with a spirit of cooperation (offering to set up a meeting, supply additional information, or provide any other assistance that might be needed). Keep your conclusion brief, as in Figure 14–3.

Attachment: Employee Fitness Proposal

Background

Information explaining extent of problem

The U.S. Department of Health and Human Services recently estimated that health-care costs in the United States will triple by the year 2013. Corporate expenses for health care are rising at such a fast rate that, if unchecked, in eight years they will significantly erode corporate profits.

Researchers have found that people who do not participate in a regular and vigorous exercise program incur double the health-care costs and are hospitalized 30 percent more days than people who exercise regularly. Nonexercisers are also 41 percent more likely to submit medical claims over $5,000 at some point during their careers than are those who exercise regularly.

U.S. companies are recognizing this trend. Tenneco, Inc., for example, found that the average health-care claim for unfit men was $1,003 per illness compared with an average claim of $562 for those who exercised regularly. For women, the average claim for those who were unfit was $1,535, more than double the average claim of $639 for women who exercised. Additionally, Control Data Corporation found that nonexercisers cost the company an extra $115 a year in health-care expenses.

These figures are further supported by data from independent studies. A model created by the National Institutes of Health (NIH) estimates that the average white-collar company could save $466,000 annually in medical costs (per 1,000 employees) just by promoting wellness. NIH researchers estimated that for every $1 a firm invests in a health-care program, it saves up to $3.75 in health-care costs. Another NIH study of 667 insurance-company employees showed savings of $1.65 million over a five-year period. The same study also showed a 400-percent drop in absentee rates after the company implemented a company-wide fitness program.

Proposed Solution

The benefits of regular, vigorous physical activity for employees and companies are compelling. To achieve these benefits at Acme, I propose that we choose from one of two possible options: build in-house fitness centers at our warehouse facilities, or offer employees several options for membership at a national fitness club.

In-House Fitness Center

Explanation of proposed solution

Building in-house fitness centers would require that Acme modify existing space in its warehouses and designate an area outside for walking and running. To accommodate the weight-lifting and cardiovascular equipment and an aerobics area would require a minimum of 4,000 square feet. Lockers and shower stalls would also have to be built adjacent to the men's and women's bathrooms.

1

Figure 14–2 Body of an Internal Proposal (continued)

Required equipment and materials

Attachment: Employee Fitness Proposal

The costs to equip each facility are as follows:

1	Challenger 3.0 Treadmill	$4,395
3	Ross Futura exercise bicycles @ $750 each	$2,250
1	CalGym S-370 inner thigh machine	$1,750
1	CalGym S-260 lat pull-down machine	$1,750
1	CalGym S-360 leg-extension, combo-curl	$1,650
1	CalGym S-390 arm-curl machine	$1,950
1	CalGym S-410 side-lat machine	$1,850
1	CalGym S-430 pullover machine	$1,950
1	CalGym S-440 abdominal machine	$2,000
1	CalGym S-460 back machine	$2,000
1	CalGym S-290 chest press	$1,600
1	CalGym S-310 pectoral developer	$1,700
10	5710321 3-wide lockers @ $81 each	$810
4	5714000 benches and pedestals @ $81 each	$324
	Carpeting for workout area	$3,000
3	showers each, men's/women's locker room	$10,000
	Men's and women's locker-room expansion	$10,000
	Remodeling expenses	$350,000
	Total per Acme site	$398,979
	Grand Total	**$1,994,895**

Breakdown of costs

Required staff

At headquarters and at the regional offices, our current Employee Assistance Program staff would need to be available several hours each workday to provide instructions for the use of exercise equipment. Aerobics instructors can be hired locally on a monthly basis for classes. The Buildings and Maintenance Department staff would clean and maintain the facilities.

Explanation of proposed solution

Fitness-Club Membership

Offering a complimentary membership to a national fitness club for all employees can also help reduce company health-care costs. Aero-Fitness Clubs, Inc., offer the best option for Acme's needs. They operate in over 45 major markets, with over 300 clubs nationwide. Most importantly, AeroFitness Clubs are located here in Bartlesville and in all four cities where our regional warehouses are located.

AeroFitness staff are trained and certified in exercise physiology and will design individualized fitness programs for our employees. They offer aerobics classes for all levels, taught by certified instructors. Each club also features the latest in resistance exercise equipment from Nautilus, Universal, Paramount, and Life Fitness. Most AeroFitness facilities provide competition-size swimming pools, cushioned indoor running tracks, saunas, whirlpools, steam rooms, and racquetball courts.

-2-

Figure 14–2 **Body of an Internal Proposal** (continued)

Attachment: Employee Fitness Proposal

Aerofitness offers a full range of membership programs that include corporate discounts. The basic membership of $400 per year includes:

- Unlimited use of exercise equipment
- Unlimited aerobics classes
- Unlimited use of racquetball, sauna, and whirlpool facilities
- Free initial consultation with an exercise physiologist for exercise and nutrition programs
- Free child care during daytime working hours

The club offers a full range of membership programs for companies. Acme may choose to pay all or part of employee membership costs. Three membership program options are available with AeroFitness:

- *Corporate purchase.* Acme buys and owns the memberships. With 10 or more memberships, Acme receives a 35-percent discount.

    Acme costs: $400 per employee × 1200 employees – 35% discount = $312,000 per year.*

- *Corporate subsidy.* Employees purchase memberships at a discount and own them. With 10 or more memberships, employees and the company each pay one-half of annual membership dues and receive a 30-percent discount off annual dues. The corporation also pays a one-time $50 enrollment fee for employees.

    Acme costs: $200 per employee × 1200 employees – 30% discount = $168,000 per year. The one-time enrollment fee of $50 per employee adds $60,000 to first-year costs.*

- *Employee purchase.* Employees purchase memberships on their own. With five or more memberships, employees receive 25 percent off regular rates. Club sales representatives conduct an on-site open-enrollment meeting. Employees own memberships.

    Acme costs: None.

Breakdown of costs

*Assumes that all employees will enroll.

-3-

Figure 14–2   Body of an Internal Proposal (continued)

Conclusion restates recommendation

Conclusion closes with spirit of cooperation

Attachment: Employee Fitness Proposal

Conclusion and Recommendation

I recommend that Acme, Inc., participate in the corporate membership program at AeroFitness Clubs, Inc., by subsidizing employee memberships. By subsidizing memberships, Acme shows its commitment to the importance of a fit workforce. Club membership allows employees at all five Acme warehouses to participate in the program. The more employees who participate, the greater the long-term savings in Acme's health-care costs. Building and equipping fitness centers at all five warehouse sites would require an initial investment of nearly $2 million. These facilities would also occupy valuable floor space—on average, 4,000 square feet at each warehouse. Therefore, this option would be very costly.

Enrolling employees in the corporate program at AeroFitness would allow them to attend on a trial basis. Those interested in continuing could then join the club and pay half of the membership cost, less a 30-percent discount on $400 a year. The other half of the membership ($140) would be paid for by Acme. If an employee leaves the company, he or she would have the option of purchasing Acme's share of the membership. Employees not wishing to keep their membership could buy the membership back from Acme and sell it to another employee.

Implementing this program will help Acme, Inc., reduce its health-care costs while building stronger employee relations by offering employees a desirable benefit. If this proposal is adopted, I have some additional thoughts about publicizing the program to encourage employee participation. I look forward to discussing the details of this proposal with you and answering any questions you may have.

-4-

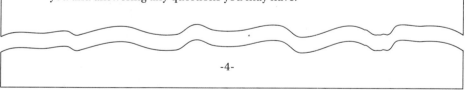

Figure 14–3   Conclusion of an Internal Proposal

Figure 14–4 shows a typical internal proposal. It was written as a memo by a plant safety officer to the plant superintendent and recommends changes in specific safety practices at the company.

Memo

To: Harold Clurman, Plant Superintendent
CC: Carla Hernandez, Supervisor Group 333
From: Fred Nelson, Safety Officer   *FN*
Date: August 4, 2003
Subject: Safety Practices for Group 333

Many accidents and near-accidents have occurred in Group 333 because of the hazardous working conditions in this area. This memo identifies those hazardous conditions and makes recommendations for their elimination.

Hazardous Conditions

Employees inside the factory must operate the walk-along crane through aisles that are frequently congested with scrap metal, discarded lumber, and other refuse from the shearing area. Many surfaces in the area are oil-coated.

The containers for holding raw stock and scrap metal are also unsafe. On many of the racks, the hooks are bent inward so far that the crane cannot fit into them properly unless it is banged and jiggled in a dangerous manner. To add to the hazard, employees in the press group do not always balance the load in the racks. As a result, the danger of falling metal is great as the unbalanced racks swing practically out of control overhead. These hazards endanger employees in Group 333 and also employees in the raw-stock and shearing areas because the crane passes over these areas.

Hazards also exist in the yard and in the chemical building. Dumping strip metal into the scrap bins is the most dangerous practice of all. To dump this metal, the tow-motor operator raises the rack over the edge of the scrap-metal bin and rotates the forks to permit the scrap metal to fall from one end of the rack. As the weight shifts, the rack slams into one of the tow-motor forks (raised 12 feet above the ground). This method has resulted in two tow-motor tip-overs in the past month. In neither incident was the driver injured, but injuries are very likely. Group 333 employees must also dump tubs full of scrap metal from the tow motor into the 10-foot-high scrap bins. Because of the unpredictable way in which the metal falls from the tubs, employees have received many facial cuts and body bruises. In winter weather, all employees have been cut and bruised in falls that occurred as they were climbing up on scrap bins covered with snow and ice to dump scrap from pallets that had not been banded.

Finally, nearly all Group 333 employees who handle the caustic chemicals report damaged clothing and ruined shoes. Poor lighting in the

Introduction that states a problem

Detailed explanation of the problem

Additional details

Tution fund for tech

Figure 14–4   Internal Proposal (continued)

Safety Practices for Group 333

chemical building (lights 20 feet above the floor), storage racks positioned less than two feet apart, and container caps incorrectly fastened have made these accidents impossible to prevent.

Recommendations

Recommended solution

To eliminate these hazards as quickly as possible, I recommend that the following actions be taken:

1. That Group 333 supervisors rigorously initiate and enforce a policy to free aisles of obstructions
2. That all dangerous racks be repaired and replaced
3. That the Engineering Group develop a safe rack dumper
4. That heavy wire-mesh screens be mounted on the front of all tow motors
5. That Group 333 employees not accept scrap in containers that have not been properly banded
6. That illumination be increased in the chemical building and that a compulsory training program for the safe handling of caustic chemicals be scheduled

Conclusion

I would like to meet with you and the supervisor of Group 333 before the end of the month, as your schedule permits. You will have my complete cooperation in working out all of the details of the proposed recommendations.

2

Figure 14–4   Internal Proposal (continued)

Creating Internal Proposals

☐ Prepare your proposal for someone in your organization with the power to act on it.

☐ Describe the problem clearly, providing any essential technical or historical background to clarify why the problem exists.

☐ Offer your solution in sufficient detail so that a decision-maker can evaluate your approach.

 ■ Note any resource requirements necessary for a solution (personnel, equipment, materials).

 ■ Provide a schedule for implementing the solution.

☐ Specify the benefits expected to result from your solution.

Sales Proposals

The *sales proposal,* a major marketing tool for business and industry, is a company's offer to provide specific goods or services to a potential buyer within a specified period of time and for a specified price. The primary purpose of a sales proposal is to demonstrate that the prospective customer's purchase of the seller's products or services will solve a problem, improve operations, or offer other benefits.

Sales proposals vary greatly in length and sophistication. Some are a page or two written by one person; others are many pages written collaboratively by several people; still others are hundreds of pages written by a proposal-writing team. A short sales proposal might bid for painting the outside of a single home; a sales proposal of moderate length might bid for the installation of a new network operating system; and a very long sales proposal might bid for the construction of a multimillion-dollar shopping center or sports complex. Short sales proposals are often written on standardized forms that are available from office-supply and stationery stores.

Your first task in writing a sales proposal is to find out exactly what your prospective customer needs. Then determine whether your organization can satisfy that customer's needs. If appropriate, compare your company's strengths with those of competing firms, determine your advantages over them, and emphasize those advantages in your proposal. For example, say a small biotechnology company is bidding for the contract to supply several types of medical test kits to a regional hospital. The proposal writer who believes that the company has better-qualified staff than its competitors might include the résumés of the key people who would be involved in the project, as a way of emphasizing that advantage.

Unsolicited and Solicited Sales Proposals

Sales proposals may be either unsolicited or solicited. *Unsolicited sales proposals* are those submitted to a company without a prior request and are not as unusual as they may sound: Companies often operate for years with a problem they have never recognized (unnecessarily high maintenance costs, for example, or poor inventory-control methods). You could prepare an unsolicited proposal for such a company if you were convinced that the potential customer could realize substantial benefits by adopting your solution to the problem. Many unsolicited proposals are preceded by a letter of inquiry that specifies the problem or unmet need to determine whether there is any potential interest. Once you have received a positive response, you would conduct a detailed study of the prospective customer's needs to determine whether you can meet them. You would then prepare your proposal on the basis of your study.

Solicited sales proposals are written in response to a request for bids on goods or services by another company or by a local, state, or federal governmental agency. To find the best method of doing a job and the most qualified company to do it, procuring organizations commonly issue a request for proposal (RFP) that asks competing companies such as yours to bid for a job. An RFP may be rigid in specifying how the proposal should be organized and what it should contain, but it is normally quite flexible about the approaches that bidding firms may propose. Ordinarily, the RFP simply defines the basic work that the procuring organization needs and leaves it up to the proposers to put forth their method of performing the work economically and within their stated schedule.

The procuring organization initiates a competitive bidding process by publishing its RFP in one or more journals and at its Web site, in addition to sending it to certain companies that have good reputations for doing the kind of work needed. Some companies and government agencies even hold a conference for the competing firms at which they provide all pertinent information about the job being bid for.

Managers interested in responding to RFPs regularly scan the appropriate publications and the Web. Upon finding a project of interest, an executive in the sales department obtains all available information from the procuring company or agency. This information is then presented to management for a decision on whether they are interested enough to pursue the project. If the decision is positive, the technical staff develops an approach to the work described in the RFP. The technical staff normally considers several alternative approaches, selecting the one that combines feasibility and a price that offers a profit for the bidder. The staff's concept is then presented to higher management for a decision on whether the company wishes to present a proposal to the requesting organization. If the decision is to proceed, preparing the proposal is the next step.

When you respond to an RFP, pay close attention to any specifications in the request governing the preparation of the proposal and follow them carefully. Such specifications usually state how the proposal should be organized, the kind of technical expertise required, the basis for calculating cost estimates, the location of the work site, and the like. For guidance on preparing a proposal on a tight schedule, see Meeting the Deadline: The Time-Sensitive Proposal on pages 507–509.

W **On the Web**
To locate requests for proposals for government agencies, see Chapter 14, **bedfordstmartins.com/ writingthatworks**

Writing a Short Sales Proposal

Short, uncomplicated sales proposals typically follow the introduction-body-conclusions pattern. The *introduction* should indicate the purpose and scope of your proposal. It should give the dates on which you propose to begin and complete work on the project, any special benefits of your proposed approach, and the total cost of the project. Your introduction could also refer to any previous association your company may have had with the potential customer.

The *body* of your short sales proposal should itemize the products and services you are offering. It should include, if applicable, a discussion of the procedures you would use to perform the work, any materials to be used, and drawings or diagrams to pinpoint the scope or location of the work. It may also present a schedule indicating when each stage of the project would be completed. Finally, the body should include a precise breakdown of the costs of the project.

The *conclusion* should express your appreciation for the opportunity to submit the proposal and your confidence in your company's ability to do the job. You might add that you look forward to establishing good working relations with the customer and that you would be glad to provide any additional information that might be needed. Your conclusion could also review any advantages your company may have over its competitors and specify the time period during which your proposal can be considered a valid offer. If any supplemental materials, such as blueprints or price sheets, accompany the proposal, include a list of them at the end of the proposal. Figures 14–5 and 14–6 show two examples of short sales proposals.

Jerwalted Nurseries

Ronald Malcomson, President

12 Rogers Highway West
St. Louis, MO 63101
Ph. 1-800-212-1212
Fax 314-999-1111

February 1, 2003

Ms. Tricia Olivera, Vice President
Watford Valve Corporation
1600 Swanson Avenue
St. Louis, MO 63121

Dear Ms. Olivera:

Jerwalted Nurseries, Inc., proposes to landscape the new corporate headquarters of the Watford Valve Corporation, on 1600 Swanson Avenue, at a total cost of $14,871. The lot to be landscaped is approximately 600 feet wide and 700 feet deep. Landscaping will begin no later than April 30, 2003, and will be completed by May 31.

Introduction states purpose and scope of proposal, and indicates when project can be started and completed

The following trees and plants will be planted, in the quantities given and at the prices specified.

4	maple trees	@ $110 each	$440
41	birch trees	@ $135 each	$5,535
2	spruce trees	@ $175 each	$350
20	juniper plants	@ $15 each	$300
60	hedges	@ $12 each	$720
200	potted plants	@ $12 each	$2,400
		Total Cost of Plants =	$9,745
		Labor =	$5,126
		Total Cost =	$14,871

Body lists products to be provided and cost per item

Figure 14–5 Short Solicited Sales Proposal (continued)

Conclusion specifies time limit of proposal, expresses confidence, and looks forward to working with prospective customer

All trees and plants will be guaranteed against defect or disease for a period of 90 days, the warranty period to begin June 1, 2003.

The prices quoted in this proposal will be valid until June 30, 2003.

Thank you for the opportunity to submit this proposal. Jerwalted Nurseries has been in the landscaping and nursery business in the St. Louis area for 30 years, and our landscaping has won several awards and commendations, including a citation from the National Association of Architects. We are eager to put our skills and knowledge to work for you, and we are confident that you will be pleased with our work. If we can provide any additional information or assistance, please call us at the number listed above.

Sincerely,

Ronald Malcomson

Ronald Malcomson

Figure 14–5 **Short Solicited Sales Proposal** (continued)

Aerolite Bicycle Supply

1536 Bicycle Road
Bedford, Pennsylvania 16802

aerolitecycle.com
Phone 1-800-331-1221

November 22, 2003

Mr. Eric Shoop
Shoop Bicycle Shop
Squall Valley, Utah 19542

Dear Mr. Shoop:

Introduction states the purpose and range of products offered

Aerolite would like to congratulate you on the grand opening of your bicycle shop in Squall Valley, Utah. As you know, Aerolite makes quality equipment for bicycling. We carry bicycles, shorts, jerseys, helmets, and a variety of bicycle parts. We are eager to introduce you to our line of high-quality equipment offered at an affordable price. Please read on!

Figure 14–6 **Short Unsolicited Sales Proposal** (continued)

Mr. Eric Shoop   2   November 22, 2003

Bicycles

Our high-end bicycle frames are made of titanium, which makes them the strongest and the lightest frames on the market today. All of our other bicycle frames are made of butted aluminum, a very strong, anticorrosive, patented material that is very durable for all kinds of riding.

Our dual-suspended mountain bikes are unique because we developed the only Y frame used in such bikes. This frame eliminates the "pogoing" that compresses the rear shock in normal dual-suspended bikes instead of putting the power to the ground and to forward momentum. Our design puts the power the rider puts into the pedals straight to the ground, which pushes the rider forward instead of up and down.

All of our bikes have Natsuya components, ranging from the ALUMA at the low end to the XRT at the high end. Each component has a groupo, which includes derailleurs (front and back), shifters, gears, brakes, brake levers, crank, pedals, headset, handlebars, and wheel hubs. Every bike has a groupo for its specific level. As the level of bike increases, the prices increase—but the quality goes right along with the price.

Shorts and Jerseys

Aerolite shorts are made of spandex with comfortable fleece padding in the seat. Our jerseys are made of an acrylic material that keeps the rider warm in the winter and cool in the summer. They pull the sweat away from the rider's body in summer and block the wind in winter.

Helmets

Our helmets—able to withstand a 300-foot vertical drop onto a hard surface without getting scratched—are the strongest on the market. With soft interior padding and generous vents, they're also the most comfortable.

Please Consider Our Line of Merchandise

Bikers of the rough terrain of Squall Valley know they can count on the durability of Aerolite bicycles and merchandise. If you choose to carry our line, you will be the exclusive Aerolite dealer between San Francisco and Boulder, offering equipment known around the world for its quality and performance.

I have enclosed a brochure that contains our entire line of merchandise. An Aerolite representative will visit your store in three weeks to see if you are interested in carrying the Aerolite line of merchandise and to answer any questions you may have.

Sincerely,

James Eugene

James Eugene
Sales Manager

Enclosure

Body details the product line and specific features

Persuasive conclusion describes advantages over competitors, price list, and follow-up with a salesperson

Figure 14–6 Short Unsolicited Sales Proposal (continued)

Writing a Long Sales Proposal

While the simple sales proposal is typically divided into an introduction, body, and conclusion, the long sales proposal contains more parts to accommodate the increased variety of information that it must present. The long sales proposal may include some or all of the following sections:

- Cover, or transmittal, letter (Figure 14–7)
- Title page
- Executive or project summary (Figure 14–8)
- General description of products (Figure 14–9)
- Detailed solution or rationale (Figure 14–10)
- Cost analysis (Figure 14–11)
- Delivery schedule or work plan (Figure 14–11)
- Site-preparation description (Figure 14–12)
- Training requirements (Figure 14–13)
- Statement of responsibilities (Figure 14–14)
- Description of vendor (Figure 14–15)
- Organizational sales pitch (optional) (Figure 14–15)
- Conclusion (optional) (Figure 14–16)
- Appendixes (optional)

Optional sections may be included at the discretion of the proposal-writing team. A conclusion, for example, may be added to a very long proposal as a convenience to the reader, but it is not mandatory. A site-preparation section, however, is essential if the work proposed requires construction, remodeling, or such preparatory work as building rewiring before equipment can be installed.

A long sales proposal begins with a *cover letter*—sometimes called a *transmittal letter*—which expresses your appreciation for the opportunity to submit your proposal and for any assistance you may have received in studying the customer's requirements. The letter should acknowledge any previous positive association with the customer. Then it should summarize the recommendations offered in the proposal and express your confidence that they will satisfy the customer's needs. Figure 14–7 shows the cover letter for the proposal illustrated in Figures 14–8 through 14–15—a proposal that the Waters Corporation of Tampa provide a computer system for the Cookson's chain of retail stores.

A *title page* and an *executive summary*—sometimes called a *project summary*—follow the cover letter. The title page contains the title of the proposal, the date of submission, the company to which it is being submitted, your company's name, and any symbol or logo that identifies your company. The executive summary is addressed to the executive who will ultimately accept or reject the proposal and should summarize in nontechnical language how you plan to approach the work. Figure 14–8 shows the executive summary of the Waters Corporation proposal.

The Waters Corporation

17 North Waterloo Blvd., Tampa, Florida 33607
Phone: (813) 919-1213 Fax: (813) 919-4411
waterscorp.com

September 1, 2003

Mr. John Yeung, General Manager
Cookson's Retail Stores, Inc.
101 Longuer Street
Savannah, Georgia 31499

Dear Mr. Yeung:

The Waters Corporation appreciates the opportunity to respond to
Cookson's Request for Proposal dated July 26, 2003. We would like to
thank Mr. Becklight, Director of your Management Information
Systems Department, for his invaluable contributions to the study of
your operations before preparing our proposal. Waters' close working
relationship with Cookson's has resulted in a clear understanding of
your philosophy and needs.

Our proposal describes a Waters Interactive Terminal/Retail Processor
System designed to meet Cookson's network and processing needs. It
will provide all of your required capabilities, from the point-of-sale operational requirements at the store terminals to the host processor. The
system is easily installed without extensive customer reprogramming
and is compatible with much of Cookson's present equipment. It will
provide the flexibility to add new features and products in the future.
The system's unique hardware modularity, microprocessor design, and
flexible programming capability greatly reduce the risk of obsolescence.

Thank you for the opportunity to present this proposal. We will use all
the resources available to the Waters Corporation to ensure the successful implementation of the new system.

Sincerely yours,

Janet A. Curtain

Janet A. Curtain
Executive Account Manager
General Merchandise Systems
JCurtain@netcom.TF.com

Enclosure

*Opening expresses ap-
preciation for chance
to bid on the project
and stresses success
of past working
relationship*

*Body describes purpose
of work proposed and
belief in its success
in meeting the
customer's need*

*Ending assures custo-
mer of company's
commitment to
success*

Figure 14–7   Cover Letter for a Sales Proposal

Opens with overview of the proposed system

Summarizes scope of system proposed

Ends with projected cost savings of interest to the executive reader

The Waters Proposal September 1, 2003

EXECUTIVE SUMMARY

The Waters 319 Interactive Terminal/615 Retail Processor System will provide your management with the tools necessary to manage people and equipment more profitably with procedures that will yield more cost-effective business controls for Cookson's.

The equipment and applications proposed for Cookson's were selected through the combined effort of Waters' and Cookson's Management Information Systems Director, Mr. Becklight. The architecture of the system will respond to your current requirements and allow for future expansion.

The features and hardware in the system were determined from data acquired through the comprehensive survey we conducted at your stores in February of this year. The total of 71 Interactive Terminals proposed to service your four store locations is based on the number of terminals currently in use and on the average number of transactions processed during normal and peak periods. The planned remodeling of all four stores was also considered, and the suggested terminal placement has been incorporated into the working floor plan. The proposed equipment configuration and software applications have been simulated to determine system performance based on the volumes and anticipated growth rates of the Cookson's stores.

The information from the survey was also used in the cost justification, which was checked and verified by your controller, Mr. Deitering. The cost-effectiveness of the Waters Interactive Terminal/Retail Processor System is apparent. Expected savings, such as the projected 45-percent reduction in sales audit expenses, are realistic projections based on Waters' experience with other installations of this type.

-1-

Figure 14–8 **Executive Summary of a Sales Proposal**

If your proposal offers products as well as services, it should include a *general description* of the products, as in Figure 14–9. Following the executive summary and the general description, explain exactly how you plan to do what you are proposing. This section, called the *detailed solution* or *rationale,* will be read by specialists who can understand and evaluate your plan, so you can feel free to use technical language and discuss complicated concepts. Figure 14–10 shows one part of the detailed solution appearing in the Waters Corporation proposal, which included several other applications in addition to the payroll application. Notice that the detailed solution, like the discussion in an unsolicited sales proposal, begins with a statement of the customer's problem, follows with a statement of the solution, and concludes with a statement of the benefits to the customer. In some proposals, the headings "Problem" and "Solution" are used for this section.

A *cost analysis* and a *delivery schedule* are essential to any sales proposal. The cost analysis—also called a *budget*—itemizes the estimated cost of all the products and services that you are offering; the *delivery schedule*—also called a *work plan*—commits you to a specific timetable for providing those products and services. Figure 14–11 shows the cost analysis and delivery schedule of the Waters Corporation proposal.

The Waters Proposal   September 1, 2003

GENERAL SYSTEM DESCRIPTION

The point-of-sale system that Waters is proposing for Cookson's includes two primary Waters products. These are the 319 Interactive Terminal and the 615 Retail Processor.

Waters 319 Interactive Terminal

The primary component in the proposed retail system is the Interactive Terminal. It contains a full microprocessor, which gives it the flexibility that Cookson's has been looking for.

The 319 Interactive Terminal provides you with freedom in sequencing a transaction. You are not limited to a preset list of available steps or transactions. The terminal program can be adapted to provide unique transaction sets, each designed with a logical sequence of entry and processing to accomplish required tasks. In addition to sales transactions recorded on the selling floor, specialized transactions such as theater-ticket sales and payments can be designed for your customer-service area.

Detailed breakdown of system components and functions essential for technical readers

Figure 14–9   General-Description-of-Products Section of a Sales Proposal (continued)

The Waters Proposal   September 1, 2003

The 319 Interactive Terminal also functions as a credit authorization device, either by using its own floor limits or by transmitting a credit inquiry to the 615 Retail Processor for authorization.

Data-collection formats have been simplified so that transaction editing and formatting are much more easily accomplished. Mr. Sier has already been provided with documentation on these formats and has outlined all data-processing efforts that will be necessary to transmit the data to your current systems. These projections have been considered in the cost justification.

Waters 615 Retail Processor

The Waters 615 Retail Processor is a minicomputer system designed to support the Waters family of retail terminals. The processor will reside in the computer room in your data center in Buffalo. Operators already on your staff will be trained to initiate and monitor its activities.

The 615 will collect data transmitted from the retail terminals, process credit and check authorization inquiries, maintain files to be accessed by the retail terminals, accumulate totals, maintain a message-routing network, and control the printing of various reports. The functions and level of control performed at the processor depend on the peripherals and software selected.

Software

The Retail III software used with the system has been thoroughly tested and is operational in many Waters customer installations.

Additional system details for technical specialists

The software provides the complete processing of the transaction, from the interaction with the operator on the sales floor through the data capture on cassette or disk in stores and in your data center.

Retail III provides a menu of modular applications for your selection. Parameters condition each of them to your hardware environment and operating requirements. The selection of hardware will be closely related to the selection of the software applications.

-3-

Figure 14–9   General-Description-of-Products Section of a Sales Proposal (continued)

The Waters Proposal   September 1, 2003

PAYROLL APPLICATION

Current Procedure

Your current system of reporting time requires each hourly employee to sign a time sheet; the time sheet is reviewed by the department manager and sent to the Payroll Department on Friday evening. Because the week ends on Saturday, the employee must show the scheduled hours for Saturday and not the actual hours; therefore, the department manager must adjust the reported hours on the time sheet for employees who do not report on the scheduled Saturday or who do not work the number of hours scheduled.

The Payroll Department employs a supervisor and three full-time clerks. To meet deadlines caused by an unbalanced work flow, an additional part-time clerk is used for 20 to 30 hours per week. The average wage for this clerk is $8.00 per hour.

Advantage of Waters System

The 319 Interactive Terminal can be programmed for entry of payroll data for each employee on Monday mornings by department managers, with the data reflecting actual hours worked. This system would eliminate the need for manual batching, controlling, and data input. The Payroll Department estimates conservatively that this work consumes 30 hours per week.

Hours per week	30
Average wage (part-time clerk)	×8.00
Weekly payroll cost	$240.00
Annual Savings	$12,480

Elimination of the manual tasks of tabulating, batching, and controlling can save 0.25 hourly units. Improved work flow resulting from timely data in the system without data-input processing will allow more efficient use of clerical hours. This would reduce payroll by the 0.50 hourly units currently required to meet weekly check disbursement.

Eliminate manual tasks	0.25
Improve work flow	0.50
40-hour unit reduction	1.00
Hours per week	40
Average wage (full-time clerk)	9.00
Savings per week	$360.00
Annual Savings	$18,720

TOTAL ANNUAL SAVINGS: $31,200

-4-

A primary system feature described in problem-solution form with supporting cost analysis

Figure 14–10   Detailed Solution of a Sales Proposal

COST ANALYSIS

This section of our proposal provides detailed cost information for the Waters 319 Interactive Terminal and the Waters 615 Retail Processor. It then multiplies these major elements by the quantities required at each of your four locations.

319 Interactive Terminal

	Price	Maint. (1 yr.)
Terminal	$2,895	$167
Journal Printer	425	38
Receipt Printer	425	38
Forms Printer	525	38
Software	220	—
TOTALS	$4,490	$281

615 Retail Processor

Breakdown of hardware, software, and maintenance costs

	Price	Maint. (1 yr.)
Processor	$57,115	$5,787
CRT I/O Writer	2,000	324
Laser Printer	4,245	568
Software	12,480	—
TOTALS	$75,840	$6,679

The following breakdown itemizes the cost per store:

Store No. 1

Description	Qty.	Price	Maint. (1 yr.)
Terminals	16	$68,400	$4,496
Digital Cassette	1	1,300	147
Laser Printer	1	2,490	332
Software	16	3,520	—
TOTALS		$75,710	$4,975

Store No. 2

Description	Qty.	Price	Maint. (1 yr.)
Terminals	20	$85,400	$5,620
Digital Cassette	1	1,300	147
Laser Printer	1	2,490	332
Software	20	4,400	—
TOTALS		$93,590	$6,099

-5-

Figure 14–11   Cost Analysis and Delivery Schedule of a Sales Proposal (continued)

Store No. 3

Description	Qty.	Price	Maint. (1 yr.)
Terminals	17	$72,590	$4,777
Digital Cassette	1	1,300	147
Laser Printer	1	2,490	332
Software	17	3,740	—
TOTALS		$80,120	$5,256

Store No. 4

Description	Qty.	Price	Maint. (1 yr.)
Terminals	18	$76,860	$5,058
Digital Cassette	1	1,300	147
Laser Printer	1	2,490	332
Software	18	3,960	—
TOTALS		$84,610	$5,537

Further cost breakdown and delivery schedule

Data Center at Buffalo

Description	Qty.	Price	Maint. (1 yr.)
Processor	1	$57,115	$5,787
CRT I/O Writer	1	2,000	324
Laser Printer	1	4,245	568
Software	1	12,480	—
TOTALS		$75,840	$6,679

The following summarizes all costs:

Location	Hardware	Maint. (1 yr.)	Software
Store No. 1	$72,190	$4,975	$3,520
Store No. 2	89,190	6,099	4,400
Store No. 3	76,380	5,256	3,740
Store No. 4	80,650	5,537	3,960
Data Center	63,360	6,679	12,480
Subtotals	$381,360	$28,546	$28,100

TOTAL $438,416

DELIVERY SCHEDULE

Waters is normally able to deliver 319 Interactive Terminals and 615 Retail Processors within 90 days of the date of the contract. This can vary depending on the rate and size of incoming orders.

All the software recommended in this proposal is available for immediate delivery. We do not anticipate any difficulty in meeting your tentative delivery schedule.

-6-

Figure 14–11   **Cost Analysis and Delivery Schedule of a Sales Proposal** (continued)

If your recommendations include modifying your customer's physical facilities, you would include a *site-preparation description* that details the modifications required. In some proposals, the headings "Facilities" and "Equipment" are used for this section.

If the products and services you are proposing require training the customer's employees, your proposals should specify the *required training* and its cost. Figure 14–12 shows the site-preparation section and Figure 14–13 the training-requirements section of the Waters proposal.

To prevent misunderstandings about what you and your customer's responsibilities will be, you should draw up a *statement of responsibilities* (Figure 14–14), which usually appears toward the end of the proposal. Also toward the end of the proposal is a *description of the vendor,* which gives a description of your company, its history, and its present position in the industry. The description-of-the-vendor

---

The Waters Proposal September 1, 2003

SITE PREPARATION

Details of system requirements and division of responsibilities for the work

Waters will work closely with Cookson's to ensure that each site is properly prepared prior to system installation. You will receive a copy of Waters' installation and wiring procedures manual, which lists the physical dimensions, service clearance, and weight of the system components in addition to the power, logic, and environmental requirements. Cookson's is responsible for all building alterations and electrical facility changes, including the purchase and installation of communication cables, connecting blocks, and receptacles.

Wiring

For the purpose of future site considerations, Waters' in-house wiring specifications for the system call for two twisted-pair wires and 22 shielded gauges. The length of communications wires must not exceed 2,500 feet.

As a guide for the power supply, we suggest that Cookson's consider the following:

1. The branch circuit (limited to 20 amps) should service no equipment other than 319 Interactive Terminals.
2. Each 20-amp branch circuit should support a maximum of three 319 Interactive Terminals.
3. Each branch circuit must have three equal-size conductors—one hot leg, one neutral, and one insulated isolated ground.
4. Hubbell IG 5362 duplex outlets or the equivalent should be used to supply power to each terminal.
5. Computer-room wiring will have to be upgraded to support the 615 Retail Processor.

Figure 14–12   Site-Preparation Section of a Sales Proposal

TRAINING

To ensure a successful installation, Waters offers the following training course for your operators.

Interactive Terminal/Retail Processor Operations

Course number: 8256
Length: three days
Tuition: $500.00

This course provides the student with the skills, knowledge, and practice required to operate an Interactive Terminal/Retail Processor System. Online, clustered, and stand-alone environments are covered.

We recommend that students have a department-store background and that they have some knowledge of the system configuration with which they will be working.

Employee training costs and length

Figure 14–13 Training-Requirements Section of a Sales Proposal

section typically includes a list of people or subcontractors and the duties they will perform. The résumés of key personnel may also be placed here or in an appendix. Following this description, many proposals add what is known as an *organizational sales pitch*. Up to this point, the proposal has attempted to sell specific goods and services. The sales pitch, striking a somewhat different chord, is designed to sell the company and its general capability in the field. The sales pitch promotes the company and concludes the proposal on an upbeat note. Figure 14–15 shows the vendor-description and sales-pitch sections of the Waters proposal.

Some long sales proposals include a conclusion section that summarizes the proposal's salient points, stresses your company's strong points, and includes information about whom the potential client can contact for further information. It may also end with a request for the date work will begin should the proposal be accepted. Figure 14–16 shows the conclusion of the Waters proposal.

Depending on length and technical complexity, some proposals include *appendixes* made up of statistical analyses, maps, charts, tables, and résumés of the principal staff assigned to the project. As with reports, appendixes to proposals should contain only supplemental information; the primary information should appear in the body of the proposal.

The Waters Proposal   September 1, 2003

RESPONSIBILITIES

Based on its years of experience in installing information-processing systems, Waters believes that a successful installation requires a clear understanding of certain responsibilities.

Division of tasks between customer and vendor

Generally, it is Waters' responsibility to provide its users with needed assistance during the installation so that live processing can begin as soon thereafter as is practical.

Waters' Responsibilities

- Provide operations documentation for each application that you acquire from Waters.
- Provide forms and other supplies as ordered.
- Provide specifications and technical guidance for proper site planning and installation.
- Provide adviser assistance in the conversion from your present system to the new system.

Customer's Responsibilities

- Identify an installation coordinator and system operator.
- Provide supervisors and clerical personnel to perform conversion to the system.
- Establish reasonable time schedules for implementation.
- Ensure that the physical site requirements are met.
- Provide competent personnel to be trained as operators and ensure that other employees are trained as necessary.
- Assume the responsibility for implementing and operating the system.

-9-

Figure 14–14   Statement-of-Responsibilities Section of a Sales Proposal

The Waters Proposal   September 1, 2003

DESCRIPTION OF VENDOR

The Waters Corporation develops, manufactures, markets, installs, and services total business information-processing systems for selected markets. These markets are primarily in the retail, financial, commercial, industrial, health-care, education, and government sectors.

The Waters total system concept encompasses one of the broadest hardware and software product lines in the industry. Waters computers range from small business systems to powerful general-purpose processors. Waters computers are supported by a complete spectrum of terminals, peripherals, and data-communication networks and an extensive library of software products. Supplemental services and products include data centers, field service, systems engineering, and educational centers.

The Waters Corporation was founded in 1934 and presently has approximately 26,500 employees. The Waters headquarters is located at 17 North Waterloo Boulevard, Tampa, Florida, with district offices throughout the United States and Canada. For a comprehensive listing of Waters products and services, visit our Web site at waterscorp.com.

Statements of the vendor's history and commitment to its core business to highlight its experience and reputation

WHY WATERS?

Corporate Commitment to the Retail Industry

Waters' commitment to the retail industry is stronger than ever. We are continually striving to provide leadership in the design and implementation of new retail systems and applications that will ensure our users of a logical growth pattern.

Research and Development

Over the years, Waters has spent increasingly large sums on research-and-development efforts to ensure the availability of products and systems for the future. In 2002, our research-and-development expenditures for advanced systems design and technological innovations reached the $70 million level.

Leading Point-of-Sale Vendor

Waters is a leading point-of-sale vendor, having installed over 150,000 units. The knowledge and experience that Waters has gained over the years from these installations ensure well-coordinated and effective systems implementations.

-10-

Figure 14–15   Description of Vendor and Sales Pitch of a Sales Proposal

The Waters Proposal   September 1, 2003

CONCLUSION

Waters welcomes the opportunity to submit this proposal to Cookson's. The Waters Corporation is confident that we have offered the right solution at a competitive price. Based on the hands-on analysis we conducted, our proposal takes into account your current and projected workloads and your plans to expand your facilities and operations. Our proposal will also, we believe, afford Cookson's future cost-avoidance measures in employee time and in enhanced accounting features.

Waters has a proven track record of success in the manufacture, installation, and servicing of retail business information systems stretching over many decades. We also have a demonstrated record of success in our past business associations with Cookson's. We believe that the system we propose will extend and strengthen this partnership.

Should you require additional information about any facet of this proposal, please contact Janet A. Curtain, who will personally arrange to meet with you or arrange for Waters' technical staff to meet with or send you the information you need.

We look forward to your decision and to continued success in our working relationship with Cookson's.

-11-

Figure 14–16   Conclusion of a Sales Proposal

Writing Proposals

☐ Is your audience a manager within your organization or a potential customer outside your organization?

☐ Does your proposal answer clearly the following questions?

- What problem does your proposal address?
- What do you propose to do?
- What benefits does your proposed plan offer?
- How do you plan to do it?
- When do you plan to undertake and complete it?
- How much do you estimate it will cost?

☐ Does your proposal address the functional needs of those who must evaluate it by including:

- An executive summary in nontechnical language for decision-makers?
- A summary of the proposed solution, budget, schedule, and training requirements for managers?
- Technical details and visuals of the proposed solution for the specialists who must assess your degree of expertise to perform the work?

☐ Is the language professional and respectful?

☐ Is the proposal written, organized, and submitted exactly as specified in the request for proposal?

☐ Have you carefully revised boilerplate to fit seamlessly into the proposal?

■ MEETING THE DEADLINE: The Time-Sensitive Proposal ———

Proposal writers must give top priority to meeting the procuring organization's deadline, while also producing a high-quality, persuasive proposal likely to receive favorable evaluations. The following time-management strategies can help toward meeting these goals.

1. *Hold an initial planning session.* The project manager should hold a planning meeting with the coordinator, the compiler, the budget specialist, and the key subject-matter specialists to introduce the project team members, set priorities, determine and delegate tasks, and set milestone deadlines for each task.

2. *Assign coordinators.* During the planning meeting, the project manager should choose a writing coordinator to organize the creation and production of text and graphics, and a compiler (often an administrative assistant) to integrate all sections and elements of the final proposal and to make sure that they adhere to the potential customer's requirements in the request for proposal.

3. *Set priorities.* The proposal sections or features likely to weigh most heavily during the prospective customer's evaluation of the proposal should receive the most attention from the writers and the most space in the final product. Make this determination at the beginning of the project. These sections tend to be longer than sections of lesser importance. For example, for a ten-page proposal that includes four sections, the two most important sections might be four pages each, while the two least important sections might be one page each.

4. *Delegate tasks.* To expedite research and writing, assign more than one person to work on each section, and allow them to work out a way to collaborate efficiently to meet the deadline for submitting their section. This strategy works best when the contributors have diverse schedules and areas of specialization. Often, two or three subject experts coauthor parts of a single section and the writing coordinator edits the resulting draft for clarity and coherence.

5. *Work out a schedule.* During the initial planning session, determine how much time each task is likely to require. Start work immediately on tasks likely to take longer to complete, but also begin to collect other important pieces, such as résumés, biographies, and project descriptions. Decide which tasks can be done simultaneously and which tasks must precede others. When establishing a schedule, work backward from the proposal deadline, leaving at least a day for the proposal to reach its destination by express delivery, half a day before that for collecting company signatures and making multiple copies of the proposal, and half a day before that for last-minute edits and proofreading.

6. *Use boilerplate material.* When possible, import into the proposal standard pieces of information from previous proposals, such as résumés, descriptions of past projects, and company goals and accomplishments. This is known as boilerplate material. For additional information about the use of boilerplate, see Digital Shortcuts: Sharing Boilerplate Material on page 183.

7. *Select the best media.* Choose the most efficient means for collecting information and draft sections for the proposal. For example, if you need written material immediately, use e-mail attachments or faxes; if you need

written material within a day or two, interoffice mail, Express Mail, or a delivery service might suffice. If you need information immediately that is not yet drafted, rely on phone calls or in-person meetings.

8. *Track progress and deadlines.* Use e-mail or phone messages periodically to send out reminders about deadlines or prompt someone to deliver material that you need right away. Hold interim meetings if doing so will speed up your work. If interim task deadlines are missed and you need information, materials, or finished products immediately, ask everyone on the project team to abandon other projects to devote full-time and extra hours to the proposal effort so that you can meet the final deadline.

9. *Hold a lessons-learned meeting, if necessary.* Even when these strategies are used, problems can arise that jeopardize the quality of your proposal or your ability to meet the final deadline. After sending out the proposal, hold a debriefing session in which you identify those problems and plan strategies for avoiding them when planning and writing future proposals.

Writing Proposals Under a Deadline

WRITER'S
CHECKLIST

- [ ] Hold a planning meeting with the proposal team to assign work and establish due dates for all tasks.

- [ ] Assign project coordinators to ensure that all sections and elements are complete and consistent and comply with the requirements of the request for proposal.

- [ ] Set priorities so that the most important sections of the proposal receive adequate attention.

- [ ] Delegate work to ensure that subject-area experts are available within the schedule established to meet the deadline.

- [ ] Schedule the project so that work begins on the sections that will take the longest, doing as many sections as possible simultaneously.

- [ ] Use boilerplate as extensively as possible, being careful to adapt it to the prospective customer.

- [ ] Select the best media to communicate among proposal team members.

- [ ] Track the status of each part of the proposal carefully, sending periodic reminders about upcoming deadlines.

CHAPTER 14 SUMMARY: Writing Proposals

A proposal:

- [ ] Is written to persuade a reader to follow a plan or course of action.
- [ ] Consists of the following parts (and may include additional parts, based on the needs of your topic).
    - An *introduction* that states:
    - [ ] The problem you propose to solve and your solution to it.
    - [ ] The dates on which you propose to begin and complete work.
    - [ ] Any special benefits of your proposed approach.
    - [ ] The total cost of the project.
    - [ ] Any previous positive association between your company and the potential customer (if a sales proposal).
    - A *body* that explains:
    - [ ] What products and services you are offering (if a sales proposal).
    - [ ] How the job will be done.
    - [ ] The procedures you propose to use to perform the work.
    - [ ] The materials you will use (if applicable).
    - [ ] The schedule for each stage of the project.
    - [ ] Detailed costs.
    - A *conclusion* that emphasizes:
    - [ ] The benefits of your solution, products, or services that persuade the reader to take action.
    - [ ] Your appreciation for the opportunity to submit the proposal.
    - [ ] Your confidence in your ability — or, if a sales proposal, of your company's ability — to carry out the project.
    - [ ] Your willingness to provide further information.
    - [ ] The advantages of your company over its competitors.
      and includes:
    - [ ] The time period during which the proposal is valid.
    - [ ] Any supplemental materials.

An internal proposal:

- [ ] Is written to a manager within your organization.
- [ ] Is usually written to persuade management to make a change or improvement, or to fund a project that you would like to launch.

An external (sales) proposal:

- [ ] Is written to a potential client outside of your organization.
- [ ] Is written to persuade a potential customer to purchase your company's products or services.
- [ ] May be solicited or unsolicited.
- [ ] May be short or long, depending on the complexity of the topic.

Exercises

1. Write a proposal in which you recommend a change in a procedure at work or at school, addressed to your supervisor or dean. In your proposal, state the nature of the problem and explain how the new procedure would be put into effect. Give at least three reasons for the change, and support your reasons with facts that show the advantages of your proposal.

2. Address an internal proposal to your boss recommending that your company begin a tuition-refund plan or technology-training program. Propose at least three major advantages to having either of these educational programs, and present them in decreasing order of importance.

3. You are a landscaping contractor and would like to respond to the following RFP, which appears in your local newspaper:

   - Lawn-mowing agreement for the Town of Augusta, Oregon. Weekly mowing of 5 miles of Route 24 median and sidings, 10 acres in Willoughby Park, and 23 acres at Augusta Memorial Golf Course, May 30 through September 30. Proposals are due April 30.

   Write a proposal in which you estimate the number of labor-hours the contract would require, what you would charge, the ability of your staff and equipment to do the job, your firm's experience and qualifications, and the weekly schedule that you propose to follow.

4. Write a proposal letter in which you recommend a change in a government process—for example, in the way we pay our taxes, the way the census is completed, the way we vote, or the way we become citizens. Be specific when listing the advantages of your idea. Address your short, informal proposal to a local, state, or federal legislator, as appropriate.

5. Write a proposal letter to change a specific rule or regulation of an organization to which you belong, such as your school, religious organization, professional association, or fitness club. List the current rule or regulation, then present your proposed changes and explain the advantages of your new rule. Address your short proposal to the president or head of the organization.

6. Prepare a short, internal proposal to persuade your instructor of one of the following ideas. Present as many logical reasons as possible to support your proposal.

   - Students should automatically be excused from class on Mondays immediately following school vacations.
   - There should be no penalty for missing class.
   - Students should be allowed up to three days to submit papers late without penalty.
   - If students have more than three tests in one week, they should be allowed to make up one exam the following week.
   - If students are within three percentage points of reaching the next highest grade, extra-credit opportunities should be granted for the purpose of raising the grade.

7. As a human resources coordinator of a large company, you've noticed an increase in the number of employee medical emergencies, some serious, over the past two years. Write an internal proposal memo to your supervisor, offering plans that

would (1) contribute to employees' good health and (2) help employees to respond to medical emergencies. Plans for improving employees' health could include a more comprehensive medical-benefits package, on-site health screening, stress-management and nutrition counseling, and corporate memberships to fitness centers. Plans for helping employees handle medical emergencies could include on-site cardiopulmonary resuscitation (CPR) and first-aid training. Explain the benefits of each solution you propose.

8. One of the pieces of boilerplate information often included in an external proposal is a chart showing the organizational structure of the company. Develop an organizational chart based on the following information. See Chapter 8, pages 289–291, for guidance about creating organizational charts.

   The Wesson consulting firm consists of 29 employees.

   - Principal employees:
       Joyce Maggle, President
       John Wanber, Vice President
       Sally Janes, C.P.A., Comptroller
       Sandra Mitchell, Chief Engineer
   - Senior consultants:
       John Smit, Engineer
       Debbie Williams, Ph.D.
       Mary Rober, Ph.D.
       Samuel Ebbs, 20 years of experience with the company
       Tom Jewell, 20 years of experience with the company
   - Associate consultants:
       Becky Crow, B.A.
       James Johns, B.Sc.
       Cris Widdel, M.S.
       Mark Mann, M.S.
       Fran Blackwell, M.S.

   The remaining 15 employees are support staff: two accounting personnel, two computer specialists, one office manager, nine clerical workers, and one mail clerk/maintenance chief.

   Your organizational chart, which will be included in your company's upcoming proposals, should be well designed and submitted on 8½-by-11-inch paper or in an electronic file. It may be in portrait or landscape orientation.

9. Prepare a one-page cost analysis for a sales proposal that you would submit to a prospective client. Your cost analysis should be clearly written and well formatted, and should include the following breakdown for the project:

   - Cost of personnel or labor
   - Cost of overhead
   - Cost of new equipment
   - Total cost of project

   Submit any amounts you wish in these categories and change the category titles as needed. Each category except total cost must contain at least four different line items. For example, cost of personnel or labor might include the hourly rate for the time the company president will spend on this project and the cost of other staff specialists required on the project. Overhead might include the cost of support staff, supplies, company vehicles, and so forth. The cost of new equipment would include the cost of items purchased solely for the client. Although you may use any numbers you wish in the line items, all subtotals should equal the total cost when added together.

Collaborative Classroom Projects

1. In teams of five to seven members, develop an internal proposal asking the dean's office to improve or upgrade a facility, technology, course offering, or other area. Your proposal is due in three weeks. Spend 45 minutes developing a plan for completing your group's proposal. Refer to Meeting the Deadline: The Time-Sensitive Proposal on pages 507–509.

    a. Your team will need to assign a project manager, a writing coordinator, a compiler, and a budget specialist.
    b. Once chosen, the project manager will begin the session by introducing team members, setting priorities, and determining and delegating tasks.
    c. In a collective effort, make a list of the tasks that will need to be completed.
    d. Decide what sections will be included in the proposal.
    e. Develop a timeline, including scheduling and sequencing of the tasks. Include any other details you feel are relevant as you develop your plan.

    As directed by your instructor, present your plan for how your team will meet the deadline orally to the class or submit the plan in writing to your instructor. Submit the finished proposal to your instructor.

2. In teams of three to five members, review the description of vendor included in Figure 14–15, and develop and design an organizational sales pitch. Referring back to this chapter, develop a rough draft, including an original layout and design created by your team. Set priorities for the information to be included and be creative in the manner you choose to present the information. Take 45 minutes to one hour to complete this assignment.

3. Often the appendix of a sales proposal will include a brief résumé of all the key project personnel. During the next 30 minutes, assume that you are the project coordinator of a sales proposal related to your major area of study. Using no more than six to eight lines, list your name, current educational status, relevant job experience, and a personal mission statement as if it were to be included in the personnel page of an appendix to a proposal.

4. Divide into teams with classmates who share a similar major area of study. If you have more than seven students in your group, divide into two smaller groups. During the next hour, your team assignment is to write a short proposal in the form of a persuasive letter directed to your instructor. In your letter, propose an educational field trip to a place of interest. Include the following in your proposal:

    • Why this place is of educational value to your team
    • What you expect to learn from the trip
    • Suggested mode of travel, accommodations, and arrangements for meals
    • A breakdown of costs
    • Suggested sources for funding
    • Any other relevant points

5. In teams of five or fewer members, begin work on a proposal for a new cafeteria, health club, day-care center, or other amenity for your company, which has approximately 200 employees. Appoint a project manager and a recorder, and in the next 60 minutes, develop a detailed outline for your proposal. Assume that your proposal is an unsolicited, internal proposal. Include areas that will require further research for your team to complete this assignment during future class meetings.

6. Divide into teams of six or fewer members with classmates who share a similar major area of study. As a group, investigate the continuing-education program available for your major area of study and submit to a professional association in your field a proposal detailing a specific, beneficial change.

   a. Your team will need to assign a project manager, a writing coordinator, one or more compilers, and a budget specialist.
   b. The project manager will begin the session by introducing team members, setting priorities, and determining and delegating tasks.
   c. As a group, make a list of the tasks that will need to be completed.
   d. Decide what sections will be included in the proposal.
   e. Develop a timeline, including scheduling and sequencing of the tasks.
   f. Include any other details you feel relevant as you develop your plan.

   Your instructor will advise you whether your group should meet weekly or twice monthly, your proposal due date, and the components that are required in your proposal.

■ Research Projects

1. Assume that you and three other classmates are members of an information technology (IT) group that has been asked by your company's chief executive officer to consider ways to improve communication between employees, departments, suppliers, etc. You come up with the idea of creating a company intranet, which is like a private Internet within a corporation that employees or suppliers can access either internally or through the Internet with passwords. You decide to research the feasibility of building a company intranet and begin by researching:

   a. What an intranet is and the many ways it can be useful to companies.
   b. What software and hardware is needed to set up an intranet.
   c. What technical skills and training will be necessary for those who will maintain the intranet and for those who will train others to use the intranet.
   d. What the setup and long-term costs could be to hire new or train existing computer technicians to run the intranet, and the cost involved in purchasing the software and hardware.

   Write a report of your findings and present them to your instructor.

2. Using information gathered in Research Project 1, create an internal proposal directed toward your company's chief executive officer suggesting the creation of an intranet to solve the company's communication problems. Begin by writing an introduction that establishes the current communication problems in the company and why an intranet would be a good solution to these problems. Then write the body of the proposal. Be sure to provide a detailed background on the communi-

cation problems; methods to be used to achieve a solution via an intranet; detailed information on the necessary equipment, materials, and staff requirements; a breakdown of (potential) costs; and a schedule for completing the project. Finally, write a brief conclusion that restates your recommendation and closes with offers of assistance in completing the intranet project.

3. Locate a professional in your major area of study who is involved with proposal writing. Schedule a 20-minute telephone or in-person interview with that person. Make a list of questions regarding the proposal-writing process, such as the following:

   - How does your company use proposals?
   - What is the procedure for assigning proposals? Who writes them? What portions of proposals are boilerplate?
   - Are specialists hired for writing proposals? Are all departments involved?
   - What advice would you offer about writing effective proposals?
   - What advice would you offer about writing effective proposals to meet a challenging deadline?

   Write a brief narrative summarizing the interview.

4. In groups of three or four, imagine that you are owners of a local health-food store that sells organic and international foods and also offers prepared meals, to-go sandwiches, smoothies, and juices. You are looking for ways to expand your business and attract customers from the nearby large computer corporation. You know that the company has many health-conscious employees and international employees and visitors who suffer through holiday parties, sales celebrations, and end-of-the-year award banquets that are catered by very traditional caterers with no knowledge of international or healthy foods. Instead, they serve packaged finger foods and typical cafeteria-type dishes with no consideration of health or cultural dietary restrictions. (See Chapter 9 for more details on international business.)

   You decide to research the feasibility of offering to cater the computer corporation's parties by providing healthy meals and culturally appropriate dishes. Begin by researching the following:

   a. Current health and eating habits of American workers today
   b. Impact of poor nutrition on employee health and the benefits of eating natural foods
   c. International business climate and needs of international employees and visitors
   d. Importance of accommodating the needs of guests from all cultures
   e. Costs of catering large parties.

   You may find that it is more costly to provide healthy and/or international foods; however, remember that this is an exercise in persuasion. The food may cost more, but the benefits of good international relations and employee health may be more important and valuable over time. Write a report of your findings and present them to your instructor.

5. Using the information gathered in Research Project 4, create an unsolicited sales proposal. Begin by defining the problem and solution as you see them (i.e., the computer company has many health-conscious employees and international employees and visitors who endure catered parties where food is offered with no consideration to health or cultural dietary restrictions). Remember to be creative and

persuasive; in writing any unsolicited sales proposal, you must persuade the head of the company that there is a problem and that you offer the best solution.

Begin by writing an introduction, which indicates the purpose and scope of the proposal, the dates and/or events that you propose to cater, the special benefits of your proposed approach, and the total cost of the catered projects. Also mention your expertise on the subject of healthy and international foods. Next, in the body, itemize the products and services you are offering (types of dishes, setup and cleanup, etc.). Present a schedule, indicating when each stage would be completed; include a precise breakdown of the costs of the project. In the conclusion, express your appreciation for the opportunity to submit the proposal and your confidence in your company's ability to do the job. You could also use this section to review any advantages your company may have over its competitors. If any supplemental materials, such as menus, accompany the proposal, include a list of them at the end of the proposal. Finish by writing a cover letter to your potential client.

■ Web Projects

Priojects followed by the symbol **W** are continued at **bedfordstmartins.com/ writingthatworks**, Chapter 14.

1. Assume that you are a member of an agricultural-research firm or a food-science researcher exploring how to respond to an RFP offered by a U.S. government agency. Find an RFP that interests you and read it carefully, then write a report to the class detailing the purpose of the RFP, the funds available, and, most important, the in-depth directions given on filling out the application. Discuss the importance of following these directions and estimate the time necessary to complete such an application, then create a schedule for completing the proposal (see Meeting the Deadline: The Time-Sensitive Proposal on pages 507–509). **W**

2. The Small Business Administration (SBA) offers tips on proposal writing. Cut and paste their information and, using your word processor's brochure or newsletter templates, create a professional-looking document you could hand out to your classmates. **W**

3. Many companies depend on proposal writers for much of their business, and good proposal writers are in high demand. Using online employment services, research available proposal-writing jobs and write a report to your class that describes the writing and technical skills necessary to become a successful proposal writer. **W**

4. Your high-tech company is interested in changing its security procedures to include biometric verification technology. Employees' fingerprints and/or retina patterns would now be scanned before they could enter top-secret areas. You have been asked to investigate at least three Web sites of companies that provide this kind of technology. Write a proposal letter to your boss that details how the technology works, the cost, and the advantages over traditional security methods.

5. Identify a problem that you feel needs to be solved either at work or at school. For example, the increasing number of students and limited number of parking spaces is causing a major parking problem. Or sealed windows in your office

building are creating sick-building syndrome, and many employees are getting ill more frequently and for longer periods of time. Your assignment is to write a proposal offering a solution to the problem. (Your instructor may want to approve your topic selection.) Assume that your proposal is internal, and include the following in your proposal:

- Transmittal letter
- Executive summary
- Introduction, body, and conclusion
- Cost analysis
- Timeline or schedule of delivery
- Description of vendor

Your completed proposal will be seven to ten pages long, with the executive summary less than one page single-spaced. Your introduction, body, and conclusion will be approximately three pages of text, 1.5-spaced. Insert at least two visuals within the text.

15 Giving Presentations and Conducting Meetings

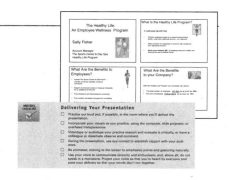

Although most of this book covers the principles of writing that works in business and industry, much workplace information is communicated orally as well, and the components of such communications—listening and responding effectively—are both critically important. Writing and presentations have much in common. Both must be logically organized and are most effective when clear and succinct. The principles of writing discussed throughout this text are also applicable to presentations in the workplace: Know your purpose and audience, organize your information, and determine the amount of information necessary to convey your message. However, there is also much that is different about presentations, and this chapter explores those elements unique to this form of communication. Oral communication is most widely used in the workplace for giving presentations and in conducting meetings. Central to the success of both is effective listening.

In the following sections, this chapter offers practical guidelines for:

- Preparing and delivering presentations.
- Listening effectively.
- Planning and conducting successful meetings.

W On the Web
For more help with giving presentations and conducting meetings, see Chapter 15, **bedfordstmartins.com/ writingthatworks**

■ Preparing and Delivering Presentations

The steps required to prepare an effective presentation parallel the steps you follow to write a document: (1) determine your purpose and analyze your audience, (2) find and gather the facts to support your point of view and proposal, and (3) logically organize your information. However, presentations are intended for listeners, not readers. Because you are giving a talk rather than writing a memo or report, your manner of delivery, the way you organize the material, and your supporting visual aids require as much attention as your content.

Determining Your Purpose

Every presentation is given for a purpose—even if it is only to share information. To determine the purpose of your presentation, use the following questions as a guide.

1. What do I want the audience to know?
2. What do I want the audience to believe?
3. What do I want the audience to do?

Then, based on the answers to these questions, write a purpose statement that answers the questions *what* and *why*.

■ The purpose of my presentation is to explain to my classmates the various tasks I performed last semester as a part-time volunteer at the Maplewood Adult Day Care Center [*what*] so that other members of the class will want to become volunteers at Maplewood [*why*].

■ The purpose of my presentation is to convince my company's chief information officer of the need to improve the appearance, content, and customer use of our company's Web site [*what*] so that she will be persuaded to include additional funds in the budget for site-development work next fiscal year [*why*].

Analyzing Your Audience

Once you determine the desired end result of the presentation, you need to analyze your audience so that you can tailor your presentation to your audience's needs. Ask yourself the following five questions about your audience:

1. What is your audience's level of experience or knowledge about your topic?
2. What is the general educational level and age of your audience?
3. What is your audience's attitude toward the topic you are speaking about, and—based on that attitude—what concerns, fears, or objections might your audience have?
4. Are there subgroups in your audience that might have different concerns or needs?
5. What questions could your audience ask about this topic?

Gathering Information

Now that you've focused the presentation, you need to find the information that will support your point of view or the action you propose. Give the audience only the information necessary to accomplish your goals; too much information will overwhelm the audience, and too little information will leave the audience either with a sketchy understanding of your topic or with the feeling that you have not

Voices from the Workplace

Paul B. Greenspan, Interland, Inc.

Paul B. Greenspan is Vice President of Channel Sales with Interland, Inc., a provider of Web-hosting and online marketing services for small businesses. Paul spends much of his time meeting with prospective and established customers, and with the staff of sales representatives who report to him. Strong oral communication and presentation skills are important to Paul's roles at Interland.

"I learned a lot of dos and don'ts in a course I took on presentation skills. One important point is that a good presenter uses techniques to minimize the amount of work the audience has to do. For example, I learned to use arresting visuals and to avoid long, bulleted lists that basically duplicate my notes. I have also learned that where a speaker stands in relation to his or her visual aids can either help or hinder the presentation. Body language is also important — how you use your arms, how you gesture. The 'big' gesture that may seem exaggerated to the presenter looks natural to the audience. Finally, you have to demand interactivity from your audience. The day of the 'droning, talking head' with an inch-thick stack of transparencies is gone forever. Insist on your audience engaging and interacting with you."

Corey Ann Eaton, Wachovia Securities

In her role as a regional liaison at Wachovia Securities, Corey Ann Eaton provides business and technology training to the company's operations personnel and financial advisers. As a trainer, Corey spends time gathering information, developing the course, and delivering presentations to small groups of employees. The topics she addresses vary from systems and software, to operations, to "soft" topics, such as phone etiquette. Corey offers the following tips for using presentation software.

"Presentation software can assist you by prompting each new topic, leading the discussion, and ensuring no point is forgotten. If the audience leads the discussion away from the intended route, the presentation slides can move the discussion back on track.

"As a presenter, you should remember that the software is there to assist with your message, not deliver it for you. The easiest way to ensure this is to keep it simple. Use the software to make the most important messages clear, and don't allow yourself to put every point you need to make in the slide presentation; include only enough to prompt the information or discussion you are delivering.

"When creating a presentation, keep in mind the importance of concise and plain language. Your audience will be attentive to the slide for only a few seconds and will shift its focus to your verbal message thereafter. The font and background color you choose is important and should be associated with the message you are relaying. However, the font should be simple, clean, and crisp. Imagine that you are sitting in the last row at the back of the room. Is the font still easy to read? If not, change it to a large, bold, or sans serif font. Regardless of how formal or creative you want to make the presentation, the slides should never distract from the message you are trying to convey."

provided enough information to support the course of action you wish them to take. (For detailed guidance about gathering information, see Chapter 7.

Structuring Your Presentation

When structuring your presentation, keep the focus on your audience as listeners. As such, they remember openings and closings best because your listeners are freshest at the outset and refocus their attention as you complete your remarks. Take advantage of this pattern. Give your audience a brief overview of your presentation at the beginning, use the body to develop your ideas, and end with a summary of what you covered and, if appropriate, a call to action.

Introduction

The introduction to your presentation may include an opening—something designed to catch and focus the audience's attention. The following opening defines a problem:

■ You have to write an important report, but you'd like to incorporate the bulk of an old report into your new one. The problem is that you don't have an electronic version of the old report. You'll have to rekey many pages. You groan because that seems an incredible waste of time. Have I got a solution for you!

You could also have used any of the following types of openings:

- *An attention-getting statement:* As many as 50 million Americans have high blood pressure.
- *A rhetorical question:* Would you be interested in a full-sized computer keyboard that is waterproof, is noiseless, and can be rolled up like a rubber mat?
- *A personal experience:* As I sat at my computer one day last month deleting my eighth junk e-mail of the day, I decided that it was time to find a solution to eliminate this time-waster that will work for you and me.
- *An appropriate quotation:* According to researchers at the Massachusetts Institute of Technology, "Garlic and its cousin the onion confer major health benefits—including fighting cancer, infections, and heart disease."

(For additional examples, see Writing an Opening on page 91 in Chapter 3.)

Following your opening, use the introduction to set the stage for your audience by giving an overview of the presentation. The overview may include general or background information that your audience will need to understand the more detailed information in the body of your presentation. It may also be an overview of how you've organized the material.

- This presentation explains the options available to you, the employees of Acme Corporation, for making contributions through payroll deductions to a long-term retirement plan—a plan that will enhance the income you will receive from Social Security and pension benefits.

- This presentation will answer your questions:
  - How much can I save?
  - How much does Acme contribute to the plan?
  - What are my investment options?

Body

In the body of your presentation, persuade your audience of the validity of your conclusion. If you are addressing a problem, demonstrate that it exists and offer a solution or range of possible solutions. If your introduction stated that the problem was low profits, high costs, outdated technology, or high employee absenteeism, use the following approach:

- Offer a solution.
  - Increase profits by lowering production costs.
  - Cut overhead to reduce costs.
  - Upgrade existing technology to improve productivity.
  - Offer employees more flexibility in their work schedules or other incentives.
- Prove your point.
  - Gather the facts and data you need.
  - Present the facts and data using easy-to-understand visual aids.
- Call for action.
  - Convince your audience to agree, to change their minds, or to do something.
- Anticipate questions ("How much will it cost?") and objections ("We're too busy now. When will we have time to learn the new software?") and be ready for them.

Closing

Your closing should achieve the goals of your presentation. If your purpose is to motivate your audience to take action, ask them to do what you want them to do; if your purpose is to get your audience to think about something, summarize what you want them to think about. Many presenters make the mistake of not actually closing—they simply quit talking, shuffle papers around, and then walk away.

Because your closing is what your audience is most likely to remember, it is the time to be strong and persuasive. Returning to the retirement savings plan example, consider the following possible closing:

- This is the first step toward your future security.
  - Decide how much you can save each month.
  - Remember Acme's contribution.
  - Choose the investment options that best fit your needs.
  - ENROLL NEXT WEEK!

This closing brings the presentation full circle and asks the audience to act on the information provided in the presentation—exactly what a closing should do.

Transitions

Transitions should appear between the introduction and the body, between the points in the body, and between the body and the closing. Transitions, simply a sentence or two, let the audience know that you're moving from one topic to the next. They also prevent a choppy presentation and provide you, the speaker, with assurance that you know where you're going and how to get there.

- Before getting into the specifics of the fund families available to you, I'd like to describe the investment goals and strategies of each. That information will provide you with the background you'll need to compare the differences among them to make an informed decision about what works best for you.

It is also a good idea to pause for a moment after you've delivered a transitional line between topics to let the audience shift gears with you. Remember, they don't know where you're headed.

The typical presentation follows a pattern made up of the components shown in Figure 15–1, although the number of slides and their content will vary depending on the speaker's topic. The complete presentation for the savings and investment program is shown in Figure 15–2. Note the conciseness and layout of the language and visuals.

Organizing a Presentation

- [ ] When preparing a presentation, follow the same guidelines that you follow for writing.
- [ ] Use a logical structure based on that of the written essay: Include an introduction, a body, and a conclusion.
- [ ] Be clear and direct, and use precise nouns.
- [ ] Support your presentation with specific examples.
- [ ] Between subtopics, use transitions to help your listeners understand how the parts are related.

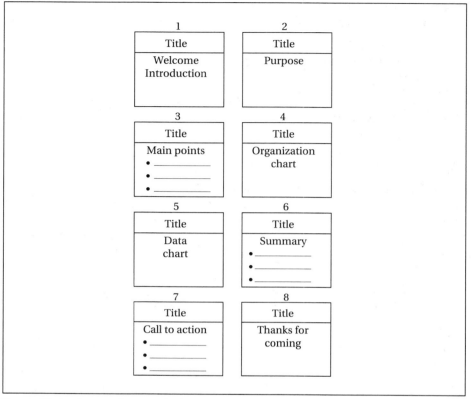

Model presentation pattern: introduce key content; support it with data; summarize content; end with a call to action

Figure 15–1   Pattern for a Typical Presentation

Cover slide for presentation information— who, what, when

Figure 15–2   Sample Presentation (continued)

Savings and Investment Program

Saving for Your Future

This slide show will explain our options for contributing to the employee savings plan through payroll deductions.

Acme Corporation considers this program a long-term retirement-oriented plan. It is intended to enhance your retirement security above the level of your pension and Social Security benefits.

-1-

Introductory slide with overview of topic and attention-getting statement

Acme Corporation
Savings and Investment Program

Questions to Ask Yourself

- How much can I save?
- How much does Acme Corporation contribute?
- What are my investment options?

-2-

Rhetorical questions to pique audience interest and announce organization of information

Acme Corporation
Savings and Investment Program

How Much Can I Save?

- Save from 2% to 20% of your gross earnings
- Elect to save on the following basis:
  - Pre-tax basis
  - After-tax basis
  - Combination of both

-3-

Response to first question

Figure 15–2   Sample Presentation (continued)

Acme Corporation
Savings and Investment Program

How Much Does Acme Corporation Contribute?

- Acme Corporation matches 25¢ of every dollar you save each month!
- Example based on earning $2,000 per month.

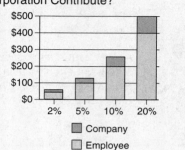

-4-

Acme Corporation
Savings and Investment Program

What Are My Investment Options?

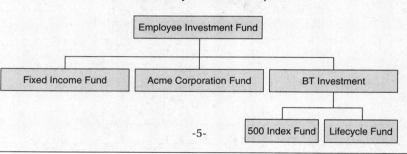

-5-

Acme Corporation
Savings and Investment Program

The Next Step to Your Future Security

- Decide how much you can save each month.
- Remember Acme's contribution.
- Choose the investment options that best fit your needs.
- ENROLL NEXT WEEK!

-6-

Figure 15–2   Sample Presentation (continued)

> ## Acme Corporation
> ## Thank You for Coming
> ___
> Your Future Is Important to Us
>
> - Consider your options.
> - Enroll next week.
> - Questions? Call or e-mail the Benefits Office:
>   - (301) 990-1200, extension 03
>   - E-mail: benefits@acme.com
>
> -7-

Instructions for response to call to action

Figure 15–2   Sample Presentation (continued)

Using Visual Aids

Well-planned visual aids can clarify and simplify your message because they communicate clearly, quickly, and vividly. They are also attention-getters that help retain audience interest. Charts, graphs, and illustrations greatly increase audience understanding and retention of the information, especially for complex issues and technical information that could otherwise be misunderstood or glossed over by your audience. A bar graph, pie chart, diagram, or concise summary of key points can eliminate misunderstanding and save many words. (Use the guidelines for preparing visuals discussed in Chapter 8.) Note that visuals in presentations require titles; however, they generally do not need figure or table numbers because the presenter refers to them in the proper sequence during the presentation.

You can create and present your visual aids in a variety of media, including computer-presentation software; flip charts, whiteboards, and chalkboards; overhead transparencies; 35mm slides; and handouts.

Using Presentation Software

Visual information in workplace presentations is frequently displayed on computer monitors, for a small audience, or by projectors connected to a laptop computer that display the computer screen, for larger audiences (Figure 15–3). Presentation software, such as PowerPoint, Corel Presentations, Freelance Graphics, and other packages, permits you simultaneously to write your presentation and to create slides. This software also allows you to import content, charts, and graphs from other files, and to format your presentation using standard templates and other aids that help you design effective visuals. These enhancements include a selection of layouts, typefaces, background textures and colors, and clip-art images. Avoid using too many enhancements, however, because they could distract

Laptop computer, projector, and pull-down screen

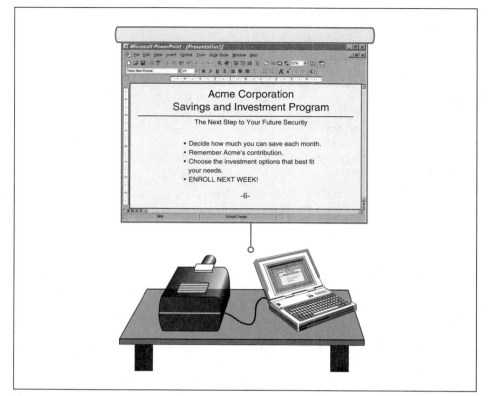

Figure 15–3   Computer-Presentation Setup

viewers from your message. (Figure 15–4 presents an example of a slide showing a bulleted text list and a clip-art image of a prize ribbon.) In addition to helping with the layout, design, and format for your slides, presentation software also permits you to add clip art, sound (including music), and video (such as animation) from outside sources, such as the Internet. You can also convert the presentation to Web format and post it to your company's intranet site, a feature that makes your slides accessible to your colleagues during or after your presentation.

Be sure to integrate your visuals with your presentation when you rehearse. Practice loading the presentation and anticipate any technical difficulties that might arise. Should you encounter a technical snag during the presentation, stay calm and give yourself time to solve the problem. If you can't, say so and move on. As a backup, carry a copy of your electronic presentation printed out as transparencies in case there's a problem with the computer projection system. Also carry an extra copy of your presentation on a disk for backup.

Using Flip Charts, Whiteboards, and Chalkboards

Flip charts are large sheets of white paper bound like a tablet and fastened to the top of an easel (Figure 15–5). The presenter writes on the sheets with colored felt-tip pens, usually during the presentation. The charts are ideal for smaller groups

Plain Language Award of the Month

What Are the Criteria for the Award?

Use "Plain Language Principles," such as:

- Common, Everyday Words
- Short Sentences
- Active Voice
- "You" and Other Pronouns (as appropriate)
- Logical Organization
- Easy-to-Read Design Features (lists and tables)

Figure 15–4   Presentation Slide with Bulleted List and Clip Art

in a conference room or a classroom. To avoid distracting your audience by writing as you speak, prepare text and sketches ahead of time on a series of sheets and flip through them during your presentation. Flip charts are also an ideal medium for brainstorming with your audience. You can fill sheet after sheet with ideas, tape them around the walls for everyone to see, and use a clean sheet or sheets to organize the ideas into an outline for follow-up work.

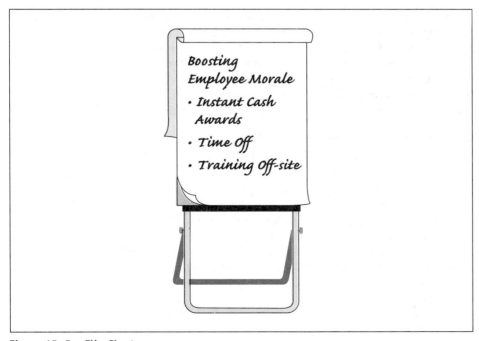

Figure 15–5   Flip Chart

Creating Slides for Presentations

☐ Use text sparingly. Instead of blocks of text, use bulleted or numbered lists and keep them parallel in content and grammatical form. Use numbers if sequence is important and bullets if not.

☐ Limit the number of bulleted or numbered items to five or six per slide. The slide should contain no more than 40 to 45 words. Any more will clutter the slide and force you to use a smaller type size that could impair your audience's ability to read it. (See Figure 15–4.)

☐ Make your slides consistent in typestyle, type size, and spacing.

☐ Use a type size visible to members of the audience in the back of the room. Type should be no smaller than 30 point bold. For headings, 45 or 50 point is even better.

☐ Use graphs and charts rather than tables to show data trends. Use only one or two graphs or charts per slide; otherwise, the data will look cluttered and may be hard to see.

☐ Ensure that the contrast between your text and background is sharp. Use light backgrounds with dark lettering and avoid textured or fancy "wallpaper" backgrounds. (See Figure 15–3.)

☐ Aim for 12 or fewer slides per presentation. More than that will tax any audience's concentration.

☐ Don't read the text on your slides word for word. Instead, summarize the content of the slide and cover salient points in detail.

Whiteboards and chalkboards, common to classrooms, are convenient for creating impromptu sketches and for jotting notes during your presentation. If your presentation requires extensive notes or complex drawings, create them before the presentation to minimize audience restlessness. Ensure before the presentation that you have ample chalk or marking pens and an eraser. If you need to keep ideas that will be erased because you're running out of space, assign someone in the audience to record them for future reference.

Using Overhead Transparencies and Slides

Transparencies are page-sized sheets of clear plastic on which the text and graphics for your presentation are copied, using a computer printer or copy machine. During the presentation, you place the transparencies on an overhead projector (Figure 15–6), and the images are projected onto a screen or blank wall. The images can be black text on clear film to multicolored computer images.

You could, depending on the complexity of the topic, create a series of overlays to cover selected areas and then remove them to reveal the next key point or illustration in the presentation. You can also lay a sheet of paper over a list of bulleted items on a transparency, uncovering one at a time as you discuss it, to focus audience attention on each point in the sequence.

Overhead transparencies are best seen in a darkened room, unlike flip charts and chalkboards or whiteboards, which are best seen in a fully lighted room.

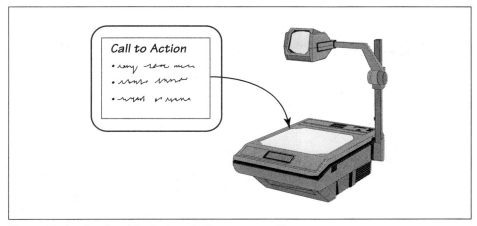

Figure 15–6 Overhead Projector and Transparency Sheet

Slides refer to 2-by-2-inch 35mm film color transparencies inserted into a slide carousel on a slide projector and projected onto a screen or a blank wall. Color transparencies are especially useful if you need to include photographs in your presentation. As with overhead transparencies, they are best viewed in a darkened room. (The individual screens produced using presentation software are also called slides.)

Using Handouts

Handouts typically are paper copies of your presentation slides, although they may be a summary of key points; supporting data in tables, charts, and graphs; or other supplementary information. They benefit you and your audience by reinforcing what is said and by permitting your listeners to take notes and retain the material for future reference. They are usually distributed before the presentation, although some presenters distribute them afterward to avoid having the handouts distract their audience during the presentation.

Delivering Your Presentation

Once you've outlined and drafted your presentation and prepared your visuals, you are ready to think about practice and delivery techniques.

Practicing Your Presentation

Begin by familiarizing yourself with the sequence of the material—major topics, notes, and visuals—in your outline. Once you feel comfortable with the content, you're ready to practice the presentation itself.

Practice on your feet and out loud.   Try to practice in the room where you'll give the presentation. Practicing here will help you learn the idiosyncrasies of the room: acoustics, lighting, how the chairs will most likely be arranged, where the electrical outlets and switches are located, and so forth. Practicing out loud is more effective than just rehearsing mentally because you process the information in your mind many times faster than you can possibly speak it. Rehearsing out loud will make clear exactly how long your presentation will take and will highlight any problems, such as awkward transitions. You can also rehearse to eliminate or reduce verbal tics, such as "um," "you know," and "like."

Practice with your visuals.   Be sure to integrate your slides, transparencies, or other visuals into your practice sessions. This will help your presentation go more smoothly. Operate the equipment (computer, slide projector, or overhead projector) until you're comfortable with it. Even if things go wrong, being prepared and having practiced will give you the confidence and poise to go on. You can also use your visuals as cues to the next point you wish to make.

Videotape your practice session.   Videotape is a very effective and sometimes painful way to catch what you are doing wrong. The tape will reveal how you present your material from the audience's perspective. If you do not have access to a videotape recorder, at the very least use an audiotape recorder to evaluate your vocal presentation. Another effective technique is to ask a friend or colleague watch you rehearse and comment on your delivery.

CONSIDERING AUDIENCE AND PURPOSE

Delivering Your Presentation

☐ Practice out loud and, if possible, in the room where you'll deliver the presentation.

☐ Incorporate your visuals as you practice, using the computer, slide projector, or overhead transparencies.

☐ Videotape or audiotape your practice session and evaluate it critically, or have a colleague or classmate observe and comment.

☐ During the presentation, use eye contact to establish rapport with your audience.

☐ Be animated, moving to the screen to emphasize points and gesturing naturally.

☐ Use your voice to communicate sincerity and enthusiasm, and, above all, do not speak in a monotone. Project your voice so that you're heard by everyone, and pace your delivery so that your words don't run together.

☐ Because the meaning of gestures differs greatly from culture to culture, carefully choose those that you use during presentations.

☐ Practice your presentation in front of colleagues or friends and have them watch for any gestures that could be misinterpreted by your audience.

Using Delivery Techniques That Work

In addition to your words and message, your nonverbal communication can engage and inspire your audience. If you want your audience to share your point of view, show them your enthusiasm for your topic. Your words will have more staying power when you deliver them with physical and vocal animation. Be sure to make eye contact; use movement and gestures; and vary your vocal inflection, pace, and projection.

Make eye contact.   The best way to establish rapport with your audience is with eye contact. For smaller audiences, make eye contact with as many people as possible. In a large audience, directly address those people who seem most responsive to you in different parts of the audience. Address each person separately, and focus your attention on him or her for several seconds before moving on. Doing so helps you establish rapport with your audience by holding their attention. It also gives you important visual cues as to how you're doing. Are people engaged and actively listening? Are they looking around or staring at the floor? These cues may tell you that you need to speed up or slow down the pace of your presentation.

Use movement and gestures.   Animate your presentation with physical movement. The easiest way to integrate movement into your presentation is to step to the screen and point to a visual as you discuss it. Touch the screen with the pointer and turn back to the audience before beginning to speak (touch, turn, and talk). If you are using an overhead projector, you can place the pointer directly on the overhead so that it casts a shadow that points to the appropriate item on the screen. Otherwise, simply take a step or two to one side or to the other after you have been talking for a minute or so. This type of movement is most effective at transitional points in your presentation, between major topics, or after pauses for emphasis. Too much movement, however, can be distracting—so try not to pace or wave your arms. Hand gestures will come more naturally during your presentation if you include them in your practice sessions.

Adjust your vocal inflection, pace, and volume.   Your voice can be an effective tool in communicating your sincerity, enthusiasm, and command of your topic. Use it to your advantage to project your credibility. *Vocal inflection* is the rise and fall of your voice at different times, such as the way your voice naturally rises at the end of a question ("You want it when?"). Keep your audience's attention by using this pattern as you would in a conversation. Do not fall into a monotone speech pattern that can hypnotize your audience and make them drowsy. Vocal variety also allows you to highlight differences between key and subordinate points in your presentation. Using a conversational delivery and making eye contact also promote the feeling among members of the audience that you're addressing each one directly.

Pace is the speed at which you deliver your presentation. If you speak too fast, your words will run together, making it difficult for your audience to follow you. If you speak too slowly, the audience will get impatient and their minds may wander.

Speak up to be heard. If anyone in the audience cannot hear you, your presentation has been ineffective for that person. If the audience has to strain to hear you, they may give up trying to listen. You can correct for these problems by practicing out loud with someone listening from the back of the room.

CONSIDERING AUDIENCE AND PURPOSE

Engaging Your Audience When Speaking

- ☐ Establish rapport and trust by looking into the eyes of as many audience members as possible.
- ☐ Hold the interest of your audience by looking at your notes as little as possible. (Never read directly from your notes.)
- ☐ Deliver your talk from a prepared outline on slides rather than memorizing it word for word. This way, it:
  - ▪ Sounds more natural and less monotonous.
  - ▪ Helps audience attention and comprehension.
  - ▪ Enables more eye contact with your audience, which helps convey your interest in and enthusiasm for the topic.

Dealing with Presentation Anxiety

Everyone experiences nervousness before a presentation. Survey after survey reveals that dread of speaking in front of others ranks among the top five fears for most people. Typical reactions to this stress include shortness of breath, a racing heartbeat, trembling, perspiration, and even nausea. Some people react by clearing their throats repeatedly, tugging at their clothing or earlobes, or moving continuously during the presentation. Instead of letting this stress inhibit you, focus on channeling your nervous energy into a helpful stimulant. That is, if you can't eliminate your stress entirely, manage it. The best way to master this feeling is to know your topic thoroughly. If you know what you are going to say and how you are going to say it, you will gain confidence and reduce anxiety as you become immersed in your subject.

Rehearsing your presentation will help. Do so alone or, if possible, in front of one or more listeners. If you're anxious because you may forget something or get lost during your delivery, you may find it helpful to write out the presentation in full, put it aside, and rehearse using only brief notes. If you falter, refer to your written version. After a practice session, imagine yourself in front of your audience delivering your material point by point. Begin by saying to yourself, "My subject is important. I am ready. My listeners are here to listen to what I have to say." If you cannot remember every point you wish to make during the practice presentation, review your notes or visuals. These will trigger your memory both as you imagine the presentation and when you're actually giving it.

You can use several techniques to quell the butterflies immediately before a presentation. Fill your lungs with a deep breath and hold it for a count of ten. Then exhale and repeat, doing so several times or until you feel your body begin to relax. Tensing and relaxing muscles is another effective stress reducer. Clench both fists tightly and count to ten while inhaling and then exhale. Repeat several times until your stress begins to diminish.

Evaluating Your Presentation

CONSIDERING AUDIENCE AND PURPOSE

☐ Have you analyzed the purpose of your presentation so that it focuses on what your audience should know, believe, or do when they leave?

☐ Do you know the makeup of your audience so that your presentation accommodates their level of knowledge of, experience with, and attitude toward your topic?

☐ Is your presentation structured in the best sequence for an audience of listeners?

☐ Are your presentation's visual aids concise, informative, and visible to everyone in the room?

☐ Have you practiced your presentation so that your delivery is animated, shows mastery of the topic, can be heard by everyone, and is not rushed?

☐ For international audiences, is your presentation free of U.S.-centered idioms, references, and jargon?

Reaching Global Audiences

The prevalence of multinational corporations and multinational trade agreements, the increasing diversity of the U.S. workforce, and even increases in immigration mean that the ability to reach audiences with varied cultural backgrounds will be essential in the years to come. The multicultural audiences for your future presentations may include clients, business partners, colleagues, and current and potential employees and customers of varied backgrounds.

Presentations to global audiences involve special challenges. As with all materials intended for global readers and listeners, keep your language simple and consistent. Don't call something a "ratio" in one place and a "rate" in another. Puns and wordplay may entertain a U.S. audience but will likely confuse foreign listeners. State the main points of your presentation often and in the identical language each time. Follow this guidance whether you are addressing an audience for whom English is a second language or speaking through an interpreter. As you deliver your presentation, speak slowly and deliberately, enunciating clearly and pausing often. Keep in mind the following additional points about delivering presentations:

- Bland is better than colorful. Avoid idioms ("dog and pony show," "barking up the wrong tree"), jargon (emoticons, debugging), and acronyms. They will put an unnecessary impediment between you and your audience.

- Avoid U.S.-centered examples of business, political, or sports figures unless they are essential to your discussion. They will not be understood and, worse, they will suggest to your audience that your perspective about the world is narrowly focused on the United States.

- Do not use the trite sports metaphors that are all too common in U.S. speech (slam dunk, touchdown, home run). They will puzzle your international audience and suggest to them that you are insensitive about their culture and customs.

- Jokes can backfire even with U.S. audiences, so they are especially tricky with foreign audiences. If you think that humor is important to your message, try it out on someone familiar with the languages and cultures of your audience beforehand and revise accordingly.

- With U.S. audiences, maintaining eye contact enhances the speaker's credibility and connectedness with the audience. In some Asian cultures, however, making direct eye contact is seen as an invasion of privacy. For these listeners, try instead to sweep your gaze across them rather than looking at anyone too long.

(For additional information and tips on communicating with multicultural audiences, see Writing International Correspondence, on page 341 in Chapter 9, and Using Graphics to Communicate Internationally, on page 295 in Chapter 8.)

MEETING THE DEADLINE: The Time-Sensitive Presentation

When working under a tight deadline to plan, create, practice, and deliver a presentation, it helps to follow a structured approach—one that will help you work efficiently, reduce anxiety caused by time constraints, and feel confident in what you have to say. As you begin this process, remember that your goal is to create and deliver a presentation that:

- Is appropriate for your audience.
- Fulfills your purpose (to inform or to persuade, for example).
- Is appropriate in scope and to the time frame set for delivery.
- Is logically organized and concise.
- Is visually appealing.

Use the following guidelines to help you plan, create, practice, and deliver a presentation that will satisfy you and your audience while meeting your deadline.

Part I: Planning Your Presentation (45 Minutes)
Focus on each of the following points as you prepare your presentation.

1. *Analyze your audience.* While considering the needs of all of your listeners, concentrate on the key decision-makers in your audience and gear your

presentation toward them. Based on your audience, decide how technical your presentation will be; use language suitable to your listeners' level of expertise, and avoid the use of jargon.

2. *Know the purpose of your presentation.* Think of what you want your audience to know or to do as a result of your presentation. Write a purpose statement just as you would if you were preparing a written document. Your purpose statement should also define the scope of your presentation; it should indicate what you plan to cover—your starting point, your key points, and your closing point. After writing your purpose statement, think about how to introduce your topic, explain your topic, and close with a clear statement to your audience.

3. *Gather your information.* Your presentation probably covers a topic you have already written about in a proposal or report. Organize all relevant information on your topic into one electronic file. If this is not possible, collect hard copies of the materials into a folder.

4. *Plan your delivery time frame.* As you plan and develop your presentation, remember that you will need to get your points across within a set time period. Whether your presentation is scheduled for five minutes or an hour, think of your main points in relation to your time frame—and also in terms of the number of slides you will need.

5. *Structure the content of your presentation.* Outline what you want to say in a logical manner that will achieve your goals and meet the needs of your listeners. As you do this, think of how many slides you will need to convey your message. For a five-minute PowerPoint presentation, you will need no more than five to ten slides. If you decide to work with five slides, plan to discuss these for about a minute each. For ten slides, plan to discuss each for about 30 seconds. Some slides—those covering key points and bene-fits—will require more time than, say, an introductory slide. Consider the following structure:

Slide 1.	Introduce yourself.
Slide 2.	Introduce your topic.
Slide 3.	State your purpose.
Slides 4–6.	State and explain your key points—points that will inform or persuade your audience.
Slides 7 and 8.	Explain how what you propose will benefit your listeners.
Slide 9.	Close by reviewing the most important parts of your pre-sentation. Choose carefully what you want your listeners to remember most.
Slide 10.	Thank your listeners for their attention. Credit outside sources, if necessary, and include your contact information.

Part II. Creating Your Presentation (90 Minutes)

Given your time frame, use your energy wisely when preparing your slides.

- Work within one of PowerPoint's basic templates.
- Create your slides.
- To write your notes simultaneously, work in the Notes Page option, available under View in the menu.
- For each slide, cover no more than five to seven ideas or "bullet points."
- Keep your slides uncluttered and easy to read, even from the back of the room.
- Import existing charts and graphs to your presentation, but don't spend time creating and designing new ones. If time permits, add clip art where appropriate or a tasteful color background. If not, focus on the clear presentation of your content. (*Note:* For visuals you are unable to import but that are important, bring printouts to hand out to your audience.) See Figure 15–7.

What Are the Benefits to Employees?

- Access The Sports Center for $20/month— includes all athletic facilities, whirlpool, and sauna.

- Support of personal trainers or massage therapists, for an additional $15/month.

- Free cholesterol and blood-pressure screening.

- Free nutrition and weight-management counseling.

- Employee incentive "wellness points" that earn discounts on fitness gear and clothing at The Sports Center Shop.

-2-

The "notes" pages of your presentation give you a space in which to expand the ideas of your slide with concrete details

The Healthy Life Program offers your employees one of the best and most affordable wellness packages available nationwide. For modest monthly fees, your employees can become members of The Sports Center and Day Spa, a facility that won the "Best of Chicago" award in 2002, and that was recently rated #1 by *In-Shape Magazine*. Here they can enjoy numerous benefits that include not only a generous offering of classes such as aerobics, spinning, kickboxing, Pilates, and yoga, all taught by top-notch instructors—but they will also enjoy the support of the highly qualified personal trainers, nutrition counselors, and health-care professionals on staff. We do all we can to make sure our members approach exercise, diet, and lifestyle change safely and sensibly.

Figure 15–7 **Notes Page of a PowerPoint Presentation**

- Once your slides are complete, work within the Notes Page (under View in your menu bar) to write the text of your presentation. You can later print out your notes for practice or for reference if you need them when delivering your presentation.

- Preview and evaluate your slides by selecting Slide Sorter (under View in your menu bar). Edit, rearrange, delete, or add to slides and visuals as needed. See Figure 15–8.

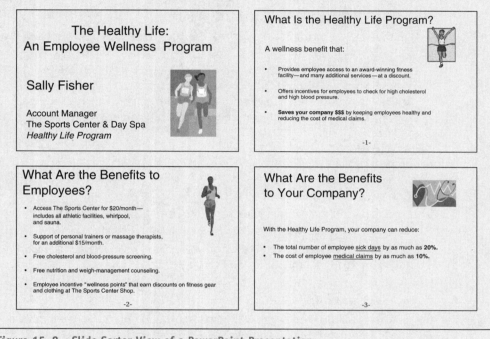

The "slide-sorter" view allows you to evaluate the structure of your presentation

Figure 15–8   Slide Sorter View of a PowerPoint Presentation

Part III. Practicing and Delivering Your Presentation (45 Minutes)

Keep the following points in mind while practicing and delivering your presentation.

- Speak energetically. Energy is the most important quality that you bring to your delivery. By this point, you are in command of your topic, your goals, and what you want to say. Let your enthusiasm come across in your voice and gestures. Conveying your authentic excitement will energize your listeners and help persuade them to consider what you propose.

- Avoid memorizing your presentation. A spontaneous delivery will be more credible and engaging to your audience. However, don't let spontaneity distract you from conveying your main points.

- As needed, refer to your slides during your presentation. However, don't read them word for word—what you say should provide detail and depth to what appears on the screen.
- Know what you want to say about each slide. If necessary, refer to the notes you created when you developed your slides. You can tape notes for each slide onto index cards for a less intrusive way to check them during the presentation.
- Make eye contact by picking out the friendly faces in the room and connecting with them from time to time.
- Use vocal inflection to emphasize key points.
- Breathe deeply. Bringing oxygen to the brain keeps you composed and mentally sharp and helps you to speak slowly and more clearly.
- Do not be upset if you say the wrong word, refer to the wrong visual, or otherwise do something unplanned. Simply take a deep breath, correct your mistake, and move forward. Do not refer to your mistake unless you must—chances are that the audience will think you are moving according to plan.

Before you give your presentation:

1. Practice your delivery at least three times.
2. Time yourself and make any necessary adjustments. If you edit your presentation at this point, practice it again at least twice.
3. Use your time constructively. If you find yourself worrying, practice again or mentally run through your slides and key points.
4. The night before your presentation, choose and prepare attire that is appropriate and professional.
5. Try to visit the room where you will be presenting beforehand, preferably a day ahead of time. If this is not possible, arrive at least 45 minutes before your presentation. Check out the presentation equipment—making sure it is in good working order and that you know how to operate it. Evaluate the setup of the room, the lighting, and the temperature, and make any necessary adjustments.

■ Listening

Active listening enables the listener to understand and then implement the instructions of a teacher, the goals of a manager, and the needs and wants of customers. It also lays the foundation for good interpersonal communication and cooperation between colleagues and members of work teams.

For communication to occur, there must be a message, a sender of the message, and a receiver of the message. At the most basic level, this model of how communication takes place works best when the sender (the speaker) and the receiver (the listener) each focus on and clearly understand the content of the message.

Because the speaker's background or cultural frame of reference may differ from the listener's, the listener needs to make sure he or she understands the message. The message may also be blocked by noise, lack of attention on the part of the listener, or impaired hearing. To the extent possible, the listener should block out distractions to focus on the message.

The listener then evaluates the message by separating fact from opinion and gauging the quality of the information in the message. The listener must be careful, however, not to dismiss the message because he or she doesn't like the speaker or because the speaker is wearing distracting clothing. Nor must the listener let preconceptions or personal biases get in the way of effectively interpreting the message.

Finally, the listener may need to respond to satisfy the speaker that the listener has understood. Accurate interpretation requires conscious effort, as well as a willingness to respond rather than simply react. A responder is a listener who can slow the communication down, if necessary, to be certain that he or she is accurately receiving the message sent by the speaker. To slow the communication down, the listener could clarify his or her understanding by asking for more information or by paraphrasing the message before offering thoughts, opinions, or recommendations. A reactor simply says the first thing that comes to mind based on limited information and might easily leave the conversation with an inaccurate version of the message.

If you are the speaker, organize and present your message logically and succinctly. The information throughout this book about understanding your audience, organizing information, and composing clear and succinct sentences will help you communicate such messages.

Fallacies about Listening

Listening is our most-used skill. Yet it is the skill we concentrate on least in our education and training, know the least about, and take most for granted. This is probably why most of us accept two fallacies about listening: (1) that hearing and listening are the same, and (2) that words mean the same to everyone.

Are Hearing and Listening the Same?

Most people assume that because they can *hear*, they know how to *listen*. In fact, listening is a skill that deserves development, just as reading, writing, and speaking do. The most basic distinction between hearing and listening is that hearing is passive and listening is active. Voices in a crowd, a ringing telephone, or a door being slammed are sounds that require no analysis, no active involvement of any kind. We hear such sounds without choosing to listen to them—we have no choice but to hear them. This kind of hearing is completely passive. Listening, however, requires effort and skill and involves related activities: interpreting the message and evaluating its value to the listener.

Do Words Mean the Same to Everyone?

Words seldom have absolute meanings—they can have multiple meanings that are determined by the context in which they are used. Meaning may be affected by the speaker's culture, education, occupation, or other factors, such as the speaker's use of idioms. The context is especially important when communicating with an international audience. Idiomatic expressions in American English cause confusion because their literal meaning is not understandable. Expressions such as "run for office" or "put up with" may not be at all clear to a non-native speaker of English. (For tips on idioms commonly used in business, see pages 751–753 in the Writer's Handbook, Section C: English as a Second Language.) Jargon, which abounds in all occupations, also creates ambiguities. A "wiki" and a "blog" make as little sense outside of an Internet context as "blue chip" and "bear market" do outside of discussions about financial markets. Homonyms—words that sound alike but differ in meaning—can also confuse non-native speakers. Such an audience will likely struggle to make distinctions between such spoken words as *brake/break*, *bear/bare*, and *sight/site/cite*. (See Section B, Spelling and Vocabulary, in the Writer's Handbook, pages 731–735, for a more complete listing of homonyms.)

Steps to More Effective Listening

To listen more effectively on the job, you should (1) consciously decide to do so, (2) take specific actions to listen more efficiently, (3) define your purpose for listening, and (4) adapt to the situation.

Make a Conscious Decision

The first step to effective listening is simply making up your mind to do so. Effective listening requires conscious effort, something that does not come naturally. Seek first to understand and then to be understood. If you follow this rule, you may find it easier to take the steps or the time required to ensure that you are indeed exerting a conscious effort to listen effectively.

Take Specific Actions

Three conscious activities will help you retain information: (1) rephrase in your own words what the speaker said, (2) demonstrate verbal and nonverbal empathy for the speaker, and (3) take notes to help you remember the message.

Your paraphrase of the message should be concise and focus on the main point or points. Paraphrasing lets the speaker know that you are listening, gives the speaker an opportunity to clear up any misunderstanding, keeps you focused, and helps you remember the discussion.

Empathy is listening in a way that puts you in the speaker's position or helps you look at things from the speaker's perspective. It means trying to understand the speaker's feelings, wants, and needs—trying to appreciate his or her point of view. When people feel they are being listened to, they tend to respond with appreciation and cooperation. Empathy by the listener can begin a mutually beneficial chain reaction—empathetic listening encourages better communication.

Taking notes while you are listening provides several benefits. It helps you stay focused on what the speaker is saying, especially during a presentation or lecture. It helps you remember what you've heard because you reinforce the message by writing it. (You can also check the notes at a later date, when you need to recall what was said.) Finally, it communicates to the speaker that you are listening and that you are interested in what he or she is saying.

Define Your Purpose

To listen effectively, you must know *why* you're listening. Focusing on your purpose will help manage the most common problems people have with listening: drifting attention, formulating a response while the speaker is still talking, and interrupting the speaker. When you know a situation will require active listening, take the time to focus on the following questions:

- What kind of information do I hope to get from this conversation or meeting?
- How will this information benefit me?
- What kind of message do I want to send while I'm listening (understanding, determination, flexibility, competence, patience)?
- Do I foresee any problems—boredom, wandering attention, anger, impatience? How can I keep these problems from preventing me from listening effectively?

Listening Effectively

CONSIDERING
AUDIENCE
AND PURPOSE

- ☐ Make a conscious decision to become a better listener.
- ☐ Define your purpose for listening in a given situation:
  - ■ What kind of information do I want from this exchange?
  - ■ How can I use this information?
- ☐ Block out background distractions to focus on the message.
- ☐ Screen out personal biases or preconceptions that may hinder an impartial evaluation of the message.
- ☐ Slow down the speaker by asking for more information or by paraphrasing the message before responding to the speaker.
- ☐ Take notes to help stay focused on what the speaker is saying.
- ☐ Adapt to the situation.

Adapt to the Situation

Listening at peak efficiency at all times is not necessary. When someone stops you in the hall for an idle conversation, you may legitimately listen without giving the conversation your full attention. Even during a lecture, you may be listening for specific information only. However, if you are on a team project where the success of the project depends on everyone's contribution, listening efficiently will enable you to gather information important to the project as well as other nuances, such as the ongoing relationships among team members.

■ Conducting Productive Meetings

A meeting is a face-to-face exchange among a group of people who have come together for a common purpose—to make a contribution to a collective effort. A meeting requires planning and preparation, just as writing and oral presentations do.

Planning a Meeting

Planning an effective meeting consists of determining the focus of the meeting, who should attend, and the best time and place to hold the meeting. You also need to prepare an agenda for the meeting and determine who should record decisions made during the meeting.

What Is the Purpose of the Meeting?

The first step in planning a meeting is to focus on your desired outcome. To do so, ask yourself what those attending want *to know*, *to believe*, or *to do* as a result of attending the meeting. Suppose you called a meeting of your sales staff to design a sales campaign for a new scanner that will result in a successful launching of the product. In response to the questions above, you could jot down the following answers:

- As a result of this meeting:
  - I want the salespeople *to know* that this is an outstanding scanner that can increase their sales considerably.
  - I want the salespeople *to believe* that this is the best scanner on the market and that their customers want it.
  - I want the salespeople *to offer* their ideas for the sales campaign.

Once you focus on your desired outcome, use the information to write a *purpose statement* for the meeting that answers the questions *what* and *why*.

- The purpose of this meeting is to gather ideas from the sales force [*what*] that will create an effective sales campaign for our new scanner [*why*].

Who Should Attend?

Invite only those to the meeting who can contribute to fulfilling your planned outcome. If a meeting must be held without some key participants, e-mail the agenda to them prior to the meeting and ask for any contributions they would like to make. If employees from regional offices or other geographic locations need to participate, they can do so by speakerphone. Before the meeting, send them the agenda and the number of the speakerphone in the conference room. Circulate the meeting minutes to everyone, including those who could not attend, following the meeting.

When Should It Be Held?

The time of day and the length of the meeting can affect its outcome. Consider the following when planning your meeting:

- People need Monday morning to focus on work after being off for two days.
- People need Friday afternoon to wrap up the week and take care of anything that must be finished before the week ends.
- During the hour following lunch, most people fall victim to a condition called *postprandial letdown*, which is the body's natural need to regroup after a meal.
- Meetings scheduled to last longer than two hours should include adequate breaks so attendees can check their messages, make important phone calls, and refresh themselves.
- You can be assured of a quick meeting during the last 15 minutes of the day—but it is likely that no one will remember what went on.

Finally, schedule the meeting at a time convenient to those participating remotely by speakerphone who are in different time zones.

Where Should It Be Held?

Having a meeting in your office or conference room can give you an advantage. You feel more comfortable, and your guests' newness to the surroundings may give you an edge. Agreeing to hold the meeting at their location, however, signals your cooperation. For balance, especially for first-time gatherings, meet at a neutral site, such as at an off-site conference center. That way, no one has a distinct advantage and attendees often feel freer to participate.

What's on the Agenda?

A tool for focusing the participants, the agenda is an outline of the issues the meeting will address. Never begin a meeting without an agenda, even if it is only a handwritten list of topics you want to cover. Distribute the agenda a day or two before the meeting so that those attending have time to prepare or gather the necessary materials. For a longer meeting in which participants will make a presentation or need to be prepared to discuss an issue in detail, try to distribute the agenda a week or more in advance. If there is no time to distribute the agenda early, however, be sure to distribute it at the beginning of the meeting.

The agenda should cover only a few major items: the names of attendees, the time and place of the meeting, and the topics to be discussed. If there are people presenting material, the agenda should indicate the amount of time allotted for each speaker. Finally, the agenda should indicate the start and stop times for the meeting so that participants can plan the rest of their day. Figure 15–9 shows a sample agenda.

If distributed in advance of the meeting, the agenda should be accompanied by a memo or an e-mail message that invites people to the meeting. The message should include the following:

- The purpose of the meeting. Everyone should know not only exactly why this meeting is being held but also what you hope to accomplish.
- The meeting start and stop time. People need to know how to budget their time. A word of warning: When you advertise an ending time for the meeting, be sure to end it on time unless everyone agrees to extend the meeting beyond the promised stop time.
- The date and place.
- The names of the people invited. Knowing the names of everyone who will be attending often has an effect on how people prepare for the meeting.

<table>
<tr><td colspan="3" align="center">Sales-Meeting Agenda</td></tr>
<tr><td>Purpose:</td><td colspan="2">To Get Input for a Sales Campaign for the New Scanner</td></tr>
<tr><td>Date:</td><td colspan="2">January 27, 2003</td></tr>
<tr><td>Place:</td><td colspan="2">Conference Room 15-C</td></tr>
<tr><td>Time:</td><td colspan="2">8:00–9:30</td></tr>
<tr><td>Attendees:</td><td colspan="2">Sales Force</td></tr>
<tr><td>Topic</td><td>Presenter</td><td>Time</td></tr>
<tr><td>The Scanner</td><td>Bob Arbuckle</td><td>Presentation, 8:00–8:15</td></tr>
<tr><td>The Sales Strategy</td><td>Mary Winifred</td><td>Presentation, 8:15–8:30</td></tr>
<tr><td>The Campaign</td><td>Maria Lopez</td><td>Presentation, 8:30–8:45</td></tr>
<tr><td>Discussion</td><td>Led by Dave Grimes</td><td>Presentation, 8:45–9:30</td></tr>
</table>

What, where, when, who details

Topics of meeting, presenters, and periods scheduled

Figure 15–9   Meeting Agenda

- Instructions on how to prepare for the meeting. Different participants may need to prepare differently, so tell them collectively and individually how to get ready for the meeting.

Figure 15–10 shows an e-mail transmitting a meeting agenda.

Subject:	Planning Meeting
Date:	Tues, 06 May 2003 13:30:12 EST
From:	Susan McLaughlin <smclaughlin@millenniumsoftware.com>
To:	**New Products Advertising Managers; Equipment Sales Representatives; Customer Service Staff; Service Managers**
Attachments:	ℓ Sales Meeting Agenda.doc (29 KB)

Purpose of the Meeting

The purpose of this meeting is to get your ideas for the upcoming introduction and sales campaign for our new software.

Date, Time, and Location

Date:	May 12, 2003
Time:	9:30 a.m.–11:00 a.m.
Place:	Conference Room E (go to the ground floor, take a right off the elevator, third door on the left)

Attendees

The groups addressed above.

Meeting Preparation

Everyone should be prepared to offer suggestions on the following items:

- Sales features of the new software
- Techniques for selling software
- Customer profile for potential business
- FAQs--questions customers may ask
- Anticipated service needs

Agenda

Please see the attached document.

E-mail announcing what, when, who, where; transmitting agenda (attached) and preparation instructions

Figure 15–10   E-mail Transmitting an Agenda

Who Should Take Minutes?

Delegate the minute-taking to someone other than the meeting leader. The minute-taker records major decisions made and tasks assigned. To avoid misunderstandings, the minute-taker must record each assignment, the person responsible for it, and the date on which it is due. For a standing committee, either rotate responsibility for taking minutes or assign someone permanently to the task.

Attending Meetings

☐ Be punctual. When attending a meeting, always arrive several minutes early. Being aware of time shows that you acknowledge the value of another person's time.

☐ Be attentive. If you are new to the organization, spend time listening and observing, but do speak.

☐ Meetings are considered an opportunity for everyone to share ideas; share yours even if they differ from those expressed by other attendees.

☐ Feel comfortable responding as your ideas come to you. Also, because meetings are considered a place for brainstorming, don't be too concerned about expressing your thoughts in complete sentences or in perfect grammatical form.

Conducting a Meeting

To conduct a successful meeting, follow your agenda—the topics that must be covered and the outcomes that you wish—and ensure that you have invited the right people with the necessary information. Equally important, keep in mind how the personalities of those attending a meeting may affect its success. Members of any group are likely to vary greatly in their personalities and attitudes. Most of the time you need only be tactful and diplomatic in your dealings with everyone in attendance, and the meeting will go well. Begin by setting an example for the group by listening carefully and by encouraging participants to listen to each other. (Review the section about listening earlier in this chapter.) To create an environment in which people listen to each other, adopt a "you" attitude by being considerate of other people's points of view.

1. Seek first to understand and then to be understood. Consider the feelings, thoughts, ideas, and needs of others; don't ignore other points of view.
2. Make others feel valued and respected by listening to them and commenting on their statements.
3. Respond positively to the comments of others as best you can.
4. Widen your acceptance level of new thoughts, different ways of doing things, and the differences between you and other people (particularly people from other cultures).

Be aware, however, that members of any group vary greatly in their personalities and attitudes. Despite your best efforts, it's not uncommon to encounter people whose personalities hinder effective communication during the meeting. The following guidelines should help you to deal with these potential impediments and keep the group's focus on successfully working through the agenda.

- *The Interruptive Person.* An interruptive person rarely lets anyone finish a sentence and can intimidate the group's quieter members, undermining the effectiveness of the group. When such a person begins to be detrimental to the group, tell him or her in a firm but nonhostile tone to let the others finish what they are saying in the interest of getting everyone's best thinking. By addressing the issue directly, you signal to the group the importance of putting its common goals first.

- *The Negative Person.* A negative person generally has difficulty accepting change and will often oppose a new idea or project. If left unchecked, this attitude can demoralize the group as a whole. Of course, not all negative views are invalid. As long as the negative person is making valid points, ask the group for its suggestions as to how to remedy the issues being raised. When these issues are outside the agenda of the meeting in progress, announce that you will schedule a separate meeting to see that the issues are addressed. Then move the meeting to the next item on the agenda. If the person's points are not valid, you may need to schedule a separate meeting with this person to sort out any misunderstandings.

- *The Rambling Person.* The rambling person cannot collect his or her thoughts quickly enough to state them succinctly. It's easy for the group to become impatient with such people and try to finish their sentences for them. Although a rambling person has trouble saying what he or she means, this doesn't mean that the thoughts are of no value. You can actively help by restating or clarifying the ideas. Quite often, the person will nod in agreement, and you can move on. Try to strike a balance between providing your own interpretation and drawing out the person's intended meaning.

- *The Quiet Person.* A quiet person may be reluctant to speak in a group setting or may be deep in thought. Your job, however, is to get everyone's best thinking, regardless of how disinclined a person is to share it. Instead of putting the person on the spot by asking directly what he or she thinks, try indirect prompting instead. You could go around the table asking everyone by name if they have any thoughts on an issue, being careful to not begin the questioning with the quiet person. This gives such a person time to collect his or her thoughts. If this approach fails, ask such a person *before the meeting* to jot down his or her thoughts for use during the meeting.

- *The Territorial Person.* The territorial person fiercely defends his or her group against all threats—real and perceived. This narrow focus can polarize a meeting by driving others to protect their own territories at the cost of pursuing the organization's goals. To deal with this situation, point out that although the individual's territorial concerns may be valid, everyone is working for the same organization and its overall goals take precedence.

Dealing with Conflict

Conflict—which can arise because of differences over issues on the agenda—is potentially valuable. When viewed positively, conflict can stimulate creative thinking, as when a person or an organization is challenged out of its complacency to achieve its goals in ways that are more efficient or economical than formerly.

Try to deal with conflict so that its benefits are retained and its negative effects are minimized. First, be sure that those involved in the conflict are aware of any areas of agreement, and emphasize these areas to establish common ground. Then identify any differences and ask why they exist. If the facts being discussed about two sides of an issue differ, determine which are correct. If the goals differ, encourage each party to try to look at the problem from the other person's point of view. You can take any of a number of approaches to resolve a conflict, including the following:

- *Noncombative tactics.* This approach involves avoiding accusations, threats, or disparaging comments and emphasizes common interests and mutual goals. You reward conciliatory acts by praising them and reciprocating, and you express a desire for harmonious relations. This can have a very disarming effect on an aggressive person.

- *Persuasion.* You could try to use persuasion to convince the other party to accept your point of view. How successful this is likely to be will depend on your credibility with the other person and his or her willingness to consider your views. Provide facts or previous practices to support your position. Point out how your position benefits the other person (if true). Show how your position is consistent with precedent, prevailing norms, or accepted standards. Tactfully point out any overlooked costs, any disadvantages, or any errors in logic in the other party's point of view.

- *Bargaining.* You could exchange concessions until a compromise is reached. Compromising means settling for half a victory rather than risking an all-out win-or-lose struggle. A compromise must provide each side with enough benefits to satisfy minimal needs.

- *Collaborating.* This approach means that each side accepts the other's goal as well as his or her own, and works to achieve the best outcome for both sides. This could be called a win-win approach. Each side must understand the other's point of view and discover the needs that must be satisfied. A flexible, exploratory attitude is a prerequisite for collaboration. Trust must be high, but collaborating to resolve conflict often leads to very creative results. Define the problem, then define alternative solutions, and then select the one that provides both sides with the most benefits.

Making a Record of Decisions and Assignments

Regardless of whether meeting minutes are necessary, it is important to record major decisions that the group makes as well as any assignments for follow-up work. (Meeting minutes are discussed on pages 551–554.) Each assignment is usually given a due date—the date by which the assignment must be completed. Be sure that the person taking these notes records each assignment, the person responsible for it, and the date on which it is due.

At a meeting, the preferable way to record decisions and assignments is to allow everyone present to see what's written. Flip charts are commonly used for this purpose (see Figure 15–5). Information on the charts can be revised for clarity later and distributed to those who attended. Another option is to use a laptop computer to record decisions and assignments and to have these notes projected on a screen so that participants can see what is being recorded. The electronic document can be revised for clarity and distributed to all attendees by e-mail or on paper. It can also serve as the basis for official meeting minutes.

Closing the Meeting

Just before closing the meeting, review all decisions and assignments by having the minute-taker read them aloud. Doing so helps the group focus on what they have collectively agreed to do. This process also allows for any questions to be raised or misunderstandings to be clarified and promotes everyone's agreement about their decisions. Set a date by which everyone at the meeting can expect to receive minutes of this meeting. Finally, thank everyone for their participation and close the meeting on a positive note.

Planning and Conducting Meetings

CONSIDERING
AUDIENCE
AND PURPOSE

- ☐ Call a meeting to address a specific need; develop a purpose statement to focus your thoughts.
- ☐ Determine who should attend; invite only those essential to fulfilling the purpose of the meeting.
- ☐ Select a meeting time and place convenient to all attendees.
- ☐ Create an agenda and distribute it a day or two before the meeting.
- ☐ Assign someone to take notes and make clear what they should include.
- ☐ Follow the agenda to keep everyone focused on the purpose of the meeting and the time available.
- ☐ Be respectful of the views of others and their ways of expressing those views.
- ☐ Review the strategies in this chapter for dealing with attendees whose style of expression in some way prevents your getting everyone's best thinking.
- ☐ Deal with conflict positively to maximize its benefits.
- ☐ Ensure that meeting minutes record major decisions, assignments, and other due dates, and, if necessary, the date, time, and location of a follow-up meeting.
- ☐ Close the meeting by reviewing all decisions and assignments so that attendees collectively agree to them.

Taking Minutes of a Meeting

Many organizations and committees keep official records of their meetings; such records are known as *minutes* and are taken by someone designated before the meeting to do so. Usually called a recording secretary, this person writes and distributes the minutes before the next meeting. At the beginning of each meeting, those attending vote to accept the minutes from the previous meeting as prepared or to revise or clarify specific items.

Because minutes are often used to settle disputes, they must be accurate, complete, and clear. When approved, minutes become the official record of decisions made at the meeting and can be used as evidence in legal proceedings.

If you are assigned to write minutes, keep them brief and to the point. Give complete information on each topic, but do not ramble—conclude the topic and go on to the next one. Following a set format, such as that shown in Figure 15–11, will help you to keep the minutes concise.

Keep abstractions and generalities to a minimum and, most important, be specific. If you are referring to a nursing station on the second floor of a hospital, say "the nursing station on the second floor," not simply "the second floor."

Remember that meeting minutes may be used, at some time in the future, by a lawyer, a judge, or a jury who probably won't be familiar with the situation you are describing—and that you may not be available to explain what you wrote or you may not remember any of the details of the situation. After all, the reason for taking minutes is to create a permanent record that will be available should it be needed.

The minutes must list all meeting attendees, so, unless you know everyone there, circulate a lined sheet of paper at the beginning of the meeting so that people can write their names and titles or organizations for you to incorporate

WRITER'S CHECKLIST

Writing Minutes of Meetings

Include the following information in meeting minutes:

- ☐ The name of the group or committee holding the meeting
- ☐ The topic of the meeting
- ☐ The kind of meeting (a regular meeting or a special meeting called to discuss a specific subject or problem)
- ☐ Names of attendees and their titles or organizations
- ☐ The place, time, and date of the meeting
- ☐ A statement that the chair and the secretary were present or the names of any substitutes
- ☐ A statement that the minutes of the previous meeting were approved or revised
- ☐ A list of any reports that were read and approved
- ☐ All the main motions that were made, with statements as to whether they were carried, defeated, or tabled (vote postponed), and the names of those who made and seconded the motions (motions that were withdrawn are not mentioned)
- ☐ A full description of resolutions that were adopted and a simple statement of any that were rejected
- ☐ A record of all ballots with the number of votes cast for and against resolutions
- ☐ The time the meeting was adjourned (officially ended) and the place, time, and date of the next meeting, if any
- ☐ The recording secretary's signature and typed name, and, if desired, the signature of the chairperson

WARETON MEDICAL CENTER
DEPARTMENT OF MEDICINE

Minutes of the Monthly Meeting of the Credentials Committee

DATE: April 18, 2003

PRESENT: M. Valden (Chairperson), R. Baron, M. Frank, J. Guern, L. Kingston,
          L. Kinslow (Secretary), S. Perry, B. Roman, J. Sorder, F. Sugihana

Meeting attendees

Dr. Mary Valden called the meeting to order at 8:40 p.m. The minutes of the previous meeting were unanimously approved, with the following correction: the
secretary of the Department of Medicine is to be changed from Dr. Juanita Alvarez
to Dr. Barbara Golden.

Meeting opening time and clarification and accep- tance of previous minutes

Old Business

None.

New Business

The request by Dr. Henry Russell for staff privileges in the Department of Medicine
was discussed. Dr. James Guern made a motion that Dr. Russell be granted staff
privileges. Dr. Martin Frank seconded the motion, which passed unanimously.

Similar requests by Dr. Ernest Hiram and Dr. Helen Redlands were discussed. Dr.
Fred Sugihana made a motion that both physicians be granted all staff privileges
except respiratory-care privileges because the two physicians had not had a sufficient number of respiratory cases. Dr. Steven Perry seconded the motion, which
passed unanimously.

Terse cover- age of topics and decisions

Dr. John Sorder and Dr. Barry Roman asked for a clarification of general duties for
active staff members with respiratory-care privileges. Dr. Richard Baron stated that
he would present a clarification at the next scheduled staff meeting, on May 15.

Dr. Baron asked for a volunteer to fill the existing vacancy for Emergency Room
duty. Dr. Guern volunteered. He and Dr. Baron will arrange a duty schedule.

There being no further business, the meeting was adjourned at 9:15 p.m. The next
regular meeting is scheduled for May 15, at 8:40 p.m.

Meeting ad- journment time

Respectfully submitted,

Leslie Kinslow   *Mary Valden*

Leslie Kinslow   Mary Valden, M.D.
Medical Staff Secretary   Chairperson

Signatures of minute-taker and com- mittee chairperson

Figure 15–11   Minutes of a Monthly Meeting

into the minutes. Be specific when you refer to people. Instead of using titles ("the chief of the Marketing Division") use names and titles ("Florence Johnson, chief of the Marketing Division"). If a member of the committee is to report to the committee at its next meeting, state the member's name and the topic so that there is no uncertainty about the assignment and who is responsible for it. Be consistent in the way you refer to people. Do not call one person Mr. Jarrell and another Janet Wilson. It may be unintentional, but a lack of consistency in titles or names may imply a deference to one person at the expense of another. Minutes should always be objective and impartial.

When you have been assigned to take the minutes at a meeting, go adequately prepared. A laptop computer is an ideal tool for this task. If you handwrite the minutes, bring more than one pen and plenty of paper. If it is convenient, you may bring a tape recorder as backup to your notes. Bring the minutes of the previous meeting and any other material that you may need. Take memory-jogging notes during the meeting and then expand them with the appropriate details immediately after the meeting. Remember that minutes are primarily a record of specific actions taken, although you may sometimes need to summarize what was said or state the essential ideas in your own words.

CHAPTER 15 SUMMARY: Giving Presentations and Conducting Meetings

In planning a presentation, ask the following questions:

- ☐ What is my purpose?
- ☐ Who is my audience?
- ☐ What amount of information should I prepare to adequately cover the topic for my audience in the time available?

In preparing the presentation:

- ☐ Gather the needed information.
- ☐ Decide how to organize the information.
- ☐ Structure the presentation around this organization.
- ☐ Decide on the types of visuals you will need.

In rehearsing your presentation:

- ☐ Become familiar with your presentation.
- ☐ Practice on your feet, out loud, and with your visuals.
- ☐ Videotape your practice sessions, if possible, and review the video for posture, gestures, and voice, as well as for content.
- ☐ Try to rehearse in the room where the presentation will take place to familiarize yourself with its layout.

When delivering the presentation:

- ☐ Remember that nervousness before a presentation is normal.
- ☐ Show enthusiasm for your topic through the effective use of movement, eye contact, gestures, and your voice.

To maximize your effectiveness as a listener:

- ☐ Adapt your level of concentration to the situation.
- ☐ Take the time to understand what the speaker is saying before speaking yourself.
- ☐ Acknowledge the speaker through questions and gestures.
- ☐ Define what you need or hope to take away from listening to someone else.
- ☐ Consciously work to control yourself from letting boredom, distractions, anger, or other impediments affect you.

In conducting effective meetings:

- ☐ Determine the purpose of the meeting.
- ☐ Decide who should be invited.
- ☐ Determine the best time and place for the meeting.
- ☐ Create and distribute an agenda before the meeting.
- ☐ Select someone to take minutes.
- ☐ Manage different types of people effectively to achieve the best outcome for the group.
- ☐ Deal with conflict positively by adopting noncombative tactics, persuasion, bargaining, or collaborating.
- ☐ Review all decisions made and assignments to participants at the close of the meeting.

To record the minutes of a meeting:

- ☐ Be prepared. Bring the necessary tools for recording the proceedings — a laptop computer is ideal. Also bring minutes from the previous meeting and any other necessary materials.
- ☐ Be accurate, complete, and clear because minutes of a meeting may be used to settle disputes or as evidence in legal proceedings. Follow a set format for taking notes.
- ☐ Be concise and avoid generalities.
- ☐ Be specific and consistent when referring to people, places, and events.
- ☐ Be objective and impartial, avoiding adjectives and adverbs that suggest either good or bad qualities.
- ☐ Record tasks and the names of attendees who will perform these tasks.
- ☐ Expand your notes immediately after the meeting, adding appropriate details, if necessary.

■ Exercises

1. Select a topic for a presentation and write a purpose statement that is based on your answers to the following three questions. When I've finished my presentation:

   - What do I want my audience to know?
   - What do I want my audience to believe?
   - What action do I want my audience to take?

Possible topics include the following:

- Should Congress censor the Internet?
- Are many heads better than one? Is collaboration essential in the workplace?
- Are printed books a thing of the past?
- What responsibility do the media have toward the public? Are the media objective?
- Should local, state, and federal governments tax Internet purchases?
- Should high school cafeterias ban hamburgers, hot dogs, pizza, and carbonated soft drinks?
- Would you and one or more partners stand a better chance of business success if you opened a coffee kiosk (in a hospital lobby, in a shopping mall, on a busy street corner, etc.) or if you invested in and ran a coffee shop for a coffee-chain franchise (Seattle's Best, Starbucks, Cosi, etc.)?

2. Complete the following statements about the audience for your presentation:

   a. The experience or level of knowledge that my audience currently has about my subject is _____. Based on their existing knowledge, I should _____.

   b. The general educational level of my audience is _____.
   Based on their general educational level, I'll need to _____.

   c. The type of information I should provide this audience to achieve my objective is _____.

   d. Some of the questions that the audience may have throughout the presentation include:
      - _____
      - _____
      - _____

3. Prepare an introduction for your presentation that includes the following:
   - An interesting opening
   - A statement of purpose
   - An explanation of how you are going to present the topic (method of development)

4. Create a closing for your presentation that asks your audience to take a specific action or that summarizes the main points and restates the purpose of your presentation.

5. Create an outline for your whole presentation.

6. Write a brief narrative describing the impact that the audience has on any presentation that you prepare. Consider the following:
   - How does the education or reading level of the audience guide your choices in what information to include and how you will convey it?
   - If the audience shares your field or major, how will that affect your choices in what information to include and how you will convey it?
   - How might your understanding of your audience affect the purpose of your presentation? How do your purpose and understanding of your audience affect the way that you organize your presentation? (It may be helpful to review The Influence of Audience and Purpose on page 31 in Chapter 2.)

7. Choose a presentation topic of interest to you and compose the following types of opening statements:

- An attention-getting statement
- A rhetorical question
- A personal experience
- An appropriate quotation
- Another example of your own (see Writing an Opening on page 91 in Chapter 3, for suggestions)

8. Assume that you are preparing a presentation that solves a problem either in your major field of study or on your campus. Decide who your audience will be, then prepare a written outline of the body that does the following:

- Offers a solution
- Proves your point
- Calls for action

Include at least two subheadings under each heading. (Refer to this chapter for additional suggestions.)

9. Sales representatives are taught that the most important part of a presentation is the closing. Considering audience and purpose, introduction, and body, why is the closing regarded as critical in sales presentations? Is it always the most important piece of a presentation? Why or why not? Write a brief narrative explaining and defending your conclusions. List at least two examples of effective closings and explain why you think they accomplish their purposes.

10. Choose an educational, work-related, or motivational presentation topic. Using an 8½-by-11 spiral notebook, draft a flip chart of sketches to accompany your presentation. Submit an outline of your presentation with your flip-chart sketches to your instructor.

11. Prepare an outline of a presentation, with at least four headings and three subheadings under each heading. Include an opening, introduction, body, and closing. Next, prepare at least six transparencies using bullet statements and keywords that will help keep the audience focused during your presentation. For this assignment, concentrate on using effective text and clip art, if desired, when preparing each transparency. You will discover that your finished product serves not only as an aid to your presentation, but as an outline for you to follow during the presentation, possibly eliminating the need for notes.

12. Add two of the following to the set of visuals you prepared for Exercise 11.

- Table
- Chart
- Graph
- Map
- Pictorial other than clip art

■ Collaborative Classroom Projects

1. Choose a presentation topic related to your area of study (or one approved by your instructor) and design an introductory transparency (or PowerPoint slide) that includes the following:

- Title of presentation
- Title of company you represent

- Your name
- Name of the person or company you are addressing
- Date
- Artwork in the form of clip art, a watermark, an original computer design, or a logo

Then, as a class, discuss the introductory visual in terms of the following:

- *Overall design:* Does the artwork fit your subject matter?
- *Effectiveness of content:* Does the visual benefit your subject?
- *Clarity and simplicity:* Is the visual easy for your audience to read or to understand?
- *Unity and balance:* Does the visual show an effective use of color, fonts, and so on?

2. Bring to class a sample of a flowchart related to your major field of study or area of professional interest. Divide into groups with classmates who share a similar area of study. Appoint a group leader and a group recorder, and review each flowchart and analyze each sample. For what audience and purpose was the flowchart intended? Is the flowchart as simple and comprehensible as it can be? Although flowcharts are excellent tools for demonstrating a process, explaining a detail, or showing a sequential order of events, they are often difficult to produce in a manner simple enough to attract and sustain an audience's attention. Choose the flowchart that achieves its purpose in the simplest, most effective manner and share it with the class. Be prepared to explain why the flowchart is an effective example.

3. During a presentation, verbal, visual, and nonverbal communications affect your audience. To make a positive impression on your audience and to keep their attention, you must convey your genuine enthusiasm for your topic. With this in mind, take turns in front of the class introducing yourselves and explaining what you plan to accomplish in your career. Speak for no more than three minutes, and pay attention to the nonverbal communication signals that you and your classmates use. Do some students seem more excited about their future careers than others? Do some seem bored? Think about which gestures and expressions work well and which should be avoided while speaking.

4. Prepare a presentation slide or transparency that you will share with the class that makes an announcement of a future event such as a meeting, a sports event, a club activity, or a public discussion. Include the following in your visual:

- Title of event
- Title of sponsoring organization
- Date
- Time
- Name of the contact person
- Any other pertinent information
- Artwork in the form of clip art, a watermark, an original computer design, or a logo

As you prepare your visual, consider the following:

- *Overall design:* Does the artwork fit your subject matter?
- *Effectiveness of content:* Does the visual benefit your subject?
- *Clarity and simplicity:* Is the visual easy for your audience to read or to understand?
- *Unity and balance:* Does the visual show an effective use of color, fonts, and so on?

Present your information and visual to the class.

5. Plan a meeting, to take place outside of class, to organize a particular class activity or trip; to decide on a specific policy; or to vote on a specific campus, national, or international issue. The meeting will require the participation of everyone in your class. As a group, determine what you expect to achieve at the meeting and prepare a short agenda. Appoint a meeting facilitator to keep the meeting focused and a meeting secretary to record the minutes. At the meeting, maintain an atmosphere in which students listen to each other and practice adopting the "you" attitude as discussed in Conducting a Meeting on pages 548–551. When the meeting is concluded and decisions are made or actions decided upon, write a brief analysis of the interaction that occurred during the session. What, if anything, could have been improved? Did the environment encourage participation?

■ Research Projects

1. Gather good and poor examples of the following types of visuals used in presentations:
   - Flip charts
   - PowerPoint (or other computer-software) presentation aids
   - Transparencies
   - Slides

   Write a brief analysis in which you compare and contrast these types of visuals, indicating the benefits and drawbacks of each style. Which is the best for your topics and audience? Why?

2. Prepare a three-minute historical perspective on a problem that affects your field of study. For example, business majors might choose financing issues; health-sciences majors could choose rising health-care costs or medical-personnel shortages; agriculture students might address the problem of failing family farms or the government-subsidy issue; engineering students could explore the question of ethics or environmental problems. You must include at least five visuals in your presentation that further your analysis. Try not to refer to notes, and be aware of your nonverbal communication. Your visuals should include the following:
   - An introduction
   - At least one map, graph, or table
   - Documentation listing resources for all visuals, if necessary

3. Prepare a six-minute presentation in which you offer a well-supported solution to the problem you researched in Research Project 2 or to another problem that has historically affected your field of study. You must include at least ten visuals in your presentation and use a pointer when presenting. Do not use notes, and remember the importance of your nonverbal communication. Dress appropriately for your presentation. Your visuals should include the following:
   - An introductory visual
   - An original computer-generated graphic
   - At least two of the following: map, graph, table, or flowchart
   - A closing visual clearly defining your solution

4. Divide into teams of four to six members each, choose a facilitator, and work on the following scenario. Your boss has asked your group to purchase new audio-visual presentation equipment for your large company. Your building has a

presentation room that seats 75. You need equipment for management to use in training, for the sales force to use in demonstrations, and for guest speakers. You have been asked to investigate available types of equipment and make a purchase recommendation to your boss. To begin, brainstorm as a team to develop a working outline. Assign team members areas to research. Include what is available, the costs, and the advantages and disadvantages of each system. Decide when you meet again to assemble the information. One or two members will need to prepare a draft to be approved by the team. Your instructor will let you know when the final equipment proposal is due; you may also be asked to prepare a presentation for your class.

5. Divide into presentation teams of three members each. Choose a current business-related problem for which you can offer a solution that you will convey in a group presentation. Determine the organization of your presentation and who will be responsible for each portion. Each team member will be required to use at least two visuals. Your instructor will give you the time limit for your presentations.

6. Learn how to use a particular type of presentation software (such as PowerPoint) and give a presentation on how to use it effectively. Your presentation should be conducted using the software.

7. Attend a meeting of an organization. Go to the meeting prepared to take careful, complete notes of the proceedings (make sure to obtain permission to do so). From the notes you have taken, write the minutes of the meeting.

8. Attend a meeting of an organization you belong to, a business meeting of a local service club (Kiwanis, Toastmasters, Jaycees, etc.), or a faculty committee meeting. Write the minutes for the meeting. (You must first, of course, obtain permission to attend the meeting and to take its minutes.)

■ Web Projects

Projects followed by the symbol Ⓦ are continued at **bedfordstmartins.com/ writingthatworks**, Chapter 15.

1. You are the CEO for a national property group interested in building a shopping mall in your state. You have several national and international chain stores interested in establishing stores in your mall, so you want to establish your mall in a county where customers of various economic and racial demographics reside. Begin by going to the U.S. Census Bureau Web site and click on the State & County QuickFacts link for your state. Look at the demographics for your state, then click on the link for counties and explore the data from several local counties. Narrow your choice down to two counties that offer the best customer base for this type of mall. Prepare a table, graph, or chart on a transparency or in PowerPoint, comparing relevant information regarding the two counties and listing the U.S. Census Bureau as your source. The transparency should be simple, with a font large enough for an audience to read it from a distance. Be ready to share the visuals and your recommendation with the class. Ⓦ

2. Search the Web to find two or three certification or degree programs offered in forensic science (e.g., crime-scene investigation). The programs may be a part of

a continuing-education program, or a junior college or college program. Prepare a table on a transparency comparing the jobs these programs would qualify you for, as well as the course work required, the application materials required, and the cost to complete each program. Include information on your sources.

3. Using the *Occupational Outlook Handbook* at the Bureau of Labor Statistics, prepare a pie chart showing the employee opportunities in your major area of study for the next five years. Use color to depict different categories. Print your finished product on a transparency and make certain that an audience would be able to read your labels. Include source information. W

4. Assume you are an administrative assistant for the director of human resources at your company. Your department is hosting four financial consultants who have come to spend a week conducting an important audit. Create a map for them that shows not only their hotels in relation to the company's location but also several restaurants and a fitness center. Begin by:

   a. Using online yellow pages to find a local company, two hotels near that company, three or four restaurants (at least one must serve breakfast), and an exercise facility in that area.

   b. Using a Web site that offers online maps and driving directions to determine the distances between the locations and collect driving directions and the respective maps.

   Then prepare a map on a transparency showing the location of all the sites in relation to each other. Include a scale for your map and indicate north, south, east, and west. To make your map easy to read, include only the necessary components and use clear labels. Include source information. W

5. Divide the class into groups of four or six (make sure they are evenly numbered). Each group will then split in half. One half of the group will pick and research a topic to present to the rest of the class, while the other half of the group will go to a public-speaking organization's Web site and compare its suggestions for a successful presentation with the advice given in this chapter. Then the two halves of the group will discuss their findings and prepare a presentation on their topic — using their best presentation strategies — for the rest of the class. Be ready to explain the sources used to collect the research and why these sources were considered credible. Also be ready to explain the sources from which your group got its presentation strategies, as well as the strategies themselves. W

16 Writing for the Web: Rhetorical Principles

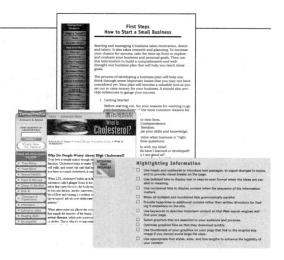

The prevalence and availability of Web technology in the workplace for news, marketing, research, and shopping may make it necessary for you to write a report, article, or introduction to a content area for a Web site. In several important ways, writing for the Web is very much like writing for print: You need to understand your purpose and your audience, carefully research your subject, organize your thoughts, use plain language, and make your text free of typographical or grammatical errors. However, writing for the Web is different from writing for other media—and more challenging—because your audience is scanning a computer screen and expects to get information quickly and efficiently. Ease of access to your content will be affected both by how it's written and organized and by the speed at which it loads to your readers' screens. This chapter offers guidance in the following areas to help you write and organize Web content, and it emphasizes the importance of collaborating closely with the site's webmaster to optimize content for speed and accessibility:[1]

---

[1]In the workplace, the webmaster or site designer maintains site-wide technical and design standards. On campus, consult your instructor or the campus computer support staff about standards for posting content.

Writing for Rapid Consumption

People read text at Web sites differently than they read paper text. Reading rates on the Web slow by 25 percent and more compared with rates for reading paper text, in part because of eyestrain caused by the flickering monitor. Few people read Web content word for word. The vast majority—up to 80 percent—scan the screen for what interests them or for what they need. They don't linger—they usually scan a page for about ten seconds before moving on, unless they find what they want.[2]

Given the reader's brief attention span and other features unique to Web sites, you must plan and organize your information to promote ease of use and comprehension.

In the workplace, content you create will likely appear on one or more pages of your organization's or company's Web site. Get familiar with the site's existing overall design and content areas. Before submitting your content, review recently published material at the site to get a sense of the site's purpose and audience and how your content works in relationship to both.

Crafting Content for the Web

Whether you plan to write original content for a Web site or adapt content from an existing document, use the following guidelines to plan and organize your text and graphics.

Using the Inverted Pyramid

As you organize and draft your information, begin with the bottom line—your conclusions—by using the inverted-pyramid method traditionally used by journalists to organize your writing. State your conclusions or most important points before providing the detailed background information—facts, data, and logic—to support them. Because the majority of Web readers do not read word for word, the inverted-pyramid presentation of information promotes speed of access to your content. By placing the most important information at the beginning, you allow readers to grasp what is significant without their having to read verbatim to the end. Of course, you still need to provide the background details, explanations, documentation, and other information essential to your content for readers wishing the additional level of detail. Figure 16–1 depicts this method in principle, and Figure 16–2 shows how it works in practice. This method is also described as "Decreasing Order of Importance" in Chapter 2, pages 45–46.

---

[2]Data pertaining to reader practices at Web sites appears in Jakob Nielson's *Designing Web Usability* (Indianapolis: New Riders, 2000), p. 106.

Malorye Branca, *Bio-ItWorld* Magazine

Malorye Branca is Senior Informatics Editor at *Bio-ItWorld* — a technology and life-sciences magazine published in print and on the Web. Malorye writes articles on developments in biotechnology, pharmaceuticals, and genomics for an international audience of technology professionals and scientists, and makes choices about how to present information to her print and online readers. At the Web site, the editors of *Bio-ItWorld* provide most of the content of the monthly print magazine, along with breaking news and additional articles and commentaries.

"Our goal online," Malorye explains, "is to provide the best, most current information. If something major happens in genomics research, for example, it has to go on the Web site within hours. By the time we publish it in the magazine, it may already be old news. Overall, the Web allows us to meet our audience's needs much better than we can in print."

Essential to Malorye's success as a writer and an editor is an understanding of her readers. "We've found that our Web audience is very different from our print audience. Web readers want shorter pieces. They are less interested in entertainment — or in elaborate layout, design, and visuals — and more interested in getting information quickly." She keeps these interests in mind as she creates content. "I'm always very careful to make my stories as short as possible. I think about how many paragraphs a story should be. I think about the headlines and keep them to one line each. I also use visuals with great care and keep them to a minimum — our readers want a clean look, and they don't want to scroll for information."

To enrich her readers' experience of her online articles, Malorye provides links to other materials on the Web — including the links within the text of the story if it is short, and at the end if it is more than 600 words. "What I like best about writing for the Web is that by using links, I can provide more information, using fewer words. And I don't have to do all the research myself." However, when linking to other online materials, she cautions, "It's very important to make sure the site or article you're linking to is responsible and accurate. You need to check the information that you find on the Web just as you would other sources." Some resources that Malorye links to include articles published by the *New York Times* and by reputable science and technology journals.

To read articles by Malorye Branca and other editors at *Bio-ItWorld* magazine, go to <bio-itworld.com>.

Annika Tamura, Boston.com

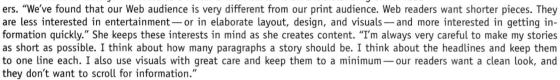

Annika Tamura is the design director at Boston.com, the nation's largest regional Web site. Along with the entire contents of the *Boston Globe,* Boston.com provides breaking news and entertainment features. "Users come to the site for information," says Annika, who, as a Web designer, understands the experience of her online audience. "People read differently online — they don't read linearly. They jump around and read short amounts of information." When Annika, the design team, and the editorial group approached the task of redesigning Boston.com, they started by focusing on their users. Annika explains: "We wanted to make the site clear and navigable, with a vibrant, fun atmosphere. We're a news site, but we're more than that." Because advertising is currently a major source of revenue for Boston.com, they also had to effectively integrate their clients throughout the user experience.

"Usability testing was key," Annika says, in achieving these goals. She and her team conducted several such tests, inviting groups of users to navigate and evaluate the site. "We asked 'What do you like about our site? What other sites do you like? How can we improve ours?'" Based on usability, they revised the design three times. "We learned that we needed to scale back on the amount of content and streamline the presentation. We needed to label and organize information into logical groupings that make it clear if a section was about news or travel. We also strive to incorporate interactive media wisely, to enhance the story in print." Of the redesigned site, Annika says, "It's now streamlined and contemporary, and it presents information in a way that is better for our users."

Annika's advice for anyone who writes or designs for the Web is, "Always keep your user in mind. Know what your content is. Use multimedia to enhance content, not to create a barrier between the information and the user. Respect that information is what people come to your site for."

W On the Web
For Web-design re-
sources recommended
by Annika Tamura,
see Chapter 16,
**bedfordstmartins.com/
writingthatworks**

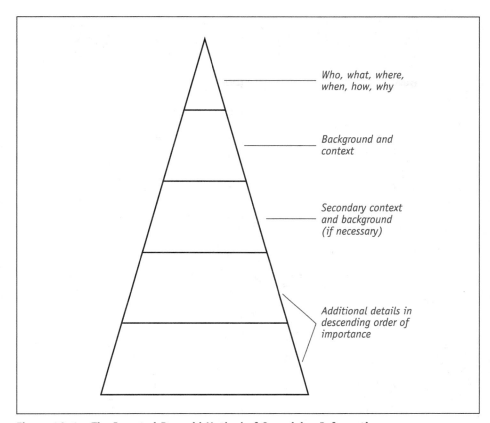

Who, what, where,
when, how, why

Background and
context

Secondary context
and background
(if necessary)

Additional details in
descending order of
importance

Figure 16–1   The Inverted-Pyramid Method of Organizing Information

Using a Simple Style and an Appropriate Tone

If you want your ideas to make an impact on the Web, your writing style must be plain, honest, and to the point. Web users are looking for information, not unsupported claims—whether you are describing a product, such as a digital camera, or a public-policy idea, such as charter schools. To this end, avoid promotional language that inflates the claims of the product or idea but provides no corroborating information to support those claims.

UNSUPPORTED CLAIM	Amco's All-in-One Mini Sound System is the best product in its class on the Internet! Buy one today!
SUPPORTED CLAIM	Amco's All-in-One Mini Sound System is a proven leader in compact systems based on <u>industry tests</u> and was voted the #1 mini sound system for 2004 by <u>*Audio Magazine.*</u>

Note that the improved version links directly to the source of the evidence (*industry tests* and *Audio Magazine*) that supports the company's claims about the

Airlines Meet FAA's Hardened Cockpit Door Deadline

Answers who, what, when, where

Washington, D.C.—The Department of Transportation's Federal Aviation Administration (FAA) today announced that more than 10,000 aircraft serving the United States are now equipped with new, hardened cockpit doors, making air travel safer for passengers and crews.

Answers why

FAA Administrator Marion C. Blakey said that the airlines met today's deadline to install doors that stop intruders and small-arms fire because of the extraordinary cooperation between the FAA and the door and airplane manufacturers. The FAA issued more than 30 design approvals for 25 airplane models, many within hours after receiving the final documentation from the manufacturer.

Provides background and context

"These hardened doors are part of Secretary of Transportation Norman Y. Mineta's system of systems, layers of dramatically increased security measures from curbside to the cockpit that make our aviation system safer than ever," said Blakey. There was a unified sense of urgency and cooperation between industry and governments worldwide.

U.S. Air Carriers

Expands context by describing scope of activity

The Aviation and Transportation Security Act (ATSA) of 2001 directed the FAA to improve airplane security both immediately (Phase I) and in the long-term (Phase II). On October 9, 2001, the FAA published the first of a series of Special Federal Aviation Regulations (SFARs) to expedite the modification of cockpit doors in the U.S. fleet. This Phase I fix included installation of steel bars and locking devices. The FAA determined that the security risk outweighed potential safety risks associated with the Phase I . . .

Foreign Air Carriers

Expands context by describing additional scope of activity

On June 21, 2002, the FAA published another final rule requiring foreign airlines to install new cockpit doors on aircraft serving the United States by today. The rule also requires that the cockpit door be closed and locked. The FAA worked closely with foreign aviation authorities and fully expects foreign airlines to meet the deadline. FAA inspectors conduct random ramp inspections of foreign airlines and may restrict flights if the FAA determines noncompliance on the part of a foreign airline. There are approximately 508 foreign (Part 129) airlines operating approximately 4,213 airplanes that are authorized to operate to the United States.

Concludes with secondary details

The purchase of each cockpit door typically costs the airlines between $30,000 and $50,000. The cost varied for each airline depending on the number of aircraft being retrofitted for each model type. Congress originally appropriated $100 million to the FAA to distribute to U.S. airlines for aircraft security enhancements, $97 million of which were given to the airlines to help defray the costs of cockpit doors (approximately $13,000 per door).

Figure 16–2   Press Release at a Web Site, Using the Inverted-Pyramid Presentation of Information   *Source:* Federal Aviation Administration (<faa.gov>).

product. To help ensure that your content meets these standards, review Defining Terms and Concepts and Explaining Cause and Effect in Chapter 3. Also review Plain Language in Chapter 4.

Like e-mail, the Web often invites informality. Remember that regardless of the technology used to reach your reader, your words and tone represent your company or project. Eliminate any biased or sexist language and resist the temptation to insert unnecessary and inappropriate humor in any writing—Web or otherwise—intended for the public. Also avoid puns, which suggest too much informality and can confuse your international readers. This guidance applies equally to the language of the captions and call-outs for graphics. See Chapter 4 for comprehensive guidance on style, tone, and the avoidance of biased language.

Writing Concisely

Revise your text for conciseness. Your readers will appreciate terseness because they are looking for useful content in a hurry. Concise content also reduces reader eyestrain caused by prolonged reading on a computer screen. Use the following guidelines to achieve conciseness:

- Cover one idea in each paragraph.
- Begin each paragraph with a topic sentence.
- Try to limit each paragraph to three or four sentences.
- Aim for short sentences with simple sentence structure; use concrete nouns and active verbs.
- Use plain language.

Figure 16–3 depicts a page at the Web site of the Argonne National Laboratory, a research facility, that describes their work in developing hydrogen-powered fuel cells. The page is effective because each paragraph is introduced by a pertinent heading, opens with a topic sentence, and covers one facet of the project in plain language. The page integrates an informative visual and closes with links to additional information and an e-mail address to which readers can submit questions.

See Chapter 4 for additional techniques to achieve conciseness and for guidelines on the use of plain language.

Chunking Content

Another way to focus reader attention is to break up dense blocks of text by chunking passages so that they stand out and can be quickly scanned and absorbed. Each chunked passage should coherently focus on one facet of your topic. Identify such passages with captions or headings that announce the topic and help the reader decide at a glance whether to read the material. Include links for more detailed secondary or background information to avoid slowing readers not interested in that level of information. Use the inverted-pyramid principle to organize these passages.

The content shown in Figures 16–2 and 16–3 both effectively divide their content into short paragraphs. Each paragraph in Figure 16–2 focuses on one point and for ease of access is set off from the others by white space. The use of headings for the short paragraphs in Figure 16–3 makes the information even easier to scan. The passages in both figures are grouped in a logical sequence for the information covered.

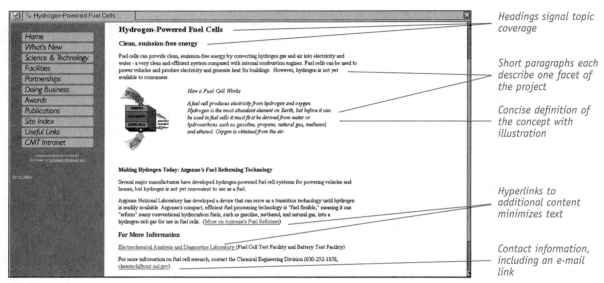

Figure 16–3   Web Page Featuring Chunked Content   *Source:* Argonna National Laboratory (<anl.gov>).

Linking to Internal Content

Use *hyperlinks*—words or images that act as gateways to other content areas—to expand access to your information. To provide facts, data, charts, glossaries, or documentation to support or expand coverage of information on the screen, create hyperlinks from your page to additional content. Hyperlinks give readers quick access to material and save them the trouble of having to scroll through screen after screen to locate content. Hyperlinks can take viewers to another page at your site or to another Web site.

If your coverage on a single page stretches beyond two or three screens, as for a short report, booklet, or pamphlet, create a table of contents for it at the top of the Web page. Hyperlink each element in the table of contents to content further down the page. Make sure these links are visible on the first screen so that readers need not scroll down to see them. Use hyperlinks to connect the headings in the table of contents to their locations in the document so that the reader can access a specific section quickly and easily. A good example of a hyperlinked table of contents is shown in Figure 16–4. Each topic is linked to paragraphs further down the

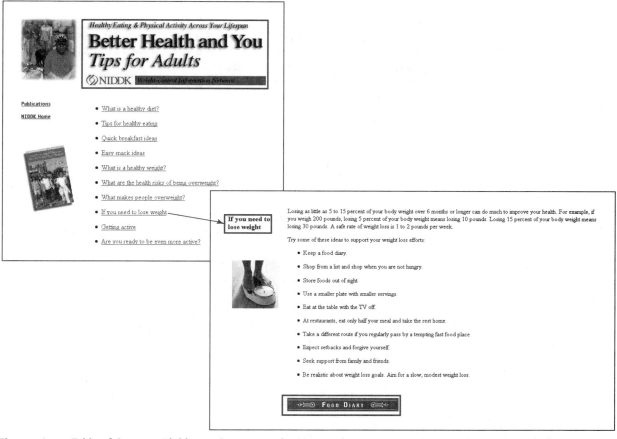

Figure 16–4   Table of Contents Linking to Content on the Same Web Page   *Source:* National Institutes of Health (<nih.gov>).

page under boldface subheadings. The reader can either scroll down to read the whole document or use the hyperlinks in the table of contents to access a piece of the information quickly and easily. Depending on the overall site design, the complete document may even be located at a different part of the site, such as in a collection of similar documents, thus eliminating the need for the reader to scroll down a single screen to review it.

For lengthy content on a single page, include helpful directional cues, such as links at convenient breaks, so that users can get to the top of the page without having to scroll.

Back to Top

These links are placed between text passages where they do not interrupt readers.

Use links to focus user attention, not distract it. Keep to a minimum hyperlinks *within* text paragraphs. Otherwise, they are visually distracting (underlined/colored) and make scanning the text difficult. Embedded links also allow readers to leave the page before reaching the end of your content. Figure 16–5 shows a page from a site that contains too many distracting links embedded in the text. Rather than embedding hyperlinks throughout the body of your text, combine them into short, well-organized lists that are introduced with explanatory text. Be sure to inform readers where the link will take them. In some cases, the title of the link is self-explanatory: <u>Glossary</u> or <u>For Additional Information</u>. At other times, you need to add a brief explanatory passage:

■ Refer to the section on <u>Plug-ins, Viewers, and Other Tools</u> for information on icons associated with document formats (e.g., PDF) used at this site.

You can place lists of hyperlinks periodically throughout your document to break up the large blocks of text, or place a list of links at the end of your document, as you would with footnotes. In Figure 16–6, the hyperlinks at the end of the document are still available without being distracting. Finally, avoid cuing readers with the phrase <u>Click Here</u>. The phrase offers no useful information and is considered a Web cliché.

AVOID   To learn more about our company, <u>Click Here</u>.

BETTER   Learn more about the <u>XYZ Corporation</u>.

Numerous embedded links distract and slow readers

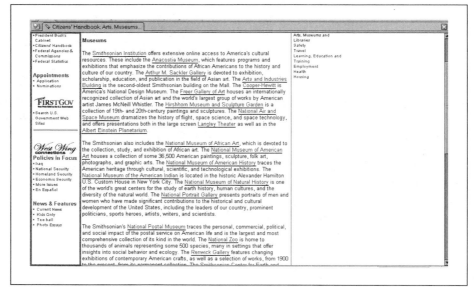

Figure 16–5   Overuse of Embedded Links (Links Underlined for Emphasis)
Source: White House Web Site (<whitehouse.gov>).

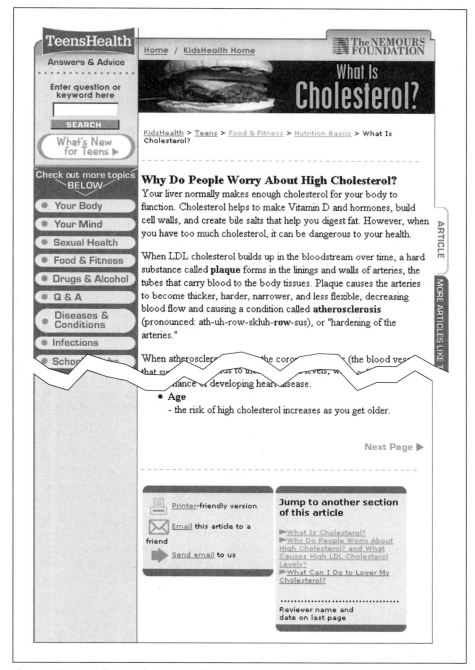

Organized links related to preceding content on the page

Figure 16–6   Well-Organized Links Following Main Text   *Source:* The Nemours Foundation © 1995–2003.

Linking to External Content

Links to external (or outside) sites can be an invaluable way of expanding your content. However, be sure to review such sites and their content carefully before activating your link to them. Is the site's author or sponsoring organization reputable? Is the content accurate and current? Does the site date-stamp its content (such as "This page was last updated on January 12, 2004")? Is the information unbiased? For detailed guidance on reviewing outside sites and other Internet sources of information, see Evaluating Online Sources on pages 215–217 in Chapter 7.

Some Web sites request that you ask their permission before linking to them. To determine a site's policy in this regard, review its <u>About Us</u> page, usually accessible from the homepage. Although linking to another site can be done electronically without the other site being aware of the link, your organization may have a policy of asking permission of outside sites before linking to them. In either case, you would e–mail a request to the site's webmaster asking for permission. Check with your site's webmaster to find out if standardized language exists for such requests.

You should link directly to the page or specific area of an external site that is relevant to your users. When you hyperlink to an external site, be sure that your writing provides a clear context for why you're sending your readers there, and what they will find. The following passage appears at a Tips for Doing Business with Us section of the Web site for the Nuclear Regulatory Commission (NRC). It directs users to a non-NRC site to obtain automatic updates about business opportunities with the agency.

- **FedBizOpps.** NRC usually publicizes proposed business opportunities valued at greater than $25,000 on the <u>FedBizOpps</u> Web site ⌞EXIT⌟. You may register on this site for automatic notification of business opportunities by product or service classification code the day they are posted.

Note the *Exit* label in this passage. Many sites place an icon or a text label next to links to outside sites to inform users that they are leaving the host site. A site's Help page may explain the purpose of the practice, such as the following passage:

- The ⌞EXIT⌟ label is placed directly after an external link to let you know that the link is going to take you away from the XYZ Corporation site. These links are provided as a service and do not imply any official endorsement of or responsibility for the opinions, ideas, data, or products presented at these locations, or guarantee the validity of the information provided.

Check with your webmaster or site administrator about site policy for these notices if your content includes links to external sites.

Once you link to another site, you are responsible for checking frequently to ensure that the content remains accurate and current—or that it hasn't disappeared. It may be corporate or organizational legal policy at your site to post a disclaimer, such as the following, to inform users that information at outside sites is not under your control and may at times be erroneous.

■   *Disclaimer:* The XYZ Corporation cannot guarantee the accuracy, completeness, or
reliability of all the information on non-XYZ servers and Web sites that are linked to
from the XYZ site.

Crafting Content for the Web

☐   Organize content from the top down — begin with your most important point,
adding supporting details and background information in descending order of
importance.

☐   Present ideas as concisely as possible and express them in plain language.

☐   Support all claims with facts.

☐   Chunk dense blocks of text into shorter passages that stand out for ease of
reading and introduce them with informative headings.

☐   Create hyperlinks to additional information to reduce content on your page and
to enrich coverage of your topic.

☐   Review hyperlinks periodically to ensure that their content continues to be relevant to your purposes.

■ Highlighting Information

Writing and organizing text for rapid consumption are essential first steps to promoting ease of access to your content. You can further augment access through a
variety of highlighting techniques, some of which are common to printed text and
some of which are unique to Web content.

Using Heads and Subheads

Headings reduce the complexity of text by highlighting structure and showing organization. They also signal breaks in coverage from one topic to the next. Readers
use them to scan rapidly for meaningful information on-screen as well as in
printed documents. Set off headings in boldface on a separate line either directly
above or in the left margin directly across from the text they describe.

Figure 16–3 uses heads effectively to introduce and divide content. See
Chapter 8, page 254, for additional guidance about the use of headings to highlight content.

Using Bullets and Numbered Lists

Like headings, bullets and numbered lists break up dense paragraphs. They also
reduce text length and highlight relevant content instead of embedding it within
paragraphs. *Bulleted lists* show readers that the items displayed are parallel in importance. *Numbered lists* inform readers immediately that the sequence of your
information is crucial. Regardless of the form the list takes, make all items in it
grammatically parallel.

Note that not all text passages should be broken into bulleted lists. Doing so would make your pages look like a PowerPoint presentation but without a speaker to fill in the context for the bulleted points. Lists without supporting explanatory text lack coherence. The bulleted items in Figure 16–7 are effective because they highlight the questions—each on a separate line—meant to be considered. They also link to additional background information about each question. See

Bulleted items encourage evaluation of each issue

First Steps
How to Start a Small Business

Starting and managing a business takes motivation, desire, and talent. It also takes research and planning. To increase your chance for success, take the time up front to explore and evaluate your business and personal goals. Then use this information to build a comprehensive and well-thought-out business plan that will help you reach these goals.

The process of developing a business plan will help you think through some important issues that you may not have considered yet. Your plan will become a valuable tool as you set out to raise money for your business. It should also provide milestones to gauge your success.

1. Getting Started

   Before starting out, list your reasons for wanting to go into business. Some of the most common reasons for starting a business are:

   • You want to be your own boss.
   • You want financial independence.
   • You want creative freedom.
   • You want to fully use your skills and knowledge.

2. Next you need to determine what business is "right for you." Ask yourself these questions:

   • What do I like to do with my time?
   • What technical skills have I learned or developed?
   • What do others say I am good at?
   • Will I have the support of my family?
   • How much time do I have to run a successful business?
   • Do I have any hobbies or interests that are marketable?

Figure 16–7   Effective Use of a Numbered List with Bullets (continued)

3. Then you should identify the niche your business will fill. Conduct the necessary research to answer these questions:

- What business am I interested in starting?
- What services or products will I sell?
- Is my idea practical, and will it fill a need?
- What is my competition?
- What is my business's advantage over existing firms?
- Can I deliver a better quality service?
- Can I create a demand for my business?

Figure 16–7   Effective Use of a Numbered List with Bullets (continued)

pages 151–152, in Chapter 5, for more information about creating numbered and bulleted lists.

Giving Directional Cues

Avoid directional cues that make sense on the printed page but not on a Web screen, such as "as shown in the example below" or "in the graph at the top of this page." Directional phrases like these can be confusing when there is no real reference for "above" and "below," and no "top" or "bottom" of the document. Instead, position links so that they are tied directly to the content to which they pertain. For example, when the terms "above" and "below" refer to content on a single page, insert links on the page that take readers to the top or bottom of your page. (See the sample <u>Back to Top</u> link on page 569.) Note in Figure 16–8 that the three bulleted items for how to locate career information by location refer readers to links elsewhere on the page: twice to the "<u>OOH Search/A-Z Index</u>" at the upper right side of the page and once to the tool bar at the right margin. These links are not apparent at a glance, especially the "<u>OOH Search/A-Z Index</u>." This information could have been written as follows to better integrate the links and so enhance user access:

■   You have three ways to locate career information by occupation at this site:

- For a *specific* occupation, enter the occupation name at "<u>OOH Search/A-Z Index.</u>"
- For a listing of *all* occupations in alphabetical order, select the appropriate letter at "<u>OOH Search/A-Z Index.</u>"
- For information about *multiple* occupations, browse the links for occupational categories at the right margin of this page.

The terms *next* and *previous* can also cause confusion. Use these terms only when you know users accessed your page from an immediately preceding page.

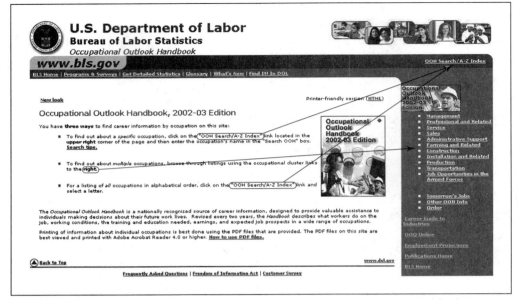

Figure 16–8 Web Page with Unnecessary Directional Cues *Source:* Bureau of Labor Statistics (<bls.gov>).

These terms are, however, used appropriately to navigate through PDF (portable document file) documents.

Providing Keywords for Content Retrieval

One challenge of writing for the Web is making sure that your desired audience can find your page. To increase the odds that Web search engines will locate your site, be specific in describing your important points. Using keywords and concepts throughout your text will help the search engine find your page.

NO KEYWORDS	We are proud to introduce a new commemorative coin honoring our company's founder and president. The item will be available on this Web site after December 1, 2003, which is the 100th anniversary of our first sale.
WITH KEYWORDS (IN ITALICS)	The new *Reynolds* commemorative coin features a portrait of *George G. Reynolds*, the founder and president of *Reynolds Corporation*. *The coin* can be purchased on our Web site (<reynoldswidgetcorp/coin.htm>) after December 1, 2003, in honor of the 100th anniversary of the sale of the first *Reynolds widget*.

By using words such as "Reynolds," "George G. Reynolds," and "the coin" instead of "our company's," "our founder," and "the item," you will give the search engines much more specific information that they, in turn, can give to users. The revised paragraph also includes a link to the company's Web site for ease of access to those wishing to purchase the coin.

Using Graphics and Typography

The way your content looks on the screen when published will be affected by the site's existing design. The page on which your content appears will likely display a banner at the top featuring the organization or company name; navigational tool bars at the top, bottom, or left side of the screen; links to other content areas; and other elements. The site's design standards may affect the line length of your text, the default type sizes and styles in use at the site, the preferred format for graphics files, and a variety of other features. To ensure that your content fits smoothly into the existing design, meet with the site's webmaster to ensure that your input is consistent with site technical and design standards.

As with print publications, your audience and purpose should determine *why* graphics are important to your content. At times, graphic elements provide visual relief from dense text and make the site attractive and appealing, as in Figure 16–4. For the most part, however, use only images that illustrate essential information, as in Figure 16–3. If users depend on the site for accessible and visually clear information, use graphics that load as quickly as possible. Large or high-resolution graphics, like color photographs or animated images, can cause long delays as they download to the user's system. If these images are gratuitous, they will frustrate your readers because they offer no relevant content to justify the slow load times. For high-resolution graphics that are essential, consider using thumbnails on your page that link to the original size image. (Thumbnails are images reduced to 10 to 15 percent of the original file size for quick access.) Work with the webmaster to optimize all graphics for speed of access. Ask about the preferred file compression format—JPEGs, GIFs, or other?—for visuals you submit. Also consider giving visitors a graphics-free option for quicker access to your content.

Font sizes and styles affect screen legibility. Computer screens display fonts at lower resolutions than in most printed text. Thus, sans serif fonts work better for text passages on-screen because serifs "fuzz out" on low-resolution monitors, adversely affecting legibility and causing eyestrain. (For background information about type sizes and styles, see Chapter 8, pages 251–254.) Consult with your webmaster about the site's font preferences and review the text of your content on an internal browser for legibility before posting it for public access. Be aware, however, that even with your best efforts to ensure legibility, the user's browser, operating system, and font preferences can affect how your text looks on the user's screen.

Line length also affects legibility. Short line lengths reduce the amount of eye movement, and hence eyestrain, necessary to scan text, with optimal length approximately half the width of the screen.[3] To achieve this length, draft text that's

---

[3]Patrick L. Lynch and Sara Horton, *Web Style Guide: Basic Design Principles for Creating Web Sites* (New Haven: Yale, 1999), p. 85.

between 50 and 70 characters, or 10 to 12 words to a line. Longer lines make it difficult for readers to locate the next line of text at the left margin, particularly for single-spaced paragraphs. Finally, as with printed material, do not use all capital letters or boldface type for blocks of text. They slow reader speed and comprehension.

For content that contains special or international characters, consult with the webmaster about the best way to submit the files for HTML coding. These characters include, among others, bullets, dashes, and asterisks; symbols for chemical and mathematical equations; or fonts and accent marks for non-English languages. In general, aim for consistency to establish a visual sense of unity and to provide visual cues that help visitors find information.

DESIGNING YOUR DOCUMENT

Highlighting Information

- ☐ Use heads and subheads to introduce text passages, to signal changes in topics, and to provide visual breaks on the page.
- ☐ Use bulleted lists to display text in easy-to-scan format when the ideas are parallel in meaning.
- ☐ Use numbered lists to display content when the sequence of the information matters.
- ☐ Make all bulleted and numbered lists grammatically parallel.
- ☐ Provide hyperlinks to additional content rather than written directions for finding it elsewhere on the site.
- ☐ Use keywords to describe important content so that Web search engines will find your page.
- ☐ Select graphics that are essential to your audience and purpose.
- ☐ Optimize graphics files so that they download quickly.
- ☐ If you cannot avoid large file sizes, use thumbnails of your graphics on your page that link to the original size image.
- ☐ Use appropriate font styles, sizes, and line lengths to enhance the legibility of your content.

■ Enhancing Access to Content

The techniques discussed in the previous sections will help you organize and present text and graphics for the Web that are easy for your audience to understand. This section describes your responsibility as a content provider to ensure that your information is accessible to people with disabilities and that it meets the needs of international users.

Ensuring Access for People with Disabilities

Many of the advantages of Web sites include colorful graphics, animation, and streaming video and audio. However, these design elements can be barriers to people with impaired vision or hearing or those who are color-blind. To overcome these barriers to your content, discuss the following strategies with the site web-master or site-accessibility specialist.

- Avoid frames, complex tables, animation, JavaScript, and other design elements that are incompatible with text-only browsers and adaptive technologies, such as voice or large-print software.[4]
- Provide HTML versions of pages and documents whenever possible because this format is most compatible with the current generation of screen readers.
- Include text-equivalent captions that describe the graphic or audio elements of your content (e.g, "Photograph of Harriet V. Sullivan, President, HVS Accounting Services").
- Design for the color-blind reader using captions and other text to make meaning independent of color (Green, labeled **G,** means **All Safe**).

Implementing these measures requires the expertise of a Web-technology specialist. However, as the content provider, you will be expected to write text captions for all graphics and sound features—as described in the third item of the preceding list. You may also want to offer different options for site visitors, such as full-graphics, light-graphics, and text-only versions of your content. Discuss these options with the webmaster.

Finally, test your pages using "Bobby" at <cast.org/bobby>, a site that will provide an on-screen analysis of a Web page to ensure its accessibility.

W On the Web
For guidelines for improving Web-site accessibility, see Chapter 16, **bedfordstmartins** .com/writingthatworks

Considering International Users

Consider the needs of international readers if they are part of your target audience. You need not write simplistic prose to do so, nor do you need to write separate versions of your content for domestic and international readers. As with other writing aimed at readers of English as a second language, you should, however, review your text to eliminate expressions and references that make sense only to someone very familiar with American English. Avoid expressions such as "throw in the towel" and "a no-brainer." Likewise, express dates, clock times, and measurements in accordance with international practices. If your content includes visuals, choose symbols and icons, colors, representations of human beings, and captions that can be easily understood. For guidelines on communicating effectively with an international audience, see Writing International Correspondence, on pages 341–347, and Using Graphics to Communicate Internationally, on pages 295–298.

---

[4]Adaptive technologies, such as screen readers, use software to activate a voice synthesizer that reads aloud the text and captions for nontext elements (e.g., graphics) on a computer screen.

CONSIDERING
AUDIENCE
AND PURPOSE

Enhancing Access to Content

☐ Work with your site's webmaster or accessibility specialist to provide content — text, graphics, audio — that is compatible with adaptive technologies used by people with disabilities.

☐ Create captions that accurately describe the graphics and audio features of your content.

☐ Describe color-coded content so that its meaning can be understood independent of color.

☐ Test your content for accessibility using the "Bobby" site at <cast.org/bobby>.

☐ Create text, graphics, and units of measurement to accommodate international readers.

■ Posting an Existing Document

This chapter has focused on how to organize and write original content or adapt existing content for Web sites. However, you may be asked to submit an existing paper document to a Web site. The document may be a report, user manual, or policy and procedure handbook, for example. In its original form, it will be organized to be read in the sequence written for paper publication. If the document is lengthy, it makes sense to retain the document's original sequence and page layout. If you shorten or revise your original document for posting on the Web, mark the Web content accordingly, as follows, so that readers will know that it differs from the original.

■ *The data in Appendix A of this report are updated monthly and vary from the data in the printed report, which is published annually each February.

Documents posted on the Web are frequently converted to PDF format, which displays the pages on-screen exactly as they appear on paper. PDFs are viewable with free, downloadable Adobe Acrobat software, which allows the pages to be enlarged for ease of online reading. Readers can read the document online, download it to a hard drive, or print it in whole or in part. Regardless of format or version used, before you prepare existing paper documents for public availability at a Web site, do the following:

- Review the document for compliance with your organization's publishing guidelines:
  - Is it appropriate for public access?
  - Is it consistent with current policies and practices for the organization's products and services?
  - Does it contain proprietary and privacy information that must be protected or deleted?

- Ensure that you obtain permission for Web publication if the document contains copyrighted text, tables, or images. (Some copyright holders require separate permissions for paper and Web publication of their content.)
- Contact the site webmaster about the preferred electronic file format in which to submit the document for coding and posting: MS Word, PageMaker, PDF, FrameMaker, or other format.
- Ask the webmaster to optimize any slow-loading graphics files for quicker access.
- Review the coded document on an internal Web site *before* it is posted to the public site to ensure that it is the correct version, that no information is missing, and that all links work and go to the right places.

If your document is long, assume that users will print it to read offline. Consult your site's webmaster about creating a single-file version of the document to optimize printing.

■ Protecting the Privacy of Your Users

You may find it necessary to collect information on your page submitted by site users. You may ask them, for example, to respond to a questionnaire that you've posted, to subscribe to a service, to comment on a document, or to give you general feedback about your page. Many users also submit unsolicited e-mail questions to Web sites about some aspect of the site. Be aware that most Internet users wish to have information about themselves—name, residential and e-mail addresses, phone number, credit-card number, personal opinions, and the like—kept confidential. In response to this concern, all reputable Web sites post a *privacy notice*—usually on the homepage—informing users about how it intends to handle the solicited and unsolicited information from individuals received at the site.

If you plan to collect such information on your page or if your page has an e-mail link, contact the site webmaster about putting a link on your page to the site-wide privacy statement. As an example, the following privacy policy, excerpted from the U.S. Nuclear Regulatory Commission's Web site, appears on its homepage (<nrc.gov>) and other locations throughout the site where the public can contact or submit information to the agency.

Privacy Policy
Thank you for visiting the Nuclear Regulatory Commission's Web site and reviewing our privacy policy. . . . If you visit our site, we collect and store only the following information about you:

- The IP address . . . ;
- The pages you visit; and
- The date and time you access our site.

(continued)

> If you send us an e-mail message or online form that includes personal informa-
> tion . . . we will only use the information for the reason you provided it.
>
> **Use of Cookies**
> NRC may use "session cookies" as place-keepers to retain context during an individ-
> ual user session. They assist with . . .
>
> **What NRC Does with Site Usage Data**
> For site management, NRC maintains an operational log of site user addresses. . . .
>
> For site security purposes and to ensure that this site remains available to all users,
> NRC employs software programs . . .
>
> Except for authorized law enforcement investigations . . .

Some corporate privacy statements describe their policy for sharing user information, such as subscriber lists, to third parties for marketing purposes.
Informing users of this practice is both candid and ethical. These sites often give
users the opportunity to refuse permission to use their addresses for marketing, as
in the following example:

- **Opt Out Choice**
  Our users are given the opportunity to "opt out" of having their information used for
  purposes not directly related to our site at the point where we ask for the information. For example, our order form has an "opt out" mechanism so that users who buy
  a product from us, but don't want any marketing material, can keep their e-mail address off of our lists.

CONSIDERING AUDIENCE AND PURPOSE →

Protecting the Privacy of Your Users

☐ Provide users with a link to the site's privacy statement, particularly if you solicit
comments or provide an e-mail link for unsolicited comments.

☐ Inform users if you intend to use their information for marketing yourself or intend to share their information with third parties.

☐ Give visitors the option of refusing permission to have their information used
for marketing.

■ Documenting Sources of Information

As with print publications, you must document and acknowledge outside sources
of information or of help received—text, images, streaming video, and other multimedia material. If any of this source material is copyrighted, you must seek prior
approval before using it. Documenting sources at your site has at least two major
advantages: (1) It discloses where you obtained your information, thereby bol-
stering the site's credibility, and (2) it allows users to locate it, if necessary. The site
should also document information in the public domain, such as publications
and Web sites of the federal government. For guidance on the use and documen-

tation of source material, including electronic information, see Chapter 7, pages 222–242.

Site credibility is further enhanced by acknowledging help received in the creation or review of content at the site. Note the passage in the third paragraph of the Weight Control Information Network of the National Institutes of Health's Web site, shown in Figure 16–9. These acknowledgments attest to the accuracy, quality, and objectivity of the information provided.

U.S. DEPARTMENT OF HEALTH AND HUMAN SERVICES
National Institutes of Health
Home | Health | Grants | News | Science | Institutes | About NIH

Weight-control Information Network

> 1 WIN WAY
> BETHESDA, MD 20892-3665
> Phone: (202) 828-1025
> FAX: (202) 828-1028
> E-mail: <win@info.niddk.nib.gov>
> Internet: <niddk.nih.gov/health/nutrit/nutrit.htm>
> Toll-free number: 1-877-946-4627

The Weight-control Information Network (WIN) is a national service of the National Institute of Diabetes and Digestive and Kidney Diseases of the National Institutes of Health, which is the Federal Government's lead agency responsible for biomedical research on nutrition and obesity. Authorized by Congress (Public Law 103-43), WIN provides the general public, health professionals, the media, and Congress with up-to-date, science-based health information on weight control, obesity, physical activity, and related nutritional issues.

WIN answers inquiries, develops and distributes publications, and works closely with professional and patient organizations and Government agencies to coordinate resources about weight control and related issues.

Publications produced by WIN are carefully reviewed by both NIDDK scientists and outside experts. This publication was also reviewed by Roland Weinsier, M.D., Dr. P.H., Professor and Director, Clinical Nutrition Research Center, University of Alabama at Birmingham; Rena Wing, Ph.D., Professor of Psychiatry and Human Behavior, Brown University; and F. Xavier Pi-Sunyer, M.D., M.P.H., Director, Obesity Research Center, St. Luke's Roosevelt Hospital Center.

Detailed listing of content reviewers

This e-text is not copyrighted. The clearinghouse encourages users of this e-pub to duplicate and distribute as many copies as desired.

U.S. DEPARTMENT OF HEALTH AND HUMAN SERVICES
National Institutes of Health

NIH Publication No. 02-4992
June 2002

Figure 16–9   Page Acknowledging Expert Review of Content   *Source:* National Institutes of Health (<nih.gov>).

CHAPTER 16 SUMMARY: Writing for the Web (*continued*)

Use the following revision checklist to make sure that content you develop or adapt for the Web is crafted for ease of reading by site visitors and is accessible to people with disabilities as well as to international users.

☐ Plan, organize, and write Web content that can be grasped quickly and efficiently using the following techniques:

- Use the inverted-pyramid method to organize content "top down" so that key points and conclusions appear first.
- Develop content that is accurate, backed up by supporting evidence, and expressed in a tone appropriate for your audience.
- Write concisely and use plain-language principles consistent with your content.
- Break up dense blocks of text into coherent paragraph-length passages that are sequenced by the inverted-pyramid method.
- Expand access to your information by hyperlinking it to content at your or other Web sites.

☐ Augment access to your content using the following highlighting techniques:

- Introduce topics with heads and subheads to signal the shift from one topic to another.
- Use bullets and numbered lists to further break up dense blocks of text and focus reader attention on relevant points.
- Use directional cues appropriate to a Web page and avoid those that make sense only in printed material.
- Describe important passages using key terms and concepts that allow search engines to locate your content.
- Select graphics pertinent to your audience and purpose, and optimize them for quick access.
- Choose type sizes and fonts to enhance legibility.
- Limit line length to promote ease of scanning.

☐ Provide for the special needs of people with disabilities and international site visitors by adhering to the following guidelines:

- Create content compatible with adaptive technologies.
- Use language, units of measurements, and graphics that are consistent with the practices of international and U.S. site visitors.

☐ Submit a previously published document to a Web site according to the following guidelines:

- Submit the document in the most suitable file format for the site.
- Inform site users if the Web version is abridged or otherwise differs from the printed version.
- Obtain prior permission to publish works that contain copyrighted text or graphics.
- Examine the document on an internal Web server for accuracy and effectiveness before it is posted for public access.
- For a long document, post a single-file version for users wishing to print the document.

> **CHAPTER 16 SUMMARY: Writing for the Web**
> (*continued*)
>
> ☐ Inform site users of how or whether their privacy is protected if they submit so-licited or unsolicited information to you.
>
> ☐ Give credit to outside sources of content at your site, including approval to use copyrighted material.

■ Exercises

1. Bring in a report, a research paper, or an essay written for another course and re-work it so it is appropriately chunked for online reading. Use appropriate captions and headings.

2. Write a letter to the head of an organization or to its respective webmaster asking if you can submit a report, a research paper, an essay, or another text you have al-ready written, or would like to write, to its Web site. Review Posting an Existing Document in this chapter before you begin. You can also use your text from Exercise 1.

3. Using this textbook (or a textbook from another class that you are taking) as a model, analyze the use of heads, subheads, white space, models/examples, visu-als, and so on. Note the consistency in the use of these and other textual elements. Do they invite the reader to continue to read from section to section and chapter to chapter? Present your findings to the class.

4. Imagine that you are a writer who wants to publish an online book because it is much cheaper to present your book in a PDF format and let readers print the pages than it is to print a hard-copy book yourself. Create an idea for your book, then design the layout of the pages and text. Use your findings from Exercise 3 to help in your design choices.

5. Create a ten-item online sample questionnaire that you could use to gather infor-mation about the television and music preferences of today's college students. Create your questions, then decide how you would design the layout of this ques-tionnaire. Consider chunking, concise text, heads and subheads, bullets and num-bered lists, and so on. Present your document to the class.

■ Collaborative Classroom Projects

1. In a group of four to six students, create a table designed to analyze the text of a Web site.

   a. Sort and reorganize the following categories under these subheadings: "Audience and Purpose," "Language and Voice," "Style," "Organization," "Punc-tuation and Mechanics," and "Visual Design:"

      Document fulfills the assigned task.
      Text anticipates the reader's questions.
      Background information is sufficient.
      Terms, acronyms, and abbreviations are defined for the audience.
      Active voice is used.

Paragraphs are of appropriate length.
Sentence length is appropriate.
Transitions exist between paragraphs.
Headings and subheadings are used effectively.
Lists are parallel.
Capitalization of words, titles, headings, and subheadings is consistent.
Quotes, punctuation for quotes, and citing/documentation styles are used correctly.
Numbers, bullets and trademark symbols are used consistently.
Spelling and grammar errors are minimal or nonexistent.
Punctuation is accurate and appropriate.
Internal and external links are appropriate.
White space is appropriate.
Text is highlighted appropriately (bolded, italicized, etc.).

b. Create a table using your word-processing software's Table tool. Your table will need to have at least 24 rows (see Chapter 8 for table format guidance) to accommodate the subheadings and categories. The table will also need at least three columns. Label the first column "Tasks." Label the second column "Rank from 1 to 5." Label the third column "Comments."

c. Insert the sorted subheadings and categories in the first column (each in its own row).

2. Using the table created in Collaborative Classroom Project 1, in groups of four to six, find three Web sites from a similar field (e.g., three car manufacturers' Web sites, three university homepages) and analyze them according to the categories in your table. Rank them from 1 to 5 (with 5 being best) in the second column, and add any necessary comments on the text to help support your ranking in the third column.

3. Based on your table in Collaborative Classroom Projects 1 and 2, write a formal report to the class detailing your findings (see Chapter 12 for help with reports). Be sure to use headings and subheadings in the report and include a graph or chart that represents some of your findings. (Do not include the full table within your report; include it in the appendix.)

4. Using hard-copy newspapers, pick a current topic in the news and find three to five stories on the topic. Read these stories, then write an online article on this topic using the inverted-pyramid style. Then, using your school library's access to databases, go to LexisNexis (a database of newspaper and journal articles), or access several online newspapers, and compare your story with those already online. Report your findings to your instructor.

5. In groups of four to six students who share similar majors, brainstorm a list of classes that each student has taken that was most helpful to them so far in their academic career. These courses may have provided a strong foundation to their understanding of the field, a clearer understanding of a key concept relevant to the discipline, and so on. Then, using concise writing and bullet points, provide a summary of the group's experiences. Be ready to present your findings to the class.

■ Research Projects

Projects followed by the symbol **W** are continued at **bedfordstmartins.com/writingthatworks**, Chapter 16.

1. Bring in a research paper or an essay written for another course and rework it so that it has appropriate heads and subheads for online reading. Then go through the text and note places where you could link elements in your text to existing Web sites. Find Web sites to link to and list them on a separate page.

2. Write an online report detailing the cars, trucks, and sport utility vehicles with the best and worst gas mileage ratings. Begin by researching sites that detail vehicles and their miles per gallon. Then write your report in the inverted-pyramid style. [W]

3. Imagine that your major department has its own Web site. Write an online article that describes (a) five databases to which your college library has access that are pertinent to your field of study and (b) the newest books in your field recently acquired by your school's library.

4. Write a story for an online financial newsletter on the recent historical activity on the New York Stock Exchange (NYSE) of two specific stocks in the same field. Begin by going to stock information sites. Then pick two companies (e.g., The Home Depot, Inc., and Lowe's Companies, Inc.) and research their stock histories for the past two years. Write your story using the inverted-pyramid style. [W]

5. In groups of three or four students who share your major, bring to class information from three Web sites related to your area of study. Print out relevant pages from each site and together review the guidelines in this chapter for writing online documentation. Draft a list of questions to consider when evaluating online text as a research resource specific to your field. Evaluate and compare each of the sites that your group members have found and decide which sites would be the most valuable for your research. Write a brief group summary of your findings to share with the class.

▓ Web Projects

Projects followed by the symbol [W] are continued at **bedfordstmartins.com/ writingthatworks**, Chapter 16.

1. Different government agencies list their own recommendations for Web writing. Go to a search engine and, using words and phrases such as "Web writing and government," compare the Web-writing recommendations of government agencies in the United States and across the world. [W]

2. There are many Web sites for freelance writers that list available writing assignments and offer advice on how to write for print and online sources. Using sources that offer advice on Web writing, write an article on new opportunities in and recommendations for online writing. Remember to use quotation marks, where appropriate, and cite correctly (see Chapter 7 for help with documenting sources). [W]

3. Go to the U.S. Government Printing Office's site for historical documents and write two versions of one Web article about one of these documents. Imagine that you are trying to get the story online in time for a national holiday or the anniversary of one of the documents (if the anniversary or holiday has passed, you can still write it for publication next year). Write two versions of the online article: one for recent immigrants for whom English is a second language, and one for 9th to

12th graders. Remember that different audiences have different needs and purposes for reading a text (see Chapter 1 on audience and purpose and Chapter 9 on international communication). 🆆

4. Many local governments have city Web sites that include text that describes local attractions, listings of educational institutions in the area, recommended shopping and art areas, and so on. Go to your city or town's Web site and analyze the material already on the site. Then get the name and e-mail address of the city site's webmaster and write a letter to him or her with ideas for stories on colorful characters or events or places in the city that would be relevant for that site. 🆆

5. Assume that you have been assigned to write an article on specific types of jobs available through the U.S. Government for an online human resources or job-search site. Go to government job sites and search for a specific type of job category, like "accountant" or "writer." Be sure to review the "Vacancy Announcement" for details of each job, along with the "Summary of Duties," for the qualifications, basic requirements, and so on. Write an article on your findings and be ready to present it to the class. 🆆

17 Finding the Right Job

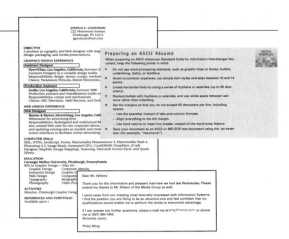

B efore you begin your search for a job, do some serious thinking about your future. Decide first what you would most like to be doing now. Then think about the kind of work you'd like to be doing two years from now and five years from now. Once you have established your goals, you can begin your job hunt with greater confidence because you'll have a better idea of what kind of position you are looking for and in what companies or other organizations you are most likely to find that position.

The search for a job can be logically divided into five steps, each of which is covered in this chapter:

- Determining the best job for you
- Preparing an effective résumé
- Writing an effective letter of application
- Doing well in the interview
- Sending follow-up correspondence

W **On the Web**
For more advice on finding a job or an internship, see Chapter 17, bedfordstmartins .com/writingthatworks

■ Determining the Best Job for You

Whether you are trying to land your first job or you want to change careers entirely, begin by assessing your skills, interests, and abilities, perhaps through brainstorming, as discussed in Chapter 1 on pages 8–9. Next, consider what your career goals and values are. Ask yourself the following questions: What courses have I most enjoyed? Does helping others interest me? How important are career stability and a certain standard of living? Do I prefer working independently or collaboratively?[1]

---

[1]A good source for stimulating your thinking is the most recent edition of *What Color Is Your Parachute? A Practical Manual for Job-Hunters & Career-Changers* by Richard Nelson Bolles, published by Ten Speed Press.

Once you've reflected and brainstormed about the job that's right for you, a number of sources can help you locate the job you want:

- College career services
- Internet resources
- Networking
- Letters of inquiry
- Advertisements in newspapers
- Trade and professional journals
- Private and temporary employment agencies
- Government employment agencies

Finding the job that's right for you may take many months. If you face unemployment during this period, consider working for a temporary employment agency, as described on page 594.

College Career Services

Visiting your school's career center—and working with a counselor who understands your strengths and interests—is a great way to begin your job search. Recruiters from business, industry, and government often visit college job-placement offices to interview prospective employees. Recruiters will also keep your school's career counselors aware of current employment needs and current job openings. Not only can career counselors help you in the brainstorming phase of your career selection, but they can also put you in touch with important, current resources. They can identify where to begin your search and suggest ways to save you time. Career centers often hold job fairs and workshops on such topics as preparing your résumé for your particular field and doing well in an interview. (See pages 595–613 for help on résumé preparation.)

Internet Resources

In addition to providing access to job listings in newspapers and professional journals, the Web provides a wealth of sites where you can search for a job, get help with your résumé and cover letter, and apply for jobs confidentially. The following general-interest sites include job-search guidance as well as job listings.

W **On the Web**
To read C. J. Pascarella's successful résumé and cover letter, see Chapter 17, bedfordstmartins.com/ writingthatworks

- *America's Job Bank*

  Sponsored by the U.S. Department of Labor, *America's Job Bank* is a comprehensive listing of job postings categorized by state. It also contains such information as salary and demographic employment profiles for job seekers interested in relocating to a region.

Voices from the Workplace

Sherri Pfennig, University of Wisconsin–Milwaukee

Sherri Pfennig is Senior Career Counselor at the University of Wisconsin–Milwaukee's Career Development Center. Sherri stresses the importance of considering audience and purpose for effective résumé writing: "Your résumé is a commercial, just like the commercials you see on TV or anywhere else. For a commercial to be successful, the creator has to know the product and the audience inside out. Creators of commercials might change the language or the packaging to reach different audiences. Likewise, you need to know what you are trying to sell with your résumé, what your audience is buying, and how this audience talks about those qualities and skills."

In addition to advising hundreds of students seeking jobs, Sherri gives this advice for preparing for the successful interview: "There are five topics for which you need to be 'blue book' ready. This means you have sat down and thought about your strengths and weaknesses in these areas and you are ready to discuss them in depth. They are your education, work experience, career goals, personal qualities, and knowledge of the field or the specific organization. Your ultimate goal is to help your interviewer see how what you have to say about these five topics qualifies you for the job. If you aren't ready to do this, you aren't ready to interview."

To find out more about the University of Wisconsin–Milwaukee's Career Development Center, visit its Web site at <uwm.edu/Dept/CDC/index.html>.

C. J. Pascarella, Deloitte & Touche, LLP

C. J. Pascarella is a 2003 graduate of Pennsylvania State University, Altoona, where he majored in business. His writing and job-application skills helped land him a paid internship at Deloitte & Touche, a Big 4 firm that provides accounting, financial management, and other consulting services — and earned him a full-time position upon graduation in May 2003.

"During my sophomore year, my goal was to secure an internship. I knew I wanted the opportunity to experience the Big 4 accounting work environment because of the advantages that these firms offer, including networking opportunities for a broad range of industries and the chance to expand my skills. However, I was cautioned that most of the firms reserve these competitive positions for junior accounting students, so I should not be surprised if the firms put me off for a year.

"Fortunately, I was enrolled in a business writing class that required me to put together a job-application package. With the help of my professor and the models in *Writing That Works,* I was able to create a professional résumé, cover letter, follow-up letter, and responses to correspondence that helped me get my foot in the door at Deloitte & Touche. I was rewarded for my efforts by first being offered a summer externship as a junior — a position that gave me a chance to further understand the firm and its practices, and to broaden my understanding of the accounting industry — and then a paid summer internship as a senior, during which I worked as a staff auditor. Having demonstrated my accounting and writing skills, I have been offered a full-time position that I will begin after graduation."

C. J. offers this advice to students applying for internships and full-time positions. "Because of the large number of applicants each year to internship programs and the competitiveness of these programs, employers often deny a perfectly qualified candidate a position because of one minor error in his or her résumé or cover letter. To avoid such pitfalls, I encourage students to refer to the models in this book and to be sure to proofread everything." As C. J. also found, it is a good idea to share your résumé and cover letter with your instructor or a professional from your field before sending them to prospective employers. "Following these guidelines helped me achieve my Big 4 goal. If you do the same, you will increase your chances of proving yourself to the firm of your choice."

- *Monster.com*

  > One of the best-known sites, *Monster.com* contains such information as career advice and job postings (including international listings). Specialized sites cater to the interests of occupational groups.

- *CollegeGrad.com*

  > *CollegeGrad.com* is a site for the entry-level job seeker. It has user-friendly design links to sections on résumés and cover letters, interviews and negotiations, what to do when you get an offer, and an E-Zine for job hunters.

- *Riley Guide: Employment Opportunities and Job Resources on the Internet*
  <rileyguide.com>

  > The *Riley Guide* contains introductions and annotated links to resources by career field, employer type, and location. There are also sections on résumé preparation and online recruiting.

- *What Color Is Your Parachute? JobHuntersBible.com*

  > *What Color Is Your Parachute?* is a site for job seekers and career changers based on the best-selling book of the same name by Richard N. Bolles. It provides such resources as an interactive test for career counseling, tips for using the Internet, tips for preparing an effective résumé, and links to job postings and other useful sites.

W On the Web
For access to online employment resources, see Chapter 17, bedfordstmartins.com/ writingthatworks

Another option is to visit the Web sites of companies you are interested in. Most corporate Web sites offer job listings online and provide information on whom you should contact. Many include a Contact Us option that allows you to e-mail your cover letter and résumé directly to the appropriate department or person. You might also consider exploring Internet discussion groups that relate to your job specialty. Discussion groups can provide a useful way to keep up with the trends in your profession and general employment conditions over time—and some also post job openings that may be appropriate for you. One resource for finding professional discussion groups is Google Groups, organized by subject and available at <google.group.com>.

Finally, consider creating your own Web site and posting your résumé to attract potential employers. (See the introductory material on writing for the Web in Chapter 16 before you create your own site.) If you post your résumé on the Web, keep in mind the advice given on pages 603–604. If you do not have a Web site or simply don't feel confident in adapting your résumé for the Web, consider using a résumé-writing company that will put your résumé online. Spend time on the Web later in the evening or very early in the morning so that you can focus on in-person contacts during working hours. (See also the discussion of Internet research on pages 209–213.)

Networking

Networking is communicating with people who might provide useful advice or connect you with potential employers. They may be people already working in your chosen field, contacts in professional organizations and volunteer groups, professors and former employers, family members, friends, or neighbors; any of them might direct you to exactly the job lead you need. Use these contacts to develop even more contacts.

Letters of Inquiry and Informal Interviews

If you would like to work for a particular firm, write and ask whether it has any openings for people with your qualifications. Normally, you should send the letter either to the director of human resources or to the department head; for a small firm, however, write to the head of the firm. Your letter should present a general summary of your employment background or training. (See the section on writing letters of application beginning on page 613.)

In your letter of inquiry, ask if you can meet with someone in the firm for an informational interview, and whether you may bring your résumé with you. Some organizations welcome the opportunity to talk with prospective employees, even when they have no immediate job openings. It's a way for them to assess fresh talent, promote their firm, and expand their file of eligible prospects. Although the interview is informal, dress appropriately and do some homework beforehand: What's the firm's core business or mission and its size? Does the firm plan to expand? (Review the list of topics discussed in Doing Well in the Interview on pages 619–623.) Use the interview as an opportunity to practice your interview skills, to learn about accepted workplace standards, and to gain insight into the organization's expectations for prospective employees.

Advertisements in Newspapers

Many employers advertise in the classified sections of print and online newspapers. Occasionally, newspapers print special supplements that provide valuable information on résumé preparation, job fairs, and other facets of the job market. Check the Sunday editions of major newspapers for the widest selection of employment listings. Keep in mind that a position may be listed under various classifications. A clinical medical technologist seeking a job, for example, might find the specialty listed under "Medical Technologist," "Clinical Medical Technologist," or "Laboratory Technologist." Depending on a hospital's or a pathologist's needs, the listing could be even more specific, such as "Blood Bank Technologist" or "Hematology Technologist." So try to read all areas that may be pertinent to your job search.

As you read the ads, take notes on such things as salary ranges, job locations, job duties and responsibilities, and even the terminology used in the ads to describe the work. A knowledge of the words and expressions that are generally used to describe a particular type of work can be helpful when you prepare your résumé and letters of application. Using the appropriate terminology is especially important for résumés that you submit electronically. (See Electronic Résumés on page 601.)

Trade and Professional Journals

Ⓦ **On the Web**
For access to professional organizations and publications, see Chapter 17, bedfordstmartins.com/ writingthatworks

In many industries, associations publish periodicals of interest to people working in the industry. Such periodicals (print and online) often contain job listings. If you were seeking a job in forestry, for example, you could check the job listings in the *Journal of Forestry*, published by the Society of American Foresters. To learn about the trade or professional associations for your occupation, consult resources on the Web, such as Google's *Directory of Professional Organizations*, or online resources offered by your library or campus career office. You may also consult the following references at a library: *Encyclopedia of Associations*, *Encyclopedia of Business Information Sources*, and *National Directory of Employment Services*. (See also Library Research on pages 202–209 in Chapter 7.)

Private and Temporary Employment Agencies

Private employment agencies are organizations that are in business to help people find jobs — for a fee. Reputable private employment agencies provide you with job leads and help you to organize your campaign to find the job you want. They may also provide useful information on the companies doing the hiring.

Ⓦ **On the Web**
For access to employment agencies approved by the Better Business Bureau, see Chapter 17, bedfordstmartins.com/ writingthatworks

Choose a private employment agency carefully, preferably through a personal recommendation. Some are well established and quite reputable, but others have questionable reputations. Check with your local Better Business Bureau and with friends, acquaintances, or your school's career office before you sign an agreement with a private employment agency.

Before signing a contract, be sure you understand who is paying the agency's fee; if you have to pay, make sure you know exactly how much. Often, the employer pays the fee. As with any written agreement, read the fine print carefully.

Temporary employment agencies and services offer another way of determining the job that may fit you — through experience. For example, if you are interested in — but not certain about — a professional area, consider working in that area as a temporary or part-time employee. Even as a temporary member of a support staff, you can gain valuable experience that can help you decide whether a particular profession is right for you. Temporary work in a professional area will also enable you to network, as discussed on page 593.

Government Employment Services

Local, state, and federal government agencies offer many employment services. Local government agencies are listed in telephone and Web directories under the name of your city, county, or state. For detailed information on the trends of over

250 occupations, see the most recent edition of the *Occupational Outlook Handbook* published by the U.S. Department of Labor at <bls.gov/OCO>. For information about jobs with the federal government, contact the U.S. Office of Personnel Management at <usajobs.opm.gov/>.

Keep records of job ads, the dates they were published, the period during which applications will be accepted, copies of letters of application and résumés, notes requesting interviews, and the names of important contacts. Use your records as a future resource and reminder.

W On the Web
For access to government employment resources, see Chapter 17, **bedfordstmartins** **.com/writingthatworks**

■ Preparing an Effective Résumé

A résumé is a summary of your qualifications and your main tool for finding a job. Your résumé itemizes the qualifications that you can mention only briefly in your application letter. The information in your résumé is key to helping employers decide whether to contact you for a personal interview. It can also serve as the source for specific questions asked during an interview. (See also Doing Well in the Interview on pages 619–623.)

W On the Web
For job-hunting tips and sample résumés, see Chapter 17, **bedfordstmartins.com/** **writingthatworks**

Your résumé forms the basis for a potential employer's impression of you, so don't skimp when creating yours. Use a high-quality printer and high-grade paper. Take the time to make your résumé attractive, well organized, easy to read, and, above all, free of errors. Proofread it carefully, verify the accuracy of the information, and have at least one other person—preferably your instructor or someone in your professional field—review it. Experiment with the design to determine a layout that highlights your strengths. Generally, keep the résumé to one page unless you have a great deal of experience. If you are a recent college graduate, stick to one page. (See also the discussion of designing documents in Chapter 8, on pages 251–261, and proofreading on pages 731–734.)

Analyzing Your Background

In preparing to write your résumé, determine what kind of job you are seeking. Then ask yourself what information about you and your background would be most important to a prospective employer in the field you have chosen. On the basis of your answers, decide what details to include in your résumé and how you can most effectively present your qualifications. Brainstorm about yourself and your background, answering the following questions:

- What college or colleges did you attend? What degree(s) do you hold? What was your major field of study? What academic honors were you awarded?
- What internships or jobs have you held? What were your principal and secondary duties in each of them? When and for how long did you hold each job?
- What personal and professional experience have you gained that would be of value in the kind of job you are seeking?

- What extracurricular activities have contributed to your learning experience? What are your leadership skills? What collaborative experience do you have?

Use your answers as a starting point and let one question lead to another.

Organizing Your Résumé

You can organize your résumé in many different ways. A common organization is to arrange information chronologically within the following topical categories:

Heading (name and contact information)
Job objective (optional)
Education
Employment experience
Skills and activities
References
Portfolios (optional)

Whether you place education or employment experience first depends on which would most strengthen your résumé. If you are a recent graduate, you would probably list education first because you may not have much work experience. If you have years of related job experience, you would list job experience first because your interviewer will most likely be interested in the skills you gained at your previous jobs. In both cases, list the most recent education or job experience first, the next most recent experience second, and so on.

The Heading

Create a heading that clearly shows your name, address, telephone and fax numbers, and e-mail address. Do not include a date in the heading; if you do, you will have to change it every time you submit your résumé to a prospective employer. Centering your heading at the top of the page usually works best (Figure 17–1).

CONSUELA B. SANDOVAL
6819 Elm Street
Somerville, Massachusetts 02144
(617) 625-1552
cbsand@cpu.fairview.edu

Figure 17–1   Heading of a Résumé

Employment Objective

If you have a clear job or career objective, you can include it in your résumé. If you do, state not only your immediate employment objective but the direction you hope your career will take. A job objective may be particularly useful in an electronic résumé because it serves both as a screening device and as an introduction to the material in the résumé (Figure 17–2). Be aware, however, that this section is optional.

EMPLOYMENT OBJECTIVE

To obtain a position that allows me to use my computer-science training to solve engineering problems with the potential to gain valuable management experience.

Figure 17–2   Employment Objective Section of a Résumé

Education

List the college or colleges you attended, the dates you attended each one, the degree or degrees you received, your major field of study and relevant course work, and any academic honors you earned (Figure 17–3). Mention the name of your

---

EDUCATION

Georgia Institute of Technology
Bachelor of Science in Engineering (expected June 2004)
Cumulative Grade Point Average: 3.46 out of possible 4.0

College, degree, and field of study

   Major Courses
   Calculus, I, II, III, IV
   Methods of Digital Computations
   Advanced Computer Techniques
   Special Computer Techniques
   Differential Equations
   Graphic Display
   Software Design

Major courses pertinent to field of study

   Activities and Honors
   Phi Chi Epsilon — Honor Society for Women in Business
     and Engineering
   Society of Women Engineers — Secretary-Treasurer junior year
   American Institute of Industrial Engineers — Secretary junior year
   Engineering Science Club
   Doris Harlow Scholarship recipient for two consecutive years
   Dean's List six of eight semesters

Activities and honors to highlight accomplishments

Figure 17–3   Education Section of a Résumé

high school only if your attendance was relatively recent, your résumé is very sparse, or you want to call attention to awards you earned in high school or to related programs, internships, or study abroad.

Employment Experience

List all your full-time jobs, starting with the most recent and working backward in time (Figure 17–4). Even if you have little full-time work experience, list part-time

Chronological listing of job experience

EMPLOYMENT EXPERIENCE

Computer Systems International, Atlanta, Georgia
September 2003 to Present
　　As Assistant Training Director, assisted in preparing Professional Training Program for the Design, Data Entry, and Engineering Departments.

Vacationland Amusement Park, Toccoa, Georgia
April 2002 to August 2003
　　As Chief Lifeguard, trained and supervised three other lifeguards.

Figure 17–4　Employment Experience Section of a Résumé

and temporary jobs, including internships, especially if they relate to your major field of study or career goals. Provide a concise description of your duties for those jobs with duties similar to those of the job you are seeking; if a job is not directly relevant, give only a job title and a very brief description of duties that developed broad skills valued in the position you are seeking. For example, if you were a lifeguard, focus on supervisory experience, or even experience in averting disaster to highlight decision-making and crisis-management skills. If you have been with one company for a number of years, highlight your accomplishments and promotions during those years. List military service as a job, give the dates you served, your duty specialty, and your rank at discharge. Describe military duties only if they apply to the job you are applying for.

　　Résumés are often organized by type of work experience rather than by job chronology. Instead of listing the positions held in sequence, a functional résumé lists jobs by the functions performed in all jobs. If you were preparing a functional résumé you might group your experience and skills under categories such as "Management," "Project Development," "Training," and "Sales." Organization by function is useful for applicants who want to stress certain skills important to the prospective employer or industry or who have been employed at only one job and want to demonstrate the diversity of their experience in that position. Functional arrangement is also useful if you are changing careers and you want to highlight transferable skills. It can also be useful for anyone with gaps in his or her résumé caused by unemployment or illness. Although functional arrangement can be effective, prospective employers know that it is sometimes used to cover weaknesses, so use it only when you feel it is to your advantage and be prepared to explain any gaps it may reveal.

Creating a Résumé Using a Template

DIGITAL SHORTCUTS

MS Word and WordPerfect offer templates for a variety of résumé styles.

- Click on File/New and follow the guidance provided.
- Select from a variety of ways to organize the content:
  - Entry level
  - Chronological
  - Functional
- Apply an array of design features:
  - Add lines across the page.
  - Change fonts.
  - Standardize headings.
- Spell check before printing. Proofread carefully.

Skills and Activities

The skills-and-activities category usually comes near the end of the résumé. Include items such as fluency in a foreign language, writing and editing abilities, specialized technical knowledge (such as knowledge of specific computer operating systems, Web composition, or desktop-publishing programs), student or community activities, professional or club memberships, published works, or Web sites you created. Be selective; do not duplicate information given in other categories, and include only activities and skills that support your employment objective. Provide a heading for this category that fits its contents, depending on which skills or activities you want to emphasize, such as "Skills and Activities," "Professional Affiliations," or "Publications and Memberships."

References

You can include references as part of the résumé or provide a statement that references will be provided upon request. Either way, do not give anyone as a reference without first obtaining his or her permission.

Portfolios

The résumé may also state that a "Portfolio is available on request." Portfolios have traditionally been used by artists and writers to illustrate their work. However, a portfolio also may provide samples of your most impressive written work (reports, proposals, presentations), copies of letters of praise, certificates that attest to special abilities, newspaper clippings, and other items that visually display your accomplishments and potential contributions to a prospective employer. Present your portfolio professionally and attractively in a folder or binder. For an interview, it is best to bring a portfolio containing ten items or fewer. For further advice on portfolios, check the Kimeldorf Library Web site at <amby.com/kimeldorf/>.

W On the Web
For more portfolio resources, see Chapter 17, bedfordstmartins.com/ writingthatworks

Writing Your Résumé

When writing your résumé, use action verbs (for example, "managed" rather than "was the manager") and state ideas concisely. However, even though the résumé is about you, do not use the word "I."

■ ~~I was promoted~~ *Promoted* to Section Leader in June 2003.

Be truthful in your résumé. If you give false information and are found out, the consequences could be serious. In fact, the truthfulness of your résumé reflects not only your personal ethics but also the integrity with which you would represent the organization.

Do not list salary requirements on the résumé. For advice on salary negotiations for a new job, see pages 622–623.

If you are returning to the workplace after an absence, most career experts say that it is important to acknowledge the gap in your career rather than trying to hide it. That is particularly true if, for example, you are reentering the workforce because you have devoted a full-time period to care for children or dependent adults. Do not undervalue such work. Although unpaid, it often provides experience that develops important time-management, problem-solving, organizational, and interpersonal skills. Figure 17–5 illustrates how you might reflect such experiences in a résumé.

Unpaid home-care tasks feature organizational and time-management responsibilities

---

Primary Child-Care Provider, 2001 to 2003
>   Furnished full-time care to three preschool children in a home environment. Instructed in crafts, beginning scholastic skills, time management, basics of nutrition, and swimming. Organized activities, managed household, and served as block-watch captain.

Home Caregiver, 2002 to 2003
>   Provided 60 hours per week in-home care to an Alzheimer's patient. Coordinated medical care, developed exercise programs, completed and processed complex medical forms, administered medications, organized budget, and managed home environment.

Figure 17–5   Unpaid Employment Experience Included in a Résumé

If you have done volunteer work during such a period, list that experience, too. Volunteer work provides valuable experience that your résumé should reflect, as in Figure 17–6.

Volunteer tasks feature coordination, organizational, and funds-management skills

---

School Association Coordinator, 2002 to 2003
>   Managed special activities of the Briarwood Elementary School Parent-Teacher Association. Planned and coordinated meetings, scheduled events, and supervised fund-drive operations. Raised $70,000 toward refurbishing the school auditorium.

Figure 17–6   Volunteer Employment Experience Included in a Résumé

Electronic Résumés

In addition to the traditional paper résumé, you can submit an electronic résumé to a potential employer in the following ways:

- In plain-text format for ease of electronic scanning
- On disk or as an e-mail attachment
- As a posting to employment sites on the Web

You can also display and periodically update your résumé at your own Web site.

Plain-Text and Portable Document File Résumés

Large companies often electronically scan résumés into a database, which allows them a timesaving way to screen a large pool of applicants for job openings. With this practice in mind, be prepared to submit your résumé in more than one format. In addition to the traditional paper résumé, prepare and submit a no-frills or plain-text version for ease of scanning. A plain-text version is easier to scan than the traditional résumé because OCR (optical character recognition) scanning software does poorly in recognizing unusual typefaces, graphics, boxes, and other typographic and design features common in traditional paper résumés. The easiest way around these limitations is to format a version of your résumé as a plain-text file (.txt) or to use ASCII-compatible[2] characters so that it can be read accurately across most applications and systems. When creating a résumé in ASCII format, as shown in Figure 17–7, do not use underlining, italics, or boldface type.

Avoid decorative, uncommon, or otherwise fancy typefaces; use simple font styles (a sans serif font such as Ariel) and sizes between 10 and 14 points. Use white space generously because scanners use it to recognize where one topic has ended and another has begun. Although a paper résumé is best kept to one page, you need not limit an electronic résumé to a single page. However, keep the résumé as simple, clear, and concise as possible. Use white or beige paper and do not fold it for mailing because a scanner can misread a folded line.

You may also include a section in such a résumé titled "Keywords." These terms, also called *descriptors,* allow employers to search the database for a match between their job requirements and the qualifications on the résumés of candidates in the system. Be sure to use keywords identical to those used in the employer's job descriptions that best match your interests and qualifications. This section can be placed to follow the main heading or near the end of your résumé, such as before the "References" heading. The sample résumé in Figure 17–7 includes a listing of keywords.

You may also submit a traditional résumé as an e-mail attachment that the employer can print. If you need to submit a résumé with special typographic and design features, however, consider scanning it as a PDF image file and e-mailing it as an attachment in that format. PDF image files are, in effect, a snapshot of the

---

[2] ASCII (pronounced *ăs´-kēy*) is an acronym for American Standard Code for Information Interchange and is the most basic format for transferring files between different programs. In word-processing terms, it can be thought of as unformatted text.

DAVID B. EDWARDS
6819 Locustview Drive
Topeka, Kansas 66614
(913) 233-1552
dedwards@cpu.fairview.edu

JOB OBJECTIVE
Work as a programmer with writing, editing, and training responsibilities, leading to a career in information design management.

KEYWORDS
Programmer, Operating Systems, Unipro, Newsletter, Graphics, Cybernetics, Listserv, Professional Writer, Editor, Trainer, Teacher, Instructor, Technical Writer, Tutor, Designer, Manager, Information Design.

Asterisks replace bullets, and all lines begin at left margin

EDUCATION
** Fairview Community College, Topeka, Kansas
** Associate's Degree, Computer Science, June 2003
** Dean's Honor List Award (six quarters)

RELEVANT COURSE WORK
** Operating Systems Design
** Database Management
** Introduction to Cybernetics
** Technical Writing

EMPLOYMENT EXPERIENCE
** Computer Consultant: September 2002 to Present
Fairview Community College Computer Center: Advised and trained novice computer users; wrote and maintained Unipro operating system documentation.
** Tutor: January 2002 to June 2003
Fairview Community College: Assisted students in mathematics and computer programming.

SKILLS AND ACTIVITIES
** Unipro Operating System: Thorough knowledge of word-processing, text-editing, and file-formatting programs.
** Writing and Editing Skills: Experience in documenting computer programs for beginning programmers and users.
** Fairview Community Microcomputer Users Group: Co-founder and editor of monthly newsletter ("Compuclub"); listserv manager.

FURTHER INFORMATION
** References, college transcripts, a portfolio of computer programs, and writing samples available upon request.

Figure 17–7   Résumé in ASCII Format

original document, so they retain the full range of formatting options found there (boldface, italics, underlining, vertical and horizontal lines, different type sizes).

Preparing an ASCII Résumé

When preparing an ASCII (American Standard Code for Information Interchange) document, keep the following points in mind.

- Do not use word-processing elements, such as graphic lines or boxes, bullets, underlining, italics, or boldface.
- Avoid uncommon typefaces; use simple font styles and sizes between 10 and 14 points.
- Create horizontal lines by using a series of hyphens or asterisks (up to 60 characters).
- Replace bullets with hyphens or asterisks, and use white space between sections rather than indenting.
- Set the margins so that you do not exceed 65 characters per line, including spaces.
    - Use the space bar instead of tabs and column formats.
    - Align everything to the left margin.
    - Use hard returns to insert line breaks, instead of the word-wrap feature.
- Save your document as an ASCII or MS-DOS text document using the .txt extension (for example, "resume.txt").

Web Résumés

Another option is to post your résumé on your own Web site. Doing so makes it available to potential employers at their convenience—you need only send them your Web address. A Web résumé can also be updated as often as necessary without the need to mail updates to everyone. Perhaps the chief advantage of a Web résumé is that it allows you to create an electronic portfolio linked to samples of your work—reports, articles, graphics projects, presentations, and the like. An interactive résumé with links to the portfolio will only work if you create an HTML (hypertext markup language) version of your work. If you wish to post a résumé and portfolio without hyperlinks, you could use a PDF image format instead.

If you plan to post your résumé on your own Web site, keep the following points in mind:

- View your résumé on several browsers to see how it looks.
- Just below your name, you can include internal links to such important categories as "Experience" and "Education."
- Use a counter to keep track of the number of times your résumé Web page has been visited.
- If you are concerned about your privacy, include an e-mail link ("mailto") at the top of the résumé rather than your home address and phone number.

Make the most of posting your résumé on your own Web site by e-mailing links to potential employers. Keep in mind that personal Web sites are by their nature less effective than commercial services that attract recruiters with their large databases of candidates.

Sample Résumés

This section includes a number of sample résumés intended to stimulate your thinking about your own résumé, which must be tailored to your own job search. Examine as many résumés as possible and select the format that best suits your goals.

Figures 17–8 and 17–9, respectively, are résumés by a recent community-college graduate and by an applicant who has been employed for many years. The writer of the résumé in Figure 17–8 has only limited work experience and therefore puts the education section first and gives fairly detailed information about his college work. The writer of the résumé in Figure 17–9 has had many years of full-time employment, so he puts his work experience first—his work experience is much more important to a prospective employer than his educational data.

The résumé shown in Figure 17–10 is for a current college student seeking an internship. She begins with her education but also features work experience advantageous to the internship she seeks. The résumés in Figures 17–11 and 17–12 reflect work experience for an employee later in her career (one organized by job, the other by function).

During your job search, apply for as many positions as possible that are acceptable to you and for which you qualify. However, be careful to adapt your core résumé to the specific requirements of each job listing before you submit it. Note how the applicant, Joshua Goodman, tailors the two résumés in Figures 17–13 and 17–14 in response to two different job listings for a graphics designer. The ABC Services listing (Figure 17–15) describes a candidate who can use graphics and desktop publishing software to produce paper-based products ("ads, brochures, signs, flyers, etc.") for printing ("Must be familiar with print process . . ."). Joshua's résumé focuses on his experience with this work under Graphics Design Experience. For the listing in Figure 17–16, his résumé (Fig-ure 17–14) gives equal coverage to his graphics- and Web-design capabilities in response to the XYZ Group's listing for someone with both skills. He specifically inserts a new section (Web Design Experience) for this purpose. If he's interviewed by ABC Services and asked about Web design, he can discuss his background then.

DAVID B. EDWARDS
6819 Locustview Drive
Topeka, Kansas 66614
(913) 233-1552
dedwards@cpu.fairview.edu

Heading with name and contact information

EDUCATION

Fairview Community College, Topeka, Kansas
Associate's Degree, Computer Science, June 2003
Dean's Honor List Award — six quarters

Education and listing of course work appropriate for a recent graduate

RELEVANT COURSE WORK

    Operating Systems Design   Computer Graphics
    Database Management   Introduction to Web Design
    Introduction to Cybernetics   Technical Writing

EMPLOYMENT EXPERIENCE

COMPUTER CONSULTANT September 2002–June 2003, Fairview Community College Computer Center: Advised and trained novice computer users; wrote and maintained Unipro operating system documentation.

Part-time job experience relevant to a recent graduate

TUTOR January 2002–June 2003, Fairview Community College: Assisted students in mathematics and computer programming.

SKILLS AND ACTIVITIES

UNIPRO OPERATING SYSTEM: Thorough knowledge of its word-processing, text-editing, and file-formatting programs.

Activities relate to college major and job objective

WRITING AND EDITING SKILLS: Experience in documenting computer programs for beginning programmers and users.

FAIRVIEW COMMUNITY MICROCOMPUTER USERS' GROUP: Co-founder and editor of monthly newsletter; listserv manager.

PERSONAL WEB SITE: <techrite.com>

FURTHER INFORMATION

References, college transcripts, a portfolio of computer programs, and writing samples available upon request.

Figure 17–8   Résumé of a Recent College Graduate

ROBERT MANDILLO
7761 Shalamar Drive
Dayton, Ohio 45424

Home: (513) 255-4137
Business: (513) 543-3337

Fax: (513) 255-3117
mand@juno.com

EMPLOYMENT EXPERIENCE

Begins with job experience relevant to prospective employers

MANAGER, AUTO CAD DRAFTING DEPARTMENT — March 2002 to Present
Wright-Patterson Air Force Base, Dayton, Ohio

Supervise 17 Auto CAD drafters in support of the engineering design staff. Develop, evaluate, and improve materials and equipment for the design and construction of exhibits. Write specifications, negotiate with vendors, and initiate procurement activities for exhibit design support.

SUPERVISOR, GRAPHICS ILLUSTRATORS — May 2001 to February 2002
Henderson Advertising Agency, Cincinnati, Ohio

Supervised five Illustrators and four Drafting Mechanics after promotion from Graphics Technician; analyzed and approved work-order requirements; selected appropriate media and techniques for orders; rendered illustrations in pencil and ink; converted department to CAD system.

EDUCATION

Education and affiliations emphasize rigorous preparation in field and continuing professional interests

Bachelor of Science in Mechanical Engineering Technology, 2001
Edison State College, Wooster, Ohio

Associate's Degree in Mechanical Drafting, 1999
Wooster Community College, Wooster, Ohio

PROFESSIONAL AFFILIATIONS

National Association of Mechanical Engineering and Drafting Design

REFERENCES

References, letters of recommendation, and a portfolio of original designs and drawings available upon request.

Figure 17–9   Résumé of an Applicant with an Extensive Work Record

Renee T. Mitchell

94 Augusta Drive
Deerfield, IL 60015
Tel. 847-999-1234
Email:
rtmitch@northwestern.edu

JOB OBJECTIVE

Internship position in the Press Office of a public interest organization

EDUCATION

2000–present	Northwestern University, Evanston, IL
	Majoring in Journalism, and European History
	GPA: 3.7
	Academic honors, four quarters
	Member, National Society of Collegiate Scholars
	George Watt Memorial Award for history thesis

Sept. 2001–May 2002	La Universidad de Sevilla, Spain
	Concentrations: Journalism and European History
	(classes taught in Spanish)
	Economics thesis on agrarian reform in Honduras

WORK EXPERIENCE

June 2002—Sept. 2002	South Florida Sun-Sentinel, Fort Lauderdale, FL
	Three month copyediting and reporting internship
	Covered police, courts and education (wrote 35 stories)

June 2001–August 2001	Chicago Sun-Times, Chicago IL
	Contributed to weekly e-business column

Sept. 2000–May 2001	The Daily Northwestern, Evanston, IL
	Staff writer, campus desk

ADDITIONAL QUALIFICATIONS

Fluent in Spanish, strong reporting and editing skills, proficient in HTML, Javascript and Dreamweaver

FURTHER INFORMATION

References, college transcripts, and a portfolio of writing samples available upon request.

Figure 17–10   Résumé of a Student Seeking an Internship

CAROL ANN WALKER
137 Sabrina Drive
Huber Heights, OH 45424
(937) 123-4567
caw@kc.com

EMPLOYMENT EXPERIENCE

Kerfheimer Corporation, Dayton, Ohio

*Job-experience
opening highlights
promotion*

Senior Financial Analyst, July 2002–Present
Report to Senior Vice President for Corporate Financial Planning.
Develop manufacturing cost estimates totaling $30 million annually for
mining and construction equipment with Department of Defense.

Financial Analyst, November 1999–June 2002
Developed $50-million funding estimates for major Department of
Defense contracts for troop carriers and digging and earthmoving
machines. Researched funding options, recommending those with most
favorable rates and terms.

First Bank, Inc., Bloomington, Indiana

Planning Analyst, September 1995–November 1999
Developed successful computer models for short- and long-range planning.

EDUCATION

Ph.D. in Finance: expected, June 2003
The Wharton School of the University of Pennsylvania

M.S. in Business Administration, 1998
University of Wisconsin–Milwaukee
"Executive Curriculum" for employees identified as promising by their
employers.

B.S. in Business Administration (*magna cum laude*), 1995
Indiana University
Emphasis: Finance   Minor: Professional Writing

PUBLISHING AND MEMBERSHIP

Published "Developing Computer Models for Financial Planning," *Midwest
Finance Journal* (Vol. 34, No. 2, 2002), pp. 126–136.

Association for Corporate Financial Planning, Senior Member.

REFERENCES

References and a portfolio of financial plans are available upon request.

Figure 17–11   Advanced Résumé Showing Promotion within a Company

CAROL ANN WALKER
137 Sabrina Drive
Huber Heights, OH 45424
(937) 123-4567
caw@kc.com

PROFESSIONAL ACCOMPLISHMENTS

FINANCIAL PLANNING
- Researched funding options to achieve a 23% return on investment.
- Developed long-range funding requirements for over $1 billion in government and military contracts.
- Developed a computer model for long- and short-range planning that saved 65% in proposal-preparation time.
- Received the Financial Planner of the Year Award from the Association of Financial Planners, a national organization composed of both practitioners and academics.

Opens with functions organized by job accomplishments

CAPITAL ACQUISITION
- Developed strategies to acquire over $1 billion at 3% below market rate.
- Secured over $100 million through private and government research grants.
- Developed computer models for capital acquisition that enabled the company to decrease its long-term debt during several major building expansions.

RESEARCH AND ANALYSIS
- Researched and developed computer models applied to practical problems of corporate finance.
- Functioned primarily as a researcher at two different firms for over 11 years.
- Published research in financial journals while pursuing an advanced degree at the Wharton School.

EDUCATION

Ph.D. in Finance: expected, June 2004
The Wharton School of the University of Pennsylvania

M.S. in Business Administration, 1996
University of Wisconsin–Milwaukee
"Executive Curriculum" for employees identified as promising by their employers.

B.S. in Business Administration (*magna cum laude*), 1992
Indiana University
Emphasis: Finance   Minor: Professional Writing

Figure 17–12   Advanced Résumé Organized by Function (continued)

Carol Ann Walker   Page 2

EMPLOYMENT EXPERIENCE

Kerfheimer Corporation, Dayton, Ohio
November 1997–Present
   Senior Financial Analyst
   Financial Analyst

First Bank, Inc., Bloomington, Indiana
September 1992–November 1997
   Planning Analyst

PUBLICATIONS AND MEMBERSHIPS

Published "Developing Computer Models for Financial Planning," *Midwest Finance Journal* (Vol. 34, No. 2, 2002), pp. 126–136.

Association for Corporate Financial Planning, Senior Member.

REFERENCES

References and a portfolio of financial plans are available upon request.

Figure 17–12 **Advanced Résumé Organized by Function** (continued)

JOSHUA S. GOODMAN
222 Morewood Avenue
Pittsburgh, PA 15212
jgoodman@aol.com

OBJECTIVE
A position as a graphics designer with responsibilities in document design, packaging, and media presentations.

GRAPHICS DESIGN EXPERIENCE

| **Assistant Designer** |

Dyer/Khan, Los Angeles, California, Summer 2002, Summer 2003
Assistant Designer in a versatile design studio.
Responsibilities: design, layout, comps, mechanicals, pre-press production, and press inspections for all four-color posters, booklets, brochures, etc.
Clients: Paramount Pictures, Mattel Electronics, and Motown Records.

| **Photo Editor** |

Paramount Pictures Corporation, Los Angeles, California, Summer 2001
Photo Editor for merchandising department.
Responsibilities: establish art files for movie and television properties, edit images used in merchandising, maintain archive and database.

| **Production Assistant** |

Grafis, Los Angeles, California, Summer 2000
Production assistant and miscellaneous studio work at fast-paced design firm.
Responsibilities: comps and mechanicals.
Clients: ABC Television, A&M Records, and Ortho Products Division.

COMPUTER SKILLS
Photoshop 5.5, Image Ready (Animated GIFs), CorelDRAW, DeepPaint, iGrafx Designer, MapEdit (Image Mapping), Scanning, PageMaker, Illustrator, Adobe Acrobat Writer, Microsoft Access/Excel, Quark XPress, MS Word, XML, HTML, JavaScript, Forms, Macromedia Dreamweaver 3, and Macromedia Flash 4.

EDUCATION
Carnegie Mellon University, Pittsburgh, Pennsylvania
BFA in Graphics Design — May 2004.

Industrial Design	Graphic Imaging Processes
Typography	Serigraphy
Photography	Video Production
Corporate Identity	Web Design

ACTIVITIES
Member, Pittsburgh Graphics Design Society; Member, The Design Group.

REFERENCES AND PORTFOLIO
Available upon request.

Opens with job experience to high-light qualifications for graphics position described in Figure 17–15

Highlights publications experience from design through the print-production cycle

Features photography background important for graphics positions

Includes Web software to provide full range of his skills

Describes relevant course work as recent graduate

Figure 17–13   Résumé Tailored to a Job Listing for a Traditional Graphics Designer (for ABC Services, Figure 17–15)

Revised version of previous résumé to target a job listing requiring Web-design skills and experience

Separate Web section calls attention to mandatory skills for the position

Skills section highlights Web software capabilities

Describes relevant course work as recent graduate

JOSHUA S. GOODMAN
222 Morewood Avenue
Pittsburgh, PA 15212
jgoodman@aol.com

OBJECTIVE
A position as a graphics and Web designer with responsibilities in Web and document design, packaging, and media presentations.

GRAPHICS DESIGN EXPERIENCE

Assistant Designer

Dyer/Khan, Los Angeles, California, Summer 2002, Summer 2003
Assistant Designer in a versatile design studio.
Responsibilities: design, layout, comps, mechanicals, and project management.
Clients: Paramount Pictures, Mattel Electronics, and Motown Records.

Production Assistant

Grafis, Los Angeles, California, Summer 2000
Production assistant and miscellaneous studio work at fast-paced design firm.
Responsibilities: comps and mechanicals.
Clients: ABC Television, A&M Records, and Ortho Products Division.

WEB DESIGN EXPERIENCE

Web Designer

Barton & Barton Advertising, Los Angeles, California, 2004
Webmaster for advertising firm.
Responsibilities: Redesigned and maintained Barton & Barton's corporate Web site; created Web sites for two corporate clients, providing Web support by e-mail and updating existing sites as needed; and created interactive Web banners and screen interfaces to facilitate online advertising for three corporate clients.

COMPUTER SKILLS
XML, HTML, JavaScript, Forms, Macromedia Dreamweaver 3, Macromedia Flash 4, Photoshop 5.5, Image Ready (Animated GIFs), CorelDRAW, DeepPaint, iGrafx Designer, MapEdit (Image Mapping), Scanning, Microsoft Access/Excel, and Quark XPress.

EDUCATION
Carnegie Mellon University, Pittsburgh, Pennsylvania
BFA in Graphics Design—May 2004.

Industrial Design	Corporate Identity
Web Design	Graphic Imaging Processes
Typography	Serigraphy
Photography	Video Production

ACTIVITIES
Member, Pittsburgh Graphics Design Society; Member, The Design Group.

REFERENCES AND PORTFOLIO
Available upon request.

Figure 17–14   Résumé Tailored to a Job Listing for a Graphics Designer with Web Development Experience (for XYZ Group, Figure 17–16)

> **GRAPHICS DESIGNER**
> ABC Services, Inc., a hospitality management company located in Anywhere, USA, is in search of a full-time graphics designer able to multi-task and proficient in Adobe PageMaker, Illustrator, Photoshop, Acrobat, and Word to create ads, brochures, signs, flyers, etc. Must be familiar with print process and IBM platforms. ABC offers great benefits, competitive salary, and flexible work environment. Please send résumé and salary requirements to: ABC Group, etc.

Figure 17–15   Job Listing for a Traditional Graphics Designer (ABC Services)

> **GRAPHICS DESIGNER**
> The XYZ Group, a prestigious scientific organization located in Anyplace, USA, seeks a graphics designer. Position requires an experienced and creative graphics designer with strong concept and design skills to work on a wide range of projects, including logos, brochures, posters, annual reports, and Web-site design. Candidate must be able to manage many projects simultaneously and work with minimal supervision on all aspects of projects from start to finish. Must have good interpersonal skills for interaction with a wide variety of staff and volunteers to ensure timely production of all projects.
>
> Candidates must have expert-level knowledge of PageMaker, Photoshop, and Illustrator/FreeHand in the Windows environment and Macromedia Dreamweaver (current release). Must have previous print-buying experience. Web-page development, good proofreading skills, and scanner experience are essential. Bachelor's degree in graphics design, fine arts, communications, or related field with a minimum 3–5 years recent experience using all required skills. Send cover letter and résumé, including salary history, to: XYZ Group, etc.

Figure 17–16   Job Listing for a Graphics Designer with Web-Development Experience (XYZ Group)

Writing an Effective Letter of Application

The letter of application is essentially a sales letter in which you market your skills, abilities, and knowledge (see the discussion of sales letters in Chapter 10, pages 363–365). The objective of an application letter and the accompanying résumé is to attract the attention of the person who screens and hires job applicants and to obtain a job interview. You may be competing with many other applicants, so your application letter must be persuasive. It must (1) give your reader a favorable impression, (2) explain the job that interests you and why, (3) convince your reader that you are qualified for the job by drawing your reader's attention to particular elements in your résumé, and (4) request an interview.

Opening Paragraph

In the opening paragraph, provide context and show your enthusiasm.

1. Indicate how you heard about the opening. If you have been referred to a company by an employee, a career counselor, a professor, or someone else, be sure to mention this even before you state your job objective ("I recently learned from Jodi Hammel of an opening in your firm").

2. State your job objective and mention the specific job title ("Karen Jarrett informed me of a possible opening for a district manager"). Those who make hiring decisions review many application letters. To save them time while also calling attention to your strengths as a candidate, state your job objective directly in your first paragraph.

3. Explain why you are interested in the job ("Your firm's buyer training program is considered one of the most effective" or "Your position interests me because I can further develop my skills and talents").

Note how the following opening paragraph cites where the position was advertised, states the position title, and expresses interest in line with a career objective.

■ Dear Mr. Lupert:

In the February 24, 2003, issue of the *Butler Gazette,* I learned that you have summer technical training internships available. This opportunity interests me because I have the professional and educational background necessary to make positive contributions to your firm.

Body Paragraphs

In the second paragraph (and third, if necessary), show through examples that you are highly qualified for the job. Limit each of these paragraphs to just one basic point that is clearly stated in the topic sentence. For example, your second paragraph might focus on work experience and your third paragraph on educational achievements. Don't just *tell* readers that you're qualified—*show* them by including examples and details. Come across as proud of your achievements and refer to your enclosed résumé. Indicate how (with your talents) you can make valuable contributions to their company, such as "I am confident that my ability to take the initiative would be a valuable asset to your company."

Note how the following two paragraphs from the application letter for the internship position give specific examples of project experience, provide information on course work and degree goals, reference the enclosed résumé, and emphasize how these experiences can contribute to the company.

■ My professional experiences are representative of my abilities. My current project, a computer tutoring system that teaches LISP (an artificial intelligence programming language), is the first of its kind and is now being sold across the country to corporations and universities. I work with a team to test and revise our work until we have solved each problem. I have also developed leadership and collaborative skills that I could contribute to a summer position at Applied Sciences. As a co-founder of a project to target and tutor high school students with learning disabilities, I organized and implemented many of the training and tutoring sessions. My ability to take the initiative on challenging projects would be a valuable asset to your company.

Pursuing degrees in industrial management and computer science has prepared me well to make valuable contributions to your goal of successfully implementing new software. Through varied courses, described in my résumé, I have the ability to learn new skills and to interact effectively in a technical environment. I would look forward to applying all these abilities at Applied Sciences, Inc.

Closing Paragraph

In the final paragraph, request an interview. Let the reader know how to reach you by including your phone number or e-mail address. End with a statement of goodwill, even if it is only "thank you."

Proofread your letter very carefully. Research indicates that if employers notice even one spelling, grammatical, or mechanical error, they often eliminate the candidate from consideration immediately. Such errors will give employers the impression that you lack writing skills or that you are generally sloppy and careless in the way you present yourself professionally.

The closing paragraph of the internship application letter requests an interview, provides phone and e-mail contact information, and ends with a courteous "thank you."

■   I would appreciate the chance to interview with you at your earliest convenience. If you have questions or would like additional information, contact me at (435) 228-3490 any Tuesday or Thursday after 10 a.m. or e-mail me at <sennett@execpr.com>. Thank you for your time.

Sincerely,

Molly Sennett

Molly Sennett

Enclosure: Résumé

Sample Letters

The three sample application letters shown in Figures 17–17 through 17–19 follow the application-letter structure described in this section. Each is adapted according to the emphasis, tone, and style to fit its particular audience.

- In Figure 17–17, a college student seeks an internship in a retailing business.
- In Figure 17–18, a recent college graduate applies for a job in an advertising company. Note that she refers the addressee to her Web site to view her résumé and design portfolio.
- In Figure 17–19, a person with many years of work experience applies for a job as a district manager.

7188 Virginia Avenue
Pittsburgh, PA 15232
February 27, 2003

Patrice C. Crandal
Executive Recruiter
Abel's Department Stores, Inc.
599 Seventh Avenue
Pittsburgh, PA 15219

Dear Ms. Crandal:

Opens by demonstrating initiative in researching the company, locating the program, and noting its value to the applicant's career

I recently learned at your Web site that you are hiring undergraduates for summer internships. Through my own research and sources in the retailing industry, I discovered that your firm's buyer training program is one of the most effective. For this reason, I am especially interested in your company and would like to be considered for a position as a summer intern.

Continues by linking the applicant's personal characteristics to tangible accomplishments

As indicated in my résumé, I have the professional and analytical qualities necessary to excel at an innovative company such as Abel's. My experiences with the Alumni Relations Program and the University Center Committee have enhanced my communication and persuasive abilities and my understanding of compromise and negotiation. For example, in the alumni program, it was my job to convince both uninterested and friendly alumni to become more involved with the direction of the university. As a member of the University Center Committee, I worked to balance the students' demands with the financial and structural constraints of the administration. In both cases, I succeeded in achieving these important goals through persuasion.

I would appreciate the opportunity to meet with you to discuss your summer internship. If you have questions or would like to speak with me personally, please contact me at (412) 863-2289 any weekday after 3 p.m. Thank you for your time and consideration.

Sincerely,

Marsha S. Parker

Marsha S. Parker

Enclosure: Résumé

Figure 17–17   Application Letter for a Student Applying for an Internship

449 Samson Street, Apt. 19
Providence, RI 02906
September 19, 2003

Alice Tobowski
Employee Relations Department
Advertising Media, Inc.
1007 Market Street
Providence, RI 02912

Dear Ms. Tobowski:

I recently learned from Jodi Hammel, a graphics designer at Advertising
Media, Inc., and a former colleague, that you are looking for advertising
assistants. Your position interests me greatly, not only because your firm
is number one in the region but also because I feel that Advertising Media
is, as Jodi and I have discussed, the kind of place where I can further
develop my skills and talents.

Opens by referencing a personal contact at the firm

I understand that you especially need bilingual assistants because of your
zone's ethnic diversity. As noted in my enclosed résumé, I speak and write
Spanish fluently. I would welcome the chance to apply my language skills at
Advertising Media. I am aware that hundreds of applicants are applying for
this position, but I have a combination of qualities probably few can match:
in addition to my bilingual skills, I have a degree and experience in advertising, outstanding verbal and written communication skills, an innate
ability to work well with colleagues, and the common sense to solve problems. I have developed my skills by contributing to advertising for Quilted
Bear, a retail outlet chain headquartered in Providence, where we develop
campaigns for diverse audiences. I have also been promoted to leadership
positions in my jobs, schools, and community organizations, and I have
worked well both individually and in team efforts in each environment.

Continues with a strong emphasis on her bilingual and other skills to stand out from many other applicants

I would enjoy meeting with you at your convenience to discuss this career
opportunity further. Also, I have many references that I encourage you to
contact. Feel free to call me any weekday morning or e-mail me at <singh
@pcexec.com> if you have any questions, need further information, or
would like to set up an interview. My résumé and a portfolio of my graphics
design work are available at my Web site at <SarasGraphics.com>. Thank you
for your consideration.

Closes by referring to a personal Web site for her résumé and portfolio of design work

Sincerely,

Sarah Singh

Sarah Singh

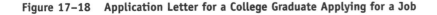

Figure 17–18   Application Letter for a College Graduate Applying for a Job

522 Beethoven Drive
Roanoke, VA 24017
November 15, 2003

Ms. Cecilia Smathers
Vice President, Dealer Sales
Hamilton Office Machines, Inc.
6194 Main Street
Hampton, VA 23661

Dear Ms. Smathers:

Opens by referencing a personal contact at the firm

During the recent NOMAD convention in Washington, one of your sales representatives, Karen Jarrett, informed me of a possible opening for a district manager in your Dealer Sales Division. My extensive background in the office-systems industry makes me highly qualified for the position.

Continues with a concise career summary

I was with Technology, Inc.'s Dealer Division from its formation in 1990 until its closing last year. During that period, I was involved in all areas of dealer sales, both within Technology, Inc., and through personal contact with a number of independent dealers. From 1996 to 2002, I served as Assistant to the Dealer Sales Manager as a Special Representative. My education and work experience are indicated in the enclosed résumé.

Closes with contact information

I would like to discuss my qualifications in an interview at your convenience. Please write to me, telephone me at (804) 449-6743 any weekday, or e-mail me at <gm302.476@sys.com>.

Sincerely,

Gregory Mindukakis

Gregory Mindukakis

Encloses a résumé

Enclosure: Résumé

Figure 17–19   Application Letter for an Applicant with Years of Experience

Writing a Letter of Application

- [ ] In the opening paragraph:
  - Indicate how you heard about the opening.
  - State your job objective and interest in the job.
  - Mention the job title.
- [ ] In the body of the letter:
  - Cite project and previous employment experiences that demonstrate your qualifications for the job.
  - Indicate how college course work, your degree, and pertinent training add to your qualifications for the job.
  - Refer to your enclosed résumé.
  - Explain how your qualifications and achievements can contribute to the prospective employer.
- [ ] In the closing paragraph:
  - Request an interview.
  - Provide your phone number and e-mail address so that you can be contacted.
  - End with a goodwill statement.

■ Doing Well in the Interview

Preparing a professional résumé and writing an effective letter of application are essential to obtaining a job interview; that preparation helps you understand your strengths as a potential employee and articulate your career objectives. Nevertheless, the interview is often the most difficult part of the job search because it is so pivotal in the hiring process. A job interview may last for 30 minutes, or it may take several hours; it may be conducted by one person or by several, either at one time or in a series of interviews, by phone, by teleconference, or in person. Because it is impossible to know exactly what to expect, it is important that you be as prepared as possible. If you are interviewed by phone, set aside a time and place where you won't be interrupted and have your résumé and note-taking tools available.

Before the Interview

The interview is not a one-way communication. It presents you with an opportunity to ask questions of your potential employer and to demonstrate your knowledge of the position and the organization itself. In preparation, learn everything you can about the company before the interview by answering the questions listed in the Writer's Checklist: Learning about Employers on page 621. You can obtain information from the company's Web site, current employees, company literature, and the business section of local and national newspapers, such as the *New York Times*, the *Los Angeles Times*, the *Wall Street Journal*, and the

Washington Post (available online and in the library). You may be able to learn about the company's size, sales volume, product line, credit rating, branch locations, subsidiary companies, new products and services, building programs, and other such information from its annual reports; publications such as Moody's Industrials at <moodys.com>, Dun and Bradstreet at <dnb.com>, Standard & Poor's at <standardpoor.com>, and Thomas' Register at <5.thomasregister.com>; and other business reference sources a librarian might suggest. What you cannot find through your own research, ask your interviewer. Now is your chance to make certain that you are considering a healthy and growing company. It is also your chance to show your interest in the company and find out as much as possible about company-employee relations, including opportunities for career growth. To that end, you may want to ask your interviewer some or all of the following questions:

W On the Web
For access to major national newspapers and other business references, see Chapter 17, bedfordstmartins.com/writingthatworks

- How often are employees formally evaluated on their performance?
- Does the company require training or certification?
- Does the company fund career-related training and outside education?
- Does the position you're applying for have promotion potential?
- Is there a probationary period for new employees?

Finally, as a way of gaining insight into how the company operates, you could ask your interviewer how he or she started at the company—if time permits.

Try to anticipate the questions your interviewer might ask, and prepare your answers in advance. Be sure you understand a question before answering it, and avoid responding too quickly with a standard answer. Be prepared to discuss answers to the interviewer's questions in a natural and relaxed manner. Interviewers typically ask the following questions:

- What are your short-term and long-term goals?
- What are your major strengths and weaknesses?
- Do you work better with others or alone?
- What do you know about our company (or organization)?
- Why do you want to work for us?
- How do you spend your free time?
- What are your personal goals?
- What accomplishment are you particularly proud of? Describe it.
- Why are you leaving your current job?
- How have you handled an unsuccessful experience?
- Why should I hire you?
- What salary do you expect?

Some of these questions are difficult. Give them careful thought, try to be as concrete as possible by offering examples when appropriate, and remember that there is no one correct answer.

Be sure that you arrive for your interview at the appointed time. In fact, it is usually a good idea to arrive early because you may be asked to fill out an application before you meet your interviewer. Read the application form before filling it out, and proofread it when you are finished. Not only does the application form provide the company with a record for its files, but it also gives the company an opportunity to see how closely you follow directions, how thoroughly you complete a task, and how well you express your ideas in writing. Always bring extra copies of your résumé and samples of your work (if applicable). Some of the people you meet may not have a copy of your résumé and it contains much of the same information the application asks for: personal data, work experience, and education.

Finally, bring a tablet and pen or personal digital assistant (PDA) to record pertinent information. Do not, however, bring a laptop computer—doing so creates a distraction and a barrier between you and your interviewer.

Learning about Employers

WRITER'S CHECKLIST

As you search for information about potential employers, use these questions as a guide.

- [ ] What kind of organization is it?
- [ ] How diversified is it?
- [ ] Is it a nonprofit organization?
- [ ] If it is government employment, at what level or sector is it?
- [ ] Does it provide a service or product? If so, what kind?
- [ ] How large is the business? How large are its assets?
- [ ] Is it locally owned? Is it a subsidiary of a larger organization? Is it expanding?
- [ ] How long has it been in business?
- [ ] Where will you fit in?

During the Interview

The interview actually begins before you are seated: What you wear and how you act make a first impression. The way you dress and groom yourself matters. In general, dress simply and conservatively. Remember, you have only one chance to make a good first impression.

Behavior

First, thank the interviewer for his or her time, express your pleasure at meeting him or her, and remain standing until you are offered a seat. Then sit up straight (good posture suggests self-assurance), look directly at the interviewer, and try to appear relaxed and confident. Never chew gum. During the interview, you may find yourself feeling a little nervous. Use that nervous energy to your advantage by channeling it into alertness. Listen carefully and record important information in your memory. Jot down a few facts and figures as needed, but do not attempt to take extensive notes during the interview. (See also the discussion of listening in Chapter 15, pages 540–544.)

Responses

When answering questions, don't ramble or stray from the subject. Say only what you must to answer each question properly and then stop, but avoid giving just yes or no answers—they usually don't permit the interviewer to learn enough about you. Some interviewers allow a silence to fall just to see how you will react. The burden of conducting the interview is the interviewer's, not yours—and he or she may interpret your rush to fill a void in the conversation as a sign of insecurity. If such a silence makes you uncomfortable, be ready to ask pertinent questions about the company from your prepared list. If the interviewer overlooks important points, bring them up.

Interviewers look for a degree of self-confidence and understanding of the field in which the applicant is applying for a job, as well as genuine interest in the field, the company, and the job. Less is expected of a beginner, but even a newcomer must show some self-confidence and command of the subject. One way to communicate your interest in the job and company is to ask questions. Interviewers respond favorably to applicants who can communicate and present themselves well.

Salary Negotiations

Although it is better to negotiate salary after you have a job offer or certainly late in the interview, you may be asked "What are your salary requirements?" You cannot answer such a question without solid preparation. Make sure that you are aware of prevailing salaries in your field so that you will be better prepared to discuss salary. If you are a recent graduate, it is usually unwise to attempt to bargain. Many companies have inflexible starting salaries for beginners.

First, your goal should be to work toward a win-win situation for you and your prospective employer. Avoid overemphasizing money because it tends to make your potential loyalty to an organization suspect. The issue is not simply one of dollar amounts but of your own job satisfaction and what value you can bring to your employer. Consider the following guidelines:

- Seek advice ahead of time from a professional with relevant experience.
- Determine the lowest salary you would accept, perhaps based on your most recent employment.
- Determine the typical salary ranges for positions in your area.
- Determine possible fringe benefits that would be valuable to you.
- Determine the firm's opportunities for promotion.

If questioned directly about salary, you can give an answer such as "I was considering a range of $--- to $---, but that would also depend on the fringe benefits available and the potential or timetable for promotions or salary increases." Remember, it's always acceptable to say to a prospective employer that you would like to think about an offer placed on the table.

Some companies study the market very carefully and give what David G. Jensen, Search Masters International, calls "First Offer, Best Offer"; that is, the offer they make is the best offer they can or will give, and there is no point in negotiating. Jensen offers further advice on negotiating on his Web site at <bio.com/hr/search/negotiation.html>.

Conclusion

At the conclusion of the interview, thank your interviewer for his or her time. Indicate that you are interested in the job (if true), and try to get an idea of when you can expect to hear from the company (do not press too hard). Reaffirm friendly contact with a firm handshake.

■ Sending Follow-up Correspondence

After you leave the interview, review your notes for accuracy and fill in any gaps while the information is fresh—it may be helpful in comparing job offers. A day or two later, send the interviewer a note of thanks in a brief letter or e-mail. If you find the job appealing, say so and state that you believe you can fill it well, as shown in Figure 17–20. If you have not heard back from the company about the status of your application in two weeks, send another brief and courteous letter or e-mail. Beyond that period, it is the responsibility of the company to contact you.

If you are offered a job you want, call or send a brief message of acceptance as

---

Dear Mr. Vallone:

Thank you for the informative and pleasant interview we had last Wednesday. Please extend my thanks to Mr. Wilson of the Media Group as well.

I came away from our meeting most favorably impressed with Information Systems. I find the position you are filling to be an attractive one and feel confident that my qualifications would enable me to perform the duties to everyone's advantage.

If I can answer any further questions, please e-mail me at pmg@home.com or phone me at (937) 964-1955.

Sincerely yours,

Philip Ming

Opens with an expression of appreciation

Continues with a strong statement of interest in the job

Ends with relevant contact information

Figure 17–20   Follow-up E-mail Thanking the Interviewer

soon as possible—certainly within a week. The organization of such a message is simple. Begin by accepting the job you have been offered. Identify the job by title and state the exact salary so that there will be no confusion on these two important points. The second paragraph might go into detail about moving dates and the time for reporting to work. The details will vary, depending on the nature of the job offer. Conclude with a statement that you are looking forward to working for your new employer, as in the acceptance letter written by a college student in Figure 17–21.

Mr. F. E. Vallone
Manager of Human Resources
Information Systems, Inc.
3275 Commercial Park Drive
Raleigh, NC 27609

Dear Mr. Vallone:

Opens by accepting job and verifying the salary, title, and organizational unit

I am pleased to accept your offer of $30,500 per year as a junior ACR designer in the Medical Group.

Continues with near-term schedule and start date

After graduation, I plan to leave Charlotte on Tuesday, June 16. I should be able to find suitable living accommodations within a few days and be ready to report for work on the following Monday, June 22. Please let me know if this date is satisfactory to you.

Ends with goodwill statement

I look forward to working with the design team at Information Systems.

Very truly yours,

Philip Ming

Philip Ming

Figure 17–21   Acceptance Letter Written by a College Student

Because you will probably have applied to more than one organization, you will need to write a letter of refusal if you receive more than one job offer. Be especially tactful and courteous because the employer you are refusing has spent time and effort interviewing you and may have counted on your accepting the job. It is also possible that you may apply for another job at this company in the future. Figure 17–22 is an example of a job-refusal letter. It acknowledges the consideration given the applicant, offers a logical reason for refusal of the offer, and then concludes on a pleasant note.

Mr. F. E. Vallone
Manager of Human Resources
Information Systems, Inc.
3275 Commercial Park Drive
Raleigh, NC 27609

Dear Mr. Vallone:

I enjoyed talking with you about your opening for a technical writer, and I was gratified to receive your offer. Although I have given the offer serious thought, I have decided to accept a position as a copywriter with an advertising agency. I feel that the job I have chosen is better suited to my skills and long-term goals.

I appreciate your consideration and the time you spent with me. I wish you the best of luck in filling the position.

Opens with a tactful reason for refusing the job offer

Closes by acknowledging the effort of the prospective employer

Figure 17–22   Letter of Refusal

Sending a Resignation Letter or Memo

When you are planning to leave a job, for any reason, you usually write a resignation letter to your supervisor or to an appropriate person in the Human Resources Department.

- Start on a positive note, regardless of the circumstances under which you are leaving.
- Consider pointing out how you have benefited from working for the company or say something complimentary about the company.
- Comment on something positive about the people with whom you have been associated.
- Explain why you are leaving in an objective, factual tone.
- Avoid angry recriminations because your resignation will remain on file with the company and could haunt you in the future when you need references.

Your letter or memo should give enough notice to allow your employer time to find a replacement. It might be no more than two weeks, or it might be enough time to put your files in order and train your replacement. Some organizations may ask for a notice equivalent to the number of weeks of vacation you receive. Check the policy of your employer before you begin your letter.

The sample resignation memo in Figure 17–23 is from an employee who is leaving to take a job offering greater opportunities. The memo of resignation in Figure 17–24 is written by an employee who is leaving under unhappy circumstances;

MEMO

To: W. R. Johnson, Director of Purchasing
From: J. L. Washburn, Purchasing Agent *JLW*
Date: January 7, 2003
Subject: Resignation from Barnside Appliances,
           effective January 21, 2003

Positive opening

My three years at Barnside Appliances have been an invaluable period of learning and professional development. I arrived as a novice, and I believe that today I am a professional—primarily as a result of the personal attention and tutoring I have received from my superiors and the fine example set by both my superiors and my peers.

Reason for leaving

I believe, however, that the time has come for me to move on to a larger company that can give me an opportunity to continue my professional development. Therefore, I have accepted a position with General Electric, where I am scheduled to begin on January 27. Thus, my last day at Barnside will be January 21. I will be happy to train my replacement during the next two weeks.

Positive closing

Many thanks for the experiences I have gained and best wishes for the future.

Figure 17–23   Resignation Memo to Accept a Better Position

MEMO

To: T. W. Haney, Vice President, Administration
From: L. R. Rupp, Executive Assistant *LRR*
Date: February 12, 2003
Subject: Resignation from Winterhaven, effective March 3, 2003

Positive opening

My five-year stay with the Winterhaven Company has been a very pleasant experience, and I believe that it has been mutually beneficial.

Reason for leaving

Because the recent restructuring of my job leaves no career path open to me, I have accepted a position with another company that I feel will offer me greater advancement opportunities. I am, therefore, submitting my resignation, to be effective on March 3, 2003.

Positive closing

I have enjoyed working with my coworkers at Winterhaven and wish the company success in the future.

Figure 17–24   Resignation Memo under Negative Conditions

notice that it opens and closes positively and that the reason for the resignation is stated without apparent anger or bitterness. For strategies concerning negative messages, see Chapter 9, pages 314–316.

CHAPTER 17 SUMMARY: Finding the Right Job

Follow these five steps for finding a job:

- ☐ Determine the best job for you.
- ☐ Prepare an effective résumé.
- ☐ Write an effective letter of application.
- ☐ Conduct yourself well during the interview.
- ☐ Send a follow-up message after the interview.

Research the following sources of information for locating jobs:

- ☐ College career center
- ☐ Internet resources
- ☐ Tips from family, friends, and acquaintances
- ☐ Letters of inquiry
- ☐ Informational interviews
- ☐ Advertisements in newspapers
- ☐ Advertisements in trade and professional journals
- ☐ Private and temporary employment agencies
- ☐ Local, state, and federal agencies

Plan your résumé carefully.

- ☐ Determine the type of job you seek and compile a list of prospective employers.
- ☐ Consider the type of information about you and your background of most importance to potential employers.
- ☐ Determine, based on this information, the details that should be included and the most effective way to present them.

Write an effective letter of application.

- ☐ Catch the reader's attention.
- ☐ Create the desire for your services.
- ☐ Include a brief summary of your qualifications for the specific job for which you are applying.
- ☐ State when and where you can be reached.

Follow these steps to prepare for a job interview:

- ☐ Learn everything you can about your prospective employer.
- ☐ Arrive on time.
- ☐ Highlight those strengths most useful to the job you are applying for.
- ☐ Demonstrate your knowledge of your field.
- ☐ Send the interviewer a brief note of thanks after the interview.

When you receive a job offer, write one of the following letters:

☐ If you plan to accept the offer, send a letter of acceptance as soon as possible after you receive the offer.

☐ If you plan to refuse, send a letter as soon as possible refusing the offer but expressing your appreciation for the organization's time and effort in considering you.

Follow these guidelines in preparing a letter or memo of resignation:

☐ Begin and end the message on a positive note.

☐ Explain the reason for your departure factually and objectively.

☐ Give at least two weeks' notice (and preferably longer) to allow your employer to prepare for your departure.

■ Exercises

1. Refer to the guidelines in this chapter to write a persuasive application letter for a summer job to a corporation, a public-interest group, a research organization, or a firm of your choosing (one page, single-spaced). Revise and enclose your current résumé.

2. Using the guidelines in this chapter, write a letter of application and a résumé in response to an advertisement for a job you will be qualified for upon graduation. Use high-quality white bond paper and make sure the letter and résumé are error- and blemish-free.

3. Assume that you have been interviewed for the job in Exercise 2. Write a follow-up letter expressing thanks for the interview.

4. Write a letter to a past or present teacher, an employer, or another appropriate person, asking permission to use him or her as a job reference. Be prepared to explain in class why you think this person is especially well qualified to comment on your job qualifications.

5. Obtain a sample résumé at your school's career-development center or local copy center. Annotate and write a brief critical analysis of the résumé for your instructor, pointing out its strong points and how it might be improved in content, organization, or design.

6. With your instructor's approval, contact an individual who works in a professional area that interests you and arrange an interview with that person. Questions you might ask include the following: What sources did you use to find your first job? your current job? What sorts of skills and abilities are needed to enter this profession? What are the starting salary and advanced salary ranges for this area? Be ready to report your findings, either as a presentation to the class or in a written report.

7. Following the guidelines in this chapter on pages 595–613, create a résumé to send in response to an electronic posting advertising a summer position in your field of study. Submit your résumé either on a disk or as an e-mail attachment, or both, as required by your instructor.

8. One way to discover if you would fit into a particular job setting or to simply learn more about how a business, a company, or an office operates is to job-shadow. With your instructor's approval, call a local job site and ask if you can observe closely for two to three hours an employee as he or she follows a regular routine. Write a brief memo to your instructor summarizing your experiences. Within two days following your visit, send a thank-you note to the company and to the employee whom you shadowed, expressing your appreciation for the visit, and give a copy of it to your instructor.

9. If your current résumé is prepared by job chronology, prepare a second résumé— a functional résumé—that not only organizes work experience by type but also helps you identify important skills, abilities, or experiences. Follow the guidelines in this chapter on pages 596–599. Your instructor may ask you to submit your chronological résumé with your functional résumé.

10. Review your existing résumé to make sure that your use of verbs and nouns in your job descriptions are consistent and parallel in structure (See Chapter 5, Parallel Structure, on pages 150–151.)

■ Collaborative Classroom Projects

1. Prepare a list of at least six job-related assets that you have and explain why and how these qualities would be useful to a potential employer. Include any honors you have received, high grade point averages, specific skills such as advanced computer knowledge or creative design talent, and unique work experience. List good work habits such as accuracy, dependability, and the ability to manage large projects, and back them up with supporting examples from your work or educational experience. Be ready to read your list aloud in class. Remember that a degree of self-confidence is a necessary tool in looking for a job, so as you relate your list to your classmates, be proud of your accomplishments.

2. Divide into groups of four to six classmates who share your major area (or a similar area) of study. Appoint a group leader and recorder. For the first 30 minutes, brainstorm a list of action words that could be used to describe your collective skills, abilities, and experiences, and which could work well in a résumé to be used in your field. During the next 15 minutes, brainstorm a list of positions that you could apply for when you graduate. Be ready to share your information with your classmates.

3. As in Collaborative Classroom Project 2, divide into groups with classmates who share your major area (or a similar area) of study to share information and ideas about job-search methods most useful to job seekers in your field. Discuss the value of Internet resources; networking; letters of inquiry; advertisements in newspapers, trade journals, and professional journals; private and temporary employment agencies, and any other sources you know of. Discuss methods of organizing job-search information and creating workable timelines for job searches.

4. As a class, discuss ways to prepare for your job search when you graduate. Brainstorm what kinds of campus organizations, part-time and summer internships or employment, other courses besides business writing, and networking you should be engaged in right now for future opportunities. Then, working in pairs,

spend 20 minutes during which you play the role of the job interviewer, while your partner plays the role of the interviewee. Then switch roles for the next 20 minutes. Begin by referring to the interview section of this chapter, and decide the name and type of company where you are interviewing, the position, and other details about the job. Include the following questions in the interview:

- What are your short-term and long-term professional goals?
- What are your major strengths and weaknesses?
- Why do you want to work for our company?
- What are your personal goals?
- What accomplishment are you particularly proud of? Describe it.
- Why should I hire you?

In conclusion, consider what answers you would change in preparation for your next interview.

■ Research Projects

1. After brainstorming about your career goals and career-related assets, search to find positions that you will be qualified for (1) while you are in school and (2) when you graduate. Use the library, the campus placement center, job fairs, networking opportunities (with individuals already working in the field), and government sources like the *Occupational Outlook Handbook* at the Bureau of Labor Statistics to identify as many positions as you can. Try to discover the following about each of the positions:

   - Detailed job description
   - The growth potential of the job offers
   - Geographic location
   - Typical working conditions
   - Average salary
   - Other relevant details

   Summarize your findings in a brief narrative and explain which jobs appealed to you and why.

2. Interview a counselor in your school's career development center to learn what mistakes students tend to make when they seek employment and to get any specific advice or tips that help in the job search. Write a report on what you learn, then make a presentation to the class; provide a handout of relevant information for the class.

3. Research three major employers in your field and, in an outline format, answer the following questions about each:

   a. What kind of an organization is it?
   b. Is it a profit or nonprofit organization?
   c. Does it provide a service or services? If so, what kind(s)?
   d. What does its mission statement reveal?
   e. How large is the business? How large are its assets?
   f. Is it locally owned? Is it a subsidiary of a larger operation? Is it expanding?
   g. How long has it been in business?
   h. If it is government employment, at what level or sector is it?
   i. Where would you fit in?

You can obtain information from the Internet, current employees, company literature such as employee publications, and the business section of back issues of local and national newspapers (available in the library and on the Web).

4. Beginning your career is important, but knowing what to expect in terms of future advancement and promotion is also important. Building on Research Project 1, pick one position that you researched and find answers to the following questions:

   a. Typically, how often do job-changing promotions come in this career?
   b. Is it important to be geographically flexible to advance in this field?
   c. What kind of travel is expected with promotions?
   d. What salary increases can be expected and when?
   e. Are advanced degrees necessary to remain competitive in this career?
   f. Is continuing education required for advancement?
   g. What kind of schedule do the higher jobs in this field require?
   h. How does a family or how do children fit into this career, once advancements are made?

   Conduct further research on any specific long-term benefits or potential problems that you feel may be involved in this career. Prepare an analysis for your instructor based on your findings and be ready to share your results with your classmates.

5. Interview someone who holds a job in a field that interests you. Based on the information you obtained from the interview, prepare a job description of the position, following the guidelines in this chapter.

▓ Web Projects

Projects followed by the symbol ▥ are continued at **bedfordstmartins.com/ writingthatworks**, Chapter 17.

1. Find information about the future employment potential of graduates in your major field of study by using at least five Web sources. In a brief memo to your instructor, answer the following questions about your major field:

   a. Based on current indicators, what are the job projections in your field in this country?
   b. Is there a worldwide demand for people in your field?
   c. Do employees in your field have an opportunity to advance?
   d. In your field, is there a wide range in salary expectations based on geographic location?
   e. What other relevant information can you provide?

2. Using the Web, find three firms that you would consider working for and compare working conditions and opportunities as presented at their Web sites. Make a list of important factors to consider as you evaluate these potential employers. For example, if you choose to compare positions for registered nurses at two different hospitals, look at the size of the facilities, the number of beds, the number of registered nurses employed, the career opportunities and benefits advertised by the hospitals, and so forth. Try to find information about as many items on your list as possible, then write a brief analysis about your findings. Determine which is the

more attractive employer and explain why. Be ready to share your narrative with your classmates.

3. Search the Web to find sites that are specifically appropriate to your career path and area of study. For example, the Small Business Administration is available to help small business owners. Or, you may search for links at the nation's largest public library devoted to business and finance, the Business Library of the Brooklyn Public Library, or the Horn Library at Babson College—both offer business links to magazine and newspaper articles, library sources, and other electronic sources. Write a brief analysis of at least two Web sites that you would recommend as helpful to you and other students enrolled in your major field of study. Report your findings to the class.

4. Search the Web for positions available in your major field outside the United States. For example, find links to international companies using Google's directory <google.com/directory>. Then determine and report on what language skills are required for the various positions, what travel experience is expected, and what cross-cultural experience is expected.

5. Review the Web sites of at least three online college or university placement centers, including the one hosted by your school. These centers offer links and general job-search information and can be helpful as you plan your own specific job search. Begin with the Center for Career Opportunities at Purdue University <purdue.edu>. Write a brief analysis of at least three career-planning sites you reviewed (including the URLs). Be ready to share your results with the class.

6. Review several general job sites to become familiar with job seeking via the Web. Sites may include College Grad Job Hunter, America's Job Bank, Monster.com, and CareerTech.com. Write a brief narrative stating which two sites seemed to be the most helpful for your field of study and why. 🅦

PART FOUR

A Writer's Handbook

Grammar, Punctuation, and Mechanics

Parts of Speech

Part of speech is a term used to describe the class of words to which a particular word belongs, according to its function in a sentence. If a word's function is to name something, it is a noun or a pronoun. If it indicates action or existence, it is a verb. If its function is to describe or modify something, the word is an adjective or an adverb. If it joins or links one element of a sentence to another, it is a conjunction or a preposition. If it expresses an exclamation, it is an interjection.

■ 1. Nouns

A *noun* names a person, a place, a thing, a concept, an action, or a quality. The two basic types of nouns are proper nouns and common nouns.

1.1 Proper Nouns

Proper nouns name specific persons, places, things, concepts, actions, or qualities. They are usually capitalized.

PROPER NOUNS   New York, Abraham Lincoln, U.S. Army, Nobel Prize, Montana, Independence Day, Amazon River, Butler County, June, Colby College

1.2 Common Nouns

Common nouns name general categories of persons, places, things, concepts, actions, or qualities; they include all types of nouns except proper nouns. Many nouns can be placed in more than one category.

Concrete nouns identify those things that can be detected by the five senses — by seeing, hearing, tasting, touching, or smelling. Concrete nouns can be either count nouns or mass nouns. *Count nouns,* as the term suggests, name things that can be counted or divided; their plurals often end in *s.* (See Section 37 for an explanation of using count and noncount nouns.)

COUNT NOUNS   human, college, house, knife, bolt, carrot

Mass nouns name things that are not usually counted and do not usually appear in the plural.

MASS NOUNS   water, sand, air, copper, velvet

Many words, of course, can serve either as count nouns or as mass nouns, depending on the context in which they are used. If you were to say "I need one brick," *brick* would be a count noun. If you were to say "The building is built of brick," *brick* would be a mass noun.

Abstract nouns refer to things that cannot be detected by the five senses.

ABSTRACT NOUNS   love, loyalty, pride, valor, peace, devotion, harmony

Collective nouns indicate groups or collections of persons, places, things, concepts, actions, or qualities. They are plural in meaning but singular in form when they refer to groups as units.

COLLECTIVE NOUNS   audience, jury, brigade, staff, committee

1.3 Functions of Nouns

Nouns may function as subjects of verbs, objects of verbs and prepositions, complements, or appositives.

NOUN AS SUBJECT   The *metal* bent as *pressure* was applied to it.

[*Metal* and *pressure* are both subjects of a verb, naming the thing about which the verb makes an assertion.]

NOUN AS
DIRECT OBJECT   The bricklayer cemented the *blocks* efficiently.

[*Blocks* is the direct object of a verb, naming the thing acted on by the verb.]

NOUN AS
INDIRECT OBJECT   The company awarded our *department* a plaque for safety.

[*Department* is the indirect object of a verb, naming the recipient of the direct object.]

NOUN AS OBJECT
OF PREPOSITION   The event occurred during the last *year.*

[*Year* is the object of a preposition, naming the thing linked by the preposition to the rest of the sentence.]

NOUN AS SUBJECTIVE COMPLEMENT	An equestrian is a *horseback rider.*
	[*Horseback rider* is the subjective complement, renaming the subject of the sentence.]
NOUN AS OBJECTIVE COMPLEMENT	We elected the sales manager *chairperson.*
	[*Chairperson* is the objective complement, renaming the direct object.]
NOUN AS APPOSITIVE	George Thomas, the *treasurer,* gave his report last.
	[*Treasurer* is the appositive, amplifying the noun that precedes it.]

With the general exception of mass nouns and abstract nouns, nouns can show number (singular or plural) and possession.

1.4 Singular and Plural Nouns

The singular form of a noun refers to one thing; the plural form refers to more than one. Most nouns form the plural by adding *-s.*

■   *Dolphins* are capable of communication with humans.

Nouns ending in *s, z, x, ch,* and *sh* form the plural by adding *-es.*

■   Our company supplies cafeterias with *dishes* and *glasses.*

Those ending in a consonant plus *y* form the plural by changing the *y* to *ies.*

■   The store limits the number of *deliveries* scheduled on a single day.

Some nouns ending in *o* add *-es* to form the plural; others add only *-s.*

■   We installed two *dynamos* in the plant.

Some nouns ending in *f* or *fe* add *-s* to form the plural; others change the *f* or *fe* to *ves.*

■   cliff/cliffs; fife/fifes; knife/knives; leaf/leaves

Some nouns require an internal change to form the plural.

■   goose/geese; man/men; mouse/mice; woman/women

Some nouns do not change in the plural form.

■   Several *fish* swam in the brook while *deer* mingled with the *sheep* in the meadow.

Most compound nouns joined by hyphens form the plural in the first noun.

■   He provided jobs for his two *sons-in-law.*

If you are in doubt about a plural form, check a good dictionary. Most dictionaries give any plural formed other than by adding *-s* or *-es*.

1.5 Possessive Nouns

The possessive case, indicating ownership, is formed by using an *of* clause, as in "the core *of* the problem," or by adding *-'s*, generally to animate nouns.

- The *director's* statement was forceful.

- The installation of the plumbing is finished except in the *men's* room.

Singular nouns ending in *s* may form the possessive by adding either an apostrophe alone or *-'s*. The latter is now preferred.

- a *seamstress'* alterations *or* a *seamstress's* alteration

Plural nouns ending in *s* add only an apostrophe to form the possessive.

- The *architects'* design manual is heavily illustrated.

With word groups and compound nouns, add *-'s* to the last noun.

- The *chief operating officer's* report was distributed.

- My *son-in-law's* address was on the envelope.

To show individual possession with a pair of nouns, use the possessive with both.

- *Mary's* and *John's* presentations were the most effective.

To show joint possession with a pair of nouns, use the possessive with only the latter.

- *Mary and John's* presentation was the most effective.

Occasionally you will use both an *of* phrase and an *'s* construction.

- Mary is a colleague of *John's*.

■ 2. Pronouns

A *pronoun* is used as a substitute for a noun that is called its *antecedent*. Pronouns fall into several categories: personal, demonstrative, relative, interrogative, indefinite, reflexive, intensive, and reciprocal.

2.1 Personal Pronouns

The *personal pronouns* refer to the person or persons speaking (*I, me, my, mine; we, us, our, ours*), the person or persons spoken to (*you, your, yours*), or the person or thing (or persons or things) spoken of (*he, him, his; she, her, hers; it, its; they, them, their, theirs*).

■ I wish *you* had told *me* that *their* cost estimates were in error.

2.2 Demonstrative Pronouns

The *demonstrative pronouns* (*this, these, that, those*) indicate or point out the thing being referred to. They also serve as adjectives. In writing, replace demonstrative pronouns that lead to ambiguity with adjectives that are not only acceptable but useful.

■ *This* is my workstation. *These* are my coworkers.

2.3 Relative Pronouns

The *relative pronouns* (*who, whom, which, whose, that*) perform two functions simultaneously. They substitute for nouns or preceding ideas, and they connect and establish the relationships between parts of sentences. (See Sections 10.2 and 10.3 for further discussion of independent and dependent clauses.)

■ The human resources manager told the applicants *who* would be hired.

Understanding Relative Pronouns

A relative pronoun (*who, whom, which, whose, that*) introduces a dependent clause and also points back to the noun being referred to.

■ The warehouse *that* stocks those books is located in Georgia.

ESL TIPS

Relative pronouns are sometimes "understood."

■ The things [*that*] *we know best* are the things [*that*] *we haven't been taught.*

2.4 Interrogative Pronouns

Interrogative pronouns (*who, whom, which, whose, what*) ask questions.

■ *Which* copier does two-sided copying? *Who* knows how to operate it?

2.5 Indefinite Pronouns

Indefinite pronouns do not refer to a particular person or thing. They include *all, another, any, anyone, anything, both, each, either, everybody, few, many, most, much, neither, nobody, none, several, some,* and *such.*

■ Not *everybody* liked the new procedures; *some* even refused to follow them.

2.6 Reflexive Pronouns

The reflexive pronouns (*myself, yourself, himself, herself, itself, oneself, ourselves, yourselves, themselves*) always end with the suffix *-self* or *-selves*. Reflexive pronouns refer to the subject of the sentence, clause, or phrase in which they appear and turn the action of the verb back on the subject.

- I asked *myself* the same question.

2.7 Intensive Pronouns

The intensive pronouns are identical in form to the reflexive pronouns, but they perform a different function. They emphasize or intensify their antecedents.

- I *myself* asked the same question.

2.8 Reciprocal Pronouns

The reciprocal pronouns (*one another, each other*) indicate relationships among people or things. Use *each other* with two persons or things and *one another* with more than two.

- Sam and Ruth work well with *each other.*
- The four crew members work well with *one another.*

Grammatical Properties of Pronouns

2.9 Person and Pronouns

Person refers to the forms of a personal pronoun that indicate whether the pronoun represents the speaker, the person spoken to, or the person (or thing) spoken about (Table A–1). If the pronoun represents the speaker, the pronoun is in the first person.

- *I* followed the directions in the manual.

If the pronoun represents the person or persons spoken to, the pronoun is in the second person.

- *You* should report to Ms. Cooper before noon.

If the pronoun represents the person or persons spoken about, the pronoun is in the third person.

- *They* followed the procedure that *he* had outlined.

Identifying pronouns by person helps you avoid illogical shifts from one person to another. A common error is to shift from the third person to the second person.

Table A–1   Identifying Pronouns by Person

Person	Singular	Plural
First	I, me, my	we, ours, us
Second	you, your	you, your
Third	he, him, his, she, her, hers, it, its	they, them, their

INCORRECT	*Employees* must sign the logbook when *you* enter a restricted area.
CORRECT	*Employees* must sign the logbook when *they* enter a restricted area.
CORRECT	*You* must sign the logbook when *you* enter a restricted area.

2.10 Gender and Pronouns

Gender refers to forms that designate words as masculine, feminine, and neuter (for objects considered neither masculine nor feminine). The pronouns *he, she,* and *it* indicate gender; only a few nouns (such as *seamstress*) do so. Writers must be sure that nouns and pronouns within a grammatical construction agree in gender.

■ Because Wanda Martin supervised *her* sales staff as effectively as Frank Martinez supervised *his,* the company doubled *its* profits.

(See also Section 2.13 for a discussion of how sexist language is best avoided.)

Assigning Gender

ESL TIPS

The English language almost completely lacks gender distinctions, which can be confusing if your native language marks gender. In the few cases in which English does make a gender distinction, the gender assigned closely connects with the sex of the subject.

Subject pronouns	*he/she*
Object pronouns	*him/her*
Possessive adjectives	*his/her(s)*
Some nouns	*king/queen; boy/girl; cow/bull*

When a noun, such as *doctor,* can refer to a person of either sex, you need to know the sex of the person to which the noun refers to determine the pronoun.

■ The doctor gave *her* patients lots of attention.

[Doctor is female.]

■ The doctor gave *his* patients lots of attention.

[Doctor is male.]

When the sex of the noun antecedent is unknown, follow the guidelines for nonsexist writing in Chapter 4, page 121. (*Note:* Some English speakers refer to vehicles and countries as *she,* but contemporary and nonsexist usage tends to use *it.*)

2.11 Number and Pronouns

Number signifies how many things a word refers to. A singular pronoun substitutes for a noun that names one thing; a plural pronoun replaces a noun that names two or more things.

■ The manager took *her* break after the employees took *their* breaks.

All singular pronouns (*I, he, she, it*) change form in the plural (*we, they*) except *you.*

■ Because *he* organizes and *she* supervises well, *they* are both valuable employees.

A few indefinite pronouns (*each, either, neither,* and those ending with *-body* or *-one,* such as *anybody, anyone, everybody, everyone, nobody, no one*) are normally singular; they require singular verbs and are referred to by singular pronouns.

■ *Everyone* at work that day had *his or her* blood pressure checked.

2.12 Case and Pronouns

Pronouns have forms to show the subjective, objective, and possessive cases (Table A–2). A pronoun in the *subjective case* is used as the subject of a clause or sentence, representing the person or thing acting or existing or after a linking verb, such as *to be.* (A linking verb connects the pronoun with the subject it renames.)

■ *He* is my boss.

■ My boss is *he.*

A pronoun in the *objective case* indicates the person or thing receiving the action of a verb, or it follows a preposition.

■ Mr. Davis hired Tom and *me.* [not *I*]

■ Between *you* and *me,* his facts are questionable.

A pronoun in the *possessive case* expresses ownership.

■ He took *his* notes with him on the business trip.

Table A–2 Subjective, Objective, and Possessive Pronouns

Subjective	*Objective*	*Possessive*
I	me	my, mine
we	us	our, ours
you	you	your, yours
he	him	his
she	her	her, hers
it	it	its
they	them	their, theirs
who	whom	whose

To test whether a pronoun is in the subjective case or the objective case, try using it with a transitive verb that requires a direct object—a person or thing to receive the action expressed by the verb. *Hit* is a useful verb for this test. If the form of the pronoun can precede the verb, it is in the subjective case. If it must follow the verb, it is in the objective case.

- *She* hit the baseball. [subjective case]

- The baseball hit *her*. [objective case]

If compound pronouns cause problems in determining case, try testing each separately.

- In his letter, John mentioned *you* and *me*.

- In his letter, John mentioned *you*.

- In his letter, John mentioned *me*.

To determine the case of a pronoun that follows *as* or *than*, try mentally adding the words that are normally omitted.

- The director does not have as much formal education as *he* [does].

  [You would not write, "Him does."]

- His friend was taller than *he* [was tall].

  [You would not write, "Him was tall."]

An appositive is a noun or noun phrase that follows and amplifies another noun or noun phrase. A pronoun appositive takes the case of its antecedent.

- Two systems analysts, Joe and *I*, were selected to represent the company.

  [*Joe and I* is in apposition to the subject, *systems analysts*, and therefore must be in the subjective case.]

- The systems analysts selected two members of our department—Joe and *me*.

  [*Joe and me* is in apposition to *two members*, the object of the verb *selected*, and therefore must be in the objective case.]

The reverse situation can also present problems. To test for the proper case when the pronouns *we* and *us* are followed by an appositive noun that defines them, try the sentence without the noun.

- (*We/Us*) pilots fly our own planes.

- *We* fly our own planes.

  [You would not write, "*Us* fly our own planes."]

- He addressed his remarks directly to (*we/us*) technicians.

- He addressed his remarks directly to *us*.

  [You would not write, "He addressed his remarks directly to *we*."]

2.13 Pronoun-Antecedent Agreement

Pronouns must agree with and clearly refer to their antecedents. The noun for which a pronoun substitutes is called its *antecedent*. A personal pronoun in the first or second person does not normally require a stated antecedent.

- *I* like my job.

- *You* were there at the time.

- *We* all worked hard on the project.

A personal pronoun in the third person usually has a clearly stated antecedent.

- John presented the report to the directors. *He* [John] first read *it* [the report] to *them* [the directors] and then asked for *their* [the directors'] questions.

A pronoun must agree, or correspond in form, with its antecedent in person, gender, and number. (Sections 2.9, 2.10, and 2.11 describe these properties further.)

A pronoun must agree with its antecedent in *person*. For example, use either the third person or the second person. Don't mix them. The first sentence in the following examples suggests that the technicians are preparing data for someone else (you).

INCORRECT	If *laboratory technicians* do not update *their* records every day, *you* will not have accurate data.
CORRECT	If *laboratory technicians* do not update *their* records every day, *they* will not have accurate data.
CORRECT	If *you* do not update *your* records every day, *you* will not have accurate data.

A pronoun must agree with its antecedent in *gender*.

- *Isabel* was wearing *her* identification badge, but *Tom* had to clip *his* on before they could pass the security guard.

Traditionally, a masculine pronoun was used to agree with antecedents that include both sexes, such as *everybody, nobody, one, person, someone,* or *student.*

- *Anyone* who meets this production goal will double *his* bonus.

However, because most people are sensitive to the implied sexual bias in such usage, it is more common to use the following alternatives:

GENDER BIAS	*Everybody* completed *his* report on time.
FREE OF BIAS	*Everybody* completed *his or her* report on time.
FREE OF BIAS	*Everybody* completed a report on time.

Often, the best solution is to rewrite the sentence in the plural. Do not, however, resort to a plural pronoun when the antecedent is singular.

INCORRECT	*Everybody* completed *their* reports on time.
	[The antecedent, *Everybody,* is singular, but the pronoun, *their,* is plural.]
CORRECT	The *employees* completed *their* reports on time.
	[The antecedent, *employees,* is plural; the pronoun, *their,* is also plural.]

A pronoun must agree with its antecedent in *number.*

INCORRECT	Because the *copier* has been used so much, *they* have been overheating.
	[The antecedent *copier* is singular, but the pronoun *they* is plural.]
CORRECT	Because the *copier* has been used so much, *it* has been overheating.
	[The antecedent *copier* is singular; the pronoun *it* is also singular.]

In formal English, use a singular pronoun with the following singular antecedents:

anybody	everybody	none
anyone	everyone	no one
anything	everything	somebody
each	neither	someone
either	nobody	something

CORRECT	*Everyone* returned to *his or her* department.
	[The antecedent *Everyone* and the pronouns *his or her* are singular.]

Sometimes a plural pronoun mistakenly refers to a singular antecedent:

INCORRECT	When *someone* has conducted research, *they* are likely to write an effective report.
	[*Someone* is a singular antecedent; *they* is a plural pronoun and does not agree with the singular *someone.*]

You can use the following options for revision:

1. Replace the incorrect plural pronoun with *he or she* (or *his or her*).

   ■ When *someone* has conducted research, ~~they are~~ _{he or she is} likely to write an effective report.

2. Make the antecedent plural.

   ■ When _{writers have} ~~someone has~~ conducted research, *they* are likely to write an effective report.

3. Rewrite the sentence so that no problem of agreement exists.

   ■ ~~When someone~~ _{A writer who} has conducted research, ~~they are~~ _{is} likely to write an effective report.

Collective nouns may be singular or plural, depending on meaning.

| CORRECT | The *staff* prepared *its* annual report. |
| CORRECT | The *staff* returned to *their* offices after the meeting. |

A compound antecedent joined by *or* or *nor* is singular if both elements are singular and plural if both are plural.

CORRECT	Either the *supervisor* or the *foreman* should present *his or her* report on the accident.
	[The antecedents *supervisor* and *foreman* are singular, and the pronouns *his or her* are also singular.]
CORRECT	Neither the *stockholders* nor the *executive officers* wanted *their* company to be taken over by Coast International.

When one of the antecedents connected by *or* or *nor* is singular and the other plural, the pronoun agrees with the nearer antecedent.

CORRECT	Either the *receptionist* or the *secretaries* should go on *their* lunch breaks.
	[The plural pronoun *their* agrees with the nearest antecedent, *typists,* which is plural.]
CORRECT	Either the *secretaries* or the *receptionist* should go on *his or her* lunch break.
	[The singular pronouns *his or her* agree with the nearest antecedent, *receptionist,* which is singular.]

A compound antecedent with its elements joined by *and* requires a plural pronoun.

CORRECT   The *architect* and the *designer* prepared *their* plans.

                   [Because the antecedents *architect* and *designer* are meant to be under-
                   stood together and thus are plural, the pronoun *their* is also plural.]

If the two elements refer to the same person, however, use the singular pronoun.

CORRECT   The *architect and designer* prepared *his* plan.

                   [The *architect and designer* are the same individual, and therefore the
                   antecedent is singular, as is the pronoun *his.*]

2.14 Pronoun Reference

The noun to which a pronoun refers must be unmistakably clear. Pronoun references may be unclear if they are general, hidden, or ambiguous.

A *general* (or *broad*) *reference,* one that has no real antecedent, may confuse
your reader.

UNCLEAR   He sold plumbing supplies in Iowa for eight years. *This* has helped him
                   in his present job as sales manager.

IMPROVED   He sold plumbing supplies in Iowa for eight years. His contacts across
                   the state have helped him in his present job as sales manager.

A *hidden reference,* one that has only an implied antecedent, is another problem.

UNCLEAR   Electronics technicians must continue to study because *it* is a dynamic
                   technology.

IMPROVED   Electronics technicians must continue to study *electronics* because *it* is
                   a dynamic technology.

The third basic problem is an *ambiguous reference,* one that can be intepreted
in more than one way.

UNCLEAR   Susan worked with Jeanette on the presentation, but *she* prepared most
                   of the slides.

                   [Who prepared most of the slides, Susan or Jeanette?]

IMPROVED   Susan worked with Jeanette on the presentation, but Jeanette prepared
                   most of the slides.

Ambiguous references frequently occur with the pronouns *it* and *they.*

UNCLEAR   The fire marshal examined the stairway and inspected the basement
                   storage room; *it* had suffered extensive smoke damage.

IMPROVED   The fire marshal examined the stairway, which had suffered extensive
                   smoke damage, and inspected the basement storage room.

| UNCLEAR | The inspector checked the scales and the time clocks; *they* needed to be leveled again. |
| IMPROVED | The inspector checked the scales and the time clocks; the scales needed to be leveled again. |

Do not repeat an antecedent in parentheses following the pronoun. If you feel that you must identify the pronoun's antecedent in this way, you need to rewrite the sentence.

| AWKWARD | The cardiologist met the patient's mother as soon as she (the cardiologist) arrived at the hospital emergency room. |
| IMPROVED | As soon as the cardiologist arrived at the hospital emergency room, she met the patient's mother. |

■ 3. Adjectives

An adjective modifies or describes a noun or pronoun.

3.1 Types of Adjectives

An adjective makes the meaning of a noun or pronoun clear by pointing out one of its qualities (descriptive adjective) or by imposing boundaries on it (limiting adjective).

| DESCRIPTIVE ADJECTIVE | a *hot* iron | He is *cold*. |
| LIMITING ADJECTIVE | *ten* automobiles | *his* desk |

Limiting adjectives include some common and important categories:

Articles (*a, an, the*)
Numeral adjectives (*one, two, first, second*)
Indefinite adjectives (*all, any, each, no, some*)
Demonstrative adjectives (*this, that, these, those*)
Possessive adjectives (*my, his, her, its, your, our, their*)
Interrogative and relative adjectives (*whose, which, what*)

3.2 Comparison of Adjectives

The three degrees of comparison are called the *positive* (the basic form of the adjective), the *comparative* (showing comparison with one other item), and the *superlative* (showing comparison with two or more other items). Most adjectives add the comparative suffix *-er* and the superlative suffix *-est*.

Using Adjectives

In English, unlike many other languages, adjectives have only one form. Do not add *-s* or *-es* to an adjective to make it plural.

- the *long* trip
- the *long* letters

Likewise, adjectives in English do not change to show gender.

- The *tall* man (masculine noun)
- The *tall* woman (feminine noun)
- The *tall* building (neuter noun)

Capitalize adjectives of origin (city, state, nation, continent).

- the *Venetian* canals
- the *French* government
- the *Texan* hat
- the *African* continent

In English, verbs of feeling (for example, *bore, interest, surprise*) have two adjectival forms: the present participle (*-ing*) and the past participle (*-ed*). Use the present participle to describe what causes the feeling. Use the past participle to describe the person who experiences the feeling.

- We heard the surprising election results.

  [The *election results* cause the feeling.]

- Only the candidate was surprised by the election results.

  [The *candidate* experienced the feeling of surprise.]

ESL TIPS

Adjectives follow the noun in English in only two cases: when the adjective functions as a subjective complement, as in:

- That project is not *finished*.

and when an adjective phrase or clause modifies the noun, as in:

- The project *that was suspended temporarily* has a new deadline.

In all other cases, adjectives are placed before the noun.

When there are multiple adjectives, the order illustrated in the following example would apply in most circumstances, but there are exceptions. (Normally, do not use a phrase with so many stacked modifiers.)

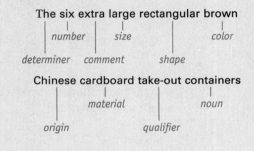

The six extra large rectangular brown

| | |
number | size | | color
determiner | comment | shape

Chinese cardboard take-out containers

| | |
| material | | noun
origin | qualifier

POSITIVE DEGREE	The first ingot is *bright.*
COMPARATIVE DEGREE	The second ingot is *brighter.*
SUPERLATIVE DEGREE	The third ingot is *brightest.*

Many two-syllable adjectives and most three-syllable adjectives, however, are preceded by *more* or *most* to form the comparative or the superlative.

COMPARATIVE DEGREE	The new facility is *more impressive* than the old one.
SUPERLATIVE DEGREE	The new facility is the *most impressive* in the city.

A few adjectives have irregular comparative and superlative degrees (*much, more, most; little, less, least*).

Absolute words (such as *unique, perfect, exact,* and *infinite*) are not logically subject to comparison. After all, something either is or is not unique; it isn't more unique or most unique. Language, however, is not always logical, so these words are sometimes used comparatively.

COMPARATIVE DEGREE   Phase-locked loop circuits make FM tuner performance *more exact* by decreasing tuner distortion.

3.3 Placement of Adjectives

When limiting and descriptive adjectives appear together, the limiting adjectives precede the descriptive adjectives, with the article usually in the first position.

■   *the ten gray* cars

      [The article *the* is followed by the limiting adjective *ten*, which is followed by the descriptive adjective *gray*.]

Within a sentence, an adjective can precede its noun or follow its noun.

CORRECT   The *small* jobs are given priority.

       [The adjective *small* precedes the noun *jobs*.]

CORRECT VARIATION   Priority is given when a job is *small*.

       [The adjective *small* follows the noun *job*.]

In a larger, more complex construction, an adjective may shift from preceding its noun to following it.

CORRECT   We negotiated a *bigger* contract than our competitor did.

       [The adjective *bigger* precedes the noun *contract*.]

CORRECT VARIATION   We negotiated a contract *bigger* than our competitor's.

       [The adjective *bigger* follows the noun *contract*.]

An adjective is called a predicate adjective when it follows a linking verb, such as a form of the verb *to be*. By completing the meaning of a linking verb, a predicate adjective describes, or limits, the subject of the verb.

PREDICATE ADJECTIVE   The job is *easy*.

       [The adjective *easy* follows the linking verb *is*.]

PREDICATE ADJECTIVE   The manager was very *demanding*.

       [The adjective *demanding* follows the linking verb *was*.]

An adjective also can follow a transitive verb and modify its direct object (the person or thing that receives the action of the verb).

MODIFIES DIRECT   They painted the office *white*.
OBJECT   [The adjective *white* modifies the direct object *office*.]

3.4 Functions of Adjectives

Nouns can sometimes function as adjectives, especially when precise qualification is necessary.

NOUN AS ADJECTIVE   The *test* conclusions led to a redesign of the system.

Frequently, business and technical writing is weakened by too many nouns strung together as modifiers. Exercise caution when you use nouns as adjectives.

WEAK   The test control group meeting was held last Wednesday.

IMPROVED   The meeting of the test control group was held last Wednesday.

MORE IMPROVED The test control group met last Wednesday.

Avoid general adjectives (*nice, fine, good*) and trite or overused adjectives (a *fond* farewell). Select adjectives that express your meaning as exactly as possible.

■ 4. Verbs

A *verb* is a word, or a group of words, that specifies an action or affirms a condition or a state of existence.

■ The antelope *bolted* at the sight of the hunters.

■ She *was saddened* by the death of her friend.

■ He *is* a wealthy man now.

A verb is the part of a sentence that makes an assertion about the action or existence of its subject, the someone or something that is its topic. Within a sentence, a verb alone is called a simple predicate; a verb with its modifiers and complements forms a complete predicate. When a subject and a predicate convey a complete thought, they form a sentence (or an independent clause). When a subject and a predicate do not convey a complete thought, they form a dependent clause. In contrast to a clause, a phrase is a group of words without the subject-predicate combination.

Verbs may be described as either transitive or intransitive; the intransitive verbs include linking verbs.

4.1 Transitive Verbs

A transitive verb requires a *direct object* to complete its meaning. The direct object normally answers the question *whom* or *what* by naming the person or thing that receives the action of the verb.

TRANSITIVE VERB AND DIRECT OBJECT	They *laid* the *foundation* on October 24.

Some transitive verbs (such as *give, wish, cause,* and *tell*) may be followed by an indirect object and then a direct object. The indirect object is usually a person and answers the question "to whom or what?" or "for whom or what?"

TRANSITIVE VERB AND INDIRECT OBJECT	Georgiana Anderson *gave* the *treasurer* a *letter*.

4.2 Intransitive Verbs

An intransitive verb does not require an object to complete its meaning. It makes a full assertion about the subject by itself (although it may have modifiers).

- The water *boiled*. The water *boiled* rapidly.
- The engine *ran*. The engine *ran* quietly.

4.3 Linking Verbs

Although intransitive verbs do not have objects, some may take complements. Linking verbs link the subject of a sentence to words following the verb. When the following complement is a noun (or pronoun), it refers to the same person or thing as the noun (or pronoun) that is the subject.

- The conference table *is* an antique.
- Maria *should be* the director.

When the complement is an adjective, it modifies the subject.

- The study *was* thorough.
- The report *seems* complete.

Such intransitive verbs as *be, become, seem,* and *appear* are almost always linking verbs. Others, such as *look, sound, taste, smell,* and *feel,* may function either as linking verbs or as simple intransitive verbs.

AS LINKING VERB	Their antennae *feel* delicate. [*Feel* is a linking verb meaning that the antennae seem fragile to the touch.]
AS SIMPLE INTRANSITIVE VERB	Their antennae *feel* delicately. [*Feel* is a simple intransitive verb meaning that the antennae have a delicate sense of touch.]

4.4 Finite Verbs

A *finite verb* is the main verb of a clause or sentence. It makes an assertion about its subject and can serve as the only verb in its clause or sentence. Finite verbs may be transitive or intransitive (including linking) verbs. They change form to reflect person (I *see*, he *sees*), tense (I *go*, I *went*), and number (he *says*, they *say*).

■ The telephone *rang*, and the secretary *answered* it.

■ When the telephones *ring*, you *answer* them.

A *helping verb* (sometimes called an *auxiliary verb*) is added to a finite or main verb to help indicate mood, voice, and tense. (See the discussions of mood, voice, and tense on pages 655–660.) Together, the helping verb and the main verb form a verb phrase.

HELPING VERBS	The work *had* begun.	I *will* go.
	I *am* going.	I *should have* gone.
	I *was* going.	I *must* go.

The most commonly used helping verbs are the various forms of *have* (*has, had*), *be* (*am, is, are, was, were*), *do* (*did, does*), *can* (*could*), *may* (*might*), *shall* (*should*), and *will* (*would*). Phrases that function as helping verbs often include *to:* for example, *am going to* and *is about to* (*will*), *has to* (*must*), and *ought to* (*should*).

■ I *am going to* quit. ■ I *will* quit.

■ She *has to* get a raise. ■ She *must* get a raise.

The helping verb always precedes the main verb, although other words may come between them. (See also ESL Tips on page 750.)

■ Machines *will* [helping verb] never completely *replace* [main verb] people.

4.5 Nonfinite Verbs or Verbals

Nonfinite verbs are the verbals (gerunds, infinitives, and participles) derived from verbs but that function as nouns, adjectives, or adverbs.

When the *-ing* form of a verb functions as a noun, it is called a *gerund*.

■ *Seeing* is *believing*.

An *infinitive*, which is the root form of a verb, can function as a noun, an adverb, or an adjective. Because the word *to* usually precedes an infinitive, it is considered the sign of an infinitive.

- He hates *to complain*.

  [*To complain* functions as a noun and direct object of the verb *hates*.]

- The valve closes *to stop* the flow.

  [*To stop* functions as an adverb and modifies the verb *closes*.]

- This is the proposal *to select*.

  [*To select* functions as an adjective and modifies the noun *proposal*.]

A *participle* is a verb form that functions as an adjective. The *present participle* ends in *-ing*.

- *Declining* sales forced us to close the branch office.

The *past participle* may end in *-ed, -t, -en, -n, or -d.*

- What are the *estimated* costs?

- Repair the *bent* lever.

- Here is the *broken* printer.

- What are the *known* properties of this metal?

- The story, *told* many times before, was still interesting.

The *perfect participle* is formed with the present participle of *have* and the past participle of the main verb.

- *Having received* [perfect participle] a large raise, the *smiling* [present participle], *contented* [past participle] employee worked harder than ever.

Grammatical Properties of Verbs

Verbs can show person and number, mood, voice, and tense.

4.6 Person and Number of Verbs

Verbs must agree with their subjects in *number* (singular or plural) and *person* (first, second, or third). In the present indicative of regular verbs (see Section 4.7), only the third-person singular differs from the infinitive stem. The verb *to be*, however, is irregular: I *am*, you *are*, he *is*, we *are*, they *are*. (See Section 4.10.)

- I *see* [first-person singular] one van, but he *sees* [third-person singular] another.

- I *am* [first-person singular] convinced, and they *are* [third-person plural] convinced; unfortunately, he *is* [third-person singular] not convinced.

4.7 Mood and Verbs

Mood refers to the functions of verbs: making statements or asking questions (indicative mood), giving commands (imperative mood), or expressing hypothetical possibilities (subjunctive mood).

The *indicative mood* refers to an action or a statement that is conceived as fact.

- *Is* the setting correct?

- The setting *is* correct.

The *imperative mood* expresses a command, suggestion, request, or entreaty.

- *Install* the wiring today.

- Please *let* me know if I can help.

The *subjunctive mood* expresses something that is contrary to fact, is conditional, or is hypothetical; it can also express a wish, a doubt, or a possibility. Only the verb *be* preserves many changes in form to show the subjunctive mood.

- The senior partner insisted that he [I, you, we, they] *be* in charge of the project.

- If the sales representative [I, you, we, they] *were* to close the sale today, we would meet our monthly quota.

Most other verbs do not change form for the subjunctive. Instead, helping verbs show the subjunctive function.

- *Had I known* that you were here, I would have come earlier.

Determining Mood

ESL TIPS

In written and especially in spoken English, there is an increasing tendency to use the indicative mood where the subjunctive traditionally has been used. Note the differences between traditional and contemporary usage in these examples:

Traditional Use of the Subjunctive Mood

- I wish he *were* here now.
- If I *were* going to the conference, I would room with him.
- I requested that she *show* up on time.

Informal Use of the Indicative Mood

- I wish he *was* here now.
- If I *was* going to the conference, I would room with him.
- I requested that she *shows* up on time.

As a non-native speaker of English, you are faced with a choice: Do you use the subjunctive and, in some circles, sound sophisticated or intellectual? Or do you use the indicative and, in other circles, sound uneducated? In business and technical writing, it is best to use the more traditional expressions.

If you wish to express a contrary-to-fact condition or a highly doubtful hypothesis, use the subjunctive; if not, use the indicative.

SUBJUNCTIVE MOOD	If I *were* president of the firm, I would change several policies.
INDICATIVE MOOD	I *am* president of the firm, but I don't control all the policies.

Do not shift haphazardly from one mood to another within a sentence; to do so makes the sentence unbalanced as well as ungrammatical.

INCORRECT	*Put* the clutch in first [imperative]; then you *should put* the truck in gear [indicative].
CORRECT	*Put* the clutch in first [imperative]; then *put* the truck in gear [imperative].
CORRECT	You *should put* the clutch in first [indicative]; then you *should put* the truck in gear [indicative].

4.8 Voice and Verbs

The grammatical term *voice* refers to whether the subject of a sentence or clause acts or receives the action. A sentence is in the active voice if the subject acts, in the passive voice if the subject is acted upon. The passive voice consists of a form of the verb *to be* and a past participle of the main verb.

ACTIVE VOICE	The aerosol bomb *propels* the liquid as a mist.
PASSIVE VOICE	The liquid *is propelled* as a mist by the aerosol bomb.

In your writing, the active voice provides force and momentum. The verb identifies what the subject is doing, thus emphasizing the subject and the action. However, the passive voice emphasizes what is being done to the subject, rather than the subject or the action. Use the active voice unless you have good reason not to.

PASSIVE VOICE	The report *was written* by Joe Albright in only two hours. [The emphasis is on *report* rather than on Joe and the writing.]
ACTIVE VOICE	Joe Albright *wrote* the report in only two hours. [Here the writer and writing receive the emphasis.]
PASSIVE VOICE	Things *are seen* by the normal human eye in three dimensions: length, width, and depth. [The emphasis is on *things* rather than on the eye's function.]

ACTIVE VOICE   The normal human eye *sees* things in three dimensions: length, width, and depth.

         [Here the eye's function—which is what the sentence is about—receives the emphasis.]

Sentences in the passive voice may state the actor, but they place the actor in a secondary position as the object of a preposition ("*by* the normal human eye").

Choosing Voice

ESL TIPS

Different languages place different values on active-voice and passive-voice constructions. In some languages, the passive is used frequently; in others, hardly at all. As a non-native speaker of English, you may have a tendency to follow the pattern of your native language. But remember, even though business writing may sometimes require the passive voice, active verbs are highly valued in English.

The passive voice has its advantages, however; when the doer of the action is not known or is not important, use the passive voice.

■ The firm *was established* in 1929.

Avoiding Shifts in Person, Number, Voice, Mood, and Tense

ESL TIPS

To write clearly, maintain consistency and avoid shifts. A shift occurs when there is an abrupt change in person, number, voice, mood, or tense. When you edit your writing, check for the following types of shifts.

Person

■ *Students* must get financial clearance before ~~you~~ *they* can attend class.

[This sentence incorrectly shifted from third-person *students* to second-person *you*.]

Number

■ *Everyone* must turn in ~~their~~ *his or her* timecards.

or

■ *All employees* must turn in *their* timecards.

[When possible, use a plural antecedent so a concise plural pronoun can be used. The pairing *his*

or *her* or *he or she* can be awkward and difficult to follow.]

Voice

■ The captain permits his crew to go ashore, but ~~they are not permitted~~ *he does not permit them* to go downtown.

[The entire sentence is now in the active voice.]

Mood

■ Reboot your computer, and ~~you should~~ empty the cache, too.

[The entire sentence is now in the imperative mood.]

Tense

■ I was working quickly, and suddenly a box ~~falls~~ *fell* off the conveyor belt and ~~breaks~~ *broke* my foot.

[The entire sentence is now in the past tense.]

When the doer of the action is less important than the receiver of the action, use the passive voice.

■   Police Officer Bryant *was cited* for heroism by Chief of Police Colby.

Be careful about shifting voice within a sentence.

INCORRECT   We *worked* late last night, and all the tests *were* finally *completed*.
CORRECT   We *worked* late last night and finally *completed* all the tests.

4.9 Verb Tense

Tense is the grammatical term for verb forms that indicate time distinctions. The six simple tenses in English are present, present perfect, past, past perfect, future, and future perfect. Each of these tenses has a corresponding progressive form that shows action in progress and is created by combining the helping verb *be*, in the appropriate tense, with the present participle (*-ing*) form of the main verb. (See Table A–3 and Table C–2, Forming Tenses: A Timeline, on page 744.)

Table A–3   Forming the Simple and Progressive Tenses

Simple	*Progressive*
I begin (present)	I am beginning (present)
I began (past)	I was beginning (past)
I will begin (future)	I will be beginning (future)
I have begun (present perfect)	I have been beginning (present perfect)
I had begun (past perfect)	I had been beginning (past perfect)
I will have begun (future perfect)	I will have been beginning (future perfect)

The *simple present tense* represents action occurring in the present, without any indication of time duration.

■   I *use* the calculator.

A general truth is always expressed in the present tense.

■   He learned that "time *heals* all wounds."

The present tense can present actions or conditions that have no time restrictions.

■   Water *boils* at 212°F.

The present tense can be used to indicate habitual action.

■   I *pass* the paint shop on the way to the office every day.

The present tense can be used as the *historical present* to make things that oc-curred in the past more vivid.

■   It is 1910, and the founder of our company is pushing his cart through Philadelphia. He *works* hard, *expands* his business, and *builds* the firm that still bears his name.

The *simple past tense* indicates that an action took place in its entirety in the past. The past tense is usually formed by adding -*d* or -*ed* to the root form of the verb.

■   We *closed* the office early yesterday.

The *simple future tense* indicates a time that will occur after the present. The helping verb *will* (or *shall*) is used along with the main verb.

■   I *will finish* the job tomorrow.

The *present perfect tense* describes something from the recent past that has a bearing on the present—a period of time before the present but after the simple past. The present perfect tense is formed by combining the present tense of the helping verb *have* with the past participle of the main verb.

■   He *has retired,* but he visits the office frequently.

■   We *have finished* the draft and are ready to begin revising it.

The *simple past perfect tense* indicates that one past event preceded another. It is formed by combining the helping verb *had* with the past participle of the main verb.

■   He *had finished* by the time I arrived.

The *future perfect tense* indicates an action that will be completed at the time of or before another future action. It is formed by linking the helping verbs *will have* to the past participle of the main verb.

■   He *will have driven* the test car 400 miles by the time he returns.

Using the Progressive Form

English uses the progressive form, particularly the present progressive, more frequently than other languages do. The progressive form of the verb is composed of two features: a form of the helping verb *be* and the *-ing* form of the base verb.

PRESENT PROGRESSIVE	I *am rewriting* the memo.
PAST PROGRESSIVE	I *was rewriting* the memo last week.
FUTURE PROGRESSIVE	I *will be rewriting* that memo forever!

The present progressive is used in three ways:

1. To refer to an action that is in progress at the moment of speaking or writing

   - The conference chair *is* constantly *interrupting* the speakers.

2. To highlight that a state or action is not permanent

   - The office temp *is helping* us for a few weeks.

3. To express future plans

   - The summer intern *is leaving* to return to school this Friday.

The past progressive is used to refer to a continuing action or condition in the past, usually with specified limits.

- I *was failing* calculus until I got eyeglasses.

The future progressive is used to refer to a continuous action or condition in the future.

- We *will be monitoring* his condition all night.

Verbs that express mental activity or the senses of sight, smell, touch, sound, and taste are generally not used in the progressive.

- I *believe* the defendant's testimony.

Other such verbs include:

appear	contain	need	resemble
appreciate	forget	own	see
be	have	prefer	seem
believe	hear	recognize	sound
belong	know	remember	think
consist of	mean	represent	understand

4.10 Conjugation of Verbs

When a verb is conjugated, all of its forms are arranged schematically so that the differences in tense, number, person, and voice are readily apparent. In the conjugation of the verb *drive,* its principal parts, used to construct its various forms, are *drive* (infinitive and present tense), *drove* (past tense), *driven* (past participle), and *driving* (present participle). Table A–4 shows each conjugated form in both the active voice and the passive voice.

Table A–4   Conjugating Verbs

Tense	*Number*	*Person*	*Active Voice*	*Passive Voice*
Present	Singular	1st	I drive	I am driven
		2nd	You drive	You are driven
		3rd	He drives	He is driven
	Plural	1st	We drive	We are driven
		2nd	You drive	You are driven
		3rd	They drive	They are driven

(continued)

Table A–4 Conjugating Verbs

Tense	Number	Person	Active Voice	Passive Voice
Progressive present	Singular	1st	I am driving	I am being driven
		2nd	You are driving	You are being driven
		3rd	He is driving	He is being driven
	Plural	1st	We are driving	We are being driven
		2nd	You are driving	You are being driven
		3rd	They are driving	They are being driven
Past	Singular	1st	I drove	I was driven
		2nd	You drove	You were driven
		3rd	He drove	He was driven
	Plural	1st	We drove	We were driven
		2nd	You drove	You were driven
		3rd	They drove	They were driven
Progressive past	Singular	1st	I was driving	I was being driven
		2nd	You were driving	You were being driven
		3rd	He was driving	He was being driven
	Plural	1st	We were driving	We were being driven
		2nd	You were driving	You were being driven
		3rd	They were driving	They were being driven
Future	Singular	1st	I will drive	I will be driven
		2nd	You will drive	You will be driven
		3rd	He will drive	He will be driven
	Plural	1st	We will drive	We will be driven
		2nd	You will drive	You will be driven
		3rd	They will drive	They will be driven
Progressive future	Singular	1st	I will be driving	I will have been driven
		2nd	You will be driving	You will have been driven
		3rd	He will be driving	He will have been driven
	Plural	1st	We will be driving	We will have been driven
		2nd	You will be driving	You will have been driven
		3rd	They will be driving	They will have been driven
Present perfect	Singular	1st	I have driven	I have been driven
		2nd	You have driven	You have been driven
		3rd	He has driven	He has been driven
	Plural	1st	We have driven	We have been driven
		2nd	You have driven	You have been driven
		3rd	They have driven	They have been driven
Past perfect	Singular	1st	I had driven	I had been driven
		2nd	You had driven	You had been driven
		3rd	He had driven	He had been driven
	Plural	1st	We had driven	We had been driven
		2nd	You had driven	You had been driven
		3rd	They had driven	They had been driven
Future perfect	Singular	1st	I will have driven	I will have been driven
		2nd	You will have driven	You will have been driven
		3rd	He will have driven	He will have been driven
	Plural	1st	We will have driven	We will have been driven
		2nd	You will have driven	You will have been driven
		3rd	They will have driven	They will have been driven

(continued)

4.11 Subject-Verb Agreement

Agreement, grammatically, means the correspondence in form between different elements of a sentence. Just as a pronoun must agree with its antecedent in person, gender, and number (see Section 2.13), so a verb must agree with its subject in person and number.

■ I *am* going to approve his promotion.

[The first-person singular subject, *I,* requires the first-person singular form of the verb, *am.*]

■ His colleagues *are* envious.

[The third-person plural subject, *colleagues,* requires the third-person plural form of the verb, *are.*]

Do not let phrases and clauses that fall between subject and verb mislead you.

■ Teaching proper oral hygiene to children, even when they are excited about learning, *requires* patience.

[The verb *requires* must agree with the singular subject of the sentence, *teaching,* rather than with the plural subject of the preceding clause, *they.*]

Avoid making the verb agree with the noun immediately before it if that noun is not its subject. This problem is especially likely to occur when a modifying phrase containing a plural noun falls between a singular subject and its verb.

■ Each of the engineers *is* experienced.

[The subject of the verb is *each,* not *engineers.*]

■ Only Bob, of all the district managers, *has doubled* his sales this year.

[The subject of the verb is *Bob,* not *managers.*]

■ Proper cleaning of the machines and tools *takes* time.

[The subject of the verb is *cleaning,* not *machines and tools.*]

Words such as *type, part, series,* and *portion* take singular verbs even when such words precede a phrase containing a plural noun.

■ A *series* of meetings *was* held to decide the best way to market the new product.

Subjects expressing measurement, weight, mass, or total often take singular verbs even though the subject word is plural. Such subjects are treated as a unit.

■ *Four years is* the normal duration of the apprenticeship program.

However, when such subjects refer to the individual items that make up the unit, a plural verb is required.

■   If you're looking for oil, *three quarts are* on the shelf in the garage.

Similarly, collective subjects take singular verbs when the group is thought of as a unit. They take plural verbs when the individuals are thought of separately.

■   The *committee is* holding its meeting on Thursday.

■   The *majority are* opposed to delivering their reports at the meeting.

A relative pronoun (*who, which, that*) may take either a singular or a plural verb depending on whether its antecedent (the noun to which it refers) is singular or plural.

■   He is an *employee* who *takes* work home at night.

■   He is one of those *employees* who *take* work home at night.

A compound subject is composed of two or more elements joined by a conjunction such as *and, or, nor, either . . . or,* or *neither . . . nor.* Usually, when the elements are connected by *and,* the subject is plural and requires a plural verb.

■   *Chemistry and finance are* prerequisites for this position.

A compound subject with a singular and a plural element joined by *or* or *nor* requires that the verb agree with the element closer to it.

■   Neither the office manager nor the *accountants were* there.

■   Neither the accountants nor the *office manager was* there.

A book with a plural title requires a singular verb.

■   *Monetary Theories is* a useful source.

Some abstract nouns are singular in meaning though plural in form: examples include *mathematics, news, physics,* and *economics.*

■   Textiles *is* an industry in need of import quotas.

Some words are always plural, such as *pants* and *scissors.*

■   His pants *were* torn by the machine.

However, a pair of pants or a pair of scissors is singular.

■   A pair of pants *is* on order.

Modifiers such as *some, none, all, more,* and *most* may be singular if they are used with mass nouns or plural if they are used with count nouns. Mass nouns identify things that cannot be separated into countable units; count nouns identify things that can be separated into countable units (see Section 1.2).

- Most of the oil *has* been used.

- Most of the drivers *know* why they are here.

One and *each* are normally singular.

- One of the brake drums *is* still scored.

- Each of the original founders *is* scheduled to speak at the ceremony.

Following a relative pronoun such as *who, which,* or *that,* a verb agrees in number with the noun to which the pronoun refers (its antecedent).

- She is an employee who *is* rarely absent.
  [*Who* refers to *employee.*]

- She is one of those employees who *are* rarely absent.
  [*Who* refers to *employees.*]

A *subjective complement* is a noun or an adjective in the predicate of a sentence following a linking verb. The number of a subjective complement does not affect the number of the verb—the verb must always agree with the subject.

- The topic of his report *was* rivers.
  [The subject of the sentence is *topic,* not *rivers.*]

Inverted word order can confuse agreement between subject and verb.

- From this work *have come* several important improvements.
  [The subject of the verb is *improvements,* not *work.*]

A compound subject is composed of two or more elements joined by a conjunction such as *and, or, nor, either . . . or,* or *neither . . . nor.* Usually, when the elements are connected by *and,* the subject is plural and requires a plural verb.

- Education and experience *are* valuable assets.

There is one exception to the *and* rule. Sometimes the elements connected by *and* form a unit or refer to the same person. In this case, the subject is regarded as singular and takes a singular verb.

- Peaches and cream *is* his favorite dessert.

- His accountant and business partner *prepares* the tax forms.
  [His accountant is also his business partner.]

A compound subject joined by *or* or *nor* requires a singular verb with two singular elements and a plural verb with two plural elements.

■   Neither the doctor nor the nurse *is* on duty.

■   Neither the doctors nor the nurses *are* on duty.

A compound subject with a singular element and a plural element joined by *or* or *nor* requires that the verb agree with the element nearest to it.

■   Neither the doctor nor the nurses *are* on duty.

■   Neither the doctors nor the nurse *is* on duty.

■ 5. Adverbs

An adverb modifies the action or condition expressed by a verb.

■   The recording head hit the surface of the disk *hard*.
    [The adverb tells *how* the recording head hit the disk.]

An adverb may also modify an adjective, another adverb, or a clause.

■   The graphics department used *extremely* bright colors.
    [The adverb *extremely* modifies the adjective *bright*.]

■   The redesigned brake pad lasted *much* longer than the original model.
    [The adverb *much* modifies the adverb *longer*.]

■   *Unexpectedly,* the machine failed.
    [The adverb *unexpectedly* modifies the clause *the machine failed*.]

5.1 Functions of Adverbs

An adverb answers one of the following questions:

- Where?
  - ■   Move the throttle *forward*.
- When?
  - ■   Replace the thermostat *immediately*.
- How?
  - ■   Add the solvent *cautiously*.
- How much?
  - ■   I *rarely* work on the weekend.
  - ■   I have worked overtime *twice* this week.

Some adverbs (such as *however, therefore, nonetheless, nevertheless, consequently, accordingly,* and *then*) can join two independent clauses, each of which could otherwise stand alone as a sentence.

■ I rarely work on the weekend; *nevertheless,* this weekend will be an exception.

Other adverbs, such as *where, when, why,* and *how,* ask questions.

■ *How* many hours did you work last week?

5.2 Comparison of Adverbs

Adverbs, like adjectives, show three degrees of comparison: the positive (the basic form), the comparative (showing comparison with one other item), and the superlative (showing comparison with two or more other items). One-syllable adverbs use the comparative ending *-er* and the superlative ending *-est.*

■ This copier works *faster* than the old one.

■ This copier works *fastest* of the three tested.

Most adverbs with two or more syllables end in *-ly,* and most adverbs ending in *-ly* are compared by inserting the comparative *more* or *less* or the superlative *most* or *least* in front of them.

■ He moved *more* [*less*] *quickly* than the other company's salesperson.

■ Of all the salespeople, he moved *most* [*least*] *quickly.*

A few irregular adverbs require a change in form to indicate comparison.

■ Our training program functions *well.*

■ Our training program functions *better* than most others in the industry.

■ Our training program functions the *best* in the industry.

5.3 Adverbs Made from Adjectives

Many adverbs are simply adjectives with *-ly* added, such as *dashingly* and *richly.* Sometimes, the adverb form is identical to the adjective form; examples are *early, hard, right,* and *fast.* Resist the temptation to drop the *-ly* ending from such adverbs as *surely, differently, seriously, considerably, badly,* and *really.*

■ The breakdown of the air conditioner damaged the computer system
         considerably
   ~~considerable~~.
        ^

However, resist the temptation to coin awkward adverbs by adding *-ly* to adjectives (*firstly, muchly*).

■ ~~Firstly~~ *First*, I'd like to thank our sponsor; ~~secondly~~ *second*, I'd like to thank all of you.

5.4 Placement of Adverbs

An adverb may appear almost anywhere in a sentence, but its position can affect the meaning of the sentence. Avoid placing an adverb between two verb forms where it will be ambiguous because it can be read as modifying either.

INCORRECT   The man who was making calculations hastily rose from his desk and left the room.

[Did the man calculate hastily or did he rise hastily?]

CORRECT   The man who was making calculations rose hastily from his desk and left the room.

An adverb is commonly placed in front of the verb it modifies.

■ The accountant *meticulously* checked the figures.

An adverb may follow the verb (or the verb and its object) that it modifies.

■ The accountant checked the figures *meticulously*.

An adverb may be placed between a helping verb and a main verb.

■ He will *surely* call.

If an adverb modifies only the main verb, and not any accompanying helping verbs, place the adverb immediately before or after the main verb.

■ The alternative proposal has been *effectively* presented.
■ The alternative proposal has been presented *effectively*.

An adverb phrase, however, should not separate the parts of a verb.

■ This suggestion has ~~time and time again~~ been rejected. *time and time again*

To emphasize an adverb that introduces an entire sentence, you can put the adverb before the subject of the sentence.

■ *Clearly,* he was ready for the promotion when it came.

In writing, such adverbs as *nearly, only, almost, just,* and *hardly* are placed immediately before the words they limit. A speaker can place these words earlier and avoid ambiguity by stressing the word to be limited; a writer, however, can ensure clarity only through correct placement of the adverb.

         costs
- The punch press almost ~~costs~~ $50,000.

■ 6. Conjunctions

A *conjunction* connects words, phrases, or clauses. A conjunction can also indicate the relationship between the two elements it connects. (For example, *and* joins together; *or* selects and separates.) Conjunctions may be coordinating, correlative, or subordinating. In addition, certain adverbs act as conjunctions.

6.1 Coordinating Conjunctions

A coordinating conjunction joins two sentence elements that have identical functions. The coordinating conjunctions are *and, but, for, nor, or, so,* and *yet.*

- Bill *and* John work at the Los Angeles office.

  [*And* joins two proper nouns.]

- To hear *and* to obey are two different things.

  [*And* joins two phrases.]

- He would like to include the test results, *but* that would make the report too long.

  [*But* joins two clauses.]

6.2 Correlative Conjunctions

Correlative conjunctions are used in pairs: *either . . . or, neither . . . nor, not only . . . but also, both . . . and,* and *whether . . . or.* To ensure not only symmetry but also logic in your writing, follow correlative conjunctions with parallel sentence elements that are alike in function and in construction.

- Bill will arrive *either* on Wednesday *or* on Thursday.

6.3 Subordinating Conjunctions

A subordinating conjunction connects sentence elements of different weights, normally independent clauses that can stand alone as sentences and dependent clauses that cannot. The most frequently used subordinating conjunctions are *so, although, after, because, if, where, than, since, as, unless, before, that, though, when,* and *whereas.*

- He left the office *after* he had finished writing the report.

6.4 Conjunctive Adverbs

A conjunctive adverb has the force of a conjunction because it is used to join two independent clauses. The most common conjunctive adverbs are *however, moreover, therefore, further, then, consequently, besides, accordingly, also,* and *too.*

■ The engine performed well in the laboratory; *moreover,* it surpassed all expectations during its road test.

6.5 Placement of Conjunctions

Coordinating conjunctions generally appear within a sentence. There is, however, no rule against beginning a sentence with a coordinating conjunction. In fact, such conjunctions can be strong transitional words and provide emphasis.

■ I realize that the project was more difficult than expected and that you have also encountered personnel problems. *But* we must meet our deadline.

Starting sentences with conjunctions is acceptable in even the most formal English. But like any other writing device, this one should be used sparingly lest it become ineffective and even annoying.

■ 7. Prepositions

A preposition links a noun or pronoun (its object) to another sentence element. (See also Prepositions on page 741.)

7.1 Functions of Prepositions

Prepositions express such relationships as direction (*to, into, across, toward*), location (*at, in, on, under, over, beside, among, by, between, through*), time (*before, after, during, until, since*), or figurative location (*for, against, with*). Although only about 70 prepositions exist in the English language, they are used frequently. Together, the preposition, its object, and the object's modifiers form a prepositional phrase, which acts as a modifier.

Many words that function as prepositions also function as adverbs. If a word takes an object and functions as a connective, it is a preposition; if it has no object and functions as a modifier, it is an adverb.

■ The manager sat *behind* the desk in his office. [preposition]

■ The customer lagged *behind;* then she came in and sat down. [adverb]

7.2 Use of Prepositions

Do not use unnecessary prepositions, such as "off *of*" or "inside *of.*"

　　Inside
■ ~~Inside of~~ the cave, the spelunkers turned on their headlamps.
　　^

Avoid adding the preposition *up* to verbs unnecessarily.

■   *Call*
~~Call up~~ and see whether he is in his office.
       ^

However, do not omit needed prepositions.

           to
■   He was oblivious and not distracted by the view from his office window.
           ^

If a preposition falls naturally at the end of a sentence, leave it there.

■   I don't remember which file I put it *in*.

Be aware, however, that a preposition at the end of a sentence can indicate that the sentence is awkwardly constructed.

AWKWARD   Corn was the crop that the wheat was planted *by*.

IMPROVED   The wheat was planted next to the corn.

The object of a preposition—the word or phrase following the preposition—is always in the objective case. Despite this rule, a construction such as "between you and *me*" frequently and incorrectly appears as "between you and *I*."

                                                    him
■   The whole department has suffered because of the quarrel between ~~he~~ and Bob.
                                                    ^

Certain verbs (and verb forms), adverbs, and adjectives are used with certain prepositions. For example, we say "interested *in*," "aware *of*," "devoted *to*," "equated *with*," "adhere *to*," "conform *to*," "capable *of*," "comply *with*," "object *to*," "find fault *with*," "inconsistent *with*," "independent *of*," and "interfere *with*."

■ 8. Interjections

An *interjection* is a word or phrase of exclamation that is used independently to express emotion or surprise or to summon attention. *Hey! Ouch! Wow!* are strong interjections. *Oh, well,* and *indeed* are mild ones. An interjection functions much as *yes* or *no,* in that it has no grammatical connection with the rest of the sentence in which it appears. When an interjection expresses a sudden or strong emotion, punctuate it with an exclamation mark.

■   His only reaction was a resounding *"Wow!"*

Punctuate a mild interjection with a comma.

■   *Well,* that's done.

■   *Oh, well,* that's done.

Because their expressive force comes from sound, interjections are more common in speech than in writing. They are rarely appropriate in business or technical writing.

Phrases, Clauses, Sentences, and Paragraphs

Good writing relies on the writer's ability to put together words that effectively convey a message to a reader. The writer can use many tools to help communicate ideas, among them phrases, clauses, sentences, and paragraphs.

■ 9. Phrases

Although a phrase is the most basic meaningful group of words, it does not make a full statement. Unlike a clause, it does not contain both a subject (words that name someone or something) and a predicate (words that make an assertion about the subject). Instead, a phrase is based on a noun, a verbal (that is, a gerund, an infinitive, or a participle), or a verb without a subject.

- by August fifth [phrase based on a noun]

- operating the machine [phrase based on a verbal]

- has been working [phrase composed of a verb without a subject]

9.1 Functions of Phrases

A phrase may function as an adjective, an adverb, a noun, or a verb.

ADJECTIVE	The subjects *on the agenda* were all discussed.
ADVERB	We discussed the project *with great enthusiasm.*
NOUN	*Hard work* is her way of life.
VERB	The chief engineer *should have been notified.*

Even though phrases function as adjectives, adverbs, nouns, or verbs, normally they are named for the kind of word around which they are constructed—preposition, verb, noun, or the three verbals. For definitions of the parts of speech, refer to pages 635–670.

9.2 Prepositional Phrases

A *preposition* shows the relationship between the noun or pronoun that is its object and another sentence element. Prepositions express relationships such as direction, location, and time. A preposition, its object, and the object's modifiers form a prepositional phrase, which acts as a modifier.

- *After the meeting,* the regional managers adjourned *to the executive dining room.*

9.3 Verb Phrases

A verb phrase consists of a main verb preceded by one or more helping verbs.

■ The secretary *had discovered* that a fax machine *was sending* pages twice.

9.4 Noun Phrases

A noun phrase consists of a noun and its modifiers.

■ Have *the two new employees* fill out *these forms.*

9.5 Participial Phrases

A participial phrase consists of a participle plus its object and any modifiers. A participial phrase functions as an adjective, so it must modify a noun or pronoun and must be placed so that this relationship is clear.

■ *Looking very pleased with himself,* the sales manager reported on the success of the policies he had introduced.

9.6 Infinitive Phrases

An *infinitive* is the root form of a verb (*go, run, talk*), one of the principal parts that is used to construct the various forms of a verb. An infinitive generally follows the word *to,* called the *sign of the infinitive.* An infinitive phrase consists of the word *to* plus an infinitive and any objects or modifiers.

■ *To succeed in this field,* you must be willing *to assume responsibility.*

9.7 Gerund Phrases

When the -*ing* form of a verb functions as a noun, it is called a *gerund.* A gerund phrase, which also functions as a noun, consists of a gerund plus any objects or modifiers.

■ *Preparing an annual report* is a difficult task.

■ She liked *running the department.*

■ 10. Clauses

A *clause* contains both a subject (the word or group of words that name someone or something as a topic) and a predicate (the main verb and its modifiers and complements that make an assertion about the subject).

10.1 Functions of Clauses

Every subject-predicate word group in a sentence is a clause. Unlike a phrase, a clause can make a complete statement because it contains a finite verb (as opposed to a nonfinite verb or verbal) as well as a subject. Every sentence must consist of at least one clause.

A clause that conveys a complete thought and thus could stand alone as a sentence is an *independent clause.*

■ *The scaffolding fell* when the rope broke.

A clause that could not stand alone without the rest of its sentence is a *dependent* or *subordinate clause.*

■ I was at the St. Louis branch *when the decision was made.*

A dependent clause may function as a noun, an adjective, or an adverb in a larger sentence; an independent clause may be modified by one or more dependent clauses.

■ While I was in college, I studied differential equations.

[*While I was in college* is a dependent clause functioning as an adverb; it modifies the independent clause *I studied differential equations.*]

A clause may be connected with the rest of its sentence by a coordinating conjunction, a subordinating conjunction, a relative pronoun, or a conjunctive adverb. (Refer to Sections 2 and 6 for discussions of pronouns and conjunctions.)

COORDINATING CONJUNCTION	Peregrine falcons are about the size of a large crow, *and* they have a wingspan of three to four feet.
SUBORDINATING CONJUNCTION	Mission control will have to be alert *because* the space laboratory will contain a highly flammable fuel at launch.
RELATIVE PRONOUN	It was Robert M. Fano *who* designed and developed the earliest "Multiple Access Computer" system at MIT.
CONJUNCTIVE ADVERB	It was dark when we arrived; *nevertheless,* we began to tour the factory.

10.2 Independent Clauses

Unlike a dependent clause, an independent clause is complete in itself. Although it might be part of a larger sentence, it always can stand alone as a separate sentence.

■ *We abandoned the project* because the cost was excessive.

10.3 Dependent Clauses

A dependent (or subordinate) clause is a group of words that has a subject and a predicate but requires a main clause to complete its meaning. A dependent clause can function in a sentence as a noun, as an adjective, or as an adverb.

As nouns, dependent clauses may function as subjects, objects, or complements.

SUBJECT	*That human beings can learn to control their glands and internal organs by direct or indirect means* is now an established fact.
DIRECT OBJECT	I learned *that drugs ordered by brand name can cost several times as much as drugs ordered by generic name.*
SUBJECTIVE COMPLEMENT	The trouble is *that we cannot finish the project by May 30.*

As adjectives, dependent clauses can modify nouns or pronouns. Dependent clauses are often introduced by relative pronouns and relative adjectives (*who, whom, whose, which, what, that*).

ADJECTIVE	The man *who called earlier* is here. [The clause modifies *man.*]

As adverbs, dependent clauses may express relationships of time, cause, result, or degree.

EXPRESSES TIME	You are making an investment *when you buy a house.*
EXPRESSES A CAUSE	A title search was necessary *because the bank would not otherwise grant a loan.*
EXPRESSES A RESULT	Consult an attorney *so that you will be aware of your rights and obligations.*
EXPRESSES DEGREE	Monthly mortgage payments should not be much more *than the buyer earns in one week.*

Dependent clauses clarify the relationships between thoughts. As a result, dependent clauses can present ideas more precisely than can simple sentences (which contain one independent clause) or compound sentences (which combine two or more independent clauses).

IMPRECISE	The sewage plant is located between Millville and Darrtown. Both villages use it. [These sentences convey two thoughts of approximately equal importance.]
IMPROVED	The sewage plant, *which is located between Millville and Darrtown,* is used by both villages. [Here, one thought, the plant's location, is subordinated to the other, its service area.]

IMPRECISE   He arrived at his office early, and he was able to finish the report with-
              out any interruptions.

              [These sentences convey two thoughts of approximately equal im-
              portance.]

IMPROVED   *Because he arrived at his office early,* he was able to finish the report
              without interruptions.

              [Here, one thought, his early arrival, is subordinated to the other, his
              completion of the report.]

Dependent clauses effectively express thoughts that describe or explain another statement. They can state where, when, how, or why an event occurred, thus
supplying logical connections that may not be obvious. Too much subordination,
however, may be worse than none at all. A string of dependent clauses, like a string
of simple sentences, may obscure important ideas.

IMPRECISE   He had selected classes *that* had a slant *that* was specifically directed
              toward students *who* intended to go into business.

              [This sentence contains three dependent clauses of approximately
              equal importance.]

IMPROVED   He had selected classes *that* were specifically directed to business
              students.

              [One dependent clause emphasizes the most important of the three
              points.]

■ 11. Sentences

A *sentence* is a sequence of words that contains a subject and a predicate and conveys a complete thought. A sentence ordinarily requires at least two words: a subject (something or someone) and a predicate (an assertion about the action or
state of existence of the subject). (See also ESL Tips: Using Common Sentence
Patterns on page 108.)

■   Sales [subject] declined [assertion about the subject].

To the basic sentence can be added modifiers—words, phrases, and clauses that
expand, limit, or otherwise clarify the meanings of other sentence elements.

■   *Laptop computer* sales declined *in August.*

In most sentences, the subject is a noun phrase rather than a single word, and
the predicate is a verb or verb phrase with appropriate modifiers, objects, or
complements.

■ A good human resources department [subject] screens job applicants carefully [predicate].

Sentences may be classified according to structure (simple, compound, complex) and intention (declarative, interrogative, imperative, exclamatory). A simple sentence often makes its content stand out in the reader's mind. A compound sentence shows that the clauses in the sentence are of equal importance. A complex sentence shows that the clauses in the sentence are of unequal importance.

11.1 Simple Sentences

A simple sentence has one clause. In its most basic form, the simple sentence contains only a subject and a predicate.

■ Profits rose.

■ The strike ended.

Both the subject and the predicate may be compounds that include several items without changing the basic structure of the simple sentence.

COMPOUND SUBJECT	*Bulldozers and road graders* have blades.
COMPOUND PREDICATE	Bulldozers *strip, ditch, and backfill.*

Likewise, although modifiers may lengthen a simple sentence, they do not change its basic structure.

■ The *recently introduced* procedure works *very well.*

11.2 Compound Sentences

A compound sentence combines two or more related independent clauses that are of equal importance. These clauses may be joined by a comma and a coordinating conjunction, by a semicolon, or by a conjunctive adverb preceded by a semicolon and followed by a comma.

■ The plan was sound, *and* the staff was eager to begin.

[The independent clauses are joined by a comma and coordinating conjunction.]

■ The plan was sound; the staff was eager to begin.

[The independent clauses are joined by a semicolon.]

■ The plan was sound; *therefore,* the staff was eager to begin.

[The independent clauses are joined by a conjunctive adverb.]

11.3 Complex Sentences

A complex sentence contains one independent clause and at least one dependent clause.

- We lost some of our efficiency [independent clause] when we moved [dependent clause].

A dependent clause may occur before, after, or within the independent clause and can function within a sentence as a subject, an object, or a modifier.

SUBJECT   *What he proposed* is irrelevant.

OBJECT   We know *where it is supposed to be.*

MODIFIER   Fingerprints, *which were used for personal identification in 200 B.C.E.,* were not used for criminal identification until about 1800.

Because complex sentences offer more variety than simple ones, changing a compound sentence into a complex one can produce a more precise statement. When one independent clause becomes subordinate to another, the relationship between the two is more clearly established.

- We moved, *and* we lost some of our efficiency.

  [This sentence contains a compound sentence with a coordinating conjunction.]

- *When* we moved, we lost some of our efficiency.

  [This is a complex sentence with a subordinating conjunction.]

A complex sentence indicates the relative importance of two clauses and expresses the relationship between their ideas. Normally, the independent clause states the main point, and the dependent clause states a related but subordinate point.

- Although the warehouse was damaged by the fire, all the employees escaped safely from the building.

Intention of Sentences

By intention, a sentence may be declarative, interrogative, imperative, or exclamatory. A *declarative sentence* conveys information or makes a factual statement.

- This motor powers the conveyor belt.

An *interrogative sentence* asks a direct question.

- Does the conveyor belt run constantly?

An *imperative sentence* issues a command.

■ Start the generator.

An *exclamatory sentence* emphatically expresses feeling, fact, or opinion.

■ The heater exploded!

Construction of Sentences

11.4 Parts of Sentences

Within a sentence, every word or word group functions as a sentence element. A *subject* names (and perhaps includes words that describe) the person or thing that is the topic of the sentence.

■ *The new machine* ran.

A *verb* describes an action or affirms the condition or state of existence of its subject.

■ The new machine *ran.*

A *complement* is used in the predicate (with the verb) to complete the meaning of a sentence. The four kinds of complements are the direct object, indirect object, objective complement, and subjective complement. The direct object names the person or thing on which a transitive verb acts, and it normally answers the question *what* or *whom.*

■ He wrote *a letter.*

The indirect object names the recipient of the direct object—the person or thing that something is done to or for.

■ He wrote *the company* a letter.

The objective complement describes or renames a direct object.

■ I like my coffee *hot.*

The subjective complement describes or renames the subject.

■ The director seems *confident.*

A *modifier* expands, limits, or refines the meaning of other sentence elements.

- *Automobile* production decreased *rapidly.*

A *connective* (a conjunction, a conjunctive adverb, or a preposition) ties together parts of sentences by indicating subordination or coordination.

- I work hard each week, *but* I relax *when* I play racquetball.

An *appositive* is a noun or noun phrase that follows and renames another noun or noun phrase.

- Bob, *the human resources director,* just interviewed another engineer.

An *absolute* is a participial or an infinitive phrase that modifies a statement as a whole and is not linked to it by a subordinating conjunction or preposition.

- *To speak bluntly,* the proposal is unacceptable.

An *expletive* is a word such as *it* or *there* that serves as a structural filler and reverses standard subject-verb order.

- *It* is certain that he will go.

11.5 Sentence Patterns

Subjects, verbs, and complements form the basic sentence patterns with which a writer works.

- The cable snapped. [subject-verb]
- Generators produce electricity. [subject-verb-direct object]
- The test results gave us confidence. [subject-verb-indirect object-direct object]
- Repairs made the equipment operational. [subject-verb-direct object-objective complement]
- The metal was aluminum. [subject-linking verb-subjective complement]

Most sentences follow the subject-verb-complement pattern. In "The company dismissed Joe," for example, you recognize the subject (*company*) and the object (*Joe*) by their positions before and after the verb. In fact, readers interpret what they read more easily because they expect this sentence order. As a result, departures from it can be effective if used sparingly for emphasis and variety but annoying if overdone.

An inverted sentence places the elements in other than normal order.

- A better job I never had. [direct object-subject-verb]

- More optimistic I have never been. [subjective complement-subject-linking verb]

Inverted sentence order also can be used in questions and exclamations.

- Have you a pencil? [verb-subject-complement]

- How heavy your book feels! [complement-subject-verb]

In sentences introduced by expletives (*there, it*), the subject comes after its verb because the expletive occupies the subject's normal location before the verb. Because expletives are fillers, they are generally avoided in concise writing.

WORDY	There are certain principles of drafting that must not be ignored.
IMPROVED	Certain principles of drafting must not be ignored.
	[The meaningful verb of the sentence, *be ignored,* which was buried in a relative clause in the expletive construction, becomes the only verb; the meaningless *are* is unnecessary.]
WORDY	It is difficult to work in a noisy office.
IMPROVED	Working in a noisy office is difficult.

Unusual word order can add emphasis or variety but cannot be used often without tiring or puzzling the reader. Instead, a sentence that moves quickly from subject to verb to complement is clear and easy to understand. The writer's goal is to preserve this clear and direct pattern while using more complicated forms to present more information. A skillful writer depends on subordination—the relative weighing of ideas—to make sentences clearer. The following sentence lacks subordination:

- The city manager's report was carefully illustrated, and it covered five typed pages.

It can be rewritten in several ways by subordinating the less important ideas to the more important ones.

ADJECTIVAL CLAUSE	The city manager's report, *which covered five typed pages,* was carefully illustrated.
PARTICIPIAL PHRASE	The city manager's report, *covering five typed pages,* was carefully illustrated.
PARTICIPIAL PHRASE	The *carefully illustrated* report of the city manager covered five typed pages.

MODIFIER   The *five-page* report of the city manager was carefully illustrated.

APPOSITIVE PHRASE   The city manager's report, *five typed pages,* was carefully illus-
                       trated.

The effective subordination of words, phrases, and clauses produces varied, concise, and emphatic sentences.

Common Sentence Problems

The most common sentence problems are faulty subordination, run-on sentences, sentence fragments, and dangling and misplaced modifiers.

11.6 Faulty Subordination

Faulty subordination occurs when a grammatically subordinate element, such as
a dependent clause, actually contains the main idea of the sentence or when a
subordinate element is so long or detailed that it overpowers the main idea.

You can avoid the first problem, expressing the main idea in a subordinate element, by deciding which idea is the main idea. Both of the following sentences,
for example, appear logical, but each emphasizes a different point.

- Although the new filing system saves money, many of the staff are unhappy with it.

  [This sentence emphasizes the staff's unhappiness and downplays the savings.]

- The new filing system saves money, although many of the staff are unhappy with it.

  [This sentence emphasizes the savings.]

In this example, if the writer's main point is that *the new filing system saves money,*
the second sentence is better. If the main point is that *many of the staff are unhappy,* the first sentence is better.

The other major problem with subordination occurs when a writer puts so
much detail into a subordinate element that it overpowers the main point by its
sheer size and weight. Omitting or moving the detail streamlines the sentence.

- If company personnel do not fully understand what the new contract ~~that was
  drawn up at the annual meeting of the district managers this past month in New
  Orleans~~ requires of them, they should call or write the vice president for finance.

11.7 Run-On Sentences

A *run-on sentence,* sometimes called a *fused sentence,* is made up of two or more
sentences that are not separated by punctuation. The term sometimes includes
independent clauses separated by only a comma, although these are usually

called *comma faults* or *comma splices*. Both types can be corrected by (1) making two sentences, (2) joining the two clauses with a semicolon (if they are closely related and of equal weight), (3) joining the two clauses with a comma and a coordinating conjunction, or (4) subordinating one clause to the other.

INCORRECT	The training division will offer three new courses interested employees should sign up by Wednesday. [run-on sentence]
INCORRECT	The training division will offer three new courses, interested employees should sign up by Wednesday. [comma fault or comma splice]
CORRECT	The training division will offer three new courses. Interested employees should sign up by Wednesday. [two sentences]
CORRECT	The training division will offer three new courses; interested employees should sign up by Wednesday. [semicolon]
CORRECT	The training division will offer three new courses, *so* interested employees should sign up by Wednesday. [comma plus coordinating conjunction]
CORRECT	*When* the training division offers the new courses, interested employees should sign up for them. [one clause subordinated to the other]

11.8 Sentence Fragments

A sentence that is missing an essential part (subject or predicate) is called a *sentence fragment*.

- She changed jobs. [sentence]

- And earned more money. [fragment, lacking a subject]

But having a subject and a predicate does not automatically turn a clause into a sentence. The clause must also make an independent statement. "I work" is a sentence; "If I work" is a fragment because the subordinating conjunction *if* makes the statement a dependent clause.

Sentence fragments are often introduced by relative pronouns (*who, whom, whose, which, that*) or subordinating conjunctions (such as *although, because, if,* and *while*). When you use these introductory words, you need to combine the dependent clause that follows with a main clause to form a complete sentence.

- The department received several new computers. ~~After~~ *after* its order was processed.

A sentence must contain a main or finite verb; verbals (gerunds, participles, and infinitives) cannot replace main or finite verbs. The following examples are sentence fragments because they lack main verbs. Their verbals (*working, to skip, expecting*) cannot function as finite verbs.

FRAGMENT   *Working* overtime every night during tax season.

FRAGMENT   *To skip* the meeting.

FRAGMENT   The manager *expecting* to place an order.

Fragments may reflect incomplete or confused thinking. The following examples illustrate common types of sentence fragments.

INCORRECT   Health insurance rates have gone up. *Because medical expenses have increased.* [adverbial clause]

CORRECT   Health insurance rates have gone up because medical expenses have increased.

INCORRECT   The engineers tested the model. *Outside the laboratory.* [prepositional phrase]

CORRECT   The engineers tested the model outside the laboratory.

INCORRECT   *Having finished the job.* We submitted our invoice. [participial phrase]

CORRECT   Having finished the job, we submitted our invoice.

INCORRECT   We met with Jim Rodgers. *Former head of the sales division.* [appositive]

CORRECT   We met with Jim Rodgers, former head of the sales division.

INCORRECT   We have one major goal this month. *To increase the strength of the alloy without reducing its flexibility.* [infinitive phrase in apposition with *goal*]

CORRECT   We have one major goal this month: to increase the strength of the alloy without reducing its flexibility.

Sometimes a writer intentionally uses an incomplete sentence. This kind of deliberate fragment makes sense in its context because the missing element is clearly implied by the preceding sentence or is clearly understood without being stated.

■ In view of these facts, is new equipment really necessary? *Or economical?*

■ You can use the one-minute long-distance rates anytime between eleven at night and eight in the morning. *Any night of the week.*

Minor sentences are elliptical expressions that are equivalent to complete sentences because the missing words are obvious from the context.

■ How much?

■ Ten dollars.

■ At last!

Common in advertising copy, fictional dialogue, and informal e-mails, minor sentences are not ordinarily appropriate in business or technical writing.

11.9 Dangling and Misplaced Modifiers

A *dangling modifier* is a word or phrase that has no clear word or subject to modify. Most dangling modifiers are phrases with verbals (gerunds, participles, or infinitives). Correct this problem by adding the appropriate noun or pronoun for the phrase to modify or by making the phrase into a clause.

- After finishing the negotiations, ~~dinner was relaxing.~~ *we relaxed at dinner.*

- ~~Entering~~ *As you enter* the gate, the administration building is visible.

A *misplaced modifier* refers, or appears to refer, to the wrong word or phrase.

- Our copier was used to duplicate materials ~~for other departments~~ that needed to be reduced *for other departments*.

You can avoid this problem by placing modifiers as close as possible to the words they modify. Position each modifier carefully so that it says what you mean.

- We ~~just~~ bought *just* the property for expansion.

A *squinting modifier* is located between two sentence elements and might refer to either one. To eliminate the ambiguity, move the modifier or revise the sentence.

- ~~The~~ *During the next week, the* union agreed ~~during the next week~~ to return to work.

- The union agreed during the next week *to return to work* ~~to return to work.~~

Occasionally, a subject and verb are omitted from a dependent clause; the result is known as an *elliptical clause*. If the omitted subject of the elliptical clause is not the same as the subject of the main clause, the construction dangles. Simply adding the subject and verb to the elliptical clause solves the problem. (Or, you can rework the whole sentence.)

INCORRECT	When ten years old, his father started the company.
	[Could his father have started the company at age ten?]
CORRECT	When *Bill Krebs was* ten years old, his father started the company.
CORRECT	*Bill Krebs was* ten years old when his father started the company.

11.10 Other Sentence Faults

The assertion made by the predicate of a sentence about its subject must be logical.

- Mr. Wilson~~'s job~~ is a forensic technician.

- Jim~~'s height~~ is six feet tall.

Do not omit a required verb.

- The floor is swept$\overset{\wedge}{,}$ and the lights $\overset{are}{\wedge}$ out.

- I never have $\overset{written}{\underset{\wedge}{}}$ and probably never will write the annual report.

Do not omit a subject.

- Although he regarded price-fixing as questionable, he engaged in it until $\overset{it\ was}{\underset{\wedge}{}}$ abolished by law.

Avoid compound sentences containing clauses that have little or no logical relationship to each other.

- My department is responsible for all company publications$\overset{\wedge}{\underset{:}{}}$ ~~, and the~~ $\overset{The}{\wedge}$ staff includes ten writers, three artists, and four composition specialists.

Effective Sentences

Effective sentences engage the reader's attention. They can alert a reader to ideas weighted equally (through parallel structure) or differently (through subordination). When carefully constructed, they clarify ideas for the reader. Besides highlighting significant information, sentences can be varied in length, pattern, and style to avoid boring the reader. Most writers wait until they are revising to concentrate on effective sentences. Then they try to build clear, precise, and varied sentences that eliminate confusion and monotony.

11.11 Sentence Parallelism

Express coordinate ideas in similar form. The very construction of a sentence with parallel elements helps the reader to grasp the similarity of its parts.

- As a working team, we understand that our project is a collaborative effort; as members of a team, we recognize that each person's assignment is his or her responsibility.

11.12 Emphatic Sentences

Subordinate your minor ideas to emphasize your more important ideas.

■ *Because we*
We had all arrived, ~~and~~ we began the meeting early.

The most emphatic positions in a sentence are the beginning and the end. Do not waste these spots by burying the main idea in the middle of the sentence between less important points or by tacking on phrases and clauses as afterthoughts.

INEFFECTIVE SENTENCE	Sales declined by 3 percent in 2003, but nevertheless the company had the most profitable year in its history, thanks to cost savings that resulted from design improvements in several of our major products; and we expect 2004 to be even better, since further design improvements are being made.
	[The sentence begins with the bad news, buries the good news, and trails off at the end.]
IMPROVED, EFFECTIVE SENTENCE	Cost savings from design improvements in several major products not only offset a 3-percent sales decline but made 2003 the most profitable year in the company's history. Further design improvements now in progress promise to make 2004 even more profitable.
	[The first sentence emphasizes *cost savings* and *design improvements;* the second stresses profits.]

Occasionally, reversing normal word order also can achieve emphasis.

NORMAL WORD ORDER	I will never agree to that.
REVISED FOR EMPHASIS	*That* I will never agree to.
REVISED FOR EMPHASIS	*Never* will I agree to that.

11.13 Clear Sentences

Uncomplicated sentences most effectively state complex ideas. Readers may be confused if they must unravel a sentence in addition to a complex idea.

CONFUSING SENTENCE	Burning fuel and air in the production chamber causes an expansion of the gases formed by combustion, which in turn pushes the piston down in its cylinder so that the crankshaft rotates and turns the flywheel, which then transmits to the clutch the power developed by the engine.
IMPROVED, CLEAR SENTENCE	Burning fuel and air in the production chamber causes an expansion of the gases formed by combustion. These gases push the piston down in its cylinder so that the crankshaft rotates. Then the flywheel on the end of the crankshaft transmits to the clutch the power developed by the engine.

Just as simpler sentences can make complex ideas easier to understand, so more complex sentences can make groups of simple ideas easier to read.

| CHOPPY, NOT INTEGRATED | The industrial park was designed carefully. A team of architects and landscape designers planned it. It has become a local landmark. |
| IMPROVED, INTEGRATED | The carefully designed industrial park, planned by a team of architects and landscape designers, has become a local landmark. |

11.14 Sentence Length

Variations in sentence length avoid monotony, making writing more interesting to read. Short sentences often can be combined by converting verbs to adjectives.

■ The steeplejack *exhausted* ~~was exhausted. He~~ collapsed on the scaffolding.

Sentences that string together short, independent clauses may be just as tedious as a series of short sentences. Vary some of the clauses by adding subordinating connectives or turning them into separate sentences.

POOR	This river is 60 miles long, *and* it averages 50 yards in width, *and* its depth averages 8 feet.
IMPROVED	This river, *which* is 60 miles long and averages 50 yards in width, has an average depth of 8 feet.
IMPROVED	This river is 60 miles long. It averages 50 yards in width and 8 feet in depth.

Although too many short sentences make your writing sound choppy and immature, a short sentence can effectively end a passage of long ones.

■ As a working team, we understand that our projects are collaborative efforts; as individual members of the team, we recognize that each person's assignment is his or her responsibility. Put more simply, team members should complete their respective tasks on time and be willing to comment on their teammates' work. Successful collaboration requires that we do our best for each other as a group and for ourselves as individuals. *There is no other way.*

In general, short sentences are good for emphatic statements. Long sentences are good for detailed explanations and support. Nothing is wrong with a long sentence, or even a complicated one, as long as it is clear and direct. In fact, a sentence that is noticeably short or long will draw the reader's attention. When varied for emphasis or contrast, sentence length becomes an element of style.

11.15 Word Order

When successive sentences all begin in exactly the same way, the result is likely to be monotonous. You can make your sentences more interesting by occasionally starting with a modifying word, phrase, or clause.

ADJECTIVE	*Fatigued,* the project director slumped into a chair.
ADVERB	*Lately,* our division has been very productive.
PARTICIPLE	*Smiling,* he extended his hand to the irate customer.
INFINITIVE	*To learn,* you must observe and ask questions.
ABSOLUTE CONSTRUCTION	*Work having already begun,* there was little we could do.
PREPOSITIONAL PHRASE	*In the morning,* we will finish the report.
PARTICIPIAL PHRASE	*Following the instructions in the manual,* she located and repaired the faulty parts.
INFINITIVE PHRASE	*To reach the top job,* she introduced constructive alternatives to unsuccessful policies.
ADVERB CLAUSE	*Because we now know the results of the survey,* we will proceed with the reorganization.

Use this technique in moderation; overusing it can cause monotony.

Avoid confusing separations of subjects and verbs, prepositions and objects, and the parts of verb phrases. Your reader expects the usual patterns and reads more quickly and easily when they are clear.

CONFUSING	The manager worked closely with, despite personality differences, the head engineer.
	[The preposition and the object are separated.]
IMPROVED	Despite personality differences, the manager worked closely with the head engineer.

This is not to say, however, that a subject and verb never should be separated by a modifying phrase or clause.

■ John Stoddard, who founded the firm in 1963, is still an active partner.

Vary the positions of modifiers in your sentences to achieve variety and different emphases or meanings, as the following examples illustrate.

■ Gently, with the square end up, slip the blasting cap down over the time fuse.

■ With the square end up, gently slip the blasting cap down over the time fuse.

■ With the square end up, slip the blasting cap gently down over the time fuse.

■ With the square end up, slip the blasting cap down over the time fuse gently.

11.16 Loose Sentences

A loose sentence follows a natural and easy pattern. It makes its major point at the beginning and then adds subordinate phrases and clauses to develop that major point. A loose sentence could seem to end at one or more points before it actually ends, as the periods in brackets illustrate in the following example.

- It went up [.], a great ball of fire about a mile in diameter [.], an elemental force freed from its bonds [.] after being chained for billions of years.

11.17 Periodic Sentences

In contrast to loose sentences, a periodic sentence delays its main idea until the end by presenting subordinate ideas or modifiers first. Skillfully handled, a periodic sentence lends force, or emphasis, to the main point by arousing the reader's anticipation and then presenting the main point as a climax.

- During the last decade or so, the attitude of the American citizen toward automation has undergone a profound change.

Do not use periodic sentences too often, for overuse may irritate a reader who tires of waiting for your point. Likewise, avoid the singsong monotony of a series of loose sentences, particularly coordinate clauses joined by conjunctions. Instead, experiment during revision with shifts from loose to periodic sentences.

12. Paragraphs

12.1 Function of Paragraphs

A *paragraph* is a group of sentences that supports and develops a single idea. Like an essay in miniature, it expands on the central idea stated in its topic sentence (italicized in the following paragraph).

- *The cost of training new employees is high.* In addition to the cost of classroom facilities and instructors, an organization must pay employees a salary to sit in the classroom while they are learning. We have determined that for the company to break even on professional employees, those employees must stay in the job for which they have been trained for at least one year.

Paragraphs perform three essential functions: (1) They develop the central ideas stated in their topic sentences; (2) they break material into logical units; and (3) they create physical breaks on the page, which visually assist the reader.

12.2 Topic Sentences

A *topic sentence* states the central idea of a paragraph; the rest of the paragraph then supports and develops that statement with pertinent details. The topic sentence is most often the first sentence of the paragraph. In this position, it lets the reader know immediately what idea the paragraph will develop. On rare occasions, the topic sentence (italicized in the following paragraphs) logically falls in the middle of a paragraph.

ESL TIPS

Understanding Paragraph Structure

North American readers expect writers to present ideas directly. A typical paragraph in English will begin with a topic sentence containing the subject and a claim about the subject that will be developed throughout the paragraph. After the topic sentence, readers expect to find specific examples that support the topic sentence and help to clarify the writer's point.

■ It is perhaps natural that psychologists should awaken only slowly to the possibility that behavioral processes may be directly observed, or that they should only gradually put the older statistical and theoretical techniques in their proper perspective. But it is time to insist that science does not progress by carefully designed steps called "experiments," each of which has a well-defined beginning and end. *Science is a continuous and often a disorderly and accidental process.* We shall not do the young psychologist any favor if we agree to reconstruct our practices to fit the pattern demanded by current scientific methodology. What the statistician means by the design of experiments is design which yields the kind of data to which *his* techniques are applicable. He does not mean the behavior of the scientist in his laboratory devising research for his own immediate and possibly inscrutable purposes.[1]

Although an early topic sentence is usually most effective, a paragraph can lead up to it to achieve emphasis. When a topic sentence (italicized) ends a paragraph, it also can serve as a summary or conclusion, based on the details that led up to it.

■ Although Merton does construct his book as a delightful romp through the intellectual life of medieval and Renaissance Europe, he does have a serious point to make. For Merton has devoted much of his work to the study of multiple discoveries in science. *He has shown that almost all major ideas rise more than once, independently and often virtually at the same time—and thus, that great scientists are embedded in their cultures, not divorced from them.*[2]

Because several paragraphs are sometimes necessary to develop different aspects of an idea, not all paragraphs have topic sentences. In this situation, transitions between paragraphs are especially important so that the reader knows that the same idea is being developed through several paragraphs.

TOPIC
SENTENCE

The software's style feature lets you insert styles that format your text for an entire document or for specific sections of text within a document. Because styles contain formatting codes that are grouped under one structure, you can save time and ensure consistency by using styles throughout your document.

TRANSITION

For example, suppose you write books. You might want to create several styles that will help you format these books. Here are some examples of the kinds of styles you might want to create:

- A Chapter Heading style. This text could be a centered, 24-point font with italics. You could add extra lines to the style to control the space between the heading and the text that follows.

---

[1] B. F. Skinner, "A Case History in Scientific Method."

[2] Steven Jay Gould, *The Panda's Thumb: More Reflections in Natural History.*

- A Text style. The text of the book could be formatted in a 10-point font with two columns and a first-line indent for each paragraph.
- A Long Quotes style. The text for long quotes from other sources could be similar to the text style, but in 9-point type instead of 10, single-spaced and indented on both sides.

TRANSITION   *When you reach a place in your book where you want to create a chapter heading or a long quote,* you can easily apply the style to text rather than reinserting the same formatting codes every time. And if you want to change any of the formatting codes, all you have to do is edit the style, and the change will affect all text to which the style has been applied.

The reader can more easily assimilate the two separate parts of the main idea in the topic sentence when it is developed in three paragraphs, rather than one.

12.3 Paragraph Unity and Coherence

A good paragraph has unity and coherence. *Unity* means singleness of purpose, based on a topic sentence that states the central idea of the paragraph and subsequent sentences that contribute to it. *Coherence* means being logically consistent throughout the paragraph. All the parts naturally connect with one another as carefully chosen transitional words tie together ideas as they are developed. (Table A–5 contains a list of common transitions.) In the following paragraph, the topic sentence and the transitions are italicized.

◼ *It turns out to be very difficult to devise a theory to describe the universe all in one go. Instead,* we break the problem up into bits and invent a number of partial theories. Each of *these* partial theories describes and predicts a certain limited class of observations, neglecting the effects of other quantities, or representing them by simple sets of numbers. *It may be that this approach is completely wrong. If* everything in the universe depends on everything else in a fundamental way, *it might be* impossible to get close to a full solution by investigating parts of the problem in isolation. *Nevertheless,* it is certainly the way that we have made progress in the past. The classic example again is the Newtonian theory of gravity, *which* tells us that the gravitational force between two bodies depends only on one number associated with each body, its mass, *but* is otherwise independent of what the bodies are made of. *Thus* one does not need to have a theory of the structure and constitution of the sun and planets in order to calculate their orbits.[3]

A good paragraph often uses details from the preceding paragraph, thereby preserving and advancing the thought being developed. Appropriate conjunctions and the repetition of keywords and key phrases can help to provide unity and coherence among, as well as within, paragraphs.

◼ Ten years ago, choosing to educate your child at *home* was a sure sign of crankiness. Today it is a growing *movement.* The department of education estimates that the number of *school*-age children being taught at home has risen from 15,000 at the

---

[3] Steven J. Hawking, *A Brief History of Time: From the Big Bang to Black Holes.*

Table A–5 Common Transitions

To add information			
also	besides	moreover	furthermore
in addition	finally	next	additionally
first, second, etc.	last		

To give an example or to illustrate a point			
for example	for instance	to illustrate	specifically
in particular	in this case	to demonstrate	notably

To compare or contrast			
on the other hand	on the contrary	likewise	however
although	similarly	nevertheless	meanwhile
whereas			

To prove			
because	moreover	furthermore	besides

To show time			
initially	eventually	during	thereafter
finally	then	later	previously
formerly	first, second, etc.	next	afterward
at last	before	at the same time	currently

To show sequence			
next	now	finally	simultaneously
first, second, etc.	after	consequently	concurrently
thus	therefore		

To conclude			
in conclusion	therefore	thus	as a result
finally	all in all		

Conjunctions			
and	or	nor	so
yet	for	but	

start of the 1980s to 350,000 in 1992. The *Home School* Legal Defense Association puts the figure even higher, at 500,000 or more. The reason for the discrepancy, according to Scott Somerville, a lawyer with the association, is that *home-schoolers* are not over-keen on owning up to census-takers.

In general, *home-schoolers* have slightly higher incomes and much more stable families than the average American. Apart from that, they are a fairly mixed bunch. In the Northwest, where the *movement* has been growing for 15 years, they tend to be New Age types, intoxicated by the *anti-schooling* ideas of A. S. Neill and Ivan Ilich. Elsewhere, particularly in the South, they are usually evangelical Christians, angry at the constitutional ruling that keeps God out of the classroom.[4]

---

[4] "Classless Society," *The Economist.*

Punctuation

Punctuation is a system of symbols that helps the reader to understand the intention of a sentence and the structural relationships within it. Misuse of punctuation can cause your reader to misunderstand your meaning. Marks of punctuation may link, separate, enclose, terminate, classify, and indicate omissions from sentences. Most of the 13 punctuation marks can perform more than one function. Their use is determined by grammatical conventions and by the writer's intention.

apostrophe	'
brackets	[ ]
colon	:
comma	,
dash	—
exclamation mark	!
hyphen	-
parentheses	( )
period	. (including ellipses and leaders)
question mark	?
quotation marks	" " (including ditto marks)
semicolon	;
slash	/

■ 13. Commas

The comma (,) is used more often than any other mark of punctuation because it has such a wide variety of uses: it can link, enclose, separate, and show omissions. Used with care, the comma can clarify and emphasize how ideas fit together; used carelessly, it can cause confusion.

Commas That Link

13.1 Commas and Coordinating Conjunctions

Coordinating conjunctions (*and, but, for, or, so, nor, yet*) require a comma immediately preceding them when they are used to connect independent clauses.

■   Human beings have always prided themselves on their unique capacity to create and manipulate symbols, but today computers are manipulating symbols.

Exceptions to this rule sometimes occur when the two independent clauses are short and each has a single subject and a single predicate. However, even in such cases, a comma is preferred.

UNLINKED CLAUSES	The cable snapped and the power failed.
IMPROVED	The cable snapped, and the power failed.

Commas That Enclose

13.2 Commas and Nonessential Elements of Sentences

Commas are used to enclose nonrestrictive and parenthetical sentence elements. Nonrestrictive elements add nonessential information about the things they modify; parenthetical elements also insert extra information into the sentence. Each is set off by commas to show its loose relationship with the rest of the sentence.

NONRESTRICTIVE CLAUSE	Our new Detroit factory, *which began operations last month,* should add 25 percent to total output.
PARENTHETICAL ELEMENT	We can, *of course,* expect their lawyer to call us.

Similarly, commas enclose nonrestrictive participial phrases.

NONRESTRICTIVE PHRASE	The lathe operator, *working quickly and efficiently,* finished early.

In contrast, restrictive elements—as their name implies—restrict the meaning of the words to which they apply and cannot be set off with commas.

RESTRICTIVE ELEMENT	The boy *in the front row* is six years old.
NONRESTRICTIVE ELEMENT	The boy, *who is sitting in the front row,* is six years old.

In the first sentence, *in the front row* is essential to the sentence: The phrase identifies the boy. In the second sentence, the relative clause *who is sitting in the front row* is incidental: The main idea can be communicated without it.

Phrases in apposition follow and amplify an essential element; they are enclosed in commas.

■ Our company, *the Blaylok Precision Company,* is doing well this year.

13.3 Commas and Dates

When complete dates appear with sentences, the year is enclosed in commas.

■ On November 11, 1918, the Armistice ending World War I went into effect.

However, when only part of a date appears, do not use commas.

■ In November 1918 the armistice ending World War I went into effect.

When the day of the week is included in a date, the month and the number of the day are enclosed in commas.

■ On Friday, November 11, 1918, the Armistice ending World War I went into effect.

13.4 Commas and Direct Address

A direct address is enclosed in commas unless it begins or ends a sentence.

■ You will note, *Mark,* that the brake shoe complies with this model's specifications.

Commas That Separate

Commas are used to separate introductory elements from the rest of the sentence, to separate items from each other, to separate subordinate clauses from main clauses, and to separate certain elements for clarity or emphasis.

13.5 Commas and Introductory Phrases or Clauses

In general, use a comma after an introductory clause or phrase unless it is very short. This comma helps indicate where the main part of the sentence begins.

■ *Because many rare fossils never occur free from their matrix,* it is wise to scan every slab with a hand lens.

When long modifying phrases precede the main clause, they should always be followed by a comma.

■ *During the first field-performance tests last year at our Colorado proving ground,* the new motor failed to meet our expectations.

When an introductory phrase is short and closely related to the main clause, the comma may be omitted.

■ *In two seconds* a 20°C temperature rise occurs in the test tube.

Certain types of introductory words must be followed by a comma, including a name used in direct address at the beginning of a sentence.

■ *Bill,* enclosed is the statement you asked me to audit.

A mild introductory interjection (such as *oh, well, why, indeed, yes,* and *no*) must be followed by a comma.

■ *Yes,* I will make sure your request is approved.

An introductory adverb, such as *moreover* or *furthermore,* must be followed by a comma.

■   *Moreover,* this policy will improve our balance of payments.

Occasionally, when adverbs are closely connected to the meaning of an entire sentence, they should not be followed by a comma. (Test such sentences by reading them aloud. If you pause after the adverb, use the comma.)

■   *Perhaps* we can still solve the balance-of-payments problem. *Certainly* we should try.

13.6 Commas and Items in a Series

Commas should be used to separate words in a series.

■   Basically, plants control the wind by *obstruction, guidance, deflection,* and *filtration.*

Phrases and clauses in coordinate series, like words, are punctuated with commas.

■   It is well known that plants *absorb noxious gases, act as receptors of dust and dirt particles,* and *cleanse the air of other impurities.*

Although the comma before the last item in a series is sometimes omitted, it is generally clearer to include it and avoid any confusion.

■   Departments within the company include *Operations, Finance, Mergers* and *Benefits.*
    [Is *mergers and benefits* one department or two? *Operations, Finance, Mergers, and Benefits* removes the doubt.]

When adjectives modifying the same noun can be reversed and make sense, or when they can be separated by *and* or *or,* they should be separated by commas.

■   The *dull, cracked* tools needed to be repaired.

When an adjective modifies a noun phrase, no comma is required.

■   He was investigating the *damaged radar-beacon system.*
    [*Damaged* modifies the noun phrase *radar-beacon system.*]

Never separate a final adjective from its noun.

■   He is a conscientious, honest, reliable/ worker.

Commas are conventionally used to separate distinct items. Use commas between the elements of an address written on the same line.

■   Walter James, 4199 Mill Road, Dayton, Ohio 45401

Use commas to separate the elements of geographical names.

■   Toronto, Ontario, Canada

Use a comma to separate the numerical elements of a complete date. When the day is omitted, however, the comma is unnecessary. (When a date appears in a sentence, a comma also follows the year. See Section 13.3.)

■   July 2, 1949   ■   July 1949

Use commas to separate the elements of Arabic numbers.

■   1,528,200

Use a comma after the salutation of a personal letter.

■   Dear Juan,

See ESL Tips: Punctuating Numbers on page 717.
        Use a comma to separate names that are reversed.

■   Smith, Alvin

13.7 Commas and Subordinate Clauses

Use a comma between the main clause and a subordinate clause when the subordinate clause comes first.

■   While the test ramp was being inspected a final time, the driver reviewed his checklist.

Use a comma after an independent clause that is only loosely related to the dependent clause that follows it.

■   The plan should be finished by July, even though I lost time because of a hospital stay.

13.8 Commas and Clarity or Emphasis

Two contrasting thoughts or ideas can be separated by commas for emphasis.

■   The project was finished on time, but not within the cost limits.

■   The specifications call for 100-ohm resistors, not 1,000-ohm resistors.

Use a comma to separate a direct quotation from its introduction.

■   Morton and Lucia White said, "Men live in cities but dream of the countryside."

Do not use a comma, however, when giving an indirect quotation.

- Morton and Lucia White said that urban dwellers continue to long for the country.

Sometimes commas simply clarify something otherwise confusing.

- The year after ˆ Xenox and 3M outproduced all the competition.

If you need a comma to separate the same word used twice, rewrite the sentence.

- *We were surprised at the*
  ~~The~~ assets we had~~, had surprised us~~.

Other Uses of Commas

13.9 Commas and Omission

In certain coordinate constructions, a comma can replace a missing, but implied, sentence element.

- Some were punctual; others, late. [Comma replaces *were*.]

13.10 Commas with Other Punctuation

In American usage, a comma always goes inside quotation marks.

- Although he called his presentation "adequate," the audience found it superb.

Except with abbreviations, a comma should not be used with a period, question mark, exclamation mark, or dash.

- "I have finished the project/," he said. [omit period]

- "Have you finished the project?/" I asked. [omit comma]

Comma Problems

The most frequent comma problems are the comma splice and the use of superfluous commas.

13.11 Comma Splices

Do not attempt to join two independent clauses with only a comma; this is called a *comma splice* or *comma fault*. (See also Section 11.7.)

INCORRECT   The new medical plan was comprehensive, the negotiator was pleased.

Such a comma fault could be corrected in several ways:

- Substitute a semicolon.
  - ■ The new medical plan was comprehensive; the negotiator was pleased.
- Add a conjunctive adverb preceded by a semicolon and followed by a comma.
  - ■ The new medical plan was comprehensive; *therefore,* the negotiator was pleased.
- Add a conjunction following a comma.
  - ■ The new medical plan was comprehensive, *so* the negotiator was pleased.
- Create two sentences. (Be aware, however, that putting a period between two closely related and brief statements may result in two weak sentences.)
  - ■ The new medical plan was comprehensive. The negotiator was pleased.
- Subordinate one clause to the other.
  - ■ *Because* the new medical plan was comprehensive, the negotiator was pleased.

13.12 Superfluous Commas

Writers often add commas where they do not belong because they assume that a pause should be indicated by a comma. It is true that commas usually signal pauses, but it is not true that pauses *necessarily* call for commas.

Be careful not to place a comma between a subject and its verb or between a verb and its object.

■ The wet weather across the region/ makes spring planting difficult. [omit comma]

■ The firm employs/ four writers, two artists, and one photographer. [omit comma]

Do not use a comma between the elements of a compound subject or a compound predicate consisting of only two elements.

■ The chairman of the board/ and the president prepared the press release. [omit comma]

■ The manager revised the schedules/ and improved morale. [omit comma]

Placing a comma after a coordinating conjunction (such as *and* or *but*) is an especially common error.

■ We doubled our sales, but/ we still did not dominate the market. [omit comma]

Do not place a comma before the first item or after the last item of a series.

■ We purchased new office furniture, including/ desks, chairs, and tables. [omit comma]

■ 14. Semicolons

The *semicolon* (;) links independent clauses or other sentence elements that are of equal weight and grammatical rank. The semicolon indicates a longer pause than a comma would, but not so long a pause as a period would.

The independent clauses of a compound sentence can be linked by a semicolon.

■ No one applied for the position; the job was too difficult.

The relationship between the two statements should be so clear that a reader will understand why they are linked without further explanation. Often, such clauses balance or contrast with each other.

■ Our last supervisor allowed only one long break; our new supervisor allows two short ones.

Use a semicolon between two main clauses connected by a coordinating conjunction (*and, but, for, or, nor, yet, so*) if the clauses are long and contain other punctuation.

■ In most cases these individuals are corporate executives, bankers, Wall Street lawyers; but they do not, as the economic determinists seem to believe, simply push the button of their economic power to affect fields remote from economics.[5]

A semicolon should be used before conjunctive adverbs (such as *therefore, moreover, furthermore, indeed, in fact, however*) that connect independent clauses.

■ I won't finish today; moreover, I doubt that I will finish this week.

Do not use a semicolon between a dependent clause and its main clause. Elements joined by semicolons must be of equal grammatical rank or weight.

■ No one applied for the position; even though it was heavily advertised.

A semicolon may be used to separate items in a series when they contain commas within them.

■ Among those present were John Howard, President of the Omega Group; Carol Martin, President of Alpha Corporation; and Larry Stanley, President of Stanley Papers.

---

[5]Robert Lubar, "The Prime Movers," *Fortune*, February 1960, 98.

■ 15. Colons

The *colon* (:) is a mark of anticipation and introduction that alerts the reader to the close connection between the first statement and the one following.

■   We carry three brands of watches: Timex, Bulova, and Omega.

A colon may be used to introduce a list.

■   The following corporations manufacture many types of computers:
      International Business Machines
      NCR Corporation
      Unisys Corporation

Do not, however, place a colon between a verb and its objects.

■   The three fluids for cleaning pipettes are: water, alcohol, and acetone. [omit colon]

Do not use a colon between a preposition and its object.

■   I would like to be transferred to: Tucson, Boston, or Miami. [omit colon]

A colon can link one statement to another that develops, explains, amplifies, or illustrates the first, including two independent clauses.

■   Any large organization must confront two separate, though related, information problems: It must maintain an effective internal communication system, and it must maintain an effective external communication system.

Occasionally, a colon may be used to link an appositive phrase to its related statement if special emphasis is needed.

■   Only one thing will satisfy Mr. Sturgess: our finished report.

Colons are used to link numbers in biblical references and time designations.

■   Genesis 10:16 [refers to chapter 10, verse 16]
■   9:30 a.m.

In a ratio, the colon indicates the proportion of one amount to another. (The colon replaces *to.*)

■   The cement is mixed with the water and sand at a ratio of 7:5:14.

A colon follows the salutation in business letters or formal e-mail messages, as opposed to personal letters or informal e-mails, where a comma may be used.

■ Dear Ms. Jeffers:

The first word after a colon may be capitalized if it begins a complete sentence, a formal resolution or question, or a direct quotation.

■ The conference attendance was low: We did not advertise widely enough.

Begin a subordinate element following a colon with a lowercase letter.

■ We have only one way to stay within our present budget: to reduce expenditures for research and development.

■ 16. Periods

A *period* (.) usually indicates the end of a declarative sentence. Periods also link (when used as leaders) and indicate omissions (when used as ellipses).

16.1 Uses of Periods

Although their primary function is to end declarative sentences, periods also end imperative sentences that are not emphatic enough for an exclamation mark.

■ Send me any information you may have on the subject.

Periods occasionally end questions that are polite requests or that assume an affirmative response.

■ Will you please send me the specifications.

Periods end minor sentences (deliberate sentence fragments), common in advertising but rarely appropriate in business or technical writing.

■ The spreadsheet that started it all is taking it to the next level—via the Internet. *The easiest to use, best-connected spreadsheet. Ever.*

Do not use a period after a declarative sentence quoted in another sentence.

■ "The project has every chance of success," she stated.

A period, in American usage, is placed inside quotation marks.

■ He liked to think of himself as a "tycoon."

■ He stated clearly, "My vote is yes."

Use periods after initials in names.

- ◾ W. T. Grant   ◾ J. P. Morgan

Use periods as decimal points with numbers. (See also ESL Tips: Punctuating Numbers on page 717.)

- ◾ 109.2   ◾ $540.26   ◾ 6.9 percent

Use periods to indicate abbreviations.

- ◾ Ms.   ◾ Dr.   ◾ Inc.

Use periods following the numbers in numbered lists.

- ◾ 1.
    2.
    3.

16.2 Period Faults

The incorrect use of a period is sometimes called a *period fault*. When a period is inserted prematurely, the result is a sentence fragment. (See Section 11.8.)

- ◾ After a long day at the office when we finished labeling the catalogs. We left hurriedly for home.

(edit mark above "catalogs. We": insert "; we")

When a period is left out, the result is a run-on sentence.

- ◾ The work plan showed the underground utility lines they might interfere with construction.

(edit mark above "lines they": insert ". They")

16.3 Periods as Ellipses

When you omit words from quoted material, use a series of three spaced periods — called *ellipsis marks* — to indicate the omission. Such an omission must not change the essential meaning of the passage.

- ◾ "Technical material distributed for promotional use is sometimes charged for, particularly in high-volume distribution to education institutions, although prices for these publications are not uniformly based on the costs of developing them." [without omission]

- ◾ "Technical material distributed for promotional use is sometimes charged for . . . although prices for these publications are not uniformly based on the costs of developing them." [with omission]

When a quotation starts in the middle of a sentence, you do not need ellipsis marks; the lowercase letter with which you begin already indicates an omission.

- "When the programmer has determined a system of runs, he must create a systems flowchart to trace the data flow through the system." [without omission]

- The booklet states that the programmer "must create a systems flowchart to trace the data flow through the system." [with omission]

If an omission follows the end of a sentence, retain the period at the end of the sentence and add the three ellipsis marks.

- "During the year, every department participated in the development of a centralized computer system. The basic plan was to use the computer to reduce costs. At the beginning of the year, each department received a booklet explaining the purpose of the system." [without omission]

- "During the year, every department participated in the development of a centralized computer system. . . . At the beginning of the year, each department received a booklet explaining the purpose of the system." [with omission]

16.4 Periods as Connectors (Leaders)

When spaced periods are used in a table to connect one item to another, they are called *leaders*. The purpose of leaders is to help the reader align the data.

- *Weight*   *Pressure*
  150 lbs . . . . 1.7 psi
  175 lbs . . . . 2.8 psi
  200 lbs . . . . 3.9 psi

■ 17. Question Marks

The *question mark* (?) indicates a question. Use it to end a sentence or any statement that asks a direct question.

- What file name did you give the specifications?

Use a question mark to end an interrogative clause within a declarative sentence.

- It was not until July (or was it August?) that we submitted the report.

With quotations, the question mark may indicate who is asking the question. When the writer doing the quoting asks the question, the question mark is outside the quotation marks.

- Did she say, "I don't think the project should continue"?

If the quotation itself is a question, the question mark goes inside the quotation marks.

■ She asked, "Will healthcare premiums increase next fiscal year?"

If the writer and the person being quoted both ask questions, use a single question mark inside the quotation marks.

■ Did she ask, "When will the improved safety data be posted on our Web site?"

Question marks may follow each item in an interrogative series.

■ Do you remember the date of the contract? its terms? whether you signed it?

A question mark should never be used at the end of an indirect question.

■ He asked me whether sales had increased this year？

When a directive is phrased as a question, a question mark usually is not used. A request (to a customer, for instance) would require a question mark.

■ Will you please make sure that the machinery is operational by August 15. [directive]
■ Will you please telephone me collect if your order does not arrive by May 10? [request]

■ 18. Exclamation Marks

The *exclamation mark* (!) indicates strong feeling. It can signal surprise, fear, indignation, or excitement but should not be used for trivial emotions or mild surprise. It cannot make an argument more convincing, lend force to a weak statement, or call attention to an intended irony.

■ Hurry! The gas line is leaking! Clear the building!

When used with quotation marks, the exclamation mark goes outside unless an exclamation is quoted.

■ The boss yelled, "Get in here!" Then Ben said, "Yes, sir"!

■ 19. Parentheses

Parentheses ( ) are used to enclose words, phrases, or sentences. Parentheses can suggest intimacy, implying that something is shared between the writer and the reader. Parentheses deemphasize (or play down) an inserted element. The material within parentheses can clarify a statement without changing its meaning. Such information may not be essential but may interest or help some readers.

- Aluminum is extracted from its ore (called bauxite) in three stages.

Parenthetical material pertains to the word or phrase immediately preceding it.

- The growth of IBM (International Business Machines) is an American success.

Parentheses may be used to enclose the figures or letters that mark items in a sequence or list. Enclose them with two parentheses, not one parenthesis.

- The following sections deal with (1) preparation, (2) research, and (3) organization.

Parenthetical material does not change the punctuation of a sentence. A comma that follows appears outside the closing parenthesis.

- These oxygen-rich chemicals, including potassium permanganate ($KMnO_4$) and potassium chromate ($KCrO_4$), were oxidizing agents.

If a parenthesis closes a sentence, the ending punctuation appears after the parenthesis. When a complete sentence within parentheses stands independently, however, the ending punctuation goes inside the final parenthesis.

- The institute was founded by Harry Denman (1902–1972).
- The project director outlined the challenges faced by her staff. (This was her third report to the board.)

Avoid parentheses where other marks of punctuation are more appropriate.

■ 20. Hyphens

The hyphen (-) functions primarily as a spelling device, joining compound words. Check your dictionary if you are uncertain about whether to hyphenate a word.

- able-bodied, self-contained, brother-in-law

A hyphen is used when writing out compound numbers and fractions.

- twenty-one, one-fifth

Two-word and three-word unit modifiers that express a single thought are frequently hyphenated when they precede a noun (a *clear-cut* decision), but not when they follow the noun. If each of the words could modify the noun without the other word or words, do not use a hyphen (a *new digital* copier—no hyphen).

If the first word is an adverb ending in -*ly,* do not use a hyphen (*hardly* used, *privately* owned).

- Our office equipment is *out of date.*

- Our *out-of-date* office equipment will be replaced next month.

A hyphen is always used as part of a letter or number modifier.

- 40-cent stamp, nine-inch ruler, e-business, T-square

When each item in a series of unit modifiers has the same term following the hyphen, this term need not be repeated throughout the series. For smoothness and brevity, add the term only to the last item in the sequence, retaining the hyphen, however.

- The third-~~floor~~, fourth-~~floor~~, and fifth-floor offices have been painted.

When a prefix precedes a proper noun, use a hyphen to connect the two.

- pre-Internet, anti-Stalinist, post-Newtonian

A hyphen may (but does not have to) be used when the prefix ends and the root word begins with the same vowel. When the repeated vowel is *i,* a hyphen is almost always used.

- re-elect, re-enter, anti-inflationary

A hyphen is used when *ex-* means "former."

- ex-partners, ex-wife

The suffix -*elect* is connected to the word it follows with a hyphen.

- president-elect, commissioner-elect

Hyphens identify prefixes, suffixes, or syllables written as such.

- *Re-, -ism,* and *ex-* are word parts that cause spelling problems.

Hyphens separate letters showing spelling (or misspelling).

- In his letter, he spelled "believed" b-e-l-e-i-v-e-d.

To avoid confusion, some words and modifiers should always be hyphenated. *Re-cover* does not mean the same thing as *recover,* for example; the same is true of *re-sent* and *resent, re-form* and *reform, re-sign* and *resign.*

A hyphen can stand for *to* or *through* between letters, numbers, and locations.

- pp. 44-46   ■ The Detroit-Toledo Expressway   ■ A-L and M-Z

Hyphens are used to divide words at the end of a line. Avoid dividing words if possible; however, if you must divide them, use the following guidelines for hyphenation (or consult a dictionary). Divide:

- Between syllables (but leave at least three letters on each line): let-ter.
- Between the compound parts of compound words: time-table.
- After a single-letter syllable in the middle of a word: sepa-rate.
- After a prefix: pre-view.
- Before a suffix: cap-tion.
- Between two consecutive vowels with separate sounds: gladi-ator.

Do not divide:

- A word that is pronounced as one syllable: shipped.
- A contraction: you're.
- An abbreviation or acronym: NCAA.

Divide a word spelled with a hyphen only after the hyphen. If the hyphen is essential to the word's meaning, do not divide the word.

■ 21. Quotation Marks

Quotation marks (" ") are used to enclose direct repetition of spoken or written words. Normally, they should not be used to show emphasis. Enclose in quotation marks anything quoted word for word (direct quotation) from speech.

- She said clearly, "I want the progress report before three o'clock."

Do not enclose indirect quotations—usually introduced by *that*—in quotation marks. Indirect quotations paraphrase a speaker's words or ideas.

- She said that she wanted a copy of the progress report by three.

Handle quotations from written material the same way: Place direct quotations within quotation marks, but not indirect quotations.

- The report stated, "During the last five years in Florida, our franchise has grown from 28 to 157 locations."
- The report indicated that our franchise now has 157 locations in Florida.

Material quoted directly and enclosed in quotation marks cannot be changed from the original unless you show the change in brackets. (See Section 25 for how to use brackets.)

When a quotation is longer than four typed lines, indent each line ten spaces (two tabs) from the left margin. Do not enclose the quotation in quotation marks.

Use single quotation marks (the apostrophe key on a keyboard) to enclose a quotation that appears within another quotation.

■   John said, "Jane told me that she would 'hang in there' until the deadline."

Using Quotation Marks with Other Punctuation   ESL TIPS

The use of quotation marks and other punctuation in North American English may differ from usage in your native language.

■   Style of quotation marks
    "exceptional" *not* „exceptional" or <<exceptional>>
■   Comma inside closing quotation mark
    "as a last resort," *not* "as a last resort",

■   Period inside closing quotation mark
    "to the bitter end." *not* "to the bitter end".
■   Semicolon or colon outside closing quotation mark
    "there is no doubt"; *not* "there is no doubt;"

Slang, colloquial expressions, and attempts at humor, although infrequent in business and technical writing, are seldom set off by quotation marks.

■   Our first six months in the new office amounted to little more than a *"*shakedown cruise*"* for what lay ahead. [omit quotation marks]

Use quotation marks to point out particular words or technical terms used in context for a special purpose.

■   What chain of events caused an "unsinkable" ship such as the *Titanic* to sink on its maiden voyage?

Use quotation marks to enclose titles of short stories, articles, essays, radio and television programs, short musical works, paintings, and other artworks. Titles of books and periodicals are *italicized.* (See Section 32.1.)

■   Did you see the article "No-Fault Insurance and Your Motorcycle" in last Sunday's *Journal?*

Commas and periods always go inside closing quotation marks.

■   "We hope," said Ms. Abrams, "that the merger will be announced this week."

Semicolons and colons always go outside closing quotation marks.

■   He said, "I will pay the full amount"; this was a real surprise to us.

■   The following are his favorite "sports": eating and sleeping.

All other punctuation follows the logic of the context: If the punctuation is part of the material quoted, it goes inside the quotation marks; if the punctuation is not part of the material quoted, it goes outside the quotation marks.

■ 22. Dashes

The *dash* (—) is a versatile, yet limited, mark of punctuation. It is versatile because it can perform all the functions of punctuation (to link, to separate, to enclose, and to show omission). It is limited because it is especially emphatic and easily overused. Use the dash cautiously, therefore, to indicate more informality, emphasis, or abruptness than the conventional marks would show. In some situations, a dash is required; in others, a dash is a forceful substitute for other marks.

A dash can indicate a sharp turn in thought.

■ That is the end of the project—unless the company provides additional funds.

A dash can indicate an emphatic pause.

■ Consider the danger of a household item containing mercury—a very toxic substance.

Sometimes, to emphasize contrast, a dash is also used with *but*.

■ We may have worked quickly—but our results have never been more impressive.

A dash can be used before a thought that completes the meaning, a final summarizing statement, or a repetition that suggests an afterthought.

■ It was hot near the ovens—steaming hot.

■ We try to speak as we write—or so we believe.

A dash can be used to set off an explanatory or appositive series.

■ Three of the applicants—John Evans, Mary Stevens, and Thomas Brown—seem well qualified for the job.

Dashes set off parenthetical elements more sharply and emphatically than commas or parentheses, which tend to reduce the importance of what they enclose. Contrast the following sentences.

■ Only one person—the president—can authorize such activity.

■ Only one person, the president, can authorize such activity.

■ Only one person (the president) can authorize such activity.

Use dashes for clarity when commas appear within a parenthetical element.

■ Retinal images are patterns in the eye—made up of light and dark shapes, in addition to areas of color—but we do not see patterns; we see objects.

A dash can be used to show the omission of words or letters.

■ Mr. A— told me to be careful.

The first word after a dash is never capitalized unless it is a proper noun. When keying in the dash, use two consecutive hyphens (--), with no spaces before or after the hyphens.

■ 23. Apostrophes

The *apostrophe* (') shows possession; marks the omission of letters; and sometimes indicates the plural of numbers, letters, and acronyms.

23.1 Apostrophes and the Possessive Case
An apostrophe is used with an *s* to form the possessive case of many nouns, acronyms and initialisms, and indefinite pronouns. (See Section 1.5.)

■ *New York City's* atmosphere [proper noun]

■ the *lawyer's* case [common noun]

■ *NASA's* investigation [acronym]

■ the *SEC's* proposed rule [initialism]

■ *everyone's* responsibility [indefinite pronoun]

Indicating Possession: -'s or *of*?   ESL TIPS

English expresses possession in two ways: apostrophe *s* (-'s) and *of*.

Use -'s with personal names, personal nouns, collective nouns, and animals. (Use just an apostrophe for plural nouns that end with *s*.)

■ *Joan's* class
■ the *secretary's* lunch hour
■ the *government's* pension plan
■ the *dog's* tail
■ the employees' stock portfolios

You can also use -'s (or just an apostrophe) with some inanimate nouns: geographical and institutional names, nouns that refer to time, and nouns of special interest to human activity.

■ the *company's* investors
■ *today's* agenda
■ a *week's* rest
■ *business'* influence on politics

Use *of* with inanimate objects and measurements.

■ the title *of* the monthly report
■ a cup *of* coffee
■ the length *of* the memo

Indicating Possession: Parts of the Body and Personal Belongings

English uses possessive pronouns to express possession of parts of the body and personal belongings.

- Ms. Winters broke *her* leg skiing.
- Mr. Sommers leaves *his* briefcase in the boardroom after every meeting.

English also uses apostrophe *s* to express possession of parts of the body and personal belongings.

- Ms. *Smith's* arm was broken in a car accident.
- Mr. *Gonzalez's* briefcase was lost in the shuffle.

English gives you the option of using the definite article *the* in prepositional phrases that refer to the object of a sentence.

- Dr. Meehan led me by *the* arm into the conference room.

  [*by the arm* is a prepositional phrase]

- The stockroom clerk was struck on *the* leg by a box that fell from the shelf.

  [*on the leg* is a prepositional phrase]

However, it would also be correct to write *by my arm* and *on her leg*.

Singular nouns ending in *s* may form the possessive either by an apostrophe alone or by -'s. The latter is now preferred.

- a waitress' uniform, a waitress's uniform

Use only an apostrophe with plural nouns ending in *s*.

- a managers' meeting, the technicians' handbook, a motorists' rest stop

Proper nouns and ancient names (*Moses, Ramses, Xerxes*) that end in consecutive *s* or *z* sounds form the possessive by adding only an apostrophe.

- Jesús Castillo was assigned to the new Global Systems Division. *Jesús'* responsibilities will include expanding our European operations.

With word groups and compound nouns, add -'s to the last noun.

- The *chairman of the board's* statement was brief.

- My *daughter-in-law's* business has been thriving.

With compound nouns, the last noun takes the possessive form to show joint possession.

- Michelson and *Morley's* famous experiment on the velocity of light was made in 1887.

To show individual possession with a series of nouns, each noun should take the possessive form.

- *Bob's* and *Susan's* promotions will be announced Friday.

The apostrophe is not used with possessive pronouns. (*It's* is a contraction of *it is,* not the possessive form of *it.*)

- yours, its, his, ours, whose, theirs

In names of places and institutions, the apostrophe is usually omitted.

- Harpers Ferry, Mystery Writers Book Club

23.2 Apostrophes and Contractions

An apostrophe is used to mark the omission of letters in a word, producing a *contraction.* Contractions are most often shortened forms of common helping verbs. In addition, contractions can reflect negation, combining elements of *not* with elements of the helping verb (*don't* for *do not,* for example). Although contractions are in no sense wrong, they are less formal than the longer forms and should be used sparingly in writing.

23.3 Apostrophes and Abbreviated Dates

An apostrophe can also stand for the first two digits of a year when these digits can be inferred from the context. Avoid this usage in formal writing.

- the class of '61   - the crash of '29

23.4 Apostrophes and Plural Forms

The trend for indicating the plural forms of words mentioned as words, of numbers used as nouns, and of abbreviations shown as single or multiple letters is currently to add only -*s* rather than -*'s.*

When a word (or letter) mentioned as a word is italicized, it is current usage to add *s* in roman type.

- There were five *and*s in his first sentence.

Rather than using italics, you may place a word in quotation marks. If you choose this option, use an apostrophe and -*s.*

- There were five "and's" in his first sentence.

To indicate the plural of a number, add -*s* (7*s,* the 1990*s*). If the letter and the *s* form a word, you may want to consider using an apostrophe to avoid confusion (*A*'s). Use -*s* to pluralize an abbreviation that is in all capital letters or that ends with a capital letter (IOU*s*). However, if the abbreviated term contains periods, some writers use an apostrophe to prevent confusion.

- The university awarded 34 Ph.D.*'s* last year.

Whatever practice you follow, be consistent.

24. Slashes

Although not always considered a punctuation mark, the *slash* (/) separates and shows omission. The slash has various names: slant line, virgule, bar, shilling sign, and diagonal.

The slash is often used to separate parts of addresses in continuous writing.

■ The return address on the envelope was Ms. Rose Howard/62 W. Pacific Court/Claremont, California 91711.

The slash can indicate alternative items.

■ David's telephone number is (504) 549-2278/2335.

The slash often indicates omitted words and letters.

■ miles/hour (for "miles per hour")   ■ w/o (for "without")

The slash separates the numerator from the denominator of a fraction.

■ 2/3 (2 of 3 parts); 3/4 (3 of 4 parts); 27/32 (27 of 32 parts)

In informal writing in the United States, the slash is used in dates to separate day from month and month from year.

■ 2/28/98

Do not use this form for international writing because the order of items varies (29 May 2004).

25. Brackets

The primary use of brackets ([ ]) is to enclose a word or words inserted by an editor or a writer into a quotation from another source.

■ The text stated, "Hypertext systems can be categorized as either modest [not modifiable] or robust [modifiable]."

Brackets are used to set off a parenthetical item within parentheses.

■ We have all been inspired by the energy and creativity of our president, Roberta Jacobs (a tradition she carries forward from her father, Frederick Jacobs [1910–1966]).

Brackets are also used in academic writing to insert the Latin word *sic,* which indicates that the writer has quoted material exactly as it appears in the original, even though it contains an error.

- Dr. Smith wrote that "the earth does not revolve around the son [*sic*] at a constant rate."

If you are following MLA style in your writing, use brackets around ellipsis dots to show that some words have been omitted from the original source.

- "The vast majority of the Internet's users are [. . .] between the ages of eighteen and thirty-four" (5).

Mechanics

Certain mechanical questions tend to confound the writer on the job. Such questions as whether a number should be written as a word or figure, how acronyms should be used, whether a date should be stated day-month-year or month-day-year, and many others frequently arise when you are writing a letter or report. This section will help you answer these and other perplexing questions.

■ 26. Numbers

26.1 Writing Out Numbers

The general rule is to write numbers from zero to ten as words and numbers above ten as figures. There are, however, a number of exceptions.

Express page numbers of books and figure and table numbers as figures.

- Figure 4 on page 9 and Table 3 on page 7 provide pertinent information.

Units of measurement are expressed in figures.

- 3 miles   ■ 45 cubic feet   ■ 9 meters

- 27 cubic centimeters   ■ 4 picas

Numbers that begin a sentence should always be spelled out, even if they would otherwise be written as figures.

- One hundred fifty people attended the meeting.

If spelling out such a number seems awkward, rewrite the sentence so that the number does not appear at the beginning.

- *Last month, 273*
  ~~Two hundred seventy-three~~ defective products were returned ~~last month.~~

When several numbers appear in the same sentence or paragraph, they should be expressed alike regardless of other rules and guidelines.

■ The company employed 271 people, owned 150 trucks, and rented 7 warehouses.

When numbers measuring different quantities appear consecutively, write one as a figure and the other as a word.

■ The order was for ~~12~~ 6-inch pipes.
    twelve

Approximate numbers may be spelled out but are more often written as figures.

■ More than 200 people attended the conference.

In business or technical writing, percentages are normally given as figures, with the word *percent* written out except when the number appears in a table.

■ Exactly 87 percent of the stockholders approved the merger.

On manuscript pages, page numbers are written as figures, but chapter or volume numbers may appear as figures or written out.

■ page 37   ■ Chapter 2 *or* Chapter Two   ■ Volume 1 *or* Volume One

Do not follow the word for a number with the figure in parentheses.

■ Send five ~~(5)~~ copies of the report.

26.2 Dates

The year and day of the month should be written as figures. Dates are usually written in month-day-year sequence, but businesses and industrial corporations sometimes use the European and military day-month-year sequence.

■ August 24, 2003   ■ 24 August 2003

The month-day-year sequence is followed by a comma in a sentence.

■ The November 24, 2003, issue of *Smart Computing* has an article . . .

The day-month-year sequence is *not* followed by a comma.

■ The 24 November 2003 issue of *Smart Computing* . . .

The slash form of expressing dates (11/24/03) is used in informal writing only.

26.3 Time

Hours and minutes are expressed as figures when a.m. or p.m. follows (11:30 a.m., 7:30 p.m.). When not followed by a.m. or p.m., however, times should be spelled out (four o'clock, eleven o'clock).

26.4 Fractions

Fractions are expressed as figures when written with whole numbers (27 1/2 inches, 4 1/4 miles). Fractions are spelled out when they are expressed without a whole number (one-fourth, seven-eighths). Numbers with decimals are always written as figures (5.21 meters).

26.5 Addresses

Numbered streets from one to ten should be spelled out unless space is restricted.

- East Tenth Street

Building numbers are written as figures, except the number *one*.

- 4862 East Monument Street
- One East Tenth Street

Highway numbers are written as figures.

- U.S. 70, Ohio 271, I-94

Punctuating Numbers

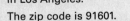

The rules for punctuating numbers in American English are summarized as follows:

Use a comma to separate numbers with five or more digits into groups of three, starting from the right.

- 57,890 cubic feet
- $187,291

The comma is optional in numbers with four digits.

- 1,902 cases *or* 1902 cases

Do not use a comma in years, house numbers, zip codes, and page numbers.

- The Boeing 777 was first flown commercially by United Airlines in June 1995.

- Autotech Industries is located at 92401 East Alameda Drive in Los Angeles.
- The zip code is 91601.
- The citation is located on page 124.

Use a period to represent the decimal point.

- Their stock values increased at a monthly rate of 4.2 percent.
- The jackpot for last week's lottery was $3,742,097.43.

26.6 Plurals of Numbers

The plural of a written number, like any other noun, is formed by adding *-s* or *-es* or *-ies* after dropping *y*, depending on the last letter.

■ elevens, sixes, twenties

The plural of a figure should be written with *s* alone.

■ 5s, 12s

■ 27. Acronyms and Initialisms

An *acronym* is an abbreviation formed by combining the first letter or letters of two or more words and pronounced as a word.

■ radar (*ra*dio *d*etecting *a*nd *r*anging)

■ LAN (*l*ocal *a*rea *n*etwork)

■ scuba (*s*elf-*c*ontained *u*nderwater *b*reathing *a*pparatus)

An *initialism* is an abbreviation formed by combining the initial letter of each word in a multiword term. Initialisms are pronounced as separate letters.

■ e.o.m. (*e*nd *o*f *m*onth)　　■ COD (*c*ash *o*n *d*elivery)

In business and industry, acronyms and initialisms are often used by people working together on projects or having the same specialties—such as engineers or accountants. When such people communicate with one another, the abbreviations are easily recognized. However, if the same acronyms or initialisms were used in correspondence outside the group, they might be incomprehensible to those readers. Convenient as acronyms and initialisms can be, avoid overusing them in a misguided attempt to be concise.

Two guidelines apply in deciding whether to use acronyms and initialisms. If these conditions do not exist, always spell out the full term.

1. If you must use a multiword term an average of once each paragraph, introduce the term and then use its acronym or initialism. For example, use PSOA instead of repeating "primary software overlay area" again and again.

2. If something is better known by its acronym or initialism than by its formal term, use the abbreviated form: a.m., for example, for *ante meridiem*.

The first time an acronym or initialism appears in a written work, write out the complete term and then give the abbreviated form in parentheses.

■ The Capital Appropriations Request (CAR) controls expenditures.

Thereafter, you may use the acronym or initialism alone. In a long document, however, you will help save your reader the trouble of searching back if you repeat the full term in parentheses after the acronym or initialism when the term has not been mentioned for some time.

■ As noted earlier, the CAR (Capital Appropriations Request) controls spending.

Write acronyms in capital letters without periods. The only exceptions are acronyms accepted as common nouns, which are written in lowercase letters.

■ laser, scuba, sonar

Initialisms that do not stand for proper nouns may be written either uppercase (generally without periods) or lowercase (always with periods). Two exceptions are geographic names and academic degrees.

■ COD/c.o.d., FOB/f.o.b., CIF/c.i.f., EOM/e.o.m.

■ CIA, FBI   ■ U.S.A., U.K.   ■ B.A., M.B.A.

Form the plural of an acronym or initialism with a lowercase *s*, but no apostrophe.

■ PACs, CD-ROMs

■ 28. Abbreviations

An abbreviation shortens a word by omitting some of its letters and is usually written with a period. In technical and business writing, abbreviations of measurements are generally an exception; if they might be confused with an actual word, the period is used.

■ September/Sept.

■ inch/in. [the abbreviation *in* could be misread as the word *in*]

Abbreviations, like symbols, can be important space savers especially in charts, tables, graphs, and other illustrations. Use them only if you are certain that your readers will understand them as readily as the terms for which they stand. Remember also that a memo or report addressed to a specific person may be read by others, and you must consider those readers as well. Take your reader's level of knowledge into account, and do not use abbreviations that might inconvenience the reader. When in doubt, spell it out.

Normally you should not make up your own abbreviations, for they will probably confuse your reader. Except for commonly used abbreviations (U.S.A., p.m.), spell out a term to be abbreviated the first time you use it, with the abbreviation in parentheses following the term. Thereafter, the abbreviation may be used alone.

- The annual report of the National Retail Dry Goods Association (NRDGA) will be is-sued next month. In it, the NRDGA will detail shortages of widely used textiles.

28.1 Measurements

The following list contains some common abbreviations used with units of mea-surement, but be sure your reader is familiar with the abbreviated form. Except for *in.* (inch), *bar.* (barometer), and other abbreviations that might be mistaken for other words, abbreviations of measurements do not require periods. These abbre-viations also are identical in the singular and plural: 1 *cm* and 3 *cm* (not 3 *cms*).

amp	ampere	km	kilometer
bar.	barometer	lb	pound
bbl	barrel	mg	milligram
Btu	British thermal unit	min	minute
C	Centigrade, Celsius	oz	ounce
cal	calorie	ppm	parts per million
cm	centimeter	rad	radian
doz or dz	dozen	rev	revolution
F	Fahrenheit	rpm	revolutions per minute
fig.	figure (illustration)	sec	second or secant
ft	foot (or feet)	T	tablespoon
gm	gram	tsp	teaspoon
hp	horsepower	yd	yard
in.	inch	yr	year
kg	kilogram		

28.2 Personal Names and Titles

Personal names should generally not be abbreviated.

INCORRECT   Chas., Thos., Wm., Marg.

CORRECT   Charles, Thomas, William, Margaret

An academic, civil, religious, or military title should be spelled out when it does not precede a name.

    doctor
- The ~~Dr.~~ asked for the patient's chart.

When it precedes a name, the title may be abbreviated.

- Dr. Smith, Mr. Mills, Capt. Hughes

Reverend and *Honorable* are abbreviated only if the name includes a first name.

- The Reverend Smith, Rev. John Smith (but not Rev. Smith)

- The Honorable Commissioner Holt, Hon. Mary J. Holt

An abbreviation of a title may follow the name; however, be certain that it does not duplicate a title before the name.

INCORRECT	Dr. William Smith, Ph.D.
CORRECT	Dr. William Smith
CORRECT	William Smith, Ph.D.

Following are common abbreviations for personal and professional titles.

Atty.	Attorney
D.D.	Doctor of Divinity
D.D.S.	Doctor of Dental Science
Dr.	Doctor (used with any doctor's degree)
Ed.D.	Doctor of Education
Hon.	Honorable
Jr.	Junior (used when a father of the same name is living)
LL.B.	Bachelor of Law
LL.D.	Doctor of Law
M.D.	Doctor of Medicine
Mr.	Mister (spelled out only in the most formal contexts)
Mrs.	Married woman
Ms.	Woman of unspecified marital status
Ph.D.	Doctor of Philosophy
Rev.	Reverend
Sr.	Senior (used when a son with the same name is living)

29. Ampersands

The *ampersand* (&) is a symbol used to represent the word *and,* especially in the names of organizations. However, when writing the name in sentences or an address, spell out *and* unless the ampersand appears in the company's official name.

- Procter & Gamble/Johnson & Johnson

- Sears, Roebuck, *and* Co.

An ampersand must always be set off by normal word spacing but should never be preceded by a comma.

- Carlton, Dillon/ & Manchester, Inc. [omit comma]

Do not use an ampersand in the titles of articles, journals, books, or other publications.

- Does the bibliography include Knoll's *Radiation Detection & Measurement*?
  and
  ^

The ampersand may be used in notes, bibliographies, lists, and references if it appears in the name being listed.

Some styles, such as MLA, prohibit the use of ampersands. However, other styles, such as APA, allow ampersands in contexts in which space is limited, such as footnotes, reference lists, and tables.

■ 30. Capital Letters

The use of capital (or uppercase) letters is determined by custom and tradition. Capital letters call attention to certain words, such as proper nouns and the first word of a sentence. Use them carefully to eliminate ambiguity (march/March, china/China, turkey/Turkey).

30.1 First Words

The first letter of the first word in a sentence is always capitalized.

- Of all the plans you mentioned, the first one seems the best.

The first word after a colon may be capitalized if the statement following is a complete sentence or if it introduces a formal resolution or question.

- Today's meeting will deal with only one issue: What is the firm's role in environmental protection?

ESL TIPS

Using Capitalization

The rules of capitalization vary from language to language. Following are some terms that must be capitalized in English.

Days of the Week
- Every *Monday* we have a meeting at noon.

Months of the Year
- The fiscal year ends in *June*.

The Pronoun I
- My sister and *I* went grocery shopping last week.

Begin a subordinate element following a colon with a lowercase letter.

■   We had to keep working for one reason: pressure from above.

The first word of a complete sentence in quotation marks is capitalized.

■   He said, "When I arrive, we will begin."

Complete sentences contained as numbered items within a sentence may also be capitalized.

■   He recommended two ways to increase sales: (1) Next year we should spend more on television advertising, and (2) Our quality control should be improved immediately.

The first word in the salutation or complimentary close of a letter is capitalized.

■   Dear Mr. Smith: ■   Sincerely yours,

30.2 Personal Names and Groups
Capitalize all personal names.

■   Walter Bunch, Mary Fortunato, Bill Krebs

Capitalize names of ethnic groups and nationalities.

■   Native American, Italian, Jew, Chicano

Do not capitalize names of social and economic groups.

■   middle class, working class, unemployed

30.3 Places
Capitalize the names of all political divisions.

■   Chicago, Cook County, Illinois, Ontario, Iran, Ward Six

Capitalize the names of geographical divisions.

■   Europe, Asia, North America, the Middle East

Do not capitalize geographic features unless they are part of a proper name.

- Mountains such as the Great Smoky Mountains impair broadcast television transmission.

The words *north, south, east,* and *west* are capitalized when they refer to sections of the country. They are not capitalized when they refer to directions.

- I will travel north when I relocate to Delaware, but my family will remain in the South.

Capitalize the names of stars, constellations, galaxies, and planets.

- Sirius, Leo, Milky Way, Saturn

Do not capitalize *earth, sun,* and *moon,* however, except when they are used with the names of other planets.

- The phases of the moon are included on my calendar.

- The effects of the Sun on Earth and the Moon were discussed at the symposium.

30.4 Institutions, Events, and Concepts

Capitalize the names of institutions, organizations, and associations.

- The American Management Association and the Department of Housing and Urban Development are cooperating in the project.

An organization usually capitalizes the names of its internal divisions and departments.

- Faculty, Senate, Board of Directors, Accounting Department

Types of organizations are not capitalized unless they are part of an official name.

- When we formed a writers' association, we called it the American Association of Writers.

- I attended Whitman High School. What high school did you attend?

Capitalize historical events.

- Dr. Jellison discussed the basis for the Boston Tea Party at the last class.

Capitalize words that designate specific periods of time.

- Labor Day, the Renaissance, January, Monday, the Great Depression

Do not, however, capitalize seasons of the year.

- spring, autumn, winter, summer

Capitalize scientific names of classes, families, and orders, but do not capitalize species or English derivatives of scientific names.

- Mammalia, Carnivora
- mammal, carnivorous

30.5 Titles

Capitalize the initial letters of the first and last words of a title of a book, article, play, or film, as well as all major words in the title. Do not capitalize articles (*a, an, the*), conjunctions (*and, but, if*), or short prepositions (*at, in, on, of*) unless they begin the title. Capitalize prepositions that contain more than four letters (*between, because, until, after*). These guidelines also apply to the titles of reports and to the subject lines of memos.

- The author wrote *Capital Markets in Eastern Europe* over a three-year period.
- The article "Year After Year" describes the life of a turn-of-the-century industrialist.
- The report, titled "Alternate Sites for Plant Location," was submitted in February.

30.6 Personal Titles

Titles preceding proper names are capitalized.

- Ms. March, Professor Wallach, Senator Arnold, Sister Margaret Anne

Appositives following proper names are not normally capitalized. (However, the word *President* is usually capitalized when it refers to a nation's chief executive.)

- Frank Jones, senator from New Mexico (but Senator Jones)

The only exception is an epithet, which actually renames the person.

- Alexander the Great, Richard the Lion-Hearted

Job titles used with personal names are capitalized, but those appearing without personal names are not.

- John Holmes, Division Manager, will meet with us on Wednesday. The other division managers will not be there.

Use capital letters only for family relationships before or in place of a name.

- One of my favorite people is Uncle Fred.

- My uncle is one of my favorite people.

- Jim and Mother went along.   - Jim and my mother went along.

30.7 Abbreviations

Capitalize abbreviations if the words they stand for would be capitalized.

- OSU (Ohio State University)   - p. (page)

- Ph.D. (Doctor of Philosophy)

30.8 Letters

Certain single letters are always capitalized. Capitalize the pronoun *I* and the interjection *O* (but do not capitalize *oh* unless it is the first word in a sentence).

- When I say writing, O believe me, I mean rewriting.

- When I say writing, oh believe me, I mean rewriting.

Capitalize letters that serve as names or indicate shapes.

- vitamin B, T-square, U-turn, I-beam

30.9 Miscellaneous Capitalization

The word *Bible* is capitalized when it refers to the Judeo-Christian Scriptures; otherwise, it is not capitalized.

- His article cited passages from the Bible, and from Blackstone, the *lawyer's bible*.

All references to deities (Allah, God, Jehovah, Yahweh) are capitalized.

- God is the One who sustains us.

A complete sentence enclosed in dashes, brackets, or parentheses is not capitalized when it appears as part of another sentence.

- We must promote sales this year (last year's sales were down 10 percent).

- We must promote sales this year. (Last year's sales were down 10 percent.)

When certain units, such as chapters of books or rooms in buildings, are specifically identified by number, they are normally capitalized.

- Chapter 5, Ch. 5   - Room 72, Rm. 72

Minor divisions within such units are not capitalized unless they begin a sentence.

- page 11, verse 14, seat 12

When in doubt about whether to capitalize, check a dictionary.

31. Dates

In business and industry, dates have traditionally been indicated by the month, day, and year, with a comma between the figures and after the year. (See also Section 13.3.)

- The project began on October 26, 2003.

The day-month-year system used by the military does not require commas.

- The project began on 26 October 2003.

The strictly numerical form for dates (10/26/03) should be used sparingly, and never in business letters or formal documents, because its meaning is less immediately clear. When this form is used, the order in American usage is always month/day/year. For example, 5/7/03 is May 7, 2003. Do not use this order for international correspondence, where dates are usually written in day-month-year sequence.

Confusion often occurs because the spelled-out names of centuries do not correspond to the numbers of the years.

- The twentieth century is the 1900s (1900–1999).
- The fifth century is the 400s (400–499).

32. Italics

Italics are a style of type: *This sentence is printed in italics.* Italics are sometimes used for words that require special emphasis in a sentence.

- Contrary to projections, sales have *not* improved.

Do not overuse italics for emphasis, however.

OVERUSE OF ITALICS	This will hurt *you* more than *me.*
IMPROVED	This will hurt you more than me!

32.1 Titles

Italicize the titles of books, periodicals, newspapers, movies, and paintings.

■ The book *Applied Statistical Methods* was published in 1999.

■ The *Journal of Marketing* is published monthly for those engaged in marketing research.

Italicize abbreviations of such titles if their spelled-out forms would be italicized.

■ The *WSJ* is the business community's journal of record.
  [The reference is to the *Wall Street Journal*.]

Put titles of chapters or articles that appear within publications and the titles of reports in quotation marks, not italics.

■ The article "Does Advertising Lower Consumer Prices?" was published in the March 2003 issue of the *Journal of Marketing*.

Do not italicize titles of holy books and legislative documents.

■ The Bible and the Magna Carta changed the history of Western civilization.

Italicize titles of long poems and musical works, but enclose titles of short poems and musical works and songs in quotation marks.

■ Milton's *Paradise Lost* (long poem)

■ Handel's *Messiah* (long musical work)

■ T. S. Eliot's "The Love Song of J. Alfred Prufrock" (short poem)

■ Elton John's "Candle in the Wind" (song)

32.2 Proper Names

Italicize ships, trains, and aircraft, but not companies that own them.

■ U.S. aircraft carrier *Independence*; U.S. space shuttle *Endeavor*

Exceptions, not italicized, are craft known by model or serial designations.

■ DC-10, Boeing 777

32.3 Words, Letters, and Figures

Italicize words, letters, and figures that are discussed as such.

■ The word *inflammable* is often misinterpreted.

■ Spell checkers stop at words containing numbers (*"will"* with two *1*'s, not two *l*'s).

32.4 Foreign Words

Italicize foreign words that have not been assimilated into English.

- *sine qua non, coup de grâce, in res, in camera*

Do not italicize foreign words that have been fully assimilated into the language.

- cliché, etiquette, vis-à-vis, de facto, siesta, taco, crepes

When in doubt about italicizing a foreign word, consult a current dictionary.

32.5 Subheads

Subheads in a report are sometimes italicized.

- In those early days, there was no publications department as such, and the writing groups were duplicated at each plant or location.

  Training Writers

  We are leading the way in developing first-line managers (or writing supervisors) who not only are technically competent but can train writers under their direction.

33. Symbols

Use symbols such as %, ¢, @, ", +, and = only in graphs and tables, not in the body of a paper. The one exception is the dollar sign ($), which may be used with specific dollar amounts *($4.75, $120 million)* in the text. (See also Section 29.)

34. Proofreaders' Marks

Publishers have symbols, called *proofreaders' marks,* which writers and editors use to communicate with compositors in the production of publications. These symbols make it easy for you to communicate your changes to others. (See Table A–6.)

Mark in Margin	Instruction	Mark on Manuscript	Corrected Type
ℓ	Delete	the ~~lawyer's~~ Bible	the Bible
lawyer's	Insert	the bible	the lawyer's bible
stet	Let stand	the ~~lawyer's~~ bible	the lawyer's bible
cap	Capitalize	the bible	the Bible
lc	Make lowercase	the Law	the law
ital	Italicize	the lawyer's bible	the *lawyer's* bible
tr	Transpose	the bible lawyer's	the lawyer's bible
⊂	Close space	the Bi ble	the Bible
sp	Spell out	2 bibles	two bibles
#	Insert space	the Bible	the Bible
¶	Start paragraph	¶ The lawyer's . . .	The lawyer's . . .
run in	No paragraph	. . . marks. Below is a . . .	. . . marks. Below is a . . .
sc	Set in small capitals	the bible	the BIBLE
rom	Set in roman type	the *bible*	the bible
bf	Set in boldface	the bible	the **bible**
lf	Set in lightface	the **bible**	the bible
⊙	Insert period	The lawyers have their own bible	The lawyers have their own bible.
⌃	Insert comma	However we cannot . . .	However, we cannot . . .
=/=/	Insert hyphens	half and half	half-and-half
⊙	Insert colon	We need the following	We need the following:
;	Insert semicolon	Use the law don't . . .	Use the law; don't . . .
⌄	Insert apostrophe	Johns law book	John's law book
⌄/⌄	Insert quotation marks	The law is law.	The "law" is law.
(/)/	Insert parentheses	John's law book	John's (law) book
[/]/	Insert brackets	(John Martin 1920–1962 went . . .)	(John Martin [1920–1962] went . . .)
⊥/N	Insert en dash	1920 1962	1920–1962
⊥/M	Insert em dash	Our goal victory	Our goal—victory
⌄	Insert superior type	3 = 9	$3^2 = 9$
⌃	Insert inferior type	HSO₄	H_2SO_4

Table A–6   Proofreaders' Marks

B Spelling and Vocabulary

■ 35. Spelling

Human resources managers often reject candidates who make spelling errors on employment applications, résumés, and application letters. Consider, for example, the story of a college graduate who applied for the position of assistant director of human resources and was rejected for misspelling the word *resources*.

Potential employers react strongly to spelling errors because poor spelling reflects negatively on an employee—and, by association, on the employer as well. Everyone makes an occasional error, of course, but a human resources manager may conclude that someone who has overlooked a spelling mistake on something as important as a job application may be careless in his or her work, too. After all, when you apply for a job, an employer must make a judgment based primarily on your résumé, letter of application, and interview.

More important, learning to be a careful speller can help you, as a writer, keep your bargain with readers: to assist them in understanding what you are saying. Spelling errors, because they can confuse and slow down readers, create roadblocks on the path of communication between you and your readers.

As you write a first draft, you should focus on what you are saying; to worry about spelling when drafting would be a distraction. You can correct spelling errors when you revise; in fact, you should proofread once *just for spelling*.

Use your spell checker as you make your final revisions. Spell checkers scan the text, stopping at each instance of a misspelled word, a repeated word ("the the"), words with numbers ("wi11" spelled with two *1*'s rather than with two *l*'s), and common errors in capitalization ("THere" for "There"). Most spell checkers also allow you to add acronyms, names, and specialized terms commonly used in your writing but not included in the spell checker's standard dictionary.

Although a spell checker is an invaluable tool, you should not rely on it completely for proofing your document. For example, a spell checker cannot tell in a given context whether you meant *it* or *if*. It simply recognizes both words as correctly spelled whenever they occur. Nor can you count on a spell checker to help you proof numbers. You still must check your document carefully yourself.

The following system will help you improve your spelling:

- If you are unsure about the spelling of a word, don't rely on memory or guesswork—consult the dictionary. Keep a standard dictionary or a small-format spelling dictionary handy. Or, consult an online dictionary such as *Merriam-Webster Online* at <m-w.com>, the *Encarta World English Dictionary* online at <encarta.msn.com>, or *The American Heritage Dictionary of the English Language* available at Bartleby.com: Great Books Online at <bartleby.com>.

- After you have looked up the spelling of a word, write the word from memory several times. Then check the accuracy of your spelling. If you have misspelled the word, repeat this step. Writing the word from memory is essential to retain it for future use.

- Keep a list of the words you commonly misspell, and work regularly at whittling it down. Do not load the list with exotic words like *asphyxiation* or *pterodactyl.* Concentrate instead on frequently used words such as *calendar, maintenance,* and *unnecessary.* Leave them on your list until you have learned to spell them.

- Study the following sets of words that sound alike but differ in spelling and meaning. Simple meanings are given here for identification only.

  accept (verb: to agree or receive)

  except (preposition: other than)

  affect (verb: to influence)

  effect (noun: a result)

  all ready (We are *all ready* to go.)

  already (Have you finished the work *already?*)

  ascent (noun: a movement up)

  assent (noun: an agreement)

  brake (noun: device for stopping)

  break (verb: to crack; noun: period of relaxation)

  cent (noun: coin)

  scent (noun: smell)

  sent (verb: past tense of *send*)

  cite (verb: to refer to)

  sight (noun: view, something to look at)

  site (noun: location)

  coarse (adjective: rough)

  course (noun: direction of study; adverb in *of course*)

  complement (noun: something that completes something else)

compliment (noun: praise; verb: to give praise)

fair (noun: exhibition; adjective: light-hued, beautiful)

fare (noun: cost of a trip, or food served)

foreword (noun: introduction to a book)

forward (adjective and adverb: near or toward the front)

hear (verb: to listen to)

here (adverb: in this place)

its (possessive pronoun: Has the team set *its* agenda?)

it's (contraction of *it is: It's* good to see you.)

knew (verb: past tense of *to know*)

new (adjective: not old)

lead (noun: a metal—rhymes with *bread*)

lead (verb: to be first—rhymes with *breed*)

led (verb: past tense of verb *to lead*)

may be (verb: It *may be* true, but it's hard to believe.)

maybe (adverb: perhaps—*Maybe* he will visit us.)

pair (noun: set of two)

pare (verb: to trim)

pear (noun: fruit)

patience (noun: tolerance)

patients (noun: people who are receiving medical attention)

peace (noun: absence of war)

piece (noun: small amount)

plain (adjective: ordinary-looking, simple; noun: large field)

plane (noun: aircraft; verb: to make smooth)

principal (adjective: primary, main; noun: school official)

principle (noun: a controlling idea or belief)

right (adjective: correct, or a direction)

rite (noun: ritual)

write (verb: to create with words)

road (noun: passageway for vehicles)

rode (past tense of verb *to ride*)

rowed (past tense of verb *to row*—to propel a small boat)

stationary (adjective: not moving)

stationery (noun: writing paper and envelopes)

their (possessive pronoun: Do you know *their* telephone number?)

there (adverb: at that place)

they're (contraction of *they are: They're* going to meet us.)

threw (verb: past tense of *to throw*)

through (preposition: by way of)

thru (informal form of *through:* avoid in business writing)

to (preposition: toward)

too (conjunction: also; adverb: excessively)

two (number)

weak (adjective: not strong)

week (noun: seven days)

weather (noun: atmospheric conditions)

whether (conjunction: if)

who's (contraction of *who is:* Do you know *who's* coming?)

whose (possessive pronoun: *Whose* coat is this?)

your (possessive pronoun: Is this *your* laptop?)

you're (contraction of *you are: You're* a fine friend!)

ESL TIPS

Selecting a Bilingual Dictionary

Some comprehensive ESL dictionaries include the following:

- *Oxford ESL Dictionary: For Students of American English.* Oxford University Press.
- *Oxford American Wordpower Dictionary.* Oxford University Press.
- *Longman Dictionary of American English.* Longman Press.

The following ESL dictionaries specialize in business English:

- *Longman Business English Dictionary.* Longman Press.
- *NTC's American Business Terms Dictionary.* National Textbook Company.
- *Oxford Dictionary of Business English. For Learners of English.* Oxford University Press.

ESL TIPS

Using a Bilingual Dictionary

Here are some tips for using a bilingual dictionary:

1. Look up the word in your first language.
2. Carefully review the dictionary entry. What part of speech are you interested in? A noun? A verb? A participle? You can usually find the abbreviations for the parts of speech at the bottom of the page or in the introduction to the dictionary.
3. If your dictionary lists fields of knowledge, scan the entry to see if any field seems particularly suited to your situation.
4. Once you have located the correct English word, turn to the English section of the dictionary and look up that word. Does the meaning of the definition in your first language match your intended meaning in English? If not, continue to look the word up in your native-language section until you find the appropriate equivalent.
5. As you write, make sure you have used the appropriate form of the new word.

■ 36. Vocabulary

Trying to get along with a limited vocabulary is like trying to prepare a five-course meal with only one utensil and a pan. The limited equipment prevents you from dealing successfully with the range of situations you'll find yourself in. A limited vocabulary is a problem, but it is one you can overcome systematically over time. This section provides a system; you must provide the time and desire.

If you stop to think about it, you'll realize that you use at least three different vocabularies, perhaps four. Your largest vocabulary is your *recognition vocabulary*, which includes all the words you recognize and understand in your reading. Next largest is your *writing vocabulary*, which takes in all the words you use in your writing. The third largest is your *speaking vocabulary;* it is smaller than your writing vocabulary because you may consider some words you'd write too formal for conversation. Finally, you may have a limited vocabulary of 50 to 1,000 words unique to the trade or profession in which you are (or will be) engaged.

You will probably have no trouble in learning your trade, or professional, vocabulary, but you may need to work on improving the other three—especially your writing and recognition vocabularies. An excellent way to improve your vocabulary is by increasing the amount of reading you do and keeping a good dictionary nearby for looking up unfamiliar words.

The following are considered good desk dictionaries. (See also the discussion of dictionaries in Chapter 7, page 207.)

- *The American Heritage Dictionary of the English Language.* 4th ed. New York: Houghton Mifflin, 2000.
- *The Random House Webster's College Dictionary.* Indexed ed. New York: Random House, 2000.
- *Merriam Webster's Collegiate Dictionary.* 11th ed. Springfield, MA: G. & C. Merriam Company, 2003.
- *Webster's New World College Dictionary.* 4th updated ed. Cleveland and New York: Simon & Schuster, 1999.

(See also ESL Tips: Selecting a Bilingual Dictionary on page 734.)

C English as a Second Language (ESL)

Learning to write well in a second language takes a great deal of effort and practice. The best and easiest way to improve your written English is to read widely beyond reports and professional articles: Read newspapers, magazine articles, novels, biographies, short stories, or any other writing that interests you.

This section is a guide to some of the common problems non-native speakers experience when writing English. For specific help when you are writing a memo or report, ask a native speaker or refer to earlier sections of this Handbook.

Persistent problem areas for non-native English speakers include the following:

- Distinguishing between count and noncount nouns (see below)
- Using articles (see pages 737–741)
- Using prepositions (see pages 741–742)
- Distinguishing between gerunds and infinitives (see pages 742–743)
- Forming adjective clauses (see page 743)
- Determining verb tenses (see pages 743–748)
- Using helping verbs and writing conditional sentences (see pages 749–750)
- Using idioms (see pages 751–753)

■ 37. Count and Noncount Nouns

Count nouns refer to things that can be separated into countable units: *tables, pencils, boys, dentists*. Noncount nouns identify things that comprise a mass that cannot be counted: *electricity, water, oil, air, wood*. Noncount nouns also describe abstract qualities: *love, loyalty, pride, harmony*.

The distinction between whether something can or cannot be counted is important because it determines the form of the noun to use (singular or plural), the kind of article that precedes it (*a, an, the*, or no article), and the kind of limiting adjective it requires (*fewer* or *less, many* or *much*, and so on). This distinction can be confusing with words such as *electricity* or *oil*. Although you can count kilowatt hours of electricity or barrels of oil, counting does not apply to the words *electricity* or *oil* in a general sense, as in "oil is a limited resource." When you learn a noun in English, you need to learn whether it is count, noncount, or both. Some ESL dictionaries will provide this information.

1. *Count nouns* refer to things that can be separated into countable units. Count nouns have plurals:

   - *tables, pencils, boys, dentists*

   A concrete noun may be countable:

   - *Six cats* live in the apartment complex.

   A collective noun is countable:

   - There are many baseball *teams* in the United States.

2. *Noncount nouns* refer to things that comprise a mass or collection of items that cannot be counted separately. Noncount nouns do not have plurals:

   - *electricity, water, oil, air, wood*

   An abstract noun is uncountable:

   - *Honesty* is the best policy.

   Many concrete nouns are uncountable:

   - *Rice* is a staple food in China.

3. Many uncountable nouns can be made countable, but the meaning changes:

Uncountable	**Countable**
- *Life* is full of surprises.	- She lived a long *life*.
[Here, *life* is an abstract noun.]	[Here, *life* refers to a specific life and is countable.]
	- A cat has nine *lives*.
	[*Lives* are distinguished as countable.]
- *Art* can be thought-provoking.	- The *arts* can enrich a person's life.
[*Art* is meant in a general sense.]	[The *arts* refers to components of art as a whole, such as literature, music, painting, etc.]

■ 38. Articles

38.1 Use of Articles

Most count nouns are preceded by an article (*a, an, the*), a demonstrative adjective (*this, that, these, those*), a possessive adjective (*my, her, their,* and so on), or some expression of quantity (such as *one, two, several, many, a few, a lot of, some*).

The article, adjective, or expression of quantity appears either directly in front of the noun or in front of the whole noun phrase.

- Mary read *a* book last week.

    [The article *a* appears directly in front of the noun *book*.]

- Mary read *a* long, boring book last week.

    [The article *a* precedes the noun phrase *long, boring book*.]

- *Those* books Mary read were long and boring.

    [The demonstrative adjective *those* appears directly in front of the noun *books*.]

- *Their* book was long and boring.

    [The possessive adjective *their* appears directly in front of the noun *book*.]

- *Some* books Mary read were long and boring.

    [The indefinite adjective *some* appears directly in front of the noun *books*.]

38.2 Indefinite and Definite Articles

A and *an* are indefinite articles. *A* is used with singular nouns or adjectives that begin with consonant sounds.

- *a* dog, *a* long walk, *a* cat

An is used before a singular noun or an adjective that begins with a vowel sound.

- *an* hour, *an* apple, *an* unhappy child

A and *an* do not precede a plural countable noun or an uncountable noun.

- Women are a large group in the workforce.

    [You would not write *"An/a women,"* because *women* is a plural countable noun.]

The indefinite articles *a* and *an* are used with nouns that refer to any one thing out of the whole class of those items. The definite article *the* refers to a specific item.

INDEFINITE ARTICLE   Bill has *a* pen.

    [Bill could have *any* pen.]

DEFINITE ARTICLE   Bill has *the* pen.

    [Bill has a *specific* pen; both the reader and the writer know which one it is.]

The only exception to this rule occurs when the writer is making a generalization using a count noun. Then the writer can use either *a* or *an* with a singular count noun or no article with a plural count noun (see Table C–1).

Table C–1   Determining Whether to Use an Article

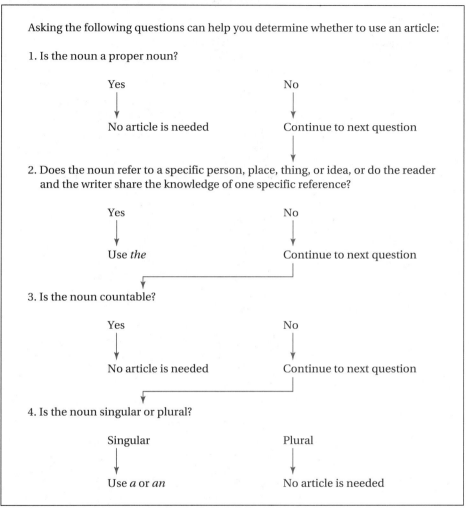

Asking the following questions can help you determine whether to use an article:

1. Is the noun a proper noun?

    Yes → No article is needed

    No → Continue to next question

2. Does the noun refer to a specific person, place, thing, or idea, or do the reader and the writer share the knowledge of one specific reference?

    Yes → Use *the*

    No → Continue to next question

3. Is the noun countable?

    Yes → No article is needed

    No → Continue to next question

4. Is the noun singular or plural?

    Singular → Use *a* or *an*

    Plural → No article is needed

- *An* egg is a good source of protein.

  [Generalization using an article: *any egg, all eggs, all in general*]

- Eggs are good sources of protein.

  [Generalization with a plural noun using no article: *any egg, all eggs, eggs in general*]

When making a generalization with a noncount noun, do not use an article.

- Sugar is bad for your teeth.

Choosing Definite or Indefinite Articles

Whether to use a definite or an indefinite article is determined by what you can safely assume about your audience's knowledge. Do your readers have enough information — either from their knowledge about the world *or* from the context of your writing — to identify the noun that will be modified by the article? If the answer is yes, use a definite article; if no, use an indefinite article.

In these sentences, you can assume that the reader can identify the noun.

- *The* sun rises in the east.

  [There is only one *sun*.]

- Did you know that yesterday was *the* coldest day of the year so far?

  [The modified noun refers to *yesterday*.]

- *The* man who left his briefcase under the table was a very bright man.

  [The relative phrase *left his briefcase under the table* restricts and, therefore, identifies the *man*.]

In this sentence, you cannot assume that the reader can identify the noun:

- *An* ice storm is on the way.

  [It is impossible to identify specifically which *ice storm* is meant.]

Using the Indefinite Articles a *and* an

Use *a* when a singular count noun is indefinite and the article is followed by a noun or an adjective beginning with a consonant sound.

- *a* cat, *a* delicious apple

Use *an* when a singular count noun is indefinite and the article is followed by a noun or an adjective beginning with a vowel sound.

- *an* apple, *an* appetizing apple

Do not use *a* or *an* with plural nouns.

  Women
- ~~A women~~
  ^

Do not use *a* or *an* with noncount nouns.

  Electricity
- ~~An electricity~~
  ^

Using the Definite Article the

Do not use *the* with plural or noncount nouns that mean "all" or "in general."

  Power
- ~~The power~~ corrupts.
  ^
  [This sentence means that all power corrupts, in general.]

Use *the* with the following phrases:

- in *the* afternoon, in *the* evening

but not with:

- at ~~the~~ night

Use *the* when the noun that follows has been previously mentioned.

- A van filled with children cut in front of our car.
  the
  When ^ van turned left, we followed it.

Use *the* when a phrase or clause that follows the noun restricts its identity.

  the
- The scientist warned me that ^ beaker on the top shelf was filled with poison.

  [The phrase *on the top shelf* identifies the beaker.]

Use *the* with the superlative form.

  the
- His report was ^ best the board ever read.

Do not use *the* with the comparative form.

- Which of these two restaurants is ~~the~~ better?

Use *the* with the word *same*.

  the
- She works ^ same shift as her husband.

Use *the* with plural names.

  the
- She went to visit ^ Smiths.

Do not use an article with the names of streets, avenues, roads, lanes, boulevards, squares, cities, states, counties, most countries, bays, single lakes, single mountains, or islands.

- ~~the~~ Miami, ~~the~~ Trafalgar Square, ~~the~~ Mt. Everest

(continued)

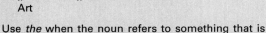
But do use *the* for united countries, large regions, deserts, peninsulas, oceans, seas, gulfs, canals and rivers, mountain ranges, and groups of islands.

■ _the_ United Arab Emirates, _the_ Sahara, _the_ Iberian Peninsula, _the_ Dead Sea, _the_ Panama Canal, _the_ Alps, _the_ Solomon Islands

Use *the* with the names of hotels, motels, theaters, bridges, and buildings.

■ _the_ Park Plaza Hotel, _the_ Golden Gate Bridge, _the_ Empire State Building

but do not use an article with the names of hospitals.

■ ~~the~~ Mt. Sinai Hospital

Use *the* with the names of zoos, gardens, museums, and institutes.

■ _the_ Bronx Zoo, _the_ Museum of Modern Art

Use *the* when the noun refers to something that is the only one that exists.

■ _the_ Eiffel Tower

Do not use an article with the names of most diseases.

■ ~~the~~ AIDS, ~~the~~ heart disease, ~~the~~ osteoporosis

But do use an article for the following:

■ _the_ measles, _the_ mumps, _the_ flu

■ 39. Prepositions

Prepositions are words that help connect nouns or pronouns to other parts of a sentence. They help to specify a relationship between items.

39.1 Prepositions of Time

The word *on* is used with days of the week.

■ We have staff meetings *on* Mondays.

At is used with hours of the day and with noon, night, and dawn.

■ We leave work *at* 5:00.

■ Lunch will be served *at* noon.

In is used with other parts of the day and with months, years, and seasons.

■ I check e-mail *in* the morning.

■ I started to work for the firm *in* May.

39.2 Prepositions of Place

The word *on* indicates a surface on which something rests.

- The files are *on* the desk.

At refers to an area or to a place.

- My assistant is *at* her desk.

In indicates a place that is inside an enclosure.

- The documents are *in* the file folder.

■ 40. Gerunds and Infinitives

Non-native writers are often puzzled by which form of a verbal (a verb used as a noun) to use as the direct object of a verb. No consistent rule exists for selecting an infinitive or a gerund as an object. Sometimes a verb takes an infinitive as its object, sometimes a gerund, and sometimes it takes either an infinitive or a gerund. At times, even the base form of the verb is used.

40.1 Gerunds as Complements

- He enjoys *working*.
- She denied *saying* that.
- Did Alice finish *reading* the report?

40.2 Infinitives as Complements

- He wants *to attend* the meeting in Los Angeles.
- The company expects *to sign* the contract soon.
- He promised *to fulfill* his part of the contract.

40.3 Infinitives or Gerunds as Complements

- It began *to rain* soon after we arrived. [infinitive]
- It began *raining* soon after we arrived. [gerund]

40.4 Base Forms of Verbs as Complements

- Let Maria *finish* the project by herself.
- The president had the technician *reassigned* to another project.

To make these choices accurately, you must rely on what you hear native speakers use or on what you read. Many ESL texts contain chapters on infinitive and gerund usage that list verbs with their appropriate complements.

■ 41. Adjective Clauses

Because of the many ways adjective clauses are constructed in different languages, they can be particularly troublesome to form correctly.

First, place the adjective clause directly *after* the noun it modifies.

■ The tall man *who is standing across the room* is a vice president of the company ~~who is standing across the room.~~

[The adjective clause *who is standing across the room* modifies *man*, not *company*, and thus comes directly after *man*.]

Second, do not omit the relative pronoun when it is in the subject position of its clause. If, however, the relative pronoun is in the object position in its clause, it may be omitted. Notice the difference in these two sentences.

■ The man *who sits at that desk* is my boss.

[The relative pronoun *who* is in the subject position.]

■ The man *whom we met* at the conference is on the board of directors.

[The relative pronoun *whom* is in the object position.]

■ The man we met at the conference is on the board of directors.

[The relative pronoun is omitted.]

Finally, avoid using a relative pronoun with another pronoun in an adjective clause.

■ The man who ~~he~~ sits at that desk is my boss.

■ The man whom we met ~~him~~ at the conference is on the board of directors.

■ 42. Verb Tenses

To determine which verb tense to use, consider the time in which the action you are describing occurs in relation to other actions. (Using the verb-tense timelines in Table C–2 will help you choose which tense to use.)

The "X" marks on the timelines of Table C-2 indicate points in time when action takes place. Arrows extending from the past and future labels further identify the activity of the verb. For example, the first timeline indicates that the accounting department currently works late, has worked late in the past, and will work late in the future.

Table C–2   Forming Tenses: A Timeline

Present Tense (verb + -*s* or -*es*)

The **present tense** expresses activities that occur on a regular basis and indicates facts.

■   The accounting department *works* late every Tuesday.

  [The accounting department does work, has worked, and will continue to work late every Tuesday.]

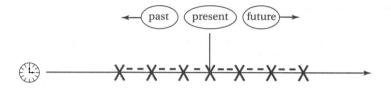

Present Progressive Tense (*am* / *is* / *are* + verb + -*ing*)

The **present progressive tense** describes an action that is occurring at the moment of speaking.

■   Mr. Greczek *is speaking* to the new employees.

  [The speaking is taking place in the present.]

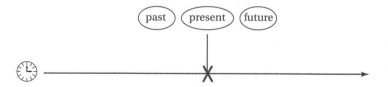

Past Tense (verb + -*ed* or irregular form of verb)

The **past tense** describes a completed action.

■   The file clerk *worked* in the new office on Monday.

  [The working took place in the past.]

■   The assistant *ran* to answer the phone.

  [The running took place in the past.]

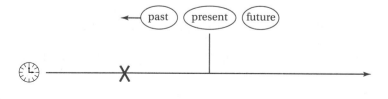

(continued)

Table C–2 Forming Tenses: A Timeline

Past Progressive Tense (*was/were* + verb + *-ing*)

The **past progressive tense** is used to specify a continuous action in the past that was interrupted by another action.

- My assistant *was typing* the report when I walked in the office.

  [The typing took place in the past, when something else also took place.]

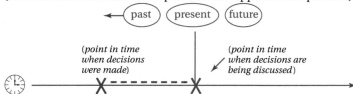

Present Perfect Tense (*have/has* + *-ed* or irregular form)

The **present perfect tense** describes an action that occurred at an unspecified time in the past and continues into the present moment. (See ESL Tips: Forming the Present Perfect Tense on page 748.)

- Mrs. Carols *has decided* to take early retirement.

  [The decision was made in the past and also applies to the present.]

- The manager *has* already *made* his decision.

  [The decision was made in the past and also applies to the present.]

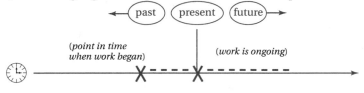

Present Perfect Progressive Tense (*have/has* + *been* + verb + *-ing*)

The **present perfect progressive tense** specifies a continuous action that started in the past and continues to the present.

- I *have been working* on the fiscal-year report for two weeks.

  [The working began in the past and continues into the present and future.]

(continued)

Table C–2 Forming Tenses: A Timeline

Past Perfect Tense (*had* + *-ed* or irregular form)

The **past perfect tense** is used to specify that an action occurred in the past before another past action occurred.

- The chairperson *had* already *started* the meeting when Celia arrived.

  [The meeting began; Celia arrived sometime later (both in the past).]

- James *had taken* the applicant to lunch before he offered her the job.

  [The applicant was taken out to dinner and later offered the job.]

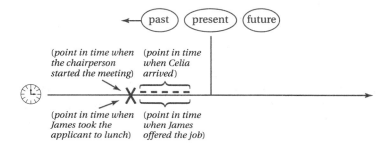

Past Perfect Progressive Tense (*had* + *been* + verb + *-ing*)

The **past perfect progressive tense** specifies an action that occurred for a time in the past but was completed before another action in the past.

- The assistant manager *had been working* for three hours before anyone else arrived.

  [The working took place; others arrived sometime later (both in the past).]

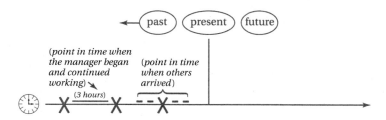

Future Tense (*will* + verb) or (*is/are* + *going to* + verb)

The **future tense** describes an action that will occur in the future.

- Mr. Williams *will coordinate* this year's conference.

  [The conference will be coordinated in the future.]

  or

- Mr. Williams *is going to coordinate* this year's conference.

(continued)

Table C–2   Forming Tenses: A Timeline

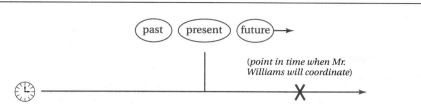

(*point in time when Mr. Williams will coordinate*)

Future Progressive Tense (*will* + *be* + verb + *-ing*)

The **future progressive tense** is used to specify a continuous action in the future that will be occurring when another action takes place.

■   He *will be working* when we arrive.

   [The working will already be taking place when we arrive.]

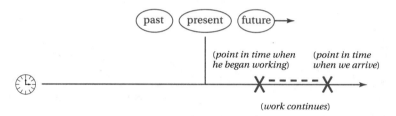

Future Perfect Progressive Tense (*will* + *have* + *been* + verb + *-ing*)

The **future perfect progressive tense** specifies an action in the future that will be finished before another action occurs in the future.

■   Ms. Stuart *will have been speaking* for two hours by the time you arrive.

   [The speaking will already be taking place (will have been going on for some time) before you arrive.]

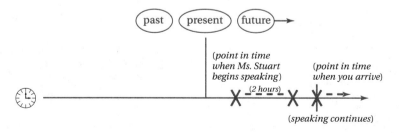

(continued)

Table C–2   Forming Tenses: A Timeline

Future Perfect Tense (*will* + *have* + -*ed* or irregular form)
The **future perfect tense** is used to specify that an action will occur in the future before another future action occurs.

■ Because Mr. Santiago arrived at work early, he *will have finished* his work before noon.

[The working, which began in the morning (past), will be finished before noon (future).]

■ Because of the company's use of flextime, Mr. Santiago *will* already *have left* when Ms. Patrick arrives.

[The leaving by Mr. Santiago will take place before the arrival of Ms. Patrick.]

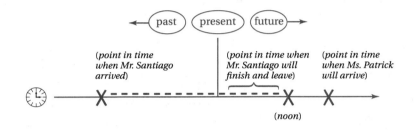

(*point in time when Mr. Santiago arrived*)

(*point in time when Mr. Santiago will finish and leave*)

(*point in time when Ms. Patrick will arrive*)

(*noon*)

(continued)

ESL TIPS

Forming the Present Perfect Tense

Because it is so closely related to the past tense, the present perfect tense remains one of the most problematic of all tenses. As a general rule, use the present perfect tense when referring to events completed in the past, but at unspecified times. When a specific time is mentioned, use the simple past tense.

SIMPLE PAST
TENSE

I *wrote* the letter yesterday.

[*Wrote* is the simple past tense of *to write.*]

PRESENT
PERFECT TENSE

I *have written* the letter.

[*Have written* is the present perfect tense of *to write*. No specific time is mentioned in this sentence. The writing could have taken place yesterday, last week, or ten years ago.]

Also use the present perfect tense to describe actions that were repeated several or many times in the unspecified past.

■ She *has revised* that report three times.
■ The president and his technical adviser *have met* many times over the past few months.

Finally, use the present perfect tense with a *since* or *for* phrase when describing actions that began in the past and continue to the present.

■ This company *has been* in business *for* ten years.
■ The company *has been* in business *since* 1993.

■ 43. Helping Verbs and Conditional Sentences

Modal verbs are helping verbs that have a variety of meanings. They precede a base form of the verb. (See ESL Tips: Using Helping Verbs on page 750.)

In *conditional sentences,* clauses that follow the words *if, when,* and *unless* show whether the result is possible or real, depending on other circumstances. Conditional sentences have two parts: a subordinate clause that begins with *if, when,* and *unless,* and a main clause that expresses a result. The following are types of conditional sentences.

A *prediction* foretells something based on conditional circumstances. Use a present tense verb within the *if* clause. The clause that expresses the result is formed with a modal helping verb (usually *will*) and the base form of the verb.

■ *If* you treat employees fairly, they *will be* better workers.

A *fact* explains a factual relationship between two or more occurrences. Use the same verb tense in both the conditional clause and the result clause.

■ When it *snows,* I *leave* for work an hour earlier.

■ When the chairperson *started* the meeting, he *welcomed* all new employees.

A *hypothetical sentence* explains that a result is impossible, did not happen, or is unlikely to happen. Use a past tense verb within the *if* clause, and *would, could,* or *might* in the result clause.

■ *If* I were CEO, I *would take* three months' vacation every year.

ESL TIPS

Using Helping Verbs

In English, 23 helping verbs (forms of *have, be, do*) may also function as main verbs. In addition, nine modals (*can, could, may, might, must, shall, should, will, would*) function only as helping verbs. *Have, be,* and *do* change form to indicate tense; the nine modals do not.

Can

- He *can* type fast. [ability]
- Bill, you *can* still improve. [possibility]

Could

- He *could* type fast before he broke his wrist. [past ability]
- Bill, you *could* still improve. [possibility]

May

- Juanita *may* show up for the meeting. [possibility]
- You *may* come and go as you please. [permission]

Might

- Juanita *might* show up for the meeting. [possibility]
- *Might* I go home early today? [very formal; permission]

Must

- We *must* finish this report by the end of the week. [necessity]
- You *must* see his new office. [recommendation]
- You *must* be hungry; you haven't eaten all day. [inference]

Shall

- *Shall* we go? [intention]

  [In American English, *shall* is used only for questions seeking agreement.]

Should

- You *should* apologize immediately. [advisability]
- Prentiss *should* be here any minute. [expectation]

Will

- Greg *will* finish as soon as he can. [intention]

Would

- *Would* you excuse me? [permission]
- He *would* repeatedly check his work when he first started working here. [habitual past]
- That *would* be a good guess. [probability]

The following guidelines will help you determine the proper use of modals.

One-word modals do not change form to show a change in subject.

- I *could* quit. She *could* quit.

Most two- and three-word modals do change form, like other helping verbs.

- I *have to* finish the project. She *has to* finish the project.

Never use *to* between a one-word modal and the main verb.

- I can type, *not* I can to type.

  [Most of the two- and three-word modals include *to,* as in *ought to drive.*]

Never use two one-word modals together.

- I could work tomorrow, *not* I might could work tomorrow.

When several helping verbs occur simultaneously, they must be in the following order:

modal perfect progressive participle

- He may have been being defrauded for several years.

■ 44. Idioms Used in Business

An *idiom* is a term that expresses something different from its literal meaning. An idiom such as "it's raining cats and dogs" (meaning much rain is falling) is not understandable from the individual meaning of each word.

The following are common idioms used in American English.

bottom line	the last figure on a financial balance sheet; the result or final outcome or ultimate truth
break down	to stop working properly
break up	to separate into smaller parts
bring about	to cause
bring up	to raise in a conversation
brush up on	to review (informal English)
call back	to return a phone call
call off	to cancel (informal English)
call on	to visit
call up	to telephone
carry out	to obey orders
check on	to inquire
come up with	to imagine; to think up (informal English)
count on	to depend on
cut down	to decrease the consumption of
cut off	to abruptly stop
deal with	to negotiate with; to take care of
decide on	to choose
do over	to repeat an action usually with corrections
do without	to manage without
drag on	proceed slowly (informal English)
drop off	to deliver (informal English)
fall behind	to not keep up with a job or a project (informal English)
fall through	to fail
figure out	to solve; to understand
fill out	to complete by writing
find out	to discover
finish up	to finish completely
get away with	to commit a bad act without being punished (informal English)

get by	to manage (informal English)
get in touch with	to call or to contact
get through	to finish (informal English)
go out of business	to stop doing business forever
go over	to review; to look over (informal English)
hang up	to replace a telephone receiver or to place an article of clothing on a hook
help out	to assist
hold on	to wait (informal English)
iron out	to solve a problem (informal English)
keep up	to maintain
lay off	a permanent or temporary dismissal of employees
lay over	to be delayed because of an airplane problem
lock up	to lock completely
look into	to investigate
look over	to examine carefully
look through	to search
make up one's mind	to make a decision (informal English)
on the table	open for discussion
pass around	to hand around to a group of people
pick out	to select
point out	to indicate
pull out	to break an agreement
put off	to postpone
run across	to find unexpectedly; to meet by chance
run into	to meet by chance
run up	to increase a bill
see about	to consider
send out	to mail
shape up	to improve (informal English)
size up	to analyze (informal English)
sort out	to classify
speak of	to mention
speak out	to say aloud
stand by	to wait for

stick with	to stay with (informal English)
take charge of	to assume responsibility for
take place	to occur
talk over	to discuss
think up	to imagine or to invent
try out	to test
turn down	to reject
wear out	to use until old; to exhaust
wrap up	to complete (informal English)
zero in (on)	to focus in on (informal English)

Comprehensive dictionaries of North American idioms include the following:

NTC's American Idioms Dictionary. 3rd ed. NTC Publishing Group.
A Dictionary of American Idioms. 3rd ed. Barron's.
Cambridge International Dictionary of Idioms. Cambridge University Press.
Longman's American Idioms Dictionary. Longman Publishing.

Acknowledgments *(continued from the copyright page)*

Scott Adams. **Dilbert** cartoon. Copyright © 1999 by United Feature Syndicate. Reprinted by permission of United Feature Syndicate, Inc.

Cartoonbank email document. © 2003 from cartoonbank.com. All rights reserved.

Steve Coffel and Karyn Feiden. Excerpt and figure from *Indoor Pollution* by Steve Coffel and Karyn Feiden. Copyright © 1990 by Steve Coffel and Karyn Feiden. Used by permission of Ballantine Books, a division of Random House, Inc.

Subscriber email from *The Wall Street Journal Online*. Copyright 2002 Dow Jones and Company, Inc. All Rights Reserved. Reprinted with permission.

Google.com Figures 7–9 & 7–10, Google screen shots. © 2003 Google. Courtesy www.google.com.

Micron Electronics, Inc. "Poster Depicting Visual Instructions to Set Up a Computer." Reproduction rights granted by MPC Computers, LLC—all other rights reserved.

Salem State College website screen shots. The content of these pages (under the addresses http://www.salemstate.edu and http://www.noblenet.org. Courtesy of The Salem State College Library, 352 Lafayette St., Salem, Massachusetts, USA. (p) 978-542-6665; (f) 978-542-6596.

Figure 13–2: "Installation of Kenmore Waste Disposers." Reprinted with the permission of Sears, Roebuck and Company.

TeensHealth.org screen shot. This information was provided by KidsHealth, one of the largest resources online for medically reviewed health information written for parents, kids, and teens. For more articles like this one, visit www.KidsHealth.org or www.TeensHealth.org. Reprinted with permisson of Nemours.org. (Fig. 16–6)

Figures 13–10, 13–11 & 13–12: "VR542 User's Guide" instructions. Courtesy of Thompson Consumer Electronics, Inc., 1995. Indianapolis, IN.

Index

Boolean operators, 212
boxes
    on business forms, 266
    for highlighting, 253, 255
boxhead, 270
brackets, 709, 714–15
    with quoted material, 218, 219
brainstorming, 8–9, 10, 194, 333, 529
Bramlage, Steve, 25
Branca, Malorye, 564
bulleted lists, 152, 530, 573–75
bulletin boards, electronic, 215
business correspondence, 305
    acceptance letters, 623–24
    accuracy in, 318
    acknowledgments, 356
    adjustment letters, 373–76, 377, 378
    business letters, 308, 319–25, 340
    collections, 376–81
    complaints, 369–73, 374
    covers or transmittals, 356, 358, 359, 421
    e-mail messages, 308–9, 334–41
    faxes, 309
    goodwill writing, 311–14
    guidelines for, 348–49, 382
    inquiries and responses, 356–62
    international, 341–47
    job application letters, 613–19
    memos, 308, 325–32, 340
    negative messages, 314–16
    openings and closings in, 317
    recommendations, 366–67
    refusals, 367–69, 370, 371, 372, 624–25
    resignation letters, 625–27
    routine and positive, 355–67
    sales and promotional, 363–65
    selecting appropriate medium, 306–11
    sensitive and negative messages, 367–81
    special considerations for, 311
    tone in, 311–14
    writing style in, 317–18
    See also business letters; e-mail messages;
        memos
business forms, 261–66
    entry lines in, 265–66
    evaluating design of, 266
    guidelines for, 266
    instructions and captions, 262–63
    planning for responses, 263–65
    sequencing data for, 263–65
    spacing in, 266
business letters, 311–18
    body of, 323
    building goodwill with, 311–14
    complimentary close in, 323, 723
    defined, 308, 348
    end notations in, 324–25
    faxing, 309
    format guidelines for, 319–25, 340, 349
    full-block style for, 319, 320

headings, 319
    for informal reports, 389
    inside address, 322
    for investigative reports, 396
    modified-block style for, 319, 321
    negative messages, 314–16
    organizational stationery for, 308, 319, 324
    organization of, 25
    paragraph length in, 141
    salutation, 322–23, 702
    second page of, 324
    "you" viewpoint in, 311–14
    See also business correspondence
Business Periodicals Index, 208
business resources, online, 213

capitalization, 722–27
    of abbreviations, 726
    all, for emphasis, 153, 254
    with colons, 702, 722–23
    in e-mail messages, 336
    ESL tips for, 722
    of first words, 722–23
    of institutions, events, concepts, 724–25
    of job titles, 725–26
    of letters, 726
    miscellaneous, 726–27
    of personal names and groups, 723
    of personal titles, 725–26
    of proper nouns, 635
    of specific places, 723–24
    in subject-line titles, 332
    of titles of works, 725
captions
    for business forms, 262–63
    for graphic elements, 275
    for highlighting, 254
    for Web graphics, 579
career services, college, 590. *See also* job search
case, pronoun, 642–43
cause-and-effect analysis
    in definitions, 85
    evidence in, 87–89
    goals of, 87
cautions. *See* warnings
CD-ROM publication, documenting, 228, 238
chalkboards, 530
charts, 267
    documenting, 229, 238
    flip charts, 528–29
    flowcharts, 288–89
    for oral presentations, 527, 528–29, 530, 538
    organizational, 289–91
    See also graphs; visuals
checklists. *See* menu of tips and checklists
check box, in business forms, 266
chemistry style manuals, 242
chronological organization, 12, 34, 35, 38,
        39, 54
chunking content, in Web writing, 567–68

Mark in Margin	Instruction	Mark on Manuscript	Corrected Type
l	Delete	the ~~lawyer's~~ Bible	the Bible
lawyer's	Insert	the ∧bible	the lawyer's bible
(stet)	Let stand	the ~~lawyer's~~ bible	the lawyer's bible
(cap)	Capitalize	the bible	the Bible
(lc)	Make lowercase	the Law	the law
(ital)	Italicize	the lawyer's bible	the *lawyer's* bible
(tr)	Transpose	the bible lawyer's	the lawyer's bible
⊂	Close space	the Bi ble	the Bible
(sp)	Spell out	②bibles	two bibles
#	Insert space	theBible	the Bible
¶	Start paragraph	¶ The lawyer's . . .	The lawyer's . . .
(run in)	No paragraph	. . . marks. ⌐ Below is a . . .	. . . marks. Below is a . . .
(sc)	Set in small capitals	the bible	the BIBLE
(rom)	Set in roman type	the (bible)	the bible
(bf)	Set in boldface	the bible	the **bible**
(lf)	Set in lightface	the (**bible**)	the bible
⊙	Insert period	The lawyers have their own bible∧	The lawyers have their own bible.
⌐	Insert comma	However∧we cannot . . .	However, we cannot . . .
⌐=⌐=⌐	Insert hyphens	half∧and∧half	half-and-half
(:)	Insert colon	We need the following∧	We need the following:
⌐;	Insert semicolon	Use the law∧don't . . .	Use the law; don't . . .
⌐'	Insert apostrophe	John✗s law book	John's law book
⌐"/⌐"	Insert quotation marks	The∧law∧is law.	The "law" is law.
(/)/	Insert parentheses	John's ∧law∧ book	John's (law) book
[/]/	Insert brackets	(John Martin ∧1920–1962∧ went . . .)	(John Martin [1920–1962] went . . .)
⌐N	Insert en dash	1920∧1962	1920–1962
⌐M	Insert em dash	Our goal∧victory	Our goal—victory
³	Insert superior type	3∨= 9	$3^2 = 9$
₂	Insert inferior type	HSO₄∧	H_2SO_4

Menu of Tips and Checklists